KT-404-413

1993   0801674425

GC 034826   GRIMSBY COLLEGE

MANAGEMENT OF
Physical Education and Sport

MANAGEMENT OF
Physical Education and Sport

CHARLES A. BUCHER

Professor, School of Health, Physical Education,
 Recreation and Dance
University of Nevada, Las Vegas
Former President, National Fitness Leaders Council
Consultant to the National Fitness Foundation

MARCH L. KROTEE

Faculty of Kinesiology and Leisure Studies
University of Minnesota, Minneapolis
Fellow, Research Consortium and Past Chair
International Relations Council and Sport Sociology Academy
American Alliance of Health, Physical Education and Dance
Consultant to the President's Council on Physical
 Fitness and Sports
Educational Mentor, Athlete Educational Mentoring Network
United States Olympic Committee
Kellogg/Partners of the Americas Fellow
Fulbright Scholar

TENTH EDITION

with 228 illustrations

 Mosby Year Book

St. Louis Baltimore Boston Chicago London Philadelphia Sydney Toronto

Mosby Year Book
Dedicated to Publishing Excellence

LOCATION HE
CLASS
ACC
No. 034826
WITHDRAWN

Editor-in-Chief: Jim Smith
Acquisitions Editor: Vicki Malinee
Assistant Editor: Cathy Waller
Project Manager: Patricia Tannian
Production Editor: Ann E. Rogers
Designer: Julie Taugner

TENTH EDITION

Copyright © 1993 by Mosby–Year Book, Inc.

A Mosby imprint of Mosby–Year Book, Inc.

Previous editions copyrighted 1955, 1958, 1963, 1967, 1971, 1975, 1979, 1983, 1987

All rights reserved. No part of this publication may be reproduced, stored in a retrieval system, or transmitted, in any form or by any means, electronic, mechanical, photocopying, recording, or otherwise, without prior written permission from the publisher.

Permission to photocopy or reproduce solely for internal or personal use is permitted for libraries or other users registered with the Copyright Clearance Center, provided that the base fee of $4.00 per chapter plus $.10 per page is paid directly to the Copyright Clearance Center, 27 Congress Street, Salem, MA 01970. This consent does not extend to other kinds of copying, such as copying for general distribution, for advertising or promotional purposes, for creating new collected works, or for resale.

Printed in the United States of America

Mosby–Year Book, Inc.
11830 Westline Industrial Drive
St. Louis, Missouri 63146

Library of Congress Cataloging in Publication Data

Bucher, Charles Augustus, 1912–1988
    Management of physical education & sport / Charles A. Bucher,
March L. Krotee.—10th ed.
        p.   cm.
    Rev. ed. of: Management of physical education & athletic programs.
9th ed. 1987.
    Includes index.
    ISBN 0-8016-0904-6
    1. Physical education and training—Administration.   2. Sports—
Organization and administration.   I. Krotee, March L.   II. Bucher,
Charles Augustus, 1912–1988   Management of physical education &
athletic programs.   III. Title.   IV. Title: Management of physical
education and sport.
GV343.5.B77   1992
613.7′068—dc20   92-5500
                                                           CIP

94 95 96 97 UG/DC 9 8 7 6 5 4 3 2

To my wife
Leslie
and my children
Chip *and* Rob
without whose love and support such an undertaking would be impossible.

I love you.

GRIMSBY COLLEGE
LIBRARY
NUNS CORNER, GRIMSBY

Preface

The tenth edition of *Management of Physical Education and Sport* is designed to provide a comprehensive, contemporary text for administration and management courses dealing with physical education and sport in the educational setting. The text has been carefully revised based on developments and trends that have taken place within our dynamic profession and therefore reflects the most current thinking and research available. As in past editions, seminal works have been maintained and referenced to provide a solid foundation from which newer management concepts, skills, and techniques may be built.

NEW TO THIS EDITION

This tenth edition has maintained the conceptual framework of the previous editions; however, the content has been rewritten and shaped to reflect the most current patterns concerning the organization and management of physical education and sport. Where appropriate, crucial issues such as race, ethnicity, gender, age, and disability have been addressed and contemporary educational initiatives concerning multiculturalism and internationalization have been included.

Changes in the text include the introduction of the management process and framework to the introductory chapter within the context of renewed managerial skills, functions, and roles. Sections concerning leadership, decision making, conflict resolution, and philosophical dimensions have also been added. The objectives and organizational structures contained in Chapter 2 have been revised, as have the

management guidelines for school and college physical education and sport programs in Chapter 3. Current Title IX and adapted physical education concepts were also reconstructed and presented in this section, as were concepts dealing with cooperative learning and instructional goal structuring.

The chapters concerning recreational, interscholastic, and intercollegiate sport have been extended in scope. New tournament structures and information concerning coaching certification, students with disabilities, academic counseling, and Title IX compliance have been inserted. The chapter dealing with alternative physical education and sport programs has been reshaped to include physical education and sport in the public and private sector. Career opportunities, as well as representative organizational and managerial models exploring corporate or workplace health and fitness, the commercial fitness industry, and community-based physical education and sport programs, are now included. The domain of personnel management and supervision for teachers and coaches has also been revised and contains new guidelines for staff recruitment, sections concerning burnout and stress management, and information concerning affirmative action and due process. The program development chapter incorporates new approaches to organizing outcome-based curriculum experiences, and the facility and fiscal management chapters have also been reconstructed. Detailed planning systems and sample budgets cutting across the Physical Activity and Sport Continuum provide the student with concrete examples of the fiscal components of physical education and sport programs.

Chapters 11 and 12 have also been reshaped to include the most current information and trends concerning purchase and care of supplies and equipment and athletic training. The legal liability chapter has been brought up to date and enlarged in scope. One of the reviewers stated that it was "the most thorough and complete" treatment in the professional literature.

The public relations chapter includes new guidelines and promotional activities used to generate support for physical education and sport programs. The final chapter concerning office management includes a section on computer contributions to management, as well as a sample list of beginning computer software programs.

PEDAGOGICAL FEATURES

To facilitate use by instructors and students, several pedagogical aids have been incorporated into this volume. These include the following:

Instructional objectives. Each chapter begins with instructional objectives that introduce the main points of the chapter. Attaining these objectives indicates fulfillment of the chapter's intent.

Introductory paragraphs. A short introduction is provided for each chapter. This provides students with a transition when progressing from the previous chapter.

Summaries. Each chapter ends with a brief review of the critical material presented in the chapter. This will assist the student in understanding and retaining the most important concepts covered.

Self-assessment activities. Each chapter includes a set of activities that will enable students to determine whether they understand the main points in the chapter. This serves as an evaluation for both the student and instructor.

References. Each chapter provides both foundational and contemporary references that may be used to acquire further information concerning the material presented.

Suggested readings. Additional readings have been selected and annotated for students to further inquire into the related and relevant material.

INSTRUCTOR'S MANUAL

The *Instructor's Manual* provides instructors with additional material to facilitate the conduct of the course. The *Instructor's Manual* contains the following features for each chapter:

Chapter overview. This provides a brief review of the main points covered in the chapter.

Instructional objectives. These provide a framework for preparing lesson plans. They are designed to focus on the objectives and competencies to be gained by the student.

Topical teaching outlines. These provide a point of reference for organizing lectures and presentations.

Multiple choice and discussion test questions. These are based on the objectives and competencies presented in each chapter. An answer key is also provided for use by the instructor.

ACKNOWLEDGMENTS

I would like to thank Paul F. Blair, Leslie L. Krotee, Linda Pleissner, and Jonathan Sweet for their assistance in the preparation of the manuscript. Special thanks are also accorded to Vicki Malinee, Cathy Waller, and Loren Stevenson of Mosby–Year Book for their confidence, patience, and diligence while bringing this project to completion. In addition I would like to personally thank the reviewers who provided invaluable input in order to ensure the integrity of the text:

Frank Ashley
Texas A&M University

Maureen Fitzgerald
University of Missouri

Mark Fohl
University of Minnesota—Morris

Diana Gray
Indiana University

Graham Hatcher
University of North Carolina—Wilmington

Keith Lambrecht
Northern Illinois University

Kathleen McCann
University of North Dakota

Ralph Sabock
Pennsylvania State University

Vernon Vradenburg
University of Wisconsin—Platteville

Jim Wasem
Eastern Washington University

I would like to acknowledge the assistance of Wendell Vandersluis, Men's Intercollegiate Athletics, University of Minnesota; Gerry Vuchetich, Women's Intercollegiate Athletics, University of Minnesota; The School of Kinesiology and Leisure Studies, University of Minnesota; The Department of Recreational Sports, University of Minnesota, The University of Nevada, Las Vegas; Special Olympics International, Washington, D.C.; Donald Krotee, Partnership, Planning and Architecture, Santa Ana, CA; Hellmuth, Obata, and Kassabaum, Inc., Sports Facilities Group, Kansas City, MO; and Dr. Thomas C. Slettehaugh, Commissioner, Minneapolis Arts Commission, for their assistance in se-

curing photographs for this tenth edition. All other key contributors of photographs are listed on the credits page in the back of the book.

I would also like to thank the many friends and professional colleagues who helped in many ways with the revision of the tenth edition—from answering crucial questions to proofing to loaning reference books. Thus the tenth edition was truly a team effort of many who continue to pursue excellence and strive to provide a quality educational experience for both students and teachers.

Finally, as you know, this tenth edition will go to press without a good friend and colleague, Charles Bucher. Charlie did much to shape the roots of the profession, specifically management and administration of physical education and sport, and through his dedicated career touched the lives of many young aspiring professionals. For this I dedicate this tenth edition to him and hope that "our" text continues to reflect the spirit of this truly great man.

March L. Krotee, Ph.D.
Fulbright Professor
University of Minnesota

Contents

PART **I**

The Management Process

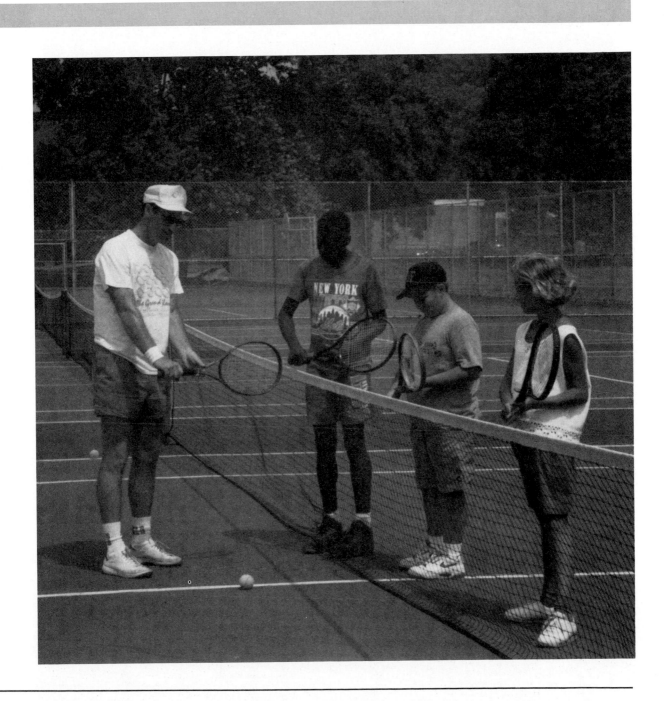

CHAPTER 1

The Management Process

> ► **Instructional Objectives and Competencies To Be Achieved**
>
> *After reading this chapter the student should be able to*
>
> - Describe and contrast the traditional and modern views of management.
> - Appreciate the advantages and problems concerned with a democratic and participatory management.
> - Discuss a modern philosophy of management.
> - Identify the factors and qualifications essential for effective physical education and sport management.
>
> - Enumerate the major duties of a manager in a physical education and sport setting.
> - Outline the preparation necessary to be an effective manager.
> - Explain why the study of management is important to the physical educator, athletic director, or sport manager.

This text is concerned with the study of management as it is applied to the domain of physical education and sport.* Although management skills and concepts are applicable over this broad continuum of organizational and institutional settings, the primary focus of the text remains the management of the traditional delivery systems of school physical education, interscholastic, intercollegiate, and recreational sports. Management is a crucial ingredient in any physical education or sports program and must be soundly implemented if that program is to be conducted in an effective and meaningful fashion. Man-

*For the purposes of the text, the terms physical education and sport will be thought to include a comprehensive spectrum of movement as adapted from the Physical Activity and Sport Continuum developed by Krotee in 1980. The continuum ranges from play to professional and performing sport and dance, and is illustrated below.

agement involves the interaction between those who administer and those who participate in the physical education and sporting processes. It involves, but is not limited to, such important matters as personnel, long-range planning, programming, facilities, budget, legal liability, and public relations. This text explores these managerial dimensions and examines ways in which they can be effectively and efficiently employed.

WHAT IS MANAGEMENT?

DuBrin, Ireland, and Williams define management as the coordinated and integrated process of utilizing an organization's resources (e.g., human, financial, physical, information, technical) to achieve specific objectives through the functions of planning, organizing, staffing, leading, and controlling[3] (Figure 1-1).

Hersey and Blanchard note that management is "working with and through individuals and groups to accomplish organizational goals."[4] The American Association of School Administrators further de-

scribes management as "the total of the processes through which appropriate human and material resources are made available and made effective for accomplishing the purpose of an enterprise."[1]

The antecedents of the theory and practice of management as we think of it today have their roots in the ancient civilizations of humankind. Leakey's diggings of the hand-axe man (predating 3000 BC) of Olorgesailie (Kenya) and Olduvai Gorge (Tanzania), the cuneiform tablets of the Sumerian society (circa 2500 BC), the physical evidence of Machu Picchu (Peru), the pyramids, and the Great Wall each serve as testimony to the management processes requisite to accomplish various societies' sociocultural objectives. Other often-cited examples of early management mastery include the Roman Empire (circa 753 BC to 476 AD), the Chinese civil service system (circa 165 BC), and the Roman Catholic Church (circa 110 AD). Thus management is recognized as a fundamental integrating process designed to achieve organized, purposeful, and meaningful results.

The term *management* was derived from the

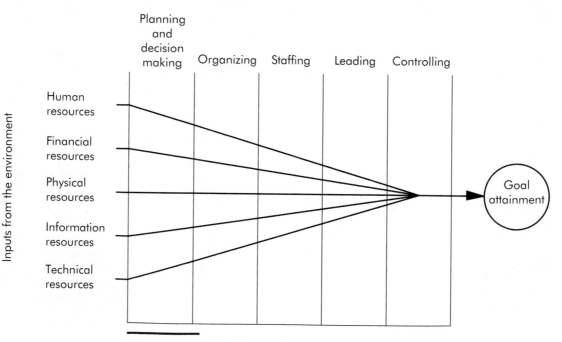

FIGURE 1-1   The management process.

French word *menager,* meaning "to use carefully" and the Italian word *maneggiare,* meaning "to handle." The term was originally employed concerning the training of horses and later was extended to the operations of war, referring to the general notion of taking charge or control. Contemporary management implies an ongoing process by which managers create, direct, maintain, and operate purposive organizations through coordinated, cooperative human effort.

WHAT IS A MANAGER?

A manager is someone whose primary activities are part of the management process. Specifically, a manager is someone who plans, makes decisions, organizes, staffs, leads, motivates, and controls organizational resources. Managers may be physical education teachers or department chairs; athletic directors; commissioners of leagues; general managers of professional teams; directors of health, golf, or racquet clubs; managers of country clubs, corporate or community fitness centers, Ys, or ski areas; or involved in any number of positions of responsibility within a traditional education system or the estimated $63 billion sporting industry.

It has been estimated that there are more than six million individuals in the United States who hold managerial positions, and as technology and information continue to expand and packaging and promoting become more sophisticated, even more well-trained and prepared individuals will be called on to perform the myriad managerial duties required to effectively and efficiently manage successful physical education and sporting operations. There is little doubt that the art of management is now becoming a science.

There are many different kinds of managers. Some possess warm, friendly personalities that foster a relaxed working environment and are popular with their staffs, whereas others are cold and unresponsive to human needs. Managers carry out their responsibilities in various ways. Some will shape members of their staffs; others are known for their inaction (seemingly waiting for problems to solve themselves); some are despots and authority figures;

and others believe in providing democratic and situational leadership for their organization. Each manager is different, influenced by such characteristics as training and preparation, personality, experience, beliefs, and values. These managerial characteristics often play a significant role in determining how managers utilize the resources at their disposal (Table 1-1).

In today's marketplace, it appears that some managers are not sufficiently trained to assume managerial roles. Although this trend seems to be reversing itself within the profession, it is still apparent that contemporary managers need to equip themselves with the necessary conceptual, human, and technical skills that are required for what Peter Drucker[2] has noted as a most "crucial resource" for developed nations, as well as one of the most needed resources in countries that are struggling to develop.

WHY PURSUE A MANAGEMENT CAREER?

Many reasons motivate individuals to pursue a career in management. Some persons like the recognition and prestige that frequently accompany a person who is a chairperson, dean, athletic director, or corporate fitness manager. The fact that management positions usually carry a higher salary than other positions in the organization can be a strong motivating factor for some. Authority and power may also be reasons for seeking a management position.

The manager usually controls functions such as recommending salary increases and promotions, making personnel decisions, and determining workloads, all of which appeal to some individuals. Some persons prefer management duties to those of teaching and coaching. Others seek to create, build, and put into operation their own ideas for helping the organization grow and gain a better identity. Clearly, individuals enter management and become managers for many different reasons.

Whether individuals are successful in getting into the field of management (e.g., department chair, principal, head coach, athletic director) depends on the particular situation and other factors. A physical education teacher who is experienced, respected by

TABLE 1-1.   Examples of resources employed by sports organizations

Organization	Human	Financial	Physical	Informational	Technical
Minneapolis Public Schools	Athletic Director Coaches Municipal employees	Tax revenue Gate receipts	Municipal building Parade stadium	Scheduling Transportation	Open enrollment PL 94-142
University of Minnesota Division of Kinesiology	Physical education students Sport and exercise science students Faculty and staff	State funding Grants Contributions Endowed Chairs	Aquatic center Golf course Fieldhouse Laboratory of sport sciences	Publications Public relations Development Funding opportunity	WATSMART System computers Equipment repair
University of Minnesota Athletic Departments	Student athletics Faculty representatives Academic counseling Sport psychology	Government grants Alumni contributions	Williams Arena Golf course Training complex	Public relations Publications Media guides	Lexicon system Drug testing protocol
Eden Prairie Community Center	Director Aquatics coordinator	Rental of ice time Bond issues	Ice arena Aquatic center Racquetball courts	Shared utilization Senior citizens programs	Energy cost Pool operation and maintenance
Clark Hatch Fitness Centers	Fitness director Business manager Staff	Corporate memberships Guests	Computers Weight training equipment	Promotional packages Nutritional programs	Computers Equipment repair
Minnesota Vikings	Players Corporate executives and board members Scouts	Television profits Stockholder investments Parking and concessions	Metrodome Training complex Weight training and rehabilitation center	Sales forecasts Playoff revenue	NFL Players' Association Contracts

students and faculty, and provides leadership in the school, or a coach who is experienced, popular with players and staff, and active in the community may be selected. The reasons people are selected for managerial positions should depend on factors such as academic preparation and certification for the posi-tion, maintaining a thorough knowledge concerning the position, experience in the field, management skills, and philosophy. Other valuable managerial commodities that may assist one in gaining a managerial position might include social and communi-cation skills, problem-solving and decision-making

The modern management process utilizes cooperative effort and up-to-date technology.

skills, poise and self-discipline, self-confidence, a co-operative demeanor, motivational skills, in-house political savvy, and technical skills (e.g., computer, legal, or financial).

THE IMPORTANCE OF MANAGEMENT

How well an organization such as a school, community center, fitness or racquet club, or aquatic complex charts its course and achieves its objectives depends on how well managers perform their jobs. Therefore it is imperative that all physical educators and sports personnel thoroughly understand the importance of effective and efficient management. Some of management's important contributions follow.

The way in which organizations are managed determines the course of human lives. Human beings are affected by management. It influences the type of program offered, the climate in which the program takes place, the goals that are sought, and the health and happiness of members of the organization.

Management provides an understanding and appreciation of the underlying principles of the science of this field. Methods, techniques, strategies, and procedures employed by the manager can be evaluated more accurately and objectively by staff members if they possess managerial understanding. Also, sound management will be better appreciated and unsound practices more easily recognized.

Studying management will help a person decide whether to select this field as a career. Increased understanding and appreciation of the management process will help individuals evaluate their personal qualifications and potential within the field.

Most physical educators perform some type of management work; therefore an understanding of management will contribute to better performance. Management is not restricted to one group of individuals. Most staff members have reports to complete, equipment to order, evaluations to make, and other duties to perform that are managerial in nature. An understanding of management will help in efficiently carrying out these assignments.

Management is fundamental to associated effort. Goals are stated and reached, ideas are implemented, and *esprit de corps* is developed with planning and cooperative action. A knowledge of management facilitates the achievement of such aims.

An understanding of management helps ensure continuity. A fundamental purpose of management is to carry on what has proved successful rather than destroy the old and attempt a new and untried path. An appreciation of this concept by all members of an organization will help to ensure the preservation of the best traditional practices that exist in the organization.

A knowledge of management helps further good human relations. An understanding of sound management principles will ensure the cooperation of the members of the organization and produce optimal efficiency and productivity.

Managers contribute to the realization of a better society. Because managers influence productivity and establish organizational policies and goals, they collectively influence a nation's standard of living and quality of life.

Management is gradually becoming a science, and the study of this science is essential to everyone. It can result in a better-ordered society through more effectively and efficiently run organizations. Every individual belongs to formal organizations. Through a democratic and cooperative approach to management the individual can aid in carrying on what has proved to be successful in the past.

MANAGEMENT IN TRANSITION

The role of management has changed markedly in recent years. The role of the manager has evolved from where "the manager" most often possessed the only voice in the governance of the organization (including such key decision making as hiring, salary, assignment, and advancement) to today's team-oriented management approach. The contemporary manager has become keenly aware of the importance of the individual within the organizational framework. This awareness has developed because of the complexity of the tasks involved in managing a classroom, gymnasium, sport club, or team or suc-

cessfully operating a ski area or a community or fitness center. Physical education and sport have become a "shared" or team-related phenomenon. The manager is part of that team whose job might be to facilitate, implement, or remove constraints to help other team members within the organizational framework achieve their respective goals. Today's manager must be thoroughly informed, and an expert in group dynamics, role differentiation, motivation, goal-setting, decision making, and positive reinforcement. These types of interpersonal processes must be masterfully exercised if the individual, the organization, and management are to be successful.

Despite managerial roles being in a perpetual state of transition and adaptation, there are some characteristics that seem to remain somewhat stable concerning the work of the manager. Managers often work long hours at an unrelenting pace. Some seem to never catch up! Their day is broken up into a large number of brief, diverse, and fragmented managerial activities. Managers meet, interact, and maintain contact with a large number of people.

Fitness professionals learn new activities at Southeastern Regional Clinic on Physical Fitness and Sport.

They often have little time for reflective thinking or planning, and many seem to prefer oral to written communication. Much of the manager's work is initiated by others, and often times managers do not control their own destiny.

If prospective managers of physical education and sport programs are thinking about being in a position to possess power over other individuals, force personal ideas on other members of the organization, or provide opportunities for making unilateral decisions, then they should not go into management, because they are doomed to failure. The formula for success is to be creative, adapt ideas, set goals, motivate, and make shared decisions with members of the organization. The power of the *organization* is crucial, not the power of the *individual*.

Dynamic leaders help shape the direction of interscholastic and intercollegiate sport.

MANAGERIAL FRAMEWORK AND FUNCTIONS

The conceptual framework for the study of management has evolved since classical school management pioneers such as Frederick W. Taylor (1911) and Henri Fayol (1929) proposed various ingredients, possessions, duties, and responsibilities that served to shape the management process. Thus the modern manager's makeup, which may be characterized as dynamic, continuous, fluid, and controlling in nature, has grown into a complex interrelated spectrum of duties and responsibilities influenced and tempered by the manager's personality, capability, and experience, as well as the environment in which the organization must function (Table 1-2).

Within this framework, some of the commonly identified functions of management follow.

Planning

Planning is the process of logically and purposefully outlining the work to be performed, together with the methods to be used and the time allotted for the performance of this work. The total plan will result in the accomplishment of the purposes for which the organization is established. Of course this requires a clear conception of the aims of the total organiza-

TABLE 1-2. A framework for the shaping of the management process		
Ingredients	**Possessions**	**Duties and responsibilities**
People personality and needs (affiliation, aspiration, power, attitude, achievement, motivation)	Dynamic Continuous	Leadership, motivation, and communication Training programs and delegation of tasks
Environmental influences (social, cultural, political, economic, race, gender)	Fluid (continually changing and adapting)	Effectiveness and performance evaluation
Physical and mental ability and experience (education, knowledge, opportunity, training)	Directs and controls (the nature, extent, and pace of the organization)	Goal setting, decision making, and feedback

tion. To accomplish this planning, the manager must have vision to look into the future and prepare a strategy for what is seen. He or she must forecast the influences that will affect the organization in order to arrive at prudent decisions concerning future organizational challenges.

Organizing

Organizing refers to the development of the formal structure of the organization whereby the various management coordinating centers and subdivisions of work are arranged in an integrated manner with clearly defined lines of authority. The purpose behind this structure is the effective accomplishment of established objectives through a coordinated marshalling of human and physical resources.

The structure should be set up to avoid red tape and provide for the clear assignment of every necessary duty to a responsible individual or cooperative work unit. Whenever possible, standards should be established for acceptable performance for each assigned duty.

The coordinating centers of authority are developed and organized primarily on the basis of the work to be done by the organization, services performed, individuals available in light of incentives offered, and efficiency of operation. A single manager cannot perform all the functions necessary, except in the smallest organizations. Hence responsibility must be logically assigned to others. These individuals occupy positions along the line, each position being broken down in terms of its own area of specialization. The higher up the line an individual goes, the more general the responsibility; the lower down the line the individual, the more specific or focused the responsibility.

Staffing

The management function of staffing refers to the entire personnel duty of selection, assignment, training and staff development, and providing and maintaining favorable working conditions for all members of the organization. The manager must have thorough knowledge of staff members. He or she must select employees with care and ensure that each subdivision in the organization has a competent

leader and that all employees are assigned to jobs in which they can be of greatest service. Personnel should possess energy, initiative, and loyalty. The duties of each position must be clearly outlined. All members of the organization must be encouraged to use their own initiative. They should be praised and rewarded fairly for their services, and informed (and perhaps reprimanded) if performance is not up to standards. Vested interests of individual employees must not be allowed to endanger the general interests of the majority. Work environment and conditions should be made as pleasant and as ideal as possible. Both physical and social factors should be provided for. Personnel who feel good about themselves and their work environment produce significant results.

Leading

Leading is a responsibility that falls to the manager as head of the organization. The manager must lead, positively motivate, and influence the individuals who make up the organization and therefore will affect the operations and conduct of the program. This means implementing and carrying out approved plans through work of employees and staff to achieve or exceed the organization's objectives. A good leader is influenced by the nature of organizational plans and structures as he or she elicits behavior that will support the achievement of the organization's objectives. A good leader maintains sound interpersonal relationships while developing systems and structures that motivate employees and satisfy their needs.

The ability to motivate is an integral part of leadership in order for the employee, organization, and manager to develop to their fullest potential. Motivation is associated with the "why" of human endeavor. Motivation in physical education and sport involves effort, persistence, and purposeful and goal-directed behavior as they relate to governing choices that affect achievement and productivity. Factors such as discipline, satisfaction, achievement, recognition, and advancement may all contribute to the enhancement of human potential.

Managerial effectiveness is determined by the ability to guide, assist, and direct others successfully toward established goals. Mangers who are good leaders receive high marks in determination, persistence, endurance, and courage. They clearly understand the organization's purposes and keep them in mind while guiding the way. Through leadership, managers maximize communication, cooperation, and shared decision-making to ensure the integrity and success of the management process.

Controlling

Controlling ensures the proper execution of plans and consists of several factors. Job standards or expectations should be set, and methods and procedures for measuring whether standards are met should be established. This should be done in light of the goals of the organization. When goals are not met, or in anticipation that they may not be met, corrective action should be taken. Controlling also means interrelating all the various phases of work within an organization; therefore the organization's

structure must clearly provide close relationships and competent leadership in the coordinating centers of activity. The manager should meet regularly with chief assistants to make arrangements for unity of effort to eliminate obstacles to coordinated work.

There should also be coordination with management units outside the organization when such responsibilities are necessary. Controlling means that subordinates must be kept informed through regular reports, research, monitoring, and evaluation concerning performance in relation to expected standards and outcomes. In this respect the manager is a point of intercommunication. In addition to accepting the responsibility for reporting to a higher authority, managers must continually know what is going on in the area under their jurisdiction. Members of the organization must be informed on many topics of general interest, such as goals to be achieved, progress being made, strong and weak points, and new areas proposed for development.

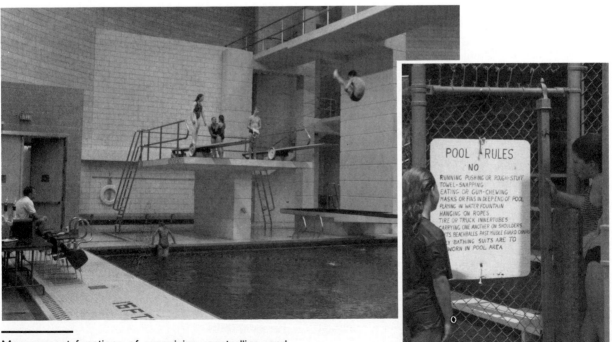

Management functions of organizing, controlling, and communication are crucial to physical education and sport activities.

OTHER MANAGEMENT FUNCTIONS

There are myriad other interrelated and associated managerial functions found throughout the literature. Those often mentioned include the following:

- *Decision Making:* the sequence of steps completed to select a course of action from two or more alternatives. This may include various interpretive phases by the management team.
- *Problem solving:* approaching a problem in a systematic way in order to enhance the probability of arriving at the proper decision.
- *Budgeting:* strategic planning to allocate resources required to support institutional objectives. The budget is most frequently associated with the control function.
- *Evaluating:* the process of measuring progress, comparing it with objectives, and taking needed corrective action.
- *Communicating:* the ability to articulate a clear and concise viewpoint or message to others. Effective communication leads to respect, trust, and increased performance outcome.
- *Reporting:* the ability to provide meaningful feedback, including analysis of data, in a clear and concise fashion in order to determine if organizational goals are being met.
- *Delegating:* the process by which authority is distributed by the manager downward in the organization. Delegating should be a form of positive motivation if planned and properly conducted.
- *Innovating:* the ability to introduce a new idea, technique, method, or purpose into the management process.
- *Coordinating:* the ability to interconnect the aims of the organization with the aspirations and needs of the participants.
- *Representing:* serving as the spokesperson, figurehead, or liaison for the organization or team to various outside organizations, groups, or individuals.
- *Creating:* the ability to originate, envisage, fashion, devise, or design a new system or strategy concerning the management process.
- *Motivating:* the process by which behavior is mobilized and sustained in the interest of achieving organizational objectives.

FUNCTIONAL, EFFECTIVE, AND EFFICIENT MANAGEMENT
Qualifications

The qualifications of physical education and sport managers are many and varied. Sound health and fitness for the job is requisite for any physical education or sport position. It is not uncommon, because of the stress of managerial positions, to find health (including burnout) to be a contributing factor to resignation. A thorough knowledge and understanding of the tasks, and associated risks, of the position are also keys to not only job qualification, but also job satisfaction. Clearly, possession and command of the managerial skills associated with the position and the willingness to accept responsibility are crucial qualifications at any managerial level, including teaching, coaching, or directing a sport program.

Other associated qualifications include, but are not limited to, the following:

Experience
  Teaching skill
  Previous and continued involvement in physical education and sport
  Coaching at various levels, or other managerial, practicum, or internship experience
  Community relations
Education
  College or university preparation and degree
  Communication skills, computer skills, as well as coursework related to the job position, including child development, legal issues, and human relations
  Certification (e.g., First Aid, CPR, WSI, Life Guard Training, Pool Operator's License, Teaching and Coaching License or Certification, or Adapted/Developmental Certification)
  Attendance at clinics, workshops, and job-related conventions, seminars, and conferences
Personal traits
  Honest, trustworthy, fair, cooperative, intelligent, creative, original, personable, dedicated, professional, ethical, and decisive, among others

Qualifications such as experience, teaching and communication skills, and personal integrity are requisite to good leaders.

Just as the qualifications and abilities of managers vary, so do the tasks and responsibilities. To complete managerial tasks successfully, certain skills are required, whether from a top, middle, or front-line manager. The three primary skill areas deemed crucial to effective and efficient management practice are technical, human (interpersonal), and conceptual.[5]

Skills and Levels
Technical Skills

Technical skills involve the ability to employ specialized knowledge and expertise with various equipment, procedures, methods, and techniques to perform the given task. The manager must understand the product (e.g., physical education, interscholastic ice hockey, or Special Olympics) or service that is being managed and the processes involved by which the product is created, packaged, marketed, and delivered. Front-line managers often rely heavily on technical skills to make certain the organization provides its services as effectively and efficiently as possible.

Human Skill

Human skill deals with the ability and judgment to work with and through people. Communication, attitude shaping, cooperative effort (team work), and motivation are key ingredients that a manager must master in order to achieve the organization's goals and objectives. Knowledge and understanding, sound judgment (predicting, diagnosing, and attributing), common sense, and ability to influence behavior (behavior modification and stress management) are just some of the skills especially critical to middle managers as they attempt to integrate the work of first-level employees and staff with the desires of top management.

Conceptual Skill

Conceptual skill implies the ability to see the "whole picture" of the organization and the environment in which the organization must function. It entails the ability to think in the abstract and analyze and understand the cause-and-effect relationship of the various interrelated organizational interests and interdependent functions. Conceptual skills are used to formulate and implement an organization's strategic plans and are most often associated with top-level management.

Leadership

Another often-mentioned management skill or trait is leadership. Leadership is the skill of influencing the activities of an individual or group in an effort to have them willingly strive for goal attainment in a given situation.

Knezevich[6] recognizes three kinds of leadership: (1) *symbolic leadership,* which is primarily a personality attribute; (2) *formal leadership,* which involves the use of a title, status, or position denoting a leadership role in a formal organization; and (3) *functional leadership,* or the role performed in an organized group. Knezevich points out that leadership is a social process that involves working with

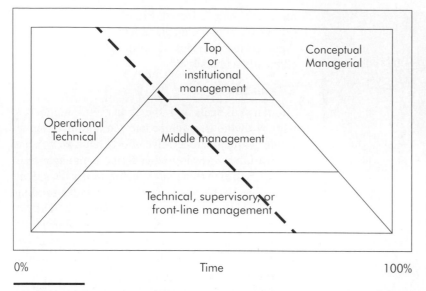

0%   Time   100%

FIGURE 1-2   Management skill schematic. A dual schematic reflecting managerial levels (top, middle, and front-line), the amount (in percentage) of managerial skill functioning (human skills held constant and crucial at each level), as well as the decrease in managerial positions as the educational, athletic, or corporate ladder is climbed.

people. Personality traits will not in themselves result in leadership. Furthermore, conferring a title does not necessarily induce leadership. Instead, the existing situation and the ability of the person to lead in that situation are critical. People usually function best under leadership that is dynamic, creative, and imaginative. Leadership cuts across all levels of management and is present in any situation in which someone is trying to influence the behavior of another.

The management domain is structured in a number of ways and consists of various interrelated systems, stages, and levels. The following is a dual schematic reflecting various managerial levels (top, middle, and front line), the amount of time in percentage (%-time) that a manager at a particular level might engage in human, technical, and conceptual skill functioning, as well as the apparent decreasing managerial opportunity as one climbs the management ladder (Figure 1-2).

Roles

The roles that managers play in physical education and sport organizations are varied and multidimen-

sional in nature. Mintzberg[7] offers ten distinct roles of an effective administrator, which have been adapted to the physical education and sporting process (Table 1-3).

Other Considerations

Regardless of where physical education and sport is delivered (e.g., schools, private clubs, community), the need for the development of a functional, effective, and efficient management scheme is required. This means developing an organizational structure that lends itself to delegating authority, resolving organizational conflict, making meaningful decisions, and forming sound policies and procedures for safe and efficient conduct of the programs set forth by the organization.

Delegating Authority

The effective manager delegates responsibilities and, with them, the authority to make the necessary decisions for carrying out such responsibilities.

Many managers are overwhelmed with their assigned duties. In many cases it is impossible for one person to discharge all of these duties. Therefore it

TABLE 1-3.   Ten physical education and sport managerial roles

Role	Description	Management activities of teachers, coaches, athletic directors, officials, sport managers, and administrators
Interpersonal roles		
Figurehead	Symbolic head; obliged to perform a number of routine duties of a legal or social nature	Ceremonies and banquets, fund-raising solicitations, alumni outings
Leader	Responsible for the motivation and activation of subordinates; responsible for staffing, training, and associated duties	Virtually all managerial activities involving subordinates
Liaison	Maintains self-developed network of outside contacts and informers who provide resources and information	Acknowledgment of correspondence; internal and external work; other activities involving external sources such as conferences, media, as well as local, state, regional, and international visitations
Informational roles		
Monitor	Seeks and receives wide variety of special information (much of it current) to develop a thorough understanding of other organizations and environments; emerges as nerve center of internal and external information of the organization	Handling all correspondence and contacts categorized as concerned primarily with receiving information (e.g., periodical news, conference newsletters, rule guidelines, legal matters)
Disseminator	Transmits information received from outsiders or from other subordinates to members of the organization; some information factual, some involving interpretation and integration of diverse value positions of organizational influencers and shapers	Forwarding correspondence into organization for informational purposes, verbal contacts involving information flow to subordinates (e.g., review sessions, instant communication, flow of facts)
Spokesperson	Transmits information to outsiders on organization's plans, policies, actions, results, etc.; serves as expert on organization's industry and posture	Staff meetings; handling correspondence and contacts involving transmission of information to external sources such as the community, and printed and electronic media
Decisional roles		
Entrepreneur	Searches organization and its environment for opportunities and initiates "improvement projects" to bring about change; supervises and designs certain projects	Strategy and review sessions involving initiation or design of improvement projects (e.g., facilities, media production)
Disturbance Handler	Responsible for corrective action when organization faces important, unexpected disturbances or problems	Strategy and review sessions involving disturbances and crises (e.g., eligibility lawsuits, harassment charges)
Resource Allocator	Responsible for the allocation of organizational resources of all kinds; in effect the making or approval of all significant organizational decisions	Scheduling; requests for authorization; any activity involving budgeting and the programming of subordinates' work
Negotiator	Responsible for representing the organization at major negotiations	Negotiation (e.g., facility rental, travel, media contracts)

Adapted from Mintzberg H, The nature of managerial work, New York, 1973, Harper & Row.

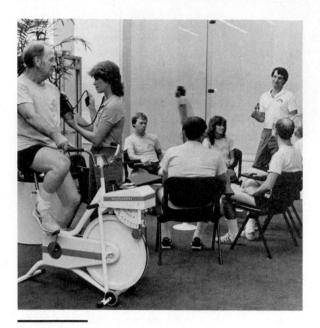

Tenneco Inc. fitness program.

is important to delegate responsibilities to qualified people who can perform effectively on behalf of the organization.

There should be a clear understanding between the manager and the people to whom the duties are being delegated. The latter must be willing to assume such responsibilities and must know exactly what their responsibilities are.

In physical education programs the director or chair of physical education often delegates to others responsibilities for the physical activity program, recreational sports, and curriculum development. The director of athletics frequently delegates authority to coaches, trainers, and equipment supervisors. The manager should recognize that in delegating responsibilities, he or she is still responsible for the conceptual and overall functioning of the unit, whether it is a school division, department, or program.

Resolving Organizational Conflicts

Wherever human beings and the variant of social change or "development" are involved, conflicts may develop. Conflicts may arise around such human needs as security, status, esteem, or self-actualization. When certain needs are not satisfied, conflict may arise. People have basic needs that can represent physical needs, such as the need for physical comfort; psychological needs, such as a feeling of belonging and recognition; or social needs, such as the desire to work with a certain group of people. Organizational conflict might occur when employees perceive a lack of consistent supervisory practice or fail to see how they "fit" into their assigned roles. Reward, recognition, status, job assignment input, and job task equity are often other trouble spots for managers. Conflict often results in poor performance, absence, frequent turnover, and organizational dissociation.

Organizational conflicts, as far as possible, should be solved swiftly and effectively by the manager. This means creating an environment in which employees want to work and can achieve self-esteem and self-actualization. It means providing opportunities for personal growth and opening channels of communication to improve both situational and employee relations. It means making work as interesting and challenging as possible to ensure positive and productive performance. It also means involving employees in decisions that affect their well-being, morale, and job effectiveness.

Organizational conflicts are kept to a minimum if the management is aware of human needs and tries to satisfy these needs in the best interest of all concerned. It is mandatory that the manager be a master of conflict resolution.

DECISION MAKING

Decision making in the management process requires that certain steps be followed to bring about meaningful action. This problem-solving approach usually includes recognizing a problem, defining the problem, gathering relevant data, analyzing the data, identifying a set of alternative solutions, and finally arriving at a decision. Management, however, must not stop at the point of arriving at a decision. Figure 1-3 presents a model of sequential phases that extend the problem-solving and deci-

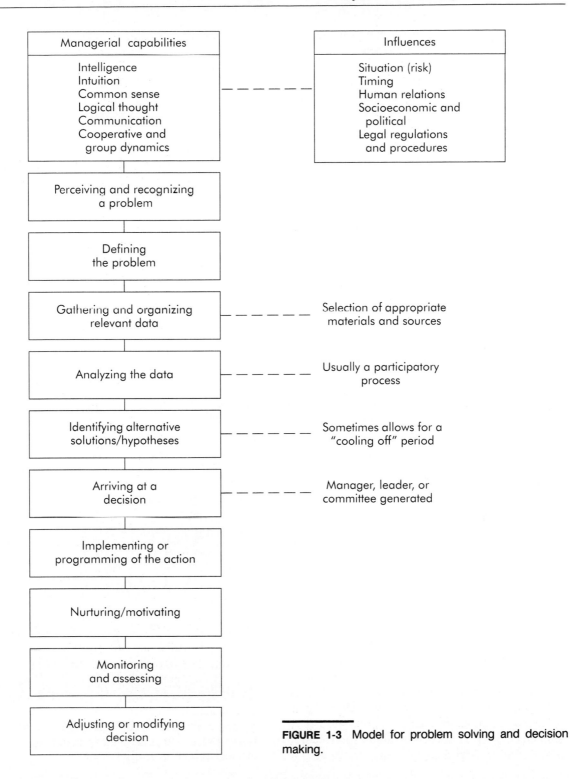

FIGURE 1-3 Model for problem solving and decision making.

sion-making processes to ensure effective and meaningful decisions are being implemented. The model includes the following phases:

Perceiving. The process of recognizing that a problem exists is the starting point of successful decision making.

Defining. Defining the problem is sometimes not an easy task. Conflicting facts requiring skillful interpretation, as well as personal reluctance to address a delicate problem, often arise. Managers need an understanding of norms, standards, and ethics that govern the selection and definition of problems.

Gathering relevant data. This may be accomplished by observation, interviewing, production of special reports by task forces or committees, and distributing questionnaires, personnel evaluations, or other appropriate sources. Information close to the source is desirable even though such sources may contain bias.

Analysis of data. After the significant and relevant information is gathered, the data is evaluated using either an objective or a qualitative approach. Decisions that are made for appearance or for the enhancement of the management record rather than for inherent validity or logic should be avoided.

Identifying alternative solutions. A set of solutions should be studied, if possible, before arriving at the final decision. This is necessary because of the ramifications that the decision itself may generate. This process should allow for creativity, brainstorming, and group participation, especially when developing new projects, programs, and proposals. This synergistic approach may yield a large number of creative solutions to complex decision situations.

The decision. Decisions are often affected by the environment, personalities of decision makers, timing, and communication, as well as by those who will be affected by the decision. Decisions are sometimes made by the manager alone; however, often times ad hoc, advisory, or standing committees play a significant role. Participation and due process should always be part of sound decision making. Often times "satisficing" occurs when a manager selects a good, but not optimal or perfect, solution because of circumstances such as time constraints or innaccuracy of information. Satisficing is related to the need for

sub-optimization, which occurs because organizational objectives cannot be pursued independently since they are interdependent and often in conflict.[8]

Implementation. After the decision is made, resources in the form of planning, budget, equipment, personnel, etc. should be mobilized to support the decision.

Motivation. As the program or position is set into operation, continued motivational support (i.e., funds, reward structures, increased commitment) should be visible. This nurturing and continued interest and support will assist in the development of proper organizational attitude and add to the productivity of the program or individual.

Monitoring and assessment. This dimension of the problem-solving process may be established over a prescribed time period (e.g., monthly or quarterly) and is an attempt to determine whether the decision was effective. This input in the form of monthly or

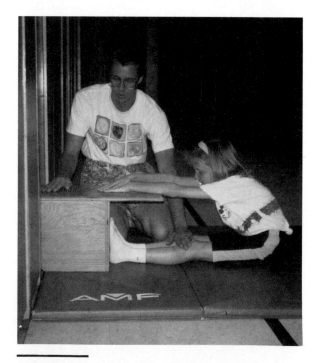

Sit and reach assessment, part of the Physical Best Health-Related Physical Fitness test. Crest View Elementary School, Brooklyn Park, Mn.

quarterly reports will serve as a primary source of data to determine if "the decision" might be adjusted, modified, or allocated more resources to continue to be productive.

Managerial decisions are rarely as rational and calculated as managers like to believe. Most decisions are a result of "bounded rationality" because of the myriad influences that pervade the decision-making process (e.g., conflicting goals, ill-defined problems, missing facts, laws, regulations, contracts). Managers become effective decision makers through exercise (trial and error), and sometimes less than desirable results will occur. The manager must accept the reality and learn from past omissions or errors, yet not become too cautious, since this might lead to lost opportunities for both the organization and the decision maker.

Tips for Decision Makers

1. Prudent planning should minimize the number of decisions with which the manager must contend.
2. Insist that subordinates (e.g., division heads of physical education, coaches, aquatics directors) assume responsibility for their programs and line staff.
3. Assess the impact of organizational politics, biases, and attitudes when others are invited into the decision-making process.
4. View problems as opportunities to demonstrate problem solving and decision making prowess.
5. Seek out the best alternatives rather than the most convenient. Be creative when generating alternative solutions and do not critically analyze while the generation process is underway.
6. Decision making involves risk, and a manager who never makes a wrong decision is often short-changing the organization, as well as the decision maker.

Forming Sound Policies

The efficient management of a physical education or athletic department requires the establishment of sound policies if it is to achieve its goals. Policies are essential to the efficient and effective management of any department, school program, business, or other organization. Without policies, there is little to

guide the activities and conduct of the organization in the pursuit of its goals. With well-reasoned policies the organization can function efficiently and effectively, and its members will better understand what is expected of them. Policymaking is decision making that restricts managers' discretion and provides limits within which acceptable decisions and behavior must fall.

Policies are guides to action that reflect procedures which, when adhered to, fulfill the best interests of the organization and the purposes for which it exists. If properly selected and developed, policies enable each member of the organization to know what duties are to be performed, the type of behavior that will result in the greatest productivity for the establishment, the best way the departmental goals can be accomplished, and the procedure by which accountability can be established and evaluated.

Management policies are statements of procedures that represent the legalistic framework under which the organization operates. As such, they are not frequently changed and possess some sense of permanence. Therefore they are not developed on short notice or hastily drafted without the input of the management team and those charged with organizational compliance.

Although policies are considered and formulated carefully, they should be reviewed periodically in light of any new developments that occur. For example, at present some high schools are involved with open enrollment. This new freedom for students makes some existing policies concerning athlete participation outdated and obsolete. Therefore, policy review and change are needed.

How policy is developed. Policy emanates as a result of many phenomena. For example, the Constitution of the United States sets forth various conditions that affect policy development in organizations throughout the country. Educators, for example, must comply with such conditions as equal rights for all in the public schools, separation of church and state, various conditions inherent in the democratic process, and those included in such legislation as Title IX and Public Law 94-142.

Because education is a state responsibility, the state government also issues policies that must be adhered to by local education authorities. These policies include such items as the number of days schools must be in session, certification qualifications, core subject requirements, and salary schedules for teachers and coaches. Within the framework of these policies or guidelines established by federal and state agencies, however, local education authorities, such as school boards, are permitted freedom to develop their own policies. Thus they establish policies pertaining to students' driving to school, attendance, chemical abuse, physical education requirements, student-athlete eligibility, and many other crucial factors. Sometimes local policies conflict with state policies, in which case the local policies are declared invalid.

Policy is developed in many ways in physical education and athletic departments. In some organizations it is done autocratically, with a manager establishing policy unilaterally. The process is devoid of deliberations and creative input from the members of the organization. The trend now, however, is toward greater involvement of staff members in developing policy.

As a general rule, the expression "many heads are better than one" is true of policy development. Policies must be carefully researched and thought through before they are drafted and presented to authorities. Therefore it is usually better to involve people who look at problems affecting policies from many different angles. Although staff members may participate in policy development, it should be recognized that the formulation and development of policy is different from the execution of the policy. Execution of policy is usually a management responsibility and should be recognized as such.

Writing policies. Before a policy is written, much research must be done to determine what goes into the substance of that policy. This can be accomplished in several ways. One method is for the director of physical education or athletics to appoint a committee to research or strategically plan and to recommend policy to the management. When the committee has been formed to recommend policy, the members will want to gather and investigate the facts thoroughly. They may decide to research the status of policies regarding this problem; what other similar organizations are doing; what policies already exist; the stand taken by selected national professional and athletic associations; views of other managers; the position of the American Civil Liberties Union, teachers' unions, and school board lawyers; and other specialized sources of information. After gathering the data, the committee will want to consider carefully and then make a recommendation. If the recommendation is approved, the director of physical education or athletics may then recommend it to his or her superior for approval, who in turn may recommend it to the school board, regents, or other responsible group for the final approval as the policy governing the organization.

The policy that finally emanates from the committee should be written clearly and concisely. There should be no ambiguities or possibilities for misinterpretation of what is intended by the policy statement. The statement of policy formulated by the committee should be reviewed carefully by the staff members, management, and compliance experts to further determine that the statement clearly says what the organization's position is on this particular issue.

When policy is needed. Only the most important items facing the department or organization should have policy statements. Policies on trivial matters should not be carried on the books, because confusion and failure to adhere to many of the policies can result when they are not known or understood. Furthermore, if there are too many policies, the important ones may be obscured by the proliferation of those less important. It is usually better to have only a few carefully researched policies that cover major management functions. The other matters, if they need attention, can be covered by rules and regulations or in some other manner.

PHILOSOPHICAL AND THEORETICAL DIMENSIONS OF MANAGEMENT

One of the fundamental components of management, and one that is often neglected, is the establishment of a sound philosophy concerning physical education and sport. Philosophy is the process of critical examination, reasoning, and insight undertaken in an effort to arrive at truth and reality. It promotes the development and clarification of beliefs and values that serve as a foundation for the behavior and, ultimately, the performance outcome of the management team and organization.

Critical to the multidimensional management process are philosophical and theoretical questions that might be raised by a master manager. These might include the following:

- Does the present management process positively affect the manager and others involved?
- Does the process include meaningful integration and interaction between the individuals involved and the environment?
- Are management actions based on accomplishing the most good for the majority of those involved?
- Do management's actions positively contribute to the improvement of the quality of life of humankind and society?
- Does management strive for "inclusion" and fair and equitable opportunity, or "exclusion"?

Of course these questions and the management process are strongly tempered by contemporary philosophical and theoretical constructs, values, politics, economics, nationalism, education, religion, ecology, and numerous other sociocultural forces that play a significant role in shaping the management process.

Management has traditionally been divided along a bipolar authoritarian–democratic continuum (Figure 1-4). Managers, for the most part, acquired their management style or orientation from prior experience, former mentors, schooling or formal training, and/or environmental or situational circumstance. Traditional management evolved from its initial stages of classical and scientific management where the employee was technically trained and required to improve task and outcome performance to the behavioral or "human relations" phase. This behavioral approach focuses on staff feelings, attitudes, and needs, and on a more integrative approach where philosophical and theoretical constructs forge a new multileveled and "eclectic" approach.

Traditional theories of philosophical and theoretical managerial orientation include authoritarian, democratic, and laissez-faire. From these, as well as the more recent systems and eclectic approaches, future managers can adopt, develop, and refine their own personalized management orientation or style.

Authoritarian

The authoritarian orientation implies one-person leadership with decision making imposed on group members by the manager. An example of this theory is the chairperson of a physical education department who seldom holds a staff meeting. Instead, directives are issued from the office dictating the policy and procedures that each staff member is expected to follow. Authority seems to reside in the position as the head of the administrative unit. As a result, staff members frequently hesitate to disagree, and their creativity is often stifled.

Democratic

The democratic or egalitarian philosophy implies a manager who submits important matters to group discussion and involves group members in both the input and output (decision-making) process.

An example of this orientation is the secondary school athletic director who holds regular staff meetings in which items that affect the sport programs and student-athletes are discussed. Each member of the staff is respected as a person, as well as for his or her expertise, creative suggestions, and ideas. The staff helps in formulating goals and procedures that influence the operation of the sport program. The athletic director realizes that for the organization to achieve its goals, the staff must cooperate and feel like an integral part of the organization.

Laissez-faire

The laissez-faire orientation is thought of as an extension of the democratic approach in which little guidance is provided, and decision making is frequently left to group members.

An example of this is the physical education chairperson who does not provide active leadership. He or she believes that problems will solve themselves if given time. This individual frequently

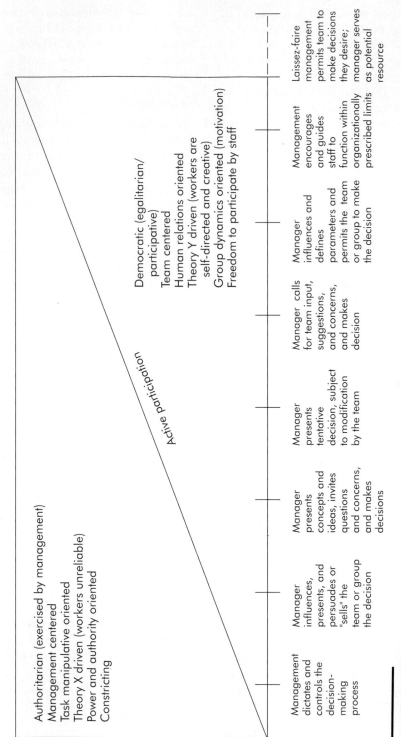

FIGURE 1-4 Management, philosophical and theoretical orientation continuum.

spends much time in activities that are personal in nature or do not have significant importance in the management of the organization. To a great degree staff members function on their own because of the absence of leadership in the organization. This fragmentation often leads to low morale and ineffectiveness.

Systems

The systems theory of management has stemmed from the rapid growth of technology and management in recent years. By borrowing techniques from the business world, managers have constructed models that bring together the many facets of an organization. The systems theory is defined as a method designed to collect data on interrelated and interacting components that, when working in an integrated manner, help accomplish a predetermined goal or goals. The application of this strategy is called a systems theory of management.

Eclectic

The eclectic approach might be considered the offspring of management's traditional philosophical and theoretical constructs and systems theory. In this regard, the eclectic approach is adaptable, fluid, and situational in nature and might build on any number of the best and most appropriate management orientations (i.e., a mixture of democratic and laissez-faire). The manager must therefore be aware of the spectrum of contemporary management orientations in order to ensure that the eclectic approach functions at full effectiveness. This spectrum might range from Ouchi's Theory Z (knowledge and understanding of international management philosophy and theory) to Management Science (the quantitative orientation focusing on mathematical and network modeling, as well as computer and information systems) to support management's decisions. Knowledge, understanding, and appreciation of the systems approach, in which the organization is viewed as an interrelated set of subsystems working synergistically, as well as contingency theory, which suggests that organizational behavior cannot always be generalized or extrapolated from the "apparent" situation, should also be an integral part of

the manager's philosophical and theoretical repertoire.

A PHILOSOPHY OF MANAGEMENT FOR PHYSICAL EDUCATION AND SPORT

Humankind and the environment in which we live represent the most important considerations in the world. The real worth of a field of endeavor, organization, or idea is found in what it does for people. The most important and worthwhile thing that can be said about a particular vocation, organization, or movement is that it contributes to the betterment of humankind.

Individuals possess goals that represent a variety of human objectives. They include the need for health and security for oneself and one's family, the desire to obtain an education and to be employed in a worthwhile, meaningful, and gainful occupation, and the right to engage in a free society and to enjoy leisure pursuit.

People do not miraculously work together. They do not spontaneously band together and strive to accomplish common objectives. Because many groups and individuals possess common goals, however, through associated effort they help each other achieve goals that would be impossible for them to accomplish alone. No one person, for example, can establish a school for his or her children's education, but through cooperative effort and support many people join together to make education possible. Thus individuals possess similar goals that they will strive together to attain.

Organizations, to function effectively, need machinery to help them run efficiently, to organize and execute their affairs, and to keep them operating smoothly, so that the goals for which they have been created will be achieved. This machinery is management—the framework of organizations and the part that helps organizations implement the purposes for which they have been established.

Management, therefore, exists to help individuals achieve the goals they have set to live happy, productive, healthful, and meaningful lives. It is not an end in itself; rather, it is a means to an end—the welfare of the people for whom the organization exists.

Effective management leads to positive outcomes.

Management exists for people, not people for management. Management can justify itself only as it serves the individuals who make up the organization, helping them to achieve the goals they possess as human beings and members of society.

SUMMARY

Management is the process by which key personnel provide leadership so that an organization functions efficiently and effectively in achieving the goals for which the organization exists. It involves such functions as planning, organizing, staffing, leading and motivating, and controlling. Problem solving and decision making are also important facets of the management process. A philosophy of management for physical education and sport should recognize that the needs and welfare of the human beings who make up the organization are paramount to success.

The contemporary manager also needs special qualifications, as well as skills (technical, human, and conceptual) that take into account various philosophical and theoretical underpinnings of management. These skills, combined with the appropriate measure of knowledge, experience, and training, will prepare the contemporary manager to achieve success and satisfaction.

◆ SELF-ASSESSMENT ACTIVITIES

These activities will assist students in determining if material and competencies presented in this chapter have been mastered.

1. Take a sheet of paper and divide it into two halves as indicated here. On the left half, list the skills and functions of a manager, and on the right side, list specific preparation you would undertake to acquire these skills.

Skills and Functions of a Manager	Preparation for Skill Acquisition

2. Assume you are a manager who believes in participatory management. Describe how you would implement this orientation as the manager of a program of physical education.
3. Discuss your philosophy of management.
4. You are superintendent of schools of a large school system interviewing applicants for the position of director of athletics. What qualifications would you look for among those who apply for the position?
5. List what you consider to be the major roles performed by a manager of a physical education and sport program.
6. You aspire to be the manager of a community fitness center. Briefly describe the steps in the decision-making process that you would employ to solve a major conflict.
7. A classmate indicates that a study of management will not be of any use as a physical educator. Prepare a rebuttal to your classmate's statement.

REFERENCES

1. American Association of School Administrators: *Staff relations in school administration,* Washington, DC, 1955.
2. Drucker PF: *Management in turbulent times,* New York, 1980, Harper & Row.
3. DuBrin AJ, Ireland RD, Williams JC: *Management and organization,* Cincinnati, 1989, Southwestern.
4. Hersey P, Blanchard KII: *Management of organizational behavior: utilizing human resources,* Englewood Cliffs, NJ, 1982, Prentice-Hall.
5. Katz RL: Skills of an effective administrator, *Harvard Business Review* 90-102, Sept-Oct 1974.
6. Knezevich SJ: *Administration of public education,* New York, 1981, Harper & Row.
7. Mintzberg H: *The nature of managerial work,* New York, 1973, Harper & Row.
8. Simon HA: Theories of decision making in economics and behavioral science, *The American Economic Review,* 49:253-283, June 1959.

SUGGESTED READINGS

- Blanchard K, Johnson S: *The one minute manager,* New York, 1982, William Morrow.
  Presents a compilation of findings and management implications from medicine and behavioral science.
- Brassie PS: Guidelines for programs preparing undergraduate and graduate students for careers in sport management, *Journal of Sport Management* 3(2):158-164, 1989.
  Discusses programmatic training and experiences necessary to become an effective manager of human resources as they pertain to physical education and sport.
- Douglas J, Klein S, Hunt D: *The strategic management of human resources,* New York, 1985, John Wiley and Sons.
  Presents a thorough overview of the converging forces that play a significant role in the management process. Motivation and other psychological concerns are well represented.
- Kraus RG, Curtis JE: *Creative management in recreation and parks,* St Louis, 1986, Mosby–Year Book.
- Scott B, Soderberg S: *The art of managing,* Hampshire, England, 1985, Wildwood House.
  Reviews the essentials of job management and suggests a balanced approach to the art of management. Offers interesting case examples.
- Sergiovanni TJ: *Handbook for effective department leadership,* Boston, 1984, Allyn & Bacon.
  Discusses resources and views of such theorists as Peter Drucker, Abraham Maslow, and Max Weber as applied to leadership at the department level.

CHAPTER 2

Management Organization to Achieve Objectives of Physical Education and Sport

---

▶ **Instructional Objectives and Competencies To Be Achieved**

After reading this chapter the student should be able to

- Discuss how and why management organization is important to the effectiveness of physical education and sport programs.
- Identify the objectives of physical education and sport for which the organization and structure exist.
- Outline the principles that should be followed in establishing an effective organization for physical education and sport programs.
- Describe a formal and an informal type of organization and structure and provide rationale for each.

- Outline the factors that need to be considered to develop a functional organization.
- Describe the organization and structure of physical education and sport programs that exist in elementary and secondary schools, colleges and universities, and other representative organizations responsible for the delivery of physical education and sport.
- Prepare a management organization chart for a physical education and sport program.

The first chapter was concerned with the nature and scope of the management process. Such things as managerial functions, skills, roles, qualifications, and philosophy were presented. This chapter discusses the objectives of physical education and sport, and the management organization and structure needed to accomplish these goals.

Schools, colleges, and other organizations do not function efficiently without some element that holds

them together and gives them direction so that they can achieve the goals for which they exist. This element is management. Management is the glue that bonds the various units and provides the control, communication, motivation, and leadership needed to achieve success. To accomplish these functions, a structure is needed that provides an efficient and effective way of operating and carrying out the various duties and responsibilities existing within the organization. The structure illustrates the roles various members of the organization play in achieving established goals. The structure indicates to whom each member reports and who is responsible for carrying out duties. It presents a blueprint or plan of action for getting the job done.

The primary purpose of structure in physical education and sport is to make it possible to achieve goals and objectives. Unless the organization and structure perform this function as efficiently and effectively as possible, it is headed for failure and should be abandoned. The structure is a means to an end, not an end in itself. Because this is true, it follows that the goals or objectives of physical education and sport must be clear in the mind of management before the establishment of the organizational structure takes place. Therefore the first task is to clarify the objectives that are being sought for physical education and sport.

PHYSICAL EDUCATION OBJECTIVES TO BE ACHIEVED

The objectives of physical education discussed here pertain, in general, to all educational levels—elementary, junior high or middle school, secondary, and college—although there could be further delineation of goals for each level. In addition, they also relate to most other agency and institutional programs.

A study of humankind reveals four general directions or phases in which growth and development take place: physical development, neuromuscular development, cognitive development, and social-emotional-affective development. Physical education can significantly contribute to each of these phases.

Physical Development Objective

The physical development objective[2] deals with the program of activities that builds power in an individual through the development of the various organic systems of the body. It results in the ability to sustain adaptive effort, to recover, and to resist fatigue. The value of this objective is based on the fact that an individual will be more active, perform better,

and be healthier if the organic systems of the body are adequately developed and functioning properly. It is sometimes called the physical fitness objective.

Muscular activity plays a major role in the development of the organic systems of the body, including the digestive, circulatory, excretory, heat regulatory, respiratory, and other body systems. Participating in activities such as hanging, climbing, running, throwing, leaping, striking, carrying, kicking, and lifting helps these systems function more efficiently. Health is also related to muscular activity.

Vigorous muscular activity also produces several other beneficial results. Krotee and Hatfield[4] point

Weight training and conditioning, Lyons Township High School, LaGrange, IL.

out that the various aspects of health-related fitness—cardiovascular and cardiorespiratory endurance, body composition, muscular strength, endurance and power, and flexibility and relaxation—represent basic elements essential to proper functioning. Research supports the fact that these components, when developed, can serve to improve quality of life. The trained heart provides better nourishment to the entire body. It beats more slowly and pumps more blood per stroke, delivering more food to the cells and more efficiently removing waste products. During exercise the trained heart's speed increases more slowly and has a longer rest period between beats, and after exercise it returns to normal much more rapidly. The end result of this state is that the trained individual can perform work for a longer period of time, expend less energy, and operate more efficiently than the untrained individual. Whether for participating in physical education class, performing routine tasks, or responding to emergencies, this trained condition serves to facilitate a vigorous and active quality of life. Therefore physical education should aid in the development of the trained individual so that he or she will be able to live a healthful, happy, and productive life.

Neuromuscular Development Objective

The neuromuscular development objective[8] is concerned with developing body awareness, making purposeful physical movement with as little expenditure of energy as possible, and being proficient, graceful, and aesthetic in this movement. This has implications for work, play, and other activities that require physical movement.

Effective motor behavior results in aesthetic qualities of movement and in the development of a movement sense, which in essence is the development of motor skill together with appropriate knowledge and understanding about the skill and a positive attitude toward its development and use. In other words, proper control of movement during life's patterns and routines takes place in the movement-educated person.

Effective movement depends on a harmonious working relationship of the muscular and nervous systems. It results in greater distance between fatigue and peak performance; it is found in activities involving running, hanging, jumping, dodging, leaping, kicking, striking, bending, twisting, carrying, and throwing; and it will enable one to perform daily work efficiently without reaching the point of exhaustion so quickly.

In physical education activities the function of efficient body movement, or *neuromuscular skill* as it is often called, is to provide the individual with the ability to perform with a degree of proficiency, which results in greater enjoyment of participation. Most individuals enjoy doing those particular things in which they have acquired some degree of mastery or skill. For example, if a person has mastered the ability to throw a ball consistently at a designated target and has developed batting and fielding prowess, he or she will be likely to choose to play baseball or softball. If the person can kick and trap a ball with some degree of effectiveness, then soccer might provide the challenge. Few individuals enjoy participating in activities in which they have little skill. Therefore it is the objective of physical education to develop in all individuals as many physical skills as possible so that the participants' interests will be wide and varied. This will not only result in more enjoyment for the participant, but at the same time will allow for better adjustment to the group situation. Other values of neuromuscular skill are that it reduces expenditure of energy, contributes to confidence, promotes affiliation and recognition, enhances physical and mental health, makes participation safer, and contributes to the aesthetic sense.

The neuromuscular objective also has implications for the health and recreational outcomes of the program. The skills that are acquired during physical education will help to determine how leisure time will be spent. If a person excels in swimming, much leisure time may be spent in a pool or lake, or pursuing another aquatic endeavor. If the person is successful in racquet sports, he or she may be found frequently on the courts. Physical educators should develop in all individuals an understanding and appreciation of human movement as well as each individual's unique movement potential.

When considering the value to young people who are in school of having fundamental skills that will

Golf instruction provides insight into neuromuscular control.

afford them maximal satisfaction and happiness throughout life, it is important to consider the balance that should exist in any physical education program between team, dual, individual, and lifetime sports. Team sports such as football, basketball, soccer, volleyball, and softball perform a great service by providing an opportunity for students to develop physical prowess and enjoy exhilarating competition. However, in many school physical education programs team sports dominate the curriculum at the expense of individual and dual sports, such as tennis, badminton, swimming, weight training, and golf, not to mention dance. In such cases, students are being deprived of the opportunity to develop skills in activities in which they can participate throughout their life span. It has been estimated that only 1 out of every 1000 students who play football, for example, ever play the game again after they leave school, whereas many students will swim, jog, dance, and play tennis, racquetball, or golf well into their older years. Only through a well-balanced program of exercise and team, dual, individual, and life-

time sports will it be possible to develop a well-rounded individual.

Physical educators can and should be proud of the contribution they make to humankind. It is within their power to help many individuals learn physical skills and thus help them to lead healthier, happier, and more meaningful and productive lives. The world is a better place in which to live as a result of the work of competent and committed physical educators because the development of neuromuscular skill has significant value.

Cognitive Development Objective

The cognitive development objective[1] involves the accumulation of knowledge and the ability to think and interpret this knowledge.

Physical education possesses a subject matter that is concerned with human movement. Physical education's body of knowledge has its roots in the sciences, humanities, and other sources that interpret the nature of human movement and the impact of movement on the growth and development of the individual and on his or her culture. Scientific principles regarding movement, including those that relate to such factors as time, space, flow, and how humankind interfaces with machines, should be considered. This subject matter should be part of the education of each individual who comes in contact with a physical education program.

Physical activities must be learned; hence thinking on the part of the intellectual mechanism is needed. The coordinations involved in various movements must be mastered and adapted to the environment in which the individual lives, whether it be walking, running, driving an automobile, or stroking a forehand in tennis. These movements require the participant to think and coordinate the muscular and nervous systems. Furthermore, this type of knowledge is acquired through trial and error, practice and affordance, and opportunity and then, as a result of this experience, meaning and sophistication in the movement situation (for example, pattern, performance outcome) changes.

The individual should not only learn coordination, but should also acquire a knowledge of rules, techniques, and strategies involved in physical activities.

Using basketball as an example, the participant should know the rules; the strategies for offense and defense; the tactics involved in the transition game; the various types of passes; the difference between screening, blocking, and blocking out; and finally, the values that may be derived from participation. Techniques learned through experience result in knowledge that should also be acquired. A ball travels faster and more accurately if one steps while making the pass, and time is saved when the pass or shot is made from the same position in which it was received. Furthermore, a knowledge of followership, leadership, courage, cooperation, self-reliance, assistance to others, interdependence, safety, and adaptation to group patterns should be transmitted in each class meeting.

Knowledge concerning health should also play an important part in the program. All individuals should know about their bodies, the importance of cleanliness, factors in disease prevention, the merits of exercise, the necessity of a well-balanced and nutritious diet, the importance of adequate rest, values of sound health attitudes and habits, and facts concerning substance abuse and which community and school agencies provide health service and counsel. With the accumulation of knowledge of these and other relevant facts, participation in physical education activities acquires a new meaning, and health practices are associated with definite purposes.

Physical educators can and should intellectualize their activities more. Physical activities are not performed in a vacuum. Physical educators should continually provide appropriate knowledge and information for participants and encourage them to ask "Why?" *Why* is it important to participate in this activity? *Why* should an hour be devoted to physical education each day? *Why* is exercise important? *Why* is it important to play by the rules? Physical educators should also provide participants more opportunities to think; that is, allow them to make choices, plan strategies, and select appropriate activities instead of usurping all of this responsibility themselves. *The more thinking that takes place on the part of the participant, the more educating the activity becomes.*

Social-Emotional-Affective Development Objective

The social-emotional-affective development objective[3] is concerned with assisting an individual in making personal and group adjustments, as well as adjustments as a member of society. Physical education activities can offer valuable opportunities for making these adjustments if proper management is provided.

Physical educators should find as many ways as possible to positively influence human behavior. The rules of the game often reflect the standard of the democratic way of life. In games, one sees democracy in action and an individual is evaluated on the basis of ability and performance. Ethnicity, economic status, cultural background, race, gender, or

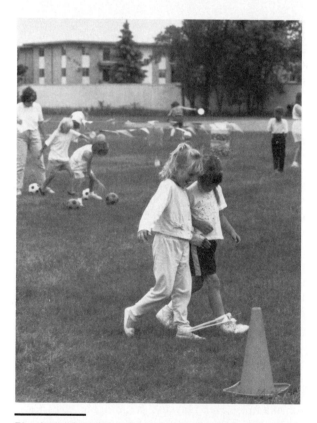

Physical education contributes to social-emotional-affective development; Crest View Elementary School, Brooklyn Park, Mn.

other characteristics should not play a role. Performance and participation are the criteria of success.

Another aspect of the social objective of physical education that is being recognized is the need for each individual to develop an approapriate self-concept. Participants need to develop wholesome attitudes toward themselves as maturing persons. During the various stages of physical growth and development that young people experience, they are often accepted or rejected by classmates because of physical characteristics and/or physical prowess. It is therefore important for individuals to develop themselves physically, not only for reasons of their own self-awareness, but also because of the implications that their physique and physical skills have for their psychosocial image.

Each individual has certain basic social needs that must be met. These include a feeling of belonging (affiliation), recognition, self-respect, and love. When these needs are met, the individual becomes well adjusted socially. When they are not met, antisocial characteristics and negative behavior may develop. For example, the aggressive bully may be seeking self-respect, the gang member may be seeking affiliation, and the substance abuser may be seeking recognition. The "needs" theory has implications for the manner in which physical education programs are conducted. The desire to win, for example, should be subordinated to meeting the needs of the participants. Students today "need" more support, more success, and more positive experiences than at any time in history. Physical education *must* contribute its fair share.

All human beings should experience success. This factor can be realized through physical education. Through successful encounters in physical activities, people develop a positive self-concept and satisfaction in their achievements. Physical education can provide for this successful experience by offering a variety of challenges and invigorating activities, as well as developing the skills necessary for successful participation in these activities.

In a democratic society all individuals must develop a sense of cooperative consciousness. This should be one of the most important objectives of the program. Therefore in various activities the following factors should be stressed: assistance for the less skilled participant, respect for the rights of others, subordination of one's desires to the will of the group, and realization of cooperative living as essential to the success of society. Individuals should be made to feel that they belong to the group and have the responsibility of directing and contributing their actions in the group's behalf. The rules of sportsmanship, followership, and leadership should be developed and practiced in all activities offered in the program. Qualities such as courtesy, sympathy, fairness, ethical behavior, honesty, respect for authority, and abiding by the rules will help considerably in the promotion of social efficiency.

Another factor that should not be overlooked is the "plus factor" of affective development. Physical educators cannot be content once they have developed the physical body, mapped the skills in the nervous system, and developed the amenities of social behavior. Something else still remains—affective development—and this represents one of the greatest challenges to the field in which so many young people have a drive to engage.

Affective development is involved with attitudes, appreciations, values, and beliefs. Therefore physical education should be concerned with such things as helping individuals to develop a healthy response to physical activity and to recognize the contribution that physical education can make to health, performance, and to the worthy pursuit of leisure. The individual should develop a positive attitude toward physical education, respect for others, self-discipline, and a wholesome attitude toward cooperative group work and play.

Members of the physical education profession should be concerned with helping young people to set goals and to clarify and think through their value judgments, appreciations, and attitudes. Although physical educators should not indoctrinate students with their own value systems, they should recognize their position as role models, and realize much can be done to motivate and facilitate boys and girls, and young men and women, to formulate, analyze, and reevaluate their own values and attitudes.

THE OBJECTIVES OF SPORT

Although the theoretical relationship between physical education and sport in the educational setting becomes increasingly complex as we move through the Physical Activity and Sport Continuum, each maintains many of the same general objectives already presented. At the same time, sport has additional goals that relate directly to the achievement of a high degree of skill and competitive success. In certain situations some physical educators feel that the goals of sport programs are not compatible with the goals of physical education. Furthermore, the goals of highly competitive sport differ in various respects for each educational level and each institutionalized sport program.

Sport in the Elementary School

The sports program in the elementary school should stress what is good for the child and provide opportunities for a variety of positive experiences. All sports activities should be geared to the developmental level of each child and not just to his or her weight, grade level, or chronological age. Children at this stage vary greatly in physical and psychosocial development; therefore an informal program and policies that recognize individual differences should be initiated.

The sports program should provide a wide variety of developmental (physical, motor, and psychosocial) experiences and should focus on lower organizational games and large muscle activity (e.g., running and jumping). Sports offerings that are selected should be broad based and diverse, and opportunity for all to participate should be encouraged. There should not be undue concentration on developing skill in just a few sports or sport-specific positions; nor should children be pressured into conforming to adult standards in a rigid, authoritarian, highly organized, and highly competitive sport program. Contact sports, particularly tackle football, are considered by many experts to be injurious for children of this age. Indeed, many football programs have been phased out of elementary school environs and picked up by myriad community-based organizations.

Sports activities—including playdays, clubs, and field trips—should be part of an overall well-organized and integrated school and community education program. Competent personnel, medical supervision, and safety procedures should be emphasized.

Sport in the Junior High or Middle School

The junior high or middle school sports program should be adapted to the needs of boys and girls in grades 6, 7, 8, and 9. This is a period of transition from elementary to senior high school and from childhood to adolescence. It is a time when students are trying to understand their bodies, gain independence, achieve social status, acquire self-confidence, and establish a system of values. It is a time when a sport program is needed to challenge the abilities and broadening interests of the student.

Interscholastic sport of a varsity type, if offered, should be provided only after the prerequisites of sound physical education (including adapted) and recreational sport programs have been developed and implemented. Selected varsity sports should be permitted only if special controls in regard to such items as qualified management (coaches and officials), medical supervision, health status, safety, facilities, game adaptations, and classification of play-

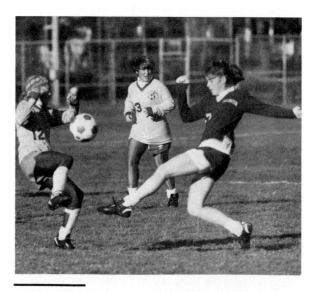

High school soccer; Lexington High School, Lexington, MA.

ers are assured. Some worthy goals at this level are to build team spirit, nurture the competitive drive, teach self-discipline and self-control, and develop pride in accomplishment and hard work. There should be room for everyone on the team, and playing time should be planned for maximal participation. The governance of the sports programs should also lie within the same educational structure as that of physical education.

Sport in the Senior High School

Representative goals of sport at the senior high school level are usually articulated by each school district. Common goals often espoused by high school officials include promoting physical excellence; engendering an appreciation of competition and the will to win, instilling morale, honesty, fair play, and self-discipline; achieving goals such as self-assurance, group loyalty, and responsibility; providing a wholesome channel for expression of emotions; integrating various aspects of the self (social, emotional, physical, and intellectual) into action; and developing qualities of good citizenship and other valuable personal qualities such as leadership ability. Other goals include providing an outlet for the release of personal energies in constructive ways, the use of sports as a unifying force for school and community, and the provision for activities that will help students live a balanced life.

Sport in College, University, and Associated Programs

The objectives of highly organized and competitive sports programs in many colleges, universities, and associated programs include developing excellence in sports competition; providing a program that is financially self-sufficient; establishing a leadership position in sports among other colleges and universities; satisfying needs of the spectators, athletes, community, and coaches; and providing sports programs for the gifted student-athlete. In some colleges (Division III) and associated programs, sports may take on a low profile. Programs at this level often foster student participation and may not depend on spectators and gate receipts for their existence.

Overall Objectives of Physical Education and Sport

It is crucial to realize that the overall objectives of physical education and sport across the totality of the Physical Activity and Sport Continuum have traditionally been embodied in the goals of education as set forth in 1918 by the Commission on the Reorganization of Secondary Education. The Commission's Seven Cardinal Principles include the following: (1) health, (2) command of fundamental processes, (3) worthy home membership, (4) vocational competence, (5) effective citizenship, (6) worthy use of leisure, and (7) ethical character.

These principles, together with the 1938 *Purposes of Education in American Democracy* tenets of self-realization, human relationships, economic efficiency, and civic responsbility, have set the tone for physical education and sport in the United States. The tone, however, has evolved from traditional subject-oriented (content and skill) physical education and sport curriculum to student-athlete–centered objectives.

The aim of organized physical education and sport programs is to create an environment that stimulates selected movement experiences resulting in desirable responses that contribute to the optimal development of the individual's potentialities in all phases of life.[6] Shepphard and Willoughby[9] further articulate what education should encompass:

A growing commitment to the full realization of human potential will place permanent emphasis upon the development of competent, productive, responsible, inquiring, questioning, value-judging, sensitive, compassionate, loving, humane individuals and their individuality as expressed by the concept of self: self-esteem, self-direction, self-control, and self-actualization. Along with this will go the preparation to play many and varied societal roles—citizen, spouse, lover, parent, colleague, worker, player—and an emphasis on skills which are of life-long importance. Schools will actually attempt to prepare students to live a life, not merely to educate them.

It is an education that should be available to, and meet the needs of, all citizens. It should furthermore be delivered in a dynamic, diverse, and professional fashion.

DEVELOPING A MANAGEMENT STRUCTURE THAT WILL ENABLE OBJECTIVES OF PHYSICAL EDUCATION AND SPORT TO BE ACCOMPLISHED

After the goals and objectives for physical education and sport programs have been identified, a management structure that will contribute to the achievement of these goals should be developed.

The structure refers to the framework whereby such things as titles of positions, role assignments, task allocations, functions, and relationships are graphically illustrated. The structure implies lines of communication, coordination, cooperation, and decision making.

Planning, developing, and organizing the structure for a physical education or sport program are important management responsibilities. Efficient organization and structure result in proper delegation of authority, effective assignment of responsibilities to staff members, adequate communication among the various units of the organization, clarification of the tasks assigned, and a high degree of morale among staff members. All of these factors determine whether the organization's goals are achieved.

Loen[5] suggests guidelines for developing a management blueprint that are organized around activities rather than around people. His suggestions include the following:

- Review the program and its objectives at least once a year since realignments in duties and responsibilities may be necessary.
- Design each position so that a short label describes its primary responsibilities. Each title should be descriptive, yet short enough to use in normal conversation.
- Assign each person clear-cut duties, responsibility, and authority, so that each position holder will possess freedom to act. When people know what they are responsible for and exactly to whom to report, they can concentrate on getting things accomplished rather than wondering if they are infringing on someone else's prerogatives.
- Establish line and staff positions that will en-

able management to realize the advantages of both centralization and decentralization.
- Establish each position on the basis of the knowledge and skills likely to be found in an individual.
- Design each position so that the position holder can make maximal use of his or her knowledge, understanding, and skills.
- Design positions so that decision-making authority is as close as possible to the scene of the action. Routine decisions should be made by the individuals "on the line."
- Give managerial staff responsibility for as many positions as possible. This is both economically and organizationally efficient and effective.

PRINCIPLES FOR MANAGEMENT ORGANIZATION AND STRUCTURE

Experts in many areas have developed principles to aid in effective management organization. Some of the most significant principles include the following:

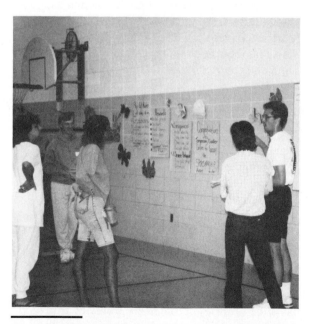

Organization is necessary for every physical education staff.

The management structure of an organization should clarify the delegation of authority and responsibility. For the goals of the organization to be met efficiently and successfully, management must delegate some of its powers to responsible individuals. These powers and the associated tasks should be clearly defined to avoid overlapping authority.

Management work may be most effectively organized by function. The "doctrine of unity" maintains that all personnel engaged in a particular type of work should function under a single authority.

Span of control should be considered in organizational structure. The number of subordinates who can be supervised adequately by one individual determines the span of control.

Successful management depends on communication. Communication is essential to effective management, because it helps avoid waste and duplication and promotes cooperation among departments and staff.

Coordination and cooperation among various departments in an organization are essential to effective management. Coordination among departments keeps each subsystem well informed and working together in a complementary and synergistic manner.

The manager must be an effective leader. An effective leader appreciates both the goals of the organization and the personnel working for the organization. Both are essential for the success of the organization.

Staff specialization aids effective management. To achieve objectives, organizations must perform many different tasks that require the abilities of various area specialists.

Authority must be commensurate with responsibilities, and lines of authority must be clearly drawn. An organizational chart is useful to illustrate the lines of authority. These lines should be well defined and unambiguous.

Organization and social purpose cannot be separated. The structure of an organization is a means to an end, and not an end in itself.

There is no single correct form of organization. Such factors as size, personnel, and economic constraints often determine the most appropriate organizational structure for a particular situation.

TRANSLATING THE MANAGEMENT STRUCTURE INTO GRAPHIC FORM (ORGANIZATIONAL CHARTS)

Once the desired type of management structure has been determined, the next step is to prepare it in graphic form so that it can be easily understood by members of the organization and by other interested individuals.

Organizational charts are frequently used to illustrate and clarify the structure of an organization. These charts clearly depict the management setup of an organization and the key management positions and their functions. Management uses these organizational graphic representations to orient new staff members to their responsibilities and their place in the total structure of the organization. They also serve as a public relations instrument to show the community how it is intimately linked to the physical education and sport process.

Peterson and associates[7] outline a six-step procedure for the development of organizational charts.

1. *Identify the objectives of the organization.* These objectives are designed to meet the goals of the organization, which in turn determines the structure that must be developed.
2. *Arrange objectives into meaningful functional units.* This step requires assessing the organization with its differentiated parts and units and organizing it to bring about a harmonious and integrated whole. If this step is successfully accomplished, it reduces friction and fragmentation and brings about a closely coordinated, smoothly functioning organization.
3. *Arrange the identified functional units into appropriate management units, such as departments.* This step varies in each organization, but it should represent the most effective and meaningful relationships for achieving the goals of the organization.
4. *Prepare a model of the structure of the organization and perform a trial run.* To make sure that the model represents the best management structure for the organization, it should be used initially on a trial basis.
5. *Revise the model in light of input received.* Views from personnel within and outside the organization should be sought and the model

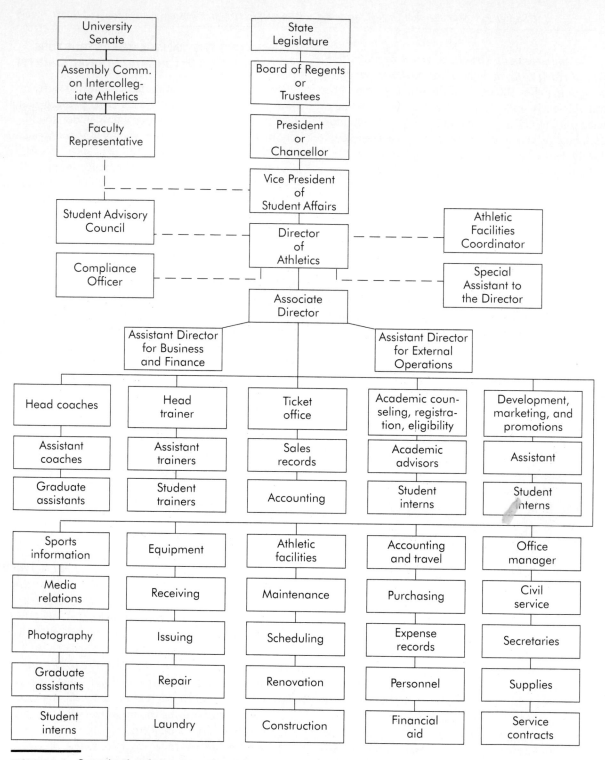

FIGURE 2-1 Organizational structure of an athletic department at a large college or university.

revised where necessary to achieve the most satisfactory, efficient, and effective structure possible.

6. *Evaluate the final design, and assign staff who work within the organization to appropriate functional units.* As a result of this final step, each member of the organization can see where and how he or she fits into the total organizational structure.

Line and Staff Organization

The most common type of organizational chart is a line and staff chart (Figure 2-1). A person in a line position has direct responsibility and authority for a specific objective or objectives of the organization. For example, an associate director of athletics would be in a line position, with direct responsibility for duties assigned by the director and, in turn, would report directly to the director. A person in a staff position has an indirect relationship to a specific objective or objectives of an organization. Staff personnel often have advisory positions or are in positions that are not responsible for carrying out the central mission of the organization. An example would be a facilities coordinator in the athletic department of a university or college program. Staff personnel do not have authority over line personnel. Line positions are related to, and derive authority from, the management head. In charts, staff positions are usually indicated by broken lines and line positions by solid lines. Line personnel are depicted in a vertical line in an organizational chart reflecting the hierarchy of power, whereas staff personnel are often depicted in a horizontal line.

In small management units such as interscholastic departments of physical education or athletics that have limited staff, there is frequently little distinction between line and staff since very few, if any, staff positions per se exist.

FORMAL AND INFORMAL ORGANIZATION AND STRUCTURE

Organizational theory and structure require that first, there must be a need for an organization to exist, and second, the organization must know the

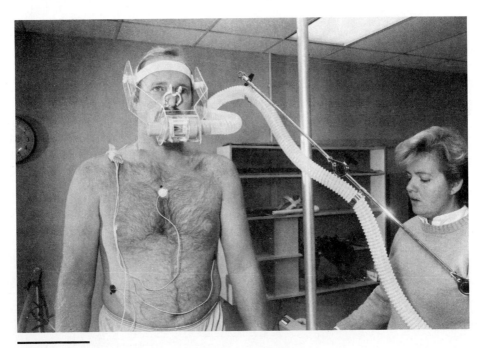

Research is vital to physical education and sport programs.

GRIMSBY COLLEGE
LIBRARY
NUNS CORNER, GRIMSBY

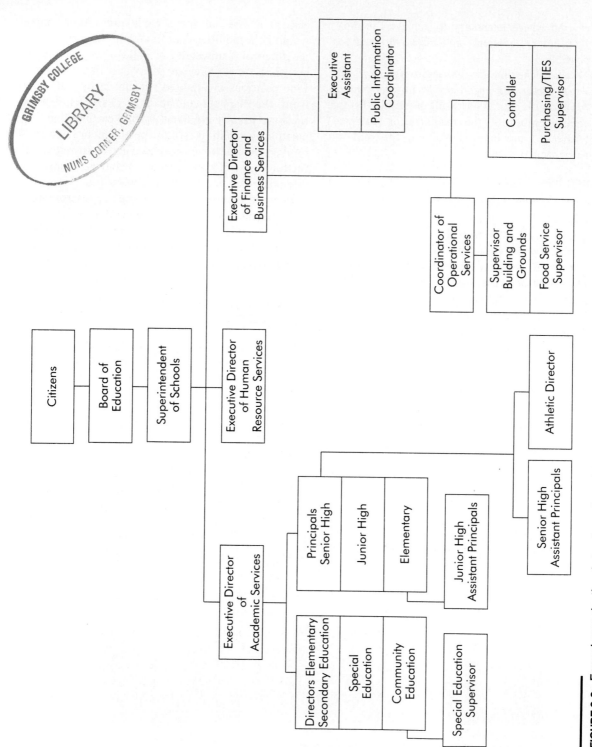

FIGURE 2-2   Formal organizational structure of a public school system athletic department.

goals it is trying to achieve. To accomplish these objectives a structure should be provided that enables the management to plan and make decisions, organize, staff, lead, motivate, control, and evaluate. These tasks can be performed through either a formal or an informal organization.

Formal Organization

A formal organization is based on a hierarchical job structure, with tasks assigned by the manager to the subordinate, concomitant with their job-task hierarchy and communications network. Figure 2-2 illustrates an interscholastic athletic department and its formal relationship within a public school setting. Such an organizational structure is concerned first with the positions to be filled (coaches) and tasks to be accomplished (the conduct of sport programs), and then with the persons to be assigned to these positions and tasks. Clearly delineated lines of authority and formal rules and regulations are earmarks of formal organization, as are dependence, obedience, discipline, reward, and chain of command.

A formal organization is employed because it provides a clear picture of the positions that exist and the tasks to be performed. It represents a way to get things done by the use of authority and chain of command. It places subordinates in a position where they must perform as instructed; thus things get done. It assumes that control of behavior is accomplished through rational judgment and that the manager is the person most qualified to make decisions and solve problems. It assumes that people should be instruments of production and is authoritarian by nature and design.

Informal Organization

An informal organization realizes that many relationships exist that cannot be illustrated in an organizational chart. In other words, things get done outside the formal relationships that a chart reflects. It assumes that relationships occur in many informal settings where ideas are generated; productivity is enhanced; and cooperation, loyalty, and high morale are developed. Figure 2-3 represents such an informal structure concerning the articulation of

physical education, recreational sport, and intercollegiate athletics at a large university.

Those who advocate informal organization contend this is how things are actually accomplished and thus oppose the formal, authoritarian type of organization. They also maintain that people who hold rank in an organization do not always behave rationally, nor do they have complete access to reliable information at all times. Advocates of informal organization also believe that members of an organization are not merely instruments of production, but instead have desires, values, needs, and aspirations that must be taken into consideration.

Modern theories of organization and structure indicate a shift away from the formal organizational structure toward an informal orientation recognizing the value of the human relations perspective. These modern theories and approaches (i.e., systems, behavioral management, contingency, etc.) are based on the fact that although most persons agree that some type of organizational framework is usually needed, most individuals are capable of some self-direction and self-motivation to perform admirably on the job.

One aspect of informal organization is the formation of subgroups that do not appear on organization charts. For example, employee unions represent an important group with whom managers must interact. In some organizations committees, commissions, councils, and task forces also represent influential subgroups. Therefore management must understand and appreciate what a staff member wants or desires and needs from his or her position, whether it is increased wages or benefits, job security, improved working conditions, a share in the decision-making process, or some other condition.

Modern theories of management are moving more and more toward an eclectic and participatory philosophy in which staff members and managers both are involved in many organizational decisions. Employees will better identify with an organization if they are involved in the decision-making process, and research suggests that performance outcome may also be significantly enhanced.

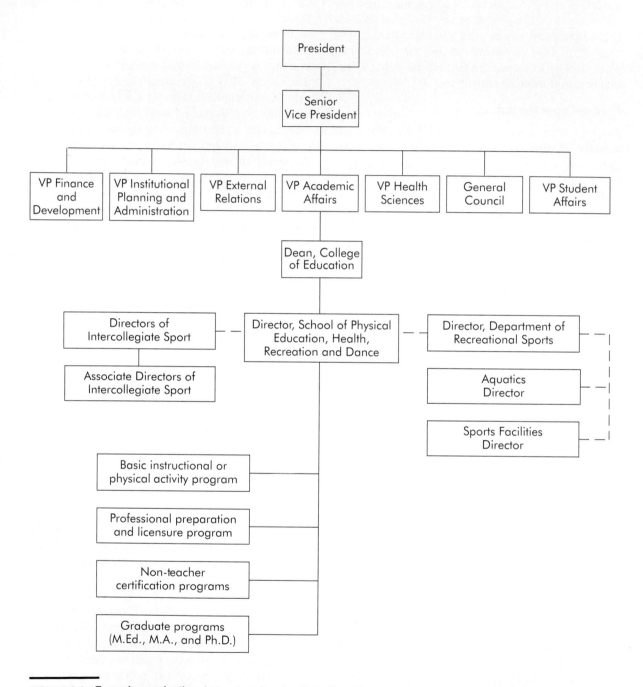

FIGURE 2-3 Formal organizational structure for physical education at a large college or university.

MANAGEMENT STRUCTURES FOR PHYSICAL EDUCATION AND SPORT PROGRAMS

The management structures currently employed for physical education and sport programs in elementary, junior high or middle school, secondary schools, colleges and universities, and community organizations are presented and discussed on the following pages. The examples offered are models and may be adapted and modified to fit each individual physical education and sport-specific circumstance.

The Organization and Structure of Physical Education and Sport in Elementary, Junior High or Middle Schools, and Secondary Schools

The school district is the basic management unit for the operation of elementary, junior high or middle schools, and secondary schools, and is a quasi-municipal corporation established by the state. In the United States this basic educational unit ranges from a one-teacher rural system to a large metropolitan system serving thousands of students. A system may be an independent governmental unit or part of a state or county government or other local administrative unit. The governing body of the system is the school board.* The chief administrative officer is the superintendent of schools.

The school board is the legal management authority created by the state legislature for each school district, and usually consists of a chair, vice chair, clerk of the board, and treasurer. The chair works intimately with the superintendent and is responsible for conducting school board meetings. The vice chair serves in this capacity in the absence of the chair. The clerk of the board is legally responsible for the board's records and documents, and the treasurer works closely with the executive director of finance and business. The responsibility of the elected board is to act on behalf of the residents of the district. It has the duty of appraising, planning, and initiating state-mandated educational programs (i.e.,

---

*The term *school board* is used throughout the text although *board of education, school committee, community-school board,* and *board of directors* are used in some regions of the United States.

special education, birth-to-age-21, Assurance-of-Mastery, etc.). It selects executive personnel and performs duties essential to the successful operation of the schools within the district. The board develops policies that are legal and in the interest of the people it serves. It devises financial means within its legal framework to support the cost of education. It keeps its constituents informed concerning the effectiveness and needs of the total program, and it solicits citizen advice and counsel.

An example of a mission statement for a school board would be to prepare all students for the future by providing a challenging education that builds academic competence, encourages creativity, promotes life-long learning, advances critical thinking skills, instills commitment to personal wellness, and fosters respect for self and others.

The key management personnel charged with carrying out the mission of the school district within each school system usually consist of the superintendent of schools, executive directors or assistant superintendents, principals, and directors (Figure 2-4).

Superintendent of Schools

Within a large school system a superintendent has management responsibility of the school program. Executive directors or assistant superintendents are in charge of academic services, resource management, and various other phases of the program, such as elementary and secondary education. There is also usually a superintendent's position associated with smaller schools. These managers are known as district superintendents; they are often responsible for many schools within a wide geographical area.

The superintendent's job is to carry out the educational policies of the state and the school board. The superintendent acts as the leader in educational matters in the community and also provides the board of education with the professional advice it needs as a lay organization. The superintendent also supervises the executive assistant, who manages the daily functions of the superintendent's office. The executive assistant attends all meetings, functions, and retreats of the school board and serves to ensure that the operations of the school board are in com-

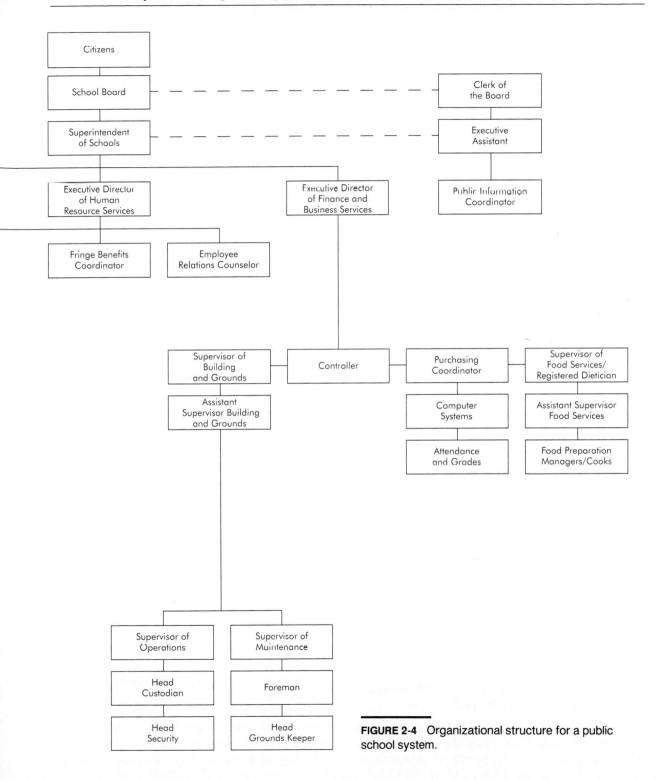

FIGURE 2-4 Organizational structure for a public school system.

pliance with the legal requirements, policies, and procedures set forth by the school board and the state.

Executive Director of Academic Services

The executive director of academic services supervises the divisions of elementary education, secondary education, special education, athletics, community education, and summer school education, and is responsible for the staff development of teachers and all district employees. The principals of elementary, junior high or middle schools, and secondary schools, as well as directors of physical education and directors of athletics, fall within the academic services director's domain. The executive director of academic services is also involved in the development and evaluation of curriculum and the organization and supervision of instruction and preservice and in-service teacher training. The executive director of academic services is first in line to perform the duties of the superintendent of schools in the event of the superintendent's absence.

Executive Director of Human Resource Services or Director of Personnel Services

The executive director of human resource services is the chief personnel officer of the district, and as such manages the personnel functions for all licensed (teachers, coaches, administrators, etc.) and classified (secretaries, clerks, etc.) staff. The executive director also assists the superintendent in district management and represents the district in assigned school–community relations. In addition, aspects of employee relations such as negotiations of union contracts, fringe benefit packages, and insurance coverage for teachers and coaches also fall within the human resource manager's domain. In the absence of the executive director of academic services, the human resource director represents the superintendent.

Executive Director for Finance and Business Services or School Business Manager

The finance and business manager serves as head of business affairs and supervises the controller, purchasing, operations, and the total information education

cational systems (district computer consortium for record keeping, grading, athletic eligibility, etc.) employed by the district. Buildings and grounds, food service, and the business office staff also usually fall under the domain of the finance and business manager. The executive director of finance and business is last in line concerning the assumption of duties during the superintendent's absence.

Principal

The position of principal is similar to that of the superintendent; it differs mainly in the extent of responsibility. Whereas the superintendent is usually in charge of all the schools within a particular community, the principal is in charge of one particular school. The duties of the principal include executing educational policy as outlined by the superintendent, appraising educational offerings, making periodic reports on various aspects of the program, directing the instructional program, promoting positive relationships between the community and the school, and supervising the maintenance of the physical plant.

Supervisor

The supervisor is generally responsible for improving instruction in a specific subject area, although sometimes a supervisor is responsible for the entire elementary or secondary instructional program.

Director

The director is responsible for functions of a specific subject matter area, such as physical education or athletics, or a particular educational level (i.e., elementary or secondary). The responsibilities have administrative and supervisory implications.

In some cases at the secondary school level the positions of *director of physical education* and *director of athletics* are consolidated into one position. There are school districts, however, where the two responsibilities are separated into two positions.

The *director of physical education* provides leadership, programs, facilities, and other essentials concerning the conduct of the program, which includes grades K-12. Specific responsibilities include the following: providing coordination between physical education and athletics; supervising inside and outside physical education facilities; overseeing equipment and supplies concerned with special areas (includes maintenance, safety, replacement, and accounting operations); maintaining liaison with community groups (includes holding educational meetings to interpret and improve the program and serving on various community committees); preparing periodic reports regarding areas of activity; and supervising the total physical education program (classroom, gymnasium, adapted, aquatic, intramural, and extramural programs). The director of physical education provides leadership for other staff members, evaluates personnel, and is responsible for long-range planning, including curriculum and program development.

A *director of athletics* assumes many duties similar to those of the director of physical education. There is, however, little organized, competitive sport (e.g., Spring Track and Field Day) at the K-6 level. Many junior high or middle schools also maintain minimal competitive sport programs (sometimes limited to football, soccer, volleyball, and basketball). In many parts of the United States, community youth sport programs have for the most part served to fill this competitive sport void.

The director of athletics serves to provide leadership, sport programs, and facilities in a coordinated and cooperative effort with the physical education department and community education or recreation department of the district, as well as other community youth sporting groups. The athletic director monitors and evaluates coaches and attends to the health status, eligibility, and behavior (e.g., awards or misconduct) of the student-athlete. The director must also budget, plan, purchase, allocate, and oversee maintenance of programs and equipment. It is necessary for the athletic director to keep up with the latest safety codes concerning equipment and facilities. Scheduling of games and officials, coordination of special game events (e.g., bands, dance lines, cheerleaders, etc.), insurance, and medical supervision also fall under the jurisdiction of the athletic director. Public relations (e.g., television, radio, and print media), marketing, production and sales, fund-raising, booster clubs, and accounting for finances provide the athletic director with a full-time position that has become an integral part of our educational system.

High School Sport Councils

In some high schools, sport councils are formed to serve in an advisory capacity to the school board and the administrative officers of the school. Membership might include principals, athletic directors, physical education directors, students, athletic trainers, coaches, and parents. The sport council performs such functions as recommending policy, awards, eligibility, budgets, and making sure that the athletic program is managed according to acceptable educational standards. Many state high school leagues/associations provide additional guidelines concerning these standards.

The Organization and Structure of Physical Education in Colleges and Universities

A college or university is characterized by a governing board, usually known as a board of regents or trustees, which is granted extensive powers of control by legislative enactment or by its charter. The governing board of a college usually delegates many of its powers of management to the administration and faculty of the institution. The chief management officers, usually headed by a president and several vice presidents, are commonly organized into such principal areas of management as academic affairs, student personnel services, business, and public relations. The members of the faculty are usually organized into colleges, schools, divisions, and departments of instruction and research. Large institutions frequently incorporate a university senate or assembly committee that is the voice of the faculty and serves as a liaison between faculty and administration.

Physical education (also referred to as kinesiology, exercise science, sport studies, etc.) is organized as one management unit for men and women in almost all colleges and universities in the United States. The management unit may be either a college, school, division, or department. The manager in charge of the physical education program may be called a director; chairperson; or division, department, or area head (see Figure 2-3). In most institutions of higher education these managers are responsible directly to a dean, but they may be responsible to the director of athletics. In some institutions recreational sport is included as a part of the physical education program. However, in many institutions recreational sport programs maintain a separate identity and often report to a vice president of student affairs, whereas physical education reports to an academic dean or vice president.

The duties of the head of a physical education department (depending on the size of the institution) may include coordinating the activities within the particular unit, requisitioning supplies and equipment, preparing schedules, making budgets, conducting meetings, teaching classes, coaching, hiring and dismissing personnel, developing community relations, supervising recreational sports and intercollegiate athletic programs, evaluating and appraising the required or basic physical activity program, representing the department at meetings, facilitating the raising of external funds, and reporting to superiors.

Physical education in colleges and universities is commonly organized in four components: (1) the basic instructional or physical activity program, (2) the teacher preparation and licensure program, (3) the non-teacher certification programs such as exercise science, athletic training, sport studies, and sport management, and (4) graduate programs (Figure 2-5). The basic instructional or physical activity program provides physical education instruction for all students, including people with varying disabilities. Basic skills, movement patterns, rules, strategies, and enjoyment of mastery are the prime focus. Surveys indicate that basic physical activity programs remain a high priority not only because of their cost effectiveness, but also their popularity among students, staff, and faculty. Many institutions have discontinued their physical activity requirements and have infused their curriculum with attractive and creative "impact" courses, ranging from aerobic dance to backpacking.

The teacher preparation program is for those interested in pursuing a teaching career and includes basic skill courses, physical education major activity and pedagogy courses, and various physical education content courses, such as applied physiology, biomechanics, history and philosophy, school law, motor behavior, sport psychology, and sport sociology. The experience usually culminates in a student teaching and practicum setting. Also associated, and often integrated, with the professional preparation program are certification and licensure programs (e.g., adapted/developmental education or coaching). These programs usually reflect current state mandates and remain integral parts of most college programs. Many colleges are in fact moving to 5-year professional training programs leading to a master's degree in teaching.

The non-teacher–certification component of physical education is rapidly expanding in many colleges. These programs provide a basic core of traditional physical education/kinesiology content courses integrated with appropriate core courses from schools of business, law, journalism, management, medicine, and health-related professions, such as physical and occupational therapy. An internship (e.g., cardiac rehabilitation center, corporate fitness center, YMCA/YWCA, professional sports organization) usually serves as the culminating experience in this non-traditional physical education delivery system. Certifications in athletic training, sport management, fitness instruction, strength and conditioning, and dance instruction are often awarded in conjunction with associations such as the National Athletic Trainers' Association (NATA), National Association for Sport and Physical Education (NASPE), American College of Sports Medicine (ACSM), National Strength and Conditioning Association (NSCA), and the International Dance Excercise Association (IDEA).

The fourth component of many college and university physical education departments is the graduate program. For the most part advanced and concentrated work in physical education major content areas (e.g., sport psychology, sport sociology, sport history and philosophy, sport management, international and comparative sport, biomechanics, motor development, exercise physiology) is prescribed with statistical methods and computer application techniques forming a research foundation

Physical Education/
Kinesiology

Basic instructional or physical activity program

Instructional
Coeducational
Sometimes required
Delivered 2-3 times/week
Credit granted
Activities include:
Team, dual, individual, and coactive
Dance and rhythms
Combative sports
Aquatics
Racquet sports
Games
Gymnastics
Movement education
Leisure pursuit
Outdoor education
Weight training and conditioning
Adapted, remedial, and developmental activities (most students are mainstreamed into programs)

Professional preparation and licensure program

Instructional
Coeducational
Required for teaching certification
Credit granted
Core courses might include a wide range of physical activities and courses such as First Aid, CPR, Anatomy, Exercise Physiology, Biomechanics, Sport Psychology, Sport Sociology, History and Philosophy, Motor Learning and Motor Development, Sport Management, School Law, Measurement and Evaluation, Administration, Curriculum and Supervision.
Student teaching and practicum
Coaching certification (required in some states)
Adapted/developmental license

Non-teacher certification programs—exercise science, sport studies, and sport management

Instructional
Coeducational
Credit granted
Sometimes required
Core courses include:
See courses listed under professional preparation with the addition of related offerings from Schools of Business, Law, Journalism, Social Sciences, Medicine, or Health-Related Professions such as Physical Therapy
Sport systems and cognitive applications
Student internship and practicum
Sport management certificate
Athletic training and fitness instructor certification

Graduate programs— M.Ed., M.A., and Ph.D.

Instructional and/or research oriented
Coeducational
Required core courses
Areas of emphasis usually include:
Exercise Science
Biomechanics
Sport Psychology
Motor Learning and Motor Behavior (Human Factors)
Sport Management
Sport Sociology
Administration
Curriculum and Supervision (Pedagogy)
Measurement and Evaluation
History
Philosophy
International and Comparative Sport

FIGURE 2-5 Organizational structure for a college or university physical education program.

or core. A minor or supporting area (e.g., law, business, marketing, international relations, counseling, special education, child development, school administration) is usually required, thus providing the potential graduate with an increased scope concerning the domain of human movement.

The Organization and Structure of Sport in Colleges and Universities

Because athletic programs are organized and administratively structured differently in colleges and universities than in high schools, the organization of sport in colleges and universities (see Figure 2-1) requires further elaboration and discussion.

The Director of Athletics

The athletic director in colleges and universities is responsible for the management of the intercollegiate athletic program. In large institutions this is a full-time position, whereas in smaller institutions it may include other responsibilities involved with physical education, teaching, administration, and coaching.

Some of the key duties of many athletic directors include scheduling contests and preparing contracts, arranging for team travel, appointing, supervising, and evaluating the coaching staff, making arrangements for home sports contests, representing the institution at athletic association and league meetings, securing officials, checking and preparing player eligibility and insurance lists, preparing the budget, fund-raising, and overseeing facility supervision and maintenance.

Faculty Athletic Committee

Most colleges and universities with sport programs of significant size have a faculty athletic committee. This committee serves in an advisory capacity to the president of the institution or, in most instances, a vice president. The membership of such committees frequently includes faculty representatives, students, coaches, student-athletes, community leaders, and alumni. The athletic director and administrative representative are usually ex officio and nonvoting members. The faculty athletic committee is involved in functions such as approving budgets,

developing eligibility standards, approving financial awards, authorizing schedules, acting on problems that arise, developing policies, investigating infractions, reviewing scholarship decisions, and deciding to what extent certain sports might be added or eliminated.

Faculty Representative

Many colleges and universities have a faculty athletic representative. The athletic representative is a member of the faculty who represents the college or university at national association meetings such as the National Collegiate Athletic Association (NCAA) and the National Association of Intercollegiate Athletics (NAIA), as well as the conference to which the institution belongs (e.g., Big Ten, Pac Ten, Big East). The faculty representative usually attends faculty athletic committee meetings as a nonvoting member, and presents periodic reports to the faculty athletic committee. The faculty representative serves at the behest of the faculty committee and usually votes according to institutional policy.

Structure of the College or University Athletic Department

The structure of athletic departments on college and university campuses usually depends on institutional enrollment, tradition, budget, funding sources, and focus of each specific institution of higher education. Figure 2-1 reflects the structure necessary for the conduct of a Division I NCAA sport program that provides balanced offerings for both men and women. The roles, duties, responsibilities, and support service personnel, of course, would have to be modified, adapted, or collapsed somewhat for institutions offering fewer sports or less competitive programs. Regardless, sport participation opportunity should be equitable across gender lines.

The Organization and Structure of Physical Education and Sport in the Private and Public Sector

Physical education and sport programs exist in settings other than school systems and institutions of higher education. Because of the current interest in

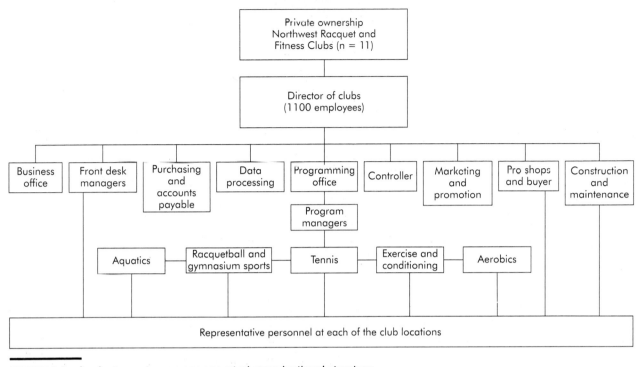

FIGURE 2-6   A private-sector, owner-operated organizational structure.

health and physical fitness, a variety of delivery structures have evolved. From executive and corporate fitness programs, to community service–oriented programs such as community centers and YMCAs, not to mention the booming "fitness club industry," the quest for enhanced physical activity and sport opportunities has developed into a multibillion-dollar enterprise. The organization and structure for such enterprises range from being operated by a private owner to being accountable to a community board of directors. Some structures are motivated by profit, whereas others might be community-service oriented, and still others might exist as part of a health-related employee fringe benefit package.

Regardless of the situational circumstances, the need to provide well-trained managers and personnel to meet the consumer demand is apparent and provides yet another attractive professional marketplace for those who are well prepared, skilled, schooled, and certified in the delivery of physical education and sport-related services. The physical education personnel involved in these programs include people trained in physical education specialties such as exercise physiology, biomechanics, sport management, coaching, athletic training, fitness training, dance, sports writing, public relations, and marketing. Figures 2-6 and 2-7 represent organizational structuring of various private-sector enterprises.

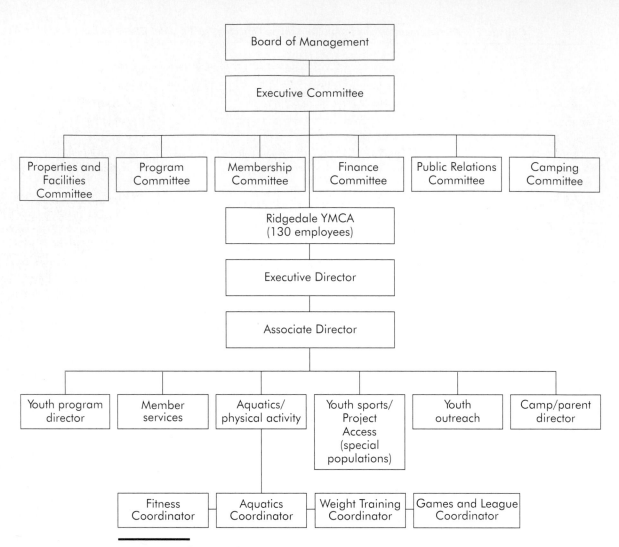

FIGURE 2-7 Organizational structure of a community Y.

SUMMARY

One of the functions of management is to develop an organizational structure through which the goals of physical edcuation and sport can be accomplished in an effective and efficient manner. The physical education and sport objectives to be achieved include physical, neuromuscular, cognitive, and social-emotional-affective development. To meet the needs of all students, including those with varying disabilities, the objectives of physical education and sport will vary at each educational and institutional level.

Management structures for physical education and sport are organized differently for elementary, junior high or middle schools, secondary schools, and colleges and universities. Fitness centers, YMCAs, and organizations other than schools and colleges also maintain their own organizational schemata. Furthermore, it is important to recognize that an informal as well as a formal management organization and structure affect most programs. It is therefore crucial in developing organizational structures that management principles and guidelines be incorporated.

◆ SELF-ASSESSMENT ACTIVITIES

These tests are to assist students in determining if material and competencies presented in this chapter have been mastered.

1. You have been asked by the head of a governmental organization to identify the objectives that physical education will be able to achieve for the members of that country and to show what management structure you would recommend to help achieve these objectives. Prepare a written statement for presentation before the country's legislative body.

2. Write an essay on the topic "Developing and organizing the structure for a sport program is an important management responsibility."

3. Cite at least six principles that should be observed in developing an effective management organization. Show how each of the following elements is essential to a sound management structure: delegation of authority, span of control, communication, and staff specialization.

4. You are a consultant with expertise in management organization and structure who has been hired by an organization with a physical education and sport program to give advice about whether it should implement a formal or informal structure. What advice would you give to this organization? Defend your decision.

5. Prepare a model for the management structure of a physical education or sport program in an organization of your choice, and describe why it is a sound structure.

6. Draw a structural organizational chart for your college, showing the various management components, and discuss their responsibilities and relationships.

7. Tell how the management organization and structure you recommended in item 4 would provide for each of the following: *delegating authority* to the heads of the instructional program, the program concerning individuals with varying disabilities, recreational sport, and varsity sport; *resolving a conflict* between the directors of athletics and physical education; *determining budget allocations* for athletics; and *formulating policies* regarding Title IX.

REFERENCES

1. Barrow HM, Brown JP: *Man and movement: principles of physical education,* Philadelphia, 1988, Lea & Febiger.
2. Bucher CA, Prentice WE: *Fitness for college and life,* St Louis, 1985, Mosby–Year Book.
3. Gensemer RE: *Physical education: perspectives, inquiry, applications,* Philadelphia, 1985, Saunders.
4. Krotee ML, Hatfield FC: *The theory and practice of physical activity,* Dubuque, Ia, 1979, Kendall/Hunt.
5. Loen RD: *Manage more by doing less,* New York, 1971, McGraw-Hill.
6. Nixon, JE, Jewett AE: *An introduction to physical education,* Philadelphia, 1980, Saunders.
7. Petersen E, Plowman EG, Trickett JM: *Business organization and management,* Homewood, Il, 1962, Richard D Irwin.
8. Sage GH: *Motor learning and control—a neuropsychological approach,* Dubuque, Ia, 1984, Wm C Brown.
9. Sheppard WC, Willoughby RH: *Child behaviors: learning and development,* Chicago, 1975, Rand McNally.

SUGGESTED READINGS

■ American Alliance for Health, Physical Education, Recreation, and Dance: *Basic stuff series I and II,* Reston, Va, 1987, AAHPERD.
The views of the profession concerning application of physical education to the curriculum.
■ Jewett AE, Bain LL: *The curriculum process in physical education,* Dubuque, Ia, 1985, Wm C Brown.
Contains theoretical and practical considerations for the implementation of school physical education programs.
■ La Point JD: *Organization and management of sport,* Dubuque, Ia, 1980, Kendall/Hunt.
Provides a significant overview of many dimensions involved in competitive sport. Discusses sport-related issues and problems encountered by student-athletes, parents, coaches, athletic directors, and school boards.
■ National Association for Sport and Physical Education: *Directory of professional fitness certifications,* Reston, Va, 1988, AAHPERD.
A guide to opportunities for certifications in the profession of physical education and sport.
■ Peters T: *Thriving on chaos,* New York, 1987, Alfred A Knopf.
A guide on goal setting, power, accelerated change, and leadership. The author also delves into creativity and innovation.
■ Vroom VH, Deci EL: *Management and motivation,* New York, 1981, Penguin.
Presents an overview of motivation including theoretical constructs concerning attitude formation, job satisfaction, and performance. Organizational change is also covered.
■ Wuest DA, Bucher CA: *Foundations of physical education and sport,* St Louis, 1991, Mosby–Year Book.
Provides an overview of physical education and sport including philosophy, history, and core content. Career patterning and issues in the profession are also explored.

PART II

Management of Physical Education and Sport Programs

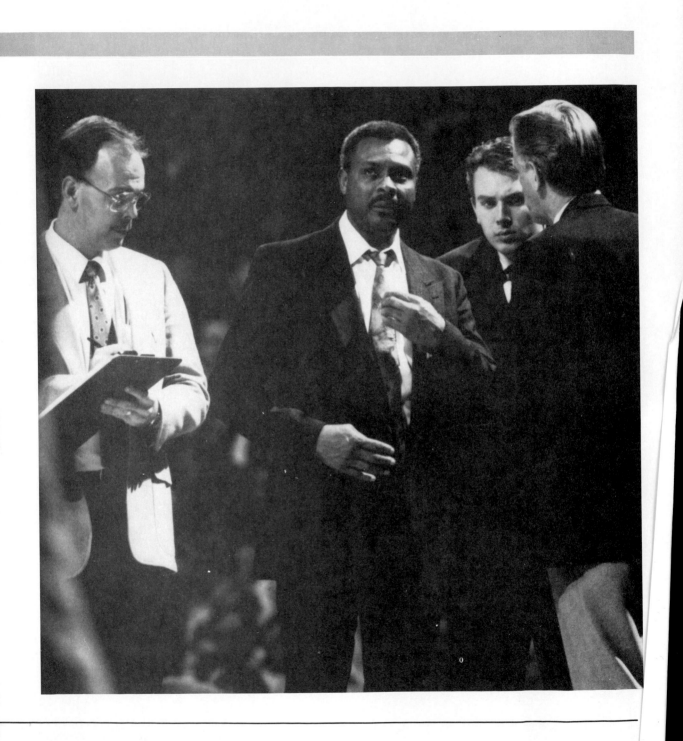

CHAPTER 3

Physical Education Instructional Programs

▶ **Instructional Objectives and Competencies To Be Achieved**

After reading this chapter the student should be able to

- Provide a description of the nature, scope, purpose, and worth of instructional programs in physical education.
- Outline management guidelines for preschool, elementary school, secondary school, and college and university physical education instructional programs.
- Describe management instructional strategies for physical education programs resulting from Title IX legislation.
- Justify the need for certain management procedures, such as scheduling, time allotment for classes, size of classes, instructional loads, class management, uniforms, taking roll, selecting physical education activities, grouping, and area of student involvement.

- Understand the professional nature of selected management problems in instructional programs such as required or elective physical education, substitutions, credit, class attendance, excuses, instruction by specialist or classroom teacher, dressing and showering, records, and evaluation.
- Discuss what is meant by an adapted/developmental program of physical education.
- Describe the various elements that make up an individualized education program (IEP).
- Describe administrative procedures to comply with and implement Public Law 94-142.

Thus far in this text we have concerned ourselves with the nature and scope of management as they relate to physical education and sport. We have also discussed the objectives these programs are designed to achieve and the organizational structure needed to efficiently and effectively pursue and accomplish these goals. This chapter delves into the instruc-tional physical education program and identifies associated guidelines, issues, and concerns.

By tradition, the basic instructional physical education program was graphically represented at the base of an isosceles triangle. The part immediately above the instructional base was the recreational sports program, and at the apex of the triangle was the varsity athletic program. What the isosceles triangle symbolized in the past is still true to the effect that a sound physical education program should serve as a firm and solid base for all other school and community physical activity and sport programs (Figure 3-1). The instructional program in physical education is the place to teach skills, strategies, concepts, and essential knowledge concerning the relationship of physical activity to physical, neuromuscular, cognitive, and social-emotional-affective development. It is a place to challenge, build competence, encourage creativity, promote lifelong activity, advance critical action skills, instill commitment to personal wellness, and foster respect for others. It is also a place to introduce an awareness concerning the development and maintenance of optimal levels of physical fitness.

Skills should be taught from a scientific, theoretical, and progressive approach so that the various biomechanical factors that affect human movement are clearly understood by the participant. Demonstration, films, video tapes and disks, computers, posters, and other audiovisual aids and materials enhance instruction and are required for optimal learning.

The physical education program presented throughout the school years should be sequential in development and progressive in application. A physical fitness program should also be developmental and progressive in nature, starting with the individual's present state of mental and physical fitness and gradually moving to higher levels.

Performance objectives should be established and targeted for individual student achievement. When boys and girls advance from one grade to another, they should have achieved certain objectives in various physical education activities, just as they master various levels of skills, knowledge, and competencies in other school subjects. A plan for assurance of mastery in physical education must be developed and implemented.

Physical education should involve more than physical activity. As the participant understands more fully the importance of human movement; what happens to the human body during exercise and stress; the relationship of physical activity to one's biological, psychological, and sociocultural development; the history of various activities; and the role of physical activity in the interdependent global community, physical education will take on a new meaning, grow in intellectual respectability, and be able to more fully contribute to building a more healthy and productive society.

Just as textbooks, handouts, and resource materials are employed within other courses in the educational system, so should they be used in the physical education program. Textbooks should not only contain material pertaining to physical skills, but should also explore the subject matter of physical education.

Grading and developmental records that follow a student from grade to grade should be maintained throughout his or her school life. These records will indicate the degree to which the objectives of the program have been achieved by the student. The level and degree of physical skill and fitness achievement, involvement in outside activity, health status, and social conduct may all serve to interpret what role physical education has played for the students as they meet the challenges of an ever-growing and complex society.

The basic instructional physical education program cannot be conducted in a "hit-or-miss" fashion. It must be planned in accordance with the needs

FIGURE 3-1 A traditional view of the relationship between the basic instructional or physical activity program, recreational sports, and varsity athletics.

Karate class; University of Nevada, Las Vegas.

and interests of the individuals it serves, as well as the society in which they will become contributing members.

MANAGEMENT GUIDELINES FOR SCHOOL AND COLLEGE PHYSICAL EDUCATION PROGRAMS

Physical education programs in schools and colleges have played a prominent role in educational systems since the turn of the century. Physical education programs exist at the preschool, elementary, junior high, middle, and senior high school levels, as well as at the college and university educational level.

Preschool Physical Education Programs

The concept of early schooling is no longer regarded as a custodial or compensatory undertaking. Instead it is viewed as a necessary provision for the normal growth and development of children. Research by psychologists, child development specialists, and sociologists has indicated that the early years are cru-

cial for the child intellectually, physically, socially, and emotionally. In light of such findings, as well as the return of many mothers to the workforce, nursery schools and child day-care centers have gained wide popularity.

Preschool educational programs involve indoor and outdoor play-learning activities. Physical education activities are crucial at this age and should include the development of fundamental movement skills, fitness and self-testing activities, music and rhythmic activities, rhymes and story plays, and low organizational games. A sound program of selected physical activities helps the child develop a positive self-concept, practice and develop social skills, enhance physical fitness, and improve cognitive and sensorimotor skills. Research maintains that a relationship exists between perception and motor development and that perception is related to cognition; therefore physical movement experiences play a crucial role in cognitive development.

Preschool programs are becoming an integral part

of educational systems in this country, and physical education is playing an important role in such programs.

Elementary School Physical Education Programs

The elementary schools of the nation are stressing movement education. Experts do not agree on a single definition for movement education. They do agree, however, that movement education depends on physical factors in the environment and on the individual's ability to react intellectually, socially, and physically to these factors. Movement education assists students in becoming more mentally and physically aware of their body movements. It is based on a conceptual approach to human movement. Through movement education, the individual develops his or her own techniques for dealing with the environmental factors of force, time, space, and flow as they relate to various movement experiences.

Movement education employs the problem-solving approach. Each skill to be explored presents a challenge to the student. Learning results as the stu-

dent accepts and solves increasingly more difficult problems. For this reason, the natural movements of childhood are considered to be the first challenges that should be presented to the student.

Physical education also emphasizes the learning of specific skills through demonstration, sustained practice, and positive reinforcement. Movement education emphasizes learning skill patterns through individual exploration of the body's movement potential. Physical education at this level should promote the individual child's standard of performance and establish a physical activity comfort level so that each child may develop to his or her fullest potential.

Elementary schools stress perceptual motor development and, in some schools, an interdisciplinary approach is utilized, whereby the subject matter of physical education is integrated with certain other subjects such as music, science, history, and art.

Some management guidelines that should be recognized in elementary school physical education programs follow. The program should meet the needs of all children, including those with learning or physical disabilities, the culturally or environ-

Movement exploration is a key ingredient in elementary physical education.

mentally deprived, and the gifted, as well as the normal. The program should focus on movement education, perceptual-motor development, and interdisciplinary analysis. It should include a variety of experiences that will help the child form a sound foundation on which to build more complex skills, techniques, strategies, and concepts. The program should provide developmental and progressive experiences in a safe and wholesome environment. It should foster creativity, self-expression, social development, positive self-concepts, and appreciation for the importance of health and fitness.

Secondary School Physical Education Programs

The junior high, middle, and senior high schools of the nation should build on the physical education foundation provided at the elementary school level. Some management guidelines that represent important considerations in secondary school physical education programs follow. Most of the guidelines set for the elementary school also have merit in developing programs for secondary schools. The secondary program should be based on the developmental tasks of secondary school students. The program should consist of a variety of activities, including gymnastics; self-testing activities; rhythm and dance; movement skills; aquatics; physical fitness activities; and individual, dual, and team sports. The program should provide a thorough understanding of the human body and the impact of physical activity on its various organic systems. The Basic Stuff Series I and II developed by AAHPERD's National Association for Sport and Physical Education (NASPE) contains concepts, principles, and developmental ideas extracted from physical education's body of knowledge, and might serve as a valuable K-12 programmatic guide. The program should teach a variety of skills progressively, eliminate excessive repetition of activities, and ensure the inclusion of lifetime sports and fitness concepts. The program should be open to all students, including those with varying disabilities, who should be provided an opportunity to function in the least restrictive environment. The program should encourage vigorous physical activity in, as well as outside of, class, including individual fitness and participation in community, recreational, and varsity sport.

In addition to these management guidelines, the following points should be stressed:

The physical education class provides the student a safe and wholesome environment in which to learn the skills, strategy, appreciation, understanding, knowledge, rules, regulations, and other material and information that are part of the program. It is not a place for free play, intramurals, or varsity practice. It is a place for pro-active instruction. Every minute of the class period should be devoted to teaching students the skills and subject matter of physical education.

Instruction should be fundamental and interesting. Skills should be broken down into basic components and presented so that each individual may understand clearly what is expected to be accomplished, and how it is to be done. Use of demonstrations, computer simulations, video tapes and discs, and other audiovisual aids and materials can help to make the instruction more meaningful and interesting.

Instruction should be progressive. There should be a definite progression from basic to complex skills. Just as a student progresses in mathematics from basic arithmetic to algebra, geometry, and calculus, so the physical education student should progress from basic skills and materials to more complex and involved skills, techniques, and strategies.

Instruction should involve definite standards. Students should be expected to reach individualized standards of achievement (assurance of mastery) in the class program. A reasonable amount of skill—whether it is in swimming, tennis, dance, or another activity—should be mastered, keeping in mind individual differences. Upon graduation from high school, students should have met definite assurance-of-mastery standards and goals that indicate that they are *physically educated.*

Instruction should involve more than physical activity. All physical education classes do not have to be conducted in the gymnasium, where physical activity predominates. A reasonable proportion of class time, perhaps as much as 10% to 20%, can be devoted to class interaction and discussion, guest

Weight training; Lyons Township High School, LaGrange, IL.

lecturers, independent study, cooperative projects, field trips (e.g., skiing, bowling, sailing, or golf), Basic Stuff Series I and II, and working on individualized fitness and learning packages. Physical activity should not be conducted in a vacuum; if it is, it has no meaning and will not be applied when the student leaves the class and school setting. As the student understands more fully the importance of physical activity and sport, what happens to the body during exercise, the roots of the various activities in which he or she engages, and the role of physical activity across cultures (such as the breaking of racial and gender barriers), physical education will take on a new meaning and, hopefully, play a significant role throughout the lifespan of each individual.

There should be records. The instructor should keep accurate records to provide tangible evidence concerning the degree to which student objectives are being met. This means that data concerning skill achievement, physical fitness level, critical knowledge, and other information, including social conduct—such as sportsmanship, cooperative effort, and out-of-class participation—should be a part of the data base.

There should be homework. It is just as reasonable to assign homework in physical education as in biology or math. Much subject matter is to be learned, many skills are to be mastered, and fitness levels must be improved or maintained. If teachers would require their students to work on various skills, endurance activities, and knowledge acquisition outside of class, there would be more time for meaningful and targeted instruction during class.

Each student should have a thorough medical examination before participating in the physical education program. An annual health examination should be regarded as a minimum, essential not only to ensure the student's safety, but to effectively prescribe the frequency, duration, and intensity of the physical activity to best meet each student's needs.

The teaching load of physical educators should be determined not only by the number of instructional class periods assigned, but also by the total number of activities handled by the teacher both in class and outside of class. To be an effective teacher, a normal daily work load should consist of not more than 5 hours of instruction, or five class periods. In addition, provisions should be made to ensure 1 hour of class-preparation time.

Trends and Innovative Ideas in Secondary School Physical Education

Many innovative instructional programs are being employed in physical education at the secondary school level.[1] These include programs stressing personalized, individualized, and cooperative learning; those emphasizing performance objectives, competency packages, and goal setting; those concerning career and leadership opportunities; those stressing flexibility in scheduling; and those concentrating on specialized electives and group experiences such as camping, sailing, skiing, backpacking, and outdoor and wilderness leadership activities during which the student interacts with the environment, as well as other cultures.

College and University Physical Education Programs

Colleges and universities should provide instruction in physical education that meets the following management criteria:
- The program should be available to all students.
- The program should not be a repetition of the high school program, but should offer more advanced work in physical education. However, instruction in the development of basic skills should continue to be an integral part of the program.
- The program should include innovative features to meet the needs of students and at the same time be interesting and challenging.
- The program should not allow athletics, band, ROTC, recreational sports, or other activities to serve as a substitute for physical education.
- The program should provide a wide range of course selection including individual, dual, and team activities, as well as dance and outdoor pursuit.
- The program should stress knowledge and understanding of the value of physical activity and its relationship to the environment.

- The program should stress the study and practice of the science and art of human movement.
- The program should focus on lifetime activities.
- The program should be conducted by well-trained and fully certified faculty and staff members.

Since the 1970s, many (approximately 50%) colleges and universities in the United States have moved physical education from a mandatory to an elective status. Institutions still requiring physical education typically do so for a 1- to 2-year period. Classes usually meet two or three times per week, with some colleges still requiring standards of achievement (most often swimming and basic fitness). The trend in today's physical activity programs is toward more emphasis on lifetime sports, outdoor pursuit, and fitness activities, including aerobics, conditioning, and weight training.

The growth of community and junior colleges has been significant. In many respects the activities for these institutions are the same as those for colleges and universities. Many community and junior colleges require students to take physical education at least 1 year. Most of the programs require 2 hours each week and stress the successful completion of physical education as a requirement for awarding of the associate degree.

The college and university physical education program is the end of formal physical education for many students. Student age range in colleges and universities is wide, incorporating those from ages 16 to 60 and beyond. However, most college students are in their late teens or early twenties, and have matured in many ways. Many hold part-time jobs. They are entering the period of greatest physical efficiency and possess many interests, including physical activity and sport. Many want to prepare themselves for successful vocations, an objective that requires the physical educator to show how physical education can contribute to success in their future profession. College students are also interested in developing socially, and coeducational activities help provide a training ground for gender-free experiences in a wide variety of settings. In addition, students are interested in developing skills that they can use and enjoy throughout life, as well as becoming physically fit and looking good.

Dance class; University of Nevada, Las Vegas.

In formulating a program at the college and university level, one needs to remember that many students enter with limited physical activity backgrounds. Therefore the program should be broadly based and varied at the start, with opportunities to elect more advanced activities later. Considerable opportunity should exist for instruction and practice in those activities in which a student desires to specialize. As much individual attention as possible should be given to ensure necessary safety, as well as skill, fitness, and attitude development.

The program of activities should be based on the interests and needs of students, as well as the availability of facilities and staff. Some colleges have introduced "Foundations" courses, which cover the basic subject matter, including the philosophical underpinnings of physical education.[2]

In college physical education programs, physical skill and fitness achievement tests should be employed to assess student needs, set reasonable goals, and ensure progress. Special assistance and individually prescribed programs should be offered to help all students develop to their fullest potential.

MANAGEMENT FACTORS RELATING TO ONE OR MORE EDUCATIONAL LEVELS

Certain management factors relate to one or more educational levels (elementary, secondary, college and university). Some of the more pertinent factors include interrelationships of elementary, secondary, and college and university programs; instructional aids and materials; class management; interpretation of Title IX regulations for instructional strategies; and implications of Public Law 94-142 for adapted/developmental physical education programs for persons with varying disabilities.

Interrelationships of Elementary, Secondary, and College and University Programs

The physical education programs from the K-12 through the college and university level should be interrelated. Continuity and progression should characterize the program from the time the student enters kindergarten until graduation. Overall planning is essential to ensure that each student becomes physically educated and to guarantee that duplication of effort, time management, curricular omissions, and shortages do not occur.

Continuity and progression do not exist today in many of the school systems in the United States. Instead, to a great degree, each institutional level is autonomous, setting up its own program with curriculum-writing teams and consultants responsible for course content and development. If the focus of attention is on the student—the consumer of the product—then curriculum planning will provide the student with a continuous program, developed to meet the dynamic needs and interests from the beginning to the end of the formal educational process (K-12 through college or university).

Consideration and cooperative planning should also exist for the entire community to ensure that each child's needs are met. Many communities have directors of school and community physical education, and recreation program managers, who regularly meet to ensure an integrated, coordinated, and continuous program of physical activity for the entire community.

Management Guidelines for Selecting Instructional Aids and Materials

When selecting audiovisual aids or other resources and materials, physical educators should consider the following principles that make using these aids effective, meaningful, and valuable:

Materials should be carefully selected and screened. The teacher should preview the materials to determine if they are appropriate for the unit and age level of the students and to ensure that they present information in an interesting, progressive, and stimulating manner.

Proper preparation of materials should be made. The teacher or responsible school official should check all equipment that may be necessary for the presentation of materials to make sure that it is in operating condition. Computers, cam-corders, videotape players, record players, and movie and overhead projectors, in particular, need to be carefully checked before each use. Maintenance schedules and records should also be maintained on equipment.

The presentation of materials should be planned and integrated into the lesson. Students should be properly introduced to the topic, and materials should be strategically placed so that they influence the learning process and the student understands their relationship to the unit of study.

Materials should be presented to the students in a proper learning environment. Students should be prepared and located so that all may hear, see, and learn from the material being offered. They should realize that they will be held responsible for the information being presented.

Materials should be varied. Different types of materials should be chosen for presentation to stimulate and motivate the students. A teacher using videotapes or slides exclusively does not take full advantage of other supplementary materials that may have widespread appeal.

Use of supplementary materials should be limited. The teacher should place a reasonable limit on the use of supplementary teaching materials in order to maintain a balance between time involved in physical activity and time engaged in, for example, viewing the serving technique of a professional tennis player.

Care should be taken to avoid excessive expenses. A reasonable part of the instructional budget should be set aside for supplementary materials. This amount should be in accordance with the emphasis placed on this phase of the teaching program, and items selected should possess long-term redeeming value.

Records and evaluations should be maintained. All supplementary materials should be carefully catalogued and kept on computer file for future reference. This should save the unnecessary time and expense involved in reordering or duplicating materials and in culling outdated materials.

By following these principles the teacher is able to supplement learning with materials that are interesting, meaningful, and valuable to the students. The following are various types of materials, activities, and personnel that can be used in the instructional process:

- *Reading materials:* textbooks, magazines, rulebooks, pamphlets, journals, news clippings, handouts
- *Audiovisual aids:* motion pictures, slides, learning loops, television, videotapes, record players, audio-tapes and disks
- *Special aids:* computers, charts, photographic materials, bulletin boards, magnetic boards
- *Professional personnel:* from professional associations and organizations
- *Community activities:* recreational activities, PTA/PTO-sponsored events, Special Olympics, Red Cross, Partners of the Americas, and other private volunteer organizations (PVOs)
- *Clinics:* special games and programs conducted by visiting teams, professional teaching organizations, community organizations, foundations such as the Women's Sport Foundation, sports federations, and state high school leagues/associations.

Class Management[5]

Sound management does not just happen. It requires careful thought, good judgment, and planning before the class begins. Management practices help to ensure that the class functions as a coordinated group in order to effectively and efficiently accomplish the goals and tasks that have been established. Quality management leads to enjoyable, satisfying, and worthwhile experiences. The teacher who is in charge of a class where optimal learning conditions exist has spent considerable time planning the details of the class from start to finish.

Behavior modification through physical activity presentation to physical educators at the International Special Olympic Games Symposium; University of Minnesota.

The following reasons for good organization should be recognized by every teacher and administrator:

- It helps to eliminate discipline problems.
- It gives meaning and purpose to instruction and to the assigned activities.
- It results in efficiency, provides proper focus, and allows the best use of precious time.
- It more fully ensures that the needs and interests of the participants will be protected and satisfied.
- It ensures meaningful progression and continuity in the program.
- It provides for measurement and evaluation of objectives, as well as timely feedback of results.
- It ensures the participant's health, safety, and maximal performance outcome.
- It encourages program adaptations to meet each individual's needs and interests.
- It reduces errors and omissions.
- It helps conserve the teacher's time and energy, and provides the teacher with a sense of accomplishment.

Management Guidelines

- Strategic and long-term planning for the semester and the year, as well as daily, weekly, and seasonal planning, should be prepared.
- A definite time schedule should be planned for each period, considering learning objectives and the priorities concerning dressing for class, taking roll, safety, warm-up, class activity, cooldown, and other pedagogical essentials.
- The activity should be carefully planned so that class proceeds with precision and dispatch, with a minimal amount of standing around and a maximal amount of activity for each student.
- The classroom environment should be one that is safe yet unrestricted, and creative movement should be encouraged. The equipment should be in proper condition and placed appropriately for safe activity. Field and gymnasium markings, equipment arrangements, logistics for activities, and other essential details should be attended to well before class.
- Procedures to be followed in the locker room should be clearly established to provide for traffic, valuables, clothes, and showering and dressing.
- The instructor should always be early for class.
- Participants should be encouraged and motivated to do their best at all times.
- A planned program of assessment and evaluation should be provided to determine progress being made by participants and the effectiveness of teaching strategies.
- The instructor should wear appropriate clothing.
- The instructor should possess a thorough command of the subject, recognizing the value of demonstrations, visual aids, cooperative goal structuring, and other techniques and strategies that promote learning.
- Desirable attitudes toward and understanding of physical fitness, learning skills, sportsmanship, safety, vigorous participation, and other concepts inherent in physical education should be continually stressed.

TITLE IX

On May 27, 1975, President Gerald Ford signed into law Title IX[3] of the Education Amendments Act of 1972, which states that no person, on the basis of sex, be excluded from participation in, be denied the benefits of, or be subjected to discrimination under any educational program or activity receiving federal assistance. The effective date of the regulation was July 21, 1975. Title IX affects nearly all the nation's 16,000 public school systems and nearly 2700 postsecondary institutions. As a first step, the regulation provides that educators (including physical educators) should perform a searching self-examination of policies and practices in their schools and institutions and take whatever remedial action is needed to bring them into compliance with federal law.

Reason for Title IX

The primary reason for the enactment of Title IX was testimony before Congressional and other committees to the effect that females were frequently denied enrollment in traditionally male courses and activities and that girls and women were continually denied equal participatory opportunity. A national survey conducted by the National Education Association showed that although women constituted a majority of all public school teachers, they accounted for only 3.5% of the junior high school principals and 3% of the senior high school principals. It was believed that by instilling and perpetuating traditional gender roles and sexual differentiation, educational institutions have, over time, denied women equal educational and employment opportunity, and therefore, equal participation in the sociocultural process. Title IX was legislated to correct this fundamental problem.

Implications of Title IX for Physical Education Instructional Strategies

Physical education classes must be organized on a coeducational basis. This regulation does not mean that activities must be taught coeducationally. Within classes, students may be grouped by sex for such contact sports as wrestling, basketball, ice hockey, rugby, and football. Also, within physical education classes, students may be grouped on an ability basis even though such grouping may result in a single-sex grouping. However, sex must *not* be the criterion for grouping. Furthermore, if an evaluation standard has an adverse impact on one sex, such as a standard of accomplishment in a physical fitness test, different evaulation requirements must be utilized.

Schools and colleges must provide equal opportunities for both sexes. Equal opportunity in this respect means that the activities offered must reflect the interests and abilities of students of both sexes. Adequate course offerings, facilities, and equipment must be available for both sexes in physical education and sport programs. Furthermore, one sex cannot dominate the facilities or the new equipment. In addition, adequate time for practice and instructional assistance must be provided for both sexes. Again, one sex cannot dominate.

Schools and colleges must spend funds in an equitable manner. Although equal aggregate expenditures are not required, an educational institution cannot discriminate on the basis of sex in providing proper equipment, supplies, and associated services.

Title IX takes precedence over all state and local laws and conference regulations that might be in conflict with this federal regulation.

If an institution receives federal aid, it must be in compliance with Title IX, even though its athletic or physical education program does not directly receive any of this aid.

There can be no discrimination in respect to personnel standards. No discrimination can exist in respect to personnel standards by sex, including marital or parental status, for employment, promotion, retention, salary, recruitment, job classification, or fringe benefits.

Financial aid must be awarded equitably. The regulations require an institution to select students to be awarded financial aid on the basis of criteria other than a student's sex.

Interpretation of Title IX Regulations

Some interpretations of Title IX regulations that affect physical education instructional strategies are listed here. Interpretations such as the following

Coeducational dance; Oak View Elementary School, Fairfax, VA.

have come from various sources. Sex designations associated with class schedules, activities, and budgets are not permitted. The term *girls' gymnasium* can be used; however, the scheduling of this facility must be nondiscriminatory in respect to each sex. Policies and procedures in regard to items such as uniforms and attendance must apply to both sexes. Sex-segregated administrative units, such as departments, do not necessarily have to be merged, although having faculty men and women in integrated offices in newly combined administrative units is encouraged. If a significantly greater number of one sex is enrolled in a particular physical education class, the administration, if called on, should be prepared to provide the rationale for such organization. Supervision of locker rooms may be assigned to teacher aides, paraprofessionals, or teachers in other departments. Marks or grades given in physical education classes should reflect individual growth and performance and not compare sexes with one another. Standards of performance that provide an unfair comparison for one sex should not be employed. In some cases, separate standards might be used for each sex; for example, on a physical fitness rating, such as number of push-ups or chin-ups in 60 seconds, separate standards may be used.

Coeducational Physical Education Classes

Because the provision for coeducational classes is one of the key implications of Title IX regulations, this topic is discussed further here.

Problems in physical education classes concerning Title IX have been cited in the professional literature. Weber[10] indicates that problems such as the following have developed as a result of Title IX: the teacher is not professionally prepared to teach various activities in a coeducational setting; male and female teachers who traditionally made decisions on their own are finding it difficult to function as a team and share the decision-making process; students are also finding problems such as being unable to perform some activities satisfactorily in front of members of the opposite sex; and those with poor skills are excluded from participation on highly skilled coeducational teams.

Weber also points out that many of these prob-

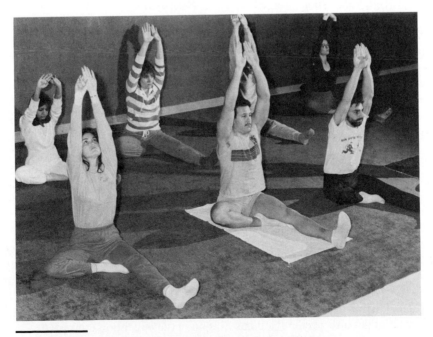

Coeducational yoga class; University of Nevada, Las Vegas.

lems can be solved by such means as teachers eliminating their personal sex biases, employing new instructional strategies and techniques, and reexamining philosophies concerning the teaching of physical education. The main consideration in establishing coeducational programs is to respond to the interests and ability levels of the participants. When conducting activities on a coeducational basis, appropriate modifications may be made in the rules and conduct of the activities to equalize competition between the sexes.

Other problems that have arisen in physical education classes as a result of Title IX include assignment of office space, scheduling of gymnasiums for various activities, teaching of activities such as wrestling, potential for sexual impropriety, supervision of locker rooms, and dressing standards.

Compliance with Title IX. Title IX is being enforced by the Office for Civil Rights of the federal government. The first step seeks to have voluntary compliance. If violations are found, federal financial support may be cut off and other legal measures taken, such as referring the violation to the Department of Justice for appropriate court action.

The Office of Civil Rights is trying to approach Title IX constructively. It wishes to achieve the goals of Title IX, that is, to end discrimination against women, in the shortest time possible. Opportunity for women is the law of the land and must be enforced. The aim will be to use the Department's enforcement machinery by giving priority to systemic forms of discrimination rather than following an approach whereby individual complaints assume priority. This means that the total picture of noncompliance will be assessed, taking into consideration information received from individuals and groups, as a means of determining enforcement priorities and compliance reviews.

Title IX regulations have been evolving since the Civil Rights Act of 1964. They should result in increased physical education opportunities for all students.

The question whether Title IX applies to all programs in an educational institution or whether it applies only to programs that get direct federal aid has been referred to the courts. The Grove City College decision ruled that Title IX applied only to programs that received direct federal aid. On March 2, 1988, the United States Senate voted to approve Senate Bill 557, The Civil Rights Restoration Act. The purpose of the act was to restore Title IX to its original intent and counteract the 1984 Supreme Court decision involving Grove City College.[4]

The Adapted/Developmental Physical Education Program

The adapted/developmental program refers to the phase of physical edcuation that meets the needs of the individual who, because of some physical inadequacy, functional defect capable of being improved through physical activity, or other deficiency, is temporarily or permanently unable to take part in the regular physical education program or the phase in which special provisions are made for students with disabilities in regular physical education classes. It also refers to students of a school or college population who do not fall into the "average" or "normal" classification for their age or grade. These students deviate from their peers in physical, mental, emotional, or social characteristics or in a combination of these traits.

The principle of individual differences that applies to education as a whole also applies to physical education. Most administrators believe that as long as a student can attend school or college, he or she should be required to participate in physical education. If this tenet is adhered to, it means that programs may have to be adapted to meet individual needs. Many children and young adults who are recuperating from long illnesses or surgery or who are suffering from other physical or emotional conditions require special consideration concerning their full and vigorous participation in physical activity programs.

It cannot be assumed that all individuals in physical education classes do not possess some type of disability. It is unfortunate that many programs are administered on this basis. An estimate has been made that one out of every eight students in our schools has a disability that requires special provision in the educational program.

Schools and colleges will always have students

who, because of many factors such as heredity, environment, disease, accident, drugs, or some other circumstance, have physical or other major disabilities. Many of these students have difficulty adjusting to the demands society places on them. The responsibility of the physical educator is to help each individual enrolled in the school to be engaged in appropriate physical education. Even though a person may possess various disabilities, this is not cause for neglect. In fact, by legal mandate and professional challenge it is required that each child enjoy the benefits of participating in physical activities adapted to his or her needs. Provision for a sound adapted/developmental program has been a shortcoming of physical education throughout the nation because of a lack of properly trained teachers, because of the financial cost of remedial instruction, and because many administrators and teachers are not aware of their responsibility and the contribution they can make in this phase of physical education. These obstacles should be overcome as the public becomes aware of the mandate to educate *all* individuals in *all* phases of the total educational process.

People With Varying Disabilities

The nation's estimated 50 million people with disabilities have engaged in an aggressive civil rights movement. These actions were aimed at obtaining

Physical education teachers instructing students with disabilities.

the equal protection promised under the Fourteenth Amendment to the Constitution of the United States.

As a result of the actions on the part of persons with disabilities, the nation is finally awakening to their needs, as well as to their human potentialities. Until recently, persons with disabilities were viewed as nonproductive, functionally disruptive, and draining on society. As a result, it has been common for persons with disabilities to be discouraged. Today, however, the picture has changed. Persons with disabilities are achieving their rights under the Constitution and the Americans With Disabilities Act of January 26, 1992 and are receiving educational opportunities, gaining meaningful employment in the public work force, and taking their rightful place in an accessible society.

Definitions Relating to the Adapted/ Developmental Program

Many terms have been used to define and classify persons with disabilities. These terms vary from publication to publication. Categories of children designated by the United States Congress in relation to legislation for persons with disabilities will be the primary classifications used in this text; however, these terms will be modified to reflect the changing view concerning persons with disabilities, such as those infected with HIV. These categories include the mentally handicapped, hearing impaired, speech impaired, visually impaired, emotionally and behaviorally disordered, learning disabled, physically disabled, and other health-impaired individuals who may require educational services out of the ordinary.

Special Education

Under federal law special education means specially designed instruction, at no cost to parents or guardians, to meet the unique needs of persons with disabilities, including classroom and "physical education instruction," home instruction, and instruction in hospitals and institutions.

Physical Education

Physical education as it relates to the persons with disabilities under federal law is the development of

(1) physical and motor fitness, (2) fundamental motor skills and patterns, and (3) skills in aquatics, dance, and individual and group games and sports (including recreational and lifetime sports). Physical educators must serve as part of the adapted students' resource team and be prepared to design specific programs of physical activity for each student.

Individualized Education Program (IEP)

The individualized education program (IEP) is the program or prescription written for each child in relation to his or her specific disability. It will be discussed in more detail later in this chapter (also see Appendix A).

Least Restrictive Environment

In essence, the least restrictive environment means persons with disabilities are placed in a class or setting that is as similar to a normal class as possible and in which the child can function safely. This location ranges from a full-time regular physical education class, to a regular physical education class with consultation from specialists in adapted physical education, to part-time regular physical education and part-time adapted physical education, to adapted physical education with regular physical education only for specific activities, to full-time adapted physical education in a regular school, to adapted physical education in a special school.

Functional Physical Education Goals for People With Disabilities

Selected goals that provide direction to the physical education program for the student with disabilities and that translate into objectives for each participant, as outlined by AAHPERD,[9] are presented here in the following modified format:

- Inform each student of his or her capacities, limitations, and potentials.
- Provide each student within his or her capabilities the opportunities to develop organic vigor, muscular strength and endurance, joint function and flexibility, and cardiovascular endurance.
- Provide each student with opportunities for social development in recreational sports and games.

- Provide each student with opportunities to develop skills in recreational sports and games.
- Help students meet demands of day-to-day living.
- Help students with disabilities in their social development.
- Help students develop personal pride in overcoming disabilities or other forms of impairment.
- Help students develop an appreciation for individual differences and being able to accept limitations and still be an integral part of the group.

Public Law 94-142

A milestone in legislative proposals providing for persons with disabilities was the passage of the Education of All Handicapped Children Act of 1975, which was signed into law by the President of the United States as PL 94-142.[8] The act, however, is now referred to as IDEA (Individuals with Disabilities Education Act). This legislation spells out the federal government's commitment to educating children with disabilities and provides for annual funding on a sliding scale for this prupose. It provides educational services to children with disabilities who are not receiving a free and appropriate public education, as well as assistance for those children receiving inadequate help.

These services have now been extended from birth through age 21. Children with disabilities, as defined in PL 94-142, are those who require some type of special education and related services. Related services, under the act, are defined as "transportation and developmental, corrective, and other supportive services, including but not limited to, occupational, speech, and physical therapy, recreation, and social, medical, and counseling services." Although gifted children might need special education and related services, they are not covered under the law.

Other specific stipulations of PL 94-142 require the following:

- State and local educational agencies initiate policies to ensure all children the right to a free and appropriate education.
- Planning of individualized educational programs, including health and physical status and motoric ability, and the scheduling of conferences including parents, teachers (including physical education and special education teachers), case managers, administrators, representatives of local educational agencies, and where appropriate, the children themselves. These conferences must be held at least once a year.
- Due process for parents and children to ensure that their rights are not abrogated.
- A per-pupil expenditure that is at least equal to the amount spent on each nondisabled child in the state or local school district.
- The state and local agency shall carry out the mandates of the law according to specific timetables provided therein.
- The development of a comprehensive system of personnel training, including pre-service and in-service training for teachers.
- That students with disabilities will be educated in the "least restrictive environment." This means that they will be placed in the regular class whenever possible.

Aspects of PL 94-142 related to physical education. Section 121a.307 of the regulations of PL 94-142 stipulates the following requirements for physical education:

121a.307 Physical Education

(a) *General.* Physical education services, specially designed if necessary, must be made available to every child with disabilities receiving a free appropriate public education. (b) *Regular physical education.* Each child must be afforded the opportunity to participate in the regular physical education program unless

1 The child is enrolled full-time in a separate facility, or
2 The child needs specially designed physical education, as prescribed in the child's Individualized Education Program (IEP).

(c) *Special physical education.* If specially designed physical education is prescribed in a child's IEP, the public agency responsible for the education of that child shall provide the services directly, or make arrangements for services to be provided through other public or private programs. (d) *Education in separate facilities.* The public agency responsible for the education of a child with disabilities who is enrolled in a separate facility shall ensure that the child receives appropriate physical education services in compliance with paragraphs (a) and (c) of this section.

Individualized Education Programs for People With Disabilities

After identification and eligiblity have been determined for students with disabilities, an individualized education program (IEP) must be developed for each individual. PL 94-142 specifies the requirements for the development of such programs. Section 4(19) provides the following guidelines (also see Appendix A):

The term *individualized education program (IEP)* means a written statement for each child with disabilities developed in any meeting by a representative of the local educational agency or an intermediate educational unit who shall be qualified to provide or supervise the provision of specially designed instruction to meet the unique needs of children with disabilities. The design of an IEP shall include:

A. An assessment of the present levels of educational performance of the child;

B. A statement of annual goals, including short-term instructional objectives;

C. A statement of the specific educational services to be provided, and the extent to which the child will be able to participate in regular educational programs;

D. The projected date for initiation and anticipated duration of the services; and

E. An outline of appropriate objective criteria and evaluation procedures and schedules for determining, on at least an annual basis, whether instructional objectives are being achieved.

The comprehensive IEP should be developed using the team approach. The following persons should be represented on the team: parent, teacher (classroom, physical education, and special education), administrator, case manager, student, and—when appropriate—the people responsible for supervising special education, related services such as guidance and counseling, and other agency representatives.

Facilities, Equipment, and Supplies

Appropriate and adequate facilities, equipment, and supplies are important to successful programs of physical education for persons with disabilities. However, these items must be emphasized for special or adapted physical education students because facilities and equipment are usually designed for students in the regular class. Adaptations are often necessary when students are mainstreamed into regular programs.

The passage of recent legislation and the results of various legal decisions have prompted school districts to make available and accessible the necessary facilities, equipment, and supplies to ensure a quality education for all students. There is some question, however, about whether students with disabilities are being provided with adequate facilities, equipment, and supplies. The types of facilities and equipment needed for adapted/developmental physical education will vary according to the nature of the program (adapted or unified sports; remedial or corrective exercises; or rest, rehabilitation, and relaxation), the student's disability, and the school level at which the program is conducted. For example, the elementary school program in adapted physical education may be taught in the regular gymnasium, or in less desirable circumstances, in the classroom. In secondary schools and colleges, however, a special facility or gymnasium for adapted physical education may be provided.

The Virginia State Department of Education, in its instructional booklet entitled *Physical Education for Handicapped Students,* outlines some of the factors that should be taken into consideration for students with disabilities. A few of these factors with other considerations are offered:

Within building

- Doors easy to open, at least 48 inches in width, and 2-way in design.
- Nonslip ramps, properly sloped, with handrails on both sides.
- Elevators or chair lifts when necessary with properly placed operating mechanisms (closing door, starting, assistance button in braille, etc.).
- Floors with nonslip surfaces.
- Restrooms with toilets at proper height (20

inches) with rails provided, and properly designed doors.

Outside building

- Loading and parking areas convenient to accessible entrances. These areas should be properly lighted, barrier- and curb-free and, if possible, covered.
- Ramps suitable for wheelchairs and accessible to all building levels.
- Doorways and sidewalks wide enough for two passing wheelchairs.
- Emergency exits for wheelchairs.

Other considerations

Certainly many other considerations are crucial in order for persons with disabilities to be able to function within the operating codes. Other considerations are listed below:

- Telephone (height, length of cord, raised numerals for visually impaired)
- Aquatic facilities (accessible dressing and changing facilities, and hair dryer at proper height)
- Safety doors at exits
- Water fountains (height and accessibility)
- Restrooms (accessibility)

All physical education and recreational sport programs must operate with sensitivity to provide every student with the opportunity to equal access. This is one area in which we must strive to do a better job.

Adaptive/Developmental Physical Education Equipment and Supplies

For the most part, equipment that is used in the regular classroom can be modified to meet adaptive needs, and certainly equipment that already exists at regular playgrounds can and should be employed. Special care and safety measures must be taken, however, to prevent children from getting struck by such items as moving swings, teeter-totters, and ropes. Of course specialized equipment can be purchased or constructed by creative school personnel. There are now myriad supplies, information, and organizations, ranging fom the Braille Sports Foundation and the National Beep Baseball Association to the Minnesota Outward Bound School for the Handicapped and the International Sports Organi-

zation for the Disabled, that can meet programmatic needs. The US Consumer Product Safety Commission (CPSC) also is a valuable resource for safety guidelines for both facilities and equipment.

MANAGEMENT MATTERS RELATED TO PHYSICAL EDUCATION INSTRUCTIONAL PROGRAMS
Scheduling

The status and role that physical education plays in the educational curriculum reflect the physical education leadership and its relationship with central administration. Physical education is more meaningful for participants when the schedule reflects their interests, rather than administrative convenience.

Scheduling should be done according to a well-conceived plan. Physical education should not be inserted in the overall master scheduling plan whenever there is time left over after all the other subjects have been scheduled. This important responsibility cannot be handled on a hit-or-miss basis because that disregards the interests and needs of the students. Instead, physical education should be scheduled first on the master plan, along with other crucial subjects that are required of all students. This allows for progression and for grouping according to the interests and needs of the individual participants. The three important items to consider in scheduling classes are (1) the number of teachers available, (2) the number of teaching stations available, and (3) the number of students who must be scheduled. This formula should be applied to all subjects on an equitable basis.

When appropriate, all students should be scheduled. If the student is able to attend school or college, he or she should be encouraged to enroll in physical education. Special attention should be provided, however, to those with disabilities or to gifted individuals to ensure that they are placed in a program suited to their individual needs. Also, attention should be accorded those students who need extra help developing physical skills, strength, and endurance, and who are searching to find their way in the psychosocial realm.

Physical educators should make a point of presenting to central administration their plans for scheduling physical education classes. The availability of facilities, equipment, supplies, weather, and student interest and attention span should be taken into consideration when preparing a master scheduling plan. The need for equitable consideration should also be discussed with the principal and the scheduling committee. Through persistent action, progress will be made. The logic and reasoning behind the formula of scheduling classes according to the number of teachers, the teaching stations available, and the number of students who must be scheduled should not be denied. The program should be planned according to these guidelines to ensure progression and safe, meaningful instruction.

Flexible scheduling. The introduction of flexible scheduling into school programs has implications for the management of school physical education programs. Flexible scheduling assumes that the traditional system of having all subjects meet the same number of times each week for the same amount of time each period is passé. Flexible scheduling provides class periods of varying lengths, depending on the course content being covered by the students, methods of instruction, and other factors pertinent to such a system. Whereas the traditional master plan makes it difficult to promote flexible scheduling, the advent of the computer has made this innovation practical and common.

Flexible scheduling also makes it possible to schedule activities for students of varying abilities at different times so that all are not required to have a similar schedule based on a standard format of the school day. Under the traditional system, all students who were academically at risk, for example, took as many courses as the brightest. Under flexible scheduling, some students may take as few as four courses and some as many as eight. In either case, physical education should be a part of every student's schedule.

Modular scheduling breaks the school day into periods of time called modules. In a high school in Illinois the school day is composed of 20-minute modules, and classes may vary from one to five modules, depending on the purpose of the course. The school is on a 6-day cycle and operates by day one,

two, or three rather than the traditional days of the week. In physical education, each grade level meets for three modules per day, 4 days each week. Each grade level also has a two-module group meeting once every cycle. In this meeting, guest speakers and classroom lectures provide students with physical education concepts.

In other schools employing modular scheduling, students frequently have unscheduled modules that can be used for aquatics or gymnasium activities. Recreational sports, open lab facilities, sport clubs, and school demonstrations or exhibitions also provide incentives for students to actively and regularly utilize the skills they have learned in physical education class.

Dress

Dress does not have to be elaborate, but it shoud be appropriate. An important concern is that the clothing ensures safety when students are engaged in physical activity. For both males and females, simple washable shorts and t-shirts or sweat shirts are suitable. Many schools still require uniforms, especially where laundry service is provided. Of course, appropriate footwear should be worn. It is important to keep the uniform clean. The instructor or physical education department should establish a policy concerning safe, clean, and appropriate attire, and work diligently to see that hygienic standards are met by all.

Time Allotment

Just as scheduling practices vary from school to school, district to district, college to college, and state to state, so does the time allotment for physical education. In some states there are laws that require a certain amount of time each day or week be devoted to physical education, whereas in others permissive legislation exists. For the most part, however, school districts set their own K-12 schedules. Some require 20 minutes daily, and others 30 minutes daily. Some districts also specify the time by the week, ranging from 50 minutes to 300 minutes. Colleges and universities do not usually require as much time in physical education as do elementary, junior, middle, or senior high schools. At the college level, requirements take the form of semesters or quarters of physical education that are usually delivered in 1-hour blocks two to three times per week. The general consensus among physical education leaders is that for physical education to be of value, it must be offered with regularity. For most individuals this means daily, or at least three times per week.

Some individuals believe that, especially in elementary schools, a program cannot be adapted to a fixed time schedule. However, as a standard, there seems to be agreement that a daily experience in physical education is needed, as well as laboratory periods where students can exercise and practice the skills they have acquired.

On the secondary level, it is recommended that sufficient time be allotted for dressing and showering in addition to the time needed for participation in physical education activities. Some leaders in physical education have suggested a double period every other day rather than a single period each day. This will assist in encouraging students to shower, which has long been a problematic issue. However, the importance of daily periods should be recognized and achieved wherever possible. Administrators should work toward providing adequate staff members and facilities to allow for a daily period of physical education. This remains a challenge in times of fiscal constraint.

The amount of time suggested for adults to spend in physical activity programs is a minimum of three times a week (not on consecutive days). However, a daily physical education regimen is considered optimal, and should be the goal of every professional physical educator.

Class Size

Some school and college administrators contend that physical education classes can accommodate more students than so-called academic content classes. This is a misconception that has developed over the years and needs to be corrected.

The problem of class size seems to be more pronounced at the secondary level than at other educational levels. At the elementary level, for example, the classroom situation represents a unit for activity assignment, and the number of students in this teaching unit is usually reasonable. However, some schools combine various units or classrooms for physical education, resulting in large classes that are not safe and provide a less than desirable teaching and learning environment.

Classes in physical education should be approximately the same size as classes in other subjects offered in the school. This is just as essential for effective teaching, individualized instruction, and optimal performance in physical education as it is in other content subjects. Physical education contributes to educational objectives on an equal basis with other subjects in the curriculum. Therefore the class size should be comparable so that its educational objectives can be attained.

After much research, many committees established a standard for an acceptable size of physical education classes. They recommend that 35 students make up a class, with enrollment never exceeding 45 for one instructor. Of course, if there is a lecture or other activity scheduled adaptable to greater numbers, it may be possible to have more persons in the class. For remedial work, a suitable class size is from one-on-one to 20 to 25 and should never exceed 30. Aquatics, gymnastics, and other high-risk activities also call for reduced student-to-teacher ratio with 20:1 being the upper limit. With flexible scheduling, the size of classes can be varied to meet the needs of the teacher, facilities, and type of activity being offered. Creative managers should employ this technique when units such as beginning swimming are introduced.

Instructional Loads and Staffing

The instructional load of the physical educator should be of prime concern to management. To maintain a high level of enthusiasm, vigor, and morale, it is important that the load be fair and equitable so that physical educators can perform to their fullest potential.

Some professional guidelines recommended that one full-time physical education teacher should be provided for every 240 elementary or 190 secondary students enrolled. Such a requirement would provide adequate professional staffing and avoid an overload for many of the teachers. This might also keep more physical education teachers involved in after-school extracurricular activities, such as intramurals and coaching.

Professional recommendations regarding teaching load at K-12 educational levels have been made that would limit class instruction per teacher to 5 hours or the equivalent in class periods per day, or 1500 minutes per week. The maximum would be 6 hours per day or 1800 minutes a week, including after-school responsibilities. A daily load of 200 students per teacher is recommended, and this should never exceed 250. Finally, each teacher should have at least one preparation period daily and other scheduled time for consultation and conferences with students.

It is generally agreed that the normal teaching load in colleges and universities should not exceed 12-16 contact hours per week. At research universities, however, the load of the physical education (kinesiology, sports studies, etc.) professor is accommodated to take into account research, publishing, and service requirements. In many institutions, including K-12 levels, professional organizations, teachers' associations, and unions prescribe the length of the workday, including the instructional work load.

The work load in a physical fitness center, which typically might open at 6 AM and close at 11 PM 7 days per week, is often 40 to 50 hours per week. Corporate fitness centers usually maintain an 8-hour working day. Some, however, stay open at night, so the staff may have to work "off-hour" shifts. Regardless of position, the profession of physical education is a "full-time" labor of love.

Differentiated Staffing

Many innovations, such as differentiated staffing, are directed toward aiding teachers in the performance of their duties. Paraprofessionals, qualified undergraduate interns, teaching assistants, and student teachers provide many schools with valuable support staff.

Differentiated staffing relates to increased responsibilities or differentiation of functions among staff members. For example, in team teaching, higher salaries are given to team leaders or head teachers.

Staff members who assume such roles as heads of departments or staff supervisors or assistants are usually compensated accordingly. In some school systems, highly competent staff members with expertise in certain areas are often assigned to special projects such as curriculum-writing teams and may also receive extra compensation for these duties.

The benefits derived from differentiated staffing are obvious from the responsibilities assigned to various staff members. In schools, for example, teachers are able to devote more time to help students, and they can also be free to work with small groups to assist them in mastering learning tasks. Differentiated staffing allows the teacher to focus on teaching and not be directly involved in time-consuming clerical and physical responsibilities.

Paraprofessionals. Responsibilities include (1) supervised instructional assistance, (2) assisting with the swimming pool, (3) clerical duties, (4) student conduct supervision, and (5) preparation of learning materials.

Qualified undergraduate interns. Responsibilities include (1) clerical assistance, (2) record keeping, (3) preparation of learning materials, (4) conduct supervision in noninstructional areas, (5) individual assistance, and (6) observation.

Student teachers. Responsibilities include (1) observation, (2) supervised clinical teaching experience, (3) assistance to supervising teachers, (4) preparation of learning materials, (5) individual assistance, and (6) extracurricular guidance.

Teaching assistants. Responsibilities may include the same as those of an instructor at the college or university level. Physical Activity Programs at many larger universities are staffed by TAs.

Taking Roll

There are many methods of taking roll. If a method satisfies the following three criteria, it is usually satisfactory. (1) It is efficient—roll taking should not consume too much time. (2) It is accurate—after class, it is important to know who was present and who was not, as well as who came late or left early. (3) It is uncomplicated—any system that is used should be easy to manage. The following provides some methods for roll taking:

1. *Having numbers on the floor.* Each member of the class is assigned a number that he or she must stand on when the signal for "fall in" is given. The person taking attendance records the numbers not covered.
2. *Reciting numbers orally.* Each member of the class is assigned a number that he or she must say out loud at the time the "fall in" signal is given. The person taking attendance then records the numbers omitted.
3. *Tag board.* Each member of the class has a number recorded on a cardboard or metal tag that hangs on a peg on a board in a central place. Each member of the class who is present removes his or her tag from the board and places it in a box. The person taking attendance records the absentees from the tags remaining on the board.
4. *Delaney system.* Involves using a folder with cards that are turned over when a person is absent. It is a cumulative system that records the attendance of pupils over time.
5. *Squad system.* The class is divided into squads and the squad leader takes the roll for his or her squad and in turn reports to the instructor.
6. *Issuing towels and equipment.* The roll is taken when a towel is issued to each student or when it is turned in, or when a basket with a uniform is issued or returned.
7. *Signing a book or register.* Students are required to write their names in a book or register at the beginning of the class. Some systems require the writing of a name at the beginning of a period and crossing it out at the end. The person taking attendance records the names not entered from the master roll.
8. *Calling the roll.* This is the most frequently observed method; it is tedious, yet effective.

Selecting Physical Education Activities

Physical education activities represent the heart of the program. They are the means for accomplishing objectives and achieving educational goals. Because activities are so important to the physical education program, they must be selected with considerable care.

Criteria for Selection

Activities should be selected in terms of the values they have in achieving the objectives of physical education. This means they should serve to promote and develop not only body awareness, movement fundamentals, and physical fitness, but also the cognitive, affective, and socioemotional makeup of the individual.

Activities should be interesting and challenging. They should appeal to the participants and present them with problem-solving activities and situations that challenge their skill, ability, and creativity. They should be adaptable to the growth and developmental needs and interests of children, youth, and adults. The needs of individuals vary from age to age. As a consequence, movement activities, the pattern of organization, and instructional delivery strategies must also change. The activity must be suited to the person, not the person to the activity. Wherever possible, participants should be allowed some choice and input into their physical education program and class.

Activities should be modifications of fundamental movements such as running, jumping, throwing, walking, striking, kicking, and climbing.

Physical education class incorporating fundamental movement; Crest View Elementary School, Brooklyn Park, MN.

Activities must be selected in light of the facilities, supplies, equipment, and other human and physical resources available in the school, college, or community. An extensive tennis program cannot be carried out if only one court is available.

Activities should be selected not only with a view to their present value while the child is in school, but also with a view to post-school and adult living. Skills learned during school and college can be used throughout life, thus contributing to enriched living. Patterns for many skills used in adult leisure hours are developed while the individual is in the formative years of childhood.

Health and safety factors must be considered when selecting activities. High-risk activities should be kept to a minimum.

The local education philosophy, policies, and school or college organization must be considered.

School activities should provide situations similar to those that children experience in natural play and competitive situations outside school.

Activities should provide the participant with opportunities for creative self-expression.

Activities selected should elicit appropriate social and moral responses through high-quality leadership and role-modeling.

Activities should reflect the democratic way of life.

Physical education activities are frequently classified into various categories. The following activities do not necessarily meet criteria that have been previously listed. They merely indicate some current offerings in physical education programs throughout the United States:

Team games

Baseball
Basketball
Codeball
Field hockey
Flag football
Football
Ice hockey
Soccer
Softball
Speedball
Team handball

Touch football
Volleyball

Outdoor winter sports

Ice hockey
Ringette
Roller skating
Skating
Skiing (Alpine and Nordic)
Snow games
Snowshoeing
Tobogganing

Other activities

Camping and outdoor activities
Combatives (judo, karate)
Correctives (posture control)
Fly-fishing
Fly-tying
Games of low organization
Jogging
Kayaking
Mountaineering
Movement education
Orienteering
Relays
Rock climbing
Self-testing activities
Yoga

Rhythms and dancing

Aerobic dance
Folk dancing
Gymnastic dancing
Modern dancing
Movement fundamentals
Rhythms
Square dancing
Social dancing
Tap dancing

Formal activities

Calisthenics
Marching

Water activities

Canoeing
Diving
Life guarding
Sailing
Scuba diving
Swimming
Rowing
Water games

Water polo
Water Safety Instructor

Gymnastics

Acrobatics
Apparatus
Obstacle course
Pyramid building
Rope climbing
Stunts
Tumbling

Dual and individual sports

Archery
Badminton
Bowling
Checkers
Cycling
Darts
Deck tennis
Fencing
Fishing
Golf
Handball
Horseback riding
Horsehoes
Paddleball
Paddle tennis
Platform tennis
Racquetball
Rifle
Rope skipping
Shuffleboard
Skeet shooting
Skish
Squash
Table tennis
Tennis
Tether ball
Track and field
Trap shooting
Weight training
Wrestling

Grouping Participants

Proper grouping of students in physical education classes is crucial to both obtaining desired results and complying with guidelines such as Title IX and Public Law 94-142. Because of considerations such as these, the physical educator needs to develop a

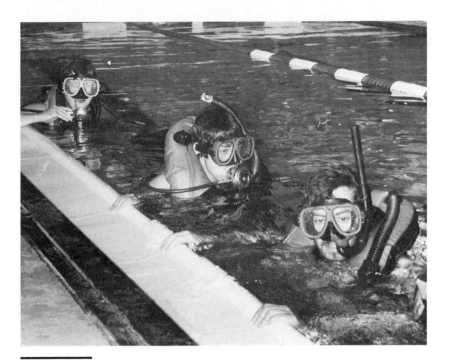

Scuba diving class; University of Nevada, Las Vegas.

broad spectrum of organizational strategies, ranging from homogeneous to heterogeneous groups.

By tradition, physical educators have tended to favor homogeneous grouping. The theory behind this strategy is that placing individuals with similar capacities and characteristics in the same class makes it possible to better meet the needs of each student. Grouping individuals with similar skill, ability, and other factors (e.g., height and weight) also aids in equalizing competition.

Current trends toward grouping students, however, take more of a heterogeneous approach. Research indicates that heterogeneous grouping promotes positive social interaction between students of differing ability, skill level, and other characteristics (e.g., race, gender, socioeconomic level, physical or mental disability) and enhances overall performance.[6] Moreover, heterogeneous grouping means that compliance with governmental mandates is easily accomplished.

Because of scheduling considerations, many schools group students by grade, which has inherent advantages as well as disadvantages. Grouping by grade provides many students with a sense of security since they are comfortable with their cohorts. On the other hand, height, weight and other developmental variations must be taken into account.

Perhaps the preferable class organizational structure is a combination of homogeneous and heterogeneous grouping. Grouping boys and girls into physical education classes by grade meets Title IX regulations and presents the physical educator with limitless possibilities for grouping strategies within the class. This, in turn, allows a variety of goal structures ranging from competitive to cooperative, with combinations thereof, to be utilized. In competitive situations where height and weight are factors, or where it is inappropriate for boys to compete against girls (and vice versa), homogeneous groups can compete against others within their group. In other circumstances, teams formed homogeneously can be pitted against other teams from within the same "skill division"; on still other occasions, teams that are developed heterogeneously can compete against like teams.

Heterogeneous grouping provides unique opportunities for students to develop physically, as well as cognitively and socially. For example, within a heterogeneous tennis class of 30 students, the instructor, after assessing skill level, can form six heterogeneous teams of five students. Each group practices as a team, teaching and coaching teammates, and when the competition round begins, the "team" plays against other teams so that number 1 players compete against other number 1s, number 2s play number 2s, and so on. This approach allows all players in the class to compete at their own level and to work toward a common goal (team victory) with

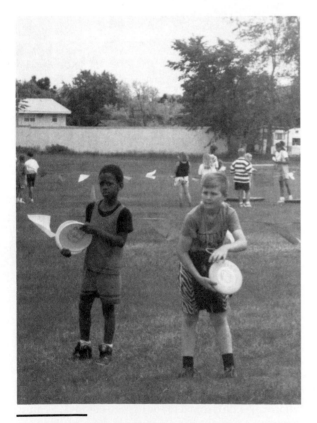

Heterogeneous grouping promotes positive social interaction; Crest View Elementary School, Brooklyn Park, MN.

students who are at different levels. It also enables the less skilled students in the class to make a meaningful contribution toward their team's success.

Many schools offer elective courses in physical education, which often is a very effective way of grouping students. Electives permit students to self-select and usually place those with similar interests and abilities in the class. Elective coursework gives the innovative physical educator many opportunities for structuring task and goal interdependence in order to stimulate students physically, cognitively, and psychosocially.

Student Leadership and Involvement

In recent years students have been demanding greater involvement in the educational process, and in most cases this increased involvement has been satisfactory to students, teachers, and administrators. Some of these areas of involvement are discussed briefly here.

General planning. Students should be involved in planning meetings that discuss scheduling, curriculum innovations, and recent changes in educational methods and instructional strategies. Students might be invited to join community task forces, attend school board and parent association meetings, and also accompany teachers and administrators to other schools where certain innovations may be directly observed. Some schools and colleges have instituted student advisory boards that meet with staff members to discuss problems, recommend changes, and participate in future strategic planning.

Curriculum planning. Student surveys sometimes reveal the extent of curriculum changes desired by the student body. Administrators, teachers, and students should carefully weigh this information in light of current literature, research, and curriculum innovations in similar schools and colleges. Student participation and feedback are essential; however, students do have limited experience in educational matters, and this must also be considered. Frequently the limited use of experimental programs can help evaluate the change before it is implemented on a larger scale.

In a high school in Massachusetts students take an active role in curriculum planning. Students, for example, plan what and how they are going to learn a gymnastics unit. Several days are set aside for students to set goals, plan the steps needed to reach a specific goal, outline the evaluation requirements, and make a commitment to learning and improvement. The students put their goals in writing and then strive to achieve them. Instruction is provided, and grading is a cooperative venture between students and teacher.

Using the Student Leader

Student leaders may be used in the physical education program in several capacities.

Class leaders. There are many opportunities in the physical education instructional class period for student leaders to be of great assistance. These include duties such as acting as squad leader; being a leader for warm-up exercises; demonstrating skills, games, and tactics to be performed; taking attendance; assisting with locker room supervision; and providing safety measures for class participation, such as serving as a spotter and checking equipment and play areas.

Officials, captains, and other positions. Student leaders can gain valuable experience by serving as officials within the class and recreational sports program; being captains of all-star or other teams; coaching recreational sport or club teams; and acting as scorers, timekeepers, referees, and equipment supervisors.

Committee members. Many committee assignments should be filled by student leaders so that they gain valuable experience. These include being a member of a *rules committee,* by which rules are established and interpreted for games and sports; serving on an *equipment and grounds committee,* where standards are established for the storage, maintenance, and use of these facilities and equipment; participating on a *committee for planning special events* in the physical education program, such as play, sports, or field days; and joining a task force on long-range strategic planning for the building of new facilities.

Supply and equipment manager. Supplies and special equipment ranging from basketballs and hockey equipment to audiovisual aids are among the

items continually required for the conduct of the physical education program. The equipment must be removed from the storage areas, transported to the place where the activity will be conducted, and then returned. The student leader can help immeasurably in this process and profit from such an experience.

Program planner. Various aspects of the physical education program need to be planned, and students should be involved. Student leaders, because of their special qualifications and interest, are logical choices to participate in such planning and curriculum development. Their knowledge and advice can ensure that the program more fully meets the needs and interests of all students who participate in the program.

Record keeper and office manager. Attendance records, test scores, and inventories must be taken, recorded, and filed; bulletin boards kept up to date; visitors greeted; and other responsibilities effectively met. These necessary functions provide worthwhile

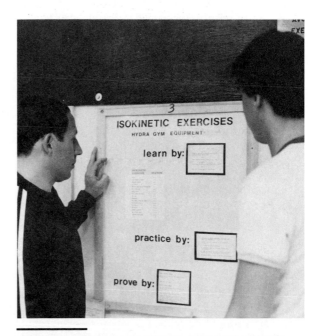

Instructor and student leader planning an isokinetic exercise program; Riverside-Brookfield High School, Riverside, IL.

experiences for the student leader to develop human and technical skills, as well as to assist the teacher.

Special events coordinator. A multitude of details always are involved in play days, sports days, demonstrations, and exhibitions. Student leaders should be involved in planning and conducting these events. This is a great way to experience sport management up close.

It is important to keep in mind that student leaders are to be accorded respect and rewarded for their work. They are invaluable volunteers whom the teacher wants to encourage, involve, and offer responsibility. They are not, however, substitute teachers; safety and legal responsibility should always remain with the teacher.

SELECTED MANAGEMENT PROBLEMS IN INSTRUCTIONAL PROGRAMS

The manager of any physical education program is continually confronted with questions such as the following: Should physical education be required or elective? Should other activities be substituted for physical education? How much credit should be awarded? What is the policy on class attendance? How should an instructor deal with excuses? What grading system should the physical educator utilize? Who should deliver physical education at the elementary school level? These questions and other issues, including dressing and showering, record keeping, and safety considerations, are addressed in the following discussion.

Should Physical Education Be Required or Elective?

General agreement is that physical education should be required at the elementary, junior high, and middle school levels. However, there are many advocates on both sides of the question of whether it should be required or elective at the secondary and college levels. Most professionals believe physical education should be required, whereas some school administrators and parents believe elective offerings are the order of the day. The following are some of the arguments presented by each.

Required

Physical education is a basic need of every student. Students need regular and vigorous physical activity to develop to their fullest potential and to release tension from the rigors of the academic setting.

The student considers required subjects most important, and if physical education is not required, many individuals who could benefit from active participation may choose not to do so.

Various subjects in the curriculum would not be provided unless they were required. This is probably true of physical education. Until mandated by state legislatures and school districts, physical education was ignored by many school administrators. This noncommittal administrative philosophy might cause physical education to suffer curtailment or possible elimination.

Even when required, physical education is not meeting all the physical, cognitive, psychomotor, and socioemotional needs of students. Therefore, an elective program would further inhibit student growth and development.

Elective

Physical education "carries its own drive." If a good basic instructional physical education program is developed in the elementary school, with students acquiring the necessary skills and attitudes, the drive for such activity will carry through to the secondary school and college. There should be no need to require physical education, because students will want to take it voluntarily.

The objectives of physical education are focused on acquiring skills and learning activities that have carry-over value, assisting in the establishment of a healthful lifestyle, and recognizing the importance of developing and maintaining one's body in its best possible condition. These goals cannot be legislated. They must become a part of each individual's attitudes and desires if they are to be realized.

Some children and young adults do not like physical education. This is indicated in their manner, attitude, and desire to get excused from the program and to substitute something else for the course. Under such circumstances the values that accrue to these individuals are not great. Therefore it would be best to place physical education on an elective basis so that those students who participate actually desire to do so. In the day and age of freedom of expression and individual choice, it seems antithetical that requirements are a part of the educational curriculum.

Should Substitutions Be Permitted for Physical Education?

A practice exists in some school and college systems that permits students to substitute some other activity for their physical education requirement. This practice should be scrutinized and resisted aggressively by every educator.

Some of the activities often used as substitutions for physical education are athletic participation, Reserve Officers' Training Corps, and band. There is no substitute for a sound program of physical education. In addition to the healthful physical activity, physical education is also concerned with developing an individual socially, emotionally, and mentally. Furthermore, the individual develops many skills that can be applied throughout life. These essentials are lost if a student is permitted to substitute some other activity for physical education.

Should Credit Be Awarded for Physical Education?

Whether credit should be awarded for physical education is another controversy with which the profession is continually confronted. Here again advocates can be found on both sides. Some think the joy of the activity and the values derived from participation are sufficient in themselves without giving credit. On the other hand, some believe that physical education is the same as any other subject in the curriculum, and therefore credit should be granted.

The general consensus among physical education leaders is that if physical education is required for graduation and if it enriches a person's education, credit should be awarded.

What Policy Should Be Established on Class Attendance?

It is important for every department of physical education to have a clear-cut policy concerning class attendance that covers absenteeism and tardiness. These regulations should be concise and clearly stated in writing so that they are recognized and understood. They should allow for a reasonable number of absences and tardies. Perfect attendance at school or college should not be stressed. Many harmful results can develop if students feel obligated to attend classes when they are ill and should be at home. There should be some provision for independent study and out-of-class activity, as well as makeup work when important experiences are missed. Makeup work should be planned and conducted so that the student derives essential values from such participation, rather than perceiving it as a disciplinary measure. There should also be written provisions for the readmission of students who have been ill or injured.

A final point to remember is the importance of keeping accurate, up-to-date attendance records to minimize administrative problems and maximize student accountability and safety.

What About Excuses?

The principal, nurse, or physical educator frequently receives a note from a parent or family physician requesting that a student be excused from participating in physical education. Many times for various reasons the student does not want to participate and obtains the parent's or family physician's support.

Most schools permit a student to be excused from daily physical education on the basis of a parental note, a memorandum from the family physician, or at the discretion of the physical education teacher. Although some schools accept the recommendation of any of these three persons, other schools might accept only an excuse from the school physician. At the college level, most programs accept the college physician's excuse or permit the instructors to use their own discretion in granting excuses to students.

Some prevalent reasons for granting daily excuses in physical education have prevailed over time. Secondary schools grant most of their excuses for participation in sports, the school band and choir, or some other school-sponsored activity. Some schools excuse athletes from physical education on game days, whereas others grant a blanket exemption from physical education for the entire sport season. Other reasons for excuses include makeup examinations, driver training, counseling, and medical considerations. Students who are excused usually are required to attend study halls or to score, officiate, or assist with the conduct of physical education class or assist the department in some meaningful task. Failure in the class usually results when too many absences accumulate.

Some school systems have attempted to control the indiscriminate granting of requests for excuses from physical education. Policies have been established, with the support of the board of education, requiring that all excuses be reviewed and approved by the school physician or nurse before they are granted. Furthermore, family physicians have been asked to state specific reasons for requesting excuses from physical education. This procedure has worked satisfactorily in some communities. In other places physical educators have taken particular pains to work closely with physicians. They have established a physical education program in collaboration with the school physician so that the needs of each individual are met, regardless of his or her physical condition. They have met with the local medical society in an attempt to clear up misunderstandings about the purpose and conduct of the program. Family physicians have been brought into the planning process. As a result of such planning, problems with excessive excuses have been reduced. In such communities the values derived from participation in the program are clearly recognized, and because most parents and physicians want children to have worthwhile experiences, they encourage rather than limit such participation.

Cooperative effort between physical educators and physicians has resulted in the formulation of a list of statements in respect to the problem under discussion:

- Orient the student, parent, and physician at an early date in regard to the objectives of the physical education program.
- Route all excuse requests through the school physician or nurse.
- Discard permanent and blanket excuses. In-

stead of being categorically excused, students can be assigned an appropriate physical activity in keeping with their special needs.
- Students involved in excuse requests should be periodically monitored as to their school performance. Parents, students, and appropriate school officials should be involved.
- Cooperation between the school physician, nurse, counselor, and the head of the physical education department needs to be emphasized, especially in the case of continuous and excessive excuse requests.

Grading and Assessment of Students

In order to determine whether students are meeting the objectives of the physical education instructional program, it is requisite that each instructor develop meaningful, effective, and efficient methods for assessment. This assessment will assist in determining a grade or mark for each student that may be reported by semester, trimester, or quarter, and usually becomes a part of the student's permanent record. Grades are a serious matter and not only serve

Assessment is crucial to the evaluation process.

to inform students concerning their class progress, but also may be used to gain admission to college, for employment, to qualify for a scholarship or to receive preferred automobile insurance rates. Students are proud of their grades!

For grades or marks to be meaningful, they should be based on established criteria (e.g., school or national norms), which are clearly presented to the student and class. A grade should reflect the student's progress toward these prescribed criteria, as well as others designed by the student and the instructor. Grading is both a science and an art and should possess the following characteristics: (1) grades should be valid—they should reflect that which is intended (e.g., muscular strength or endurance, cardiovascular endurance, the defensive clear in badminton), (2) grades should be reliable—they should be a true reflection of the student's prowess and capability to perform, (3) grades should be objective—they should be based on well-defined criteria (e.g., making 6 out of 10 foul shots reflects free throw proficiency), and (4) grades should be fair, equitable, and consistent—students performing at similar levels should receive similar grades.

There are many philosophies and methods concerning the grading of physical education skills, fitness level, knowledge, and understanding. The teacher usually assigns a Pass or Fail, Satisfactory or Unsatisfactory, A through F, or sometimes a percentage. Regardless of the grading system employed, it is important to meet with each student in order to personalize grading. Finally, it is crucial to keep each student's yearly objectives and the teacher's and student's written assessments on file.

Who Should Conduct the Elementary School Physical Education Class?

The question of who should conduct elementary school physical education class has been discussed and debated for many years. Some educators suggest that the elementary classroom teacher instruct physical education classes, whereas physical education advocates prefer a physical education specialist to assume this responsibility. The regular classroom teacher usually possesses limited professional training in physical education. Most classroom teachers are not interested in teaching physical education. Furthermore, there is renewed interest in physical education, as well as a return to mainstreaming children with disabilities into the gym, which implies that qualified and certified teaching specialists should conduct these classes. The trend is toward more emphasis on movement education, perceptual motor development, physical fitness, lifetime skill acquisition, and other aspects of education with which the profession is concerned. There is an increased emphasis on looking to the physical education specialist for help and advice in planning and conducting the elementary school program, including both the regular and self-contained classroom. These developments have implications for sound inservice programs to assist the classroom teacher do a better job in delivering physical education.

In light of the present status of physical education in the elementary schools of this country, such recommendations as the following should be very carefully considered. Each elementary school should be staffed with a specialist in physical education. Although the classroom teacher may significantly contribute to the physical education program in primary school, factors such as the growth and developmental changes and interests taking place in boys and girls and the more complex specialized program that exists at this level make it imperative to seek the help of a specialist who possesses the ability, experience, and training required to meet the needs of the students. The physical education specialist and the classroom teacher should pool their experience to provide the student with an optimal learning environment. Each professional has much to contribute and should be encouraged to do so to reach the fullest potential of each student.

Dressing and Showering

The problem of showering and dressing is not so pertinent at the elementary level where the age of the participants and type of activities usually do not require special dress and showering. Some junior high, middle, and senior high schools require physical education uniforms. Reasons for this include safety, uniformity, and name identification. Those programs that do not require physical education uniforms request that students wear comfortable, safe clothing without zippers and buttons.

In the interests of comfort and good hygiene practices, ample time and provisions should be made for showering and dressing. At the junior and senior high levels where no towel service is provided, many students choose not to shower. Therefore schools should make special provisions for secure, clean, attractive places to dress and shower. Such places should be convenient to the physical education areas, be comfortable, and afford privacy. Although boys and girls are becoming increasingly accustomed to using group showers, many still prefer private showers. In the interests of these individuals, as well as those students with disabilities, such facilities should be provided. When possible, there should also be a towel laundering service and hair drying facilities for the convenience of the students. Attractive and convenient showering facilities will lead more students to take advantage of this healthful practice.

Records

Records are essential in keeping valuable information regarding the participants' welfare. They also are essential to efficient program planning and management. They should, however, be kept to a minimum and should be practical and functional. They should not be maintained merely as busy work and for the sake of filling files.

Some of the records should be concerned directly with the welfare of the participant and others with certain programmatic and administrative variables.

- Records that concern the health status, the cumulative physical education record, attendance reports, grades, and accident reports are of prime value.
- Health records are essential. They contain information on the most current medical examination, health appraisal, health counseling, and any other data pertaining to the person's health and medical status.
- The cumulative physical education record should contain information about activity participation, physical fitness appraisals, growth and development status, and other pertinent in-

formation concerning the student's participation in the physical education program. If a student has a disability, the student's IEPs should be on record.
- There should also be special records for attendance, grades, and any other unique occurrences bearing on the participant that are not a part of other records.
- A year-end assessment for each student should also be maintained.
- If a student is involved in a physical education class accident, a full account of the circumstances surrounding the accident should be recorded. Usually special forms are provided for such purposes.
- Management records should also provide general information and equipment records, including a list of the year's events, activities, records of teams, play days, sports days, recreational sports, events of special interest, techniques that have been helpful, budget information, and any other data that would be helpful in planning for succeeding years. Memory often fails over time, with the result that many good ideas are lost and many activities and techniques of special value are not used because they are forgotten. The computer is extremely valuable for this function.
- There should be records of equipment, facilities, and supplies that show the current status, repair dates, inventory, new materials needed, and the location of various materials, so that they can be easily found. Records of such items as locker or basket assignments, lock combinations, and equipment checkout are essential to the efficient and effective running of a physical education program.

Safety Considerations

The teacher of the instructional physical education program is responsible for the basic conduct of the program. This involves ensuring that each class is operated in a safe, progressive, and prudent fashion. This means providing a safe environment in terms of facilities, equipment, supervision, selection of age- and ability-appropriate activities, as well as outlin-

Physical educators must be aware of safety and liability considerations.

ing proper procedures if an emergency should arise.

The teacher is also responsible for thoroughly explaining and demonstrating each activity, warning students of potential risks and hazards, employing proper and progressive skill techniques, requiring appropriate and safe dress, and providing prudent supervision to ensure optimal student learning and safety.

The teacher should be licensed and maintain current certification (e.g., First Aid, CPR, Life Guard Training, coaching, adapted) to ensure safety and provide the optimal learning environment for the students.

Each student should have a thorough medical examination by a qualified physician on file with the school or institution, and the physical education teacher should be aware of this health status (e.g., activity restrictions, medications, allergies).

Safety policies and procedures should be posted in several accessible and appropriate areas, and each student should be informed of these procedures and what is expected under emergency circumstances. Activity release and modified program forms, accident forms, and return-to-activity clearance forms should all be standardized and maintained in departmental records.

The teacher should also be encouraged to join the professional organization of his or her choice, because such organizations often provide insurance that covers potential professional injury, as well as legal liability.

CRITERIA FOR EVALUATING PHYSICAL EDUCATION INSTRUCTIONAL PROGRAMS

The authors have adapted the following checklist for evaluating physical education instructional programs.[7]

CRITERIA FOR EVALUATING PHYSICAL EDUCATION INSTRUCTIONAL PROGRAMS

	Poor (1)	Fair (2)	Good (3)	Very good (4)	Excellent (5)
Meeting physical education objectives					
1. Does the class activity contribute to the development of physical fitness?	☐	☐	☐	☐	☐
2. Does the class activity foster the growth of ethical character, desirable emotional and psychosocial characteristics?	☐	☐	☐	☐	☐
3. Does the class activity contain recreational value?	☐	☐	☐	☐	☐
4. Does the class activity contain carryover value for later life?	☐	☐	☐	☐	☐
5. Is the class activity accepted as a regular part of the curriculum?	☐	☐	☐	☐	☐
6. Does the class activity meet the needs of *all* participants in the group?	☐	☐	☐	☐	☐
7. Does the class activity encourage the development of leadership?	☐	☐	☐	☐	☐
8. Does the class activity fulfill the safety objective in physical education?	☐	☐	☐	☐	☐
9. Do the class activity and conduct foster a better understanding of democratic living?	☐	☐	☐	☐	☐
10. Do the class activity and conduct cultivate a better understanding of and appreciation for exercise and sports?	☐	☐	☐	☐	☐

PERFECT SCORE: 50   ACTUAL SCORE: _____

	Poor (1)	Fair (2)	Good (3)	Very good (4)	Excellent (5)
Leadership (teaching conduct)					
1. Is the teacher appropriately dressed for the class activity?	☐	☐	☐	☐	☐
2. Does the teacher know the activity thoroughly?	☐	☐	☐	☐	
3. Does the teacher possess an audible and pleasing voice?	☐	☐	☐	☐	☐
4. Does the teacher project an enthusiastic and dynamic attitude in class presentation?	☐	☐	☐	☐	☐
5. Does the teacher maintain discipline?	☐	☐	☐	☐	☐
6. Does the teacher identify, analyze and correct faulty performance in guiding students?	☐	☐	☐	☐	☐
7. Does the teacher present a sound, logical method of teaching motor skills, for example, explanation, demonstration, participation, and assessment?	☐	☐	☐	☐	☐
8. Does the teacher avoid the use of destructive criticism, sarcasm, and ridicule with students?	☐	☐	☐	☐	☐
9. Does the teacher maintain emotional stability and poise?	☐	☐	☐	☐	☐
10. Does the teacher possess high standards and ideals of work?	☐	☐	☐	☐	☐

PERFECT SCORE: 50   ACTUAL SCORE: _____

	Poor (1)	Fair (2)	Good (3)	Very good (4)	Excellent (5)
General class procedures, methods, and techniques					
1. Does class conduct yield evidence of preplanning?	☐	☐	☐	☐	☐
2. Does the organization of the class allow for individual differences?	☐	☐	☐	☐	☐
3. Does the class exhibit maximal activity and minimal teacher participation (e.g., proper emphasis on explanation and/or demonstration)?	☐	☐	☐	☐	☐
4. Are adequate motivational devices such as teaching aids and audiovisual techniques effectively utilized?	☐	☐	☐	☐	☐
5. Are squad leaders effectively employed when appropriate?	☐	☐	☐	☐	☐
6. Does the class start promptly at the scheduled time?	☐	☐	☐	☐	☐
7. Are students with medical excuses from regular class supervised and channelled into appropriate activities?	☐	☐	☐	☐	☐
8. Is the class roll taken quickly and accurately?	☐	☐	☐	☐	☐
9. Are accurate records of progress and achievements maintained?	☐	☐	☐	☐	☐
10. Are supplies and equipment quickly issued and stored?	☐	☐	☐	☐	☐

PERFECT SCORE: 50   ACTUAL SCORE: _____

	Poor (1)	Fair (2)	Good (3)	Very good (4)	Excellent (5)
Student conduct					
1. Are the objectives of the activity or sport clearly known to the learner?	☐	☐	☐	☐	☐
2. Are the students interested in the class activities?	☐	☐	☐	☐	☐
3. Do the students enjoy their physical education class?	☐	☐	☐	☐	☐
4. Are the students familiar with organizational procedures such as those for taking roll and obtaining excuses?	☐	☐	☐	☐	☐
5. Are the students appropriately dressed for the class activity?	☐	☐	☐	☐	☐
6. Does the class exhibit a spirit of cooperation in learning new skills?	☐	☐	☐	☐	☐
7. Do students avoid mischief or "horseplay"?	☐	☐	☐	☐	☐
8. Do students shower when the nature of the activity requires?	☐	☐	☐	☐	☐
9. Do lesser skilled students receive as much opportunity to participate as higher skilled classmates?	☐	☐	☐	☐	☐
10. Do students show respect for the teacher?	☐	☐	☐	☐	☐

PERFECT SCORE: 50   ACTUAL SCORE: _____

◈ **CRITERIA FOR EVALUATING PHYSICAL EDUCATION INSTRUCTIONAL PROGRAMS—cont'd**

	Poor (1)	Fair (2)	Good (3)	Very good (4)	Excellent (5)
Safe and healthful environment					
1. Is the area large enough for the activity and number of participants in the class?	☐	☐	☐	☐	☐
2. Does the class possess adequate equipment and/or supplies?	☐	☐	☐	☐	☐
3. Are adequate shower and locker facilities available and readily accessible?	☐	☐	☐	☐	☐
4. Is the equipment and/or apparatus clean and in good working order?	☐	☐	☐	☐	☐
5. Does the activity area contain good lighting and ventilation?	☐	☐	☐	☐	☐
6. Are all safety hazards eliminated or reduced where possible?	☐	☐	☐	☐	☐
7. Is first aid and safety equipment readily accessible?	☐	☐	☐	☐	☐
8. Is the storage area adequate for supplies and equipment?	☐	☐	☐	☐	☐
9. Does the activity area contain a properly equipped room for use in injury, illness, or for rest periods?	☐	☐	☐	☐	☐
10. Does the activity area contain accessible toilet facilities?	☐	☐	☐	☐	☐

PERFECT SCORE: 50   ACTUAL SCORE: _____

Criteria	Perfect score	Actual score
Meeting physical education objectives	50	_____
Leadership (teacher conduct)	50	_____
General class procedures, methods, and techniques	50	_____
Student conduct	50	_____
Safe and healthful environment	50	_____
TOTAL	250	_____

SUMMARY

The instructional program in physical education is the place to teach such vital elements as skills, strategies, and understandings concerning the contribution of physical activity to total well-being.

Physical education instructional programs exist at all educational levels and in various community agencies and private volunteer organizations. Management guidelines exist for teaching physical education in all of these settings, as well as for selecting instructional aids, guides, and materials.

Effective class operation facilitates successful management of a physical education organization.

Title IX affects the implementation of physical education instructional programs in all educational institutions receiving federal assistance. To ensure compliance, all physical educators should be sensitive to Title IX concepts.

The adapted/developmental physical education program is designed to meet the needs of all individuals with disabilities. Public Law 94-142 mandates educational services for all students in either the adapted physical education setting or within the regular physical education program.

Management matters that relate to physical education instructional programs include scheduling, grading and assessment, class size, differentiated staffing, selection of appropriate activities, grouping of and instructional strategies for participants, and student involvement.

Selected management problems related to the instructional programs involve whether physical education should be required, who should deliver physical education at the elementary level, whether to permit the substitution of other activities for physical education, and the awarding of credit. Other issues to be addressed include the development of policies concerning class attendance, excuses, grading, showering and dressing, record keeping, and safety considerations.

◆ **SELF-ASSESSMENT ACTIVITIES**

These activities will assist students in determining if material and competencies presented in this chapter have been mastered:

1. You are a member of a physical education staff in a high school where the instructional program is under attack by the faculty. It has been suggested that the program be abolished. Prepare a brief defense of the instructional physical education program that describes its nature, scope, and worth in the educational process.
2. You have been invited to speak to the PTA in your community on the topic, "The role of phys-

ical education in the community." Prepare a speech that describes the role of physical education and present it to your class.
3. Develop a model for a high school instructional physical education program and discuss how Title IX legislation has influenced your model.
4. Compare how traditional physical education instructional programs are conducted with respect to students with disabilities and how it is proposed they should be conducted as a result of mainstreaming and Public Law 94-142.
5. Develop a list of principles for physical education instructional programs that would serve as guides for each of the following: scheduling, time allotment for classes, class size, instructional loads, uniforms, taking roll, activity offerings, grouping, and student involvement.
6. You are a director of a school physical education program and have been assigned by the superintendent of schools to plan an adapted physical education program for the entire school system. Prepare the plan you will submit to the superintendent, including the objectives you will strive to achieve, the guidelines you will follow, and the activities to be offered.
7. You are a physical education faculty member and have been selected by your college to see that PL 94-142 is fully implemented in your department. Prepare a plan that will ensure that your school physical education program complies.

REFERENCES

1. Bucher CA, Keonig CR: *Methods and materials for secondary school physical education,* ed 6, St Louis, 1983, Mosby–Year Book.
2. Bucher CA, Prentice WE: *Fitness for college and life,* St Louis, 1985, Mosby–Year Book.
3. Clement A: *Law in sport and physical activity,* Indianapolis, 1988, Benchmark Press.
4. Clement A: Legal system assures women equity in sport, *The Sports, Parks, and Recreation Law Reporter,* 3:8-12, 1989.
5. Jensen CR: Administrative management of physical education and athletic programs, Philadelphia, 1988, Lea & Febiger.
6. Johnson RT, Bjorkland R, Krotee ML: The effects of cooperative, competitive and individualistic student interaction patterns on achievement and attitudes of the golf skill of putt-

ing, *Research Quarterly for Sport and Exercise,* 55:129-134, 1984.

7. Piscopo J: Quality of life: first priority, *The Physical Educator* 21:162, 1964.
8. Singer JD: 10th anniversary of PL. 94-142: a visionary law that has worked, *Education Week,* Feb 27, 1985.
9. Stein JU: A clarification of terms, *Journal of Health, Physical Education, and Recreation* 42:63, 1971.
10. Weber M: Title IX in action, *Journal of Physical Education and Recreation* 51:20, 1980.

SUGGESTED READINGS

- Allen RR, Reuter T: *Teaching assistant strategies: an introduction to college teaching,* Dubuque, Ia, 1990, Kendall/Hunt.

  Provides coverage concerning teaching roles, responsibilities, interpersonal relationships, creating learning environments, and assessment. Also included are tips on lecturing, leading class discussion, and facilitating student learning.

- Arnheim DD, Sinclair WA: *Physical education for special populations,* Englewood Cliffs, NJ, 1985, Prentice-Hall.

  Provides valuable information for the professional physical educator working in adapted or developmental physical education. Practical strategies and desirable activities for specific populations are provided. Covers areas such as teacher qualifications, competitive sports, and physical education for persons with disabilities. Sets forth guidelines for areas such as program development and financial support.

- Dunn J, Fait H: *Special physical education,* Dubuque, Ia, 1989, Wm C Brown.

  Presents valuable information concerning managing the learning environment, learning developmental patterns, and understanding the myriad disabilities that physical educators will be involved with. It also includes lists, guidelines, and organizations and associations for physical education, recreational and competitive sports.

- Harrison JM: *Instructional strategies for physical education,* Dubuque, Ia, 1983, Wm C Brown.

  Designed to help physical educators acquire skills necessary to design and carry out effective instructional programs in their field of expertise. Presents skills essential for instruction, covers classroom management, and outlines how unit planning can take place. Ties together cognitive, psychomotor, and affective learning domains as a basis for the design and implementation of instructional strategies. Provides learning aids for students and offers practical examples in such areas as performance objectives, evaluation, and discipline.

- Kleinman M: *The acquisition of motor skill,* Princeton, NJ, 1983, Princeton Book.

  Discusses theoretical foundations of motor learning and establishes the basic psychological foundations of motor learning. Covers such important items as transfer of learning, distribution of practice, knowledge of results, motor retention, and motor control. Contributes to the instructional program in physical education by providing basic information about how motor skills can best be taught.

- Payne GV, Isaacs LD: *Human motor development: a lifespan approach,* Mountain View, Ca, 1991, Mayfield.

  Presents a conceptual view of motor development throughout the lifespan. Provides various assessment suggestions, as well as managerial considerations, regarding curriculum, computer utilization, and instructional strategies.

- Rink JE: *Teaching physical education for learning,* St Louis, 1985, Mosby–Year Book.

  Promotes teaching practices that make a difference in the learning of students. Guidelines and suggestions offered will help preservice and experienced tearchers in their instructional roles. Task complexity and difficulty, learner readiness, and relatedness of sequential learning experiences are considered. Helps students become competent teachers by improving their skills and effectiveness in achieving desirable goals. Identifies the major components of the instructional process and describes, analyzes, and interprets the instructional process in light of the teacher's role.

- US Consumer Product Safety Commission: *Handbook for public playground safety,* Washington, DC, 1992, Author.

  Provides a resource guide for playground areas, facilities, equipment, and maintenance. Includes a section concerning parks and recreation for persons with disabilities.

- Willgoose CE: *The curriculum in physical education,* Englewood Cliffs, NJ, 1984, Prentice-Hall.

  Discusses the curriculum of physical education in various educational levels against a background of societal needs, educational foundations, student characteristics, and research findings. It also discusses curriculum planning, program organization, the curriculum guide, individualizing physical education, and curriculum evaluation.

CHAPTER 4

Recreational Sports: Intramural, Extramural, and Sport Club Programs

▶ **Instructional Objectives and Competencies To Be Achieved**

After reading this chapter the student should be able to

- Define *intramural, extramural,* and *sport club programs* and name the objectives each is designed to achieve.
- Prepare a list of policies that, if followed, will enable a person to organize and manage intramural, extramural, and sport club programs.
- Understand the roles played by various managerial personnel in conducting intramural, extramural, and sport club programs.
- Discuss how intramural, extramural, and sport club programs are administered in elementary, junior high or middle schools, secondary schools, colleges and universities, and other representative organizations.
- Organize various types of competition for intramural and extramural activities.
- Show the importance of and the procedures for managing sport clubs, corecreation, and programs for faculty and for persons with varying disabilities.

Chapter 3 was concerned with basic instructional physical education programs, one of the components of a well-rounded offering for students in schools and members of other representative organizations. This chapter is concerned with the second component, the intramural, extramural, and sport club programs, which are often referred to collectively as recreational sports. By tradition, the term *intramural* denotes "within" institution competition, and *extramural* depicts competition with "outside" schools; sport clubs fall in between. Recreational sports offer competition and other types of physical activities for individuals of all levels of skill and ability. In universities and colleges, as discussed in Chapter 2, intramural, extramural, and sport club activities are usually organized into a department separate from physical education. This is also the case in some secondary and elementary schools, whereas in others, recreational sports programs are considered an extension of the physical education program.

Intramurals and extramurals make up that phase

of a physical education program in a school, college, industry, or other representative organization geared to the abilities and skills of the entire student body or all the members of the organization. It consists of voluntary participation in games, sports, and other activities. Recreational sports offers intramural activities within a single school or institution, as well as extramural activities such as play days and sports days that bring together participants from several institutions.

A sport club program is usually devoted to one activity such as tennis, skiing, or mountain climbing, and it encourages students and other individuals to participate at all levels of skill. Clubs compete within their own ranks, as well as with other outside clubs. Sport clubs may be managed by members of the organization, such as students in schools and colleges, or by the central management of the organization. Members, advisors, or community volunteers usually provide instruction and coaching. Clubs are popular in schools and colleges, as well as

in other organizations. Many communities have tennis, swimming, running, racquetball, riding, and other types of clubs.

Intramurals were started many years ago as a result of student initiative in schools and colleges. At first they received little central administrative notice or support and were poorly organized. However, as student interest grew, the demand for departmental control kept pace. In 1913 intramural sports came under faculty control at the University of Michigan and Ohio State University. Since that time intramurals, extramurals, and sport club programs have continued to grow and in most educational institutions today are under the management and direction of fully trained professional personnel. The National Intramural-Recreational Sports Association (formerly the National Intramural Association founded by Dr. William Wesson at Dillard University in New Orleans) was formed in 1950 and is considered the major professional organization concerning the conduct of recreational sports.

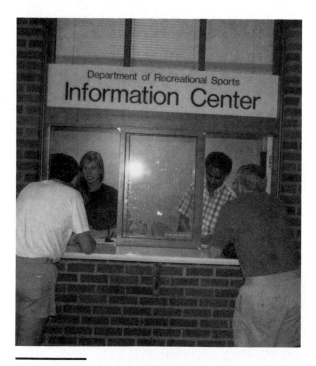

Recreational sport is an integral part of the university community.

RECREATIONAL SPORTS PROGRAMS
Objectives

The objectives of recreational sports programs are an indication of why such programs have expanded greatly throughout the country. These objectives are compatible with the overall objectives of physical education and also with those of education in general.

The objectives of the programs may be classified under four headings: (1) health, (2) skill, (3) psychosocial development, and (4) recreation.

Health. Recreational sports activities contribute to the physical, social, and emotional health of the individual. They contribute to physical health through participation in activities offering healthful exercise. Such characteristics as muscular strength, agility, flexibility, cardiovascular endurance, speed, and body control are developed. They contribute to psychosocial health through group participation and working toward achievement of group goals. Participation also contributes to emotional health by helping a person achieve self-confidence and improve his or her self-concept.

Skill. Recreational sports activities offer the opportunity for every individual to display and develop his or her skills in various physical education activities. Through specialization and voluntary participation they offer individuals the opportunity to excel and to experience the thrill of competition. It is generally agreed that an individual enjoys activities in which he or she has developed skill. Participation in recreational sports offers the opportunity to develop proficiency in group activities in which each person is grouped according to skill, thus providing for equality of competition, which helps guarantee greater success and enjoyment. These programs also enable many persons to spend leisure time profitably and happily.

Psychosocial development. Opportunities for psychosocial development are numerous in recreational sport activities. Through many social contacts, coeducational experiences, and playing on and against other teams, desirable qualities are developed. Individuals learn to subordinate their desires to the will of the group and to develop sportsmanship; they also learn fair play, courage, cooperation, group loyalty, social poise, and other desirable traits. Participation in such a program is voluntary, and people who desire to play under such conditions will do so by group codes of conduct. These experiences offer training for citizenship, adult living, and human relations.

Recreation. Recreational sports programs help develop an interest in many sports and physical education activities; this interest carries over into adult living and provides the basis for many happy leisure hours. These programs also provide excellent recreational activities and support groups during school days, when idle moments have the potential to foster less than desirable behavior.

RELATION TO BASIC INSTRUCTIONAL AND HIGHLY ORGANIZED ATHLETIC PROGRAMS

Recreational sports activities and interscholastic and intercollegiate sports are integral phases of the total sport program in a school or college. This total

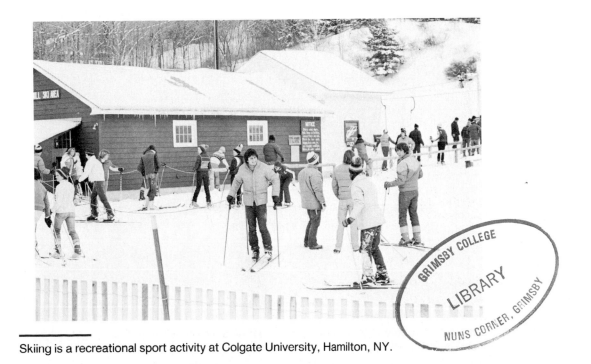

Skiing is a recreational sport activity at Colgate University, Hamilton, NY.

GRIMSBY COLLEGE LIBRARY NUNS CORNER, GRIMSBY

sporting package includes the intramural and extramural programs, sport clubs, and varsity sport, as well as the basic instructional physical education program. Each makes an important contribution to the achievement of educational and physical education objectives. It is crucial to maintain a proper balance so that each program phase enhances and does not restrict the other.

The basic instructional program in physical education is viewed by many physical educators as the foundation for recreational and competitive sport programs. The instructional program includes teaching such fundamentals as skills, concepts, and strategies. Recreational sports programs provide opportunities for all students and others to employ these concepts, skills, and strategies in games and contests that are usually competitive. This part of the total Physical Activity and Sport Continuum is sometimes referred to as the laboratory where the individual has an opportunity to experiment and test what has been learned in the physical education program.

Whereas recreational sports are for everyone, varsity sports are usually for those individuals who are highly skilled in sport-specific activities. The intramural phase of the recreational sports program is conducted on an intra-institutional basis, whereas varsity sports and extramurals are conducted on an inter-institutional basis.

Very little conflict should exist between these two phases of the sports program if the facilities, time, personnel, finance, and other factors are apportioned according to the degree to which each phase achieves the desired outcome, rather than the degree of public appeal and interest stimulated. One should not be designed as a training ground for the other. It should be possible for a person to move from one phase to the other, but this should be incidental rather than planned.

If conducted properly, each phase of the program can contribute to the other, and through an overall, well-balanced sports program the entire student body or all members of an organization will gain appreciation for sport and the great potential it has for improving physical, mental, psychosocial, and emotional growth.

The philosophical model[7] (see Figure 3-1) illustrated the placement of recreational sports within the province of physical activity. This triangular model depicted an interdependence and a building of skills from the basic instructional physical education level to the recreational sports level and, finally, to the level of varsity competition. This model conveyed the philosophy that instruction is basic to

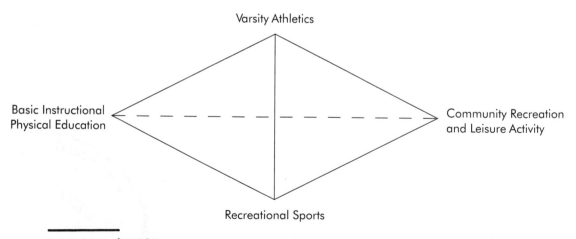

FIGURE 4-1   A modern conceptualization of the interaction of school and community physical education and sport.

the other programs and that recreational sports skills are essential to producing the high-level skills found in varsity play.

The model in Figure 4-1 is presented because of its implications for viewing the phases of the physical education program as both interdependent and equal. It establishes each phase as independent of the others. Recreational and varsity sports are placed close to each other because each is related to the other more closely than are leisure activity and instruction. Community recreation has been added to the model because of its contribution to recreational and varsity sport activities, both of which have as a primary objective the satisfaction derived from participation.

Although the basic physical education and recreational sports programs in a school or college are designed for every student, in practice they generally attract beginning students or those with moderate levels of skill. The highly skilled person usually finds a niche in the varsity program. This has its benefits in that it is an equalizer for competitive structuring. In some cases further recreational sport skill divisions (e.g., "Jag" leagues, co-rec, first division, Division I) may be instituted.

MANAGEMENT PERSONNEL

Many management personnel are needed if a recreational sports program is to be a success. Some key persons involved are the director, student leaders, student directors and unit managers, recreational sports council members, and officials.

The Director

Many larger schools, colleges, corporations, and other organizations have established the position of director of recreational sports. In some cases other titles are used. The director is responsible for establishing programs, securing adequate funding, involving the community, and evaluating the success of the program. Some of the more specific duties of the director include planning programs; organizing tournaments and other forms of competition; supervising the maintenance of facilities, equipment, and supplies; attending and planning sports council meetings; interpreting the program to the membership, the management, and the public in general; supervising the program in action; preparing budgets; and evaluating the worth of the program.

Place in management structure. The director or person in charge of recreational sports in an elementary, junior high, middle, or secondary school is usually reponsible to the director of physical education or athletics. In some cases, not all of these various components are under the same department.

At small colleges the recrcational sports department might also fall under the control of a director of physical education or athletics and in some instances a student activities director. These program administrators usually appoint one person to manage the entire campus recreational sports program of which intramurals, extramurals, and sports club activitics are integral parts. In many cases partial responsibility for recreational sports activities is delegated to students themselves.

In most larger colleges and universities, recreational sports departments maintain separate divisions, receiving consideration along with the physical education or athletic divisions concerning staff members, finances, facilities, equipment, supplies, and other departmental essentials. The department is usually headed by a director well schooled in physical education and sport or recreation management. Working with the director (when conditions warrant) should be assistant and associate directors, supervisors, student managers, and other staff members as needed, depending on the size of the organization. There should also be an adequate number of trained officials and support staff.

Student Leaders

Student involvement in all phases of education has been steadily increasing. Involvement in the management of recreational sports has been happening in high schools and on college campuses since the 1850s. Roles of student leaders may range from serving as board members to being managers, office assistants, and officials. For example, many colleges have "drop-in" centers where student supervisors are available to establish programs, reserve equipment, and arrange additional hours for the gymna-

Recreational sport provides students opportunities to participate and promote fair play and sportsmanship through officiating.

sium or swimming pool. Some schools have student managers who also supervise recreational sports activities.

Student Directors and Unit Managers

In some school programs the director of recreational sports appoints an upper-level student who has been involved with the program to be student director. This student director may have such responsibilities as contacting officials, working with managers, issuing supplies, and scheduling.

Student unit managers have an important responsibility because they are in charge of a particular sport or activity. They usually work closely with the team captains and manage supplies and equipment, team rosters, and entry sheets, and notify teams of the time and date of contests, as well as clarifying eligibility rules.

Recreational Sports Council Members

An important feature of the overall management of a recreational sports program is a recreational sports council, which is usually an elected body with representatives from the participants, central administration, and recreational sports staff. The council is influential in establishing policy and practices for a broad recreational sports program. The council assists and advises the person in charge, as well as the staff members. In some cases it plays an important role in the decision-making process.

Councils usually consist of representatives from the various participating units who disseminate information to the participating teams or individual membership. The council also helps make decisions about program operation and serves as a sounding board for ways in which the program may be improved.

Officials

Excellent officials are necessary for a quality recreational sports program. They should have special qualifications, including a knowledge of the activity, the participants, the goals of the program, and the organization's philosophy of competition. Some of the responsibilities of the managers of the recreational sports program are to find sources for competent officials and then to recruit, select, and train them so that they enhance the program. Some of the duties performed by officials are to have game equipment ready before the contest, see that accurate score sheets are prepared, check for any safety hazards, prepare accident reports if needed, and officiate the game or activity objectively and impartially. Some institutions put officials through training sessions, supervise them during the playing season, and evaluate their performance after the season is over. Whereas most colleges pay their officials, elementary and secondary schools usually do not have the budget to provide compensation. Many schools seek voluntary help from students, staff, parents, and community workers. At the same time it is recognized that these volunteers also need close supervision and should be offered some in-service training.

POLICIES AND PROCEDURES FOR ORGANIZATION AND MANAGEMENT

A list of policies and procedures governing the various features of the program should be in writing and well publicized, perhaps in handbook form. The National Intramural-Recreational Sports Association (NIRSA)[10] serves as an excellent resource for this undertaking.

Policies and procedures for recreational sports should be developed in at least the following areas: student involvement in program organization and management, health and welfare of all participants, activities that meet the interests and needs of the participants, officiating, protests, eligibility standards, fees, forfeits, postponements, point systems, and awards. Policies and procedures concerning user groups, guest fees, rental structure, noise, food consumption, key control, equipment control, and facility use should also be on record. The health and safety of the participants must be a top priority, and policies concerning emergency procedures should be well publicized.

MANAGEMENT CONCERNS IN K-12 SCHOOLS

The management of recreational sports at the elementary, junior high or middle, and secondary school levels presents some problems that are peculiar to these programs. Whereas in many colleges and universities students live in dormitories and on campus, this is not the case in K-12 systems. Some students have to work after school or catch a bus to take them home and cannot stay after school to participate in recreational sports, whereas college students more often are able to participate because they are not faced with such a problem, at least in institutions with dormitory living. Also, many times the parents of elementary, junior high or middle, and secondary school students do not see the value of recreational sports and so do not encourage their children to participate after school. College students, on the other hand, make their own decisions in most cases. Another problem faced by managers of K-12 recreational programs is the lack of facilities. Most schools have limited gymnasium and outdoor space. Varsity sports are often given priority in the use of these facilities, which causes a hardship on the recreational sports program. The question of financial and human resource support also exists in many schools.

In light of these problems managers of school recreational sport programs need to be creative when trying to initiate such programs. Some schools, for example, use community parks and centers, YWCA swimming pools, and Boys' Clubs to provide facilities that meet the programmatic needs of their students.[6]

MANAGEMENT CONCERNS FOR COLLEGES AND UNIVERSITIES

Recreational sport has grown so large on the college campus that it presents a different pattern of concerns and challenges than that of the school setting. It is estimated that 40% to 80% of most college students participate in recreational sports. Despite this increase in participation, finances remain a prime concern. Most programs' primary sources of revenue are institutional funds and student fees. A trend in decrease of institutional funding has challenged many programs to create alternative sources of funding (e.g., opening facilities to the public, providing instructional classes, operating sport camps).

Facility development, however, remains alive and well—one just has to visit Central Michigan University, the University of Nebraska–Lincoln, Vanderbilt University, or the Universities of Minnesota, Illinois, or Arizona to mention a few that have invested in architectural showcase facilities. Furthermore, with the development of new and refurbished facilities there are myriad opportunities for qualified and well-trained professionals to provide leadership in recreational sport management.

ORGANIZATIONAL CONSIDERATIONS

The organization of a recreational sports program involves selecting activities, scheduling, determining eligibility, establishing awards and point systems, maintaining records, planning health examinations, financing, and directing publicity and promotion.

Activities. The activities constituting the recreational sports program determine the amount of resulting participation. It is therefore important to select the most appropriate activities. The following are recommended management guidelines that will help in selecting activities:

- Activities should be selected in accordance with the season of the year and local conditions and influences.
- Activities should reflect the needs and interests of the students or the members of the organization. These may include faculty and staff.

- Coeducational recreational activities and recreational activities for students with varying disabilities should be provided.
- The activities included in the school physical education program should be coordinated with the activities included in the recreational sports program, which could serve as a laboratory experience for physical education.
- Many desirable activities require little special equipment and do not require long periods of training to get the participant in appropriate playing condition.

◆ RECREATIONAL SPORTS COMPOSITE ACTIVITIES

Selected individual activities

Archery	Horseshoes	Shuffleboard
Badminton	Orienteering	Skiing (Nordic
Billiards	Paddle tennis	and Alpine)
Bowling	Physical fitness	Swimming
Curling	Racquetball	Table tennis
Cycling	Rock climbing	Tennis
Deck tennis	Rodeo	Track and field
Golf	Rope climbing	Tumbling
Gymnastics	Scuba diving	Weight lifting
Handball	Shooting	Wrestling

Selected recreational activities

Camping and cookouts	Fishing	Rifle
	Hiking	Roller skating
Canoeing	Horseback	Rowing
Cycling	riding	Sailing
Dance	Hosteling	
Figure skating	Ice skating	

Selected team sport activities

Baseball	Ice hockey	Team handball
Basketball	Lacrosse	Touch (or flag)
Broomball	Rugby	football
Field hockey	Soccer	Track and field
Touch football	Softball	Volleyball
	Speedball	Water polo
Gymnastics	Swimming	

- Consideration should be given to such recreational activities as field trips, dramatics, hiking, camping, bicycling, orienteering, and other outdoor pursuit activities.
- Activities should be selected with special attention to the ability and safety of the participant.

Self-directed recreational sports activities should also be included when organizing a program. Opportunities should be provided for students to come to a facility and work out without having to enter a competitive environment. This is particularly necessary in light of the physical fitness and health movement and today's stressful lifestyle. The following Recreational Sports Composite Activities box illustrates some offerings that have been used successfully in various recreational sports programs throughout the nation.

Scheduling. The time when recreational sports activities are scheduled will depend on student needs, student and faculty availability, facilities, season of year, community support, and budget constraints.

One of the most popular and convenient scheduling times for schools is late afternoon, especially in the fall and spring. This has proved best for many elementary, junior high or middle, and senior high schools. It is an economical time because lighting is not required, outdoor space is available, and faculty supervision is readily available.

Evenings have been used quite extensively at colleges, and this trend has followed in many high schools. This time is not recommended for elementary, junior high, or middle schools. Some schools use hours during the school day. The physical education class is primarily an instructional period, however, and use of this period for intramurals or extramurals does not conform to the standards set by the profession. However, some schools have satisfactorily used free periods, activity periods, club periods, and even before-school hours for the recreational sports program when facilities are available.

The noon hour has also been popular in some schools, especially in elementary, junior high or middle, and secondary schools and particularly in rural schools where students do not go home for lunch. Because students will be active anyway, such a period offers possibilities in selected situations, if overly strenuous activities are not offered.

Saturdays have also been used in some situations. Although the weekend is a problem in some localities because many individuals have to work or have planned this time to be with their families, weekend programs have worked successfully in many communities. On occasion, special days are set aside in many schools for field days or May Day when all the students participate in a day or a half-day devoted entirely to the program's activities. These traditional sports days remain quite popular, especially at the K-6 level.

Recreational sports activities in the corporate setting, youth-serving agencies, and other organizations are scheduled at various times to meet the convenience of the members. Activities might be scheduled at any time during the day or night. With more single parents and more dual working–parent households, afterschool activities have become standard rather than an experiment.[11]

Eligibility. A few simple eligibility rules are needed. These should be kept to a minimum, because the recreational sports programs should offer something for all students.

It is generally agreed that in schools and colleges players should not be allowed to participate in like activities when they are on the varsity team or squad. A student should be allowed to participate on only one team in a given activity during the season. Students, of course, are eligible to participate in more than one activity during a season (e.g., flag football, coeducational soccer) and should be enrolled in or affiliated with the school and conform to the institutional rules for participation.

Unsportsmanlike conduct should be handled in a manner that is in the best interests of the individual concerned, the program, and the established procedures. On occasion a student's eligibility may be forfeited for serious or repeated rules infractions.

Certain activities by their very nature are not appropriate for individuals with certain health problems. Therefore such individuals should be cleared by their personal physician or the school health de-

Trophies awarded by Youth Services Section, Los Angeles City Schools.

partment before being eligible to participate.

Several states have recently instituted policies linking academic achievement and attendance of students with their eligibility to participate in extra-curricular actvities.[1] However, some controversy has developed concerning whether a student should be denied the right to participate in such activities because of poor grades. In some cases, state officials have threatened to challenge such action in the courts.

Awards. There are arguments for and against granting awards for recreational sports involvement. Some argue that awards stimulate interest, serve as extrinsic incentive for participation, and recognize achievement. Some argue that awards make the program more expensive and that a few individuals capture most of the awards. Leaders who oppose awards also stress that there should be no expectation of awards for voluntary, leisure-time participation and

that it is difficult to present awards on the basis of all factors that should be considered. Their belief is that the intrinsic joy and satisfaction received through participation are reward enough.

Research indicates that approximately four out of five recreational sports programs give awards. If awards are presented, they should be inexpensive, such as medals, ribbons, certificates, plaques, cups, or letters. Letters, pins, cups, medals, and similar awards have been used most frequently in K-12 schools, whereas trophies and plaques are given more extensively at colleges, universities, and in other organizations. A popular and relatively recent trend, however, is the practice of giving T-shirts as awards. T-shirts can be imprinted with a school or recreational sports logo and provide excellent publicity for the program.

Point systems. Many recreational sports programs have a cumulative point system figured on an all-year basis, which maintains interest and enthusiasm over the course of the school year and encourages greater participation.

A system of keeping points should be developed that stimulates wholesome competition, sustains interest, and conforms with the objectives of the total program. The point system should be readily understood by all and easy to manage. Under such conditions, points should be awarded on the basis of contests won, championships gained, standing in a league or order of finishing, participation, sportsmanship, and contribution to the objectives of the program.

A point system might be based on the following items:

Each entry, 10 points
Each win, 2 points
Each loss, 1 point
Forfeit, 0 points
Each team championship, 10 points
Second-place team championship, 6 points
Third-place team championship, 3 points
Each individual championship, 6 points
Second-place individual championship, 4 points
Third-place individual championship, 3 points
Being homeroom or team representative, 10 points
Each meeting attended by homeroom or team representative, 2 points

Protests and forfeitures.[9] Procedures should be established in advance so that all persons involved know what the rules are when a protest is made and forfeitures of contests take place. The circumstances under which protests and forfeitures will be acted upon, the decision-making process, and the penalties that will be assessed should be clearly set forth. An attempt should be made to have established policies that help to prevent and discourage protests and forfeitures, since a great deal of time and effort are involved in such actions, and they also frequently result in bad feelings and negative public relations.

Records. Efficient management of the program will necessitate keeping records. These should not be extensive but should contain the information needed to determine the worth of the program and the progress being made.

Such records allow for comparison with other similar organizations. They show the degree to which the program is providing for the needs of the entire membership, the extent of participation, and retention and adherence rates. They track the activities that are popular, as well as those that are struggling. They focus attention on the best units of competition, needs of the program, effective management procedures, and leadership strengths and weaknesses. Record keeping is an important phase of the program that should not be overlooked.

Use of computers in recreational sports.[2] Recreational sports can be managed much more efficiently using some of the versatile software now available for the computer. Virtually all information pertaining to the recreational sports program can be managed through computer programming. Names, addresses, telephone numbers, health status, entry fee information, eligibility, dropout rates, wins, losses, facility and team scheduling, and yearly point accumulation can all be recorded on computer. Computer literacy is requisite for all future managers in order to ensure maximal efficiency, accuracy, and effective use of time, thereby rendering better service to students and other clientele.

Medical examinations. Medical examinations should be required of all participants as a safeguard to their health, as well as legal protection for the program. Sometimes this is handled through annual school medical examinations and at other times through personal medical examinations given before a seasonal activity starts. The health status of all participants must be of the utmost importance for all managers of recreational sports programs.

Finances. The monies involved in recreational sports programs are raised in various ways. Because these programs have as many, or more, contributions to make to educational objectives as other parts of the educational program, they should be financed out of board of education and central administration funds, just as other phases of the institution are financed.

Another method of financing programs that has proved satisfactory in some high schools and colleges incorporates the cost of running the programs in the regular student activity fee that may also include the school newspaper, dramatics, the interscholastic or intercollegiate athletic program, and various student organizations. This provides funds in proportion to the student enrollment and can be anticipated for future budget forecasting.

Other methods of financing used by some organizations include the use of varsity sport gate receipts, equipment rental, required participant or user entry fee, and special fund-raising projects such as sports nights, carnivals, and corporate sponsorship drives. Some argue that such practices discourage persons from participating, and that requiring special projects to raise money should not be necessary for such a valuable phase of the institution. As mentioned previously, revenue generation and self-sufficiency have become vital in the conduct of recreational sport programs.

Publicity and promotion. Members of an organization and the general public must understand the role of recreational sport programs, the individuals they service, the activities offered, and their objectives. Such information should be disseminated to the appropriate individuals through a well-planned and properly timed publicity and promotion campaign.

Newspapers and other print and electronic media should be used to provide appropriate space and publicity for the program and its activities. Brochures, bulletin boards, posters, and the school or organization's newspaper or newsletter can help focus attention on the program. Notices can be prepared and sent home to K-12 parents. A handbook can be prepared that explains the various aspects of the total program and can be distributed to all who are interested. Record boards and display cases can be constructed and placed in conspicuous settings. Clinics and workshops can be conducted on the various sports. Orientation talks and discussions can be held in school and college assemblies and at other gatherings. Special days can be slated with considerable publicity, and catch slogans such as "It Pays to Play" can be adopted. Good publicity and promotion will result in greater student participation and better public understanding and support.

At Downers Grove (Illinois) North High School, where 40 activities are offered each year, the man-

agers utilize various promotional ingredients to publicize their program. These include a *Weekly Trojans Intramural Report,* T-shirts for champions, team uniforms paid for by local merchants, pictures of winners on the Recreational Sport Bulletin Board, community-oriented events such as the Trojan mile, and an annual Intramural Champions Pizza Party.

PATTERNS OF ORGANIZATION

Recreational Sport Programs in the Elementary School

The recreational sport programs in the elementary school should be outgrowths of the physical education program. They should consist of a broad variety of activities including stunts, rhythmic activities, relays, and tumbling. They should be suited to the developmental ages and interests of children at this level and should be carefully supervised. The younger children in the primary grades probably will benefit most from simple games, lead-up activities, and low-organizational games. However, in the

Elementary school recreational sports should be fun and well supervised; Crest View Elementary School, Brooklyn Park, MN.

Intramural inner tube water polo; Lyons Township High School, La Grange, IL.

upper elementary grades, more advanced activities can take place on both intragrade and intergrade bases (see the box to the right). These programs should also be broadly based, varied, and progressive. Special field days and theme days such as the Olympics and the Pan-American Games can also add an international educational component to the program.

Guidelines for recreational sport programs in the elementary school follow.

- A basic instructional offering geared to the needs, interests, and growth and developmental levels of primary school children is prerequisite to and foundational for recreational sport programs.
- Qualified leadership should be provided, characterized by competencies involving understanding the physical, mental, emotional, and social needs of the child.
- Competition should involve only those children who are developmentally compatible (e.g., maturity, size, and ability).

SUGGESTED PROGRAM OF ACTIVITIES FOR ELEMENTARY SCHOOLS[5]

Fall and Spring

Beat the runner	Foursquare	Soccer
Bicycle distance race	Hopscotch	Soccer kick
	Kickball	Softball
Bocce	Longball	Speedball
Cosom hockey	Playdays	Stealing sticks
Dodge ball	Prisoner out	Tetherball
Endball	Punchball	Track and
Fitness day	Relays	field
Flag football	Rope jumping	Wiffleball

Winter

Badminton	Dodge ball	Rope climbing
Basket shooting	Gym scooters	Shuffleboard
Basketball	Gymnastics	Tug-of-war
Battleball	Ice skating	Tumbling
Bowling	Newcomb	Volleyball
Cageball	Relays	Wiffleball
Cosom bowling	Rhythms	Wrestling
Cosom hockey		

- Cooperative games and large-muscle activities should be integral parts of the program.
- In the elementary school, recreational sport competitions should be limited to grades 4 through 6. Grades kindergarten through 3 (K-3) should focus on the basic instructional physical education program, which should provide sufficient organized activity.
- Desirable social, emotional, physical, and health outcomes for students should be the goal of recreational sport programs.
- Activities such as tackle football and other dangerous contact activities should not be permitted.
- The planning of the program should involve students, parents, administrators, and the community.

Recreational Sport Programs in the Junior High or Middle School

The junior high and middle schools provide a setting where many students develop a keen interest in sport. This is a time of limitless energy, physiological change, and immense psychosocial challenge. A full concentration of challenging recreational sport activities should be made available for all those who are not involved in seasonal interscholastic competition. In fact, many professional groups favor recreational sport programs at this level and are opposed to high degrees of competition. Activities conducted after school (see the box on p. 107) should provide the student with the opportunity to develop skills, gain self-confidence, have fun, socialize, gain recognition, develop self-worth, and break down cliques as well as racial and gender stereotypes.

The program should be well structured, properly supervised and managed by the school's physical education teachers, and "student-run." Challenges by homeroom, grade, neighborhood, academic interest area, or school club are often used as motivators for maximal student participation. Weekends, lunch hours, and special event days featuring faculty challenges should not be overlooked as a means of building school pride, as well as healthful, wholesome,

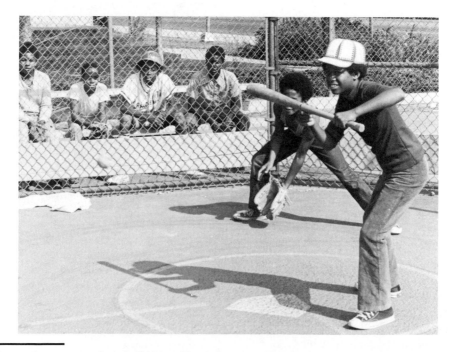

Recreation program baseball game; Youth Services Section, Los Angeles City Schools, CA.

SUGGESTED ACTIVITIES FOR JUNIOR OR MIDDLE AND HIGH SCHOOLS

Team sports

A	Basketball	W	Gymnastics	S	Softball
S	Baseball	W	Ice hockey	A	Speedball
W	Broomball	FS	Kickball	F	Touch (or flag) football
A	Dodge ball	W	Newcomb	S	Track and field
S	Fieldball	W	Ringette	F	Tug-of-war
FS	Field hockey	A	Soccer	W	Volleyball

Individual and dual sports

A	Aerobic dance (varying levels of impact)	W	Gymnastics	A	Rope climbing
		A	Handball (1-wall)	F	Rowing
FS	Archery	FS	Horseshoes	A	Shuffleboard
A	Badminton	A	Jogging	A	Table tennis
A	Basketball free throw and field goal shooting	FS	Paddle tennis	FS	Tennis
		A	Paddleball	A	Tetherball
A	Bounce ball	FS	Paddle tetherball	FS	Track and field
A	Bowling	A	Quoits	AW	Tumbling
FS	Cross country	A	Racquetball	W	Wrestling
W	Deck tennis				

Corecreational activities

A	Badminton	F	Flag football	W	Skiing (Alpine, Nordic)
A	Bicycling	FS	Golf	W	Swimming
A	Bowling	FS	Horseshoes	A	Table tennis
FS	Canoeing	W	Ice skating	FS	Tennis
A	Dance (social and folk)	FS	Roller skating	FS	Track and field
W	Deck tennis	A	Shuffleboard	AW	Volleyball

Club activities

A	Bicycling	FS	Fishing	FS	Rock climbing
S	Canoeing	FS	Golf	FS	Roller skating
A	Dance (social, folk, square, modern)	A	Hiking	A	Tumbling
		W	Ice skating		

Special events

FS	Track-and-field meet	FS	Field day	WS	Relay carnival
WA	Basketball skills contest	A	Fitness day	FS	5K Fun Run
		S	Baseball and softball		

F, fall; W, winter; S, spring; A, all seasons.

physically active lifestyles which, it is hoped, will carry over into adulthood. The program should also be "open" to all students with any type of special need regardless of disability or physical limitation, and provision should be made for "inclusion versus exclusion."

Recreational Sport Programs in the High School

At the senior high level, recreational sports should continue the pattern that has been laid down at the junior high or middle school.[3,6] Recreational sport activities should be varied and should focus on skill development, fun, building positive self-images, cooperation, and friendly competition, as well as setting a positive tone for lifetime participation. At this level, activities can be conducted not only at noon, during prescribed activity hours during the day, and in the afternoon, but also in the evenings. The activities should cut across age, grade, and gender barriers, although wholesome rivalries by grade still seem to permeate the high school environs.

Personnel for the conduct of recreational sport programs should be well-trained professionals. Sound, creative leadership is needed if the programs are to prosper. Each school should be concerned with developing a plan in which proper supervision and guidance are available for afterschool hours. Recreational sport clubs may be initiated to help train students to take an active role in the planning and conduct of the high school program. Qualified officials are also a necessity to ensure safe, equal, and wholesome competition. Facilities, equipment, and supplies should be apportioned equitably for the entire recreational sport program. No part of any group or any program should monopolize facilities and equipment, and a cooperative effort of the school and community is crucial to having a first-class high school recreational sport program.

Recreational Sports in Colleges and Universities

College and university recreational sport programs offer an ideal setting for both men and women to participate in a wide range of physical activity.[4,8] These activities range from individualized activity such as weight training to a full complement of team and individual sports, from corecreational endeavor to carnival or special event days and from aerobic dance to outdoor pursuit. The recreational sports center on a college or university campus is a place to gather, work out, and socialize, and should offer a wide range of physical activity for the entire university community. It is a place that can and should bring a "sense of community" to the institution.

At this level, the fastest growing area of recreational sport programming endeavor is in sport clubs. These organizations provide participants with opportunities for high-level competition in many different activities. The University of Minnesota offers a wide range of opportunities that may be available for the college sport club participant (Table 4-1). Many club sports ranging from skiing to rugby and from rowing to soccer sponsor national championship competitions.

Sport clubs, however, are only one component of the college and university recreational sport program. Intramurals (e.g., Competitive A, B, and C; recreational and corecreational leagues), extramurals, open recreation (e.g., fitness, aerobics, weight training, running), faculty and staff leagues, and even summer sport camps are integral parts of the contemporary college recreational sports scene. Activities for men, women, corecreational sport, graduate students, staff and faculty, family and guest participation, fitness assessments and counseling, and instructional activities are all delicately woven into the collegiate recreational sports endeavor (Table 4-2). Safety, health status, eligibility, and responsibility for the conduct of the program and funding and facilities continue to be the salient issues to be addressed by sound management.

At many colleges and universities, student involvement in the management process is integral and ranges from the formulation of recreational sport constitutions to officiating. Many colleges still structure much of their recreational sport programming around units such as residence halls and dormitories, the Greek system (fraternities and sororities), or academic departments, although the traditional practice of competitions between teams that are arbitrarily formed at registration under "la-

TABLE 4-1. University of Minnesota sport clubs

Team	Men's	Women's	Co-ed	Club intercollegiate	Recreational instructional
Aikido			☑		☑
Aikido, Yoshinaki			☑		☑
Archery			☑	☑	☑
Badminton			☑	☑	☑
Ballroom dance			☑		☑
Bowling	☑	☑		☑	☑
Boxing	☑			☑	☑
Crew, men's	☑			☑	
Crew, women's		☑		☑	
Cycling			☑	☑	☑
Fencing	☑	☑		☑	☑
Gymnastics			☑		☑
Ice hockey, women's		☑		☑	☑
Judo	☑	☑		☑	☑
Juggling					☑
Karate, int'l league			☑		☑
Karate, Japanese			☑		☑
Karate, Tai KwonDo			☑	☑	☑
Kung Fu, Chinese			☑	☑	☑
Kung Fu, Vo Lam			☑		☑
Marlinettes (synchro)		☑		☑	☑
Rodeo	☑	☑		☑	☑
Rugby, men's	☑			☑	
Rugby, women's		☑		☑	
Sailing	☑	☑		☑	☑
Scuba			☑		☑
Ski, Alpine	☑	☑		☑	
Ski, Nordic	☑	☑		☑	
Skydiving	☑	☑		☑	☑
Soccer, men's	☑			☑	
Soccer, women's		☑		☑	
Swim Club			☑		☑
Tai Chi			☑		☑
Team handball	☑	☑		☑	
Tennis, men's	☑			☑	☑
Tennis, women's		☑			☑
Ultimate frisbee			☑	☑	☑
Volleyball	☑	☑		☑	
Water polo	☑	☑		☑	
Water ski			☑		☑

TABLE 4-2. University of Tennessee recreational sports

Men	Women	Faculty/staff	Corecreation
Fall			
Team			
Football	Football	Football	Paddleball
Bowling	Tug-of-war	Golf	Racquetball
Handball	Volleyball	Handball	Tennis
Tug-of-war	Badminton	Paddleball	Badminton
Volleyball		Racquetball	
Golf		Squash	
		Tennis	
		Badminton	
		Turkey trot	
Individual and dual			
Handball	Paddleball		
Paddleball	Racquetball		
Racquetball	Squash		
Squash	Tennis		
Tennis	Golf (par 3)		
Golf (par 3)	Pass, punt, and kick		
Pass, punt, and kick	Turkey trot		
Turkey trot			
Winter			
Team			
Basketball	Basketball	Three-player basketball	Paddleball
Racquetball	Racquetball	Handball	Racquetball
Inner tube water polo	Inner tube water polo	Paddleball	Badminton
Swimming and diving	Swimming and diving	Racquetball	Table tennis
Track relays	Bowling	Squash	
Individual and dual			
Handball	Paddleball		
Paddleball	Racquetball		
Racquetball	Squash		
Squash	Badminton		
Badminton	Basketball free throw		
Basketball free throw			
Wrestling			
Spring			
Team			
Softball	Softball	Softball	Paddleball
Paddleball	Tennis	Handball	Racquetball
Tennis	Golf putting	Paddleball	Tennis (2 male/2 female)
Track and field		Squash	Basketball
		Three-player basketball	Softball (5 male/5 female)
		One-on-one basketball	Volleyball (3 male/3 female)
		Table tennis	Horseshoes

TABLE 4-2. University of Tennessee recreational sports—cont'd

Men	Women	Faculty/staff	Corecreation
		Billiards	Shuffleboard
		Golf	
		Golf putting	

Individual and dual

Men	Women		
Handball	Paddleball		
Paddleball	Racquetball		
Racquetball	Squash		
Squash	Three-player basketball		
Three-player basketball	One-on-one baskctball		
One-on-one basketball	Table tennis		
Table tennis	Shuffleboard		
Billiards	Horseshoes		
Shuffleboard	Golf		
Horseshoes	Golf putting		
Golf			
Golf putting			

Summer

Team

Men	Women	Faculty/staff	Corecreation
Softball	Softball	Softball	Baskctball (2 male/2 female)
Basketball	Basketball	Basketball	Softball (5 male/5 female)
Volleyball	Volleyball	Volleyball	Volleyball (3 male/3 female)
		Handball	Paddleball
		Paddleball	Racquetball
		Racquetball	Tennis
		Squash	Horseshoes
		Tennis	Shuffleboard
		Billiards	
		Table tennis	
		Golf putting	
		Golf	
		Horseshoes	
		Shuffleboard	

Individual and dual

Men	Women		
Handball	Handball		
Paddleball	Paddleball		
Racquetball	Racquetball		
Squash	Squash		
Tennis	Tennis		
Billiards	Billiards		
Table tennis	Table tennis		
Golf putting	Golf putting		
Golf	Golf		
Horseshoes	Horseshoes		
Shuffleboard	Shuffleboard		

bels" ranging from the Nerds to MASH still seem to permeate "rec sports" registration.

Recreational Sport Programs in Other Organizations

Recreational sport programs play a major role in many organizations outside the educational domain. For example, in the corporate setting there are many recreational sport leagues for employees in a variety of sports and other physical activities. In many instances softball diamonds, basketball and volleyball courts, jogging areas, platform and lawn tennis courts, swimming pools, fitness centers, and even golf courses are provided. In some instances, employees are compensated for joining nearby public-sector fitness clubs, and in other situations, businesses subcontract their recreational sport commitment to a private-sector enterprise. Employees usually take an active role in these programs, which contribute much to their morale, health, and physical and mental well-being; research attests to the increased work productivity and reduction of absenteeism.

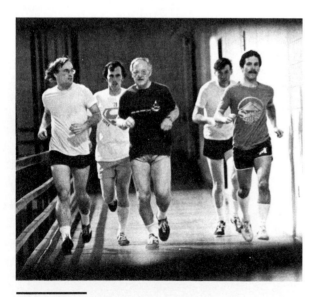

Faculty and staff jog during open recreation at Dow Health and Physical Education Center, Hope College, Holland, MI.

Recreational sport programs may also be found in YMCAs, Boys' Clubs, community centers, park and recreation districts, church organizations, military installations, and other youth- and adult-serving agencies. The NCAA and many sports federations such as those of golf and tennis are also beginning to sponsor inter-city youth programs. Recreational sports represent an important part of many organizations' curricular and educational offerings.

The same types of formats for structuring multi-dimensional and creative physical activity and sport competition employed in schools and colleges are used in these non-school organizations.

COMPETITIVE STRUCTURING

There are several different ways of structuring competition within most recreational sports programs. Three of the most common are leagues, tournaments, and meets. These modes of structuring take many forms, with league play popular in the domain of team sports, elimination tournaments used to a great extent after culmination of league play, and meets held to recognize the closure of a season or year of sports activity.

Various types of tournament competition have been employed extensively in recreational sports; descriptions of some competitive tournament structures will be included here.

The round robin tournament is probably one of the most widely used and one of the best types of competitive structures, because it allows for maximal play. It is frequently used in leagues, where it works best with no more than eight teams. Each team plays every other team at least once during the tournament. Each team continues to play to the completion of the tournament, and the winner is the one who has the highest percentage, based on wins and losses, at the end of scheduled play (Figure 4-2, *A*).

The single or straight elimination tournament is set up so that one defeat eliminates a player or team (Figure 4-2, *B* and *C*). This structure does not allow for maximal play; the winners continue to play, but the losers drop out. A team or individual is automatically out when it or he or she loses. However,

I. 1 vs. 5
   2 vs. 6
   3 vs. 7
   4 vs. 8

II. 1 vs. 2
   3 vs. 5
   4 vs. 6
   8 vs. 7

III. 1 vs. 3
   4 vs. 2
   8 vs. 5
   7 vs. 6

A

IV. 1 vs. 4
   8 vs. 3
   7 vs. 2
   6 vs. 5

V. 1 vs. 8
   7 vs. 4
   6 vs. 3
   5 vs. 2

VI. 1 vs. 7
   6 vs. 8
   5 vs. 4
   2 vs. 3

FIGURE 4-2 A, Round robin tournament for eight teams. Team 1 remains fixed while the remaining teams rotate clockwise. **B,** Single elimination tournament with 13 entrants. **C,** Single elimination tournament with seedings.

VII. 1 vs. 6
   5 vs. 7
   2 vs. 8
   3 vs. 4

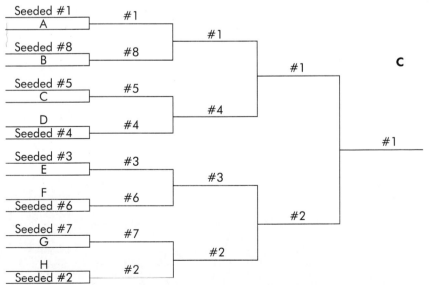

this is the most economical form of organization from the standpoint of time in determining the winning player or team. Usually a drawing for positions takes place, with provisions for seeding the better players or teams on the basis of past performance. Such seeding provides more intense competition as the tournament moves toward the finals. Under such

a structure, byes are awarded in the first round of play whenever the number of entrants does not fall into units to the power of two (i.e., 2, 4, 8, 16, 32, 64, etc.). The number of byes is determined by subtracting the number of entrants from the next higher power of two. Figure 4-2, *B* has 13 entrants (16 − 13 = 3 byes). Although such a tournament is a time-

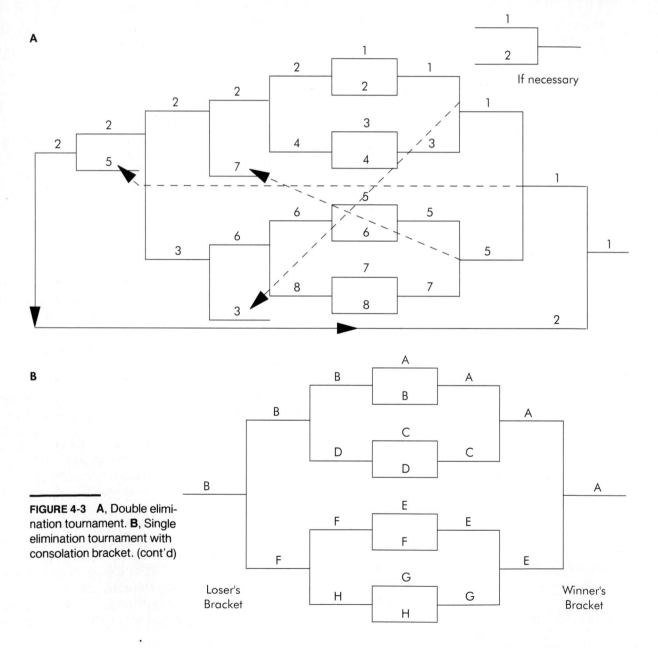

FIGURE 4-3   A, Double elimination tournament. **B,** Single elimination tournament with consolation bracket. (cont'd)

saver, it possesses a flaw because it does not adequately select the second- and third-place winners. The second or third best player may meet the best player, and eventual winner, in the first round of play, which often dampens the enthusiasm for the remaining games or matches in the tournament. Another weakness is that the majority of participants play only once or twice in the tournament.

The double elimination tournament does not have some of the weaknesses of the single elimination, because it is necessary for a team or individual to lose twice before being eliminated. This is also characteristic of various types of consolation elimination tournaments that permit the player or team to play more than once.

In some consolation tournaments all players who lose in the first round and those who, because they received a bye, did not lose until the second round get to play again to determine a consolation winner. In other similar tournaments any player or team who loses once, regardless of the round in which the loss occurs, is allowed to play again. There are also other tournaments, such as the Mueller-Anderson Playback, in which the competitors continue to play until all places of finish have been determined in the tournament (see Figure 4-3, *C*) and the Bagnall-Wild Elimination Tournament (Figure 4-3, *D*), which is a form of single elimination tournament that focuses on more accurately selecting the second- and third-place finishers. The theory is that it

FIGURE 4-3 (cont'd)   C, Mueller-Anderson playback. D, Bagnall-Wild brackets of a single elimination tournament. E, Ladder tournament.

is possible for the second or third best player to be eliminated in an early round by the eventual winner. In the Bagnall-Wild, the players eliminated by each finalist participate in separate consolation tournaments.

The ladder tournament (Figure 4-3, *E*) adapts well to individual competition. Here the contestants are arranged in ladder, or vertical, formation, with rankings established arbitrarily or on the basis of previous performance. Each contestant may challenge the one directly above or in some cases two above, and if he or she wins, the names change place on the ladder. When a contestant loses to a challenger from below, he or she may not immediately rechallenge the winner, but must accept another challenge from below. This is a continuous type of tournament that does not eliminate any participants. However, it is not ideal, because it may drag and interest may wane.

The pyramid tournament is similar to the ladder variety (Figure 4-4). Here, instead of having one name on a rung or step, several names are on the lower steps, gradually pyramiding to the top-ranking individual. A player may challenge anyone in the same horizontal row, and then the winner may challenge anyone in the row above.

The spider web tournament takes its name from the bracket design, which is the shape of a spider's web (Figure 4-5). The championship position is at the center of the web. The bracket consists of five (or any other selected number) lines drawn radially from the center, and the participants' names are placed on concentric lines crossing these radial lines. Challenges may be made by persons on any concentric line to any person on the next line closer to the center. A player must defeat someone on his or her own level after losing a challenge in the immediate inner tier of the web. This tournament provides more opportunity for competitive activity.

The type of tournament structure adopted should be the one deemed best for the unit, group, activity, or local interests. The goal should be maximal participation within facility and time constraints. Tournaments encourage participant interest and enthusiasm and are an important part of the recreational sport experience.

RECREATIONAL SPORT CONSIDERATIONS

Recreational sport has the potential to make significant contributions to all levels of education (K-12

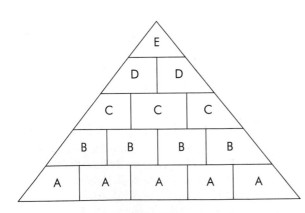

Any A may challenge any B.
Any B may challenge any C.
Any C may challenge either D.
Either D may challenge E.

FIGURE 4-4 Pyramid tournament.

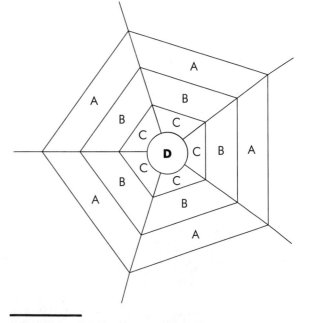

FIGURE 4-5 Spider web tournament.

and college and university), as well as to the private and public sectors. In light of recent legislation, such as Title IX and PL 94-142, special sensitivity is warranted and effort mandated to include opportunities for women and persons with varying disabilities, as well as other diverse populations. Recreational sports has led the way concerning opportunity in regard to corecreational activities, and now recreational sports' overall objectives must be further extended. Objectives should include provisions for: (1) opportunities for both sexes, as well as minorities and persons with disabilities (in the least restrictive environment) to participate in wholesome play experiences, (2) cooperative experience through physical activity for all in order to enhance self-esteem and develop interdependence, (3) participants to enjoy themselves, develop friendships, improve personal skills, and gain mutual respect through both traditional and new activities, (4) participants to

gain the skills, information, and the support network needed for spending leisure hours constructively in physical pursuits.

The goal of having persons with disabilities participate in the least restrictive environment and to join the regular recreational sport program is challenging, to say the least. Programs such as "Special Friends" and "Unified Sports" (a program instituted by Special Olympics International) should also be included. Special populations' participation in sports days, playdays, and invitational days, which have long been traditional extramural recreational sports activities endorsed by the American Alliance of Health, Physical Education, Recreation, and Dance and the National Association of Girls and Women in Sport, should also be encouraged.

At the college and university level, recreational sport managers should not forget the graduate student (many older students are now returning to

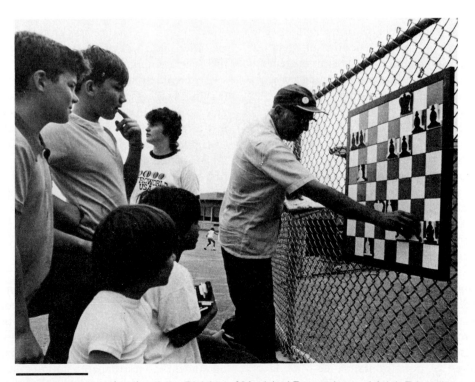

Chess as a recreational activity; Division of Municipal Recreation and Adult Education, Milwaukee, WI.

school), faculty and staff, and those individuals' families and significant others. Research suggests that an attractive recreational sport program assists in retaining and recruiting both faculty and students. Inclusion of significant others will contribute to sustained participation in physical activity throughout the lifespan. Certainly these are worthy considerations for all managers of both physical education and recreational sport to not only address, but to actively promote (see recreational sport checklists in the boxes on pages 119 and 120–121).

RECREATIONAL SPORT PROGRAM PLANNING

One of the most important functions of the recreational sports manager is the continuous planning and evaluation of the program to see if its goals are being met. The program must also be evaluated in terms of budget and numbers of persons participating. In today's competitive climate a program must be cost effective or it faces the probability of being phased out.

Evaluation is a crucial component of the planning process of any well-managed organization. The planning process involves a number of steps or phases that can be modified for most management circumstances. The following planning process phases are offered for consideration:

A mission or vision of accomplishment. This is a statement of what should be accomplished and how this fits into the conceptual and philosophical view of the organization.

Overview of the situation. A managerial analysis of the conditions and complexities of the task that will serve as a guide to set realistic goals is necessary.

Specification of goals. Goals must be realistic, reasonable, challenging, achievable, and quantifiable when possible (e.g., to increase the number of students with disabilities in the program from 16 to 50 participants). Goals may be long range, intermediate, or short term in nature. Growth, profitability, client satisfaction, retention, and social awareness are examples of areas in which organizational goals might be established.

Identification of constraints. A description of the conditions and barriers that may hinder goal at-

tainment, including alternative pathways toward goal attainment, should be outlined. Constraints may be human, technical, environmental, economic, or sociopolitical.

Identification of resources. Closely linked to the development of any plan of action is the establishment of criteria for information gathering to assist in the generation of sound ideas. Research, consultants', and student and community input is vital to this phase.

The plan. For any plan to be effective, the manager needs to involve all the workers (human resources) who are necessary for its implementation. Clearly defined tasks and roles, job descriptions and expectations, how the parts relate to the whole, timetables, cost, individual feelings, and direct input are vital to "The Plan."

Evaluation. Evaluation techniques will differ but generally should include (1) definition of the program goals, (2) data collection (e.g., number of participants, number of teams, games played), (3) an appraisal of players, coaches, officials, game scores, facility utilization, etc., (4) recommendations from internal and external review groups, (5) consultant visitation, and (6) participant opinion and rating forms concerning the overall program.

On completion of the evaluation phase of the planning process, the recreational sports director and the program staff may want to revise, modify, or institute new programs to further meet the cognitive, psychomotor, sociocultural, and affective demands of the population being served. The realization of the need for careful and prudent planning, as well as the total involvement of all recreational sport program participants, leads to sustained and successful programs.

SUMMARY

Recreational sport programs represent a very important component of the total educational process. They contribute to important qualities such as health, feelings of self-worth, skill, and social development. In addition, they provide an opportunity for all students to participate and interact on a voluntary basis. Activities should be selected that reflect

◈ CHECKLIST FOR RECREATIONAL SPORT PROGRAMS		
	Yes	No
1. Is the recreational sport program a normal outgrowth of the regular school program?	_____	_____
2. Are there clearly stated objectives for the program?	_____	_____
3. Does the program supplement the formal curriculum by increasing knowledge and skills?	_____	_____
4. Are recreational sport activities, including clubs, organized in terms of educational value rather than administrative convenience?	_____	_____
5. Does the administration set adequate policies to guide the program?	_____	_____
6. Have the aims and objectives of the program been determined?	_____	_____
7. Can any student participate?	_____	_____
8. Is a student limited to the number of recreational sport activities he or she may join?	_____	_____
9. Does each club have a simple constitution and bylaws that can guide students in the conduct of the organization?	_____	_____
10. Does recreational sport participation prepare the student for democratic living?	_____	_____
11. Do the activities help to develop school or organizational spirit?	_____	_____
12. Does the school schedule recreational sport activities so that they do not conflict with regularly scheduled school activities?	_____	_____
13. Does the school administrator support the program with adequate space, staff, and funds to carry on a worthwhile program?	_____	_____
14. Can a student discover and develop special attitudes and abilities through the recreational sport program?	_____	_____
15. Does the program offer opportunities for vocational exploration?	_____	_____
16. Is the individual student able to develop socially acceptable attitudes and ideals through the program?	_____	_____
17. Does the recreational sport experience provide situations that will contribute to the formation of improved behavior patterns in the student?	_____	_____
18. Do members actively participate in program planning?	_____	_____
19. Are the projects and activities of the program initiated primarily by the students?	_____	_____
20. Do all the activities performed pertain to the club purpose?	_____	_____
21. Are the students allowed to select recreational sport activities according to interests?	_____	_____
22. Are students issued a calendar of events?	_____	_____
23. Does the school library make available books and periodicals needed by the program's participants?	_____	_____
24. Does the faculty advisor enlist the confidence of both boys and girls?	_____	_____
25. Is a faculty advisor willing to give time and thought to make the recreational sport or club program a success?	_____	_____
26. Is a faculty advisor able to find his or her chief satisfaction in student growth and not in appreciation of personal efforts?	_____	_____
27. Does the administration of the school evaluate the program periodically?	_____	_____
28. Does the recreational sport program allow time for the evaluation of activities?	_____	_____

◆ RECREATIONAL SPORT PROGRAM EVALUATION CHECKLIST

A program can be evaluated in terms of the stated principles and objectives or according to prevalent acceptable standards.

How does the recreational sport program measure up to the acceptable minimum standards? By taking a few minutes to check off the items listed below, a quick evaluation can be made of the present status of the excellence of the program.

Philosophy and objectives   Yes   No

1. Is a written philosophy or a set of objectives available to the participants?   _____   _____

Organization and administration

1. Is the director professionally qualified to administer the program?   _____   _____
2. Does the director devote sufficient time per week to administering the program?   _____   _____
3. Are participants included in the management of the program?   _____   _____
4. Is there an advisory committee?   _____   _____

Units of competition

1. Are participants classified according to ability, age, height, or weight within the competitive unit?   _____   _____
2. Within the basic unit, are participants permitted to choose the members of their teams?   _____   _____

Program activities

1. Does the director consult with the participants to make sure that their interests are of prime consideration in the selection of activities for the program?   _____   _____
2. Are there both strenuous and nonstrenuous sports in the program?   _____   _____
3. Are there both team and individual sports in the program?   _____   _____
4. Are there at least five different sports making up the program?   _____   _____
5. Do corecreational activities make up part of the program?   _____   _____
6. Are there programs for persons with disabilities?   _____   _____

Time periods

1. Do the hours that participants are free receive top priority for scheduling?   _____   _____
2. Is the noon hour used for programming?   _____   _____

Methods of organizing competition

1. Is the round robin tournament used whenever possible in preference to others?   _____   _____

Point system of awards

1. Is recognition of any kind given to the participants for their achievements?   _____   _____
2. Is the award primarily for achievement instead of incentive for participants?   _____   _____

Rules and regulations

1. Are the rules defining such things as eligibility, health, safety, forfeits, postponements, and team membership distributed to all participants?   _____   _____
2. Is the lack of good sportsmanship regarded as a rule violated?   _____   _____
3. Is equipment provided for all activities offered?   _____   _____
4. Is proper supervision required for all activities offered?   _____   _____

◆	**RECREATIONAL SPORT PROGRAM EVALUATION CHECKLIST—cont'd**

Publicity

1. Is there a special bulletin board for recreational sport information?   ——   ——
2. Does a newsletter exist that carries recreational sport information?   ——   ——

Finances

1. Does the organization provide funds for the operation of the program?   ——   ——

Rating scale

A "yes" answer must be given in each category if a program is to be considered good or excellent.

Excellent	17 to 25
Good	14 to 16
Fair	11 to 13
Poor	10 or less

---

and extend the basic physical education instructional program, as well as student interests. The activities should be in consort with the laws of the land. The management of recreational sports programs at lower education levels is sometimes difficult because of a lack of transportation for students during after-school hours, as well as a lack of facilities, finances, staffing, and parental support. To have a well-run program, the management of recreational sports should be concerned with things such as safety, supervision, health of participants, scheduling, awards, point systems, eligibility requirements, and officials so that the best interests of the student and the educational process will be served. There are many different types of tournaments that can be employed in the recreational sports setting to increase the flavor of the competition. Programs should be carefully planned and evaluated periodically to determine if they meet the goals of the system in which they are housed and how they can be improved to better serve the clientele for which they have been established.

◆ SELF-ASSESSMENT ACTIVITIES

These activities will assist students to determine if material and competencies presented in this chapter have been mastered.

1. In terms of their objectives and activities, justify the place of intramural, extramural, and sport club programs in the total educational plan of a school, college, or other organization.
2. Imagine you are the director of physical education in a high school, college, or other organization. You have been requested by your superior to develop a list of policies for a newly organized recreational sport program in your organization. Prepare the policies and submit them to your class for their critical evaluation.
3. Conduct a job analysis of the roles played by various management personnel involved with the recreational sport program of the college you are attending. Compare it with the personnel roles discussed in this chapter.
4. Develop what you consider to be a model sports club for an elementary school, high school, college, and large corporation.
5. Identify each of the following: round robin tournament, straight elimination tournament, ladder tournament, pyramid tournament, and double elimination tournament. Using one of these tournaments, prepare a hypothetical competitive league for 16 volleyball teams.
6. Describe the planning process you would employ for organizing a scuba diving club in your school.

REFERENCES

1. Bridgman A: Backlash: its efforts to tie achievement with extracurriculars, *Education News* Mar 13, 1985.
2. Dougherty NJ, Bonanno D: *Management principles in sport and leisure activities,* Minneapolis, 1985, Burgess.
3. Hammitt SA, Hammitt WE: Campus recreation activities— planning for better use, *Journal of Physical Education, Recreation and Dance* 56:23, Jan 1985.
4. Henderson KA, Bialeschki MD: Girls' and women's recreation programming—constraints and opportunities, *Journal of Physical Education, Recreation and Dance* 62(1):55-58, 1991.
5. Hyatt RW: *Intramural sports: organization and administration,* St Louis, 1977, Mosby–Year Book.
6. Jaundris, T: Possibilities and potentials—high school intramurals, *Journal of Physical Education, Recreation and Dance* 51(3):49, 1980.
7. Jones, TR: Needed, a new philosophical model for intramurals, *Journal of Health, Physical Education, and Recreation* 43:34, 1971.
8. Matthews DO: Intramural administration principles, *The Athletic Journal* 46:82, 1966. Reproduced courtesy of The Athletic Journal. Adapted and updated, 1979.
9. Mueller CE, Reznik JW: *Intramural-recreational sports: programming and administration,* New York, 1979, John Wiley and Sons.
10. NIRSA: *General and specialty standards for collegiate recreational sports,* 1989, Oregon State University.
11. Vannoy W: Latchkey intramurals, *Journal of Physical Education, Recreation and Dance,* 59:82-84, Apr 1988.

SUGGESTED READINGS

- Fairman LS, Nitchman J: A complete bowling program in our gymnasium, *Journal of Physical Education, Recreation and Dance* 54:59, Mar 1983.

  Presents an innovative approach to bowling that is being used at Sheffield Middle School, Lorain, Ohio. The authors brought the gymnasium to their students rather than paying the expense of taking them to the bowling alley. Describes how to build a complete, portable, eight-lane bowling alley for use in school's physical education and recreational sports program.

- Imergot LS: Get those skeletons out of the closet . . . and use them in intramurals, *Journal of Physical Education, Recreation and Dance* 54:64, June 1983.

  Rather than being held on a specific date and time, recreational sports were scheduled with a deadline date with one week to complete contests. This change increased time for other activities such as corecreational badminton, made it easier to supervise matches, and decreased the number of forfeits because players could play at their convenience. Provides good suggestions about scheduling recreational sports.

- McLellan RW: Intramural-recreational programs—selecting qualified coordinators, *Journal of Physical Education, Recreation and Dance* 55:57, Aug 1984.

  Traces the roots of organized intramural sport programs and how they have become the recreational sport programs of today. Points out the many educational values of such programs.

- Ross JG, Dotson CO, Gilbert GG, Katz SJ: Physical activity outside of school physical education, *Journal of Physical Education, Recreation and Dance* 56:35-39, Jan 1985.

  Provides the results and cites national trends and patterns of physical activity participation for students outside the school physical education program. Discusses the amount of time spent in such places as community or youth sport organizations and the types and trends of activity available outside the school setting.

- Turner ET: Helter-skelter tournament, *Journal of Physical Education, Recreation and Dance* 54:61, Mar 1983.

  Indicates how the most appropriate tournament should be selected in order to promote maximum participation and interest. Describes the Helter-Skelter Tournament, which is designed for classroom use. The Helter-Skelter Tournament provides the student with maximum participation in tournament play, as well as many opportunities to experience success-failure situations. A meaningful, flexible, enjoyable, and educationally sound tournament.

- NIRSA: *Instructional programs: A resource manual,* 1987, Oregon State University.

  Describes the general standards and procedures for certification, contracts, safety, liability, scheduling, and fee assessment as they pertain to recreational sport instructional programs. Goals, expectations, and evaluations, as well as potential intradepartmental and interdepartmental conflict are discussed.

- Special Olympics International, *Special Olympics Unified Sports,* Washington, DC, 1989, Special Olympics International.

  Presents an overview of SOI's integrated sports offerings and strategies.

CHAPTER 5

Interscholastic, Intercollegiate, and Other Competitive Sport Programs

▶ **Instructional Objectives and Competencies To Be Achieved**

After reading this chapter the student should be able to

- Discuss the purpose of and the values derived from participating in competitive sport programs.
- Specify the duties performed by such key management personnel in competitive sport programs as the athletic director, coach, athletic trainer, and members of the sport council.
- Explain some of the management considerations involved in sport programs relating to scheduling, providing for the health of participants, contracts, officials, transportation, game management, crowd control, protests and forfeitures, awards, and records.
- Understand some of the central issues involved in such management problems concerned with

competitive sport as recruitment, eligibility, proselytizing, scouting, finances, and extra compensation for coaching.
- Describe the nature and scope of competitive sport programs in elementary schools, junior and senior high schools, colleges and universities, and other organizations.
- Identify some of the key athletic associations and the role they play in influencing organized sport competition in schools, colleges, and other organizations.
- Outline key provisions of Title IX concerning the conduct of interscholastic and intercollegiate sport.

Two primary components of the Physical Activity and Sport Continuum have been presented: the basic instructional physical education program, and the recreational sports program, which included intramural, extramural, and sport club offerings. This chapter will focus on competitive sport in schools, colleges, and other organizations.

Interscholastic, intercollegiate, and other organized sport programs represent an integral part of the total spectrum of human movement experience. In some cases involvement in competitive sport programs evolves from active participation in school physical education and recreational sports, as well as the myriad sport programs that are housed elsewhere in the community.

Competitive sports, with their appeal to all age-groups, should play an integral role in the movement experience and help achieve the goals that have been discussed in previous chapters. They should also aid individual growth and development, and help all participants realize their full potential.

The competitive sport program is usually designed for those individuals most competent in sport-specific endeavors. It is the domain of the most talented and highly skilled, and it receives more attention and publicity than most other phases of the physical activity and sport continuum. The reason for this is not that it is more important or renders a greater contribution; instead, it is largely the result of popular appeal. It is that print and electronic media, alumni, parents, and others discuss it in glowing terms and that it involves competition of one school or college against another. This increases public awareness and creates enthusiasm and often a spirit of rivalry, which seems to be pervasive as sport plays out its role in society. The competitive spirit is not only a local phenomenon, but is nationwide, and indeed has worked its way to the international sporting scene.

Interscholastic and intercollegiate sport programs concomitantly have had more attendant difficulties than most other phases of the sport continuum. The desire to win and to generate revenue has resulted in some unfortunate practices, such as unethical recruitment procedures, altering transcripts to make players eligible, admitting students to colleges and universities who may be academically unqualified, and the relaxing of academic and behavioral standards for varsity athletes, not to mention substance abuse and player exploitation issues and concerns. Large stadiums and sports complexes that require huge capital outlay and substantial revenue for their upkeep have been constructed. Indeed, many collegiate and some school programs have been enticed off campus in hope for the big payday.

The challenge of providing sound educational programs in competitive or "varsity" interscholastic and intercollegiate sports is one that all physical education professionals recognize. The challenge can be met and resolved if physical educators and other professionals bring to the attention of administra-

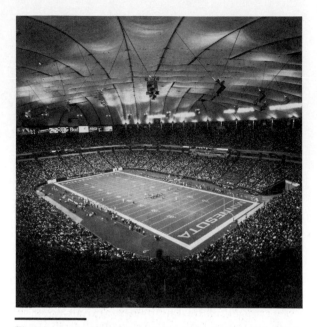

The Hubert H. Humphrey Metrodome, home of the University of Minnesota football team.

tors, the community, and the general public the true purposes of sports in their respective schools and institutions of higher education. It is important to emphasize that a need exists for maintaining competitive sport programs within the school that meet the needs of everyone; that are professionally organized and managed with the welfare of the individual in mind; and that are conducted in a manner by which educational objectives are not compromised even when exposed to pressures from parents, alumni, community members, and the media.

THE ROLE OF SPORT IN SOCIETY

It is no secret that millions of Americans engage in competitive sport (more than 5 million young girls and boys participate in interscholastic sport) on a yearly basis. Indeed, serving as testimony to the status of sport in contemporary society are the facts that sport is a multibillion-dollar industry, that more than one tenth of the *World Almanac* is devoted to sport, and that more people watched the World Cup than watched Neil Armstrong take the first step on the moon.

Sport's magnetism has been chronicled and debated by many who concentrate their effort on sport-specific exploration of our limits and inner selves; however, Wilkerson and Dodder[18] contend that sport possesses the following seven societal functions:

Emotional release. Sport releases emotions and relieves stress, serves as a safety valve, and provides a catharsis to relieve aggressive tendencies.

Affirmation of identity. Sport offers opportunities to be recognized and to express one's individual qualities.

Social control. Sport provides a means of control over and containment of people.

Socialization. Sport serves as a means of socializing those individuals who identify with it.

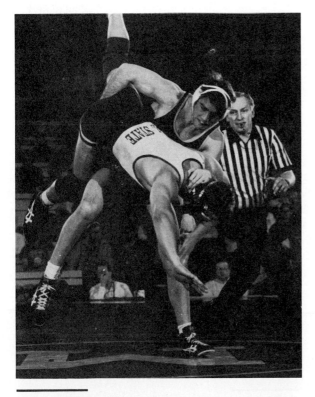

NCAA Champion Marty Morgan, University of Minnesota, Minneapolis.

Change agent. Sport results in social change and new behavior patterns and is a factor that may contribute to changes in the course of history (e.g., interaction of classes, upward socioeconomic mobility based on ability, Ping-Pong diplomacy, the demise of apartheid).

Collective conscience. Sport creates a communal spirit that brings people together in search of common goals.

Success. Sport provides a feeling of success both for the participant and for the spectator when a player or team with whom one identifies achieves. To win in sport is also to win in life, and winning seems to be glorified by all.

BENEFITS OF COMPETITIVE SPORT

The values of participation in competitive sports are discussed under the headings of physical fitness, sport skill and knowledge, individual development, and social development.

Physical Fitness

Competitive sports contribute to physical fitness by developing organic vigor, cardiovascular and cardio-respiratory endurance, neuromuscular skill, muscular strength and endurance, flexibility, and agility, as well as desirable psychosocial attitudes toward play and exercise. To develop and sustain a high degree of physical fitness, the individual must voluntarily submit to a vigorous program of exercise. Perhaps the most powerful force capable of motivating a person to engage in strenuous training regimens is the desire to excel in the competitive sport situation.

Sport Skill and Knowledge

To achieve success in sport, individuals must develop neuromuscular skills that will enable them to respond instantly and effectively in a competitive sports situation. The resulting skill development will enable individuals to successfully respond to situations requiring strength, endurance, speed, and coordination, and to fit their skills within the framework of the sport decision-making process.

Acquiring skill through sport also leads to a high

level of proficiency and a further desire to engage in physical activity. Some research indicates that persons who participate in sports when they are young are more likely to lead physically active lives as they age. The development and mastery of physical skill holds many other benefits, such as feelings of accomplishment, recognition, and affiliation, as well as contributing to a more positive self-image.

Individual Development

Self-realization, self-sufficiency, self-control, and self-discipline are individual qualities frequently developed through competitive sport experience. Self-image and self-confidence are also enhanced through comparison of one's competitive interaction with others .

Participation in competitive sports facilitates the development of leadership, cooperation, sportsmanship, and loyalty. Furthermore, commitment, decision making, and self-worth seem to be enhanced through the rigors of the competitive sport process.

Social Development[7]

Competitive sport provides opportunities for competition, cooperation, and individualistic participation. Although competition is a part of life, at the same time life demands cooperation, self-sacrifice, and respect for other people (e.g., race, ethnicity, gender, age, disability). Competition, cooperation, and individualistic sport behaviors, therefore, must be interdependent. Sport provides a natural opportunity to achieve this multifaceted objective, because individuals must be both competitive and cooperative in some situations, whereas under other circumstances, the sport environment may require individualistic behaviors. Fairness, adherence to the rules of the game, the ability to accept defeat, gaining respect for others, and the love of the game con-

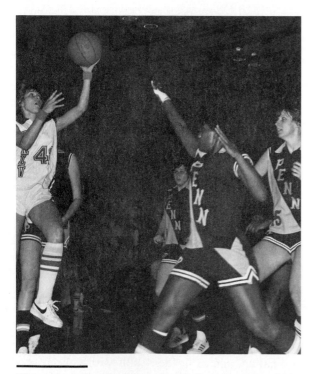

Women's intercollegiate basketball; University of Nevada, Las Vegas.

Varsity athletes gain valuable social skills.

tinue to shape the player as the player shapes the game.

There are, however, critics of the competitive sporting process, and Table 5-1 offers some popular arguments for and against it.

MANAGEMENT PERSONNEL INVOLVED IN SPORTS PROGRAMS

Key management personnel involved in sports programs include the director of athletics, the coach, the athletic trainer, and members of the sport council. In addition, the following personnel are also involved in sport programs, particularly at the college level: assistant or associate athletic director, academic counselor, sports information director, athletic business manager, facility director, travel coordinator, administrative assistant, fund raiser, sport psychologist or educator, equipment manager, game manager, ticket manager, and coordinator of special events. For the purposes of this chapter, however, only the major sport management positions applicable to both high school and college competitive sport programs will be presented.

The Director of Athletics

The director of athletics implements the athletic policies as established by the state, school board, or institution. Responsibilities and duties of the athletic director include preparing the budget; employing and evaluating coaches (Figure 5-1); purchasing equipment and supplies; scheduling; arranging for officials; supervising eligibility and health status requirements; arranging transportation; seeing that medical examinations, insurance coverage, and medical treatment are available and adequate; and generally supervising the total conduct of the program.

The athletic director should be professionally trained and possess a background in physical education and sport. Qualifications might include a major in physical education, with additional preparation in sport management and business. Experiences as a player, manager, or coach should also remain experiential requisites. Although the scope of duties and responsibilities might vary from school to university level and from Division III to Division I, the conceptual, human, and technical skills remain constant.

In a well-organized school, college, or other organization with a large sports program, the athletic director might work closely with a business manager whose responsibilities might include hiring and scheduling of officials, office personnel, and security, as well as keeping financial records, paying guarantees, and other contractual arrangements (e.g., in-

---

TABLE 5-1. Arguments for and against interscholastic sport programs[7]

Arguments for	Arguments against
1. Involves students in school activities and increases interest in academic activities.	1. Distracts the attention of students away from academic activities.
2. Builds the responsibility, achievement orientation, and physical vigor required for adult participation in society.	2. Perpetuates dependence and immaturity and focuses the attention of students on a set of values no longer appropriate in industrial society.
3. Stimulates interest in physical activities among students in the school.	3. Relegates most students to the role of spectator rather than active participant.
4. Generates the spirit and unity necessary to maintain the school as a viable organization.	4. Creates a superficial transitory spirit subverting the educational goals of the school.
5. Promotes parental, alumni, and community support for all school programs.	5. Deprives educational programs of resources, facilities, staff, and community support.

From Coakley JJ: *Sport in society,* ed 3, St Louis, 1986, Mosby–Year Book.

DEPARTMENT OF ATHLETICS

Name_____ SCHOOL DISTRICT NO. 48   Evaluator _____

Beaverton, Oregon

Assignment _____   COACH'S EVALUATION   Date _____

COACH'S SELF-EVALUATION (To be completed prior to the start of coaching assignment.)

1. Statement of personal goals and/or program goals as they relate to your coaching assignment.

   _____

   _____

   _____

2. Statement of self-evaluation on applicable criteria relative to completion of goals statement. (To be completed at the conclusion of your coaching assignment.)

   _____

   _____

   _____

3. ATHLETIC COORDINATORS EVALUATION (To be completed subsequent to the coaching assignment then reviewed with the coach.)
   CODE: Scale of 1 to 5, with 5 highest competency. If blank, not applicable.

   A. Administration   Circle one
      1. Care of equipment (issue, inventory, cleaning, etc.)   1 2 3 4 5
      2. Organization of staff   1 2 3 4 5
      3. Organization of practices   1 2 3 4 5
      4. Communication with coaches   1 2 3 4 5
      5. Adherence to district and school philosophy and policies
         (eligibility reports, inventories, budgets, rosters,
         insurance forms, and follow-up, scores reported)
      6. Public relations   1 2 3 4 5
      7. Supervision   1 2 3 4 5
   B. Skills
      1. Knowledge of fundamentals   1 2 3 4 5
      2. Presentation of fundamentals   1 2 3 4 5
      3. Conditioning   1 2 3 4 5
      4. Game preparation   1 2 3 4 5
      5. Prevention and care of injuries (follow-up with parents) 1 2 3 4 5
   C. Relationships
      1. Enthusiasm   1 2 3 4 5
         a. For working with students   1 2 3 4 5
         b. For working with staff (support of other programs)   1 2 3 4 5
         c. For working with academic staff   1 2 3 4 5
         d. For the sport itself   1 2 3 4 5
      2. Discipline   1 2 3 4 5
         a. Firm but fair   1 2 3 4 5
         b. Consistent   1 2 3 4 5
      3. Communication with players
         a. Individual   1 2 3 4 5
         b. As a team   1 2 3 4 5
   D. Performance
      1. Appearance of team on the field or floor   1 2 3 4 5
      2. Execution of the team on the field or floor   1 2 3 4 5
      3. Attitude of the team   1 2 3 4 5
      4. Conduct of coach during game   1 2 3 4 5
   E. Self-improvement
      1. Attends in-district meetings and clinics   1 2 3 4 5
      2. Attends out-of-district clinics   1 2 3 4 5
      3. Keeps updated by reading current literature   1 2 3 4 5
4. Review by Building Athletic Coordinator with Coach
   (District Athletic Coordinator will review all evaluations before
   forwarding to principal.)

   _____

   _____

   _____

5. To be placed in working papers of principal and forwarded to the personnel office
   with yearly teaching evaluation.

Original-Building Principal
  Canary-District Athletic Coordinator   _____
  Pink-Building Athletic Coordinator   Signed by Coach
  Gold-Coach

                                          _____
                                              Signed by Evaluator

---

FIGURE 5-1 An example of a form for evaluating coaches.

surance and media contracts, gate receipts, and guarantees).

The director of athletics in some complex Division I programs usually has an associate and assistants to help with such responsibilities as scheduling, staff supervision, eligibility, fund raising, budgets, insurance, purchasing, travel, and academic counseling. There might also be a sports information director (SID) who prepares media releases, develops brochures, and handles such things as photography, media, and public relations.

The Coach

One of the most challenging management positions within the physical activity and sport continuum is that of coaching. Indeed, there are more than 350,000 high school coaches, many of whom have no sport-related education. Many students who show exceptional skill in an interscholastic sport feel they would make good candidates for various coaching positions.[13] They believe that because they have proved themselves outstanding athletes in high school, their skills will carry over into the coaching

domain. This, however, is not necessarily true. There is insufficient evidence to indicate that exceptional skill in sport will necessarily guarantee success in the teaching and coaching profession. Many qualities and properties such as a thorough knowledge of the sport, educational degree, coaching license, professional attitude, and teaching prowess, combined with such personal characteristics as personality, intelligence, fairness, flexibility, integrity, leadership, and a sincere interest in working closely with youth and young men and women must provide the foundation for coaching success.

Coaching should be recognized as a form of teaching. Because of the nature of the profession, a coach is in a powerful position to affect participants more than most other members of a school faculty. Youths, in their inherent drive for activity and action and the quest for the excitement of sports competition, often look up to the coach and, in many cases, believe that the coach is a person to emulate. Coaches should recognize this role modeling concept, and strive to instill such values as character, honesty, self-discipline, and integrity. Although a

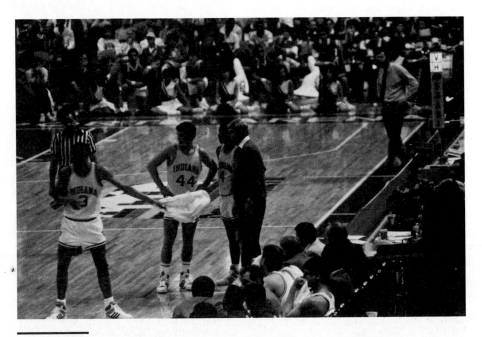

Coaching offers a challenging and rewarding career for many individuals.

coach must be a student and an expert of the game, these other characteristics are equally important.

Coaching is regarded by many as a position of insecurity, political or parental jockeying, and a hotseat of psychosocial turmoil. On the other hand, coaching offers an interesting and satisfying career for many individuals who seem to become permanent fixtures on the sidelines. However, the coach should recognize the possibility of finding himself or herself in a situation where the pressure to produce winning teams may be so great as to cause unhappiness, insecurity, and job discomfort. One need not look at a school like Notre Dame or into the professional ranks to examine these coaching concerns, since they exist within every local community.[9] Lopiano suggests that if the competent, ethical, and well trained coach is the key to elimination of undesirable behavior for which sport is now being criticized, it seems obvious that the better organized we are in training this individual and the more reflective we are in employing a coach, the better our programs will be.[10]

Of the qualifications needed to function as a credible coach, there are four that are paramount. First, the coach must be a good teacher who is able to teach the fundamentals and strategies of the sport. Second, the coach needs to understand the player—how a person functions at a particular level of development, with a full appreciation of human growth and development, including psychosocial parameters. Third, the coach must understand the game; a thorough knowledge of techniques, rules, strategies, and tactics is basic. Fourth, the coach must possess a desirable personality and character. Patience, understanding, kindness, honesty, sportsmanship, sense of right and wrong, courage, common sense, solid communication skills, cheerfulness, affection, humor, enthusiasm, and unending energy are imperative.

It should be noted that many times the coach may work part time at the school and, in many cases, men are coaching girls and young women. This presents certain logistical problems and is further reason why the contemporary coach must be a thorough professional in all regards.

Coaching Certification and Licensure

In some situations, the only qualification some coaches possess is that they have played the game or sport in high school, college, or sometimes, as a professional. It is generally recognized, however, that the best preparation for a coach is training in physical education. In light of this, many states are requiring, or at least attempting to require, that coaches, particularly at the precollege level, have at least some training in physical education.

Standards for coaching certification have been identified by the AAHPERD through their Task Force on Certification of High School Coaches. The essential areas identified were (1) medical, health, and safety aspects of coaching; (2) psychological and sociological dimensions; (3) theoretical and technical aspects of coaching; (4) motorical and biomechanical foundations; and (5) physiological foundations of training.[12]

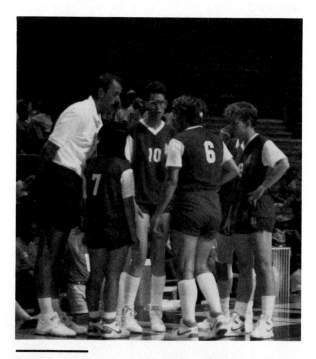

Special Olympics International provides excellent coaching preparation; 1991 Special Olympics International Summer Games, Minneapolis, MN.

Coaches should be encouraged to seek training, even if certification standards have not yet been required by their particular state or institution. Many coaching federations, such as the United States Soccer Federation, the United States Volleyball Association, and The Athletic Congress, provide outstanding coaching licensure programs. Private concerns such as the American Coaching Effectiveness Program (ACEP), the North American Youth Sport Institute (NAYSI), the National Youth Sport Coaches Association (NYSCA), and Special Olympics International also provide excellent coaching preparation opportunities. Although the trend toward certification is increasing, the thorough training of all coaches remains essential for the health, safety, and enhanced performance of each athlete.

Sisley and Wiese's[14] survey of the 50 states and District of Columbia provides the following information regarding coaching certification:

- 25 states require all coaches to hold a valid teaching certificate
- 6 states require only the head coaches to hold a teaching certificate
- 2 states require only major sport head coaches to hold a teaching certificate
- Arkansas, Iowa, Minnesota, New York, and Wyoming also require a coaching certificate
- 9 states reported that coaches must be employed by the school district; Florida and Louisiana reported that only the head coaches must be employed by the school district
- 12 states require neither a teaching certificate nor coaching licensure

Tables 5-2 and 5-3 illustrate some of the various states' teaching and coaching certification and licensure requirements.

The State of Minnesota and University of Minnesota have instituted one of the most comprehensive coaching certification programs, details of which are included in Table 5-4.

TABLE 5-2. States requiring a teacher certificate for some or all of their coaches, 1986-1987[15]

All coaches	Head coaches	All major sport coaches	Major sport head coaches
Alabama	Arizona	Florida	Iowa
Alaska	Idaho	Louisiana	Montana
Arkansas	Minnesota		
Colorado	New Mexico		
Delaware	North Carolina		
Georgia	South Carolina		
Illinois			
Kansas			
Kentucky			
Maryland			
Mississippi			
Missouri			
Nebraksa			
Nevada			
New Jersey			
New York			
Oklahoma			
South Dakota			
Tennessee			
Texas			
Utah			
Virginia			
West Virginia			
Wisconsin			
Wyoming			

TABLE 5-3. States requiring neither a teaching certificate nor a coaching certificate for some or all of their coaches, 1986-1987[15]

All coaches	Assistant coaches	Minor sport coaches
Hawaii	Arizona	Florida
Indiana	Idaho	Louisiana
Maine		
Massachusetts		
Michigan		
New Hampshire		
North Dakota		
Ohio		
Oregon		
Pennsylvania		
Rhode Island		
Vermont		

TABLE 5-4.   Course requirements for the coaching minor and Minnesota public secondary school coaching licensure program for boys' and girls' interscholastic sports (18 credits)

Course number	Course name
CBN 1027	Anatomy for Physical Education Students (4) or KIN 3110 Human Anatomy (3)
Hlth 1500	American Red Cross Standard First Aid and Personal Safety (1) or current American Red Cross Standard First Aid card
2 credits	KIN 3169 Volleyball Coaching (2), 3170 Baseball Coaching (2), 3171 Basketball Coaching (2), 3172 Football Coaching (2), 3173 Golf Coaching (2), 3174 Gymnastics Coaching (2), 3175 Ice Hockey Coaching (2), 3176 Swimming and Diving Coaching (2), 3177 Tennis Coaching (2), 3178 Track and Field Coaching (2), 3179 Wrestling Coaching (2), 3371 Soccer Coaching (2)
KIN 3111	Mechanics of Movement (3) or KIN 3115 Physiological Application of Sports (3) or KIN 3386 Exercise Physiology (4)
KIN 3114	Prevention and Care of Injuries (3) or KIN 5620 Practicum: Prevention and Care of Athletic Injuries (3)
KIN 3143	Organization and Management of Sport (3)
KIN 3624	Student Teaching: Coaching (3)

The now defunct Association of Intercollegiate Athletics for Women (AIAW) recommended a code of ethics for coaches from which any coach may benefit.[4] Ethical considerations for the coach include the following:

1. Respect each player as a special individual with unique needs, experience, and characteristics, and develop this understanding and respect among players.
2. Have pride in being a good example of a coach in appearance, conduct, language, and sportsmanship, and teach the players the importance of these standards.
3. Demonstrate and instill in players a respect for courtesy toward opposing players, coaches, and officials.
4. Express appreciation to the officials for their contribution and appropriately address officials regarding rule interpretations of officiating techniques. Respect their integrity and judgment.
5. Exhibit and develop in one's players the ability to accept defeat or victory gracefully without undue emotionalism.
6. Teach players to play within the spirit of the game and the letter of the rules.

7. Develop understanding among players, stressing a spirit of team play. Encourage qualities of self-discipline, cooperation, self-confidence, leadership, courtesy, honesty, initiative, and fair play.
8. Provide for the welfare of the players by:
   a. Scheduling appropriate practice periods
   b. Providing safe transportation
   c. Scheduling appropriate number of practice and league games
   d. Providing safe playing areas
   e. Using good judgment before allowing injured, fatigued, or emotionally upset players to play
   f. Providing proper medical care and treatment
9. Use consistent and fair criteria in judging players and establishing standards for them.
10. Treat players with respect, equality, and courtesy.
11. Direct constructive criticism toward players in a positive, objective manner.
12. Compliment players honestly and avoid exploiting them for self-glory.
13. Emphasize the ideals of sportsmanship and fair play in all competitive situations.

14. Maintain an uncompromising adherence to standards, rules, eligibility, conduct, etiquette, and attendance requirements. Teach players to understand these principles and adhere to them also.

15. Be knowledgeable in aspects of the sport to provide an appropriate level of player achievement. Have a goal of quality play and excellence. Know proper fundamentals, strategy, safety factors, and training and conditioning principles, and understand rules and officiating.

16. Attend workshops, clinics, classes, and institutes to keep abreast with and informed of current trends and techniques of the sport.

17. Obtain membership and be of service in organizations and agencies that promote the sport and conduct competitive opportunities.

18. Use common sense and composure in meeting stressful situations and in establishing practice and game schedules that are appropriate and realistic in terms of demands on players' time and physical condition.

19. Conduct practice opportunities that provide appropriate preparation to allow the players to meet the competitive situation with confidence.

20. Require medical examinations for all players before the sports season and follow the medical recommendations for those players who have a history of medical problems or who have sustained injury during the season.

21. Cooperate with administrative personnel in establishing and conducting a quality athletic program.

22. Accept opportunities to host events and conduct quality competition.

23. Contribute constructive suggestions to the governing association for promoting and organizing competitive experiences.

24. Show respect and appreciation for tournament personnel and offer assistance when appropriate.

25. Be present at all practices and competitions. Avoid letting other appointments interfere with the scheduled team time. Provide time to meet the needs of the individual players.

26. Encourage spectators to display respect and hospitality toward opponents and officials and to recognize good play and sportsmanship. When inappropriate crowd action occurs, the coach should assist in curtailing the crowd reaction.[4]

Athletic Trainer/Sports Medicine

The profession of athletic training has taken on greater significance in recent years because of the guidance of the National Athletic Trainers Association (NATA) and the concomitant increase in sports programs and the recognition that the health and safety of the student-athlete is a top priority. The role of the athletic trainer is the prevention and management of injuries at all levels of competitive sport.

The contemporary athletic trainer needs special preparation to carry out training duties, which include prevention of injuries, first aid and post-injury treatment, and rehabilitation. Such preparation, if possible, should include a major in physical education, NATA certification, or being a registered physical therapist. Also needed are such personal qualifications as emotional stability under stress, ability to act rationally when injuries occur, and a standard of ethics that places the welfare of the participant above the pressures for approval to play.

Many schools and colleges whose financial situation does not permit hiring a full-time athletic trainer are strongly encouraged to provide a part-time athletic trainer at the very minimum.

Qualifications for Athletic Trainers

Athletic trainers should complete a 4-year college curriculum that emphasizes the biological and physical sciences. The courses required in professional preparation programs for athletic trainers also indicate some of the competencies needed. These courses include anatomy, physiology, exercise physiology, applied anatomy, biomechanics, sport psychology, sport sociology, organization and management of sport, first aid and safety, nutrition, remedial exercise, health, techniques of athletic training, and a laboratory of internship in the techniques of athletic training.

The trainer is part of the sports management team

and must work closely with administrators, coaches, physicians, school medical personnel, athletes, and parents in a cooperative effort to provide the best possible health care. In some community situations, the trainer is also responsible for staff development, in-service training, and supervision of a student athletic training staff.

Arnheim[3] lists the following as the personal qualifications requisite for athletic trainers: good health, sense of fair play, maturity and emotional stability, good appearance, leadership, compassion, intellectual capacity, sense of humor, kindness and understanding, competence and responsibility, and a sound philosophy of life.

Additional information concerning the management of athletic training programs is provided in Chapter 12.

The Sport Council

Most colleges and many schools have some type of sport council, board, or committee that establishes and is responsible for the conduct of sport policies and procedures for the institution. Such councils, boards, or committees are responsible for providing proper direction as sport operates in the educational context of the organization.

The composition of such committees or councils varies widely from school to school and college to college. In a school, the superintendent or principal may serve as chairperson, or the director of physical education and/or athletics or other faculty member may hold this position. The committee may include coaches, members of the board of education, faculty, students, parents, and members of the community at large. In a college or university, the committee may consist of administrators, faculty, students, athletic directors, coaches, alumni, community leaders, and others.

Some of the functions of sport councils at the high school and college levels include making and reviewing policy, approving awards and eligibility, advising the athletic department on issues or concerns, endorsing and approving schedules and budgets, evaluating the athletic program, investigating complaints, interviewing and recommending to athletic

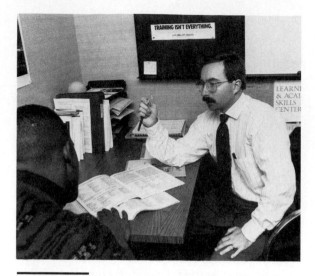

Academic counseling services; University of Minnesota, Minneapolis.

directors potential athletic personnel for hiring, approving codes of ethics, reviewing scholarship programs, approving post-season play and international educational competitions, and deciding if various sport programs should be added or discontinued.

Academic Counseling

In the last decade, many colleges and universities have made a concerted effort to improve their academic image and the graduation rates of student-athletes. These program support services have as their mission to enable each student-athlete to become an educated, self-reliant, and self-confident member of the campus community. With the stress of sport and the pursuit of sporting excellence permeating all education levels, academic counseling is now becoming an integral part of high school programs as well.

SELECTED MANAGEMENT FUNCTIONS IN COMPETITIVE SPORTS PROGRAMS

Many management functions are pertinent to the directing of a competitive sport program, including the following concerns: event, game, and practice scheduling; contracts; health and safety of players; injuries and insurance; officials; transportation; game management; crowd control; protests, forfeitures, and "called" games; awards and honors; and recordkeeping.

Event, Game, and Practice Scheduling

Scheduling involves maintaining a proper balance between home and away contests, seeking contests with organizations and institutions of approximately the same size and caliber of play, and trying to restrict the scope of the geographical area where contests are conducted to minimize transportation costs.

Where leagues and conferences are in place, schedules are usually made many months or years in advance, leaving the athletic director or coach few windows of opportunity for nonconference matches. In most instances, the high school league or association, NCAA, NAIA, or other appropriate governing body limits the number of matches, as well as the length of the season. All contests, games, and competitive sport events should have the sanction and approval of school, college, or other organizational authorities. Season lengths should be arranged so that they interfere as little as possible with institutional academic priorities. Practice schedules before the first game should be adequate so that the players are in match or game condition.

Some factors that may affect scheduling include environmental conditions, maximizing gate receipts, number of participants, state playoffs and invitational tournaments, transportation and logistics, availability of facilities, different sports that appeal to the same students, limitations concerning number of games or contests permitted, religious considerations, paid guarantees to travel and play, and potential educational impact on the student-athlete, ranging from tournament participation in Hawaii to number of class days missed.

Games, events, and practices should be scheduled equitably and according to Title IX guidelines. All coaches and other personnel involved in facilities utilization and travel scheduling should be involved in management's decision-making process.

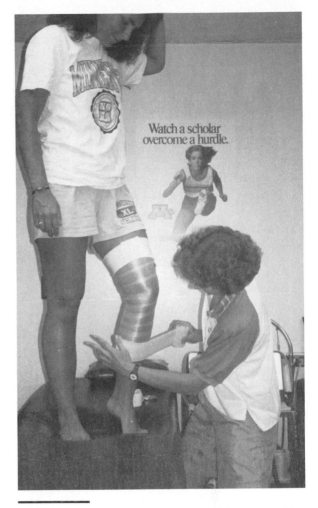

Athletic trainer at work; University of Minnesota, Minneapolis.

Contracts

Written contracts are usually essential in the management of interscholastic and intercollegiate sports programs (Figure 5-2). On the college level, in particular, games are scheduled many months, and sometimes years, in advance. Memories and facts tend to fade and become obscure with time. To avoid misunderstanding and confusion, it is best to have a written contract between the schools or colleges and all those concerned, as well as interested third parties (e.g., officials, hotels, transportation companies).

ATHLETIC EVENTS AGREEMENT
Department of Intercollegiate Athletics
University of Nevada, Las Vegas

ATHLETIC ACTIVITY _____

_____ VS UNIVERSITY OF NEVADA, LAS VEGAS

I. THE PARTIES HERETO HEREBY AGREE AS FOLLOWS:

(1) _____
       (Location)   (Date)   (Time)

(2) _____
       (Location)   (Date)   (Time)

(3) _____
       (Location)   (Date)   (Time)

(4) _____
       (Location)   (Date)   (Time)

II. THE FINANCIAL AGREEMENT SHALL BE SPECIFIED SUBSEQUENTLY:

(1) _____
     (Financial Sum)

(2) _____
     (Complimentary Tickets)

(3) _____
     (Other)

FOR: UNIVERSITY OF NEVADA, LAS VEGAS   **FOR: VISITING TEAM**

Signature: _____   Signature: _____

Title: _____   Title: _____

Date: _____   Date: _____

DISTRIBUTION:

   WHITE: University of Nevada, Las Vegas
   PINK: Visiting Team

FIGURE 5-2   Athletic events agreement.

Contracts should be properly executed and signed by official representatives of both schools or colleges. Many sport associations, federations, and conferences provide specially prepared forms for use by member schools or colleges. Such forms usually contain the names of the schools, dates, times, and circumstances and conditions under which the contests will be held. In addition, they usually provide for penalties if contracts are breached by either party.

Health and Safety of the Players

Competitive sport should contribute to the health and well-being of the players. Through wholesome physical activity the participant should not only become more aware of the benefits of exercise, but also become more physically, cognitively, emotionally, and psychosocially healthy.

One of the first requirements for every participant involved in a sport program should be a thorough medical examination by a trained physician to determine physical health status before engaging in strenuous activities. The nature of competitive sport and the sometimes stressful demands placed on the participant make this examination imperative.

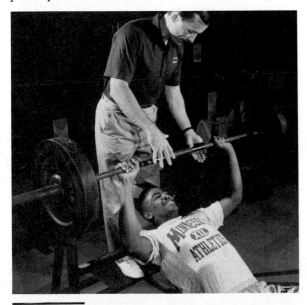

Strength training and conditioning play an important role in contemporary sport; University of Minnesota, Minneapolis.

Everything possible should be done to protect the health and safety of the participant. A coach should always conduct the program with these objectives in mind. The coach should possess current certification in first aid and CPR, and strictly adhere to progressive and prudent measures of training.

Proper conditioning and training should take place before any player is subjected to competition. Such conditioning and training should always be progressive and gradual. There should be ample players on the squad to allow for substitutions in the event a person is not physically fit or is otherwise unable to compete.

Proper facilities and equipment should be available to ensure the safety and health of the players. This means that facilities are constructed according to recommended standards concerning size, surfacing, and various safety features. Protective equipment meeting all current safety specifications (e.g., for football, lacrosse, and ice hockey) should be provided as required in the various sports. If appropriate facilities and equipment are not available, competition should be immediately suspended.

Games should be scheduled that result in equal and safe competition. The desire of small schools to compete against larger schools, in which case the competition is not equal, often brings potentially disastrous results in regard to the health, safety, and welfare of the players (primarily in the case of collision sports). Under such circumstances, one often hears the remark, "They really took a beating." Competition should be as equal and fair as possible.

Proper sanitary measures should be taken. Individual towels and drinking cups or bottles should be provided. The day of the team towel and the team water bottle has passed. Equipment should be well maintained, uniforms should be laundered as often as necessary, and facilities (e.g., weight training stations and mats) kept clean and up to code. Locker, dressing, shower, toilet, and other facilities used by participants should be kept clean and sanitary.

Playing areas should also be kept clean and safe. Gymnasiums, pools, and other facilities should be maintained at the proper temperature, and every measure must be taken to ensure safe, healthful, and maximal performance conditions.

Injuries and Insurance

Prompt attention should be given to all injuries. Injured players should be examined by a physician and administered proper treatment. There should be complete medical supervision of the entire sports program. A physician should be present at all games and practices involving the most strenuous contact sports. The athletic trainer is not a substitute for a physician. The physician should determine the extent of injury. After being ill or hurt, a player should not be permitted to participate again until the coach receives an approved statement from the family, school, or college physician. The coach should make sure that, even though such permission is granted, the athlete is psychosocially and physically prepared for match or game conditions.

In many states, the state high school association sponsors an athletic insurance plan. Some insurance companies have plans that allow a sports participation rider to be added to the student's basic student insurance policy. Such plans pay various medical, x-ray examination, dental, hospitalization, and other expenses according to the terms of the plan. The amount of any payment for an injury is usually only the amount of the actual expenses incurred, but not in excess of the amounts listed in the schedule of allowance for such injury. To collect benefits, plan requirements must be met.

The insurance provided by various state and independent plans usually includes benefits for accidental death or dismemberment, hospital expenses, x-ray examination fees, physicians' fees, and surgical and dental expenses, as well as emergency transportation. Dental benefits may or may not be included in the schedule of surgical benefits. In some plans catastrophe benefits are also available for injuries requiring extensive medical care and long-term hospitalization. Coverage is normally provided on a deductible basis, with the insurance company paying 75% to 80% of the total cost over the deductible amount up to a maximum amount.

Every school, college, or organization involved in the delivery of competitive sport should have a written policy concerning health, safety, injury and insurance, and other concerns relating to the competitive sport process. Furthermore, the administrator, coach, athletic trainer, team physician, parents, and players should be thoroughly familiar with the legal responsibilities, rights, and due process concerning all phases of the competitive sport program.

Officials

Officials play an integral role in any competitive sport program; therefore they should be well qualified, certified, and hold membership in their respective officiating association. They should know the rules and be able to interpret them accurately, recognize their responsibility to the players, be good sportspersons, and be courteous, honest, friendly, cooperative, impartial, and able to control the game at all times.

To ensure that only the best officials are employed, procedures should be established to register officials and determine which are qualified. Officials should be medically fit and required to pass examinations on rules and to demonstrate their competence. Rating scales have been developed to help make such assessments. Most sports associations have some method of registering and certifying acceptable officials. The National Association of Girls and Women in Sport of AAHPERD has a rating committee that certifies officials, as do State High School Associations or Leagues. In some states the officials who are used then rate the schools or colleges regarding facilities, environment, and circumstances surrounding the game. Officials' ratings can provide important feedback on coaching behavior and site management, and, in turn, coaches should rate every official.

Subject to contract differences, officials are frequently chosen by the home team with approval of opponents or the conference. The practice of the home team selecting officials without any consideration concerning the wishes of other organizations has on occasion resulted in relations that have not been in the best interests of sport. The growing practice of having the conference or association select officials has nullified many of these situations.

Officials should be duly notified of the date and time of the contests to which they have been assigned and contracts awarded. Officials' fees vary from school to school and sport to sport, although

Umpires play a major role in baseball competition.

some associations have assigned standard rates. It is usually considered best to pay a flat fee that includes both salary and expenses, rather than to budget them separately.

Transportation

Transporting athletes to and from sporting contests presents many management problems, such as the following: Who should be transported? In what kinds of vehicles should athletes be transported? Is sport part of a regular day-school program? Should private vehicles or school- and college-owned vehicles be used? What are the legal implications involved in transporting athletes to and from school- and college-sponsored events?

The present trend is to view competitive sport as an integral part of the educational program so that public funds may be used for transportation. At the same time, however, statutes vary from state to state, and persons managing sport programs should carefully examine the statutes and policies concerning their own circumstance.

Many managers believe that athletes and representatives of the school or college concerned, such as band members and cheerleaders, should travel only in transportation provided by the school. When private cars belonging to coaches, students, or other persons are used, the manager should be sure to determine whether the procedures are in conformity with the state statutes regarding liability. Under no circumstances should students or other representatives be permitted to drive unless they are licensed drivers, and under most circumstances students should not be used as drivers.

> ### ◆ ONE DAY IN A MONTHLY SCHEDULE OF SPORTING EVENTS
>
> **April 8**
> Depart: 3:00 PM
> From: Senior High School Parking Lot, West Exit
> Team: Junior Varsity Baseball
> To: Jones High School, 3 Oak St., Plymouth, MN 55447
> Phone: 612-123-4567
> Students: 25
> Pickup: 5:30 PM at Jones High School Baseball Field
> Remarks: Construction on Route 12 may require travel on Route 55. Please check before trip.

The business manager is generally responsible for transportation. This usually involves a great deal of advance planning, and the coach, athletic director, and department representative assigned to handle transportation must work in consort both to provide for the safety of the participants, as well as to minimize the costs associated with travel. The director of athletics should submit a monthly calendar of athletic events, listing the date, time and place of departure, event, destination, number of participants, time of pickup, mode of transport, and remarks (see the box above). These should be posted and sent to all coaches and athletes involved.

After the transportation has been scheduled with the appropriate school department or transportation company, a copy of the transportation contract is distributed to the athletic director involved, the coach, and the principal (or college manager). The procedure for submitting transportation requests varies in different schools and colleges, but written records should always be confirmed and scrutinized by the athletic director and coach involved.

Event and Game Management

Because so many details are associated with event or game management, it is possible to include only a brief statement of some of the more important items.[17] To have an effectively and efficiently conducted event, good organization is important. Someone must be responsible. Advance planning must be done. Many details must be attended to, including (1) pregame responsibilities, (2) game responsibilities, (3) post-game responsibilities, and (4) preparation for away games. Before an event or game, details such as contracts (e.g., officials, transportation, and facilities), eligibility records, equipment, facility availability, tickets, public relations, medical supervision, and medical examinations must be thoroughly checked. Responsibilities for home games might include checking such items as supplies and equipment, pregame and halftime entertainment, tickets and ushers, scoreboards, public-address system, emergency care procedures, availability of physician and trainers, and quarters for visiting teams and officials. The responsibilities after a home game consist of checking such items as payments to officials and visiting school, evaluation of officials, attendance and participation records, and financial records and deposits. Preparations for an away game include such important details as parents' permissions, missed classes, transportation, funding, contracts, travel group, and records. In addition, after an away game, forms must be completed in order to accurately account for travel expenses (Figure 5-3).

Crowd Control

Crowd control at sports contests is becoming increasingly important in light of potential security problems and incidents (as few as they may be when compared with recent international sporting events) that have occurred at high school and college campuses, as well as at neutral sports venues. The elimination of evening sports events at the high school level has been on the increase, particularly in metropolitan areas. School districts and college authorities are taking increased precautions to avoid crowd problems at sporting contests. Sportsmanship assemblies are being conducted, townspeople are being informed, and administrators are discussing the matter. Awards are now presented at most state high school association competitions, as well as at

UNIVERSITY OF NEVADA, LAS VEGAS

Controller's Office
Accounts Payable Department
CLAIM FOR GROUP TRAVEL EXPENSES

Note: Do not use this form for submitting Travel expenses for individual faculty/staff of UNLV.

Department to Travel: _____

Destination: _____

Dates of Travel: _____

Number of Students and Staff Members: _____

SUMMARY OF EXPENDITURES

Transportation:

  Method: _____

  Cost (Do not enter cost of any agency vehicle.) _____

Meals, lodging, and miscellaneous.

Dates						Total
Breakfasts						
Lunches						
Dinners						
Lodging						
Other						
Student Allowance						

Total Meals, Lodging, and Miscellaneous: ....

Total All Expenditures and/or Student Allowances.......................
  (Must be substantiated by receipts)

Advance Received: ....

Balance Due or to be reimbursed.......................................
  (If balance is to be reimbursed to the traveler submit a request
  for check in the amount of reimbursement.)

Account to be Charged: _____

Signed by: _____

Approved by: _____
                   Department Head

UNLV AP 270 4-76

(1) Controller's Office
(2) Controller's Office
(3) Department

FIGURE 5-3 Claim for group travel expenses.

college level tournaments, for sportspersonship. After several years of research into crowd control problems, the National Conference of City and County Directors, under the auspices of AAHPERD, have suggested guidelines concerning crowd control, which are outlined in Appendix B. These approaches to crowd control should also be extended to include crowd emergencies such as lightning storms, tornadoes, and other environmental disasters in which crowd communication and safety are paramount.

Protests, Forfeitures, and "Called" Games

Procedures for handling protests and forfeitures in connection with sports contests should be a matter of written policy. Of course, careful preventive action should be taken beforehand to avoid a situation in which such protests and forfeitures occur. Proper interpretation of the rules, good officiating, elimination of undue pressures, and proper education of coaches concerning the philosophy and objectives of competitive sport will help prevent such action. However, the procedure for filing protests and forfeitures should be established. This procedure should be clearly stated in writing and contain all the details, such as the person or responsible organization to whom the protest should be addressed. Time limits and time frame involved, person or group responsible for action, legal counsel, and any other necessary information should be readily available for the parties involved. One of the most frequent reasons for a protest is the use of ineligible players, which usually results in the forfeiture of any game in which ineligible players participated.

Calling games because of environmental (e.g., rain, snow, cold, lightning, tornado, earthquake) or other unforeseen conditions (e.g., sickness or tragic circumstance) also requires following the policies and procedures set down by the management concerned. Often times, short notice is the great concern, which is why communication via phone, fax, and walkie-talkie must be readily available.

Awards and Honors

The basis for awards in interscholastic and intercollegiate sport is similar to that in recreational sport,

except some limitations might exist in respect to high school or NCAA limitations. There are arguments for and against granting awards. Some individuals believe that the intrinsic values derived from playing a sport—joy and satisfaction, physical and psychosocial benefits, among others—are sufficient and that no materialistic awards should be given. Others argue that awards have been a symbolic recognition of achievement since the time of ancient Greece, and they should be an integral part of the competitive sport program.

The awards policy should be determined by the sport council at each sporting level. The practice of granting awards in the form of letters, insignia, plaques, medals, or some other symbol is almost universal. Along with traditional sporting honors, many organizations are beginning to recognize the academic achievement of student-athletes (e.g., ban-

Extrinsic rewards are commonplace in competitive sport programs.

quets for academic excellence). This practice is strongly encouraged.

When awards are given they should be modest and meaningful. Some state athletic associations and other governing bodies have placed financial limits on awards to student-athletes. Furthermore, it seems wise not to distinguish between so-called major, or revenue-producing, and minor, or non-revenue–producing, sports when granting awards. Award criteria should call for equal treatment among potential recipients. Awards and honors (e.g., All-State, MVP, All-Academic, captain) are personally meaningful for those student-athletes who receive them. College admissions officials or prospective employers often request such information and sometimes admission and financial aid are directly related to such achievements.

Record Keeping

Management of any competitive sporting endeavor requires accurate records of all the details concerned with the sport-specific situation. The following records should be considered for inclusion in the computer or file: medical status, parents' insurance information and permission to participate, academic eligibility, budget, travel, conference schedules, and transportation. Records on the conduct of various sports from year to year so that they can be compared over time or with other organizations; statistical summaries of player and game performance that may assist the coach in determining weaknesses in game strategy or in quantifying players' performances vs. stated objectives, and other pertinent information essential to well-organized game preparation should also be "on-line." Moreover, sound management practices demand records concerning equipment and supplies, officials, financial reports, and other accountability items requisite for conducting a top-notch program.

SELECTED MANAGEMENT PROBLEMS ASSOCIATED WITH COMPETITIVE SPORT

Contemporary competitive sport at both the school and college levels has become a quagmire of seemingly ever-changing rules and regulations.[7] Needless to say, the sport management team (athletic director, coaches, student-athletes, the sport council, school and college personnel, etc.) is responsible for the conduct of a program of integrity. The management team is bound to encounter problems related to recruitment, eligibility, scholarships, proselytizing, scouting, finances, substance abuse, and compensation for coaching.

Recruitment

Recruiting athletes is a controversial issue. Some educational institutions indicate that they do not condone recruiting for the primary purpose of developing winning teams. They feel the admission process should be the same for all students, regardless of whether they are athletes, merit scholars, minority students, or others gifted in music, art, or architecture. No special consideration should be shown to any particular group. The same standards, academic and otherwise, should prevail. This idealistic view, however, seems to be in constant conflict with most pragmatic practices at both the high school and college levels.

Some educational institutions, however, actively recruit athletes for their varsity teams. One has only to identify the country's leading football, basketball, or ice hockey high school teams to gain a realistic view of big-time high school recruiting. The main consideration here is to live up to rules of the state high school association or league, the conference, the NCAA, or other organizations in which the institution participates. To do otherwise should not be condoned.

In high school and college sports, teams should be made up of matriculated students attracted to the school or college because of its educational offerings, not its sports reputation. In some states, high school open enrollment continually causes problems, which have not truly been addressed. At the college and university level, there is a population of student-athletes on whom millions of dollars are spent during the recruitment process. Management can do much to see that acceptable academic standards are observed in the recruitment process, and that the cost of attracting qualified student-athletes is reduced. It should be made clear in writing that established rules will be observed and that any violation by the coaching staff will be dealt with severely. Also, at many universities, sport departments are hiring consultants to conduct seminars for the management team, including coaching staffs, concerning effective and legal recruiting practices.

Eligibility

Standards regarding the eligibility of participants are essential. These should be in writing, disseminated widely, and clearly understood by all concerned so that players, coaches, and significant others will not become emotional when they "suddenly" realize they cannot use a star player who is ineligible to compete.

Standards of eligibility in interscholastic circles usually include an age limit of not more than 19 or 20 years; a requirement that an athlete be a bona fide student; rules concerning transfer students that frequently require them to be residents in the community served by the school; rules concerning international and exchange students; satisfactory attendance, academic standing, and grades in school; a limit of three or four seasons of competition permitted per sport (playing in one game might constitute a season); permission to play on only one team during a season; playing on an outside all-star or select team during or after the season; and a requirement that the participant have a medical examination, amateur status, and parent's consent. These eligibility regulations vary from school to school, conference to conference, and state to state.

The National Federation of State High School Athletic Associations considers a student ineligible for amateur standing if the student (1) has accepted money or compensation for playing in an athletic contest, (2) has played under an assumed name, (3) has competed with a team whose players were paid, or (4) has signed a contract to play with a professional team.

Eligibility requirements at the college and university level include rules concerning core courses, academic test scores, residence, undergraduate status, academic grade point average and progress, limits of game participation, transfer, substance abuse, and amateur status, including hiring of agents and pro-

fessional tryouts. These rules have become quite complex, and athletic directors, coaches, counselors, and compliance officers must remain current.

Scholarships

Should athletes receive scholarships or special financial assistance from schools and colleges? Those in favor of scholarships and financial assistance claim that a student who excels in sport deserves to receive aid just as much as one who excels in various other academic pursuits. Those opposed point out that scholarships should be awarded on the basis of the need and academic qualifications, rather than physical prowess in some sport.

The NCAA has recently reduced the number of allowable scholarships, which has caused a controversy concerning further limitations on students who without athletic scholarships would be unable to afford a Duke, Georgetown, or Stanford education. The complex web of sport scholarships is not confined to the college campus. The situation even extends into the private high schools and preparatory schools, which seem to be in steady supply of high-powered athletes, whether in football, basketball, soccer, or ice hockey.

The controversy is a difficult one; however, with competitive sport being an integral part of the educational process, it seems that if sport can enable young people to further their education or can assist them in gaining admission to highly selective institutions, the student-athletes should have those opportunities.

Proselytizing

Proselytizing is a term applied to a high school or college that has so strongly overemphasized sport that is has stooped to unethical behavior to secure outstanding talent or winning teams. High schools are not immune to this problem, and colleges seem to receive a lot of attention as well as visitations from the staff of the NCAA office. Between open enrollment, international exchange students, and gracious financial incentives offered by private high schools, there are legitimate concerns regarding the management of competitive sport at the high school level. For the most part, however, state high school ath-

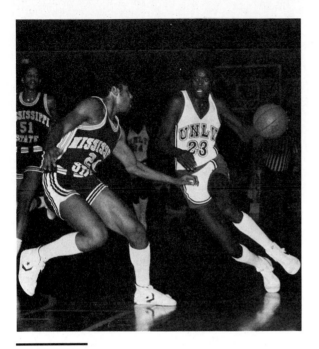

Intercollegiate basketball; University of Nevada, Las Vegas.

letic associations and leagues have attempted to legislate and control these problems, and have realized a fair amount of success. The NCAA, however, seems to be continuously investigating unscrupulous proselytizing practices.

Scouting

Scouting has become an integral part of competitive sport at both the high school and college levels. By watching another team perform, one can learn the formations and plays used, as well as discover certain team or individual player tendencies or weaknesses. This might range from watching players to determine mannerisms they possess that might "give away" a certain play to evaluating the "personality" of the opponent under stress.

Many schools and colleges are spending considerable money and time on scouting. Some scout a rival team every game during the season, using three or four persons on the same scouting assignment, and some study endless footage of "exchanged" vi-

deos. It is felt by many that money could be spent more wisely if used to enhance the value of the game for the participants.

Scouting is considered an important part of the game and, if scouting does occur, the head coach at the institution has direct responsibility for the action. Prior arrangements should be made concerning the game to be scouted, or videos to be exchanged with the opposing team's sports department. Although one hears stories of coaches falling out of trees while observing "closed" practices, for the most part scouting has been ethical and remains an important facet of game preparation.

Finances

Interscholastic and intercollegiate sport programs throughout the country are financed through many different sources. These include gate receipts, board of education and central university funds, donations and gifts, endowments, special projects, students' fees, physical education department funds, magazine subscriptions, and concessions.

It has long been argued by leaders in physical education that competitive sport programs have great educational potential. They are curricular in nature rather than extracurricular. This means they contribute to the welfare of students like any other subject in the curriculum. On this basis, therefore, the finances necessary to support such a program should come from board of education or central university funding sources. Sport programs should not be self-supporting or used as a means to support part or all of the other so-called extracurricular activities of a school or college. They represent an integral part of the educational program and as such deserve to be treated the same as other aspects of the program. This procedure is followed in some schools and colleges with benefits, as well as limitations, to all concerned.

Gate receipts are a primary source of funding for many competitive sport programs. Too often they become the point of emphasis rather than the vehicle that provides valuable educational opportunities and experiences to the participant. When this occurs, sport cannot justify its existence in the educational process.

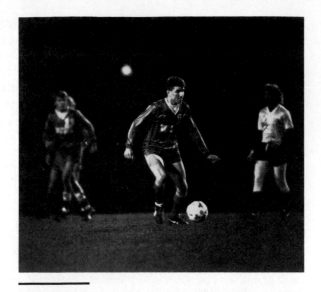

Interscholastic evening soccer match, Wayzata High School, Wayzata, MN.

Recent trends indicate that one out of every five US schools has cut back sport programs, or may soon do so, as a result of fiscal difficulty. It has come to the point where gate receipts alone cannot support the number of men's and women's sport programs that are being offered at many institutions.

In some school districts, a student fee, which is collected from the interscholastic sport participant, has managed to keep competitive sport programs intact. Schools, colleges, and universities will have to creatively address this fiscal issue as the decade of the 1990s hits full stride.

Substance Abuse

Substance abuse among junior high or middle and high school, as well as college students is a reality that must be recognized, treated, and combatted with preventive measures. The student-athlete has no immunity to the use of drugs among students. Indeed, athletes and anabolic steroid abuse are often mentioned in the same breath, which tarnishes the traditional belief that the athlete was somehow "above" substance abuse.

The substance abuse problem in the world of pro-fessional and college sports is of great concern to all. The news media, public, parents, student-athletes, and particularly educators and coaches, should be even more concerned about the young athlete. Substance use and addiction are not limited to the adult world; they endanger the entire younger generation.

The Drug Education Committee of the National Collegiate Athletic Association has indicated that most athletes bring their substance use habits with them when they come to the college campus.

Therefore they concluded that "it may be more effective to deal with the problem at the secondary school level."

Alcohol is the most commonly abused drug, with 93 out of every 100 young athletes 11 to 14 years of age coming in contact with this element. Marijuana is the next most popular drug on the list. The United States Department of Health and Human Services has pointed out that approximately one out of every three high school seniors had tried marijuana before entering high school.

Young athletes who hope to give themselves more energy use agents such as cocaine, including its derivatives "crack" and "ice," and "uppers" such as amphetamines, caffeine, and ephedrine. Anabolic steroids are also being used by these sport neophytes who hope to make themselves bigger, quicker, and stronger for sport competition.

These drugs are taking their toll on our young athletes, as well as on the community as a whole. Growth potential and maturity are being hampered, and side effects are causing poor health, not to mention impairment of motor function, slower reaction times, improper coordination with poor execution of movement, altered perception of speed, and withdrawal and loss of friends. In addition, they are resulting in academic, psychosocial, and vocational failure.

According to the report in the September 1984 *Athletic Business,*[5] the Milton, Wisconsin, School District is coming to grips with drug abuse. Its program is designed to identify those students who come to school under the influence of alcohol or other drugs. Those students who exhibit overt behavior of drug abuse are referred to the principal of the school. If they voluntarily admit use of drugs, they are then referred to the student assistance and counseling program. However, if they claim they are not involved, they are given a urinalysis. If the test is positive, they are assigned to a state-licensed assessment program. If students refuse to take the test, they are placed on a 3-day suspension and assigned to a licensed assessment program and must get treatment before returning to school. The Milton, Wisconsin, program applies to all students. Voluntary self-referral to the student assistance program for drug abuse is not a violation of the athletic code. In many high schools, however, substance abuse is forbidden, and immediate suspension from the team for various time lengths is prescribed.

Bruce Durbin, Executive Director of the National Federation of State High School Associations (which represents 20,000 schools and 93,000 individual members), believes that a drug program should stress education rather than enforcement. Such programs should reach coaches, officials, parents, students, and educators in general.

The state of Minnesota is using an education program with the help of the Hazelden Foundation, the Kroc Foundation, and the Minnesota State High School League. As a cooperative team they are sponsoring several projects such as chemical awareness seminars. This program is building a model for other state high school associations, colleges, and professional leagues to follow. The drug abuse program called Operation Cork was founded by Joan Kroc, widow of McDonald's founder Ray Kroc, for the purpose of coping with the problems of athletes and drugs. The Hazelden and Kroc Foundations are now investing $7 million in a facility that will focus its efforts on drug education and the prevention of drug abuse.

Many universities and high schools have also taken a pro-active stance toward substance abuse; some of those relevant ideas are offered in Appendix C.

Coaching Compensation

A frequent topic of discussion at school meetings is whether teachers should receive extra pay for extra services. Parents, taxpayers, school boards, and administrators have been trying to decide whether

sport coaches, adapted coaches, dance line coaches, cheerleading advisors, band leaders, dramatics supervisors, yearbook advisors, and others who perform services in addition to their teaching load should receive additional compensation.

A sensible solution to this problem is essential to the morale of a school staff. Because most school systems are demanding more and more services, most have formulated pay scales to cover the extra duties. These scales often include compensation formulas including hours spent, length of season, number of participants, and experience, which may culminate in as much as $4000 to $5000 for a head coach of football or basketball and $1500 to $3500 for an assistant coach in a typical suburban junior or senior high school.

Coaching loads should be equalized as much as possible. If inequalities exist that cannot be corrected through extra pay, then extra staff and, sometimes, release time may be considered.

The compensation involved in competitive sport at the college or university level is not as clear cut as in high school. At the NCAA Division III level, coaching might be part of the teaching or administrative responsibilities, whereas at the Division I

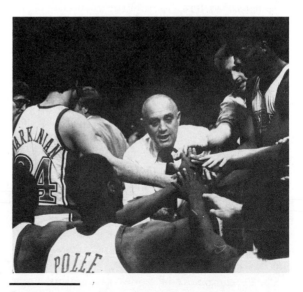

Coaching at the elite level can be a lucrative profession.

level, coaching and its associated duties may be the only assignment. Within sport, differences range from six-figure salaries, radio and television shows, cars, shoe contracts, and country club privileges to the "no perks club" of many non–revenue-producing sports. There seems to be a distinction between revenue-producing and non–revenue-producing sport coaches' compensation, not to mention gender-based salary equity concerns.

For the majority of coaches, however, at both the school and college level, compensation for coaching is similar to pay for teaching. It needs to improve and should be a top priority.

MANAGEMENT GUIDELINES FOR COMPETITIVE SPORT PROGRAMS

Competitive sport programs have existed in schools, colleges, and universities since 1852 when the Harvard and Yale crews dueled on the calm water of the Winnipesaukee River in New Hampshire.

Elementary, Junior High, and Middle Schools

Since competitive sport was first introduced to college campuses throughout the United States, high schools have embraced sport as part of their educational offerings. As a result, most high schools in America today have some form of interscholastic sport. It did not take long for our junior high and elementary schools to feel the impact of interscholastic sport programs. A survey made by the National Association of Secondary School Principals (which included 2296 junior high schools) revealed 85.2% had some program of interscholastic sport.

For the most part, interscholastic sport has been phased out of the elementary school level, where educators agree that physical activities should be concerned with the development of basic motor skills and positive attitudes toward physical activity. An informal recreational sport program should be a part of all elementary programs, as should traditional May Days and Field Days at which competitive intramural and extramural sport may be introduced.

The special nature of grades seven through nine, representing a transition period between the elementary school and the senior high school and between

childhood and adolescence, has raised a question in the minds of many eductors about whether an interscholastic sport program is in the best interests of the students concerned. Many junior high and middle schools do, however, have football, soccer, basketball, volleyball, and track and field for young boys and girls.

Management Guidelines for Elementary School Sport

Many of the guidelines of the American Academy of Pediatrics may be applied at the elementary school level and to the type of sport competition that should be offered:

- All children should have opportunities to develop skill in a variety of activities.
- All such activities should take into account the age and developmental level of the child.
- Sport activities of elementary school children should be part of an overall school program.
- Competent medical supervision of each child should be ensured.
- Health observation by teachers and others should be encouraged and help given by the physician.
- Sport activities outside the school program should be on an entirely voluntary basis without undue emphasis on any special program or sport and without undue emphasis on winning. These programs should also include competent medical supervision.
- Competition is an inherent characteristic of growing, developing children; therefore, competitive programs organized at the school, neighborhood, and community levels that meet the needs of children should be provided. State, regional, and national tournaments, bowl games, and charity and exhibition games are not recommended for this age-group. Commercial exploitation in any form should be avoided.
- Body-contact sports, particularly tackle football and boxing, are considered a physical risk and should have no place in programs for children of this age.
- All competitive sport programs at this level should be organized with the cooperation of in-

terested medical groups, who will ensure adequate medical care before and during such programs. This should include thorough physical examinations at specified intervals, advising parents and coaches about such factors as (1) injury, (2) response to fatigue, (3) individual emotional needs, and (4) the risks of undue emotional strains.

With a proper blend of common sense and sound management and leadership, competitive sport activities at the elementary school level can lay the foundation for a lifetime of wholesome physical activity. The primary consideration should be a diversity of wholesome childhood experiences that will aid in the proper physical and emotional development of the child rather than highly organized competition.

Low organized sport focusing on skill development; Brooklyn Park, MN.

Management Guidelines for Junior High and Middle School Sport

The research regarding a highly organized sport program at the junior high or middle school level indicates the following points of substantial agreement:

- This age range is a period of transition from elementary school to senior high school and from childhood to adolescence. It is a time when students are trying to understand their bodies, gain independence, achieve adult social status, acquire self-confidence, and establish a system of values. It is a time when a program of education unique to this age-group is needed to meet the abilities and broadening interests of students.
- The best educational program at the junior high school level provides for enrichment that meets the needs of students in grades 7 through 9. A distinct and separate educational climate for these grades is needed to ensure that the program will not be influenced unduly by either the elementary or the senior high school.
- Coaches are needed whose full responsibilities lie in the junior high or middle school and whose training is appropriate to the needs of these students.
- The junior high school should provide for exploratory experiences with specialization delayed through the completion of senior high school.
- The junior high school competitive sport environment should provide for the mental, physical, social, and emotional development of students, as well as the concern for the development of a sound standard of values.
- The principal and other members of management have the responsibility for providing sound educational leadership in all school matters. The type of physical education and competitive sport programs offered will reflect the type of leadership provided.

The interscholastic sport program, if offered at this level, should be provided only after the prerequisites of physical education, adapted/developmental, and recreational sport programs have been developed, and only if special controls regarding health and safety, facilities, game adaptation and supervision, classification of players, leadership, and qualified, certified coaches and officials have been provided.

The competitive sport program should provide a favorable social and emotional climate for the student. There should be freedom from anxiety and fear, absence of tensions and strains, a feeling of belonging for each student, a social awareness that contributes to the development of such important traits as respect for the rights of others, and an atmosphere conducive to growing into social and emotional maturity.

All sport activities should be professionally supervised and a physician or athletic trainer should be intimately involved to ensure optimal health and safety conditions.

Competition itself is not the factor that makes sport dangerous to the student. Instead, items such as the manner in which the program is conducted, type of activity, facilities, leadership, and physical condition of students are the crucial factors.

Competitive sport, if properly conducted, has the potential for satisfying such basic psychological needs as recognition, belonging, self-respect, and the feeling of achievement, as well as providing a wholesome outlet for the physical activity drive. However, if conducted in light of adult interests, community pressure, and other questionable influences, it can prove psychosocially harmful.

Interscholastic sports, when conducted in accordance with desirable standards of leadership, educational philosophy, activities, and other pertinent factors, have the potential for realizing beneficial social effects for the student; but when not conducted in accordance with desirable standards, they can be socially detrimental to all involved.

Management Guidelines for Interscholastic and Intercollegiate Sport Programs[11]

Selected recommended standards for high school and college sport programs follow:

Organization

The wholesome conduct of the sport programs should be the ultimate responsibility of the school administration along with the school board or board of regents.

Sport policy should be developed, evaluated, and supervised by a faculty committee.

Sport policy should be implemented by the director of athletics.

Sport should be organized as an integral part of the department of physical education at the high school level and should maintain strong positive relationships with associated departments (e.g., physical education, public health, physical therapy) at the collegiate level.

Staff

All members of the coaching staff should be members of the faculty.

Coaches should be hired based on their qualifications to assume educational responsibilities and not on their ability to produce winning teams.

Coaches should enjoy the same privileges of tenure, rank, and salary accorded other similarly qualified faculty members. This remains a major point of contention at many large universities.

Public school coaches should be certified educators and hold a coaching minor or coaching certification including First Aid and CPR training.

Finances

The financing of interscholastic and intercollegiate sport should be governed by the same policies that control the financing of all other educational activities within an institution.

Gate receipts should be considered a supplemental source of revenue, as should the myriad fund raising enterprises undertaken by both schools and colleges.

Health and Safety

An annual medical examination should be requried of all participants; a physical examination on a seasonal basis would be preferable.

Each school should have a written policy concerning the responsibility for sport-related injuries and should provide or make available athletic accident insurance.

Good officiating is requisite for the protection and safety of the participant; Minnesota State High School League playoff, Wayzata vs. Park Cottage Grove.

Each school should have a written policy for the implementation of an injury-care program.

A physician and trainer should be present at all sport contests.

Only equipment that is fully certified as offering the best protection for the student-athlete should be purchased and utilized.

All protective equipment should fit players properly.

Competition should be scheduled between teams of comparable ability.

Games should not be played until players have had a minimum of 3 weeks of physical conditioning and training.

Playing fields and surfaces should meet standards for size and safety for the participants.

Eligibility

All schools should join, and fully participate, honor, and respect the eligibility rules and regulations of, respective local, state, and national sport associations.

Recruiting

The sport teams of each school should be composed of bona fide student-athletes who live in the school district or who were attracted to the institution by its educational program.

All candidates for admission to a school should be evaluated according to similar standards.

All financial aid should be administered with regard to need and according to the same standards for all students. The recipient of financial aid should be provided a statement of the amount, duration, and conditions of the award.

Sport scholarships, when possible, should be allocated on a full basis to avoid inequitable distribution among team members.

Awards and Honors

The value of sport awards and honors is sometimes questioned. However, when the program is properly managed and kept in perspective, awards are a meaningful part of high school and college sport programs and are a positive recognition of hard work, dedication, skill, and school commitment. Many institutions have developed broadly based

Awards can play a meaningful role in recognizing hard work and significant sport achievement.

◆ **EVALUATION OF A HIGH SCHOOL SPORT PROGRAM**[11]

	Yes	No

1. Sport program as an integral part of total curriculum
   a. The sports are an outgrowth of the physical education program
   b. A variety of sports is available for all students
   c. The educational values of sport are foremost in the philosophy
   d. All students have an opportunity to participate in a sport
   e. Sports are used appropriately as a school's unifying force
   f. Athletes are not excused from courses, including physical education, because of sport participation
2. Coaches as faculty members
   a. Coaches have an adequate opportunity to exercise the same rights and privileges as other faculty members in determining school and curricular matters
   b. Coaches attend, and they are scheduled so that they may attend, faculty meetings
   c. Coaches are not expected to assume more duties of a general nature than are other faculty members
   d. Teaching tenure and other faculty privileges are available to coaches
   e. Assignments for extra duties are made for coaches on the same basis as for other teachers
3. Participants encouraged to perform adequately in academic areas
   a. Athletes are held accountable scholastically at the same level as other students
   b. Practices are of such length and intensity that they do not deter students' academic pursuits
   c. Game trips do not cause the students to miss an excessive number of classes
   d. Counseling services emphasize the importance of academic records in regard to career education
   e. Athletes are required to attend classes on days of contests
4. Meeting philosophy of school board
   a. New coaches are made aware of the board policies and informed that they will be expected to follow them in spirit, as well as to the letter
   b. All coaches are regularly informed by the principal and athletic director that they must conduct their programs within the framework of board policy
   c. A procedure is available for the athletic director and coaches to make recommendations regarding policy change
   d. Noncoaching faculty members are made aware of board policy regarding sport so that they may discuss it from a base of fact
   e. The philosophy of the board is written and made available to all personnel
5. Awards
   a. Only those awards authorized by local conferences, state high school athletic associations and NCAA or similar organizations are given
   b. Diligence is exercised to ensure that outside groups do not cause violations of the award regulations
   c. Care is taken to assure that athletes are not granted privileges not available to the general student body

---

◆ **EVALUATION OF A HIGH SCHOOL SPORT PROGRAM[11]—cont'd**

	Yes	No
6. Projected program outcomes		
a. It is emphasized that participation in sport is a privilege	____	____
b. Development of critical thinking, as well as sport performance, is planned into the program	____	____
c. Development of self-direction and individual motivation is a real part of the sporting experience	____	____
d. The athletes are allowed to develop at their own cognitive, psychomotor, and affective readiness level	____	____
e. The accepted social values are used as standards of behavior both on and off the playing area	____	____
7. Guarding against student exploitation		
a. The student is not used in sport performance to provide an activity that has as its main purpose entertainment of the community	____	____
b. The student's academic program is in no way altered to allow continued eligibility with less than normal effort and academic progress	____	____
c. The students are not given a false impression of their ability through the device of suggesting the possibility of a college scholarship or professional career	____	____
d. The athletes are not given a false image of the value of their athletic prowess to the material and cultural success within the school and community	____	____

---

award programs in which scholar-athlete and all-academic honors share the spotlight with traditional sport awards, such as all-state, all-district, all-conference, and most valuable player.

Management Guidelines for Competitive Sport Programs in Other Organizations

Competitive sport programs also exist in forms other than the formal educational setting. Community organizations and businesses, Recreation and Park Districts, YMCAs, and the traditional golf and tennis clubs offer tremendous opportunities for all age-groups to compete. State games, Olympic Festivals, Police Athletic Leagues, church leagues, aquatic clubs, Athletes in Action, and the military are just some of the many sports delivery systems available to the competitive sport consumer.

The main consideration in such sport programs is to gear them to the age and needs of the participants. Youth-serving agencies, for example, should ob-serve the established standards for interscholastic programs, whereas adults and seniors might follow the standards applicable at the college and university level. Many advantages accrue from belonging to leagues and conferences rather than playing independently. Leagues and conferences often promote established procedures, rules, and regulations that are more likely to benefit the participant than if a team were organized independently.

Usually sports sponsored by educational institutions take special pains to provide for the health and safety of the participants. They frequently provide insurance options, physicians and athletic trainers, access to transportation, and other provisions that help guarantee safer participation.

Sometimes in highly competitive sport programs in other organizations, especially as the participant gets older (e.g., senior leagues), there is not the same concern for the safety and well-being of the players; as a result, players sometimes participate more at their own risk than players in institutionalized school sport.

It would be helpful if all sport organizations would examine and apply many of the procedures and standards set forth in this chapter for educational institutions.

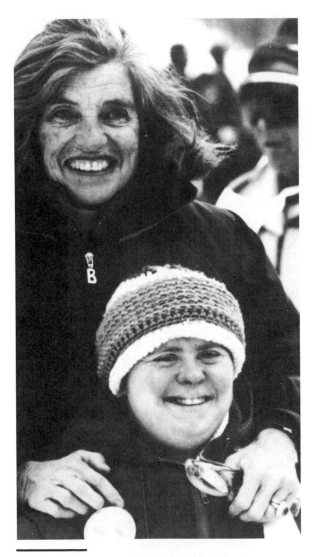

Eunice Kennedy Shriver, founder of Special Olympics International.

Management Guidelines for Sport for People with Varying Disabilities

Persons with disabilities can receive the same benefits, as well as harm, from a program of competitive sport as their nondisabled peer group. The following reasons for including adapted or unified sport activities in the school sport programs are listed by Auxter and Pyfer.[6]

Many students assigned to an adapted physical education class are unable to correct an existing condition and also are unable to participate in regular physical education. A program of adapted sport would be ideal for such students because it would provide them additional opportunities to participate in various forms of physical activity.

Students in the adapted/developmental sport program need activities that have carry-over value. They may continue exercise programs in the future, but they also need training in sports and games that will be useful in later life.

Adapted sports and games should help the person with disabilities learn to handle his or her body under a variety of circumstances and assist in the physical conduct of daily living.

A certain amount of emotional release also takes place in sport activities, and this is just as important to the student-athlete with a disability as it is for the nondisabled student-athlete.

The Joseph P. Kennedy, Jr. Foundation probably has focused more attention on sport for persons with disabilities (mentally retarded) than any other single organization or legislation. The most visible activity promoted by the Kennedy Foundation is the Special Olympics, which was organized in 1968. It was designed to provide mentally retarded youths, 8 years of age and over, with opportunities to participate in a variety of sports and games on local, state, regional, national, and international levels.

The basic objectives of the Special Olympics follow:

- Encourage development of comprehensive physical education and recreation programs for the mentally retarded in schools, day-care centers, and residential facilities in every community.
- Prepare the retarded for sport competition—

particularly where no opportunities and programs now exist.

- Supplement existing activities and programs in schools, communities, daycare centers, and residential facilities.
- Provide training for volunteer coaches to enable them to work with youngsters in physical fitness, recreation, and sports activities.[16]

Since the enactment of the Amateur Sports Act of 1978, P.L. 95-606, the Committee on Sport for the Disabled (COSD) was established by the United States Olympic Committee, and other groups and associations have taken up the challenge to provide sport opportunities for athletes with disabilities (see Appendix D).

TITLE IX AND THE CHANGING ROLE OF GIRLS' AND WOMEN'S SPORT COMPETITION

Proponents of equality in girls' and women's sport and Title IX have opened the window of opportunity concerning participation in women's sport in recent years. Women have become accepted as athletes, with full rights to experience the competitive urges so long restricted by our gender-dominated society.

Procedures and practices concerning interscholastic and intercollegiate sport competition for females vary from school to school, state to state, and university to university. Some schools and colleges have wide-ranging programs of interscholastic and intercollegiate sports, whereas others still have few opportunities to compete at the varsity level. Most states have not set up specific requirements for girls' sport, but many believe that their established regulations apply to both girls and boys. Some states have athletic associations for girls that are similar to those for boys, and there are a few universities that still maintain independent men's and women's athletic departments (e.g., University of Iowa, University of Minnesota).

The National Association for Girls and Women in Sport (NAGWS)[2] of AAHPERD believes that op-

Title IX has provided increased opportunity for girls and women to participate in sport.

portunities should be provided for all girls and women who want to participate in competitive sport. Adequate and equitable funds, facilities, and staff should be provided for these programs.

Title IX*

One of the major reasons for the passage of Title IX was to ensure that girls and women receive the same educational rights as boys and men. Testimony before congressional committees before the enactment of this legislation indicated that girls and women were being discriminated against in many education programs, including physical education and sport. Indeed, even after enactment, suits were levied concerning baseball, soccer, tennis, track, golf, and basketball in states ranging from New York to California.

Although Title IX applies to all types of educational programs, probably the most dramatically affected have been those associated with sport and physical education programs. Girls' and women's sports programs have grown rapidly since the early 1970s when there were comparatively few varsity interscholastic and intercollegiate sport opportunities. Today, however, girls' and women's interscholastic and intercollegiate sport teams are in full evidence throughout the nation, providing athletes with the challenges and championships on an equal basis with their male counterparts. Sport once again has contributed to breaking down discriminatory social barriers (e.g., gender, race, ethnicity, age).

---

*Parts of this section have been taken directly from government documents relating to Title IX, particularly the following documents:

US Department of Health, Education, and Welfare, Office of Civil Rights: *Final Title IX regulation implementing Education Amendments of 1972—prohibiting sex discrimination in education,* Washington, DC, July 1975, US Government Printing Office.

US Department of Health, Education, and Welfare, Office for Civil Rights: *Memorandum to chief state school officers, superintendents of local educational agencies and college and university presidents; subject: elimination of sex discrimination in athletic programs,* Washington, DC, Sept 1975, US Government Printing Office.

Provisions of Title IX Affecting Sport Programs

Chapter 3 contained some background information concerning Title IX of the Education Amendment Act of 1972. The following section offers some of the provisions of Title IX specifically affecting sport programs.

- Separate teams for boys and girls, or a coeducational team, must be provided in schools and colleges. For example, if there is only one team in a particular sport, such as swimming, then students of both sexes must be permitted to try out for this team.

- Equal opportunities must be provided for both sexes in the educational institution in terms of competitive training facilities, equipment and supplies, facilities for practice and games, medical and training services, coaching and academic tutoring, travel allowances, housing and dining facilities, compensation of coaches, and publicity. Equal aggregate expenditures are not required; however, equal opportunity for men and women is mandated. Where men are given the opportunity for athletic scholarships, women must be given the same opportunity. Contact sports such as football, basketball, boxing, wrestling, rugby, and ice hockey may be offered either separately or on a unitary basis.

- The emphasis of Title IX is to provide equal opportunity for both sexes. In determining whether equal opportunity is provided, it is important to know whether the interests and abilities of students of both sexes have been met and whether such things as adequate facilities and equipment are equally available.

- Title IX guidelines provide that expenditures on men's and women's sport be proportional to the number of men and women participating. This standard of substantially equal per capita expenditures must be met unless the institution can demonstrate that the differences are based on nondiscriminatory factors, such as the costs of a particular sport (e.g., the equipment required in football) or the scope of the competition (national rather than regional or local). This proportional standard applies to athletic scholarships, recruitment, and other readily measurable financial benefits such as equipment, supplies, travel, and publicity.

- According to the Department of Health and Human Services, the policy is designed to eliminate, over a reasonable period of time, the discriminatory effects, particularly at the college level, of the historic emphasis on men's sport and to facilitate the continued growth of women's sport. It requires colleges and universities to take specific steps to provide additional competitive sport opportunities for women—opportunities that will fully accommodate the increasing interest of women participating in sport.

Procedures for Assuring Compliance With Title IX

To make sure the provisions of Title IX have been complied with by an educational institution, certain procedures should be followed. Each educational institution usually has some member of the faculty or staff coordinate a self-evaluation and ensure compliance. Some universities have employed a full-time compliance officer.

The steps that have been followed in some sport programs involve first developing a statement of philosophy that provides a guide for equality of opportunity for both sexes. Then student interest is determined regarding the activities in which they desire to participate. In addition, all written materials concerned with items such as mission statements, curriculum, employment, job descriptions, and organizational structures are reviewed to see that needed changes are made to ensure that equal and fair inclusion is described. Also, such things as practice times for all teams, provision for supplies and equipment, travel expenses, number of coaches assigned to teams, and salaries of coaches are examined to see if any discrepancies exist between the sexes. The membership requirements for clubs and other student organizations associated with sport are also reviewed. The amount of publicity and information services provided for physical education and sport programs are checked. Eligibility requirements for

scholarships and financial aid, medical and accident policies, award systems, and employment procedures are examined. Teaching loads, coaching assignments, coaches' gender, and facility assignments are also included in such an appraisal.

According to AAHPERD,[2] many questions can be asked to determine if equality exists for men's and women's programs. For example, regarding *employment conditions* the question might be asked, "Are men and women compensated the same for essentially the same work for both teaching and coaching?" Under *physical education classes* the question might be asked, "Are physical education requirements for graduation the same for boys and girls, men and women?" Under *recreational sport opportunities,* "Are recreational sport programs provided for both sexes?" Under *competitive sport,* "Does the total budget reflect comparable support to both the men's and women's programs?" Many other questions are listed in their publication to determine if equality exists.

In some cases where equality does not exist between men and women, litigation is initiated. For example, in one case a high school girl wanted to participate on the boys' golf team. There was no girls' golf team, and the court ruled in favor of the plaintiff. Another case involved girls who wanted to play on the high school football team, thus challenging a state athletic association rule excluding girls. The court ruled in favor of the girls and said the association rule discriminated on the basis of sex.

A project of the Women's Equity Action League Educational and Legal Defense Fund[13] has offered the following pros and cons of bringing a legal suit.

Some pros of filing a complaint. It is possible to win! You may convince others to take legal action for other complaints. You may change discriminatory practices at your school or college. Many girls and women may benefit from your action. Your action may result in the Title IX compliance plan at your school becoming the subject of scrutiny. Schools that have been cited for complaints are more likely to come closer to compliance.

Some cons of filing a complaint. You can lose! You may lose your position or scholarship and be labeled a troublemaker. You may become frustrated in dealing with the many organizations' legal concerns involved. The procedure sometimes takes years to resolve.

Organizations that may be of help in case it is found that inequality exists are the Department of Health and Human Services; Office for Civil Rights; Equal Employment Opportunity Commission; Office of Federal Contract Compliance; and the U.S. Department of Labor–Wage and Hour Division of the Employment Standards Administration.

Title IX sport complaints have been filed against numerous institutions. The complaints are usually filed with the regional Office of Civil Rights (OCR) and have been referred to the national OCR headquarters office in Washington, DC.

Coeducational Sport and Title IX

Coeducational sport should be provided for students in schools and institutions of higher education because of the benefits that can accrue from such participation. In instances in which highly skilled females would not otherwise have the opportunity to participate in a particular sport, they must be allowed to participate on male teams. However, coeducational sport, in most cases, should be limited to the recreational sport level.

The primary reason for not advocating coeducational sport participation on interscholastic and intercollegiate levels in many sports is the physical difference between males and females. The ratio of strength to weight is greater in males than in females. Females thus would be at a decided disadvantage in those sports requiring speed, power, strength, and impact. As a consequence, teams would be male dominated.

The Impact of Title IX on Girls and Women in Sport

During the year before the birth of Title IX, 3,366,000 boys and 294,000 girls competed in interscholastic sport in the United States. After 7 years the figures increased to 4,109,000 boys and 1,645,000 girls in the same activities. The figures are even greater today. Girls' participation in interscholastic sport increased 460% during the interim. Fur-

thermore, the participation of girls increased from 7% of the total number of students involved to 29%. In addition, approximately 500 colleges offer sport scholarships to women athletes. The Association for Intercollegiate Athletics for Women (AIAW), now defunct, had more than 1000 member schools a decade ago and was the largest collegiate athletic association in the United States. Since that time, however, the NCAA has taken over control of women's sport in many colleges and universities and for more than 10 years has provided opportunities for young women to participate in myriad championship events.

The National Federation of State High School Associations indicates there are approximately two million female participants in competitive sport teams on the high school level. Girls participate in a total of 29 high school sports. The three most popular sports, in terms of schools sponsoring teams and number of participants, are basketball, track and field, and volleyball. Budgets for boys' sport activities at the interscholastic level were on the average larger than the budgets for girls' sport activities.

Although sport programs for men and women are still not equal in terms of funding, legislation such as Title IX has had a positive impact. One negative impact concerning Title IX is that the number of female coaches in girls' and women's sport programs has decreased dramatically, from about 90% in the early 1970s to around 50% in the mid-1980s.[1]

However, sport programs for male and female student-athletes on all levels are far more equal, as well as more numerous, in the 1990s than ever before. It is unfortunate that financial constraints are now also equally affecting men's and women's programs, resulting in some loss of both men's and women's sports, especially at the collegiate level.

Title IX, the Courts, and Prospects for the Future

The courts have caused some changes in Title IX. The 1984 United States Supreme Court decision regarding Grove City College changed the interpretation of Title IX as formerly held.[8] The court ruled that only the student aid office at Grove City College was covered by law barring sex bias, because the

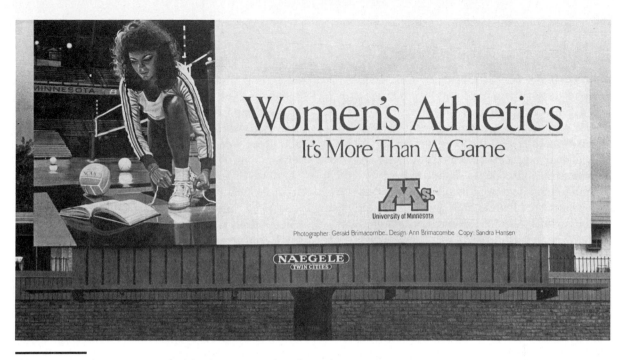

Women have become accepted in the community of sport.

only federal money that the institution received came through student Pell Grants. In the case of private institutions that received direct federal aid, the U.S. Commission on Civil Rights said that only the program or activity that actually received the aid need abide by Title IX regulations. In other words, the federal law barring sex discrimination in education, according to the Grove City ruling, did not apply to schools and colleges as a whole, but only to those parts of an institution that directly received federal aid. The court ruling meant, for example, that if the sport programs do not receive federal aid directly, they are not covered by Title IX. This ruling raised a storm of protest from the Office of Civil Rights and other organizations supporting the original concept of Title IX—if an institution received federal aid, then all programs within that organization are covered by Title IX regulations.

After the Grove City decision there was action in Congress to introduce new language to resurrect and restore the kinds of protection afforded by Title IX. This legislation finally passed the Senate (75-14) to become the Civil Rights Restoration Act of 1988.

Each institution and each educational program will face continued challenges in complying with Title IX. This is true particularly in light of the budget crises that many schools and colleges face at present. For example, it will be difficult for many institutions to increase, or even maintain, items such as support services, budgets, and facilities for an expanded sport program for girls without curtailing some other parts of the educational program at the same time. More realistically, it will become even more difficult to bear the increased costs of our present sport programming that now provide females and males with comparable sport programs. If proportioned equally, however, reductions in programs of compliance would further serve to reduce the opportunities for girls and women to participate.

Regardless, many changes have taken place to comply with the spirit of Title IX. These are positive steps in breaking down the myth that women are either physically or psychosocially inferior to men either in or out of the arena of competitive sport. Title IX has thus cleared the way for behavioral change to take place concerning women's participation not only in the domain of competitive sport, but also in all of society.

SELECTED SPORTING ASSOCIATIONS

An individual school or college, by itself, finds it difficult to develop standards and control sport in a sound educational manner. However, uniting with similar schools and colleges makes such a formidable task possible. This has been done on local, state, and national levels in the interest of better sport for high schools and colleges. Establishing rules, policies, and procedures well in advance of playing seasons provides educators and coaches the necessary guidelines and control for conducting sound competitive sport programs. It aids them in resisting pressures of alumni, students, spectators, townspeople, media, and others who do not always have the best interests of the student-athlete and the program in mind.

Various types of sport associations exist. The ones most prevalent in high schools and colleges are student athletic associations, local conferences or leagues, state high school associations or leagues, the National Federation of State High School Athletic Associations, the National Association for Intercollegiate Athletes, the National Collegiate Athletic Association, and their respective conferences that exist throughout the nation.

The student athletic association or board is an organization within a school designed to actively promote and participate in the conduct of the school sport program. It is usually open to all students who elect to pay fees, which further help support the competitive sport program. Such associations are found in many high schools and colleges throughout the country. These associations assist in the mobilization of ticket sales, programs, and overall school enthusiasm. Once initiated they add another educational component and dimension to the management structure of a well-managed sport program.

Various associations or boards, conferences, or leagues also bind together to facilitate sport competition and scheduling and to reduce travel. Usually several high schools within a particular geographical area will become members of a conference in order to construct schedules, assign officials, handle disputes, and maintain general guidance over the sport programs of the member schools.

The state high school athletic association or league that now exists in almost every state is yet another major influence in high school sport. The state association is usually open to all professionally accredited high schools within the state. It operates under a constitution, employs an administrative core of officers to conduct business, and usually possesses a board of directors. The number of members on the board varies widely but usually has a representative from each district or region. Fees or dues are usually assessed by the association on a per school basis or sometimes according to the size of the school or number of sports offered. In some states there are no fees, because the necessary revenue is derived from the gate receipts and/or television revenue from tournament competition. State associations are interested in sound programs of sport competition within the confines of the state. They concern themselves with the usual problems that have to do with sport, such as eligibility of players, certification of officials, conduct of coaches, handling of protests and disputes, and the organization and conduct of state tournaments. These state associations are interested in promoting sound high school sport practices, equalizing athletic competition, protecting participants, and guarding the health and welfare of players. In some states, such as Minnesota, they operate drug awareness programs throughout the state. State associations have generally been a positive influence and have won the respect of school administrators, coaches, and educators.

National Association for Girls and Women in Sport

The National Association for Girls and Women in Sport (NAGWS) is one of the six associations of the American Alliance for Health, Physical Education, Recreation, and Dance and is concerned with the governance of sports for girls and women.

The specific functions of the NAGWS follow:

- To formulate and publicize guiding principles and standards for the administrator, leader, official, and player
- To publish and interpret rules governing sports for girls and women
- To provide the means for training, evaluating, and rating officials

- To disseminate information on the conduct of girls' and women's sports
- To stimulate, evaluate, and disseminate research in the field of girls' and women's sports
- To cooperate with allied groups interested in girls' and women's sports in order to formulate policies and rules that affect the conduct of women's sports
- To provide opportunities for the development of leadership among girls and women for the conduct of their sport programs

The National Council of Secondary School Athletic Directors

The American Alliance for Health, Physical Education, Recreation, and Dance's National Association for Sport and Physical Education (NASPE) established the National Council of Secondary School Athletic Directors. The increased emphasis on sport and the important position of athletic directors in the nation's secondary schools warranted a council by which increased services could be rendered to enhance the services offered to the nation's youth. The membership in the National Council is open to members of AAHPERD who have primary responsibility in directing, administering, or coordinating interscholastic sport programs.

The purposes of the Council follow:

- To improve the educational aspects of interscholastic sport and their articulation in the total educational program
- To foster high standards of professional proficiency and ethics
- To improve understanding of sport throughout the nation
- To establish closer working relationships with related professional groups
- To promote greater unity, good will, and fellowship among all members
- To provide for an exchange of ideas
- To assist and cooperate with existing state athletic directors' organizations
- To make available to members special resource materials through publications, conferences, and consultant services

The National Federation of State High School Athletic Associations

High school competition for boys began in Michigan in the late 1890s and, subsequently, a Michigan state athletic association was developed. By the turn of the century, Illinois and Indiana had followed Michigan's lead and inaugurated their respective state athletic associations. In New York, Luther Gulick established the New York City Public School Athletic League in 1903, which was followed in 1905 by the founding of a girls' branch under the direction of Elizabeth Burchenal.

The National Federation of State High School Athletic Associations was established in 1920 with five states participating. At present nearly all states are members. The National Federation is particularly concerned with the control of interstate sport competitions. Its constitution states this purpose:

> The object of this Federation shall be to protect and supervise the interstate athletic interests of the high schools belonging to the state associations, to assist in those activities of state associations, which can best be operated on a nationwide scale, to sponsor meetings, publications and activities which will permit each state association to profit by the experience of all other member associations, and to coordinate the work so that waste effort and unnecessary duplication will be avoided.

The National Federation has been responsible for many improvements in sport on a national basis, such as eliminating national tournaments and working toward uniformity of standards.

The National Collegiate Athletic Association

The National Collegiate Athletic Association (NCAA) was formed in 1906. The alarming number of football injuries and the fact that there was no institutional control of the game led to a conference in New York City of representatives from thirteen universities and colleges, on December 12, 1905. Preliminary plans were made for a national agency to assist in the formulation of sound requirements for intercollegiate athletics, particularly football, and the name Intercollegiate Athletic Association (IAA) was suggested. At a meeting March 31, 1906, a constitution and bylaws were adopted and issued.

The NCAA conducts 76 championships in 21 sports.

On December 29, 1910, the name of the IAA was changed to National Collegiate Athletic Association (NCAA). The purposes of the NCAA are as follows:

- To uphold the principle of institutional control of, and responsibility for, all intercollegiate athletics in conformity with the Association's constitution and bylaws
- To serve as an overall national discussion, legislative, and administrative body for the universities and colleges of the United States in matters of intercollegiate athletics
- To recommend policies for the guidance of member institutions in the conduct of their intercollegiate athletic programs
- To legislate upon any subject of general concern to the membership in the administration of intercollegiate athletics

- To study all phases of competitive athletics and establish standards therefor, to the end that colleges and universities throughout the United States may maintain their athletic activities on a high plane
- To encourage the adoption by its constituent members of eligibility rules in compliance with satisfactory standards of scholarship, amateur standing, and good sportmanship
- To establish and supervise regional and national collegiate athletic contests under the auspices of the Association and establish rules of eligibility therefor
- To stimulate and improve programs to promote and develop educational leadership, physical fitness, sports participation as a recreational pursuit, and athletic excellence through competitive intramural and intercollegiate programs
- To formulate, copyright, and publish rules of play for collegiate sports
- To preserve collegiate athletic records
- To cooperate with other amateur athletic organizations in the promotion and conduct of national and international athletic contests
- To otherwise assist member institutions as requested in the furtherance of their intercollegiate athletic programs

Membership in the NCAA numbers more than 980 colleges and universities categorized in three divisions. The NCAA requires that an institution be accredited and compete in a minimum of seven intercollegiate sports each year, with at least one sport sponsored in each of the three recognized sport seasons.

The services provided by the NCAA are as extensive as its stated purposes for existence. These services include publication of official guides in various sports, provision of a film and video library, establishment of an eligibility code for athletes and provisions for the enforcement of this code, provisions for national meets and tournaments with appropriate eligibility rules for competition, provision of financial and other assistance to groups interested in the promotion and encouragement of intercollegiate and recreational sport, and provision of administrative services for US universities and colleges concerning matters of international competition and student-athletes. The NCAA offers 76 women's and men's championships in 21 sports at the Division I, II, and III levels.

The National Association of Intercollegiate Athletics

Another sport association on the college and university level is the National Association of Intercollegiate Athletics (NAIA), which has a membership of more than 500 institutions, mostly among the smaller colleges. This organization was instituted in 1940 as a basketball tournament association and by 1952 emerged as a "total" sport association. Its primary function is to provide national championship opportunities for young men and women competing below the "big time" NCAA Division I level.

The National Junior College Athletic Association

The National Junior College Athletic Association (NJCAA) is an organization of junior colleges that has sponsored sport programs since its inception in 1937 in California. It now has regional offices with an elected regional director for each. Regional business matters are conducted within the framework of the constitution and bylaws of the parent organization. The regional directors, who are governed by an executive committee, hold an annual legislative assembly in Hutchinson, Kansas, and determine the policies, programs, and procedures for the organization. The *Juco Review* is the official publication of the organization. Standing and special committees are appointed each year to cover special items and problems that develop. The role of the NJCAA closely follows that outlined by the NCAA.

National championships are conducted in sports such as basketball, cross country, football, wrestling, baseball, track and field, golf, and tennis. National invitation events are also conducted in activities such as soccer, swimming, and gymnastics.

The NJCAA, with more than 500 institutional members, is affiliated with the National Federation of State High School Athletic Associations and the National Association of Intercollegiate Athletics. It is also affiliated with the United States Collegiate Sports Council, United States Olympic Committee and its respective federations, and the American Alliance for Health, Physical Education, Recreation, and Dance.

Some of the services offered by the NJCAA to its members include an insurance plan for athletes, recognition in official records, publications, film and video library, and participation in events sponsored by the association.

Amateur Athletic Union of the United States

Founded in 1888, the Amateur Athletic Union (AAU) of the United States is probably the oldest, as well as the largest, single organization designed to regulate and promote the conduct of amateur sport. Certainly it is one of the most influential organizations governing amateur sport in the world.

The AAU is a federation of sport and athletic clubs, national and district associations, educational institutions, and amateur athletic organizations.

Many persons associate the AAU only with track and field. However, it is concerned with many more sports and activities, including basketball, baton twirling, bobsledding, boxing, diving, gymnastics, handball, judo, karate, luge, power lifting, swimming, synchronized swimming, volleyball, water polo, weight lifting, and wrestling. In addition to governing this multiplicity of sports and activities, the AAU is vitally concerned with ensuring that the amateur status of athletes is maintained at all times when participating in the amateur sport arena. To this end, the leaders of the AAU have developed and promulgated a precise set of guidelines describing amateurism.

Some of the other activities of the AAU include registering athletes to identify and control the amateur status of participants in sport events, sponsoring national championships, raising funds for the United States' athletes for international competition and the Olympic Games, conducting tryouts for the selection of Olympic competitors, and sponsoring Junior Olympic competition. The AAU has established a number of committees (e.g., Age Group Diving, Track and Field, Youth Activities, Swimming) to help with the monumental task of performing the myriad duties associated with governing such a large number of sports and activities. An executive director housed in Indianapolis, Indiana directs and coordinates all activities of the AAU.

Other Organizations

In higher education there are also many leagues, conferences, and associations formed by a limited number of schools for sport competition. Examples are the Ivy League, Big Ten, Big East, Big Eight, PAC 10, SEC, Southland, and Atlantic Coast Conferences. These associations regulate sport competition among their members and settle problems that may arise in connection with such competition.

Other groups related to sport and the sporting process include, but are not limited to, the American Alliance for Health, Physical Education, Recreation, and Dance (AAHPERD); the National Association of Collegiate Directors of Athletics (NACDA); and the United States Olympic Committee (USOC).

SUMMARY

The standards for competitive sport in schools, colleges, and other organizations have been clearly identified. There should be no doubt in any individual's mind about the types of interscholastic and intercollegiate programs that are educationally sound and operate in the best interests of student-athletes who participate in them. It is the responsibility of managers and others concerned with such programs to implement the various standards that have been established. In every case it is not a question of de-emphasis, but a question of re-emphasis along educational lines. Sound leadership will make the interscholastic and intercollegiate programs forces for quality education that have no equal.

Competitive sport is a part of a total Physical Activity and Sport Continuum. The objectives stated earlier in this text for physical education also apply to interscholastic and intercollegiate sport. Managers should evaluate their programs in terms of the extent to which the listed objectives are being achieved.

Sport has value if it is conducted in a sound educational manner. The management in charge of competitive sport is largely responsible to see that it is conducted in accordance with the standards that have been set. In so doing, managers may be confronted with many problems that periodically occur in these programs because of their high public visibility and the economics involved. However, prudent managers know the goals to be achieved and the standards to be observed. Therefore it is their responsibility to see that the total competitive sport program is conducted accordingly.

◆ SELF-ASSESSMENT ACTIVITIES

These activities will assist students in determining if material and competencies presented in this chapter have been mastered:

1. Imagine you are at a school budget hearing where a taxpayer attacks the varsity sport program as costing too much money for the values derived. As a member of the athletic staff you are asked to react to the taxpayer's statement. What values can you cite to support the need for a varsity sport program?

2. Write a profile of what you consider to be an ideal director of athletics, coach, and athletic trainer.

3. List some essential points to keep in mind concerning each of the following: contracts, officials, protests and forfeitures, game management, awards, schedules, records, and medical examinations.

4. As a director of athletics, what administrative policy would you recommend regarding the following? Gate receipts, tournaments and championships, eligibility, scholarships, recruiting, proselytizing, and scouting.

5. Develop a set of standards that could be used to evaluate a sport program at the junior high school level.

6. Identify the sporting association that governs your institution and the role it plays in the conduct of sport on your campus.

7. Prepare a report that provides pertinent facts regarding the impact of Title IX on your competitive sport program.

REFERENCES

1. Acosta RV, Carpenter LJ: Women in athletics—a status report, *Journal of Physical Education, Recreation, and Dance,* 56(6):30-37, 1985.
2. American Alliance for Health, Physical Education, Recreation, and Dance: Equality in sports for women, Reston, Va, 1977, The Alliance.
3. Arnheim DD: *Modern principles of athletic training,* St Louis, 1989, Mosby–Year Book.
4. Association of Intercollegiate Athletic for Women: Code of ethics for coaches, *AIAW handbook,* Washington, DC, 1979, American Alliance for Health, Physical Education, Recreation, and Dance.
5. *Athletic Business,* Sept 1984.
6. Auxter D, Pyfer J: *Principles and methods of adapted physical education and recreation,* ed 5, St Louis, 1985, Mosby–Year Book.
7. Coakley JJ: *Sport in society,* ed 3, St Louis, 1986, Mosby–Year Book.
8. Evans G: Civil rights panel assails bill to override Grove City ruling, *Chronicle of Higher Education,* Mar 13, 1985.
9. Legett L: Why do coaches fail? *Journal of Physical Education, Recreation and Dance* 54:62-63, 1983.
10. Lopiano D: The certified coach: central figure, *Journal of Physical Education, Recreation and Dance* 51(9):32-33, 1986.
11. National Council of Secondary School Athletic Directors: *Evaluating the high school athletic program,* Washington, DC, 1973, American Association for Health, Physical Education, Recreation, and Dance.
12. Pflug J: Evaluating high school coaches, *Journal of Physical Education and Recreation* 51:76, Apr 1980.
13. Rosensweig M: Want to file a Title IX complaint? *In The Running* 1:1, Fall 1978.
14. Sage GH: Becoming a high school coach: from playing sports to coaching, *Research Quarterly for Exercise and Sport,* 60:81-90, 1989.
15. Sisley BL, Wiese DM: Current status: requirements for interscholastic coaches, *Journal of Physical Education, Recreation and Dance* 58(7):73-85, 1987.
16. Stein JU, Klappholz LA: *Special Olympics instructional manual,* Washington, DC, 1977, American Association for Health, Physical Education, Recreation, and Dance and The Kennedy Foundation.
17. VanderZwaag HJ: *Sport management in schools and colleges,* New York, 1984, John Wiley and Sons.
18. Wilkerson M, Dodder RA: What does sport do for people? *Journal of Physical Education and Recreation* 50:50, Feb 1979.

SUGGESTED READINGS

- Bird AM, Cripe BK: *Psychology and sport behavior,* St Louis, 1986, Mosby–Year Book.
  Introduces the student to the field of sport psychology and the basic concepts of scientific inquiry. Discusses such topics as behaviorism, cognitive sport psychology, aggression, group performance, state and trait anxiety, arousal, and coaching behavior.
- Coakley J: *Sport in society: issues and controversies,* St Louis, 1990, Mosby–Year Book.
  Provides a critical analysis of many of the salient sociological issues, concerns, and controversies in the sporting domain. Race, violence, social mobility, and politics, as well as competitive sport, are explored.
- Cratty BJ: *Psychology in contemporary sport,* Englewood Cliffs, NJ, 1989, Prentice-Hall.
  Provides guidelines for coaches and athletes regarding various aspects of the psychology of sports, including psychological assessment, leadership, motivation, activation, aggression, and group dynamics. It also discusses characteristics such as coaching behavior, behavior modification, imagery, and team cohesion.
- Frey J, editor: *The governance of intercollegiate sports,* West Point NY, 1982, Leisure Press.
  Examines the history of sport governance, sport cartels, alumni, law, and the "greening" of American athletes.
- Orlick T: *In pursuit of excellence,* Champaign, Il, 1980, Human Kinetics.
  Explores the limits of human performance including commitment, self-control, goal setting, concentration, imagery, and dealing with coaching problems.
- Paterno J. In Crystal balling with America's sports leaders, *Athletic Business,* Jan 1985.
  Nationally known sport leader predicts the future for college sports, women's sport programs, youth sport, and the Olympic Games. Discusses academic standards, recruiting, economic problems, and Title IX.
- Perry RH: Intercollegiate athletics in turmoil: so what else is new? *Journal of Sports Management,* 1:82-86, Jan 1987.
  Traces the recurring problems of intercollegiate sport and discusses sports' external power brokers. Offers a prescription for future conduct of competitive sport.
- Robinson JG: *Reaching your athletic potential,* Tigard, Or, 1981, Quality Publications.
  Written for men and women who are serious about a career in sports. Maintains that sports development is an organized process that requires planning and persistence. Discusses goals, planning, motivation, attitude, conditioning, self-image, practicing, and performing. Gives suggestions for reaching your athletic potential.
- Wuest DA, Bucher CA: *Foundations of physical education and sport,* St Louis, 1991, Mosby–Year Book.
  Presents an overview of the various academic components of physical education; discusses sports-related careers, issues, and challenges facing the profession.

PART III

Management of Physical Education and Sport Programs in the Public and Private Sector

CHAPTER **6**   Physical Education and Sport Programs in the Public and Private Sector

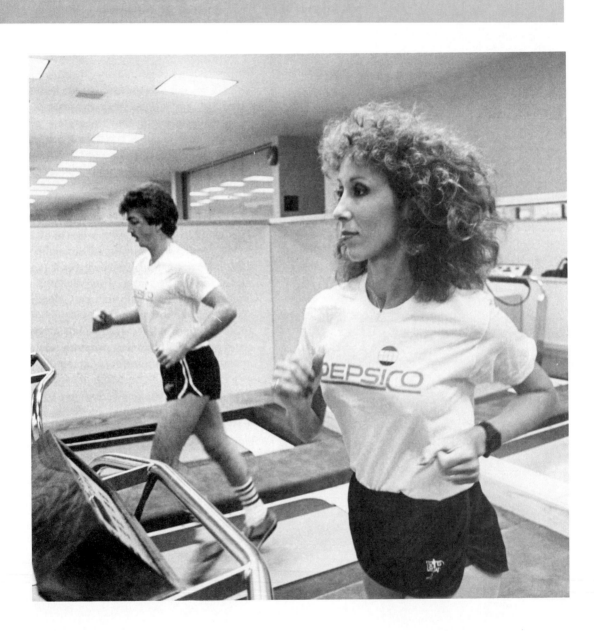

Physical Education and Sport Programs in the Public and Private Sector

---

▶ **Instructional Objectives and Competencies To Be Achieved**

After reading this chapter the student should be able to

- Identify physical education and sport careers and opportunities across the physical activity and sport continuum.
- Understand some of the management and program responsibilities involved in various employment settings.
- Identify and describe the role of physical education and sport in public and private sector settings.

- Determine qualifications and preparation needed to successfully fulfill management responsibilities in the corporate and commercial health and fitness industry.
- Illustrate organizational structures related to public and private sector physical education and sport programs.

This text is devoted in great measure to the management processes, organizational structure, and functioning of physical education and sport programs housed within educational institutions at the elementary, secondary, and college levels. However, in recent years many potentially promising careers and employment opportunities have developed in settings other than schools and colleges (Table 6-1). Corporations, businesses, athletic clubs, therapeutic centers, health clubs and spas, senior citizen centers, YMCAs, JCCs, and community centers have provided new windows of employment opportunity for physical educators.

This chapter is designed to provide the reader with information concerning representative public and private organizations where physical educators may seek employment (even ownership) as instructors, consultants, and managers.

The chapter will be divided into three sections. The first section will present corporate or workplace health and fitness career opportunities. These include Xerox Corporation, IBM, PepsiCo Inc., General Mills Inc., and Tenneco Inc. The second section will provide a glimpse into the commercial fitness industry; Bally's U.S. Swim and Fitness, Clark Hatch Physical Fitness Centers, and the Radisson Hotel

TABLE 6-1.   Physical education and sport career opportunities[4]

Teaching opportunities

School setting	Nonschool setting
Elementary school	Community recreation/
Junior high school	sport programs
High school	Corporate recreation
Junior/community college	programs
College and university	Commercial sport clubs
Basic instructional	Youth-serving agencies
programs	Preschools
Professional	Health clubs
preparation programs	Military personnel
Adapted physical	programs
education	Resort sport programs
Overseas school programs	Geriatric programs
Military school programs	Correctional institution
International school	programs
programs	State high school leagues

Coaching opportunities

Interscholastic programs	Commercial sport clubs
Intercollegiate programs	Community sport
Commercial sport camps	programs
	Military sport programs

Fitness and health-related opportunities

Cardiac rehabilitation	Space fitness programs
Sports medicine	Corporate fitness
Movement therapy	programs
Health clubs	Sports nutrition
Community fitness	Athletic training
programs	Weight control spas
Personal fitness trainer	Military personnel
	programs

Sport management opportunities

Athletic administration	Sport organization
Aquatic administration	administration
Sport facility management	Health club management
Commercial sport club	Sport information
management	Sport retailing
Community recreation/	Corporate recreation
sport management	Resort sport management
Recreational sport/	Bowl organizations
campus recreation	Sport conference
US Olympic Committee	commissioner
organizations	
Sports governing bodies	

Sport media opportunities

Sport journalism	Sport broadcasting and
Sport photography	production
Writing sport-oriented	Sport art
books	Sport product advisor

Sport-related opportunities

Sport law	Sport officiating
Professional athlete	Dancer
Entrepreneur	Sport statistician
Research	Sport consulting
Academic counseling	Compliance director

and Conference Center will be presented. The final section will explore various representative community-based programs, including the Y, Jewish Community Center, a recreation and parks department, and a local community recreation department.

CORPORATE OR WORKPLACE HEALTH AND FITNESS PROGRAMS

In the last decade, many large and small corporations and businesses have begun to offer employee health and fitness programs. These companies have found that improved fitness among their ranks leads to improved health, decreased employee medical problems and absenteeism, and higher levels of employee job satisfaction. Indeed, a survey by the United States Department of Health and Human Services[3] reported that more than half of United States companies with 750 or more employees, and almost 22% of the companies with 50 or more employees, offer some form of corporate or workplace health and fitness program. Furthermore, more than

$5 billion annually is spent in fitness-related corporate environs.

The following pages will present representative corporate or workplace programs which, as the reader will determine, go well beyond the scope of the traditional employee fitness programs. The information concerning these creative programs has been gathered from the professional literature, publications prepared by the corporations or companies, as well as directly from personnel of the respective organizations.

Xerox Corporation
Source of Information:

Peter L DeFranco, Manager
Fitness and Recreation Services

General Information:

In 1974, Xerox Corporation opened a centralized educational facility named the Xerox International Center for Training and Management Development (XICTMD) in Leesburg, Virginia. In this environment, employees learn the latest techniques of selling and servicing information systems and products, as well as developing themselves to meet the management challenges of the future. A crucial component of Xerox's Center for training and development is its Fitness and Recreation Service program.

Fitness and Recreation Services (FRS) establishes and manages program activities that contribute to effective use of employee leisure time and improve employee health and morale.

Program Goals/Objectives:

Since the opening of FRS in 1974, its primary objectives have been to: (1) provide optimal physical and mental fitness for its employees through organized and open fitness and recreation programs, (2) promote the constructive use of leisure time, and (3) provide an outlet for stress and tension.

Program Description:

Xerox Corporation offers the following programs, which are designed to promote the effective use of leisure time as well as to enhance employee wellness and lifestyle:

- **Xerox Leesburg Recreation Association (XLRA)** implements recreational and exercise programs to improve the health of, as well as to meet the leisure, intellectual, and fellowship needs of staff, employees, and their families, whether active or retired.
- **Health Quest** centers around cardiovascular benefits, health promotional materials, and related recreational exercises. Employees are tested in various fitness and exercise areas and are provided an evaluation upon completion of the assessment.
- **Xerox Health Management Program (XHMP)** is a corporate-sponsored program that publishes and disseminates a monthly health/fitness publication for all Xerox employees.

Program Specifics:

Operation hours are 10 AM to 9 PM Monday through Thursday; 10 AM to 7 PM Friday; and 12 PM to 6 PM Saturday and Sunday.

Gymnasium #1 provides areas for volleyball and aerobic workouts, weight training and exercise

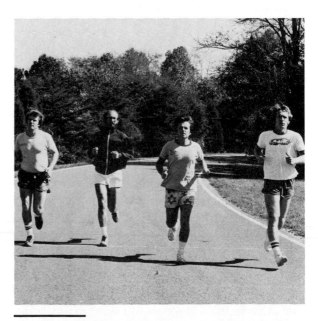

Employees jog at Xerox Corporation Fitness and Recreation Center; Leesburg, Va.

equipment, one squash and two racquetball courts, as well as a fitness assessment area and a physical activity room.

Gymnasium #2 houses facilities for basketball, volleyball, badminton, and jogging, as well as individual exercise equipment in various exercise stations.

Outdoor facilities include four tennis courts, two volleyball and paddle tennis courts, swimming pool, picnic area, jogging and bicycling trail, and an 18-station "Exer-trail."

Additional programs organized by the FRS include nutritional assessment and counseling, a body composition profile, a golf league, tennis and volleyball clubs, fishing tournaments, and myriad special events.

Personnel:

Manager of Fitness and Recreation Services
Fitness and Recreation Specialist
Equipment Coordinator
College Interns

Contact Address:

Xerox Corporation
International Center for Training and Management
    Development
P.O. Box 2000
Leesburg, VA 22075

International Business Machines (IBM)
Source of Information:

Robbin L Suess, Team Leader
Wellness Programs

General Information:

IBM United States has a tradition of concern for the health of its employees, retirees, and their families, and offers a variety of wellness programs designed to encourage health, fitness, and work performance. Management believes that healthy employees/retirees are more productive and enjoy a state of well-being that contributes to the quality of life and work in the home and company. IBM is also aware that enhanced health and fitness will slow the escalating cost of health-related corporate expense.

IBM United States has a work force of approxi-

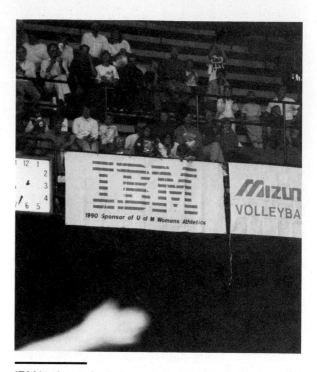

IBM is also active in sponsoring and promoting physical education and sport.

mately 200,000 employees, with more than 750,000 individuals (i.e., employees, retirees, family members) spread over 200 locations eligible to participate in its wellness and fitness programs. Because of these numbers, operations are decentralized, and implementation and communication are the responsibility of local-site general managers. Outside specialists are utilized to manage the local IBM programs and provide a high level of expertise and service. The same program format is, for the most part, offered to all employees/retirees at all IBM locations.

Program Goals/Objectives:

IBM's health promotion programs for employees, retirees, and their families grew out of a convergence of several factors—a concern for better health, the spiraling costs of medical benefits, a more fitness-oriented population, and research indicating that personal care can be as important as medical science in improving health and extending the life span.

The objectives of IBM's health promotion programs are to improve/maintain the participants' health, reduce risks of developing disease, improve employee productivity and morale, reduce absenteeism, and slow the escalation of health-care expenditures.

Program Description:

The IBM comprehensive program includes a voluntary health assessment (VHA). Since the VHA was initiated in 1968 more than 250,000 (19,000 in 1990) employees have taken advantage of this corporate benefit. The VHA provides a health profile based on age, gender, lifestyle, and family background.

The core of the IBM program, however, resides in its A Plan For Life (APFL) Health Education Program. This is a coordinated program offered at all IBM sites, enabling employees and their families an opportunity to take a variety of classes (e.g., sexuality, parenting, humor, health, and first aid), as well as fitness and health-related activities ranging from solid soft-impact aerobic exercise to water exercise. The programs are conducted by specialists at the IBM location as well as local racquet clubs, YMCAs, and other community-based fitness locations.

IBM also maintains recreation and fitness facilities at more than 30 locations across the country. These facilities vary, but many include sports fields, outdoor tennis and basketball courts, swimming pools, and exercise rooms. Flagship facilities (i.e., golf course) exist in Poughkeepsie, Endicott, and Sands Point, New York as well as in San Jose, California.

Program Specifics:

For the most part, IBM focuses on the APFL Program, which is offered at all of IBM's manufacturing, laboratory, and sales office sites. The APFL consists of a series of comprehensive health-related classes (often conducted on location). Samples of these include exercise, weight management, smoking cessation, nutrition, first aid and CPR, parenting, and legal issues in caring for the elderly, just to mention a few. The classes are conducted in the morning, during noon hour, and in the evening to encourage as many employees as possible to attend.

Other APFL components include physical activities ranging from aerobic exercise to water safety. These are conducted for the most part off-site. Usually participants pay their own way to APFL coordinated offerings and IBM provides a tuition assistance reimbursement program, which pays up to the cost of the program (e.g., $175.00 for smoking-cessation class, $65.00 for water safety). Specific program completion reimbursement fees may also be used toward the cost of a membership to, for instance, a community-based YMCA or health and fitness club.

The APFL program operates year-round, is open to all regular, part-time and retired employees, their spouses, and dependent children ages 15 to 22. There are also appropriate programs for children from ages 12 to 14, including first aid, water safety, and "Ease at Work/Safety at Home" courses.

In 1987, IBM also established a videotape library at most sites focusing on topics ranging from fitness and stress management to AIDS and substance abuse. The tapes are available to employees and other community-based organizations at no cost.

Yearly health fairs are conducted at IBM locations nationwide, where health-related assessments such as blood pressure, cholesterol, and body fat composition are developed into a health profile for each participant. IBM's Employee Assistance Program also provides counseling 24 hours a day for all eligible IBM employees and family members.

Personnel:

Because of the decentralized nature of IBM's APFL program, the personnel requirements may include an APFL site coordinator (more than 200 nationally); however, for the most part, outside specialists are contracted to conduct both the on-site and off-site activities by Johnson and Johnson Health Inc., Santa Monica, California.

Contact Address:

IBM
2000 Purchase Street
Purchase, NY 10577

Pepsi-Cola
Source of Information:

Mike Moreau, Program Manager

General Information:

Pepsi-Cola, a large soft drink producer, is under the larger PepsiCo umbrella, which also operates several restaurant/food divisions, including Frito-Lay, Pizza Hut, Taco Bell, and KFC. PepsiCo and all its divisions are committed to corporate fitness programs.

Program Goals/Objectives:

The mission of the Pepsi-Cola health and fitness program is to meet the cultural objectives of the company by focusing on family issues, employee involvement, and lifestyles conducive to better work and personal performance.

Goals include (1) the improvement of the social and physical profile of the company by increasing employee involvement over the previous year; (2) the increasing of the percentage of employees in the health, fitness, and recreation programs; (3) the promotion, internally and externally, of the Pepsi-Cola Health and Fitness Program; and (4) the identification of the needs of employees in health, fitness, and recreation.

Program Description:

Pepsi-Cola and the other divisions offer programs made up of the following five componenets:
  1) General fitness: exercise testing and prescription
  2) Recreation: intermurals and intramurals, special events
  3) Health education: lunch-time lectures and programs
  4) Behavior change: behavior modification–based counseling programs (e.g., diet, nutrition, smoking)
  5) Rehabilitation: injury prevention and care, massage therapy

Program Specifics:

Of 1200 employees at Pepsi-Cola corporate headquarters, 50% participate in the Fitness, Recreation,

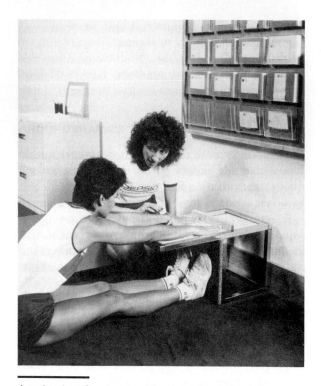

A trained professional guides a workout; PepsiCo., Inc., NY.

and Health Education programs. An annual budget of $400,000 is appropriated for the Pepsi-Cola programs. Monthly special events (e.g., Family Month, Heart Month, Nutrition Month), tournaments, corporate leagues, and fitness and health incentives are all creatively packaged and aimed at total company involvement.

The "total person" approach combines physical parameters, nutrition, psychosociological wellness, and personal safety awareness. Pepsi-Cola also supports a wide range of charities and community programs such as running and walking events and cycling tours.

Personnel:

Program manager
3 Fitness coordinators
1 Fitness instructor
1 Administrative assistant

Contact Address:

Pepsi-Cola Headquarters
Health and Fitness Program
1 Pepsi Way
Somers, NY 10589-2201

General Mills, Inc.
Source of information:

Andy Wood, Director
TriHealthalon Program

General Information:

General Mills, Inc. is a Midwest-based firm that consists of two divisions: consumer foods (e.g., Cheerios, Wheaties) and restaurants (e.g., Red Lobster, The Olive Garden).

Workplace health promotion began in earnest in the early 1980s under the title "Framework—A Healthy Lifestyle Program." In 1984, the expanded "TriHealthalon" began under the auspices of the Health and Human Services Department (Figure 6-1). General Mills' Employee Service unit also promotes leisure-time recreation and sport clubs. The corporation is furthermore a strong supporter of Special Olympics and other worthy community-based programs.

Program Goals/Objectives:

The TriHealthalon is a program developed to improve the health of General Mills employees in the areas designated by the World Health Organization. These include the focal aspects of health—physical, mental, and social well-being.

- Physical well-being signifies exercising, eating

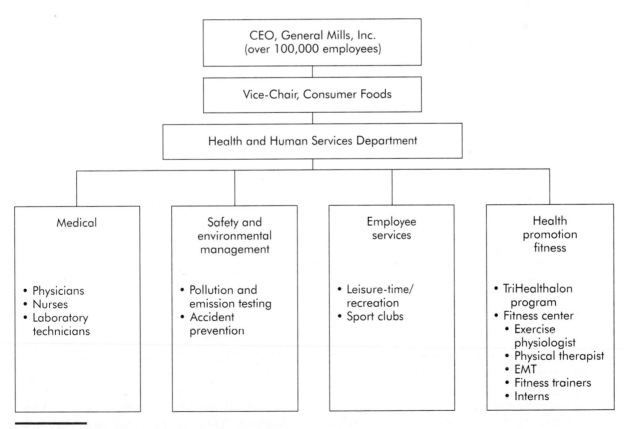

FIGURE 6-1 Organizational structure of a corporate fitness program.

Employees playing volleyball; Tenneco Health and Fitness Department, Houston, Tx.

well, controlling body weight, and being aware of the risk factors associated with cardiovascular heart disease and cancer.

- Mental well-being includes release of stress in one's life and involvement in activities that are recreational, relaxing, and entertaining.
- Social well-being focuses on improving interpersonal relations, controlling chemical usage, and being aware of personal safety.

Program Description:

Every employee who completes the Personal Medical History and Lifestyle Appraisal forms is enrolled in the TriHealthalon program. Each participant receives a fitness assessment and a computer-analyzed health recommendation plan.

Health goals are determined, and three categories of participation are outlined in terms of physical, mental, and social well-being goals:

1) physical: fitness, nutrition and weight control, and cancer prevention
2) mental: stress management, recreation, relaxation, and entertainment
3) social: interpersonal relations, chemical usage, and safety

Program Specifics:

The Fitness Center consists of 5300 square feet of space and provides services from 6 AM to 8 PM Monday through Friday and 8 AM to 12 noon on Saturday. Completion of an orientation and a fitness/medical questionnaire is required before participation.

Health classes and seminars are routinely scheduled to provide participants with information concerning physical, mental, and psychosocial well-being. In addition, the program is promoted through the dissemination of materials and fliers. Furthermore, individualized physical fitness programs are prescribed to address specific employee needs, and fitness evaluations and follow-ups are ongoing.

The Fitness Center has weight training stations, stationary bicycles, treadmills, and rowing machines, as well as other exercise apparatus. Available fitness classes range from beginning to advanced level in activities such as stretching, aerobic dance, conditioning, stepping, and progressive relaxation.

Personnel:

Director
Exercise Physiologist/Physical Therapist/
    Emergency Medical Technician
Physical Fitness Trainer
Physician
Nurses
Laboratory Technicians
University Interns

Contact Address:

General Mills TriHealthalon Program
Health and Human Services, 3C
P.O. Box 1113
Minneapolis, MN 55440

Tenneco Incorporated
Source of Information:

William Baun, Manager
Health and Fitness Program

General Information:

Tenneco's health and fitness program evolved as a result of the chief executive officer's personal positive experience with exercise. The program was implemented in 1982 at corporate headquarters in Houston, Texas in order to preserve Tenneco's most important asset—its more than 4000 innovative and highly skilled employees. Since the program's inception, many of Tenneco's divisional headquarters have set up similar programs. Tenneco was the first oil company to provide "heart-healthy" cooking on oil rigs. The company has also implemented a Pipeline-to-Health promotion program in 125 field locations along their natural gas pipeline, which extends from Midland, Texas to Emerson, Manitoba, Canada.

Program Goals/Objectives:

The Tenneco program focuses on providing employees with the opportunity to learn about and maintain good health. Each year a joint planning meeting is conducted within the medical department to determine the program goals and objectives. In 1990, the

The computer as an aid to fitness in the Tenneco Health and Fitness Department.

departmental mission statement was "a unified effort to expand our services into community and family." Step-Up-To-Health became the program name, and employee committees were reorganized around the themes of (1) Eating Right, (2) Smoke-Free, (3) Recreation, and (4) Exercise.

Program Description:

The components of the Step-Up-To-Health program (health promotion, safety, medical, and employee assistance programs) are contained in the Tenneco Inc. Medical Department. A holistic health promotion program offers employees group and individual activities, screenings and assessments, and classes concerning a variety of topics. The safety program addresses safety issues at work and in the home, as well as providing opportunities for aquatic, driving, first aid, and CPR certifications. Central to the department's success is the primary care medical clinic, which is organized under a preventative model. Employees who have medical problems, concerns, or questions come to the clinic and are seen by a nurse practitioner or physician. The 1100 to 1500 employees who are attended to each month not only get answers concerning their medical problems, but are also networked to other facets of the Step-Up-To-Health program. The employee assistance program provides psychological counseling, organizes various employee support groups, and designs classes in a wide range of personal growth topics including health and fitness.

Besides its recently initiated Pipeline-To-Health venture, Tenneco has also inaugurated a Walk-the-Pipeline Program, which adds another unique dimension to its progressive approach to employee health and physical fitness.

Program Specifics:

The health and fitness center occupies 25,000 square feet of the Tenneco Employee Center. It is equipped with weight-training equipment, bicycle ergometers, stretching areas, rowing machines, and stairclimbers. The most impressive exercise area is the ⅙ mile indoor track that encircles the entire building. A computer-based information system stores individual exercise data, provides employees immediate

Tenneco Health and Fitness Department.

feedback concerning caloric energy expenditure, and provides participants with a monthly log of exercise patterns. A new addition to the computer system allows employees to input food items for analysis and meal planning. Tenneco's system is also equipped with a health topic dictionary that provides a quick source of information concerning common health questions and topics. A drug data base provides information about both prescription and over-the-counter drugs. The system also has a goal-setting section that challenges employees in a variety of physical fitness and health-related areas.

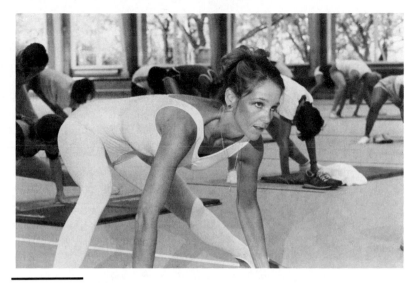

An exercise class is vital to a well-rounded fitness program.

Personnel:

Medical Director
Health and Fitness Manager
Health and Fitness Coordinator
2 Health and Fitness Specialists
Clerical Staff Member
Student Helper (Clerical)
3 Contract Exercise Teachers

Contact Address:

William B Baun, Manager
Health and Fitness Department
Tenneco Incorporated
P.O. Box 2511
Houston, TX 77252

COMMERCIAL HEALTH AND FITNESS INDUSTRY

The commercial health and fitness industry has grown significantly in the last decade. Membership campaigns have attracted millions of men and women to health clubs and fitness centers, which seem to have become a permanent part of our society.

The commercial fintess industry focuses on adult fitness and sport pursuits, although most clubs are open to all age-groups. The commercial health and fitness industry is profit motivated, which differentiates it from corporate and community-based physical education and sport programs.

Facilities at a typical center might include exercise rooms, resistive-type exercise or strength training equipment of the Universal or Nautilus design, as well as free weights, treadmills, rowing machines, stationary bicycles, stairclimbers, swimming pools, whirlpools, saunas, steam rooms, massage room, cold plunges, oil baths, tanning rooms, and locker and shower areas, not to mention courts for volleyball, basketball, tennis, racquetball, and squash.

Programs in commercial enterprises also include such items as fitness assessment and prescription, weight training, yoga, aerobics of various types and intensity levels, and sport competitions, both in-house and against other clubs. Personnel often include instructors (physical educators), business executives, and sales, marketing, and promotions specialists. The following are representative examples of the commercial health and fitness industry.

Bally's U.S. Swim and Fitness
Source of Information:

Dennis Morin, Member Representative
James Larson, Senior Fitness Instructor

General Information:

Bally's U.S. Swim and Fitness is a branch of Bally's Manufacturing, which also oversees equipment manufacturing, casinos, and the Health and Tennis Corporation of America. U.S. Swim and Fitness is one of many fitness centers under the Health and Tennis Corporation of America "umbrella" that constitutes the largest commercial fitness chain in the United States. These reciprocal-use fitness centers with transfer privileges include such clubs as Holiday, Jack LaLanne, Vic Tanny, Family Fitness, President's, Health and Tennis, Bally, and Chicago Health Club, among others.

Program Goals/Objectives:

Bally's U.S. Swim and Fitness designs a personalized physical fitness program based on the member's needs (e.g., cardiovascular, muscular strength and endurance). The company creed is "Our commitment is to positively affect the quality of life by providing the finest service and facilities in the health and fitness industry." Consonant with the creed, Bally's fitness clubs adhere to a holistic approach to exercise in order to meet each individual's specific exercise needs.

Program Description:

Each U.S. Swim and Fitness provides a wide array of programs, which include exercise and fitness, injury management, and a variety of counseling and assessment services. Exercise and aerobic classes include low-impact, intermediate, and advanced levels, as well as muscle conditioning (e.g., "30-Minute Workout," Program Advancement) and aqua-aerobics. Exercise, fitness, and aerobic classes are provided for children and senior citizens.

In the area of injury management, "Injury C.A.R.E." is a holistic program available to members. The program is designed according to the individual's physical limitations and his or her physi-

cian's recommendations for exercise. Counseling is also an integral part of the program, and is available in regard to basic nutrition, and in conjunction with body composition assessment. Other assessment services that are tailored to meet individual needs are also offered (e.g., posture, cholesterol, blood pressure). As an added service to the U.S. Swim and Fitness clientele, personalized trainers can be contracted for one-to-one instruction.

Program Specifics:

Each U.S. Swim and Fitness is well equipped with computerized resistance machines, exercise bicycles, step ergometers, and rowing machines, as well as an indoor jogging track and swimming pool. Some facilities also maintain racquetball, volleyball, and/or basketball courts.

U.S. Swim and Fitness is open 24 hours a day, except holidays. Membership fees vary according to the local economy and state laws and regulations, with the average fee being $32 to $35 per month. Women make up approximately 55% of the total member population, with men at about 45%. Each fitness center serves approximately 1000 members daily.

Personnel:

Instructional staff are professionally trained and regularly updated with the most current principles and methods of fitness training. Standard red, white, and blue sport uniforms identify U.S. Swim and Fitness staff.

Contact Address:

Bally's U.S. Swim and Fitness
4900 Excelsior Boulevard
St. Louis Park, MN 55416

Clark Hatch Physical Centers
Source of Information:

Clark G Hatch, Founder/President
William A Monsen, Senior Vice President, Operations
John L Sheppard, Senior Vice President, Development

General Information:

An international chain of fitness centers with more than 25,000 members worldwide in 14 countries, the Clark Hatch organization began in Tokyo, Japan in 1965. There are now 35 locations, which are either wholly owned, co-owned, or managed by Mr. Hatch from his flagship center in the Hawaii Building, Honolulu, Hawaii. Clark Hatch has been the pioneer for physical fitness and health in the Pacific Rim, and his impact has set the pace and established the standard of quality, excellence, and professionalism for today's health and physical fitness manager.

Programs Goals/Objectives:

Clark Hatch Fitness Centers offer in-house developmental and managerial fitness services to hotels and corporations throughout the world. The Clark Hatch program has carved out a special niche in the fitness industry with more than 25 of the centers being located in prominent world-class hotels, which serve not only the hotel clientele, but also its immediate multicultural user.

Mr. Hatch's philosophy mirrors his personal fitness, vigor, and enthusiasm for the industry, and this, in turn, is reflected in the managers and staff he employs, trains, and continually updates through yearly, if not more frequent, managerial and instructor seminars. Clark Hatch Fitness Centers, although profit driven, are grounded in the underlying philosophy of promoting health and fitness throughout the world.

Program Description:

Following an initial fitness assessment, which includes health history, injuries, nutrition, stress level, body measurements, and physical fitness appraisal, all members are scheduled for one-to-one exercise sessions. During these individualized sessions, a five-phase program of warmup, aerobic exercise, flexibility, strength/conditioning, and cooldown is introduced. This provides a sound base from which all members progressively build more personalized programs under the direction of a well-trained staff.

Clark Hatch programs provide incentives such as

motivational charts, newsletters, ongoing assessments, and program readjustments to inspire adherence as well as attainment of fitness goals. Personalized service, quality facilities, and sound managerial skill are evident throughout the Clark Hatch network.

Program Specifics:

All centers are equipped with the most modern exercise equipment, an aerobics area, and one or more

Clark Hatch Fitness Centers support a wide range of quality fitness activities.

additional facilities (e.g., swimming pool, sauna, steam room, whirlpool, massage, and tennis, squash, or racquetball courts). Furthermore, the centers also sponsor "outside" events such as fun runs, hiking, outrigger canoeing, softball, and soccer. As an added amenity, members and hotel guests are provided with complimentary use of gym clothing and towels.

Hours of operation vary from center to center (generally 6 AM to 10 PM). Members pay an initiation fee (e.g., Honolulu individual membership is $150) and monthly dues ($44 to $46), which vary from country to country and center to center. Special husband/wife, student, off-peak hours, and corporate memberships are also available. Memberships offer unlimited usage and are fully reciprocal at Clark Hatch Fitness Centers throughout the world.

Table 6-2 presents a general representative breakdown of expenses for a Clark Hatch Fitness Center which, of course, varies with country and location.

TABLE 6-2. Sample budget of a representative commercial fitness center

Clark Hatch Fitness Center budget sample

General & administration expenses	% of gross revenue
Payroll	34.0
Employee benefits	1.9
Rent	21.9
Repair/maintenance	3.2
Office expenses	1.7
Fitness center expenses	2.8
Advertisement/promotion	5.0
Entertainment/transportation/seminars	0.7
General excise tax	4.0
License fee	0.2
Insurance	1.0
Professional fees/outside services	1.3
Temporary instructors	0.2
Parking/miscellaneous	0.2
Depreciation	3.8
	84.7
PROFIT MARGIN (varies by country and site)	15.3

Personnel:

The worldwide Clark Hatch Fitness Center network is illustrated in Figure 6-2. At each location there is typically a fitness center manager, senior fitness instructor(s), aerobic dance instructors, and support personnel ranging from on-site recreational staff to locker room attendants, and from sales and marketing to maintenance. The personnel, regardless of level or location, are "people-oriented" and follow standardized corporation policies and procedures.

Contact Address:

Clark Hatch Fitness Centers
Hawaii Building
745 Fort Street
Honolulu, HI 96813

Radisson Hotel and Conference Center
Source of Information:

Bill Kirkhuff, General Manager
Barry McLaughlin, Manager

General Information:

The Radisson Hotel and Conference Center and its Fitness Center opened August 1, 1991. The fitness center caters to guests of the 243-room hotel, and its conferees who attend intensive meetings and conferences, as well as to a limited membership who work or reside in the local community (Figure 6-3).

Program Goals/Objectives:

The objective of the Radisson Fitness Center is to provide exercise facilities and fitness programs for the guests of the Radisson Hotel and Conference Center and for club members from the surrounding community. The center seeks to promote fitness and adherence to an exercise prescription program, as well as to provide physical activities during "stretch breaks" for those attending corporate seminars at the convention center. The key is availability, accessibility, and personalized cooperative programming planned in coordination with the various corporate seminar directors.

Program Description:

The Fitness Center at the Radisson Hotel and Conference Center focuses on an exercise prescription

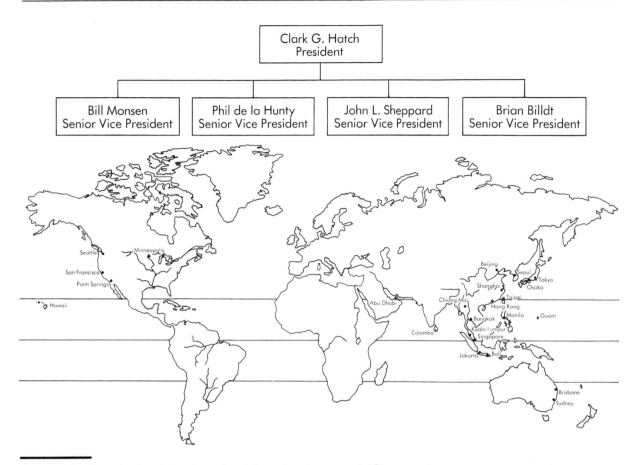

FIGURE 6-2 Organizational structure of an international commercial fitness center.

program that is offered to all members. The program consists of a nine-phase fitness regimen designed to meet individual needs and to assist members in exercise adherence.

The organization offers a wide range of membership options, including individual, joint, family, short-term, and corporate, in order to meet the varied needs of the community clientele. The Fitness Center is not as membership and profit driven as most. It is, however, intimately tied into corporate sales packages. Service and long-range planning are keys to its success.

Program Specifics:

The Radisson Fitness Center is housed in a 3-story building separated from the hotel by a 20-foot atrium entrance. The 20,000 square foot complex includes a weight room that features selectorial, free weight, and Keiser equipment, a 1200 square foot aerobic room, and an exercise room equipped with step machines, rowing machines, treadmills, stationary bicycles, and cross-country skiing machines. The facility also has a swimming pool, sauna, and whirlpool, as well as four racquetball courts, a basketball court, four outdoor lighted tennis courts, a sand volleyball court, and numerous jogging trails in the immediate area. Additional amenities include a suntan bed, massage, and a juice bar.

A schedule of aerobic dance classes provides instruction at 21 different times each week (usually mornings and evenings).

Hours of operation are 6 AM to 11 PM Monday

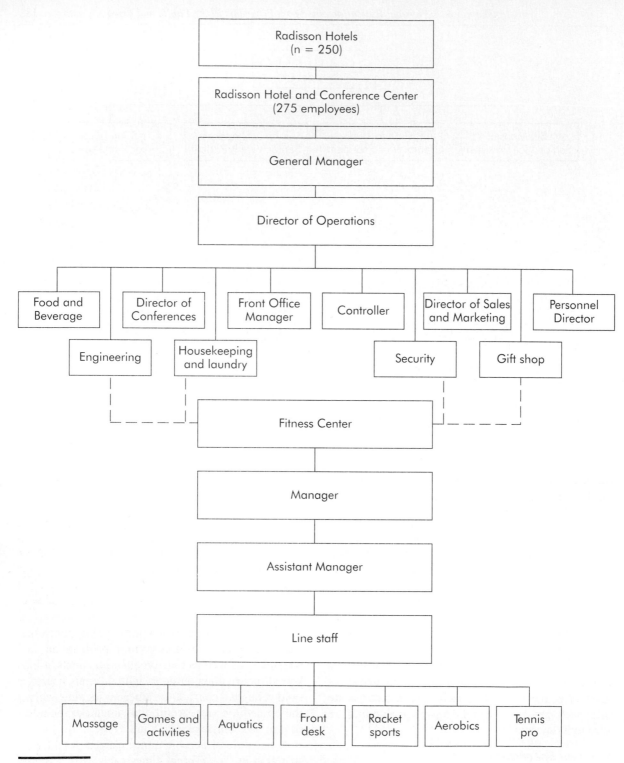

FIGURE 6-3 Organizational structure of a hotel-related fitness center.

A sample Fitness Trail found in many communities as well as corporate and hotel settings.

through Friday, 7 AM to 11 PM on Saturdays, and 8 AM to 9 PM on Sundays.

Personnel:

The fitness center is staffed by four full-time employees, which include a manager, an assistant manager, a front desk attendant, and a fitness center attendant, and three part-time (12 to 20 hours per week) employees. Responsibilities for all personnel involve front desk duties (e.g., communications/ making reservations, accessibility, and some sales), directing fitness programs, stocking the locker room and juice bar, and general maintenance and cleaning. Education, experience, appearance, and communication are requisite to employment.

Contact Address:

Radisson Fitness Center
Radisson Hotel and Conference Center
3131 Campus Drive
Plymouth, MN 55441

COMMUNITY-BASED PHYSICAL EDUCATION AND SPORT PROGRAMS

In addition to corporate fitness and commercial health and fitness centers, there are other settings in which physical educators are finding employment and assuming management responsibilities. Many of these opportunities exist in community-based programs such as YMCAs and YWCAs, Jewish Community Centers, and community education and senior centers. Other community-based delivery systems include organizations such as Recreation and Park Departments, Boys and Girls Clubs, and local sport clubs. Some representative community-based physical education and sport organizations will be described.

Young Men's Christian Association
New Hope, Minnesota
Source of Information:

Jeff Filipek, Program Director
Heather Howery, Instructor
Adult and Children Fitness Programs

General Information:

The Young Men's Christian Association (YMCA) was founded by George Williams in 1844 in London, England. Initially the YMCA offered programs designed to teach adults and children (with an emphasis on young males) the values of health and Christianity. This concept was transnationalized to Montreal, Boston, and New York in the 1850s, and spread throughout the urban centers of the United States in the 1870s when a commitment to add physical education to its educational agenda and curriculum was adopted. YMCA programs were the cradle from which sprang the inventions of basketball (1891) and volleyball (1895). The YMCA continues to play an active role in the building of strong communities through innovative programs of physical fitness and sport.

Program Goals/Objectives:

The YMCA is a worldwide fellowship united by a common loyalty with the purpose of developing a Christian personality for the members, and building a Christian society for the development of families. The goals for members include the following:
- To understand, accept, and respect themselves, as well as their families
- To accept the responsibilities of citizenship in

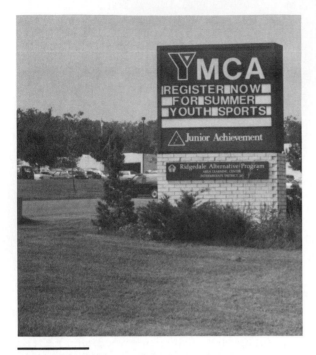

Ys have long been an integral part of many communities; Ridgedale Y, Minnetonka, MN.

the community, and to work for interracial understanding

- To develop a sense of world-mindedness
- To form habits of health and physical fitness
- To develop faith based on Christianity

Program Description:

The YMCA program promotes a mind-body-spirit approach to the health and fitness of its members. The YMCA is supported not only by its membership, but also by donations from individuals who value the ideals of the organization. Today's YMCAs are open to all users regardless of race, gender, or religion. They remain an active contributor to local communities from Minneapolis to Nairobi, and from Kingston to Hong Kong.

Program Specifics:

Hours of operation at the New Hope YMCA are 6 AM to 10 PM Monday through Saturday and 10 AM to 10 PM on Sunday.

Movement exploration in the children's gym.

The facilities consist of a swimming pool, an indoor running track, four racquetball courts, and a gymnasium that can be partitioned to form two activity areas, providing areas for basketball and/or volleyball. In addition, there is a free-weight room, as well as nautilus, exercise, and aerobic dance rooms. There is also a children's gym, and a conference and counseling area. Equipment in the exercise room includes eight stationary exercise bicycles, eight stairclimbers, four rowing machines, and a full complement of gymnastic apparatus. Added attractions of the New Hope YMCA are a sauna and large whirlpool, as well as a teen room and nursery, not to mention kitchen and classroom facilities.

Programming includes exercise instruction, classes in aerobic dance, and basketball and volleyball leagues. The YMCA also offers a children's sport program and a popular summer camp program. Most contemporary community-based YMCAs rival many of the best private fitness clubs for facilities and programming. The "atmosphere," however, is special!

Personnel:

The YMCA management structure consists of a manager, assistant manager, and staff for the service and information desk. There are Program Directors and instructional staff for aquatics, adult fitness, gymnastics, children's programs, and special events, as well as for human relations.

Contact Address:

Northwest YMCA
42nd Avenue North
New Hope, MN 55427
    or
Your local YMCA/YWCA

**Jewish Community Center
Schenectady, New York**
Source of Information:

Douglas M Black
Program Director

The Schenectady Jewish Community Center (JCC) is a committed community-oriented organization that provides exercise, sport and recreational facilities, and associated programming for a wide range of local clientele.

Program Goals/Objectives:

The objective of the JCC is to provide health and fitness, sport, and recreational opportunities for children and adults in an atmosphere of sportsmanship, cooperation, and family. These physical education objectives are couched within the overall JCC goals of enhancing the mind, body, and spirit, as well as

the cultural dimension of the Jewish faith. The JCC, however, is secular in nature, with 40% to 50% of its users being non-Jewish.

Program Description:

The JCC offers a wide range of programming to meet the physical education and recreational needs of its 1200 members, which include boys and girls, adults, senior citizens, and especially families. Programming includes instruction in aquatics, aerobics, and tennis, as well as sport leagues for soccer, basketball, softball, and volleyball. Programs for seniors (e.g., water walking), pre-school movement offerings, and a popular after-school recreation program are also cornerstones of the JCC.

Program Specifics:

The Schenectady JCC offers indoor facilities comprising a swimming pool, gymnasium, health club

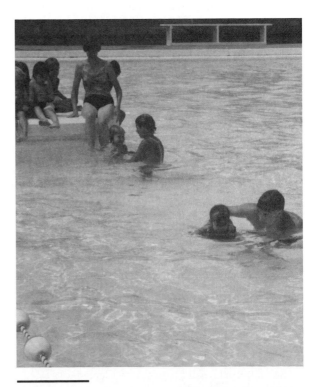

Children's aquatic programs are important to community safety.

with steam room and sauna, fitness room, television room, and kitchen area. Outdoor facilities consist of a $1.5 million Family Park Complex, which includes a 300,000 gallon swimming pool, a spray pool, tennis courts, playing fields, amphitheater, and picnic area. This beautiful area is rented for a nominal fee to many school groups who take advantage of the modern facilities.

The focus of the department is the after-school recreation program, as well as the adult recreation program. A number of activities are available on an "adults only" basis. In addition, a variety of aerobic activities is offered including "Lite Touch" (low-impact aerobics), "Bodyworks" (intensive aerobics), and "Aerobic Dance" (high-impact and dance). Aquatics ranging from Red Cross pre-school programs to YMCA certifications are also very popular, as are the myriad games and physical activities offered in the after-school program. Another well-publicized facet of the JCC program is the youth basketball team, which travels to play other youth teams.

The operational hours are 6:30 AM to 9:45 PM Monday through Friday, 9 AM to 5 PM Sundays, and 2 PM to 6 PM on Saturday (Shabbat). Saturday is devoted to family and recreation day, and no competitive activities or games are permitted. Once again, the family and cultural preservation are important parts of the JCC.

Personnel:

The Health and Physical Education Department of the Schenectady JCC is composed of a Director, who manages all recreation and fitness programming, as well as overseeing the maintenance of the facilities; an Aquatics Director, who directs the indoor pool activities, including a staff of seven lifeguards; and the certified aerobics instructors, who provide instruction and leadership for the aerobic programs. The staff is small, well-qualified, and committed to the aims and objectives of the JCC.

Contact Address:

Schenectady Jewish Community Center
2565 Baytown Road
Schenectady, NY 12309

Recreation and Parks Department
Brooklyn Park, Minnesota
Source of Information:

Jay Lotthammer, Youth Sports Coordinator

General Information:

The Brooklyn Park Recreation and Parks Department was started in 1965 by its current director, Dennis C Palm. From its inception the department has steadily grown to be one of the finest and most diverse departments in the nation and enjoys the distinction of being the first recreation program in the country to twice (1970 and 1981) receive the National Gold Medal Award for excellence in the field of Park and Recreation Management.

Department Goals/Objectives:

The basic objective of the Brooklyn Park Recreation and Parks Department program is to provide facilities and a program of wholesome leisure-time activities to as many community residents as possible. Further goals of the organization are that the activities offered can assist both adults and children in gaining satisfaction, joy, and new friendships, as well as provide an opportunity to improve skills while participating in meaningful leisure-time activities.

Program Description:

The Brooklyn Park Recreation and Parks Department is not only well known for its comprehensive and quality sport programs across all ages, but also offers more than 400 diverse recreational programs for its users. Age-group activities in the domains of art, music, drama, dance, safety, health, and wellness are also critical in promotion of a well-rounded program. The department is committed to enhancing the social, cultural, and aesthetic environment of its diverse community and serves as a focal point for many community activities.

Program Specifics:

In addition to designing and conducting the aforementioned 400 programs, the City of Brooklyn Park oversees a park system that contains 1500 acres of community park land, including 22 neighborhood

Golf lessons for children at a community course.

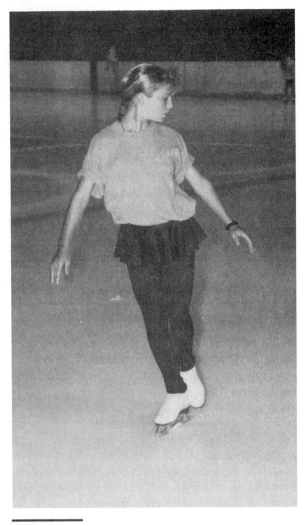

Figure skating at Brooklyn Park Community Center, MN.

parks. The system also includes 3 nature areas, a community-wide trail system, 10 school/park sites, 3 major sports complexes, 5 separate community public meeting facilities, and a Community Activity Center/Armory facility, which is one of the finest centers of its kind in the nation. The park system also operates the restored Brooklyn Park Historical Farm, which showcases an 1890s farmstead, and 2 municipal golf courses (Brookland Executive Nine and Edinburgh U.S.A., which has been selected as one of the Nation's Top 50 Public Championship Golf Courses), and sponsors a Children's Art Festival with more than 5000 participants.

The Community Activity Center is home to the department's management staff, and houses a gymnasium, ice arena, community room, racquetball, volleyball, and wallyball courts, as well as confer-

ence rooms and classrooms. These are shared with groups ranging from the Lions to the National Guard. The facility also provides a nursery and day-care facility, and programs for persons with varying disabilities are organized cooperatively with the local human service department including "Thursday Night Friendship Club."

The center opens daily at 6 AM and ice time is typically programmed to 1 AM. Summer Park hours extend daily from 8 AM to 10 PM. There are user fees for golf, tennis, racquetball, the ice arena, and the nursery, with other modest fees ($5 to $25) associated with each specific program. The center in this regard is user friendly!

Personnel:

As implied by the depth, scope, and popularity of the program, there are many opportunities for employment for qualified physical educators and recreation specialists. The center also likes to provide summer jobs for qualified young men and women (high school/college). The center employs a Director, three Assistants, two Program Supervisors, and five Program Coordinators (youth, seniors, special events, aquatics, and nursery), as well as 200 to 300 instructors and support staff necessary for providing first-class facilities and programming to all members of the community.

Contact Address:

Brooklyn Park Recreation and Parks Department
5600 85th Avenue North
Brooklyn Park, MN 55443

Hopkins-Minnetonka Recreation Department
Source of Information:

Ron Schwartz, Assistant Recreation Director
Donna Tilsner, Recreation Supervisor

General Information:

Since 1967, the neighboring cities of Hopkins and Minnetonka, as well as their respective school districts, have combined in a joint powers agreement concerning the responsibility of management of a community recreation department. The program, in fact, serves 17 communities that are housed in the two school districts. Operating costs for the recreation program are apportioned to the two cities' general fund tax base on the basis of the average user attendance. Although the program's administrative offices are housed in the Minnetonka City Hall, its facilities are primarily those of the two school districts as well as the cities.

Program Goals/Objectives:

The mission statement of this innovative organization is "to develop, promote, and provide quality op-

portunities and experiences in anticipation of, and in response to, the leisure-time needs and interests of the Hopkins-Minnetonka community."

Program Description:

The comprehensive recreation program includes league play activity ranging from T-ball to high school and senior league competition in basketball, volleyball, broomball, ice hockey, softball, football, soccer, and baseball. Year-round aquatic programs, low-impact aerobics, slimnastics, morning stretch, senior tennis league ladder, indoor soccer, and figure skating, as well as a nature environmental studies camp, are other features of this multidimensional community-based program. The recreation department also offers special programs ranging from "Fabulous 4s" (for parents and 4-year-olds) to "Over 55 and Fit," and from "New Horizons" (integration of persons with disabilities) to weekly summer "Teen Beach Party."

General activities include pool splash time, summer playground activities for preschool children, day camp experiences, a municipal swimming beach, ice skating rinks with warming houses, open gymnasiums, and an adaptive recreational program. Other services provided by the department are day centers, clubs, outings for senior citizens, group picnics, and Breakfast With Santa.

Program Specifics:

Recreation Department activities are available to all residents of Hopkins, Minnetonka, and the surrounding school districts, as well as any individuals who are employed full time in either of these cities.

Programming for the department is developed and conducted by a joint recreation staff. Sport programs are low-pressure in nature; they emphasize skill learning and development rather than highly competitive play.

An important focus for the Hopkins-Minnetonka Recreation Department is providing ample opportunity for senior citizens to engage in meaningful and enjoyable leisure-time activities. The department offers an active "Seniors" schedule that includes hiking, square dancing, ballroom dancing, swimming, softball, tennis, and tai-ji-quan, as well

As our population grays, senior physical activity is growing in popularity.

as ceramics and parlor games. In addition, senior trips, outings, and tours are organized and promoted via the "Senior Script" newsletter.

The department's programs run year-round and operate after school hours and on weekends, with the exception of summer. The fees involved typically sustain each of the programs and provide a 10% profit margin for administrative cost.

Personnel:

The Hopkins-Minnetonka Recreation Department is headed by the Recreation Director, who is supported by an Assistant, a Recreation Supervisor, clerical and support staff, and more than 300 part-time instructors who are responsible for the conduct of the various phases of the department's programs.

Contact Address:

Hopkins-Minnetonka Recreation Department
14600 Minnetonka Boulevard
Minnetonka, MN 55345

PROFESSIONAL QUALIFICATIONS AND RESPONSIBILITIES OF PUBLIC AND PRIVATE SECTOR PHYSICAL EDUCATION AND SPORT PERSONNEL

The qualifications required in the various public and private sector physical education and sport professions are similar in nature, but expanded in scope and intensity from that of the teacher, coach, or athletic director. Certainly a degree in physical education/kinesiology, recreation, sport management, exercise fitness (with basic business or counseling background) or some allied degree and certification (e.g., American College of Sports Medicine [ACSM], Institute For Aerobic Research [IAB], National Strength and Conditioning Association [NSCA], etc.) is required. An internship in a public or private sector setting is also mandatory, as well as actual work experience in a similar setting.

Other qualifications that come in handy are the ability to repair and maintain equipment, create and design a wide range of exercise/nutrition programs, and sell and promote memberships, as well as developing or adopting a "personality" and communication style conducive to the specific workplace setting. The public and private sector job market is "people-oriented," service and labor intensive, and demands a great deal from the employee.

The responsibilities of personnel involved with corporate and workplace organizations, commercial health and fitness industry, and community-based physical education and sport programs cover the total spectrum of work endeavor.

Sol[2] identifies some responsibilities of health and fitness industry specialists as follows:

- Direct the exercise program, which may be oriented to prevention and/or rehabilitation
- Train and supervise staff
- Develop and manage the program budget
- Design and manage the exercise facility and laboratories
- Market the exercise program
- Evaluate, in conjunction with a physician, each participant's medical and physical activity history, as well as performing graded exercise and pulmonary function tests and various other fitness assessment procedures
- Develop individual exercise prescriptions and packages for participants
- Evaluate and/or counsel participants, on request, about nutrition, smoking, substance abuse, weight control, and stress reduction
- Accumulate program data for statistical analysis and research
- Maintain professional affiliations

This list of responsibilities, however, must be supplemented with the following tasks, which often fall in the domain of the corporate, commercial, and community-based program manager:

- Instruct a wide variety of skills (e.g., aerobic dance, racquetball, jogging, weight training)
- Participate with members in a wide variety of physical activity
- Counsel participants on skill and technique development
- Serve as individual trainers (IEP and computer analysis)

- Clean, maintain, and repair equipment (especially in an international setting where parts are unavailable)
- Be an accountant and money collector (maintain daily, weekly, and monthly statements)
- Supervise groundskeeping, maintenance, and cleaning crews
- Supervise lifeguards
- Write newsletters, construct media guides, and design corporate health and fitness handbooks
- Sell and sustain memberships (conduct tours of facilities)
- Budget, schedule, teach, promote, advertise, supervise, and evaluate programs and personnel
- Schedule members for interclub and intraclub activities and competitions (e.g., Boston Marathon, cycling tour of France, fun runs)
- Become a stress reducer for each member

These are just some of the responsibilities and duties required of personnel employed in a public- or private-sector physical education and sport environment. This profession offers a tremendous educational, physical, and psychosocial challenge,[1] and one which requires commitment, endless vigor, and personal excellence.

SUMMARY

Physical education and sport programs are not limited to schools, colleges, universities, and other educational institutions. Many other programs and settings exist in the larger community, including the international domain. Corporate enterprises, health and fitness clubs, and other commercial fitness industry creations, as well as various community-based organizations such as YMCAs, community centers, and recreation- and park-related services now play, and will continue to play, a vital role in the delivery of health and fitness to the nation. These settings represent new, exciting, and challenging opportunities for well-trained and skilled physical educators seeking employment as instructors, managers, and potential owners.

◆ SELF-ASSESSMENT ACTIVITIES

These activities will assist students in determining if material and competencies in this chapter have been mastered:

1. Conduct a survey of your county and state to determine various public- and private-sector physical education and sport programs providing employment opportunities.
2. Prepare a set of guidelines you would follow if asked to manage a commercial health club.
3. What physical education objectives might be accomplished in public and private sector physical education and sport programs?
4. Construct a job description for a manager of a corporate fitness center.
5. Design a plan to present to hotel chain management to convince them to include a fitness center component in their management scheme.
6. Describe how a community-based fitness center may cooperate with existing school district programs.

REFERENCES

1. Ferreira RR: Effect of work shift and club size on employees, *Journal of Sport Management,* 2:1-13, 1988.
2. Sol N: Graduate preparation for exercise program professionals, *Journal of Physical Education, Recreation, and Dance,* 52(7), 76-77, 1981.
3. United States Department of Health and Human Services: *National survey of worksite health promotion activities,* Washington, DC, Summer 1987, Office of Disease Prevention and Health Promotion.
4. Wuest DS, Bucher CA: *Foundations of physical education and sport,* ed 11, St Louis, 1991, Mosby–Year Book.

SUGGESTED READINGS

- Clayton RD, Clayton JA: *Concepts and careers in physical education,* Minneapolis, 1982, Burgess.
  Designed for students who are considering a career in physical education and related professions. The appendix lists various organizations that may be of interest to physical educators.
- Flatten K: Fitness evaluation and programming for older adults, *Journal of Physical Education, Recreation, and Dance,* 60(3), 63-78, 1989.
  Discusses fitness evaluation, programming, and sport opportunities for the aging population and suggests the development of professional standards for their conduct.
- Forouzesh MR, Ratzker LE: Health promotion and wellness programs: insight into the Fortune 500, *Health Education,* 15(6):18-22, 1984-85.
  Describes the nature and the extent of health promotion and wellness programs in Fortune 500 companies.
- Kraus RG, Curtis JE: *Creative management in recreation, parks, and leisure services,* St Louis, 1986, Mosby–Year Book.
  Describes recreation, parks, and leisure service programs for various special-interest groups. Commercial and private recreation enterprises are outlined. Many of these programs focus on physical education and sport.
- Pestolesi RA, Baker C: *Introduction to physical education: a contemporary careers approach,* Glenview, Il, 1984, Scott, Foresman.
  Provides physical educators with an orientation to many diverse career pathways.
- Yiannakis A: Some contributions of sport sociology to the marketing of sport and leisure organizations, *Journal of Sport Management* 3:103-115, 1989.
  Discusses preparation and qualifications needed to be employed as a sport manager. Critical concerns of sport marketing, including product marketing features, target markets, positioning strategies, and other strategic planning phases are thoroughly addressed.

Management Functions

GRIMSBY COLLEGE

LIBRARY

NUNS CORNER, GRIMSBY

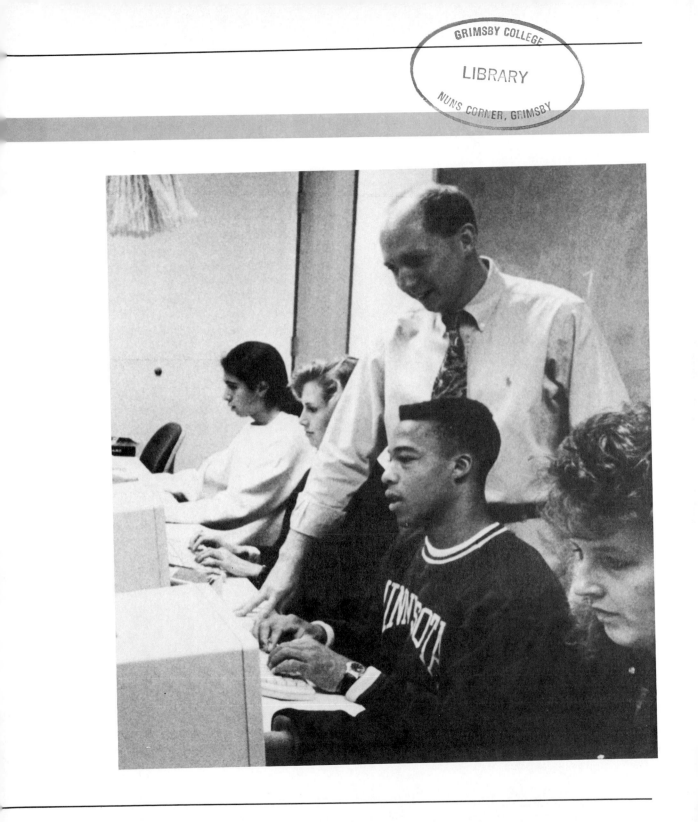

CHAPTER 7

Personnel Management and Supervision

▶ **Instructional Objectives and Competencies To Be Achieved**

After reading this chapter the student should be able to

- Understand the need for personnel policies.
- State the basic principles underlying effective personnel management.
- Summarize the qualifications needed by physical educators and coaches who work in schools, institutions of higher education, or in the private sector.
- Trace the process for recruitment, selection, orientation, pre-service and in-service training, and professional development of new staff members.

- Discuss the subject of supervision, including the qualities needed by supervisory personnel, the role of group dynamics in the supervisory process, and the basic principles that should guide effective supervisory working relationships with staff members.
- State the various steps of procedural due process to which all personnel are entitled.
- Describe various methods of evaluating physical educators, coaches, and other personnel in physical education and sport programs.

This text has been concerned thus far with a discussion of management theory, organization and structure, and the management of various kinds of physical education and sport programs. Part IV contains a discussion of the main functions and duties that managers must perform within these programs. The first of these is personnel management and supervision.

Originally personnel management was mainly concerned with selecting, placing, orienting, evaluating, and retaining people who were staff members of an organization. Contemporary personnel man-

agement, however, has taken on a more mature connotation. It does not involve manipulating people to get them to produce, but instead it involves the entire organization and the procedures by which the organization can best achieve its goals. Recruitment, selection, morale, and other considerations become the responsibility not only of management, but of all staff members. As a result, it depends on various individuals and groups understanding and accepting each other and working closely together to ultimately achieve the organization's goals.

The nature of personnel management and supervision is changing as many institutions are adopting school-based management (SBM) concepts that provide for more decentralized decision making. Managers and supervisors are consulting more closely with faculty and staff members before making final decisions on hiring, staffing, curriculum, scheduling, evaluations, and working conditions. Managers are also being required to negotiate with unions in collective bargaining sessions. Management and supervision positions are no longer considered to be isolated positions where decision making takes place. School-based management ensures that various faculty, staff members, students and those who care about quality education have a voice in departmental or institutional policy making.

For all these reasons personnel management and supervision are perhaps the most challenging responsibilities for an effective leader. Leaders who do not have the confidence and cooperation of their personnel will have great difficulty implementing any decision or policy.

PERSONNEL POLICIES

With the help of staff members, management should see that a detailed handbook of personnel policies is developed. These policies should be sound, up to date, and consistent with contemporary personnel management theory. Selected areas that might be covered by a personnel policies manual include teachers' rights, terms of employment, assignments, promotions, due process, grievance procedure, separations, evaluations, hours of service and length of school year, compensation, schedules, fringe benefits, insurance, child care, absences, leaves, travel, in-service training, and conduct on the job.

In some cases personnel policies are not developed by the management but rather by a bargaining contract or exclusive representative (e.g., union, association, or federation). In such cases the bargaining contract will probably affect the flexibility with which the manager and management may operate. It is crucial that management understand such exclusive representatives and that the guidelines prescribed are contained in full in the personnel policies manual or handbook.[4]

PRINCIPLES OF PERSONNEL AND SUPERVISORY MANAGEMENT

Productive personnel management and supervision do not just happen. They occur as a result of adhering to a prescribed set of basic principles.

Cooperation

To achieve cooperation, the talents and unique abilities of individuals must be utilized, reinforced, and rewarded to ensure that their service will be most productive and effective. Maintaining cooperation among the staff will largely depend on staff satisfaction in the work environment and fulfillment of the organization's obligations and goals. The function of management and supervision is to see that these essentials are provided and sustained.

The Individual as a Member of an Organization

Management and supervision should seek to imbue the organization with the idea that every individual has an investment in the enterprise. The undertak-

Cooperative effort between administrators, coaches, support staff, and athletes produces positive outcomes.

ings can be successful only if all persons contribute by working to their fullest potential; then success brings satisfaction to all. Submergence of self to this end is necessary for achievement of the organization's goals.

Final Authority

The existing authority of management belongs to the position and not to the person. Power and authority do not reside in one human being, but in the best thinking, judgment, and imagination that the organization can summon. This is the value of the SBM approach. Individuals possess only the authority that goes with their position. In turn, this authority is respected and appreciated by other members whose work is closely allied to achieving the objectives for which the organization exists. Final authority rests in those who, because of their positions, are responsible for ultimate decisions.

Department heads, various committees, and staff consultants issue reports interpreting the facts. Their judgments, conclusions, and recommendations contribute to the formulation of final decisions, which are the responsibility of the manager (e.g., teacher, athletic director, principal). If these interpretations, judgments, conclusions, and recommendations are not accepted, the organization is not only weakened but may fail. Furthermore, individuals cannot be induced to contribute their full efforts to an organization that has little respect for their thinking. Authority permeates any organization and should be a shared concept.

Staff Morale[7]

Management should continually strive to create conditions that facilitate good staff morale. The degree to which high staff morale exists will be in direct proportion to the degree to which such conditions are satisfied.

Leadership. The quality of management will determine staff morale to a great degree. From the top down, all leaders should be carefully selected. Other things being equal, individuals who contribute and produce more will possess better morale. These individuals usually have more respect for managers who are leaders in the true sense of the word.

Physical and social environment. A contributing physical and social environment is essential to good staff morale. The organization must provide for the physical health and safety of the employee or student-athlete. It must also make provisions for mental and emotional health, including proper supervision and counseling, opportunity for advancement through professional development, emergency plans, and avenues for intellectual enhancement.

The social environment is also an important consideration. Individuals with whom a person interacts and the activities in which they engage can strengthen or diminish the human drive for excellence. Therefore it is important to associate with those who can serve as facilitators and motivators not only to accomplish the goals of the organization, but also to build positive social relationships that are conducive to individual development and continued satisfaction.

Advancement. Each individual likes to believe that he or she is progressing in the world. Each member of an organization must be aware of what is essential for retention, progress, and promotion. Op-

A supportive physical and social environment contributes to individual development.

portunities should be provided for learning new skills and knowledge and for gaining new experiences. Encouragement and resources should be provided to those who wish to improve and are willing to devote extra time and effort to this end.

Recognition of meritorious service. Everyone possesses the need to be recognized. Those who make outstanding contributions to the organization should be so honored. Investing in this positive reinforcement dimension is important to the future of the organization, as well as to individual self-enhancement, self-esteem, and self-worth.

Individual differences. An important principle of personnel management is recognizing individual differences and different types of work. Individuals differ in many ways—abilities, skills, and training, as well as physical, mental, and social qualities. Various types of work require different skills, abilities, personalities, and training. These differences should be recognized by the manager, who must make sure that the right person is in the right position. An individual who is a square peg in a round hole does not contribute to his or her own or the organization's welfare.

The status granted any one person should be in line with the talents and capacities of that individual and importance of the function he or she performs. To be placed in a position that should be held by a person with lesser qualifications or vice versa is unjust and sometimes emotionally devastating and destabilizing. Many disruptive features can develop if individual abilities are not recognized or if proper incentives are not provided in accordance with training, qualification, and affirmative action.

Differentiated staffing. Management must recognize staff members' interests, talents, and general suitability for each position or task that is delegated. Teachers and coaches should be assigned activities that are allied to their particular skills. Schools are also employing persons such as paraprofessionals, activity specialists, interns, teacher's aides, clerks, custodians, and equipment and facility managers to perform specialized tasks. All staff members must be carefully and selectively integrated into the whole so that each may develop to their fullest potential and add to the organization's effectiveness.

PERSONNEL RECRUITMENT AND SELECTION

Personnel recruitment and selection are important functions of management. They include consideration of the special qualifications for teaching and coaching, the general qualifications of physical educators, and the unique qualifications of those working in other private and public sector physical education and sport settings. Orientation, pre-training and in-service training, and professional development are also responsibilities that go with staff recruitment and selection.

SPECIAL QUALIFICATIONS FOR TEACHING AND COACHING

It has long been recognized that the qualifications and qualities of a good teacher and coach are synonymous. Many experts include the following as being desirable qualities.

- Thorough knowledge of the subject matter.
- Expertise in making an enthusiastic presentation of the fundamentals involved.
- Ability to take a personal interest in each student.
- Well prepared and organized.
- Respected by the students.
- Ability to stimulate and motivate the students to think and act.
- Interesting and able to make the subject matter/sport come to life.
- Original thinker who is creative in his or her methods.
- Fine communicator.
- Presents a neat, well-groomed appearance.
- Possesses a good sense of humor.
- Consistent, firm, fair, and honest in dealings with students.
- Understanding and kind.
- Exemplary in conduct and adheres to school policy and procedure.
- Emotionally stable, self-controlled, and sensitive to all situations.

Beginning teachers, instructors, and coaches need considerable encouragement and help to hone their skills. Management should be aware of these needs and work to ensure that they are met. A survey of 50 instructors indicated the following problems of new practitioners in the profession:

- Difficulties arising from a lack of facilities.
- Large size of classes, making it difficult to instruct effectively.
- Instructional assignments in addition to the primary responsibility of teaching physical education and coaching.
- Discipline problems with students.
- Conflicting methods between what was learned by the beginning instructor/coach in his or her training and the established patterns and expectations of experienced instructors/coaches, as well as traditional systems.
- Difficulty keeping records, reports, and other paperwork up to date.
- Problems encountered in obtaining books, materials, and supplies.
- Problems encountered in obtaining cooperative attitude from other instructors.
- Lack of departmental meetings to discuss common problems.
- Inability to find time for personal recreation.

GENERAL QUALIFICATIONS FOR PHYSICAL EDUCATORS

One of the most important considerations in management is selecting and hiring the most qualified personnel. The members of an organization determine whether it will succeed or fail. Therefore management must recognize the following qualifications needed to meaningfully deliver physical education and sport.

The teacher/coach should be a graduate of an accredited institution that prepares professionals for a career in physical education and sport. Knowledge of the college or university that the potential employee has attended may play a part in the selection process.

Because physical education and sport is grounded in the sciences of anatomy, exercise physiology, biomechanics, sport sociology, and sport psychology, physical educators and coaches should be well versed in these disciplines, as well as in research methods that will permit the teacher or coach to survey and apply appropriate research findings to the sport-specific situation.

The general education of physical educators and coaches is under continuous scrutiny and, at times, criticism. Knowledge of world affairs, mastery of the arts, and possession of other educational attributes are imperative. Because the position also requires frequent appearances in public, appearance and communication skills are essential.

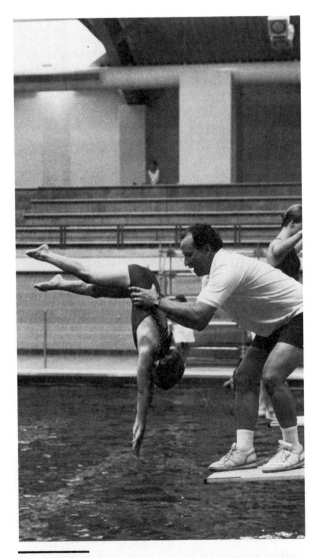

A diving instructor assists a student in a complex skill.

Physical education and coaching are strenuous and therefore demand that members of the profession be in good physical and mental condition in order to carry out their duties efficiently and effectively. Physical educators and coaches are supposed to help build healthy bodies and minds and are often expected by students, community, and management to be "role models." Therefore physical educators and coaches should be in good physical condition themselves.

Values, ethics, and morals are often developed through participation in games and other physical education activities. Therefore it is essential that the professional stress fair play, good sportsmanship, and sound values. His or her leadership should develop a recognition of the importance of high moral and ethical behavior and significantly contribute to the development and enhancement of sound human relation skills.

Physical educators and coaches should have a sincere interest in and enjoy teaching, participating in activities, helping others realize the thrill of participation, and becoming physically fit. Unless the individual has a firm belief in the value of physical ac-

An instructor guides a workout at Tenneco, Inc., Houston, TX.

tivity and a desire to help extend the benefits of such an endeavor to others, he or she will not be an asset to the profession.

The physical educator and coach should also possess an acceptable standard of motor ability and skill level. To coach and teach various games and activities to others and fully realize the discipline, stress, and anxiety, as well as the intricate finesse, that accompany such activities, it is most helpful to possess the skills and ability to participate.

UNIQUE QUALIFICATIONS FOR PHYSICAL EDUCATION PROFESSIONALS IN OTHER SETTINGS

The professional who seeks employment in settings other than schools and institutions of higher education needs to possess those general qualifications listed, and in addition, the special training and qualifications needed for work in the activity-specific agency or area in which he or she seeks employment. For example, a physical educator who seeks employment in the corporate fitness setting should have as much experience as possible in exercise physiology, nutrition, and fitness assessment, because many of the duties will involve determining the physical status of employees and planning and supervising programs to develop and maintain optimal physical fitness levels. It would also be helpful to be familiar with the various types of exercise equipment that are used in these programs. If the physical educator plans to seek a position in a community-based recreation program, he or she should have a wide variety of skills in activities that will interest adults and seniors. Furthermore, he or she will need to be familiar with program planning and structuring, scheduling, facility maintenance, public relations, and promotion.

To be successful in such settings as health and fitness clubs, ski areas, golf and tennis centers, senior centers, and youth-serving agencies, the physical educator should know the characteristics and needs of the population being served. For example, the professional working with the elderly must understand senior citizens—their lifestyles, interests, needs, physical fitness status, and the activities and programs that will contribute to their well-being.

Qualified, certified, and well-trained personnel are requisite to outstanding programs.

In a health and fitness club setting, the educator must be able to sell, promote, and market the program, and keep books, as well as be able to design individualized fitness programs for the members and supervise their implementation. The bottom line is that in order to gain meaningful employment, today's professional must be well educated, physically skilled, and multitalented.

GUIDELINES FOR STAFF RECRUITMENT

Several guidelines regarding the recruitment of qualified personnel follow.

A job description that includes the various duties and qualifications the position requires should be prepared. The job description should provide such details as the position title, a list of specific duties involved, salary, and educational and experience requirements. In addition, it is standard practice to declare that the employing organization or agency is an Equal Opportunity Employer (Equal Opportunity Employment Act, 1972), as well as to invite the application of qualified women, minorities, and handicapped, and to state that the organization complies with federal and state laws prohibiting discrimination in employment.

Notices of the position vacancy should be distributed within the organization, to professional programs and placement offices in colleges and universities, and to respected leaders and colleagues in the field, and should be advertised in professional publications such as *JOPERD,* the *NCAA News,* and the *Chronicle of Higher Education,* as well as in local and regional newspapers.

Candidates for the position should be asked to submit their resumes, including college transcripts, and confidential references (or persons who can be contacted by the employing organization). A file should be prepared on each candidate, including records of references and other pertinent information. Candidates should be duly notified when their files are complete or if something more might be needed to fulfill completion requirements. Completed files should then be forwarded to members of the search committee or personnel department who are assigned the task of selecting the most promising candidate.

GUIDELINES FOR SELECTION

Many organizations have a search or personnel committee, as well as an affirmative action officer, that recruits and interviews candidates for vacancies and makes recommendatons to the management. Guidelines for the selection of personnel follow.

The search, personnel, or other committee or individual should review the files of all candidates, select three to five viable candidates for the position, and then invite them for a personal interview. Persons within the organization who apply for the position should be evaluated by the same criteria as the outside candidates.

The personal interview offers an opportunity to meet the candidate firsthand and discuss the position with him or her. During a personal interview it is important to assess the candidate's personality, character, education, experience, and other specific qualifications. Questions asked might revolve around his or her interest in the position, qualifications, understanding of the employing organization, involvement in various professional activities, and background experience and education. Some organizations require that the candidate make a presentation before faculty, staff, and students.

Based on the personal interview and a further examination of credentials, a recommendation should be made to management that includes either one or several applicants, giving personnel or management the prerogative to select the most qualified person.

Another consideration that should be discussed is contracts. Contractual items such as salary, educational step level, length of employment, duties, tenure considerations, vacation time and sick days, as well as other job details, should be made very clear to the prospective employee. These could be the deciding factor that prompts an outstanding person to accept a position. Such benefits as health insurance, retirement benefits, sick leave, annual leave, and travel allowances are an important consideration in the minds of many prospective employees. Managers should make sure applicants clearly understand all aspects of the position for which a candidate is being hired. Offers and acceptance of employment can be made orally at first but should be followed up with a written contract.

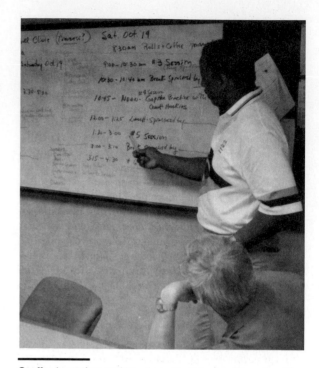

Staff orientation and in-service training are important for efficient functioning of any program.

ORIENTATION OF NEW STAFF

The new staff member needs considerable orientation and help in adjusting to a new position. On hiring a new staff member, management should provide guidance and assistance concerning housing, transportation, educational system, hospitals, church, and other items necessary to getting settled into the community. A pre-orientation familiarizing the person with the organization and management personnel should also be conducted before the opening of school in order to discuss, reinforce, and clarify the new staff member's duties and responsibilities. The new member should know the person to whom he or she is responsible, as well as the lines of communication within the organization and any protocol including due process and grievance procedures that must be observed. The new person will have many questions; these should be expected and answered quickly and frankly. Quality pre-service pre-orientation should result in a happier and more productive member of the organization.

IN-SERVICE TRAINING AND STAFF DEVELOPMENT

Because of the rapid changes occurring within the profession, staff members should attend regular in-service and staff development training programs. New methods of management, programming, teaching, and evaluation have implications for all professionals.

Some suggestions for in-service training and staff development include the following:

- Conducting workshops for staff members in which new trends and developments are examined.
- Holding faculty retreats or arranging programs that will enhance faculty and staff development by inviting consultants and professional colleagues who are specialists in facilities, curriculum development, methods, activity skills, and computer techniques to meet with staff members and share new developments.

- Developing a professional library with the latest books, journals and periodicals, films, and videos and making them readily accessible to staff members.
- Devoting some staff meetings to discussions of new developments or issues like teacher burnout, sexual harassment, or substance abuse.
- Encouraging and subsidizing staff members' attendance at professional meetings and conferences.
- Using staff members with special talents to upgrade the knowledge and competence levels of other staff members (e.g., stress management, relaxation, creative thinking, cooperative learning).
- Providing presemester or summer orientation sessions for staff members.
- Conducting research and experimentation within the organization's own program, as well as linking in-house information and research systems with local university information systems via fiber optics.
- Arranging for the local college or university to come to the school and conduct cohort group graduate classes and workshops or setting up an interactive TV link for "distance learning" opportunities.
- Providing training seminars in such activities as problem solving, teacher assistant teaming, social and emotional health issues, and mainstream collaborative modeling to enhance teacher performance.
- Encouraging sabbaticals and travel for professional enhancement.

In-service training and staff development are vital to building a cooperative team of teachers and coaches. They promote communication, enthusiasm, creativity, and sharing and build esprit de corps. Professional enhancement opportunities should play a significant role in all management structures.

SUPERVISION

Supervisors must recognize each individual staff member and the contribution he or she makes to the

Supervision is an applied art that must be learned and practiced.

organization, see that staff members are assigned to tasks in line with their abilities, be willing to delegate responsibility, establish high yet attainable standards, provide a complete analysis of each position in the organization, establish accountability for staff members, and help each member to feel a sense of accomplishment.

Supervision will be effective if sound leadership is provided within the organization.

Qualities of the Supervisor Who Is a Leader

Years ago it was believed that certain beliefs or qualities indicated who the leaders would be, that leaders are born and not made, and that some people will lead and others will follow. These statements are not valid. Instead, personal characteristics, experience, and the ability to work independently help determine the person with leadership qualities.

Research indicates that there may be a relationship between personality factors and leadership.

Group leaders were also found to outperform other staff members in such areas as scholarship, acceptance of responsibility, participation, and socioeconomic status.

Research further reveals that the closer an individual conforms to the accepted norms of the group, the better liked he or she will be; the style of the leader is determined more by the expectations of the membership and the requirements of the situation than by the personal traits of the leader. The leader will be followed more faithfully the more he or she makes it possible for the members to achieve their personal goals along with the group goals, and in a small group, authoritarian leadership is less effective than democratic leadership in holding the group together and getting its work done.

Hersey and Blanchard's Situational Leadership Theory[5] suggests that to be an outstanding leader, the individual will change behavior with each situation. The theory is based on things such as the interaction between the one who aspires to be a leader and the followers, the group's socioemotional support, two-way communication with the group, maturity level of followers, and education and experience of individuals or groups who are being led.

The physical educator or coach who desires to obtain and excel in a leadership and supervisory position in an organization should study the literature on management and supervision. This will help expose potential leaders to a variety of situations that may contribute to a greater understanding of the issues and concerns pertaining to leadership.[2]

The physical educator and coach should also recognize that various personal qualities are essential for providing supervisory leadership. These personal qualities include a sense of humor, empathy, sensitivity, feeling of adequacy, ability to win confidence and respect, enthusiasm, originality, sincerity, and resourcefulness. Supervision requires the ability to assist staff members to envisage their own strengths and weaknesses, provide assistance in helping them solve problems, resolve personnel conflicts, improve morale, objectively judge personal performance, and make recommendations for promotions and other rewards. To accomplish these tasks the supervisor must be able to promote staff development, create effective channels of communication, establish staff accountability, set goals, provide effective motivation and adequate rewards, and supply a proper dosage of positive reinforcement.

GROUP DYNAMICS

Group dynamics are important in supervision. They are concerned with understanding the nature and role of groups in modern living. In this text, group dynamics are considered in light of the supervisory role in physical education and sport programs. Research has revolved around the structure of groups, how groups operate, the relationships of members within a group and between groups, the factors that affect group attitudes and productivity, and what types of leadership are most effective in varying group relationships.

Physical educators and coaches can benefit from the study of group dynamics because they work with various groups of people in their programs and they are interested in getting groups to enter and participate in their activities and support their programs. Teamwork and cooperative effort are essential when working with organizations, agencies, and other groups. Managers and supervisors must be able to work comfortably both inside and outside the organizational framework and should be familiar with the various methodologies employed to examine group behavior.

Shaw[13] has noted the following approaches to the study of groups:

- *Formal models research:* theoretical models of the structure and behavior of groups are developed.
- *Field theory:* the behavior of groups and individuals within a group results from many interrelated and interdependent phenomena.
- *Sociometric research:* the choices of the group on an interpersonal basis among members play a major role.
- *Systems approach:* the group is viewed as a structure of interlocking elements, and group inputs and outputs are analyzed.

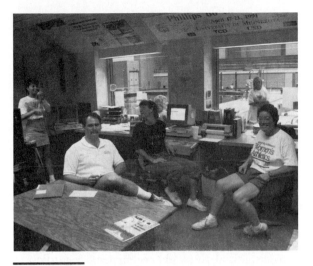

Group dynamics and cooperative effort at the University of Minnesota Aquatics Center.

- *Psychoanalytic approach:* the factors that groups and individuals use for motivation and defensive actions form the basis for investigation.
- *Empirical approach:* groups are observed, observational behaviors are recorded, and statistical procedures are used to develop basic concepts and guidelines regarding group decisions.

Research has shown that supervisors must understand certain factors concerning groups in order to work effectively with them. These factors include an understanding of the group's mission in working with other groups, the power the group has over its own members, whether the group's activities are informal or highly structured, and the satisfaction derived by members of the group as a result of such group association. Other factors include the similarities of members of the group, the relationship of members with each other, the degree to which members actively participate in group activities, the ease of access to group membership, significance of the group to its members, overall stability of the group, and the structure of the group as it affects the status of each of its members.

Shaw also suggests the following reasons why groups are effective:

- Group performance provides increased motivation over individual performance.
- Groups usually produce better solutions to problems than do people working alone.
- Groups are able to learn faster than individuals can by themselves.
- More new and different ideas are generated by both individuals and groups when there is an absence of critical evaluation.

An understanding of group dynamics can enhance the physical educator's and/or coach's role in the supervisory process. The study of group dynamics is an evolving area that has great potential for increasing the productivity and interpersonal relationships of any organization.

THE WORKING RELATIONSHIP BETWEEN SUPERVISORS AND STAFF

Effective working relationships between supervisors and staff members will be discussed in four sections: (1) responsibilities of supervisors, (2) responsibilities of staff members, (3) common points of conflict, and (4) checklist for effective working relationships.

Responsibilities of Supervisors

Supervisors should possess a sound understanding of human nature to work effectively with people. Physical educators and coaches should not look on supervising as impersonal but should always keep in mind human dimensions and give human problems high priority.

Supervisors should understand their own behavior. They should see conflicts where they exist and not fabricate them where they do not exist. They should present an accurate account of group expectations although they may not be in agreement with them. They should recognize the differences and rationale between their own views and those of others.

Supervisors should exercise wisely the authority vested in their positions. The authority goes with the position and not with the person. Supervisors should recognize that the position exists to further the goals of the organization and that it should never be used for personal gain.

Supervisors should establish effective means of communication among members of the organization. Opportunities should be readily available to discuss professional and personal (if appropriate) problems, new ideas, and ways to improve the effective functioning of the organization.

Supervisors should provide maximal opportunity for personal self-fulfillment. Each person has a basic psychological need to be recognized, to have self-respect, and to belong. Within the organizational structure, supervisors should strive to make this possible for every group member.

Supervisors should provide leadership. Supervising requires leadership qualities that bring out maximal individual effort in the context of the total coordinated effort of the group.

Supervisors should provide clear-cut procedures. Sound procedures are essential to the effective and efficient functioning of an organization. Procedures should be carefully developed; thoroughly discussed with those concerned; written and articulated in clear, concise language; implemented; and evaluated.

Supervisors should plan meaningful meetings. Staff meetings should be carefully planned and effectively conducted. Meetings should not be called on impulse or dominated by the supervisor. Agendas should be set and followed, and procedures agreed upon at such meetings should be carried out.

Supervisors should recommend promotions on the basis of merit, without politics or favoritism. Recommendations for promotions, tenure, and change of status or grade, when requested, should be attained through careful evaluation of each person's qualifications in relation to objective criteria. Each member of the staff (teaching or coaching) should be observed three to four times per year, with follow-up meetings and written evaluations being submitted to management.

Supervisors should protect and enhance the mental and physical health of staff members. In carrying out this responsibility, the supervisor should attempt to eliminate petty annoyances and worries that can weigh heavily on staff members. This in turn will increase the satisfaction each person derives from the organization, promote friendly relationships, develop esprit de corps, improve respect for the status of staff members, and establish a climate of understanding that promotes good will and personal development.

Responsibilities of Staff Members

Physical educators and coaches should support the total program. Each staff member must fulfill his or her responsibility to the program. This means serving on committees, attending meetings, contributing ideas, and giving support to worthy projects, initiatives, and developments regardless of the phase of the program to which he or she belongs. Staff members should view their own fields of specialization in proper perspective with the conceptual or total educational endeavor.

Physical educators and coaches should take an interest in supervision. By participating in policy and decision making, role playing the problems and pressures faced by the supervisor, and contributing ideas that will help cut down on red tape and thus streamline the process, they can have significant impact.

Physical educators and coaches should carry out their individual responsibilities efficiently. If each individual job is performed effectively and attention to detail is maintained, the organization as a whole will function more efficiently.

Physical educators and coaches should be prompt in completing administrative responsibilities. Purchase requisitions, attendance, excuse and accident reports, and many other administrative tasks have to be completed on schedule.

Physical educators and coaches should be loyal. Each staff member must be loyal to the organization. Disagreement about supervision and differences of opinion can exist, but loyalty to the management and the organization is essential.

Physical educators and coaches should observe proper protocol. Staff members should discuss problems with immediate supervisors before going to higher authority. Lines of authority and chains of command should be recognized and followed.

Physical educators and coaches should be professional. In relationships with colleagues, supervisors, parents, students, or the general public, a staff member should recognize that professional and ethical behavior is essential. Confidences should not be betrayed, and professional and personal problems should be settled with the appropriate people concerned.

 COMMON POINTS OF CONFLICT BETWEEN SUPERVISORS AND STAFF MEMBERS

Areas in which poor working relationships occur include the following:

- The failure of supervisors to recognize physical education and sport as a vital part of the program
- The existence of authoritarian and undemocratic supervision
- The failure to clarify goals and responsibilities for the organization and for each member of the organization
- The failure of supervisors to provide dynamic leadership
- The failure of supervisors to provide clearly defined procedures
- The practice of supervisors encroaching on classes and schedules without good reason or adequate previous announcement
- The assignment of unreasonable work loads and assignments
- The failure of staff members to read bulletins that contain important announcements
- The failure of supervisors to assume conscientiously the duties and responsibilities associated with supervision
- The existence of unsatisfactory working conditions
- The lack of adequate materials, supplies, and equipment

PERSONNEL PROBLEMS REQUIRING SPECIAL ATTENTION

Selected personnel problems that need special attention are teacher burnout, stress management, unionism, affirmative action, use of certified and noncertified personnel, grievance, and due process.

Teacher Burnout

Teacher burnout has been described as a physical, emotional, and attitudinal exhaustion. Depression, lack of concentration, anger, loss of sleep, and decreased productiveness are just some of the symptoms that seem to be prevalent in today's profession. Large classes, lack of administrative support, repetitiveness, lack of facilities, violence, shrinking employment opportunities, austere budgets, ill-conceived curricular movements, public criticism, lack of community support, heavier teaching or work loads, overemphasis on accountability, discipline problems, and inadequate salaries are a few of the conditions contributing to teacher burnout.

Some teachers and coaches are tired of their work and the many problems and pressures they face. As a result, the students are being shortchanged by teachers and coaches who are complacent, dissatisfied, restless, and suffering emotionally and sometimes physically.

What can be done to cope with burnout? How can teachers and coaches who are suffering from it be helped? What procedures will result in self-renewal and revival for overburdened teachers and "stressed out" coaches? More important, how can teacher and coach burnout be prevented?

Many suggestions have been made for eliminating and avoiding burnout. They are listed here so that beginning teachers and coaches, as well as those currently on the job, will be familiar with ways to avoid it or, if already afflicted, can find a cure for it.

Langlois[10] suggests that physical fitness is one answer. She has initiated faculty fitness classes at her college that seem to be paying dividends in helping eliminate and avoid teacher burnout.

A review of the literature suggests the following activities as antidotes to teacher and coach burnout:

reassess teaching technologies, reevaluate curricular offerings, participate in visitations and exchange programs, participate in structured learning experiences, become involved in professional organizations, reassess reading habits, contribute to professional publications, develop a quest for new knowledge, get involved in local service functions, and explore additional development opportunities.

Other potential solutions include the following: use holidays and vacations for personal and professional revitalization, change the way material is taught, transfer to another school, transfer to another position within the educational system, find a job outside education, or participate in professional development education. Horton[6] points out that burnout must be attacked on several fronts since no single cause or solution exists. Therefore a teacher or coach experiencing burnout must recognize the problem and then develop a meaningful plan of correction. These plans can range from exercise to prayer and from study leaves to hobbies. Many educational and corporate environments now provide counseling and self-help groups to alleviate this serious and growing problem.

Stress Management

Stress can be harmful or beneficial, depending on the nature of the stimulus or *stressor,* as the causal agent is called. Harmful stress affects the ability of the body to maintain stable conditions within itself. Beneficial stress can result in euphoria and greater personal achievements. Negative stress should be reduced to avoid developing physical or emotional health problems. In many cases physical activity provides an excellent means of stress reduction.

Some symptoms of stress that may represent danger signs are irritability, headaches, pain in the back, loss of appetite, nightmares, depression, emotional tension, and heart palpitations. The late Hans Selye,[12] endocrinologist, philosopher, scientist, and pioneer in modern stress theory, defined stress as the "nonspecific response of the body to any demand placed upon it." He indicated the body's response to stress follows a three-stage pattern:

Alarm State—the body mobilizes its resources to fight the hostile stressor.

◆ SELYE'S GENERAL GUIDELINES FOR STRESS REDUCTION

Try not to be a perfectionist—instead, perform and work within your capabilities.

Spend your time in ways other than trying to befriend those persons who don't want to experience your love and friendship.

Enjoy the simple things in life.

Strive and fight only for those things that are really worthwhile.

Accent the positive and the pleasant side of life.

On experiencing a defeat or setback, maintain your self-confidence by remembering past accomplishments and successes.

Don't delay tackling the unpleasant tasks that must be done; instead, get at them immediately.

Evaluate people's progress on the basis of their performance.

Recognize that leaders, to be leaders, must have the respect of their followers.

Adopt a motto that you will live in a way that will earn your neighbor's love.

Try to live your life in such a way that your existence may be useful to someone.

Clarify your values.

Take constructive action to eliminate a source of stress.

Other suggestions

Maintain good physical and mental health.

Accept what you cannot change.

Serve other people and some worthy cause.

Share worries with someone you can trust.

Pay attention to your body.

Balance work and recreation.

Improve your qualifications for the realistic goals you aspire to.

Avoid reliance on things such as drugs and alcohol.

Don't be narcissistic.

Manage your time effectively.

Laugh at yourself.

Get enough rest and sleep.

Don't be too hard on yourself.

Improve your self-esteem.

Resistance State—the body adjusts to stress by using its maximal ability to withstand the stressor.

Exhaustion State—the body becomes devitalized and loses ability to resist stress, leading to serious illness and even death. Many mental and physical reasons have been set forth proclaiming the benefits of physical activity and sport in stress reduction. Through physical activity individuals can improve mind-body harmony and thus reduce harmful stress, thereby contributing to their own health and fitness.

Exactly how physical activity reduces stress is not completely understood. It has been generally established that the mind can influence the body and the body can influence the mind. Research suggests that physical activity can result in a positive psychological response. One theory is that exercise burns up stress hormones. The human body reacts to stress by a response known as "fight or flight." As a result, a number of hormonal and physiological changes take place as stress by-products are created.

If one responds to the stressor by engaging in physical activity, the stress by-products are depleted. Selye suggested that the person who exercises regularly is able to resist stressors better, and that stressful situations do not represent as much harm to the physically active person as to the sedentary individual.

A second explanation is that activity helps to release the tension that can accumulate when one is under stress. As a result, hormone-induced tension is alleviated by engaging in physical activity. A stress-regulated and controlled lifestyle should provide a balance between work, exercise, rest, and structured relaxation training.

Krotee and Hatfield[9] suggest that activities such as jogging, bicycling, and brisk walking produce an increased target heart rate and respiration rate response, and result in significant relaxation for tense persons. Physical activity also appears to provide a mental diversion from problems and concerns that cause stress. It also provides a low-level type of stress for the adrenal glands that in turn strengthens them so that they can more effectively counter severe stress. Increased adrenal activity as a result of exercise appears to result in the creation and formation of reserves of steroids that counteract stress.

Exercise can contribute to stress reduction, as well as maintaining or improving fitness level.

Many experts report that endurance exercise promotes the secretion of hormones called endorphins that produce the "jogger's high." Endorphins are reported to be 200 times more powerful than morphine and serve as nature's way of rendering negative psychological feelings inert and producing a natural feeling of well-being.[11]

Other experts point out that regular and vigorous exercise helps reduce stress by contributing to a lower heart rate, lower blood pressure, improved condition of blood vessels, fewer circulatory disorders, and improved body composition.[11]

The negative image of the human body held by some individuals, whether it is caused by obesity, weak muscular development, poor posture, or low fitness level, can also be a stressor. Exercise can not only improve body and fitness level development, but it can also assist in enhancement of a person's self-image, self-concept, or body image.

Stress can also be managed in other ways, such as utilizing various kinds of interventions such as progressive relaxation techniques, biofeedback, and meditation. Selye's guidelines for stress reduction are provided so that teachers and coaches can take full advantage of the suggested interventions and develop successful personalized stress management programs.

Exclusive Representation, Unionism

Exclusive representation (e.g., federation of teachers, labor unions, professional organizations) is widespread, and management, teachers, coaches, and other staff members should understand the nature of such an association and be able to work effecitvely within their exclusive representative framework, including personnel and contractual agreements.

The emphasis in physical education and sport over the years has been for teachers and coaches to become involved in their professional organizations. But since the Public Employment Labor Relations Act of 1971 (PELRA), very little has been introduced to orient the manager, teachers, or coach to exclusive representation.

Managers, especially, need to understand teacher bargaining units and binding arbitration agreements to be able to work effectively with all personnel involved. Some recommendations for managers to follow if involved with exclusive representation negotiations are to look on negotiations as a time to attempt to improve relationships rather than harm such relationships, adjust to negotiations and make the best of the working relationship, advance the organization and improve its democratic atmosphere, insist on being a part of the negotiation process, protect the right to be the professional leader of the or-

ganization, and strive to promote mutual trust, understanding, respect, and cooperation. Other strategies contained in the Harvard Negotiation Project[3] and related literature should also be a part of the shared decision making in the negotiation process. Managers should know and be conversant as to their responsibilities in professional negotiations, and these should be included within their job descriptions. If managers perform within the responsibilities as stated, they should receive solid backing from those whom they represent.

Teachers and coaches should understand that pursuant to PELRA, nothing contained in any exclusive representation agreement should be construed to limit, impair, or affect their right to express a view or opinion, to grieve, or to complain, as long as their duties are conducted faithfully.

Affirmative Action

Managers need to understand and conform to affirmative action guidelines. Among other things, these guidelines indicate that no discrimination can exist on the basis of gender, race, age, religion, color, ethnic background, handicap, or creed. All individuals must be afforded equal opportunities to achieve their destinies. In hiring personnel, attention must be given to adequate and appropriate publicity of vacancies (e.g., time, appropriate journals, newspapers), equal consideration of all applications, and selection based on each individual's qualifications. No discrimination can exist against members of minority groups in employment, retention, salary, or promotion. Also, organizations should strive to achieve representative diversity, as well as to promote equal opportunity for professional growth and economic security.

Many organizations employ individuals whose responsibilities include promoting and overseeing the process of equal opportunity and affirmative action within their department, school, or division. Managers should continually consult with these individuals to see that affirmative action compliance is being met. If no such individual exists in an organization, the manager should be thoroughly familiar with and committed to affirmative action guidelines and goals.

Use of Certified and Noncertified Personnel

A recent trend has been to use noncertified personnel in physical education and sport to teach and coach activities when permanent certified personnel are not available or when work loads have become too heavy for the full-time faculty. The profession has suggested the following guidelines:

- Activities and sports in which students and other consumers are interested in participating need to be conducted by regular full-time faculty members.
- In hiring new faculty, attention should be given to applicants who have the qualifications to teach and coach. If no faculty member is available to teach or coach an activity, part-time personnel should be hired. If no certified person is available, then noncertified personnel may be considered.
- Noncertified personnel should have expertise in the activity to be taught or coached, and proper supervision should be provided for the noncertified person.
- A noncertified person should be replaced with regular full-time faculty when they become available.

There is considerable discussion in sport programs as to whether coaches should be certified. Broderick[1] and Kelly and Brightwell[8] have explored this question and, among other recommendations, believe that coaches need to be qualified and certified since tasks such as progressive training and conditioning programs, as well as risk, safety, and legal liability issues, can lead to serious problems if coaches are not well trained and well qualified.

Grievance and Due Process

In most educational organizations a prescribed procedure is set forth to be followed by a staff member or other person who has a *grievance*. Grievance implies that the person feels he or she has been wronged or a hardship, harm, or harassment has been realized and that he or she has a just cause for protest and complaint.

The established procedure usually includes discussing the grievance with persons in the chain of command and trying to solve and correct the problem at the grassroots level. If the problem cannot be solved at the lowest level, it moves on to a higher level or is submitted to a grievance committee. This committee discusses the facts in the case and attempts to arrive at a solution that is right and, if possible, satisfactory to all concerned.

Management should always be alert to situations in which grievances may occur and try to solve personal and other problems before they reach the grievance stage. At the same time, it may not always be possible to solve some problems, and therefore it is essential to have an established grievance procedure.

Due process refers to an established procedure requiring certain prescribed steps that are designed to safeguard the legal rights of the individual under the Fourteenth Amendment. For example, when a person is accused of some wrongdoing and could be fired or suspended from the job or denied the right to participate in sport, that person is protected legally by having the right to pursue a judicial procedure that enables both sides to present their facts before a final decision is made. In general, procedural due process includes the individual's right (1) to be informed of all charges and complaints, (2) to a hearing, (3) to secure counsel, (4) to have adequate time to prepare and respond to the charge or complaint, (5) to present his or her side of the issue, (6) to call witnesses and to cross-examine opposing witnesses and parties, and (7) to a fair trial.

EVALUATION

Managers and supervisors need to establish methods to accurately assess staff effectiveness; to make sound decisions for retention, salary adjustments, promotion, and tenure; and to help staff members improve and grow. Management should encourage a program of evaluation. Staff members need assistance and support to improve their effectiveness. Records should be maintained to determine and chart progress.

Some guidelines for evaluating staff members follow:

Appraisal should involve staff members themselves. Evaluation is a cooperative venture,

◆ **CHECKLIST FOR EFFECTIVE WORKING RELATIONSHIPS AMONG MANAGERS, SUPERVISORS, PHYSICAL EDUCATORS, AND ATHLETIC DIRECTORS**

	Yes	No
1. Job descriptions of all positions are formulated, written, and disseminated to each individual involved.		
2. Policies are cooperatively formulated.		
3. Staff members are encouraged to participate in the determination of policies. Management uses faculty committees to develop policies.		
4. Policies cover priorities in the use of physical education and sport facilities.		
5. Policies have been developed and are in writing for the major areas of the enterprise, as well as specifically for physical education and sport.		
6. Departmental policies and procedures are up to date and complete.		
7. Board establishes and approves policies and programs.		
8. Physical educators and coaches know the policies of their organization and work within this framework.		
9. Open channels of communication are maintained between manager, supervisor, and staff.		
10. Preservice, in-service, and staff development education is provided.		
11. Staff members are encouraged to participate in the activities of professional organizations.		
12. Supervisors act in an advisory, and not a managerial, capacity.		
13. The teaching load of all instructors is equitable in that such factors as the following are considered: work hours per week and number of clientele per week.		
14. Physical education and sport programs are open to all and conducted according to sound educational principles.		
15. Policies are in writing and disseminated and cover the organization and management of sport.		
16. Coaches are certified in physical education, teacher education, or coaching.		
17. The group process is effectively used in staff and committee meetings.		
18. There is a strong belief in and a willingness to have democratic management.		
19. Staff meetings are well organized.		
20. New staff members are oriented with respect to responsibilities, policies, and other items essential to their effective functioning in the organization.		
21. Departmental budgets and other reports are submitted on time and in proper form.		
22. Staff members attend meetings regularly.		
23. Staff members participate in curriculum studies.		
24. Class interruptions are kept to an absolute minimum.		
25. Proper management channels are followed.		
26. Relationships with colleagues are based on mutual integrity, understanding, and respect.		
27. Management is interested in the human problems of the organization.		
28. Maximal opportunity is provided for personal self-fulfillment consistent with organization requirements.		
29. Department heads are selected on the basis of qualifications rather than seniority.		
30. Staff members are enthusiastic about their work.		
31. All personnel are provided opportunities to contribute to the improved functioning of the organization.		

> ### ◈ CHECKLIST FOR EFFECTIVE WORKING RELATIONSHIPS AMONG MANAGERS, SUPERVISORS, PHYSICAL EDUCATORS, AND ATHLETIC DIRECTORS—cont'd
>
> 32. The board's executive officer executes policy.   ———— ————
> 33. Faculty and staff assignments are educationally sound.   ———— ————
> 34. Management works continually to improve the working conditions of personnel.   ———— ————
> 35. Responsibilities are equitably distributed.   ———— ————
> 36. Management provides recreational and social outlets for the staff.   ———— ————
> 37. Management recognizes and records quality work.   ———— ————
> 38. Physical educators and coaches seek to improve themselves professionally.   ———— ————
> 39. Physical educators and coaches view with proper perspective their special fields in the total enterprise.   ———— ————
> 40. Physical educators and coaches organize and plan their programs to best meet the needs and interests of the participants.   ———— ————
> 41. Physical educators and coaches continually evaluate themselves and the professional job they are doing in the organization.   ———— ————
> 42. Budgetary allocations are equitably made among departments.   ———— ————
> 43. Management is sensitive to the specific abilities and interests of staff.   ———— ————
> 44. Physical educators and coaches take an active role in planning.   ———— ————
> 45. Physical education objectives are consistent with general education objectives.   ———— ————
> 46. Management recognizes and gives respect and prestige to each area of specialization in the organization.   ———— ————
> 47. Physical educators and coaches are consulted when new facilities are planned in their areas of specialization.   ———— ————
> 48. Funds are available for professional library materials, professional travel, and quality in-service programs.   ———— ————
> 49. Physical educators and coaches carefully consider constructive criticism when given by the management.   ———— ————
> 50. Management is skilled in organization and administration.   ———— ————

and staff members should be included in developing the criteria for evaluation because they need to understand the process.

Evaluation should be centered on performance. The job to be accomplished should be the focus, with extraneous factors considered as secondary.

Evaluation should be concerned with helping staff members grow on the job. The purpose of evaluation is to help individuals evaluate themselves and develop or maintain strengths and reduce weaknesses.

Evaluation should look to the future. It should be concerned with developing an improved physical education and sport program and a better organization.

Evaluation of staff members should be well organized. A step-by-step approach with clearly outlined evaluation criteria should be provided for both teacher and coach.

Sturtevant[14] suggests that the use of management techniques can be very helpful in assessing programs. Problems such as depressed economic conditions, changing enrollments, cost effectiveness, and increased travel and competition can be analyzed more objectively by using management techniques to improve productivity, increase efficiency, and reduce costs. When such techniques are employed and departmental and programmatic assessment has taken place and has been examined, then informed decision making can take place.

METHODS OF EVALUATION

Some methods of evaluating instructors follow:

Observation of teachers/coaches. Teachers and coaches should be notified in advance that the observation will take place, and a conference should follow the observation, with the performance outcomes being discussed and evaluated.

Student progress. With this method, standardized tests are used to determine what progress the student has made as a result of exposure to the teacher or coach.

Ratings. Ratings vary and may consist of an overall estimate of a teacher's or coach's effectiveness or consist of separate evaluations of specific teacher/coach behaviors and traits. Self-ratings may also be used. Ratings may be conducted by peers, by students, or by management personnel and may include judgments based on observation of student or team progress. To be effective, rating scales must be based on criteria that maintain objectivity, reliability, sensitivity, validity, and utility.

At colleges and universities the evaluation of teacher performance is sometimes more difficult than at other schools because of the unwillingness of the faculty to permit managers or others to observe them. Various methods have been devised to rate faculty members, including statements from department heads and ratings by peers, students, supervisors, and other management personnel. The athletic director usually rates the coaches' performance.

What constitutes effective evaluation as it relates to a teacher/coach in a particular school or college? Research reveals, for example, only a slight correlation between intelligence and the rated success of an instructor. Therefore, within reasonable limits, the degree of intelligence a teacher possesses seems to have little value as a criterion. The relationship of knowledge of subject matter to effectiveness appears to depend on the particular teaching situation. A teacher's demonstration of good scholarship (e.g., publication record) appears to have little relationship to good teaching. Some evidence indicates that teachers who have demonstrated high levels of professional knowledge on National Teachers Examinations are more effective teachers. The relationship of experience to teacher/coaching effectiveness also seems to have questionable value. Experience during the first 5 years of teaching seems to enhance teacher effectiveness but then levels off. Little, if any, relationship has been found between teaching effectiveness and cultural background, socioeconomic status, gender, or marital status. More systematic research, however, must be accomplished in this domain to establish what constitutes sound teaching and coaching effectiveness.

Accountability. Accountability may be defined as a means of holding the teacher or coach (and other staff members) responsible for what the students or other individuals learn or achieve.

How can accountability be assessed? The first obstacle that must be overcome to have valid accountability is the acceptance by teachers and coaches of certain objectives that must be met. This can usually be accomplished by developing performance objectives. Once objectives have been developed, the student, coach, and instructor know what is expected of them. Accountability can be based on how well the students satisfy the stated performance objectives. Some have suggested that student performance should be a basis for merit pay increases for teachers and coaches. This method of outcome-based education has its pros and cons.

Student evaluations. The student is the one most exposed to the teacher or coach and his or her method. Therefore the student should have some input concerning the evaluation process.

Some factors that students feel relate to teacher or coach effectiveness include knowledge of subject, fairness, interest in students, patience, leadership that is amicable but firm, enthusiasm, and skill in activities.

Many teachers are using student opinion questionnaires for teacher evaluation. The student is asked to respond to multiple choice or Likert scale questions that indicate items such as (1) interest level in activity, (2) skills learned, (3) time spent outside of class on activity, (4) knowledge gained, and (5) rating of instructor concerning course objectives, understandability of instructions, organization of presentation, enthusiasm, knowledge, skill, and accessibility to students. Space is often left for students to express themselves in paragraph form concerning recommended changes in curriculum. teaching style, or method.

Self-evaluation. An area of evaluation sometimes overlooked is self-evaluation, which is often the key to self-improvement. One should ask himself or herself some of the following questions: Have I been innovative? Do I alter my teaching to meet the different ability levels? Are my classes planned well in advance to ensure adequate teaching space, equipment, and facility use? Do I involve all my students and athletes? Do I stress cognitive, psychosocial, and behavioral objectives? Do I change my activities and practices from year to year and try new concepts such as contact grading, performance objectives, and self-directed and cooperative learning? Do I continually evaluate my programs? Do I try to improve myself by continuing my education?

Questions such as these can help the teacher and coach begin the process of self-evaluation. Self-evaluation is not easy, but it can be a valuable assessment tool and may help improve both the teacher's and coach's performance.

Independent Evaluators

In recent years the trend has been moving toward using independent evaluators because they may be more objective in assessing a teacher's and coach's abilities or a program's effectiveness. Independent evaluators should be thoroughly trained and familiar with the subject they are evaluating and should have a teaching, coaching, and administrative background. Often evaluators are drawn from consultant groups, professional organizations, or colleges and universities. The evaluators should have no previous links with present organizational personnel or the institution being evaluated.

Evaluating the Prospective Teacher and Coach

The competence of the prospective teacher and coach is an important facet of the total educational evaluation system. Traditionally the undergraduate education major was evaluated in terms of grade point average, completion of required course work including student teaching experience, and a minimum grade level in major subjects. Such evaluation

techniques obviously are not sufficient to produce quality teachers. New assessment criteria must be established to include such factors as (1) comprehensive testing to ascertain mastery of both general and specific knowledge, as well as teacher education objectives; (2) performance testing based on teaching task analysis; and (3) an internship to develop teaching and coaching skills.

The prospective teacher and coach should be field oriented, with much of his or her undergraduate training spent in school-related or community-based tasks. During undergraduate years, the individual should have experience in grading papers, keeping records, individual tutoring, and teaching and coaching experience. The teacher or coach who has graduated from such an experiential-based program and has satisfied the assessment criteria will be a better teacher or coach and will also have an easier and more enjoyable adjustment to the first few years of teaching. Many teacher preparation programs are extending their programs an additional year to provide such extensive in-school training and preparation.

Performance-Based Teacher Education

The trend today, as has been pointed out earlier in this text, is toward performance- or outcome-based teacher education. Under this plan the prospective teacher or coach is evaluated, not in terms of courses taken, but in terms of certain competencies (skills, knowledge, abilities) that have been determined essential to satisfactory teaching or coaching. The prospective teacher is evaluated by scientific assessment techniques that are performance based. A major consideration is whether the individual possesses or can develop the skills requisite to changing student-athlete behavior through his or her teaching and coaching.

Evaluation of Physical Educators in Other Settings

Much of what has been said about the evaluation of teachers of physical education and coaches is also true about the evaluation of physical education professionals who work in capacities other than in school environs. They are also held accountable for the effective performance of assigned duties. This accountability is determined, for the most part, by on-the-job observation and by opinions elicited from persons who have been served by the instructors, as well as by their productivity. One form of productivity in a commercial establishment, such as a health and fitness club, unfortunately, is how many customers are attracted and the bottom line profit or loss statement. This situation is like the win-loss ratio for the coach, which although it may seem unfair, appears to be the nature of the game.

The main concern of all physical educators and coaches, wherever they are employed, is to do the best job possible and let the evaluation take care of itself. In other words, one should be enthusiastic, develop as much expertise as possible concerning the position and responsibilities one has, and provide the best experience possible to all persons being served. One should also strive to develop good human relations and rapport with everyone concerned. If these suggestions are followed, the physical educator and coach should not have to worry about the evaluation process. The satisfaction of doing the best job possible will lead to productivity, and advancement will result.

SUMMARY

One of the most important functions that management has to perform is that of personnel management. Management is responsible for such actions as establishing policies under which the staff will operate, seeing that staff morale is high, recruiting qualified members for the organization according to federal and state equal opportunity guidelines, providing adequate supervision, employing group dynamics and cooperative approaches in the achievement of organizational goals, and providing creative ways to prevent such problems as undue stress and teacher and coach burnout. Furthermore, managers must be able to work harmoniously with exclusive representatives and the various publics in general. Last, staff members need to be evaluated periodically in an objective and fair manner so that performance can be improved and deserving staff members are appropriately rewarded.

◆ **SELF-ASSESSMENT ACTIVITIES**

These activities will assist students in determining if material and competencies presented in this chapter have been mastered:

1. Define what is meant by *personnel management* and *supervision* and describe the guiding principles for a physical education supervisor.
2. If you were hiring a physical educator in a health and fitness club or corporate setting, what qualifications would you look for?
3. Prepare a step-by-step procedure for the recruitment, selection, orientation, and in-service and professional development training of a new member of a physical education staff.
4. You are scheduled to be interviewed by a superintendent of schools who is looking for a person to supervise the work of coaches employed within the school system. Discuss the evaluation technique that you would employ to retain those coaches within your program. Present to your class what you told the superintendent. Then have the class decide whether you were hired for the position.
5. Develop a performance-based outcome rating scale you would use to evaluate the work of a physical educator at a senior high school.
6. Prepare a job description for a junior high or middle school girls' volleyball coach.
7. A teacher named in a misconduct complaint by a student should be entitled to what due process steps?

REFERENCES

1. Broderick R: Non-certified coaches, *Journal of Physical Education, Recreation and Dance* 55:38, May/June 1984.
2. Case RW: Leadership in sport—the situational leadership theory, *Journal of Physical Education, Recreation and Dance* 55:15, Jan 1984.
3. Fisher R, Brown S: *Getting together—building relationships as we negotiate,* Boston, 1988, Houghton-Mifflin.
4. Hale RL, Hoelscher DR, Kowal RE: *Quest for quality,* Minneapolis, Mn, 1987, Tennant Company.
5. Hershey P, Blanchard K: *Management of organizational behavior,* Englewood Cliffs, NJ, 1982, Prentice-Hall.
6. Horton L: What to do about teacher burnout? *Journal of Physical Education, Recreation and Dance* 55:69, Mar 1984.

7. Hunter M: *Mastering coaching and supervision,* El Segundo, Ca, 1989, Tip Publications.
8. Kelley JE, Brightwell S: Should interscholastic coaches be certified? *Journal of Physical Education, Recreation and Dance,* 55:49, Mar 1984.
9. Krotee ML, Hatfield FC: *The theory and practice of physical activity,* Dubuque, Ia, 1979, Kendell/Hunt.
10. Langlois S: *Faculty fitness: a program to combat teacher burnout, Update,* March 1981, American Alliance for Health, Physical Education, Recreation, and Dance.
11. Prentice WE, Bucher CA: *Fitness for college and life,* St Louis, 1988, Mosby–Year Book.
12. Selye H: *The stress of life,* New York, 1976, McGraw-Hill.
13. Shaw M: *Group dynamics: the psychology of small group behavior,* New York, 1971.
14. Sturtevant M: Use management techniques to assess programs, *Journal of Physical Education, Recreation and Dance,* 55:48, May/June 1984.

SUGGESTED READINGS

- Iacocca L: *Iacocca—an autobiography,* New York, 1984, Bantam.
Tells the story of one of today's most successful managers in industry. As Chief Executive Officer of the Chrysler Corporation, he transformed a dying company into a great success. Relates how he works with his staff to achieve results.
- Kraus RG, Curtis JE: *Creative management in recreation, parks, and leisure services,* St Louis, 1986, Mosby–Year Book.
Outlines the scope and process of personnel management, including information concerning such items as job descriptions, competency-based approaches to hiring personnel, professional preparation, employment standards, supervisory practices, training approaches, and working with unions.
- Lehr C: Meeting staff development needs of teachers, *Journal of Physical Education, Recreation and Dance* 55:73, Aug 1984.
Presents what mature professional teachers want in the way of staff development. Such things as interaction with peers, self-awakening, and how to improve teaching and communication skills are at the forefront.
- Marburger CL: *One school at a time, school based management, a process for change,* Columbia, Md, 1988, The National Committee for Citizens in Education.
Provides parents, students, school boards, and administrators with specific information about the concept of school based management. SBM is a new approach to decentralized organization in which decisions are made by those who know and care about quality education.
- Peters T: *Thriving on chaos,* New York, 1987, Alfred Knopf.
Introduces the revolution of personnel recruiting, and covers topics such as reducing structure and the reorganization of the manager's role. Presents a model for empowering personnel and measuring what is important to the organization.
- Rogers EJ: *Getting hired,* Englewood Cliffs, NJ, 1982, Prentice-Hall.
As Vice President and Director of Personnel for a large corporation, the author illustrates the importance of such things as resumes, interviews, planning, and how to get off to a good start in a new position.
- Zaleznik A: *The managerial mystique: restoring leadership in business,* New York, 1989, Harper & Row.
The author describes the relationship of positive leadership to successful management, which can be applied to any organization or profession.

CHAPTER 8

Program Development

▶ **Instructional Objectives and Competencies To Be Achieved**

After reading this chapter the student should be able to

- Explain why program development is an important part of the management process and what programs of physical education and sport should accomplish.
- Identify the factors that influence program development.
- Outline a step-by-step process for program de-

velopment, including the personnel or groups who will be involved.
- Describe a systems- and competency-based approach to program development.
- Discuss significant elements of program development.
- Develop a procedure for evaluating a program.

Chapter 7 focused on personnel management, one of the most important functions that directors, chairs, and other individuals involved with managerial functions in physical education and sport have to assume. Chapter 8 presents another important function of management—to provide the leadership and support needed to develop a program that will achieve the objectives of physical education and sport.

The term *program development* as used in this text refers to the total learning experiences provided to consumers to achieve the objectives of physical education and sport. It is concerned with the component parts of physical education and sport programs as well as with the resources (e.g., human, physical, financial, informational, and technical) involved in implementing these learning experiences. Physical education and sport management is involved with programs in schools and colleges, as well

as various public- and private-sector organizations. Today the trend is to provide carefully planned programs based on the following considerations: (1) the needs and abilities of the participant or user, (2) the needs of society, (3) the practical usefulness of various knowledge and skills, and (4) the social psychology of learning.

WHAT PROGRAM GOALS SHOULD THE PHYSICAL EDUCATION MANAGEMENT SUPPORT?

The main goals the physical education program should strive to accomplish pertain to four areas. The physical education curriculum should (1) develop health- and motor performance–related fitness, (2) develop skill in activities, (3) develop an understanding and appreciation of physical activity, and (4) provide a meaningful psychosocial experience.

220

Develop Health- and Motor Performance–Related Fitness

The physical education program should develop such physical characteristics as adequate cardiovascular and respiratory endurance and function, proper body composition, strength, flexibility, body awareness, muscular power and endurance, coordination, speed, reaction time, balance, agility, and proper posture.

Develop Skill in Activities

The physical education program should also develop skill in activities including basic movement patterns and fundamentals (e.g., running, jumping, throwing, skipping), as well as individual, team, and lifetime sports. Gymnastics, aquatics, and rhythmic activities (such as dance) that incorporate such factors as time, space, and flow should be integral components of the program. Management should also provide support for activities that will assist in any way the development of the various components of health- and motor performance–related physical fitness (e.g., exercise, jogging, orienteering, outdoor pursuit).

Develop an Understanding of Physical Activity

The program should also foster an understanding and appreciation of, among other things, the contri-

Students learn the art of stretching.

bution of physical activity to physical health (reduction of risk factors, weight control, nutrition), of biomechanical principles (role of gravity, levers, acceleration, force), and the contribution of physical health to mental health (relief of nervous tension and stress, self-esteem). Also, physical education and sport managers should help students and other individuals assess their own fitness level and needs and assist them in setting goals that lead to a healthful lifestyle.

Provide a Meaningful Psychosocial Experience

Physical education and sport programs should provide for such psychosocial goals as the human desire for affiliation, mastery and success in play activities, cooperative effort, recognition of ability, self-reliance, respect for leadership, and followership.

IMPORTANCE OF PROGRAM DEVELOPMENT AND THE ROLE OF MANAGEMENT

Sergiovanni[8] indicates that management should pay attention to three basic concerns regarding program development. The first is what ought to be taught (the ideal program), the second is what is being taught (the real program), and the third is what can be taught (the practical program).

Program development should determine what must be learned and achieved and then should provide the means for seeing that these goals are accomplished. Because no two people are exactly alike, a wide range of physical activity and sport experiences that meet the requirements of all individuals is needed.

Management plays an important part in program planning. The goal of management is to provide quality teaching and coaching, an optimal learning environment, and healthful and safe experiences and activities to achieve the established objectives. Because problems constantly arise and unmet needs continue to exist or remain unrecognized, continuous and adaptable planning is always a management priority. The manager provides the leadership required to accomplish this dynamic task.

Program construction requires the selection, guidance, and evaluation of experiences and activities to achieve both long-term and more immediate short-term goals. It provides for a periodic evaluation of the entire program to make changes whenever necessary. It considers factors such as participants, the community, the organization, existing facilities, personnel, time allotments, national trends, and state and federal laws and regulations. Program construction sets up a conceptual framework for a progressive plan that serves as a guide to physical education and sport personnel so that they are better able to achieve organizational and educational goals.

Although program development is in many cases a staff and faculty responsibility, management plays a very important role in bringing about program reform. Management assesses the organization's needs, assigns tasks, and sees that the mechanism is set in motion to develop a quality program that meets the organization's objectives.

PROGRAM DEVELOPMENT PLAYERS

Program planning is a role and responsibility that involves the entire organization. The considerations of managers, staff members, professional agencies and groups, participants, parents and community leaders, and other significant individuals are crucial to program development.

Managers

Managers are key personnel in program planning. They serve as the catalytic force that sets curriculum and program studies into motion; the leadership that encourages and stimulates interest in providing optimal learning experiences; the barrier clearers who provide the time, place, and resources to accomplish the task; and the implementers who help carry out appropriate recommendations of such plans.

McNeil[6] points to the roles of principals and superintendents of schools in program development. The principal's role is to serve as a management link between the central office, parents, and staff when it comes to program development. Superintendents of schools influence program development by discussing curriculum with boards of education, by seeing that state and federal government mandates are implemented, and by providing for pre- and in-service training and professional staff development of teachers and coaches.

Other management obligations are to place together a team of program developers who can work cooperatively and effectively, provide this team with direction (e.g., organizational philosophy and goals), and supply the team with the necessary motivation as well as human, technical, and informational resources to accomplish the task of designing a quality program.

Staff

Staff members lie at the grass roots level of program development. The staff member can contribute his or her experiences and knowledge and provide data to support recommendations of desired programmatic changes. Teachers' and coaches' comments, based on their immediate understanding of students' needs and interests, can make a valuable contribution. Committees are an effective way to use staff members. They can be established to study specific instructional areas; identify deficiencies, weaknesses, and inequities; and recommend immediate needs of participants, as well as means of implementing changes. Staff input and perceived ownership are necessary before a program is designed and implemented.

Professional Groups and Agencies

In most states there are many groups and agencies who can help in physical education and sport planning. These include the state departments of public instruction, education, and/or health; colleges and universities; corporate groups; private voluntary organizations (PVOs); state high school associations or leagues; the NCAA; and state AAHPERD affiliates. All these organizations as well as various community-based service groups can provide meaningful input. These groups may provide program guides, courses of study, teaching aids and materials, consulting service, and advice that will prove to be invaluable in the planning of any program.

The Participant

The participants (e.g., student-athletes or senior citizens) should play a part in program development. Their thinking in regard to what constitutes desira-

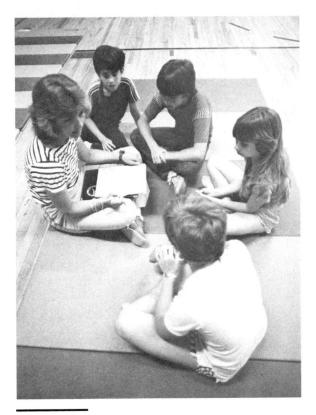

Children and teacher plan the next activity.

ble activities or instructional strategy for program delivery, for example, is vital. Participants today are more actively involved in expressing their program desires. They want to be heard, be identified, and play a part in planning the various activities and experiences that a quality program should provide.

Parents, Significant Others, and Community Leaders

Dialogue with parents and other interested citizens can sometimes help communicate to the public what the school or institution is trying to achieve. Parents and other community-minded people can make significant contributions by supplying input in terms of desired outcomes and other programmatic recommendations. Parents, students, and the community for the most part are also actively expressing their program desires and views concerning the conduct

of the program. It is vital to ensure their full participation and satisfaction in order to manage any program in an effective and efficient manner.

Other Significant Individuals

Program development should employ the services of all interested individuals. Professionals such as physicians, nurses, lawyers, architects, recreation leaders, and corporate leaders (e.g., finance and marketing executives), who reside in the community can all make worthwhile contributions by examining offerings and providing input for various programmatic initiatives. It is management's charge to ensure the full participation of all who may significantly contribute to building a quality program.

FACTORS THAT INFLUENCE PROGRAM DEVELOPMENT

Factors that directly and indirectly influence program development in physical education and sport include (1) the community; (2) federal and state legislation; (3) research; (4) professional organizations; (5) attitudes of managers, faculty, students, and consumers; (6) facilities and equipment; (7) scheduling classes; (8) class size; (9) physical education and coaching staff; (10) climate and geographical considerations; and (11) social forces.

The Community

The community has considerable influence on physical education and sport program development. In public schools and other institutions in particular, the community provides the funds for the program; therefore there are vital implications for program development. The community wants to be, and should be, involved.

In the Darien, Connecticut public schools, a task force on physical education curriculum was appointed by the board of education. The task force consisted of 13 members who were active in the community. This group established the objectives they wished to accomplish and the strategy they would use to achieve their goals. The strategy provided for a survey of 600 students in the school system, the district's coaches and staff members, 1000 Darien residents selected from tax rolls, and 40 organizations with a direct or indirect interest in sport and recreation. Furthermore, the task force established evaluation criteria for program assessment.

The result of this community involvement project was rewriting K-12 curriculum guides, setting up student advisory boards and student recreational sport councils, creating a physical education inventory system, creating faculty manager positions in the secondary school, instituting a full-day in-service workshop for physical education teachers and coaches, holding regular meetings with community agencies, and developing a coaches' handbook.[7]

Communities are becoming more aware of their role and responsibility in the planning and program development process, and good management practice allows for full and active participation. The manager in turn must be aware of the physical characteristics (boundaries, housing, parks) of the community, who lives there, and its economic base, political systems, and culture.

Federal Legislation

Although the governmental authority primarily responsible for education is the local authority and the state, the federal government is active in shaping educational programs. The Department of Health and Human Services is responsible for recommending many legislative changes in various fields, including education.

Title IX had a profound effect on physical education and sport programs by prohibiting sex discrimination in educational programs. As a result, many school districts have had to revise the curriculum to meet the mandate. Many more sports teams have also been brought into the educational fold, providing for marked increases in female participation at all levels.

PL 94-142 and its continual upgrading has also had an effect on school programs in physical education and sport by requiring schools to provide educational services for persons with disabilities from birth through age 21. The upgrading of facilities and personnel has been a direct result of these mandates. Equal opportunity laws and affirmative action continue to a play a role in the conduct and staffing of any program.

Sensitivity to issues of diversity has also brought about initiatives such as NASPE's Multicultural Education Project. Multicultural physical education shall:

- Include examination of prejudice based on race, ethicity, language, religion, gender, and exceptionality;
- Be directed toward elimination of stereotypes and biases and toward achievement of full commitment to cultural pluralism;
- Be designed for students of both minority and dominant cultures; and
- Promote equity and the maintenance of diverse cultural identities.

To further clarify the definition, the following components were established:

- Appreciation of (and pride in) a person's own unique cultural heritage, as reflected in history, philosophy and values, customs and traditions, and contemporary concerns.
- Appreciation of (and respect for) persons of different ethnic groups and their varying cultural perspectives.
- Appreciation of (and respect for) persons of

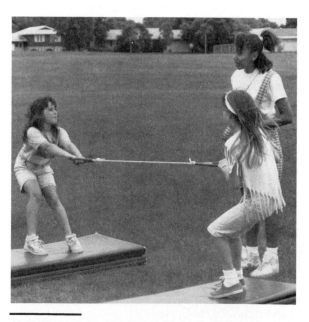

Students and peer teacher work at tug of war.

both sexes and their differing cultural perspectives.

- Appreciation of (and respect for) persons of all racial groups and their varying cultural perspectives.
- Appreciation of (and respect for) persons of other religious affiliations and their varying cultural perspectives.
- Recognition of differences in goals of individuals within a culturally diverse population.
- Recognition of common goals and concerns of all persons within a culturally diverse population, as a basis for positive personal interaction within and across cultural groups.

All programs, including those of physical education and sport, must lead the way to provide fair and equitable opportunity for all.

State Legislation

The state is the governmental authority primarily responsible for education. Local boards of education are responsible to the state for operating schools in their respective local school districts. They must adhere to the rules and regulations established by state departments of education. Most schools are also members of their state high school leagues, which in turn set regulations for participation in many extra-curricular activities including sport.

State departments of education set policies concerning credits to be earned for graduation, courses (e.g., physical education, health) to be included in the curriculum, and requirements concerning physical education including the number of hours and days per week, as well as the opportunity for participation by persons with disabilities.

In most cases, the regulations adopted by state departments of education set minimum standards. In an ideal situation, local school management sets minimum standards, and management must continue to play a pro-active role in lobbying for daily physical education initiatives and sport programs at both the state and local governmental levels.

Research

Although some school districts rely on research to assist them in developing and revising their physical education and sport programs, too many schools fail to recognize the value of the latest research concerning health, physical education, and sport.

Important research studies that affect curriculum offerings in physical education are being conducted by researchers in a variety of disciplines. An example of the results of research that have influenced physical education programs are studies relating to the fitness of American children and youths. Results have indicated that American children and youths are lacking in many fitness components, and curricula have been revised accordingly to upgrade physical fitness levels.

Relevant research in the social, psychological, and movement sciences, as they relate to human movement and learning, should guide physical education program planning. Researchers are investigating topics ranging from cooperative learning to effective movement patterns, and mainstreaming to exercise adherence; their research has implications for program development at all levels of education. The decade of the 1990s provides researchers with an opportunity and challenge to meaningfully contribute to the classroom, field, pool, and gymnasium. This research dimension for the most part must be enhanced and advanced through cooperative pro-

Visualizaton research assists student-athletes at the University of Minnesota.

gram ventures, and the gap between research and practical application must be bridged.

Professional Organizations

National, state, and local professional organizations are constantly engaged in activities that influence physical education and sport programs. Through such activities as workshops, conferences, research, and publications, these organizations provide needed information in program development.

AAHPERD for example, sponsors many national, regional, and state conferences of vital importance to physical education and sport professionals. Research studies; workshops; demonstrations of new activities, equipment, methods, and materials; and a general exchange of ideas are presented at these conferences. Also, on request AAHPERD will suggest knowledgeable consultants to work with school and college personnel in program development, evaluation, and revision. The National Education Association (NEA), American College of Sport Medicine, and various sporting and coaching organizations also provide meaningful program and personnel support services.

State and local professional organizations also provide valuable program development resources and information. These associations should be joined and supported to keep abreast of the latest trends, issues, concerns, and activities. This is not only good public relations, but also a way to keep the program in step with societal demands.

Attitudes of Managers, Faculty, Students, and Participants

In education the scope and content of physical education and sport programs are influenced by school managers and teachers. If physical education and sport are viewed as an integral part of the school program, attempts will be made to provide the necessary support, financial and otherwise, for a quality program. If, on the other hand, they are viewed as extraneous, attempts to diminish and downsize sound programs may be expected. The attitudes of teachers and students toward physical education and sport can also affect the kind of program offered.

Management has the responsibility for interpreting and setting the tone for the program to students,

Arnold Schwarzenegger, Chair of the President's Council on Physical Fitness and Sports, addresses AAHPERD members.

faculty, school boards, and the community. A written statement of philosophy and policies should be provided and included in the curriculum guide, as well as other school materials (e.g., orientation handbook).

Students' and participants' attitudes should not be overlooked by program planners. The way students and student-athletes feel about their programs will influence their participation in, and support for, the program. A well-designed needs-and-opinions questionnaire is one way of determining attitudes toward physical education and sport programs.

Facilities and Equipment

The provision of adequate physical resources (e.g., facilities, equipment, maintenance, and upkeep) can help in influencing attitudes and facilitating programmatic success. Attractive indoor and outdoor facilities entice participation and adherence and thus help in shaping a quality program. The extent and nature of the facilities depend on such factors as the number of students, financial support, and the geographical location (e.g., urban, rural) of the school. Chapter 9 will provide in-depth treatment of facility management.

Class Schedules and Sports Offered

The number of classes of physical education provided each week and the length of these classes affect the program. The minimum time for all subjects is set by state departments of education. However, local school managers can increase the amount of time spent on physical education, as with other subjects.

The number of sports offered for both males and females also depends on attitudes, financial resources, and the interests of the community, school, and participants. It is the manager's role to marshal these human resources to provide quality, equitable opportunities and programs for all.

Class Size

The type of activity being taught and the number of teachers will determine the class size. It is recommended that under normal circumstances the number of children in a physical education class not ex-

ceed 30. Size of classes in adapted/developmental physical education should be determined by the specific needs of the students. In school districts where physical education is accepted as an integral part of the school curriculum, class size is kept at a level that promotes optimal learning. The school management, and sometimes the local exclusive representative, can do much to see that class size is reasonable in order to achieve learning goals.

Physical Education and Coaching Staff

The number and qualifications of physical education and coaching staff members influence the program. Are teachers and coaches qualified and certified? Is there a supervisor of physical education and/or athletic director to coordinate physical education and sport in the school district? These are important questions that need to be considered because sound physical education and sport programs depend on the quality of the teaching and coaching staffs. The faculty of every school should include personnel who have expertise in physical education and sport.

Physical education specialists responsible for delivering the subject matter should have completed a sequence of courses relating to their specialty. Too often physical education is taught by individuals with limited physical education experiences. Coaches often are assigned because of willingness rather than qualification. Management should require that only qualified and certified personnel be employed.

Climate and Geographical Considerations

The content of the program in physical education and sport is also influenced by environmental conditions including weather and geographical location. Program designers should take advantage of the environmental aspects of school locations. For example, many outdoor activities can be scheduled in schools in areas where the weather and terrain are favorable (e.g., rock climbing, sailing). Schools in areas with an abundance of water might offer various aquatic activities, whereas those located in northern environs might include skating, alpine and nordic skiing instruction, and winter camping. Management's role is to turn climatic and environmental

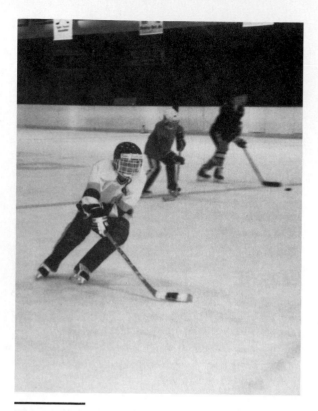

Winter activities are popular in some regions of the country.

barriers into challenges, and to transform creative ideas into program offerings.

Social Forces and Pressure Groups

Social forces such as the civil and equal rights movements, religion, booster clubs, mass communication, student activism, and sports promotion have implications for program development. Times, customs, and habits change; rules vary; and the role of schools and institutions and their responsibilities to society are also altered over time.

Influential groups ranging from the National Rifle Association to labor unions, ROTC to PTOs, and alumni boards to booster clubs should be monitored in order to reflect their positive contributions in program development and implementation.

STEPS IN PROGRAM DEVELOPMENT

The major steps involved in program development include (1) determining the objectives, (2) analyzing the objectives in terms of the program, (3) analyzing the objectives in terms of activities, (4) providing program guides and teaching aids, and (5) assessing the program.

Determining the Objectives

Determining the objectives involves studying such factors as the nature of society, developmental program trends, the learning process, and the needs of the participant so that objectives may be clearly formulated.

If the main objective of physical education and sport is to produce a physically educated person, this should be the focus of the program objectives. For example, a physically educated person[3] is one who possesses the following characteristics:

- Has sufficient skills to perform a variety of physical activities
- Participates regularly in physical activity
- Is physically fit
- Knows the benefits, costs, risks, and obligations of involvement in physical activity
- Values the effect of regular physical activity in maintaining a healthful lifestyle

Analyzing the Objectives in Terms of the Program

Having determined the program objectives, and knowing the characteristics of the participant, as well as the various constraints associated with the task, those developing a program can outline and analyze broad categories of experiences and activities and assign relative emphases to the various phases of the process. The specialized fields of physical education and sport should be viewed as part of the total educational program and process. As a consequence, their specific objectives should relate to the overall objectives of the organization.

Analyzing the Objectives in Terms of Activities

The next step is to focus attention on the activities needed to achieve the set objectives. For example, the cognitive, affective, and psychomotor needs of the participants necessitate providing a wide range of physical activities, as well as emphasizing the growth and development characteristics of participants throughout the life span. In addition, enabling participants to become self-educative throughout their lives provides a tremendous challenge to program developers.

Providing Program Guides and Teaching Aids

Curriculum and program guides and teaching aids such as books and visual aids offer opportunities to use educationally sound materials to achieve objectives. Computer software programs, videos, and behavior modification counseling are other means to support program development.

Assessing the Program

Evaluation represents the culmination of the program development process—what actually takes place in the classroom, gymnasium, fitness center, or natatorium. The learning that takes place, physical fitness level achieved, materials and human resources employed, and the outcomes accomplished detrmine the success or failure of program development.

Evaluation is a dynamic process that helps to determine the progress being made in meeting program objectives. It can identify strengths, weaknesses, and omissions, and show where needed resources or emphases might be shifted in order to improve the program. It also helps the participants determine their own progress (e.g., competence, individuality, socialization, integration) within the program and is useful to the manager for interpreting and reporting program outcomes to the public (see the box on p. 230).

SELECTED APPROACHES TO ORGANIZING CURRICULUM EXPERIENCES

Many approaches and models have been designed for the development and organization of curriculum experiences. For example, Jewett and Bain[5] describe what they believe are curriculum designs for contemporary program development. They are listed under the titles of developmental education, humanistic physical education, fitness, movement education, kinesiological studies, play education, and personal meaning.

Three approaches that have been employed to or-

Video feedback is a useful teaching aid; Omaha Public Schools, Omaha, Nebraska.

◈ MANAGEMENT PRINCIPLES TO CONSIDER IN PROGRAM DEVELOPMENT

Although program development varies from organization to organization, the following general principles are applicable to all situations:

Learning experiences and activities should be selected and developed to achieve desired outcomes.

The value of program development is determined by improved instruction and results.

Program development is a continuous and dynamic effort rather than one accomplished at periodic intervals.

The leadership in program development rests primarily with managers and supervisors.

The management should consult (wherever possible and practical) teachers, coaches, laypeople, students, participants, state consultants, and other persons who can contribute to the development of the best program possible. The work should not, however, place an unreasonable demand on any person's time and effort.

Program development depends on a thorough knowledge of the needs and characteristics, developmental levels, capacities, and maturity levels of participants, as well as an understanding of their environments and lifestyles.

Program development should permit staff members to explore sound principles of learning when selecting and developing experiences.

Physical education should be viewed in its broadest scope and include all programs provided by the physical education department, including sport and recreational activity.

Physical education and sport should be integrated with other areas in the organization.

Physical education and sport activities should be selected using valid criteria.

Working relationships should be sought with recreational sport and athletic departments, as well as with community-based and private-sector programs.

---

ganize curriculum experiences are the systems, conceptual, and competency-based approaches.

Systems Approach

In recent years physical educators have tried to develop a more logical means of determining what activities to include in a program. In some cases formulas have been created; in other instances step-by-step procedures have been developed to match activities to goals. Such methods of program development are encouraging because they represent an attempt to make program development a more scientific procedure.

A systems approach for developing a physical education program may be helpful to the physical educator because it provides a scientific, logical, and systematic method for program preparation that meets the needs of the participants. This systems approach to program development is composed of seven basic steps:

1. Identify the developmental objectives to be achieved in physical education (e.g., physical development, neuromuscular development, cognitive development, and social-emotional-affective development).

2. Divide each of the developmental objectives listed in the first step into subobjectives. Identifying the subobjectives brings into sharper focus what must be accomplished and makes the achievement of the developmental objective more manageable. The following are examples of some subobjectives of each of the development objectives:

Physical development objective
Subobjectives: health-related fitness components
Cardiovascular and cardiorespiratory endurance (e.g., 1-mile run/walk)
Muscular strength and endurance (e.g., pull-ups and sit-ups)
Flexibility
Relaxation
Subobjectives: motor performance related
Agility

Balance
Coordination
Posture
Reaction time
Speed and power

Neuromuscular development objective

Subobjectives

Locomotor (e.g., running, skipping, leaping) and nonlocomotor (e.g., stretching, pulling) skills

Movement fundamentals (e.g., throwing, catching, striking)

General motor ability and efficiency

Specific motor ability in game and sport skills (e.g., Hyde archery test, McDonald soccer test)

Cognitive development objective

Subobjectives

Understanding the principles of movement (e.g., gravity, force, time, acceleration, flow)

Knowledge of rules and strategies of games and sports (e.g., Scott badminton knowledge test)

Children use objectives chart for balance beam activity.

Knowledge of contribution of physical activity to health-related fitness

Awareness of contribution of physical activity to academic achievement

Problem-solving ability

Social-emotional-affective development objective

Subobjectives

Sportspersonship

Clarifying values

Cooperation in group work

Positive attitude toward physical education and sport

Development of self-concept

Respect for other students and management

3. Identify participant characteristics in terms of each subobjective identified in step 2. A cardiorespiratory endurance characteristic, for example, of junior high or middle school students under the physical development objective is that they may tire easily during a 1-mile run/walk activity because of their rapid, uneven growth, whereas in grades 10 to 12, students possess a more mature physiological capacity and therefore are better equipped to engage in this type of vigorous activity.

The characteristics of participants at each educational level must be determined in terms of each of the subobjectives identified in step 2. It is now possible to determine the relationship between the goals and specific participant growth and development characteristics.

4. Determine participant needs in relation to the characteristics outlined in step 3. For each subobjective, the needs of the participant must be identified. For example, a cardiorespiratory endurance characteristic of students in grades 7 to 9 indicates that they tire easily. Therefore a need exists for physical education and sport experiences that overcome fatiguing factors associated with time, distance, and game pressures. Students also need guidance concerning nutrition habits, rest, and sleep.

5. Identify appropriate activities. For example, the activities scheduled for students in grades

7 to 9 that meet their needs should include large-muscle activities such as soccer, field hockey, lacrosse, or floor hockey. Use of modified rules, including shortened periods of play, smaller playing areas, frequent timeouts, and unlimited substitutions are recommended. Health-related fitness activities such as jogging, cycling, and walking should also be utilized.

6. List specific performance objectives for the participants in relation to their objectives, characteristics, and needs and the activities appropriate to their age, fitness level, and ability. For each of the subobjectives, specific performance objectives should be listed. For example, a performance objective for the cardiorespiratory endurance subobjective for seventh to ninth grade students could be an exercise that measures cardiorespiratory endurance (e.g., the 600-yard run/walk), where the student is able to perform without undue fatigue, and to promptly achieve heart rate recovery. A performance objective for tenth to twelfth grade students might be having the student engage in a 1-mile run/walk and be able to perform without undue fatigue and with a quick recovery time as measured by pulse rate. Of course, all performance objectives should consider the characteristics and needs of the specific students involved. Performance objectives provide specific levels of accomplishment that indicate whether progression toward the desired goals occurs.

7. Identify the teaching methods, strategies, and procedures that will most effectively achieve the desired goals. These instructional strategies provide for variety and should incorporate sound learning theories (e.g., cooperative learning). They reinforce concepts related to accomplishing the objectives (e.g., follow-through contributes to accuracy, a concept in skill development).

Methods that can be employed to develop the subobjective of cardiorespiratory endurance for seventh to ninth graders include viewing a laboratory experiment comparing conditioned and nonconditioned adults. An explanation of the role and worth of cardiorespiratory endurance in physical development and physical fitness and a presentation of research that outlines the comparative physical fitness level of their United States age-group with others throughout the world may also serve to educate and motivate the participants. Participation in activities that develop this type of endurance, together with an explanation of performance objectives and guidance in practice and self-evaluation, will assist the learner and facilitate efforts toward successful achievement of the objectives.

The seven-step systems approach to curricular program development provides a logical, scientific, step-by-step method for determining the activities that will achieve the objectives, meet the characteristics and needs of participants, and provide the performance or outcome-based objectives to assess whether students are progressing or have met each objective. A systems approach may advance a meaningful physical education program aimed at helping participants become truly physically educated and making physical education a viable, well-planned offering that achieves specific educational and developmental goals.

Conceptual Approach

During the past two decades many disciplines have instituted major curriculum reforms that emphasize the conceptual approach to curriculum development. New curriculum models based on the conceptual approach have been designed for mathematics, science, biology, social studies, and health education.

In addition to studying national curriculum models, physical education curriculum planners and other educators interested in the conceptual approach should also become acquainted with the theoretical aspects of concept development.

To better understand the conceptual approach to curriculum development a definition of a concept is presented. Woodruff[11] defines a concept as "some amount of meaning more or less organized in an individual's mind as a result of sensory perception of external objects or events and the cognitive interpretation of the perceived data."

According to Woodruff, several kinds of concepts can be identified, including concepts that might be a mental construct, an abstraction, a symbolic response, or some other connotation. It should be added that although a concept might be a high-level abstraction, many concepts might also be presented as concrete, easy-to-understand ideas. For example, a concept in exercise science could be related to the cardiac response to exercise: the heart rate increases during exercise. It can be illustrated by having students take their resting pulse rate, engage in exercise, and then take their pulse rate again to note the increase as a result of exercise. Another concept is related to energy metabolism, whereby the body must provide energy compounds needed for the function of any active tissue. This concept is somewhat more abstract than the first. These and other concepts have been tested and found useful for students at the upper elementary school level.

The following example of the conceptual approach is based on movement activities. It is broken down into the key concept, the concept, and subconcepts. Some conceptual statements are then provided:

- *Key concept:* Individual development can be enhanced through movement activities.
- *Concept:* The development of locomotor skills is necessary for effective and efficient movement. These skills are also necessary for later development of competency in specialized games, sports, and other movement activities.
- *Subconcept:* Sprints and distance running are two specialized forms of one locomotor movement—running.

Examples of Conceptual Statements in Physical Education and Sport

Proper techniques and skill in starting are necessary for mastery of sprint running. The ability to understand and carry out the concept of pacing (the idea of running at a gradually increased speed to have enough energy left to sprint the last part of the race)

Starting skills are crucial to sprint running.

is necessary for distance running. Leg strength is important in sprint running. Proper leg strength, endurance, and cardiovascular-respiratory endurance are important concepts in distance running. A knowledge of the cognitive aspects related to both sprint and distance running and a positive attitude about running are necessary to the development of these running skills.

Basic Stuff Series I and II[1]

The National Association of Sport and Physical Education (NASPE) of AAHPERD has created Basic Stuff Series I and II. The purpose behind this project has been to identify the basic knowledge that applies to physical education programs and organize it in a manner that can be utilized by physical educators. It is applicable to elementary and secondary school children and youth at a time when the foundations are being laid down for adult years. It presents—in clear, concise language—basic concepts in the areas of exercise physiology, kinesiology, motor learning, psychosocial aspects of physical education, humanities (art, history, and philosophy), and motor development. A booklet has been prepared covering the basic concepts in each of the six areas; it is designed for pre-service and in-service teachers. Series I represents the body of knowledge that supports the worth and interconnectedness of physical education.

The chapters in each pamphlet in the series share a similar organizational format relating to questions asked by students, such as (1) What do you have (e.g., self-concept, health, weight control) to help me? (2) How do I get it? (3) Why does it happen this way? Concepts are presented and then the student is shown how they can best be grasped, understood, and realized or controlled. It also explains why the concepts are valid and work.

Series II, which has been designed for teachers in the field, provides learning experience booklets with examples of instructional activities for early childhood (ages 3 to 8), childhood (ages 9 to 12), and adolescence (ages 13 to 18). The scientific knowledge in the six areas in Series I is related directly to physical education and sport and enables physical educators and coaches to have at their disposal the basic information and learning activities that will make it

possible to educate the students. General concepts such as how to learn a new skill, how to better one's performance, and the beneficial effects of exercise are identified. The booklets also include ways to present the concepts in activity programs so that students may realize the importance of these concepts. This is accomplished by relating the concepts to the motives most children and young people possess. These motives are health (they want to feel good), appearance (they want to look good), achievement (they want to achieve), social (they want to develop aesthetic and affective qualities), and coping with the environment (they want to survive). Furthermore, the Basic Stuff Series makes it possible for teachers and coaches to tell and show students what concepts are important in physical education and sport, as well as how and why they are important.

Basic Stuff Series I and II have been cooperatively developed by teachers and researchers who are experts in their particular disciplines.

Competency-Based Approach

Competency-based learning has evolved because of a public and professional concern for accountability. Students are taught by means of defined performance objectives based on cognitive, psychomotor, and affective tasks. Students are not in competition with each other, but with themselves and various norms. The teacher becomes a facilitator to learning rather than a taskmaster, and each student proceeds at his or her own rate. In addition, resource materials are made available to students to help further their behavioral and cognitive skills.

How competency-based instruction or learning actually takes place can be better understood by reviewing the competency-based instruction at the high school level in Illinois. The performance objectives are developed and written by a team of physical educators and based on general physical, neuromuscular, cognitive, and social-emotional-affective goals. A competency-based learning unit for tenth-grade gymnastics, for example, is divided into a 10-day introductory unit and a 3-week advanced unit. A lecture and demonstration of the 40 selected gymnastic stunts were presented to the students, followed by an introductory unit in instruction, safety, and practice. The grading system for the introductory unit is based on performance mastery of the number of stunts as determined by the instructor:

16 to 28 stunts = A
10 to 15 stunts = B
6 to 9 stunts = C
3 to 5 stunts = D
0 to 2 stunts = F

The advanced unit might require a 3-week instruction demonstration period for the students continuing from the introductory unit. In this example, a student who satisfactorily completes 29 to 40 stunts might receive an A, 16 to 28 stunts a B, and 10 to 15 stunts a C, etc.

The Cripton Project (West Haven, Ct), entitled "Continuous Progress, K-12," provides another example of the competency-based approach. The project requires that student levels of achievement be divided into 10 blocks consisting of a total of 44 competency packages. Each student is regularly assessed, and a profile card that tracks each student's progress throughout his or her school experience is recorded, moved to computer, and kept on file.

OTHER SELECTED CONSIDERATIONS FOR PROGRAM PLANNING
Health-Related Physical Fitness/Physical Best[2]

AAHPERD, through its Task Force on Youth Fitness, has advocated the general population's need for health-related physical fitness consisting of an emphasis on cardiovascular function, body composition, muscular strength and endurance, and flexibility. These components also represent the ingredients for AAHPERD's Physical Best, a performance-related fitness program.[2] Curriculum designers will want to keep health-related and performance-related fitness in mind in developing programs for various segments of the population. Physical Best also provides for individualized goal-setting strategies in an effort to achieve lifetime commitment to fitness through physical education and sport. Other health-related physical fitness tests include the AAHPERD Youth Fitness Test, which

is composed of the 50-yard dash, standing long jump, sit-ups, shuttle run, distance run, and pull-ups (boys) and flexed-arm hang (girls), as well as the AAHPERD Health-Related Fitness Test, and the FitnessGram, examples of which may be found in the box on p. 236 and Figure 8-1, respectively. AAHPERD and the President's Council on Physical Fitness have also merged their Physical Best and President's Challenge into the "President's Youth Fitness Program."[7]

The Health and Wellness Movement

The emphasis on health and wellness has implications for curriculum development in physical education. The current trend is toward an emphasis on helping people stay healthy and fit. Individuals need to follow a personal health regimen and adopt a wholesome lifestyle that includes health-related fitness activities. Physical activity, physical fitness, and physical education programs thus have an increased value and importance for all segments of the population. Curriculum designers in physical education therefore should take into consideration such reports as the Surgeon General's *Promoting Health/Preventing Disease: Objectives for the Nation*[9] and *Promoting Health/Preventing Disease: Year 2000 Objectives for the Nation.*[10]

Mastery Learning

Mastery learning is based on the assumption that nearly all students and others can master material if they are given sufficient time and the material is presented in an understandable way. First material is presented to a group of students, for example. Then an evaluation is conducted and those students who have not mastered the material are given a second chance. The material is presented again, but in a different way and in a manner that can be better understood by the students who didn't master the material the first time. This procedure is repeated until all students have mastered the material. Mastery learning operates under the assumption that there are few failures—everyone succeeds. Curriculum designers should take this new development into consideration in developing physical education and sport programs.

◆   **AAHPERD HEALTH-RELATED PHYSICAL FITNESS TEST**

Item A: Distance run

Fitness component: Cardiorespiratory fitness
Purpose: To measure the maximal function and endurance of the cardiorespiratory system
Item description:

Procedures and norms are provided for two optional distance run tests: the mile run for time and the 9-minute run for distance. The decision as to which of the two tests to administer should be based on facilities, equipment, time limitations, and personal preference of the teacher. For students 13 years of age and older, the 1.5 mile run for time or the 12-minute run for distance may be utilized as the distance run items.

Item B: Sum of skinfolds (triceps and subscapular)

Fitness component: Body composition
Purpose: To evaluate the level of body fatness
Item description:

In a number of regions of the body, the subcutaneous adipose tissue may be lifted with the fingers to form a skinfold. The skinfold consists of a double layer of subcutaneous fat and skin whose thickness may be measured with a skinfold caliper. The skinfold sites (triceps and subscapular) have been chosen for this test because they are easily measured and are highly correlated with total body fat.

Item C: Sit-ups

Fitness component: Muscular strength/endurance.
Purpose: To test muscular strength and endurance of the abdominal muscles
Item description:

Students lie on their backs with knees flexed, feet on the floor with heels between 12 and 18 inches from the buttocks. The arms are crossed on the chest with hands on the opposite shoulder. Feet are held by a partner to keep them in touch with the testing surface. The students, by tightening their abdominal muscles, curl to the sitting position. Arm contact with the chest must be maintained. The sit-up is completed when elbows touch the thighs. Students return to down position until the midback makes contact with the testing surface. Repetitions are counted.

Item D: Sit and reach

Fitness component: Flexibility
Purpose: To test the flexibility of the low back and posterior thigh.
Item description:

The students remove their shoes and assume the sitting position with knees fully extended and feet against the apparatus shoulder width apart. The arms are extended forward with the hands placed one on top of the other. The students reach directly forward palms down, along the measuring scale. In this position, each student slowly stretches forward four times and holds the position of maximum reach on the fourth count. The position of maximum reach must be held for 1 second with knees in full extension while the feet are in contact with the apparatus.

Movement Education and Exploration

Movement education has been an integral part of K-6 school physical education programs (Figure 8-2). It focuses on the individual's exploration of the body as it relates to and reacts to the physical concepts of the environment. Movement education refers to the development of this system, whereas movement exploration refers to the methodology or process used in this problem-solving approach to developing desirable movement responses. A discussion of movement education is presented in Chapter 3.

Title IX and PL 94-142

Chapters 3 and 4 discuss at length Title IX and PL 94-142 and the manner in which they affect program development in physical education and sport. Because these are federally mandated laws, physical educators and coaches must comply with them.

TOTAL PHYSICAL FITNESS SCORE
EXCELLENT 352
ABOVE AVERAGE 316-351
AVERAGE 287-315
BELOW AVERAGE 251-286
WELL BELOW AVERAGE 0-250

NAME: John Smith
SCHOOL: South West Elementary
GRADE: 06
INSTRUCTOR: Johnson
SECTION: 03

	PULL-UP		SIT-UP		SHUTTLE		STANDING LONG JUMP		50 YD DASH		WALK/RUN*			DATE	HEIGHT	WEIGHT	TOTAL FITNESS SCORE
	NO.	% RANK	NO.	% RANK	SEC.	% RANK	FT-IN.	% RANK	SEC.	% RANK	MIN. SEC. OR YARDS	% RANK	TYPE	SEM.-YR.	FT.-IN.	LBS.	
02	02	65	025	25	11.7	35	4-09	40	8.3	40	8:54	25	1	F 92	4-07	069	297
03	03	75	028	35	11.0	55	4-11	50	7.6	60	7:58	55	1	S 93	4-08	073	309

Number of pull-ups completed by child (flexed-arm hang for girls)

Child's rank for each test based on the national norm

Information is shown from previous test dates which allows monitoring a child's growth and improvement.

Child's time to complete the test item

These activities are recommended. To improve your abdominal strength and endurance: bent knee-sit-ups, hands clasped behind head.

A composite score of all test items

"Exercise prescription" as needed

PROFILE FOR John Smith

PERCENTILE
100
90
80
70
60
50
40

PULL-UP   SIT-UP   SHUTTLE   STANDING LONG JUMP   50 YD DASH   WALK RUN

*WALK/RUN TYPE
600 — 600 YARD (MIN, SEC)
1 — 1 MILE (MIN, SEC)
1.5 — 1.5 MILES (MIN, SEC)
9 — 9 MINUTES (YARDS)
12 — 12 MINUTES (YARDS)

FIGURE 8-1 FITNESSGRAM.

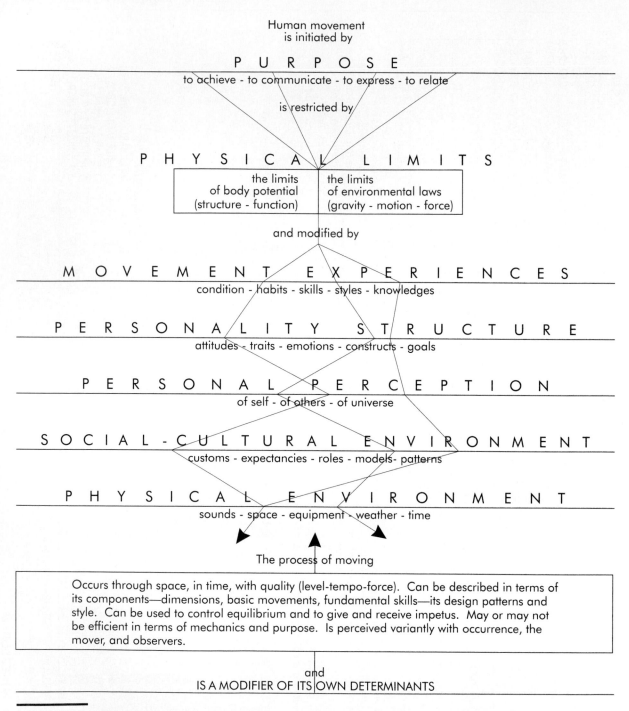

Human movement
is initiated by

P U R P O S E

to achieve - to communicate - to express - to relate

is restricted by

P H Y S I C A L   L I M I T S

| the limits of body potential (structure - function) | the limits of environmental laws (gravity - motion - force) |

and modified by

M O V E M E N T   E X P E R I E N C E S

condition - habits - skills - styles - knowledges

P E R S O N A L I T Y   S T R U C T U R E

attitudes - traits - emotions - constructs - goals

P E R S O N A L   P E R C E P T I O N

of self - of others - of universe

S O C I A L - C U L T U R A L   E N V I R O N M E N T

customs - expectancies - roles - models - patterns

P H Y S I C A L   E N V I R O N M E N T

sounds - space - equipment - weather - time

The process of moving

Occurs through space, in time, with quality (level-tempo-force). Can be described in terms of its components—dimensions, basic movements, fundamental skills—its design patterns and style. Can be used to control equilibrium and to give and receive impetus. May or may not be efficient in terms of mechanics and purpose. Is perceived variantly with occurrence, the mover, and observers.

and
IS A MODIFIER OF ITS OWN DETERMINANTS

FIGURE 8-2 Mediators of human movement. Movement education, an approach to the study of observable movement, is an objective of many K-6 education programs.

Humanistic Physical Education and Sport

The human being is the most valuable commodity in our existence. Change is needed in our society to humanize schools and other organizations so that students and others feel a sense of identity and belonging and are actively involved in the decision-making processes that affect them. Physical education and sport program planners need to be concerned with humanization and the needs and welfare of the participants. Our programs must return to the student-centered approach.

Olympic Curriculum*

The United States Olympic Committee's subcommittee on education has designed enrichment units to incorporate the ideals associated with the Olympic Movement into the curriculum of several subjects at the K-12 levels. One of the subjects in which these Olympic concepts can be taught is physical education. Program designers will want to review these materials and determine how best this material could be incorporated into their program. It is a unique way to get students thinking about the international realities of our "shrinking" global village, and to promote the need for cooperation, understanding, and communication in the world.

New Games

New Games represents an innovative approach being used by some physical educators. It is based on such concepts as "any game can be a new game," "anyone can play," "creating a new game is part of the fun," "we play for the fun of it," "it is the process of finding a game that we will want to play," and "we learn about play by playing." The New Games Foundation holds training sessions for individuals who are interested in learning more about this movement-based philosophy of "it's not what you play . . . but how you play."

Lifetime Sports

Considerable emphasis is placed on the importance of including lifetime sports in physical education

*United States Olympic Committee, *The Olympics: An educational opportunity, enrichment units K-6 and enrichment units 7-9,* Colorado Springs, Co, United States Olympic Committee.

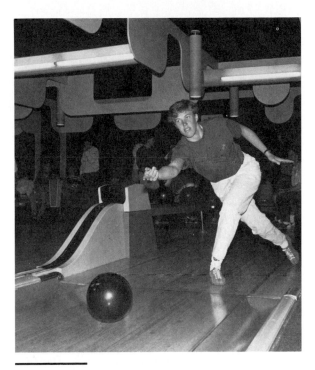

Bowling is one of the most popular lifetime sports in the United States.

programming. The term *lifetime sports* refers to activities that can be engaged in throughout a person's life span. Sports such as bowling, badminton, sailing, squash, tennis, golf, and swimming are just a few of the activities that might play a significant role in all physical education and sport program development.

Other Leisure-Pursuit Activities

More people today are engaging in such outdoor pursuit activities as skydiving, hang-gliding, and white-water canoeing. The risks involved in participating in such activities appeal to some individuals who want to be challenged and are looking for thrills and excitement. It is questionable, because of high risk and legal liability, whether such activities should be a part of any school physical education or recreational sports program.

There are, however, other outdoor leisure-pursuit activities such as hiking, winter survival camping, snow shoeing, and rock climbing that deserve full consideration when developing programs. Also, there are various challenge-related organizations such as Project Adventure, Inc. in Hamilton, Massachusetts or the Pecos River Learning Center in Sante Fe, New Mexico. The staff of these groups will assist a manager in developing these types of educational pursuits.

Nongraded Curricula

Nongraded schools are based on the premise that individual differences exist among students. Therefore traditional grade levels are removed in some subjects, and children with similar abilities study and work together regardless of chronological age. For example, a science class might have students ranging in age from 5 to 8 years. A student progresses as rapidly as desired, based on individual achievement and potential. The desirability of nongrading in physical education is controversial, and great care should be taken to protect the well-being of the students involved. It also has serious ramifications for sports programming.

Accountability Through Outcome-Based Education

Accountability generally denotes various ways of making persons answerable for their performance, be they teachers, managers, students, or student-athletes. Performance or productivity may be measured by prespecified goals, the outcomes of which must meet certain criteria-based standards. Accountability in education through outcome-based education models—because of declining test scores and lack of literacy skills, as well as substandard physical fitness levels—has come to the forefront. Physical educators involved with students with varying disabilities have long been held accountable for developing IEPs. The trend is toward extending this program format to all students and programs.

MANAGEMENT AND PROGRAM CHANGE

Because so many factors have an impact on programs, the physical educator and coach must assess the recommended changes to make informed and prudent decisions. Four questions that managers might ask themselves in evaluating changes follow:

1. *What are the functions of the organization?* How does the suggested change conform to the philosophy and purpose of the organization?
2. *Am I sufficiently well informed to make an intelligent decision?* Managers need to be knowledgeable about the learning process; health-related fitness patterns; human growth and development; current program needs, issues, and mandates; and the needs and interests of the local community.
3. *How does the change relate to staff, facility, budget, and other important managerial considerations?* The change must be practical to implement and make the best use of staff and the physical plant.
4. *What do the experts say?* What is the thinking, opinion, and position of professionals and organizations who have conducted research, thoroughly studied the problem, and piloted like programs? Expert testimony may be helpful in making sound program decisions.

Considerations in Program Change

Program revision cannot occur without considering the following:

1. *Participants.* The number of participants, their needs and interests, and other characteristics such as sociocultural background need to be considered before initiating any program change.
2. *Staff members.* Staff members play a key role in program revision. For example, the attitude of the faculty toward change, present work loads, comprehension of goals of the school, attitudes toward after-school sport programs, competencies in curriculum revision, and past training and experience are a few important considerations. Change in curriculum might mean new members being added to the faculty or a different type of competency being represented on the staff.
3. *Physical facility.* The adequacy of the physical plant and facility for present and future programs must be considered. Information

should be available on capabilities and limitations of the present physical plant (e.g., pool and field space). New demands may be placed on facilities through program revision that brings about changes in class size, scheduling, and alternative site planning.

4. *Budget.* The budget is another important consideration. What will the new sport program cost? What are the sources of support? Before staff members expend time and effort to study program change, they need reasonable assurance that proposed changes are economically feasible. In systems using a "planning-programming-budgeting-evaluation-system," or (PPBES), budgets are formulated considering the objectives of the program; PPBES also provides for evaluation techniques that may require further program change or modification if goals are not being met.

5. *Program.* Because any new program proposal is likely to reflect current practices to some degree, it seems logical that the present program needs careful scrutiny to determine what has happened over the years, the degree to which staff members have brought about change, and the general direction in which the institution is moving.

6. *Management.* Staff members must take a hard look at the managerial leadership. The philosophy of management and its views toward change should be carefully weighed. Managers will need to approve budgetary and resource allocations, as well as required expenditures, in order to affect the proposed program initiative or change.

Research in Program Changes in Physical Education and Sport

Advancing the frontiers of knowledge in physical education and sport is urgently needed. Too many unsupported claims concerning the value of physical education and sport have been set forth. There is a need to determine its worth through valid research findings: basic research that will advance knowledge and applied research that will determine the best ways to implement this knowledge.

Many questions are still unanswered, such as the following: What is the most effective way to develop physical fitness? What activities are most effective for developing muscular strength and power? How many times per week is physical education needed to enhance self-concept? What activities can the employee on the job perform to enhance his or her physical fitness level? What are the fundamental patterns of human movement? What activities are best conducted cooperatively? What is the relationship of personality development to motor performance? What is the relationship of academic achievement to physical fitness level? What is the therapeutic value of physical activity? What instructional strategies are most effective in mainstreaming?

Research opportunity abounds in both the classroom and the gymnasium. There is no question that more systematic research is crucial to the development of the profession and that many program improvements will result from such concerted research effort.

EVALUATION

Once a program has been developed, evaluation is essential to determine the extent to which the experiences provided have produced desirable outcomes, or are at least progressing toward its established goals. Unless the outcomes are acceptable, the program cannot be considered successful. Essential characteristics of an evaluation program follow.

The relationship between program planning and evaluation is recognized and understood by all individuals involved in the program. Changes are based on evaluation techniques and results. All learning experiences are evaluated. Evaluation is primarily concerned with: (1) meeting participant needs, (2) meeting the objectives of the program, and (3) considering the requirements of parents, staff members, and organization members.

Goodlad[4] indicates that program evaluation to date has used the following four means to determine the worth of a new program: (1) observing individuals who have been exposed to the new program and the progress they have made, (2) systematic questioning of people involved in the program, (3) testing participants periodically to determine their progress, and (4) comparative testing of participants under both the new and old programs to determine the progress of each.

Management may want to explore alternative evaluative models, which include utilizing desired outcomes, goal-free models, adversarial models, or artistic models.

Program Management Evaluation

Evaluation of program management may be a yearly procedure, handled by members of a department for the purpose of curriculum organization, or it may be an examination of the entire organization by a visiting team of external specialists. The process of evaluation itself involves rating or judging the program according to selected criteria and standards. Some standardized forms have been developed to evaluate various phases of the physical education curriculum (e.g., by NASPE/NCATE).

Where standardized tests are not available to judge program management, criteria based on authoritative textbook sources or the judgment of experts in the field must be established.

The following are sample questions, which may be answered "poor," "fair," "good," or "excellent" or may be scored on a scale of 1 to 10 or Likert scale wherein the respondent reacts to a five-point scale indicating "strongly agree," "agree," "uncertain," "disagree," or "strongly disagree." Program areas are listed with sample questions concerning various factors that managers must take into full consideration.

Basic Instructional Physical Education Program

- Does the program devote equitable time to team, individual, and lifetime sports, as well as rhythms, aquatics, dance, and gymnastic activities?
- Are the available equipment and facilities adequate to allow for maximal, as well as safe, participation?
- Are reasonable budgetary allotments made for the program?
- Are accurate evaluation procedures conducted, and records kept?

- Are minimal participation requirements met by all students?
- Are participants meeting proper physical education requirements in regard to participation?
- Are proper safety measures implemented in all activities?
- Are opportunities for developing student leadership being provided in the program?

Adapted/Developmental Program

- Do adequate screening and evaluation procedures exist for its participants?
- Are proper supervision and instruction afforded each individual participant?
- Are adequate facilities, equipment, time, and space made available to the program?
- Is school and parental approval obtained for each individual's regimen of activity?
- Do participants engage in regular class activity, as well as any recommended developmental classes?
- Are careful records and progress charts (e.g., IEP objectives) kept for each student?
- Is the financial allotment to the program reasonable?
- Does student achievement reflect the value of the program?

Recreational Sport Programs

- Are intramural, extramural, and club sports offered to all students, including the disabled?
- Are enough activities (e.g., level, coed) offered to the student population?
- Has the percentage of participation in these programs increased during the past 3 years?
- Is maximal supervision available to all participants?
- Is adequate financial assistance given to this phase of the program?
- Are accurate records maintained concerning the participants, their awards, protests, and conduct violations?
- Does the reward or point system emphasize the joys of participation rather than focus on the value of the reward?
- Is the equipment utilized for the program safe and adequate for the number of participants?

- Is equipment properly maintained and stored to gain the most use from it?
- Are competitive experiences wholesome and worthwhile for all participants?
- Is the level of organization appropriate to the activity?

Interscholastic and Intercollegiate Sport Programs

- Is financial support provided by the school for this program adequate?
- Is there equitable financial support for all sports in the program?
- Are equal numbers of interscholastic sports available to boys and girls alike?

◆ SUGGESTED OUTLINE OF A SCHOOL CURRICULUM EVALUATION CHECKLIST

The following evaluation checklist for physical education programs suggests methods of assessing curriculum development in this area.

	Yes	No
1. Does the physical education curriculum meet the established objectives?	___	___
2. Does the physical education curriculum provide for the keeping of records to show student progress?	___	___
3. Is evaluation used to help each student in the physical education program find out where he or she is in relation to the program objectives?	___	___
4. Are objective, as well as subjective, measures used to determine the progress of students in attaining program objectives?	___	___
5. Are the students protected by periodical medical examinations to see if they have health deficiencies?	___	___
6. Does the physical education curriculum provide for the administration of physical fitness tests to evaluate the fitness of each student?	___	___
7. Does the physical education program provide for the testing of skills and use specific ability tests?	___	___
8. Does the physical education curriculum provide for cognitive testing of students?	___	___
9. Does the physical education curriculum provide for the testing of the social adjustment of each student?	___	___
10. Are the attitudes and interests of the students evaluated?	___	___
11. If scientific methods of testing are not feasible, does the physical education curriculum provide for teacher-made tests?	___	___
12. Does the physical education program use test results in planning and asessing units of activity?	___	___
13. Does the physical education curriculum provide for mobility of students based on evaluation results?	___	___
14. Does the physical education curriculum provide for student evaluation as well as teacher evaluation?	___	___
15. Does the physical education program provide for the recognition of curriculum problems and then try to bring about change?	___	___
16. Once change in the curriculum is recognized, is it easy to bring about change?	___	___
17. Is the physical education staff receptive to change?	___	___
18. Is there a provision for ongoing evaluation of programs in reference to satisfying objectives according to an established schedule?	___	___
19. Does the physical education curriculum provide for the needs of students with varying disabilities?	___	___

- Are adequate health standards being met in respect to number of practices and games, fitness level of participants, and level of competition?
- Is competition provided by schools of a similar size?
- Is the program justifiable as an important facet of the educational process?
- Are academic standards for participants maintained?
- Are good public relations with the community furthered through this program?
- Are sport offerings healthful and safe for all participants?
- Are medical personnel available at practices and games?

Staff and Faculty

- Is the teaching and coaching staff well qualified and capable of carrying out the program?
- Is the program run efficiently, with little loss of teaching time or space, and is maximal use made of facilities?
- Are professional or exclusive representative standards maintained regarding class size and teacher/coach assignment?
- Does the departmental organization function on a democratic basis, with members sharing in the decisions?
- Do members of the staff have a professional outlook and attitudes?
- Do staff members attend professional meetings and keep up with the latest developments in the profession?
- Do staff members apply current research findings to various programmatic activities?

These are just a few sample questions that may be used in evaluating program management. A sample evaluation checklist for a school curriculum is also offered (see the box on p. 243). The key to successful evaluation of this type lies in the follow-up steps for program improvement.

Whatever method of program evaluation is selected, it should be realistic, functional, and continuous, in order to fulfill its major purpose of providing meaningful and quality programs that benefit all involved.

SUMMARY

Management has the responsibility to see that quality physical education and sport programs are developed, periodically reviewed, and changed or modified when necessary to better meet the needs of the participant. This responsibility includes deciding on what goals should be created and supported, enlisting the help of key individuals and groups in the construction of the program, taking into account the factors and groups who influence and are influenced by the program, following the proper procedures and selecting the best approach in program development, and being aware of the current trends and issues in the field for which the program is being targeted. In other words, management is responsible for providing effective leadership, as well as the resources and motivation to fully support the program development process.

◆ SELF-ASSESSMENT ACTIVITIES

These activities will assist students in determing if material and competencies presented in this chapter have been mastered:

1. Explain to the class what is meant by program development, the role of management in this process, and the ways in which program change occurs.
2. If you were an athletic director of a junior high or middle school, what factors would influence the various activities included in your program?
3. You have been assigned to chair a committee to develop a physical education program for your school. Who would you select to serve on a curriculum committee?
4. List and discuss several principles you would observe in developing a middle school curriculum.
5. Using the systems approach, trace program development for a high school.
6. You have been hired as a consultant to evaluate a physical education program in a developing nation. Describe the process you will follow in conducting this task.
7. Discuss various restrictions that may influence the shape and conduct of the physical education curriculum at your institution.

REFERENCES

1. American Alliance for Health, Physical Education, Recreation and Dance: *Basic stuff series, I and II,* Reston, Va, 1987, The Alliance.
2. American Alliance for Health, Physical Education, Recreation and Dance: *Physical best,* Reston, Va, 1988, The Alliance.
3. Franck DM: *Physical education outcomes project making progress, Update,* Reston, Va, 1989, American Alliance for Health Physical Education, Recreation and Dance.
4. Goodlad JL: *School curriculum reform in the United States,* New York, 1964, The Fund for Advancement of Education.
5. Jewett AE, Bain LL: *The curriculum process in physical education,* Dubuque, Ia 1985, Wm C Brown.
6. McNeil JD: *Curriculum: a comprehensive introduction,* Boston, 1981, Little, Brown.
7. President's Council on Physical Fitness and Sports: *Get fit: a handbook for youth ages 6-17,* Washington, DC, 1991, Department of Health and Human Resources.
8. Sergiovanni TJ: *Effective department leadership,* Newton, MA, 1984, Allyn & Bacon.
9. US Department of Health and Human Services: *Promoting health/preventing disease: objectives for the nation,* Washington, DC, 1980, US Government Printing Office.
10. US Department of Health and Human Services: *Promoting health/preventing disease: year 2000 objectives for the nation* (draft for public view and comment), Washington, DC, 1989, US Government Printing Office.
11. Woodruff AD: The use of concepts in teaching and learning, *Journal of Teacher Education* 20:84, Mar 1964.

SUGGESTED READINGS

- American Alliance for Health, Physical Education, Recreation and Dance: Special focus: playing fair, *Strategies,* 1(3):5 21, 27-29, 1988.
  Part of a series of articles dealing with coaching conduct and ethics. It provides a glimpse into coaching strategy and methodology.
- Gensemer RE: *Physical education: perspectives, inquiry, applications,* Philadelphia, 1985, Saunders.
  Discusses perspectives of the philosophies and principles of physical education. Presents information about how the knowledge base of physical education and sport relates to career potentials. Tells what physical education is, what it examines, and how it is employed.
- Lacy AC, Hastad DN: Measurement and evaluation, *Strategies,* 2(3):21-25, 1989.
  Techniques to assess student progress in meeting program goals are presented, including an easy-to-read chart that highlights the learning domains.
- Oliva PF: *Developing the curriculum,* Boston, 1982, Little, Brown.
  Provides a comprehensive analysis of the process of curriculum development, planning, and improvement. Management personnel will find the book to be a practical guide to curriculum development.
- Powell KE, Christenson GM, Kreuter MW: Objectives for the nation: assessing the role physical education must play, *Journal of Physical Education, Recreation, and Dance,* 55(6):18-20, 1984.
  Emphasizes three important aspects of the reports *Healthy People* and *Objectives for the Nation.* Realistic goals for the profession are discussed, as well as the need to garner the support of the American people. Physical educators are challenged to promote lifelong health-related physical activity for all segments of the population.
- Rink JE: *Teaching physical education for learning,* St Louis, 1985, Mosby–Year Book.
  Has implications for the implementation of the curriculum in physical education through the improvement of the efficiency of instruction, quality of teaching, and other factors that should be considered in seeing that students reap the greatest benefits from planned programs. Comprehensive coverage of sequential learning experiences are presented.
- Sanborn MA, Hartman B: *Issues in physical education,* Philadelphia, 1982, Lea & Febiger.
  Helpful for management personnel who need to make curricular decisions involving types of programs to be supported. Provides examples of the issues and resultant problems that can occur in program management.
- Willgoose CE: *The curriculum in physical education,* Englewood Cliffs, NJ 1984, Prentice-Hall.
  Provides help in the development of a curriculum in physical education for all educational levels. Includes such topics as objectives, curriculum planning, research, program organization, the curriculum guide, evaluation, and management guidelines for programs at each educational level.
- Wilmore J: Objectives for the nation: physical fitness and exercise, *Journal of Physical Education, Recreation, and Dance,* 53(3):41-43, 1982.
  Presents key points from the physical fitness and exercise section of the report *Objectives for the Nation.* Necessary preventive, promotive, legislative, and economic measures are described relative to the objectives. The specific objectives for the 1990s are delineated, as well as the challenge for physical educators to work together within professional organizations and make a personal commitment to be role models of a healthy, active lifestyle.

CHAPTER 9

Facility Management

▶ **Instructional Objectives and Competencies To Be Achieved**

After reading this chapter the student should be able to

- Prepare a list of principles that could be used by the management in planning, constructing, and utilizing facilities for physical education and sport programs.
- List the procedure involved in working with an architect.
- Describe the indoor facilities (type, size, location) needed for physical education and sport programs, and prepare guidelines for managers to follow in planning such facilities.
- Describe the outdoor facilities (type, size, location) needed for physical education and sport programs, and prepare guidelines for

managers to follow when planning such facilities.
- Compute the number of teaching stations needed, given the total number of participants, size of classes, and periods per week.
- Discuss contemporary features and developments in the construction of physical education and sport facilities.
- Show how to provide facilities that will be conducive to a healthful and safe environment for conducting physical education and sport programs.

Facility management is usually a responsibility of those persons who are in charge of physical education and sport programs. The facilities for which they are responsible include outdoor facilities—such as playgrounds, courts, and fields—and indoor facilities—such as locker and shower rooms, natatoriums, racket sport courts, weight and exercise rooms, and gymnasiums. Facility management includes not only the effective scheduling and maintenance of such facilities, but also at times planning new structures to keep pace with the demand for participation in physical education and sport programs.

Some recent developments have implications for facility management. The cost of materials and labor is rising as a result of inflation. High interest rates make it difficult to get bond issues passed for facility construction. Facilities must be accessible for persons with disabilities and must be brought up to code concerning myriad environmental standards. Energy conservation and costs must also be taken into consideration.

Community involvement and cooperation must be given priority in the construction and shared utilization of many facility projects. That little or no money is available in some situations has resulted in alternative methods for seeing that physical education and sport programs have the facilities necessary to conduct quality programs. Methods such as renovating and converting existing structures and instituting multiple use of present facilities are emerging. When funds are limited, fiscal responsibility involves following construction plans that are most economical, not only in cost, but in construction time and the use of energy.

Physical plants require careful planning and consultation with specialists in architectural planning. Managers, physical educators, coaches, program specialists, consultants, and other personnel should participate in planning new facilities. The facility manager must be knowledgeable not only about the facility's specific structure, but also its functions and maintenance. Trends and innovative structural con-

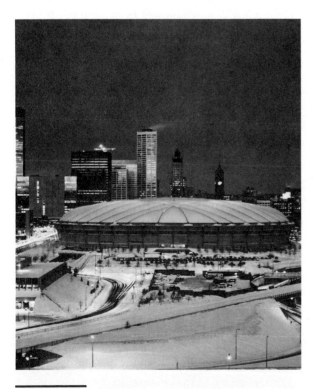

The Hubert H. Humphrey Metrodome is shared by the community, Minnesota State High School League, and the University of Minnesota, as well as the area's professional sport teams.

cepts should be thoroughly examined to provide a healthful, safe, and efficient physical plant.

The physical plant is a major consideration in most physical education and sport programs. New architectural ideas are constantly being introduced and new concepts developed that have a more economical, accessible, and functional management scheme. Some building concepts include *convertibility*, for example, where interiors are rearranged by employing movable walls, curtains, and partitions, which facilitates using the gymnasium, cafeteria, and amphitheater as multipurpose activity stations that can accommodate small or large groups. This concept provides instruction and independent study spaces for a number of varied activities and is becoming a trend as plant space and fiscal restraint become crucial to the survival of programs.

Many excellent books are devoted exclusively to facilities for physical education and sport. Some of these are listed at the end of the chapter and should be consulted by those who desire a more thorough treatment of this subject.

PLANNING THE FACILITY

At the outset two principles relating to facility management should be uppermost in the minds of physical educators: (1) facilities are built as a result of program needs, and (2) cooperative planning is essential to avoid common mistakes. The objectives; activities; teaching methods, strategies, and materials; management philosophy; policies; equipment; and supplies represent program considerations regarding facilities. The educational and recreational needs of both the school and community; the thinking of the managers, physical educators, and coaches; and the advice of architects, engineers, and lay persons are other considerations if facilities are to be planned wisely.

Management guidelines and principles for facility planning that apply to all educational levels and organizations include the following:

- Facilities should be planned primarily for the participants and user groups.
- All planning should be based on goals that recognize that the total physical and nonphysical

environments must be safe, secure, attractive, comfortable, clean, practical, and adapted to the needs of the individual.

- Facilities must be economical to operate and maintain.
- The planning should include a consideration of the total physical education and sport facilities of the community. The programs and facilities of these common areas are closely allied, and planning should be coordinated and cooperative, based on the needs of the community.
- Facilities should be geared to health and safety codes and standards, which are important in protecting the health, welfare, and safety of user groups.
- Facilities should be planned so that they are easily accessible and secure for all individuals, including those with disabilities.
- Facilities play a part in a healthful environment. The extent to which organizations provide ample play area space, sanitary considerations, and proper ventilation, heating, and cleanliness will to some extent determine how effectively health is promoted.

Managers must make plans for facilities long before an architect is consulted. Technical information can be obtained in the form of standards and guides from various sources, such as state departments of health and education, sports organizations and federations, professional journals and literature (e.g., *Athletic Business, Facility Manager, Club Industry, Aquatics*), as well as from appropriate groups such as the American Association of School Administrators, AAHPERD, NASPE, and the American Institute of Architects.

Standards may be used as guides and as a starting point; however, it is important to keep in mind that standards cannot always be implemented entirely as envisaged. They usually have to be modified in light of community needs, environmental conditions, and scarce inputs, including fiscal constraints.

Building safety and sanitation codes managed by the local and state departments of public health, as well as the technical advice and consultation services available through these sources, should be identified and implemented by managers during the planning and construction of facilities. Information concerned with quality building materials, safety specifications, minimal standards of sanitation, sound and light, and other details may be procured from these sources.

Physical education and sport personnel should play important roles in planning and operating facilities. The specialized knowldedge that such individuals have is important. Provisions should be made so that their expert opinion will be used to promote healthful, safe, optimal learning environments.

Facilities should be planned only after future forecasting is performed. Too often, facilities are constructed, outdated, and outgrown within a very short time. Building units should be large enough to accommodate peak-load participation for various activities at all user group levels. The peak-load estimates should be made with future growth of both the participant and the activity in mind.

Planning should provide adequate allotment of space to each activity and program area. Space allotment should fit into an overall plan of program priorities (e.g., weight training, dance, spectator sports). Office space and service and storage units, although important, should not be planned and developed in a spacious and luxurious manner that goes beyond efficiency and necessity.

Geographical, ecological, and climatic conditions should be considered when planning facilities. By doing this, the full potential for conducting activities outdoors as well as indoors can be realized.

Architects do not always pay as much attention as they should to the educational and health features when planning buildings and facilities. Therefore it is important that they be briefed on certain requirements that physical educators believe are essential so that the health, safety, and welfare of children, youth, and adults may be better served. Such a procedure is usually welcomed by the architect and planning committee and will aid them in rendering a greater service to the community.

Facilities should include all the safety features essential in physical education and sport programs. Health and sports medicine services and office locations near the gymnasium and other play areas,

From construction to operation, the University of Minnesota Track and Field Complex.

proper surfacing of activity areas, adequate space, temperature and humidity control, and proper lighting are a few of these considerations (see the box on p. 250).

The construction of school physical education and sport facilities often tends to set a pattern and elicit a positive reaction that will influence community, civic leaders, parents, and others. This in turn promotes a healthful and safe environment for the entire community to take pride in.

◆ ROLE OF MANAGEMENT IN FACILITY PLANNING AND DEVELOPMENT

Kraus and Curtis[8] have indicated the role of management in the planning and development of a facility, presented here in the following adapted form:

- Management should familiarize itself with background information pertinent to the facility plan and should be actively involved in all planning sessions.
- Management should meet and discuss the facility project with all people (e.g., user, community) who have a stake in the project. Management should be familiar with the views of such people and consider their suggestions carefully.
- Management should insist on being involved in selecting the architect or engineer who is going to do the plan. Management should press strongly for selecting competent and qualified people to do the job rather than the lowest bidder or firm with political connections.
- Management should be at all planning conferences to present the department's point of view on programs to be considered.
- Management should visit the site regularly after construction begins. All problems should be noted and a follow-up of recognized errors made.
- Management should insist that all details and standards incorporated in the project be carried out exactly as specified. Management should not approve any facility or authorize payment unless this has been done.

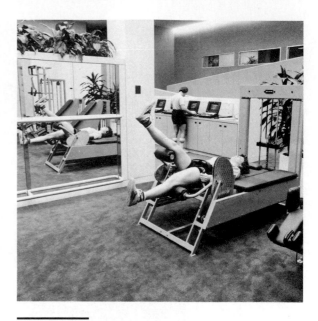

A safe and healthful psychosocial environment is provided at Tenneco's Fitness Center; Houston, TX.

HEALTH CONSIDERATIONS IN FACILITY PLANNING

The participant must be provided a safe, healthful, pleasant, and emotionally secure environment in which to participate. This environment also includes the outdoors, where everything possible should be done to protect and enhance land, water, air, and other delicate ecosystems. The total learning and working environment should be healthful and pleasant for all faculty members, staff members, and employees, as well as all user groups.

Another set of principles basic to facility planning concerns the optimal promotion of a healthful environment for not only the participants but also the community. Included in this set of principles is the provision for facilities that consider the physiological needs of the participant, including proper temperature and humidity control, lighting, water supply, and acoustic (noise) level. A second principle is to provide safe facilities. The facilities should be planned so that the danger of fire, the possibility of mechanical accidents, and the hazards involved in traffic would be eliminated or kept to a minimum. A third principle is concerned with protection against disease. This means attention to items such as proper sewage disposal, sanitation procedures, and water supply. A fourth principle is the need to provide a healthful psychosocial environment. This has implications for space, location of activities, color schemes, and elimination of distractions through such means as soundproof construction materials.

The general health features of the physical environment include site, building, lighting, heating and ventilation, plant sanitation, and acoustics.

Site.   There are many aspects to consider in selecting a suitable site. These considerations will differ, depending on the community. Whether it is a rural or an urban community will have a bearing on the location of the site. In an urban community it is desirable to have a school situated near transportation facilities but at the same time located away from industrial concerns, railroads, noise, heavy traffic, toxic fumes, and smoke. Consideration should be given to demographic trends, population movements, and future development of the area in which the buildings are planned. Adequate space for play and recreation should be provided. The play area should consist of a minimum of 100 square feet for each child. Some standards concerning schools recommend 5 acres of land for elementary schools, 10 to 12 acres for junior high or middle schools, and 20 acres for senior high schools.

Attention also should be given to the aesthetic features of a site because of their effect on the physical and emotional well-being of participants and staff members. The surroundings should be well landscaped, attractive, and free from disturbing noises or odors.

Building. The trend in schools and community-based building projects is toward one-story construction, with stress on planning from a functional rather than an ornamental point of view. The building should be constructed for *use*. The materials selected should make the building attractive and safe. Every precaution should be taken to protect against accidents, fire, slippery floors, and other dangers and risks. The walls should be painted with light colors and treated with acoustic materials. Doors should open outward. Space for clothing should be provided. Provisions for persons with disabilities, including ramps, toilet facilities, and others discussed in Chapter 3, should be major considerations when building or renovating an existing facility.

Lighting. Proper lighting is important to protect and conserve vision, prevent fatigue, and improve morale. In the past it had been recommended that natural light should come into the room from the left and that indirect artificial light should be provided as needed. There is a trend now toward allowing natural light from more than one direction. Artificial light, moreover, should come from many sources rather than one to prevent too much concentration of light in one place. Lighting intensity should be in

Proper lighting is a feature at the U.S. Olympic Sport Center; Colorado Springs, CO.

accordance with recommended standards. Switches for artificial light should be located in various parts of the room and of course lights should be recessed and enclosed for protection.[6]

In gymnasiums and swimming pools light intensity should range from 10 to 80 footcandles, depending on the activity being conducted. Glare is an undesirable hazard that should be eliminated, especially in diving wells to ensure the safety of the participant. Fluorescent lights or other multistage lights should be properly installed and adjusted for best results. Strong contrasts of color such as light walls and dark floors should also be avoided if possible.

Heating and ventilation. Efficiency in the classroom, gymnasium, special activities rooms, and other places is determined to some extent by thermal comfort, which is mainly determined by heating and ventilation.

The purposes of heating and ventilation are to remove excess heat and humidity, unpleasant odors, and in some cases, gases, vapors, fumes, and dust from the room; to prevent rapid temperature fluctuations; to diffuse the heat within a room; and to supply heat to counteract loss from the human body through radiation and otherwise.

Heating standards vary according to the activities engaged in, the participant's clothing, and the geographic location of the facility.

Concerning ventilation, the range of recommendations is from 8 to 21 cubic feet of fresh air per minute per occupant. Adequate ventilating systems are especially needed in dressing, shower, and locker rooms; toilets; gymnasiums; and swimming pools; in fact all rooms require adequate ventilation. The recommended humidity level ranges from 35% to 60%. The type and amount of ventilation will vary with the specific needs of the particular activity area.

Plant sanitation. Plant sanitation should not be overlooked. Sanitation facilities should be well planned and maintained. The water supply should be safe and adequate. If any question exists, the health department should be consulted. Concerning water supply, one authority suggests that at least 20 gallons per individual per day is needed for all purposes.

Drinking fountains of various heights should be recessed in corridor walls and should consist of material that is easily cleaned. A stream of water should flow from the fountain so that it is not necessary for the mouth of the drinker to get too near the water outlet or drain bowl.

Water closets, urinals, lavatories, and washroom equipment such as soap dispensers, toilet paper holders, waste containers, mirrors, bookshelves, and hand and hair drying facilities should be provided as needed, also keeping the person with disabilities in mind.

Waste disposal should be adequate. There should be provision for cleanup and removal and recycling of paper and other materials that make the grounds and buildings a health and safety hazard, as well as unsightly. Proper sewage disposal and prompt garbage disposal should also be provided. Weekly plant and facility sanitation audits are strongly encouraged.

Acoustics. Noise distracts, causes nervous strain, and detracts from many of the activities' benefits. Therefore noise should be eliminated as effectively as possible. This can be achieved by acoustical treatment of such important places as corridors, gymnasiums, and swimming pools.

Acoustical materials include plasters, fibers, boards, acoustic tiles, and various fabrics. Floor covering that reduces noise should be used in corridors, and acoustical material should be used in walls and ceilings. Gymnasiums, swimming pools, and racket courts need special treatment to control the various noises associated with enthusiastic play and participation.

DETERMINING NUMBER OF TEACHING STATIONS NEEDED

The teaching station concept should be considered when scheduling physical education and sport classes. A teaching station is the space or setting where one teacher or staff member can conduct physical activities for one group of students. The number and size of teaching stations available together with the number of teachers on the staff, the size of the group, the number of times the group meets, the number of periods in the school or college day, and the program of activities are important items to consider when planning.

According to the participants in the National Facilities Conference, the following formulas should be considered to help determine the number of teaching stations necessary for effective teaching and learning.[2]

Elementary Schools

The formula for computing the number of teaching stations needed for physical education in the elementary schools is:

$$\text{Minimum number of teaching stations} = \frac{\substack{\text{Number of} \\ \text{classes or units} \\ \text{of students}} \times \substack{\text{Number of Physical} \\ \text{Education periods} \\ \text{per week per class}}}{\text{Total periods in school week}}$$

For example, for an elementary school of six grades, with three classes at each level (approximately 450 to 540 students), ten 30-minute physical education periods per day, and physical education conducted on a daily basis, the teaching station needs are calculated as follows:

$$\text{Minimum number of teaching stations} = \frac{18 \text{ units} \times 5 \text{ periods/week}}{50 \text{ total periods in school week}} = \frac{90}{50} = 1.8$$

Secondary Schools and Colleges

The formula for computing the number of teaching stations needed for physical education in secondary schools and colleges is as follows:

$$\text{Minimum number of teaching stations} = \frac{\text{Number of students}}{\text{Average number of students/instructor}} \times \frac{\text{Number of periods class meets each week}}{\text{Total number of class periods in school week}}$$

For example, if a school system projects its enrollment as 700 students and plans six class periods a day with an average class size of 30 students, and physical education is required daily, the formula is as follows:

$$\text{Minimum number of teaching stations} = \frac{700 \text{ students}}{30 \text{ per class}} \times \frac{5 \text{ periods/week}}{30 \text{ periods/week}} = \frac{3500}{900} = 3.9$$

THE TEAM APPROACH TO FACILITY PLANNING

Facility planning requires a team approach that includes many crucial players. The planning team may include the architect, engineer, business manager, physical plant and maintenance staff, physical education and sport managers, coaches, and consultants in facility safety, law, and health. Flynn[5] has indicated the steps that should be followed in achieving the best results from the team approach.

First, form a planning team that will identify needs (needs assessment team) and prepare a project proposal. Included on this team may be the project coordinator for the organization for whom the facility is being planned, the architect, a representative from the physical education and sport area, a community government representative, and a budget director or business manager. Team members should understand the role each plays in the planning process.

Second, secure consultants during the early stages of the project because the other team members may not have expertise in all aspects of programming and design. Consultants can help close the gap between architectural theory and physical education and sport practice, not to mention fiscal and legal responsibility.

Third, stress faculty, staff, and community involvement to provide information about special

A rowing tank at Trinity College; Hartford, CT.

areas and facilities for which they are responsible. For example, a physical education teacher, adapted/developmental teacher, specialist in biomechanics, exercise physiologist, dance instructor, or tennis, rowing, or swimming coach could provide meaningful information about his or her projected facility or laboratory space and needs.

Fourth, visit and gather materials from other facilities and experts to obtain ideas and advice that may contribute to improving on your facility plan. Appendix E provides a thorough checklist for facility planners.

The planning team should also be alert when making facility recommendations concerning long-term maintenance and operational costs. When construction is under way, not only the architect and consultants, but also the physical education and sport specialists should monitor the work. By doing this, many potential errors may be avoided or corrected.

The architect and physical educators cooperatively planned for facilities at the University of Delaware, Newark.

WORKING WITH THE ARCHITECT

The architect is the specialist in facility planning and leads the design team in the planning and construction of new physical education and sport facilities. The architect, through his or her training and experience, is a specialist who is competent to give advisory service in most aspects of facility management.

Ferreri,[4] a chief operations officer for a group of architects in Illinois, points out that a strong, positive relationship between the architect, the school, and the community is crucial for effective planning. Lines of communication within the school, between the school and the architect, and within the architect's office must be based on mutual understanding. Communication about program and space needs and requirements must be continuous. These are the hallmarks of the satisfied and successful facility planner.

Physical educators and coaches should carefully think through their own ideas and plans for their special facilities and submit them in writing to the planning team during the early stages of planning. The architect and physical education and sports spe-

cialists should have several conferences in which they exchange views and consider architectural potentials, possibilities, and alternatives.

Many architects are limited in their knowledge about physical education and sport programs and therefore welcome the advice of specialists. The architect might be furnished with such information as the names of plants where excellent facilities exist; kinds of activities that will constitute the program; space and rules requirements for various age-appropriate activities; storage and equipment areas needed; temperature requirements; relation of dressing, showering, and toilet facilities to the program; teaching stations needed; best construction materials for activities; and lighting, noise, and accessibility requirements. The physical educator and coach may not have all this information readily available, including some of the latest trends and standards recommended for his or her specific field or sport. However, such information can be obtained through the literature from professional organizations and federations, as well as from other schools and organizations where excellent facilities have been developed, financed, and constructed.

Mr. William Haroldson, former Director of Health and Physical Education for the Seattle, Washington public schools, developed a procedural outline in cooperation with three architectural firms, which lists some essential considerations for physical educators when planning with architects. Some of the main points from this outline are discussed here.

Educational specifications. Adequate educational specifications provide the basis for sound planning by the architect:

1. General description of the program, such as the number of teaching stations necessary to service the physical education program for a total student body of approximately (n = ?) boys and (n = ?) girls. The general description should also include school or institutional philosophy, primary user group (e.g., age and developmental level), and projected popularity of physical activities to be delivered.

2. Basic criteria that pertain to the gymnasium, including the number of teaching periods per day; capacities, number, and size of courts and lockers; and total uses projected for the facility:

   a. Availability and accessibility to the community (e.g., foot, bicycle, wheelchair)
   b. Proximity to parks and community centers
   c. Parking, transportation, traffic patterns, and accessibility (e.g., persons with disabilities, medical emergency units, fire department)
   d. Popularity and type of activities for primary and other appropriate user groups
   e. Size and nature of groups and activities that will be accommodated after school hours
   f. Whether locker rooms and facilities will be made available for public use.

3. Specific description of various aspects of the physical education and sport program that affect the architects:

   a. Class size, scheduling, and number of instructors—present and future projection
   b. Preferred method of handling students—for example, flow of traffic in classrooms, gyms, pools, locker rooms, and shower rooms—and distance to outside play areas
   c. Storage requirements (e.g., size and space by square footage) and preferred method of handling permanent equipment and supplies
   d. Primary user groups and other extracurricular use of facilities (It helps the architect if the educational specifications can describe a typical week's use of the proposed facility, whcih would include a typical daily program, after-school use, and potential community integration)
   e. Rules, regulations, and safety codes concerning various user groups and physical activities should be reaffirmed. All user groups must be involved in this process.

Meeting with the architect. At this point, it is advisable to meet with the architect to discuss specifications to ensure complete understanding and to allow the architect to point out certain restrictions or limitations that may be anticipated even before the first preliminary plan is made. There is no use creating elaborate plans if the only space available is one that is directly over an earthquake fault line!

Design. The following factors might be considered in the design of the facility and discussed with the architect.

1. *Budget.* An adequate budget should be allowed for the participants and the community to be proud of the completed project.

2. *Function.* Physical education and sport facilities should be durable, multipurpose, easily maintained, functional, safe, secure, and user friendly.

3. *Acoustics.* Use the service of acoustical consultants.

4. *Public address system.* How is it to be used—for instruction, sporting events, general communication?

5. *Aesthetics.* The design and color scheme should be compatible with surrounding environs, including existing structures and the immediate community.

6. *Fenestration (window treatment).* Consider light control, potential window breakage, and

vision panel; windows in gymnasium areas and all high-traffic areas should have safety glass and be well marked.

7. *Ventilation.* The area should be zoned for flexibility of use. This means greater ventilation when a larger number of spectators or users are present, or a reduction for single class groups or in isolated areas such as locker and storage rooms. Special attention must be given to proper ventilation of uniform drying rooms, gymnasium storage areas, and locker, sauna, and shower areas. Ventilation equipment should have a low noise level and maximal efficiency rating.

8. *Supplementary equipment in the gymnasium.* Such equipment should be held to a minimum. Supplementary equipment, such as fire boxes, drinking fountains, and electrical light boxes should be recessed but accessible for all user groups.

9. *Compactness and integration.* Keep volume compact—large, barnlike spaces are unpleasant and are costly to heat and maintain. Integrate and divide the facility as far as budget permits.

10. *Mechanical or electrical features.* Special attention should be given to location of panel boards, chalk and bulletin boards, video monitors, fire alarm, folding doors, and drop nets. All must be easy to use and safe.

Further critique with the architect. The architect begins to develop plans from an understanding of the initial requirements he or she has considered in relation to the design factors listed. Aesthetics (how it looks), project budget, technology, and function will significantly determine the shape of your facility plans.

When the basic plan is set (e.g., square footage, cost estimate), the architect will usually call in consulting engineers to discuss the structural and mechanical systems before approval of the plan. These systems will have been outlined by the architect, but usually are not discussed with planning teams other than in generalities before the plan is in approximate final form.

More meetings are then conducted regarding approval of preliminary plans and proposed structural and mechanical systems, including the use of materials after the incorporation in the preliminary plans.

If supplementary financing by government or private sector agencies is involved, the plans or set of drawings will have been submitted to those agencies with a project outline or specifications as soon as the plan has been sufficiently developed to establish the area. If the agency approves the application as submitted by the architect, the final preliminary working drawings are started.

Final processing. It is advisable to settle all matters that can be settled during preliminary planning to save time and expense. If this method is employed, greater clarity is assured and less changing or misunderstanding results (see the box on p. 257). On completion of the preliminary plan and agreement of the planning committee, the plans are then submitted to higher management (e.g., School Board, Board of Regents) for approval, and competitive bids are sent out. From these a cooperative and coordinated effort between the planning team (representing the user), architect, and contractor remains in place until the facility is on line.

INDOOR FACILITIES

Several special areas and facilities are needed by physical education and sport programs. These typically include such areas as management and staff offices; locker, shower and drying rooms; gymnasiums, special activity areas; and indoor swimming pools.

Management and Staff Offices

It is important, as far as practical and possible, for physical educators and athletic directors to have a section of a building set aside for management and staff offices. At minimum, the area should be a large central office with an outer office that can serve as a waiting room and reception area. The central office provides a place where secretarial and clerical work is performed; computer systems are housed; and records, files, and office supplies are secured. The waiting room may also serve as a reception point where people can wait for staff members.

COMMON ERRORS MADE BY MANAGERS IN FACILITY PLANNING AND DEVELOPMENT

Some common mistakes made by managers and athletic directors in facility planning and development include the following:
- Failure to adequately project enrollments and program needs into the future (facilities are difficult to expand or change, so this is a significant error).
- Failure to provide for multiple use of facilities.
- Failure to provide for adequate accessibility for students in physical education and recreational sport and also for community user groups.
- Failure to observe basic health factors regarding lighting, safety, and ventilation.
- Failure to provide adequate space for the conduct of a comprehensive program of physical education and sport activities.
- Failure to provide appropriate accommodations for spectators and persons with disabilities.
- Failure to soundproof areas of the building where noise will interfere with educational functions.
- Failure to meet with the architect to present views on program needs during the early planning process.
- Failure to provide adequate staff offices.
- Failure to provide adequate storage space.
- Failure to provide adequate space for privacy for medical services.
- Failure to provide entrances large enough to transport equipment.
- Failure to observe desirable current professional standards.
- Failure to provide for adequate study of cost in terms of durability, time, money, and effective instruction.

- Failure to properly locate teaching stations with service facilities.
- Failure to provide adequate locker and dressing space.
- Failure to plan dressing and shower area so as to reduce foot traffic to a minimum and establish clean, dry aisles for bare feet.
- Failure to provide a nonskid surface on dressing, shower, and toweling room floors.
- Inadequate provision for drinking fountains.
- Failure to provide acoustical treatment where needed.
- Failure to provide and properly locate toilet facilities to serve *all* participants and spectators.
- Failure to provide doorways, hallways, or ramps so that equipment may be moved easily.
- Failure to design equipment rooms for convenient and quick check-in and check-out.
- Failure to provide mirrors and shelving for boys' and girls' dressing facilities.
- Faiure to plan locker and dressing rooms with correct traffic pattern to swimming pools.
- Failure to construct shower, toilet, and dressing rooms with sufficient floor slope and properly located drains.
- Failure to place shower heads low enough and in such a position that the spray is kept within the shower room.
- Failure to provide shelves in the toilet room.

Separate offices for the staff members should be provided, if possible. This provides a place where conferences can be conducted in private and without interruption. This is an important consideration for counseling, meeting with parents, and discussing other school-related business. If separate offices are not practical, a desk and office divider should be provided for each staff member. There should, however, be a private room available for conferences.

Other facilities that make the administrative and

staff setup more efficient and enjoyable are staff locker and dressing rooms, a staff lounge, departmental library, conference room, and private toilet and lavatory facilities.

Locker, Shower, and Drying Rooms

Physical education and sport activities require facilities for storage of clothes and uniforms, as well as for showering and drying. These are essential to good health and a well-organized program.

Locker and shower rooms should be readily accessible to all users and close to activity areas. Locker rooms should not be congested places that people want to get out of as soon as possible. Instead, they should provide ample room for storage and dressing lockers, stationary benches, mirrors, recessed lighting fixtures, scales, sauna, hair dryers, and drinking fountains.

A minimum of 20 square feet per individual at peak load, exclusive of the locker space, is generally required to provide proper locker room space.

Storage lockers should also be provided for each individual. An additional number of lockers equal to 10% of those needed should be installed for expanded enrollments or membership. Lockers are typically permanently assigned and can be used to hold essential clothing and other necessary supplies. They can be smaller than the dressing lockers; some recommended sizes are $7\frac{1}{2} \times 12 \times 24$ inches, $6 \times 12 \times 36$ inches, and $7\frac{1}{2} \times 12 \times 18$ inches. Basket lockers are not favored by many experts because of hygiene problems, because an attendant is required,

and because of the logistics involved in carting the baskets from place to place.

Dressing lockers are used by participants only when actually engaging in activity. They are large, usually $12 \times 12 \times 54$ inches or $12 \times 12 \times 48$ inches in elementary schools, and $12 \times 12 \times 72$ inches or $12 \times 15 \times 60$ for junior high, middle, and secondary schools and colleges, as well as for community recreation programs.

Locker rooms should provide dressing and storage lockers for all participants. Adequate space should be provided so that dressing is not done in cramped quarters. Lockers should also have proper ventilation, be periodically inspected, and kept clean at all times.

Shower rooms that have both group and cubicle showers should be provided. Some facility planners recommend that the number of shower heads be equal to 30% to 40% of the enrollment at peak load. Another recommendation suggests a 1:4 shower to person ratio at peak load; University National Standards insist on 10 shower heads for the first 30 users with an additional 1:40 ratio thereafter. Showers should be 4 feet apart or dispersed in a circular group pattern, and a graded change of water temperature is recommended. Shower rooms should also be equipped with liquid soap dispensers, good ventilation and heating, nonslip floors, and recessed plumbing. The ceiling should be constructed to prevent condensation. The shower area should be washed daily to prevent athlete's foot and other contaminations. A towel and laundry service should be initiated if it does not already exist.

A drying room adjacent to the shower room is essential. This should be equipped with proper drainage, good ventilation, towel bar, drinking fountain, mirrors, and appropriate hair drying equipment.

Gymnasiums

The type and number of gymnasiums that should be part of a school or physical plant depend on the number of individuals who will be participating and the variety of activities that will be conducted.

Athletic Business[1] lists some suggestions to consider when constructing or renovating a gymnasium. One of the major suggestions is to save money on the

Locker rooms should present a healthful environment.

square footage, not on dollars per square foot. The wrong time to save money, they point out, is when considering building materials. With careful planning it is possible to buy the best materials and finishes. It is important to visit other facilities and talk to management to find out the advantages and disadvantages of those in use.

It is also generally agreed that in schools it is best to have the gymnasium located in a separate wing of the building to isolate the potential noise and to provide a convenient location for community-based groups that will be anxious to use such facilities.

Many gymnasiums have folding doors or curtains that divide them into halves, thirds, or fourths and allow activities to be conducted simultaneously. This has proved satisfactory where separate gymnasiums or teaching stations could not be provided.

General construction features for gymnasiums include smooth walls, hardwood floors (maple—laid lengthwise—is preferred), recessed lights, recessed radiators, adequately screened or safety windows, and storage space for the apparatus and other equipment.

In elementary schools that need only one teaching

Dividing curtains and partitions create additional teaching stations.

station, a minimum floor space of 36 × 52 feet is suggested. Where two teaching stations are desired, floor space of 54 × 90 feet, which may be divided by a folding partition, is recommended.

In junior, middle, and senior high schools where only one teaching station is desired, a minimum floor space of 48 × 66 feet is necessary. An area 66 × 96 feet exclusive of bleachers will provide two teaching stations of minimal size. Where seating capacity is desired, additional space will be needed. If more than two teaching stations are desired, the gymnasium area may be extended to provide an additional station, or activity rooms may be added. Of course, the addition of a swimming pool also provides another functional teaching station.

Other considerations for gymnasiums might include provisions for basketball backboards, mountings for floor plates for various apparatus that will be used, places for hanging and storing mats, outlets for various instructional aids (e.g., video, computer analysis, interactive video disc), proper line markings for activities, bulletin boards, a false wall for rock climbing, and other essentials necessary for a well-rounded program.

Just as safe and properly constructed and maintained equipment should be a part of outdoor facilities, so should they be a part of indoor physical education facilities. Adequate space should be provided for all the activity phases of the program, whether they are in the gymnasium, swimming pool, or auxiliary areas. Mats should be used as a protective measure on walls, floors, and other areas where participants may be at risk. Drinking fountains and cuspidors should be recessed, and doors should open away from the playing floor. Proper flooring should be used; tile-cement floors are sometimes undesirable where activity takes place. Accessibility and appropriate space should be provided for people with disabilities so that all facilities (indoor, outdoor, locker room, etc.) are fully accessible.

Clothing and equipment used in physical education activities should meet health and safety standards. If not, odors and germs will thrive, causing an unpleasant environment that may help spread disease. Gymnasium mats, for example, should be kept clean. Regular physical education clothing, not street clothes, should be worn except in appropriate and designated activities. Clean and safe clothing, including sport footwear, should be required.

Guidelines for Gymnasium Planning

The following guidelines are valid for management, architects, board members, consultants, and other persons involved in gymnasium planning. Many of these guidelines are overlooked by those responsible for gymnasium construction.

The roof. If the roof is not properly designed before construction, costly changes in equipment installation may occur later. Ceiling support beams that may be part of the construction could also be employed by the physical educator to make maximal use of the facility. The design of the roof should allow for support beams strong enough to absorb the stress placed on them in various activities. Support beams should be placed to allow maximal flexibility concerning the placement of equipment such as scoreboards and gymnastic apparatus. Ceilings should reflect light and absorb sound and the distance from the floor to the exposed beams should be at least 22 to 24 feet.

The floor. The floor is a vital part of the gymnasium and should be constructed from hardwood, not tile. Although more expensive, hardwood is safer, more resilient, does not become slick, and is better for sports performance. Plates for floor apparatus such as the high bar or volleyball standards should be designed with safety and flexibility in mind. Floor markings should be placed after the prime coat of seal has been applied and before the application of the finishing coat.

The walls. Electrical outlets should be provided throughout the gymnasium so that audiovisual instructional strategies can be used at each teaching station. Computers, timing devices, scoreboards, public address systems, and outlets for the media should be kept in mind. Walls behind baskets should be recessed and padded. This is safer than hanging pads near glazed tile walls. It is a good idea to provide a smooth wall for participants to practice their throwing, catching, and racket skills. A line could be taped along the wall to indicate the height of the tennis or badminton net. The wall can also be used for other assorted targets and goals.

Lighting. Proper illumination that meets approved standards, with selective controls to vary intensity depending on activity, is a necessity. Durable lighting with recessed and protected fixtures is essential. This helps prevent bulb or tube breakage from ball activities.

Acoustics. Noise control should be a primary consideration in any gymnasium construction. Acoustic treatment of ceilings and walls can help reduce or eliminate noise.

Special Activity Areas

Although gymnasiums take up considerable space, there should still be additional areas for activities essential to physical education and sport programs.

Wherever possible, additional activity areas and teaching stations should be provided for remedial or adapted activities, apparatus, tennis (1 court/400 school population), handball, squash, weight training, dance, rhythms, fencing, and exhibitions and shows. The activities to be provided will depend on the interests of the user groups and type of activities involved in the program. The recommended size for such teaching stations is 30 × 50 × 24 feet, or 40 × 60 × 24 feet. A 75 × 90 foot auxiliary gymnasium is ideal. The adapted/developmental activities room, if the school is fortunate enough to have one, should be equipped with items such as horizontal ladders, mirrors, mats, climbing ropes, stall bars and benches, fixed and free weights, dumbbells, and other equipment and assessment materials suited to individual or small group instruction.

It should also be noted that regulation classrooms and other multipurpose space can be converted into additional teaching stations. This may be feasible where the actual construction of such costly facilities may not be practical.

Auxiliary rooms. The main auxiliary rooms are equipment, supply, check-out, custodial, and laundry rooms.

Equipment and supply rooms should be easily accessible from the gymnasium and other activity areas. In these rooms balls, nets, standards, and other equipment and supplies needed for the program are stored. Towels and uniforms can also be distributed from this area, as can first aid materials when necessary. The size of these rooms varies according to the number of participants, the number of activities offered, and the size of the program, as well as the physical plant.

Check-out rooms should be provided seasonally. They house the equipment and supplies used in various seasonal activities. They may be less centrally located and more proximate to fields, courts, or ice rinks.

Custodial rooms provide a place for storing some equipment and supplies used to maintain these specialized facilities. They too should be appropriately maintained, and provide a comfortable environmental setting.

Laundry rooms should be large enough to accommodate the washing and drying of such essential items as towels, uniforms, and swimsuits. They should be well ventilated and possess the shelf space necessary for a well-organized and neat appearance.

Indoor Swimming Pools

Major design decisions must be made if an organization decides to construct a pool. These include items such as the nature of the program to be conducted, philosophy of user groups, type of overflow system, dimensions and shape of pool, depth of the water, type of finish, type of filters and water treatment system, construction material, amount of deck area, types of air handling and climate control systems, illumination and sound systems, and number of spectators to be accommodated.

Some mistakes that should be avoided in the construction of a pool include entrances to the pool from the locker rooms opening onto the deep rather than the shallow end of the pool, the pool base finished with slippery material such as glazed tile, insufficient depth of water for diving, improper placement of ladders and guard rails, the placement of starting blocks in shallow water, insufficient rate of recirculation of water to accommodate peak participation loads, inadequate storage space, failure to use acoustic material on ceiling and walls, insufficient illumination, slippery tile on decks, and an inadequate overflow system at the ends of the pool.

Some trends and innovations in pool design and operation include the Rim-Flow Overflow System, inflatable roof structure, the skydome design, pool tent cover, floating swimming pool complex including moveable bulkheads, prefabrication of pool tanks, automation of pool recirculating and filter systems, regenerative cycle filter system, adjustable height diving platform, variable bottom depths, fluorescent underwater lights, underwater sound systems, automatic cleaning systems, and wave-making machines.

Swimming pools have two main objectives: to provide instructional and competitive programs and to provide recreation.

The swimming pool should be located on or above the ground level, have a southern exposure, be isolated from other units in the building, and be easily accessible from the central dressing and locker rooms. Materials that have been found most adaptive to swimming pools are smooth, glazed, light-colored tile or brick.

The standard indoor pool is 75 feet long. The width should be a multiple of 7 or 9 feet, with a minimum of 35 feet. Depths vary from 2 feet 6 inches at the shallow end to 4 feet 6 inches at the outer limits of the shallow area. The shallow or instructional area should make up about two thirds of the pool and be separated by pool lane dividers from the deeper areas, which taper to 9 to 12 feet in depth. An added important factor is a moveable bulkhead that can be used to divide a large pool into various instructional or practice areas.

Water depth under the 1- or 3-meter board should be 12 feet or more, and under any platform, 18 feet or more.

The deck space around the pool should be constructed of a nonslip material and must provide ample space for land drills and demonstrations. The area above the water should be unobstructed. The ceiling should be at least 25 feet above the water and 20 feet above the diving board height if this is part of the complex. The walls and the ceiling of the pool area should be acoustically treated.

The swimming pool should be constructed to receive as much natural light as possible, with the windows located on the sides rather than on the ends. Artificial lighting should be recessed in the ceiling. Good lighting is essential, especially near the diving board, where glare should be eliminated. Underwater lighting is attractive but not essential.

There should be an efficient system for adequately

The planning of the University of Minnesota Aquatics Complex.

The University of Minnesota Aquatics Complex now in operation.

Health Considerations for Swimming Pools

Swimming pools need special attention whether indoor or outdoor. First, the pool should be properly constructed to provide for adequate filtration, circulation, and chemical treatment. The computer can assist in planning this task. Next to water treatment, air handling is crucial to maintain a proper educational and competitive environment. A daily log should be kept on things such as water temperature, facility humidity, hydrogen ion concentration, residual chlorine, and other important factors. Regulations and rules for pool use, as well as safety and emergency procedures, should be established and appropriately posted; all user groups should be acquainted with them.

Athletic Training and Sports Medicine Facilities

Athletic training, sports medicine, and health services are an important part of the program and require adequate facilities. These facets of physical education and sport are addressed in Chapter 12.

OUTDOOR FACILITIES

The outdoor facilities discussed in this section are play areas, game areas, outdoor swimming pools, camping and outdoor pursuit, facilities for persons with disabilities, and other special activity areas.

Play Areas

Many factors must be considered when planning outdoor facilities for schools and colleges. Before a site is selected, it is important to appraise the location, topography, soil drainage, water supply and table, size, shape, and natural features. The outdoor facilities should be as near the gymnasium and locker rooms as possible, yet far enough from the classrooms so that noise will not be disturbing.

The play areas should serve the needs and interests of the students for the entire school year and at the same time provide a setting for activities during vacation periods. The needs and interests of the community must also be considered, especially in some communities where physical plants and facilities such as schools and recreation centers are

heating and circulating the water. When possible, solar and self-heating systems should be adopted to save energy and reduce pool overhead costs. The temperature of the water should range from 78° to 82° F.

An office adjacent to the pool with open vision to the pool where communication and first aid supplies can be stored is advisable. Such an office should be equipped with windows that overlook the entire length of the pool. Also, lavatory and toilet facilities should be available and, of course, the pool must be fully accessible.

The swimming pool is a costly operation. Therefore it is essential that it be planned with the help of the best advice obtainable. Specialists who are well acquainted with such facilities and who conduct aquatic activities should be brought into conferences with the architect, a representative from the public health department, and experts in essentials such as lighting, heating, acoustics, construction, and law.

shared. Because the community uses the areas after the school day is over, a joint planning team with community input is strongly recommended.

The size of the area should be determined on the basis of activities offered in the program and the number of individuals who will be using the facilities at peak load. Possibilities for expansion should also be kept in mind. Playing fields and playgrounds should have good turf and be clear of rocks, holes, and uneven surfaces. A dirty, dusty surface, for example, can aggravate conditions such as emphysema, chronic bronchitis, and allergies. Safety precautions should also be provided in terms of regular inspection of facilities and replacement of worn equipment and fenced-in playfields and playgrounds, particularly where there is heavy traffic adjoining these facilities. Rubber, asphalt, synthetic materials, and other substances that require little maintenance and help to free an area from cinders, gravel, stones, and dust are being used on many outdoor surfaces. In some sections of the country limited shelters are also being utilized to provide protection from the cold, rain, wind, and sun. All outdoor areas should have accessible sanitary drinking fountains and toilet facilities as needed.

Elementary school. The activities program in the K-6 learning environment suggests what facilities should be available. Children in the primary grades engage in large muscle activity involving adaptations of climbing, jumping, skipping, kicking, throwing, leaping, and catching. Children in the intermediate and upper elementary grades perform these fundamental skill activities and others in low organization games and various cooperative and team activities.

The playground area for an elementary school should be located near the building and should be easily accessible from the classrooms. Children in kindergarten should have a section of the playground for their exclusive use. This should be at least 5000 square feet and separated from the rest of the playground. It should consist of a surfaced area, a grass area, and a place for sand and digging. The sand area should be enclosed to prevent it from being scattered or shared by local pets. It is also wise to have a shaded area where storytelling and similar

quiet activities may be conducted. Some essential equipment includes swings, slides, seesaws, climbing structures, tables, and seats.

Elementary school children should have play space that includes surfaced and grass areas, play equipment, and a shaded area. The grass area provides space for varied and modified field and team games such as speedball, soccer, field hockey, softball, and fieldball. The play area should provide equipment such as climbing bars in the form of a jungle gym, horizontal bars, and Giant Strides. There should be ample space to provide for the safety of the participants. The shaded area may provide space for activities such as marbles, hopscotch, ring toss, and storytelling. The surfaced area may serve as a year-round activities center for both school and community. It can house basketball, tennis, and handball courts, games of minimal organization, and other creative activities. This area should be paved with material that provides resilience, safety, and durability. Rapid and efficient drainage is also essential. Lines may be painted on the area for various games. Schools should allow additional space adjacent to this area for possible future expansion.

Other community-based recreation areas that have important implications for K-6 students include any landscaped, parklike areas. These provide a place for quiet activities such as dramatics and informal gatherings, fitness trails, hiking, and a place for children to have gardening and picnic opportunities.

Junior high and middle school. The junior high or middle school play and recreation area, planned and developed for the children who attend the school and also for the adults in the community, should be located on a site that consists of 10 to 25 acres. Local conditions will determine the amount of land available.

Many of the facilities addressed in the elementary school section may be incorporated in the junior high school. In many cases, however, the various play areas should be increased in size. The necessary facilities should provide for those activities that will be part of the basic physical education, recreational sport, and varsity sport programs. Often times the community shares this space, so ample field, court, and gymnasium space with lighting is required for evening use.

A landscaped, parklike area should also be provided for various recreational activities for the students and the community. Activities such as walking, picnicking, roller skating and blading, bicycling, playing broomball, sailing, nordic skiing, and fly casting might be considered appropriate.

Senior high school. The senior high school physical education program is characterized by individual and lifetime sports, as well as team game activities. This emphasis, together with the popularity of recreational and interscholastic sport and the fact that facilities are needed for recreational use by the community, requires an even larger area than those for the two previous educational levels. Estimates range from 10 to 40 acres for such a physical plant.

Most of the environmental concepts and areas that have been listed in discussing the elementary and junior high school should be included at the senior high level. Considerably more space for physical education class instruction and the various field games is necessary to provide full-sized official fields for softball, field hockey, soccer, speedball, lacrosse, football, and baseball, because recreational sport and the interscholastic programs, as well as the community education and recreation program, usually share these facilities. Facility management is therefore a crucial issue to the conduct of an effective and efficient program.

Football, soccer, and track can be provided for in an area of approximately 4 acres, with the football/soccer field placed within an enlarged track oval. Baseball and softball need an area of about 700 square feet to allow safe participation. With so many user teams practicing, however, game space should be protected from daily wear and tear, so additional field space with lighting capacity is strongly recommended. The more field space and creative configurations that can be adapted for small-sided games, the better.

Game Areas

The recommended dimensions for game areas for school physical education and sport programs as

outlined by a group of experts are illustrated in Table 9-1. One acre will accommodate four tennis courts, four handball courts, three badminton courts, and two volleyball courts.

The game area should allow for basic instructional physical education classes and also provide fields for softball, field hockey, soccer, speedball, lacrosse, and court areas that include badminton, basketball, softball, team handball, volleyball, shuffleboard, and other activities. There should be appropriate space for track and field. A 400-meter oval, or at least a straightaway of 120 meters that is 6 to 8 meters wide, is mandatory. Most interscholastic sport complexes include a football/soccer field, a track, and baseball and softball diamonds, as well as ample practice and scrimmage fields.

Winter activities should not be forgotten. With such activities gaining popular, provisions should be made for skating, cross country skiing, broomball, and other winter activities.

One state recommends the outdoor facilities for the basic needs of a physical education and recreation program for K-12 should consist of a minimum

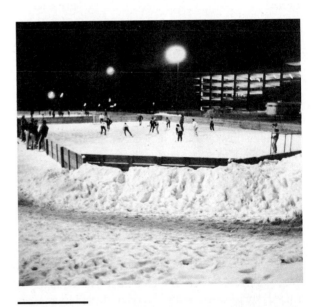

Multisport winter activities are popular in both schools and communities. Evening broomball in Minneapolis, MN.

TABLE 9-1. Recommended dimensions for game areas[2]

	Elementary	Upper grades	High school (adults)	Side and end safety space
Basketball	40′ × 60′	42′ × 74′	50′ × 84′	6′; 8′
Volleyball	69′ × 50′	25′ × 50′	30′ × 60′	6′; 6′
Badminton			20′ × 44′	6′; 8′
Paddle tennis			20′ × 44′	6′; 8′
Deck dennis			18′ × 40′	
Tennis		36′ × 78′	36′ × 78′	12′; 21′
Ice hockey			85′ × 200′	
Field hockey			180′ × 300′	8′; 8′
Horseshoes		10′ × 40′	10′ × 50′	
Shuffleboard			6′ × 52′	6′; 2′
Lawn bowling			14′ × 110′	
Tetherball	10′ circle	12′ circle	12′ circle	
Croquet	38′ × 60′	38′ × 60′	38′ × 60′	
Handball/Racquetball	18′ × 26′	18′ × 26′	20′ × 40′	
Baseball			350′ × 350′	
Archery		50′ × 150′	50′ × 300′	15′; 50′
Softball (12″ ball)	150′ × 150′	200′ × 200′	250′ × 250′	
Football—with 400-yard track— 220-yard straightaway			300′ × 600′	
Touch football		120′ × 300′	160′ × 360′	
6-person football			120′ × 300′	
Soccer	40′ × 60′	165′ × 360′	225′ × 360′	8′; 8′
Squash			18.5′ × 32′	
Wrestling/combatives			24′ × 24′	5′; 5′

of 12 acres. This area should be divided into an elementary area of 3 acres; courts area of 1 acre; high school recreational sport area of 5 acres, and an interscholastic sport area of 3 acres.

A concept in play areas is the multipurpose sports court. This small, self-contained fenced-in court provides for a variety of activities in a small area. The average sports court is 12 × 24 × 10½ feet and may be completely enclosed (including top) with a weatherproofed steel tube and link fence that rests like a box on the floor of the court. Low-cost lighting and canvas covering can be used for evening and cold weather activities. The floor is frequently a raised, weather-resistant, wooden deck playing surface that allows for quick drainage and year-round play. When needed, pads or other roll-out playing surfaces can be laid over the wooden deck. The court can then be used for basketball, volleyball, paddle tennis, pickle ball, handball, and other activities. This type of court is excellent for high-density urban school areas, corporate recreation programs, planned communities, and apartment complexes.

Outdoor Swimming Pools

The outdoor swimming pool is a popular and important facility in almost all communities. To a great degree climatic conditions determine the advisability of such a facility.

Outdoor pools are built in various shapes, including oval, circular, T-shaped, and rectangular. Rectangular pools are most popular because of easier construction and practicality of conducting competitive swimming events.

The size of pools varies, depending on the number

of persons they are to serve. One recommendation has been made that 12 square feet of water space per swimmer be allotted for swimming purposes or, if the deck is taken into consideration, 20 square feet of space for swimming and walking area per swimmer.

The decks for outdoor pools should be larger than those for indoor pools. This larger space will accommodate more people and also provide space for lounging and sunbathing.

Shower facilities should be provided to ensure that every swimmer is clean before entering the

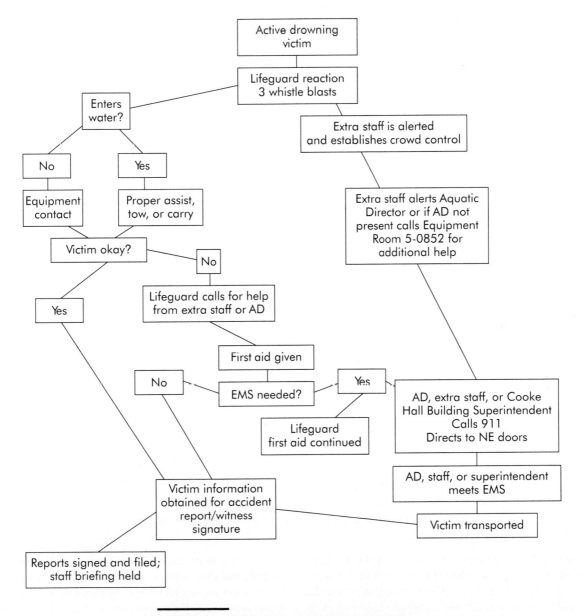

FIGURE 9-1 Active drowning emergency guidelines.

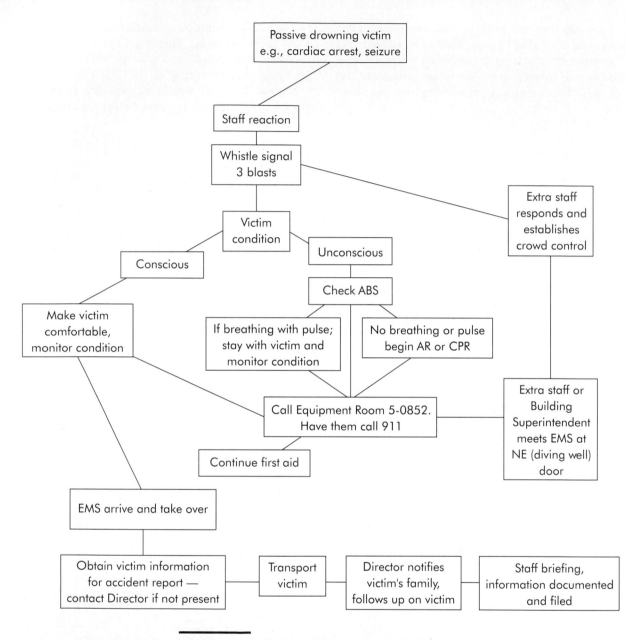

FIGURE 9-2 Passive drowning emergency guidelines.

water. A basket system for storing clothes has been found practical, but when the pool is located adjacent to a school, it is sometimes practical to use the school's locker and shower facilities. However, it is strongly advised that wherever possible, separate shower, locker, and toilet facilities be provided, and that accessibility for all participants is ensured.

Because swimming is popular at night as well as in the daytime, lights should be provided so that the community may participate in this healthful and enjoyable activity.

Diving boards generally are constructed of fiber-

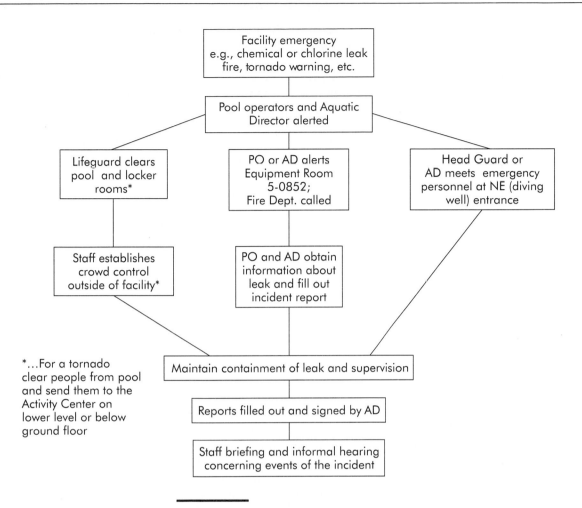

FIGURE 9-3 Facility emergency guidelines.

glass or plastic, and the standard heights of 1 and 3 meters are typically found in most outdoor aquatic facilities. The board or any diving takeoff area should have a nonskid surface, be securely fastened to the ground or foundation, and conform to state safety standards and recommendations for water depth as previously discussed.

The rules and regulations concerning the facility, including diving, should be clearly posted near the appropriate areas. Clear markings, firm dividers of shallow and deep water, and a quality guard staff are also a must for all aquatic facilities. Management should provide clear emergency guidelines (Figures 9-1, 9-2, and 9-3) concerning active and passive drowning victims, as well as facility emergency.

These sample emergency guidelines should serve as a model to develop policies and procedures that are crucial to sound facility management.

Camping and Outdoor Pursuit

Because camping and outdoor pursuit (hiking, rock climbing, skiing, small craft, etc.) are becoming increasingly popular in both school and recreational programs, they should receive full consideration for inclusion in a quality physical education program.

Camping areas should be located within easy reach of the school and community. They should be in locations desirable from the standpoints of scenic beauty, safety, accessibility, clear and unobstructed water, and natural resources pertinent to the program offered. Activities usually offered include fishing, hiking, rock climbing, orienteering, swimming, campcraft, boating and small craft, ecostudy, and appropriate winter activities (e.g., alpine and cross country skiing, snow shoeing). The natural terrain and other resources can contribute much toward such a program.

There should be housing, eating, sanitation, waterfront, and other facilities essential to camp life. These do not have to be elaborate, but they should provide adequate protection against the elements or in case of emergency. Facilities should also meet acceptable standards of health and sanitation. In general, camp structures should be adapted to the climatic and environmental conditions of the particular area in which the camp is located. It is wise to consult public health authorities, department of natural resources, or other appropriate professionals when selecting a campsite. Sometimes existing facilities can be shared (e.g., YMCA, Scouts) or converted to camp use. The campsite could also be purchased outright by the school system or community, or acquired under a long-term lease agreement by coordinating with other local user groups or school districts.

FACILITIES FOR PEOPLE WITH DISABILITIES

Since the passage of PL 94-142 more consideration has been given to the facility needs of people with disabilities. These facilities in particular are concerned with the students' programs of specialized developmental exercises, perceptual-motor ability activities, health and fitness, modified sports, stress management, rest, and relaxation. Facilities for individuals usually vary from school to school and according to the disabling conditions of those served.

Contemporary physical education and sport has the person with disabilities returning to the least restrictive environment (LRE) and to the gymnasium and activity whenever appropriate and possible. Special case teams design appropriate user IEPs, and some special equipment may be necessary; however, mainstreaming back into the gymnasium as well as the classroom is the trend of the 1990s. This trend requires accessibility, sound planning, and a committed team effort by faculty and staff.

For those schools and communities that provide people with disabilities separate developmental space, a minimum area of 40 by 60 feet is recommended. Creative teachers can construct numerous challenging, flexible goals and fitness courses utilizing much of the standard equipment and physical plant (e.g., aquatic facilities) already available.

Some schools also make use of nearby community or private facilities, and this trend will grow as more specialized resources and specific physical activity are legislated and supported by the community. With scarce financial inputs it is envisaged that the school and community will have to work even more closely together in order to meet the needs of this special user group.

OTHER SPECIAL ACTIVITY AREAS

Other special activity areas needing attention include those involving dance, gymnastics, weight training, wrestling, martial arts, racquetball, squash, and other activity areas. Research and assessment facilities, especially at colleges and universities, should also be provided not only for direct use by the students, staff, and faculty, but also to enable researchers to contribute to the body of knowledge of the profession.

Because dance has always been, and continues to be, a very popular activity, special facilities should be provided. It is recommended that a minimum of 100 square feet of space per student be provided. Full-length mirrors, a sound and video system, and practice bars on one wall at heights of 34 and 42 inches are required for a quality program. The floor is an important consideration, and it has been recommended it consist of sealed and buffed hard northern maple. Sound and video systems, proper acoustics, and other appropriate dance-specific supplies should also be available.

Gymnastics is another special activity area, and it is recommended that 120 × 90 feet of floor space, with a minimum ceiling height of 23 feet, should be provided.

Gymnastics room renovation at the University of Minnesota, Minneapolis.

Weight training is another very popular activity for both girls and boys. A minimum of 2500 square feet should be provided with both fixed and free weights available. A weight room facility design is presented in Figure 9-4.[7]

A wrestling and martial arts area of a minimum 50 × 100 feet will provide enough space for two 42 × 42 foot mats. Judo, karate, and self-defense, among other combatives, have become popular activities for all age levels and should be housed in an appropriate space that is well ventilated and cleaned daily to prevent the spread of various communicable germs (e.g., impetigo, herpes simplex).

Racquetball and handball courts are common, particularly in colleges, universities, and club settings. Each four-wall court is 40 feet long and 20 feet wide, with a ceiling height of 20 feet. Multipurpose squash courts (18.5 × 32 feet) can also be housed within this area.

Such activities as indoor tennis, fencing, archery, golf, skating, skiing, and rock climbing also deserve full consideration when designing facilities. Technology has enabled many of these activities to be delivered indoors at any time of year.

An integral part of many physical plant designs, especially at the college and university level, are research and teaching laboratories or teaching stations. Space for exercise science (e.g., biomechanics, exercise physiology), psychosocial training (e.g., behavior, performance, and skill enhancement), and resource centers, as well as sport medicine (training and first aid rooms) should be provided for all students, staff, and faculty. This space too must be accessible, well-maintained, functional, and in budgetary alignment with the mission of the department or college in which it is housed.

CONSTRUCTION TRENDS IN PHYSICAL EDUCATION AND SPORT FACILITIES

There are many new trends in facilities, supplies, and materials for physical education and sport programs,[9] including new paving and surface materials, roll-out floor systems, new types of equipment and personal storage units (lockers), air-supported structures, improved landscapes, new ceiling and lighting systems, new shapes for swimming pools, partial shelters, and synthetic grass, just to name a few. Combination indoor-outdoor pools, physical fitness equipment for outdoor use, all-weather tennis courts, and various kinds of climbing walls are other new developments that have had an impact on physical education and sport facility management, as well as program development.

In gymnasium construction some of the new features include using modern engineering techniques and materials, which has resulted in welded steel and laminated wood modular frames; arched and gabled roofs; domes that provide areas completely free from internal supports; exterior surfaces of aluminum, steel, fiberglass, and plastics; different window patterns and styles; myriad floor surfaces

FIGURE 9-4 Weight training facility and design.

The University of Idaho has a portable football field. The tartan turf is 200 × 370 feet and can be rolled up and stored on a 210-foot long steel drum.

including nonslip material; prefabricated wall surfaces; and better lighting systems with improved quality and quantity and reduced glare. Facilities are moving from using regular glass to using either a plastic and fiberglass panel or to an overhead skydome. Lightweight fiberglass, sandwich panels, or fabricated sheets of translucent fiberglass laminated over an aluminum framework are proving popular. These require no painting; maintenance, labor, and material cost is lower; shades, curtains, or blinds are not needed to eliminate glare; and the breakage problem is reduced or eliminated.

Locker rooms with built-in locks with combination changers, quiet tone control, and even coin-operated lockers have made their way into sport facilities. Ceramic nonslip tile is used extensively because of its durability and low-cost maintenance. Wall-hung toilet compartment features permit easier maintenance and sanitation with no chance for

rust to start from the floor. Odor control is being effectively handled by new dispensers and dehumidification systems. New thin-profile heating, ventilating, and air-conditioning fan coil units are now being used to provide improved ventilation, heating, and lighting. More walls and floors are being constructed of easily cleansed materials, which aids in improving sanitation.

New developments concerning indoor swimming pools include computers that have direct control over all filters, chlorinators, chemical pumps, and lever controllers; much larger deck space area constructed of nonslip ceramic tile; greater use of diatomaceous earth rather than sand filters to filter out small particles of matter including some bacteria; underwater lighting and sound; water level deck pools (the overflow gutters are placed in the deck surrounding the pool instead of in the pool's side walls, and provision is made for grating designed so that the water that overflows is drained to a trench under the deck without the possibility of debris returning to the pool); air-supported roofs that can serve as removable tops in a combination indoor-outdoor pool; and movable bulkheads.

New developments concerning outdoor swimming pools involve new shapes, including oval, wedge, kidney, figure-8, cloverleaf, and bean shaped, as well as modern accessories, including wave-making machines, gas heaters, automatic water levelers, and retractable roofs and sides. More supplemental recreational facilities (such as shuffleboard courts, volleyball, and horseshoes) and more deck equipment (including guard rails, slides, and pool covers) are being included around larger pools.

New concepts have been put to good use in the physical plants of the following schools:

Oak Grove High School, San Jose, California. This school has a movable interior partitioning system with adjustable lighting, acoustics, and air conditioning that can accommodate different types of activities on short notice.

Nova High School, Fort Lauderdale, Florida. This school spent 10% of the school's total cost on teaching aids so that all types of audiovisual materials could be used or piped into most classrooms and teaching stations in the school.

Andrews Senior High School, Andrews, Texas. Here the open court has a windowless exterior and faces inward to a concourse and a domed rotunda. Along the concourse are a swimming pool and gymnasium, and under the rotunda is an assembly area.

Holland High School, Holland, Michigan. This school constructed its plant on the multicampus plan, with four small schools sharing physical education and sports facilities.

Shattuck–St. Mary's School, Faribault, Minnesota. This school has recently expanded its ice arena to include new locker rooms. Eight tennis courts and a new synthetic track were also part of the expansion project.

Brooklyn Polytech, New York City. A bubble was erected on top of the physics building to house a gymnasium.

University of Texas at El Paso. This university covered its outdoor swimming pool with prefabricated material to have an all-weather, year-round facility.

LaVerne College, California. A "super tent," involving a cable-supported fabric roof structure made of fiberglass and Teflon, houses theater, gymnasium, cafeteria, bookstore, and health clinic.

Cuyahoga Falls, Ohio. Here a roof was installed over the swimming pool to provide residents with year-round swimming. In the summer, the roof is removed.

Thomas Jefferson Junior High School, Arlington, Virginia. This school has implemented the shared facilities concept by housing together performing arts, recreation, and physical education.

Harvard University, Cambridge, Massachusetts. A large air-supported structure for a new track facility has been erected; it is 250×300 feet, and 60 feet high.

Lewis and Clark Elementary School, St. Louis, Missouri. A physical education partial shelter has been erected with the sides of the open structure protected by banks of shrubbery.

Boston College, Chestnut Hill, Massachusetts. A roof design of hyperbolic paraboloids is used. This efficient structure spans a large area—42,000 square feet of floor space.

University of Minnesota, Minneapolis. A 16,000-pound (2000 pounds in water) moveable bulkhead is used to divide its aquatic facilities into various recreational and competitive configurations. Its filter and chemical systems are fully computerized, controlling chemical analyses and water treatment.

Limited Shelters for Physical Education

The shelter or limited shelter provides protection from extremes of climate, uses the desirable elements of the natural environment, and creates an interesting background for physical education and sport activities.

The actual design of the shelter is determined by climate, number of participants, type of activity program, and user group. Methods of controlling air movement may be developed by using natural elements (trees and plantings), architectural elements (wall, roofs, and screens), and mechanical devices (fan, moving walls, and dividers). Solar radiation

Super tent at LaVerne College, CA.

may be controlled with natural shading and moving walls. These shelters cost about half as much as the traditional gymnasium.

Air-Supported Structures

An air-supported structure consists of a large plastic bubble that is inflated and supported by continuous air pressure. It is the least expensive building that can be erected, costing from one fifth to one half of what a solid structure may cost. These facilities have housed military equipment and served as theaters, factories, swimming pools, tennis courts, indoor tracks, golf ranges, and gymnasiums.

The outside construction is usually made of vinyl-coated or Dacron polyester, which is lightweight, strong, and flexible. The fabric is flame-retardant, waterproof, tear-resistant, mildew-resistant, and sunlight-resistant. Installation is simple and may be completed in a few hours by a minimal crew. The installation process includes placement of the vinyl envelope and inflation. The bubble is supported by a blower that provides a constant flow of air pressure. The bubble may be easily dismantled by stopping the blower, opening the door, unhitching the attachments, and folding the bubble compactly.

Minigyms and Fitness Corners

Minigyms can be operated in the halls and alcoves of the school building. They may consist of climbing, pulling, and hanging apparatus that the students use between classes and at study hours, lunch, and recess. The concept is to distribute the gymnasium throughout the school. Some other suggestions include mats, chinning bars, incline benches and boards, walls to throw balls against, and carpeted corridors for stunts and tumbling.

Classrooms can also be turned into minigyms with fitness corners for exercise and equipment such as stationary bicycles, rowing machines, and stand-up desks to promote activity.

Court Games and Other Facilities

Rubber-cushioned tennis courts are being used in many facilities. They consist of tough durable material about 4 inches thick, which has the individual advantages of clay, turf, and composition courts combined in one surface. Portable roll-on surfaces are also being used by some school and community park systems for court games ranging from basketball to tennis, and from badminton to pickleball.

Other New Developments

New developments in physical education and sport facilities are numerous. Sculptured play apparatus has been produced by a number of firms. It is designed to be more conducive to imaginative movements and creativity than conventional equipment. Hard-surfaced, rubberized, all-weather running tracks; radiant heating of decks on swimming pools; heated wet rooms for teaching aquatics classes; floating roofs that eliminate non–load bearing walls; interior climate control; better indoor and outdoor lighting; new cooling systems for ice rinks; padding for use under apparatus and on walls; outdoor skating rinks; translucent plastic materials for swimming pool canopies and other uses; and electrically operated machinery to move equipment, partitions, and bleachers are just a few of the many facility enhancements that have been, and continue to be, upgraded.

Bellemare[3] lists some more of the latest facility developments for physical education and sport. Some of these are synthetic ice and snow, snowless ski hills, climbing walls, turntable skating, convertible roofs, mobile locker rooms, illuminated game lines, folding racquet courts, movable pool floors, computerized pool treatment, and myriad other challenging factors that may influence the management and planning of a physical education and sport program.

With the contemporary trend toward scarce inputs (e.g., lack of money and land), facility planning and creative and cooperative management of new and existing facilities are more crucial than ever.

FACILITY MAINTENANCE

Planning for the construction or remodeling of facilities is an important management function. An equally important responsibility of facility management is maintenance. With proper maintenance a facility will last longer, provide a healthier environment, be less costly, and provide a more satisfying experience for user groups. Planning and constructing facilities in physical education and sport are team efforts. If proper plans, construction, and materials are selected, then maintenance should be made easier. There is nothing more embarrassing than a new facility that is a maintenance nightmare because of poor management decisions in the design and planning phases of the construction process. Given an adequate facility, it is up to the physical education, sport, and custodial staffs to work together in taking pride in their facility and putting forth a special effort to see that it is maintained in as near perfect condition as possible.

SHARED FACILITIES

Schools and colleges continually receive requests to open their facilities to various community and other user groups. It is therefore imperative that management establish guidelines ensuring that appropriate precautions are taken (e.g., legal and fiscal) and that such facilities are used properly when approval is granted.

First, management should see that a written pol-

The tennis complex at Northwest Racket Club promotes the shared facilities concept; Bloomington, MN.

icy is established and approved by proper authorities regarding community use of facilities (who can use facilities, at what times, under what conditions). Second, procedures regarding outside use should be established. This usually includes such things as making a proper application, obtaining the liability insurance coverage necessary, setting the fee structure and type of payment, and making stipulations regarding maintenance and security. Third, management controls should be established to see that policies and procedures are carried out as specified in the user contract.

Schools Using Community Resources

Such facilities as parks, bowling alleys, golf courses, swimming pools, ski areas, Ys, and skating arenas can extend and enhance the school physical education program as well as related sports activities. Most community facilities can be used during off-hours or non-peak hours, and the charge is frequently nominal. Sometimes barter agreements can be arranged. Those procedures described in community use of school facilities apply in reverse.

With bond issues and fiscal inputs becoming difficult to obtain, it is imperative that management and the community (public and private sector) work together to build model programs, which might be impossible to accomplish alone. This is a challenge to management and all those intimately involved in long-range strategic facility planning.

SUMMARY

Facility management is an important managerial responsibility. It involves such things as planning based on physical education and sport program philosophy and particular needs, taking health, safety, and environmental conditions into consideration. Working with an architect and planning team, and being aware of the latest developments, issues, concerns, and laws in facility construction is also a crucial part of facility management. A basic knowledge of the requirements of both indoor and outdoor facilities is also important so that the needs of all participants, including those with disabilities, may be met. Facility management also includes establishing

sound emergency procedures and policies. Management should be concerned with the renovation, multiple use, maintenance, and cleanliness of the facilities since these are crucial to effective and efficient programming. Furthermore, most physical education and sport facilities are used by people other than just the students and members of one institution or organization. It is common practice for community residents and other community-based organizations (e.g., youth groups, seniors) to use such facilities. Therefore consideration should be given to the development of policies, procedures, and priorities for such usage. Creative and cooperative facility management is requisite in this time of scarce financial inputs.

◆ SELF-ASSESSMENT ACTIVITIES

These activities will assist students in determining if material and competencies presented in this chapter have been mastered.

1. List the basic considerations that should be followed by management in planning physical education and sport facilities.
2. As a director of a physical education program, what steps would you follow in working with an architect in the construction of a gymnasium?
3. Prepare a sketch of what you consider to be an ideal indoor weight training facility.
4. Develop a list of standards for outdoor areas in physical education and sport, including a play area and swimming pool, for a junior high or middle school.
5. You are a director of physical education in an elementary school with 500 students. There are five class periods a day with an average class size of 30 students, and physical education is required daily. What is the minimum number of teaching stations you will need?
6. Describe some new features being used in the construction of physical education and sport facilities. What are the advantages of these new features?
7. Prepare a checklist for a physical education and sport plant that will ensure that it is safe, healthful, and accessible for all participants.

From the Florida Suncoast Dome in St. Petersburg to the Londondome Arena and Exhibition Center in London, and from the Metrodome in Minneapolis to Joe Robbie Stadium in Miami, high-quality stadiums are an international statement of sport management prowess.

REFERENCES

1. Tips on gymnasium construction, *Athletic Business* 20, July 1984.
2. Flynn RB, editor: *Planning facilities for athletics, physical education and recreation,* North Palm Beach, Fl, 1985, The Athletic Institute.
3. Bellemare HK: *Athletic Purchasing and Facilities* 20, Oct 1983.
4. Ferreri JP: Successful strategies for facility planning, *Athletic Business* 64-67, Jan 1985.
5. Flynn RB: The team approach to facility planning, *Athletic Purchasing and Facilities* 5:12-24, June 1981.
6. Frier JP: Keeping users out of the dark, *Journal of Physical Education, Recreation, and Dance* 12:38-43, May 1988.
7. Hatfield FC, Krotee ML: *Personalized weight training for fitness and athletics,* Dubuque, Ia, 1984, Kendall/Hunt.
8. Kraus RG, Curtis JE: *Creative administration in recreation and parks,* ed 4, St Louis, 1986, Mosby–Year Book.
9. Turner E: Facility design, trends and innovations, *Journal of Physical Education, Recreation, and Dance* 58:34-35, Jan 1987.

SUGGESTED READINGS

- A gym by any other name is a multipurpose area, *Athletic Business* 46, Mar 1985.
  Describes how modern technology and proper design principles make it possible to have a gymnasium that is multipurpose in construction as well as in usage.
- Clayton R, Thomas DB: *Professional aquatic management,* Champaign, Il, 1989, Human Kinetics.
  Discusses a wide range of aquatic trends in facility management. Also includes a thorough overview of rules, procedures, and policies necessary for effective management.
- Dunn J, Fait H: *Special physical education,* Dubuque, Ia, 1989, Wm C Brown.
  Discusses, suggests, and provides guidelines for adapted physical education facilities. Outlines how facilities can be modified and planned to meet the needs of persons with disabilities.
- Dougherty NJ, Bonanno D: *Management principles in sport and leisure services,* Minneapolis, Mn, 1985, Burgess Publishing.
  Discusses steps in the process of facility development, including the role of the manager, the planning process, operational considerations, and policies requisite to effective management.
- McGuire M: Skylit cluster design: efficient space combined with aesthetic form, *Athletic Business* 32, July 1984.
  Describes the multipurpose 130,000 square foot physical education facility at the College of Du Page.
- Penman KA: What's what in sports surfaces? *Athletic Business* 8, Aug 1984.
  Discusses the various options in sport facility surfaces available in today's market as well as the management guidelines that should be used in selecting a surface.

CHAPTER 10

Fiscal Management

GRIMSBY COLLEGE LIBRARY NUNS CORNER, GRIMSBY

▶ **Instructional Objectives and Competencies To Be Achieved**

After reading this chapter the student should be able to

- Support the need for sound fiscal management in physical education and sport programs.
- Explain the budgeting process and formulate a physical education and sport budget.
- Apply a planning-programming-budgeting-evaluation system (PPBES) in the management of a physical education and sport program.

- Understand the role of school and college business managers or administrators in fiscal management.
- Outline principles necessary for managers to follow to ensure financial accountability in a physical education and sport program.
- Discuss zero-base budgeting as applied to a physical education and sport program.

A crucial function of management involves securing the funds necessary to provide sound physical education and sport programs. Adequate funding must be procured, programs and budgets implemented, and accountability for funds established. This chapter deals with this managerial function.

Fiscal management has become an increasingly important responsibility for management in light of current financial problems and constraints. In recent years financial problems caused by inadequate financial forecasting and monitoring, insufficient levy referendum coverage, and rising operational costs have made it much more difficult to fund physical education and sport programs even though sport is a multibillion-dollar enterprise. Other compounding reasons for fiscal difficulty include the high price of supplies, equipment, and travel; the need to finance

an increasing number of girls and women who are participating in physical activity and sport; crowd control costs at sporting events as a result of violence; expensive product liability and lawyer contingency funds; and an inflationary spiral that is resulting in rising costs for labor, teachers, coaches, trainers, officials, and other associated personnel.

An analysis of the responses of directors of physical education and athletics in New York (more than 1000 questionnaires) regarding the effect of budget cuts and austerity budget control on their programs disclosed the difficulties managers of physical education and sport programs are having today. The survey revealed the following:

- Of the directors, 67% said they had to cut supplies, transportation, specific sports, and levels of sports to balance the budget.

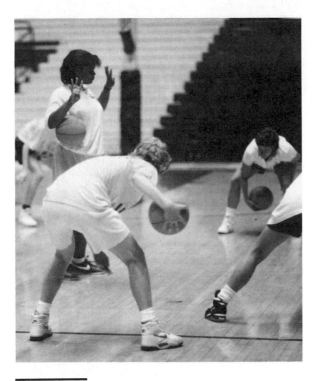

Girls' and women's physical education and sport programs are expanding.

- Athletic programs conducted with private funds during cutbacks numbered 29.
- Volunteer coaches were used by 40% of the directors in part of their programs.
- Fund-raising activities such as booster club memberships, participation fees, sales, student work projects, and promotional activities such as lotteries and raffles were instituted to support programs.
- Regarding support for sport programs, the teachers' association (exclusive representation) was found to be the least supportive and the students the most supportive. The school management and community were also highly supportive.

Efficient fiscal management is an essential management function that ensures proper budgeting and financial accountability. Therefore managers must understand thoroughly the philosophy of the organization, as well as the fiscal needs and objectives of all the departments under their supervision. Budgeting deals with departmental requests. The fiscal management of an institution, department, or program deals with goal setting, design of budget that is targeted to achieve these goals, the process of budget review and approval, and the actual management of the program. This is a critical and challenging responsibility.[1]

IMPORTANCE AND FUNCTION OF FISCAL MANAGEMENT

The services a program provides, whether personnel, facilities, or purchase of equipment, usually involve the gathering and disbursement of funds. This money must be secured from appropriate sources, be expended for proper purposes, and be accounted for item by item. The budget (from the French *bougette,* meaning bag or wallet), the master financial plan for the organization, is constructed with these purposes in mind.

Policies for raising and spending money must be set within organizational limits. Persons responsible should know the procedures for handling such funds with integrity, the basic purposes for which the program exists, as well as the laws, codes, and regulations concerning fiscal management. Only as funds are implemented wisely and in the best interests of all concerned can the outlay of monies be justified.

Place of Fiscal Management in Physical Education and Sport Programs

In schools, colleges, or other organizations, physical education and sport require a major outlay of funds. As much as 25% of many school and college physical plants are devoted to these programs. Personnel, health services, insurance, facilities, supplies and equipment, and transportation are only a few of the line items that quickly amount to significant sums of money. Probably as many as 500,000 physical educators and coaches are collectively paid millions of dollars in annual salaries, and more than 60 million students participate in school physical education and sport programs. Gymnasiums, stadium and aquatic complexes, athletic training and weight

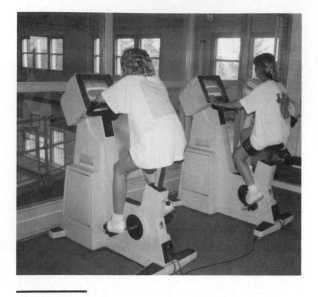

The cost of equipment, programs, and personnel is increasing.

◆   **PURPOSES OF FISCAL MANAGEMENT**

Some of the principal purposes of financial management in physical education and sport programs are the following:

To prevent misuse and waste of funds that have been allocated to these special fields.

To help coordinate and relate the objectives of physical education and sport programs with the money appropriated for achieving such outcomes.

To ensure that monies allocated to physical education and sport will be based on research, study, and a careful analysis of the pertinent conditions that influence such a process.

To involve the entire staff in formulating policies and procedures and in preparing budgetary items that will help ensure that the right program directions are taken.

To use funds to develop the best physical education and sport programs possible.

To exercise control over the process of fiscal management to guarantee that the entire financial process has integrity and purpose.

To make the greatest use of personnel, facilities, supplies, equipment, and other factors involved in accomplishing organizational objectives.

rooms, playgrounds, and other school and college facilities are being constructed at huge costs to the taxpayers.

What is true of schools and colleges regarding fiscal management is also true of community-based, corporate, and other public- and private-sector settings where physical education and sport programs exist.

Responsibility

The responsibility for fiscal management, although falling largely on the shoulders of management, involves every member of the staff. In schools and colleges, students should also play an active part. In this regard fiscal management is similar to strategic planning; it is a team effort (see the box above).

Formulating and preparing the budget are cooperative enterprises. They are based on information, reports, and forecasts that have been forwarded by staff members from various departments and subdivisions of the organization. These reports must contain accurate information on programs, projects, obligations that exist, funds that have been spent, and monies that have been received from various

sources (e.g., interest-bearing benefits, endorsements, user fees). Managers must have a conceptual or overall picture of the enterprise at their fingertips. They must be cognizant of the work being done throughout the organization, functions that should be carried out, needs and resources of every facet of the organization, and other items that must be considered in preparing the budget. The advent of the computer and its myriad software packages make budgeting a far less labor-intensive task, as well as a far more accurate management venture.

BUDGETING

Budgeting is the formulation of a financial plan in terms of work to be accomplished and services to be performed. All expenditures should be closely related to the objectives the organization is trying to achieve. In this control aspect, management plays an important part.

Budgets should be planned and prepared with thought to the future. They are an important part of management's 3-year, 5-year, or 7-year plan and the program of accomplishment outlined for a fiscal period. Projects of any size should be integrated progressively over many years. Thus the outlay of monies to realize such aims requires long-term, strategic planning. Down-sizing or budget reduction should also follow a similar planning path.

According to the strict interpretation of the word, a budget is merely a record of receipts and expenditures. As used here, however, it reflects the long-term planning of the organization, pointing up user needs and projected costs, and then ensuring that a realistic program is planned that will fit into the proposed financial plan. Budgets, forecasts, revenues, and expenses for a period of 1 year, known as the fiscal year, are the most common in school and college physical education and sport programs.

Types of Budgets

There are short-term and long-term budgets. The short-term is usually the annual budget. The long-term budget represents long-term fiscal planning, possibly for a 5- or 10-year period. Most physical education and sport personnel will be concerned with short-term or annual budgets whereby they plan their financial needs for a period covering the school year.

Budgets are also categorized into (1) object classification (e.g., supplies and equipment, travel, salaries), (2) functions (e.g., indoor, outdoor, aquatics), (3) organizational unit (e.g., football, swimming, lifetime sports), and (4) classification by fund (e.g., 0100-state, municipal bond, user fee).

Budgets are also classified into (1) operational, (2) equipment and supply, (3) personnel, and (4) capital outlay. Usually the first two types of budgets are directly managed by the chair or director of the respective physical education or sport program. Capital outlay management and personnel, however, usually reside at a higher level (e.g., principal, executive director of finances, vice-president) with top-down input usually applied.

◆ PURPOSES OF BUDGETS

They express the plan and program for physical education and sport. They determine things such as (a) size of classes, (b) supplies, equipment, and facilities, (c) methods used, (d) results and educational values sought, and (e) personnel available.

They reflect the philosophy and policies of the professions of physical education and sport. They provide an overview of these specialized areas.

They determine what phases of the program are to be emphasized and help analyze all aspects of physical education and sport programs.

They interpret the need and the funds necessary for physical education and sport.

In a school program they help determine, together with the budgets of other subdivisions, the tax levy for the school district.

They make it possible to manage the physical education and sport programs economically by improving accounting procedures.

They make it possible, on approval by officials, to authorize expenditures for physical education and sport programs.

Regardless of the type of budget, the budgeting process is a critical part of the management function and demands continuous attention to detail (see the box above).

Responsibility for Budgets

The responsibility for the preparation of the budget may vary from one locality or institution to another. In most school systems, the superintendent of schools is responsible. In colleges, budgeting may be the responsibility of the president, vice-president, dean, or athletic director. In other organizations, the department chair or head coach plays a key role. It is often possible for school managers, department heads, teachers, professors, coaches, and members of the organization to participate in preparing the budget by submitting various requests for item expenditures. In other situations a comprehensive budget may first be prepared and then submitted to the appropriate subdivisions or departments for consideration.

In some large school systems the superintendent of schools frequently delegates much of the budget responsibility to an executive director of finances, business manager, or assistant or associate superintendent.

The final official school authority concerned with school budgets is the Board of Education and, in colleges, the Board of Regents or Trustees. In some organizations other than schools, it is the controller who possesses authority to approve, reject, or amend. Beyond the Board of Education rests the authority of the people, who in most communities also have the right to approve, reject, or significantly influence budget proposals.

In colleges the budget may be handled in the dean's office, or the director or chairperson of the physical education department may have the responsibility. In most cases the director of athletics is responsible for the intercollegiate or interscholastic sport budget.

Within school departments of physical education and sport the chairperson, supervisor, or director is the person responsible for the budget. However, he or she will usually consult with members of the department to consider their input, opinions, and projections. This type of bottom-up management is most effective in schools and community-based physical education and sport programs.

Criteria for a Sound Budget

A budget for physical education and sport should meet the following criteria:

- The budget will clearly present the financial needs of the entire program in relation to the objectives sought.
- Key persons in the organization have been consulted.
- The budget will provide a realistic estimate of income to balance the expenditures anticipated.
- The budget should reflect equitable allocations to boys' and girls' physical education and sport programs.
- The possibility of emergencies is recognized through flexibility in the financial plan.

- The budget will be prepared well in advance of the fiscal year to leave ample time for analysis, thought, criticism, and review.
- Budget requests should be realistic, not padded.
- The budget meets the essential requirements of students, faculty, staff members, community, and management.

Budget Preparation and Planning

The budget process is continuous. Business management resources indicate that there are seven basic steps to this process:[8]

Planning. Management uses the input power of staff and community in creative planning, as well as to identify user needs.

Coordinating. Management coordinates and integrates staff members' and community suggestions and recommendations into a unified whole.

Interpreting. To have support for the budget, proper interpretation of plans and actions is a continual part of the budgetary process.

Presenting. Management presents the budget in a simplified version so that it can be readily understood. Pictures, diagrams, graphics, and other visual materials make such a presentation more interesting and informative.

Approving. Adoption of the budget is but the formal approval of many projects that have been studied and considered throughout the year. Management is continually planning, researching, and studying various budgetary items.

Administering. The budget, when approved, serves as management's guide throughout the year as to how monies will be allocated and spent and what activities will be conducted and supported.

Appraising. Appraisal is a continuous process indicating how the budget is functioning. Methods used include daily observation, cost accounting records and reports, surveys, audits, checklists, and staff studies.

There are four general procedures or stages in budget planning that physical education and sport personnel might consider. First is actual preparation of the budget by the chairperson of the department with his or her staff, listing the various estimated revenue, expenditures, and any other information that needs to be included. Second, the budget is presented to the principal, superintendent, dean, Board of Education, or other person or group that represents the proper authority and has the responsibility and legal authorization for reviewing it. Third, after formal approval of the budget, it is used as a guide for the execution of the financial management plan of the department or organization. Fourth, periodic critical evaluation of the budget takes place to determine its effectiveness in meeting organizational needs, with notations being made for the next year's budget.

The preparation of the budget, representing the first step, is a long-term endeavor that cannot be accomplished in 1 or 2 days. The budget can be prepared only after a careful review of last year's program effectiveness and extensive appraisal. Often times economic forecasts, projections, and fiscal targets will be passed down from the administration. However, the actual completion of the budget usually is accomplished in the early spring after a detailed inventory of program needs has been taken. The director of physical education or sport, after close consultation with staff members, coaches, athletic trainers, the principal, dean, superintendent of schools, or other responsible management, should formulate the budget.

Involvement of Staff Members

Involving staff members (teachers, coaches, trainers) in the budget-making process is very important. Klappholz[6] provides some suggestions that permit dynamic involvement:

- Teachers and coaches should maintain inventory records indicating supplies and equipment on hand.
- Teachers, coaches, and directors should keep accurate records of all expenditures for each activity, sport, or piece of equipment.
- Teaching staff and coaches should determine the items that were not a part of this year's budget, but that should be included in the budget for the coming year (e.g., new equipment, repairs, subscriptions to professional journals).
- Accurate records should be kept by staff members regarding funds allocated and spent each

year. Then it should be determined if funds were spent for purposes that were initially listed.

- When all pertinent information has been collected and analyzed, management should meet with all staff members and go over requests.
- Management should prepare total physical education or sport budgets including all valid requests. The budget should not be padded, but provision should be made for emergencies.

Klappholz[6] also stresses that management and staff members should do their homework by having the latest price lists for supplies and equipment; number of students or other personnel projected for the program; cost of such items as officials, travel, phone, recruiting, meals, lodging, insurance, and medical supervision; money needed for teaching aids, film, video, equipment repair, and other teaching and coaching materials; and cost of attending professional meetings.

Many records and reports are essential to budget preparation and should be part of a central database. The inventory of equipment and supplies on hand will be useful, and copies of inventories and budgets from previous years will provide good references and projection points. Comparison of budgetary items with those of organizations of similar size may also be of help. Accounting records will be valuable.

All records, reports, inventories, past budgets, and budget requests should be part of management's database. Lexington, Massachusetts public schools provide such a program that enables each teacher and coach to project and assess their budgetary requirements.

The budget is based on forecasts that can be overtaken by reality, therefore some flexibility for readjustment is necessary. It is difficult to accurately and specifically list each detail in the way it will be needed and executed; however, budgets should also be reasonably rigid (see the boxes on pp. 286 and 287).

The budget should represent a schedule that can be justified. This means that each budgetary item must satisfy the needs and interests of everyone concerned. Furthermore, each item that constitutes an

◆ A SCHOOL BUDGET

Proposed budget classification by major function

	Salaries, fees, and benefits	Equipment and supplies	Services and other expenses	Totals
Board of Education and district administration				
Board/district administration	$ 183,400	$ 11,400	$ 45,900	$ 240,700
District insurance			74,600	74,600
Claims, property tax, administrative costs			78,300	78,300
Category total				$ 393,600
Instruction				
Building administration	302,600	19,700	8,600	330,900
Salaries and materials	3,178,300	169,000	439,700	3,787,000
Guidance and health	264,200	2,900	14,600	281,700
Student activities	57,300	22,900	6,700	86,900
Category total				$4,486,500
Support services				
Transportation	287,600	106,500	36,300	430,400
Operation and maintenance	362,000	42,900	378,400	783,300
School lunch program			5,000	5,000
Category total				$1,218,700
Employee benefits	1,293,400			$1,293,400
Total operating expenses	$5,928,800	$375,300	$1,088,100	$7,392,200
Debt service			765,600	765,600
TOTAL BUDGET				$8,157,800

expenditure should be reflected in budget specifications. A typical high school varsity sport budget, as well as a sample intercollegiate sport budget, accompanied by the monthly budget balance and year-to-date ledger balance with transactions for supplies, equipment, and other expenses, may be found in Appendix F. Sample budgets for a recreational sport and a community-based youth sport organization are also included for consideration.

Budget Organization

Budgets can be organized in many ways. One pattern that can prove useful for the physical education

and sport manager includes a four-phased program. First, a brief introductory message enables management to present the financial proposals in terms a person outside the educational domain might readily understand. This might include the philosophy and goals of the total organization.

The second phase presents an overall graphic view of the budget, with expenditures and anticipated revenues arranged clearly and systematically so that any person can compare the two.

Phase three includes a more detailed estimate of receipts and expenditures, enabling a principal, superintendent of schools, Board of Education, or

◆ BUDGETARY ALLOCATIONS FOR REGULAR INSTRUCTIONAL PROGRAMS

The programs listed below describe the funding for regular classroom instruction. The costs of general classroom teachers in grades 1 through 5 are divided among the language arts, mathematics, and environment programs, according to the estimated percentage of instructional time each subject receives in the classroom curriculum.

Program costs in grades 6 through 12 are based on the division of staff members by academic specialization.

The unclassified group contains those general supply and equipment items that support the entire program and cannot be allocated by program.

	Salaries	Benefits	Equipment	Supplies	Services	Total
Art	$ 136,761	$ 38,434	$ 522	$ 10,401	$ 677	$ 186,795
Business education	66,465	18,681	2,150	1,638	1,350	90,284
Driver education	4,410	1,239	550	10,850	—	17,049
Environment	151,747	42,650	—	1,999	300	196,696
Health education	2,290	627	—	400	420	3,737
Home economics	39,609	11,313	—	3,341	447	54,528
Industrial arts	70,837	19,910	471	5,335	675	97,228
Kindergarten	47,203	13,267	—	1,255	—	61,725
Language arts	613,255	172,365	—	14,375	2,900	802,895
Foreign languages	158,078	44,430	—	5,361	1,715	209,584
Mathematics	452,918	127,291	710	7,489	560	588,968
Music	141,035	39,635	516	2,439	850	184,485
Physical education	233,176	65,552	2,147	6,069	2,590	309,534
Reading (special)	83,162	23,372	—	915	400	107,849
Science	333,804	87,083	3,124	11,140	1,850	437,001
Speech	10,751	3,018	—	261	—	14,030
Social studies	283,827	79,774	—	4,509	3,500	371,610
Unclassified	146,898	41,286	1,737	22,009	9,080	221,010
TOTAL	$2,976,226	$829,745	$11,927	$109,786	$27,314	$3,954,998

other interested person or group to understand the specific budget item expenditure and projected income.

A fourth phase includes supporting documentation to provide additional evidence for the requests outlined in the budget. Many times a budget will have a better chance of approval if there is sufficient documentation to support some items. For example, extra compensation for coaches may be supported by presenting salary schedules for coaches in cohort school systems.

Another form of budget organization consists of the following three parts: (a) an introductory statement of the objectives, policies, and programs of the physical education or sport department; (2) a resume of the objectives, policies, and programs inter-preted in terms of proposed expenditures; and (3) a financial plan for meeting the needs during the fiscal period.

Not all budgets are broken down into these three or four divisions. All budgets do, however, present an itemized account of receipts and expenditures.

In a physical education or sport budget common inclusions are items concerning instruction, such as extra compensation for coaches; matters of capital outlay, such as a new swimming pool or weight room; replacement of expendable equipment, such as basketballs and baseball helmets; and provision for maintenance and repair, such as refurbishing football uniforms or resurfacing the playground. It is difficult to estimate many of these items without making a careful inventory and analysis of the con-

The capital outlay for a weight room is significant for many sport programs.

dition of the facilities and equipment on hand. This can be accomplished yearly (e.g., facility and inventory audit) and supplied to the computer database. This status can then be updated each year with adjustable projections resulting.

FUND RAISING FOR PHYSICAL EDUCATION AND SPORT PROGRAMS

The sources of income for most school and college physical education and sport programs include the general school fund (e.g., local taxes, millage, state appropriations, bonds) or college fund, gate receipts, concessions, and general organization and activity fees. However, these usually do not provide sufficient monies to run quality programs.

The budget crunch in many school districts and institutions of higher education has caused physical education and sport directors to find ways of raising revenues for their programs. In Massachusetts, for example, they are getting business organizations to provide matching funds for specific programs, conducting fund-raising campaigns among alumni, soliciting local citizens to make tax-free donations and to make "gift" provisions in their wills, as well as

selling two-for-one passes to the public for sport contests.[3]

Other sources of additional revenue are special foundation, governmental, or individual grants or gifts; sale of television and radio rights; concessions at sport contests and physical education events; and special fund-raising events such as games involving faculty vs. the media or a local professional team such as the Minnesota Vikings basketball team.

Many physical educators at the college level also look to replenish and supplement their funds with grants and external funding. Local and federal sources (e.g., Department of Education, National Institute on Aging) are approached with well-written proposals, as are various private foundations, corporations, and PVOs (e.g., Bush Foundation, Kellogg Foundation, Partners of the Americas, Pacific Cultural Foundation). Such proposals outline the proposed project, goals, and outcomes of the project itself. These competitive funding channels are difficult to tap; however, all avenues to support worthwhile programs should be explored.

The principles of fund raising are simple and easy to apply. A successful campaign is the combination of a good cause, careful planning, fact finding, and skillful communication. Good public relations are essential. Secondary schools and community-based programs have a product with which many people like to be associated: sport. Physical education is not quite as attractive to many potential sponsors; however, if presented in the right fashion with students as a point of focus, it also can be a recipient of fund-raising rewards.

To be effective, a program of fund raising should have excellent organization, clearly articulated objectives, effective management, and a philosophy.

Some illustrations of successful fund raising are associated with booster clubs. The question of using booster clubs may be controversial since sometimes such clubs want to influence the operation of the physical education and sport programs. With proper guidelines and procedures, however, opportunity for this to occur is minimal.

Christian Brothers High School in Sacramento, California has the La Salle Club, which raises money for the physical education and sport programs by means such as the Old Timer Baseball Night, a golf tourney, and a fireworks booth for the 4th of July. Davis Senior High School in Davis, California has an annual Lift-A-Thon for their football program to raise money. Notre Dame High School in Sherman Oaks, California uses their booster club membership as a major contributor to their sport fund. The Dell Rapids, South Dakota school system sells advertising on their scoreboards to help finance their programs. Wayzata High School in Wayzata, Minnesota has booster clubs for almost all of their girls' and boys' sports. Pig roasts, pot lucks, and the selling of T-shirts and sweatshirts, among other items, seem to raise ample sums of money that are used to employ assistant coaches and provide needed equipment or transport.

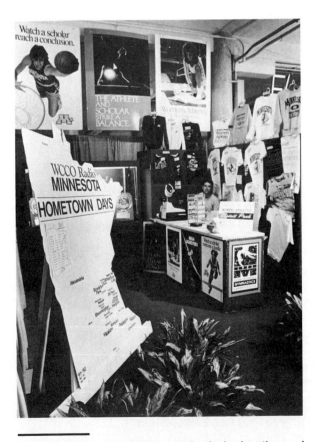

Fund raising is crucial to many physical education and sport programs. A booth at the Minnesota State Fair.

Some high schools across the country use professional organizations to do their fund raising. For example, the Revere Company has helped many schools to raise funds. Parke Techniques is a company that works through the schools selling everything from bookends to paper weights. Another company is the American Cap Company, which prints painter's caps. Win Craft Incorporated makes pom-pons, buttons, balloons, megaphones, cushions, and many other items. Most programs, however, usually have talented parents and a supportive community who are willing to get the job done in this process of budget supplementation.

PAY-TO-PLAY POLICY

A recent development in high school sport programs is to require students who wish to participate to pay fees.[7] This plan is being initiated because school sport programs have outgrown their projected budgets. The National Council of Secondary School Athletic Directors indicates that the average high school athletic budget has been reduced by at least 25% and some even by 75%. This seems to be the trend of the 1990s. Cuts in funding combined with increased costs are prompting schools to defray expenses through student participation fees ranging typically from $25 to $75 depending on the sport or activity. Some schools have been forced to drop various sport programs, as well as to reduce teaching, coaching, and supervisory staff.

Although some states such as Iowa and Michigan have ruled against such a practice, California courts have upheld user fees. A citizens' group called "The Coalition Opposing Student Fees" lost a suit against the Santa Barbara School Board. The ruling stated that fees were permissible since sport takes place outside the regular school day, students volunteer for the activity, fees are used only to pay the cost of running such a program, and fees do not violate the equal opportunity clauses of federal and state constitutions, that is, financially disadvantaged students are exempt from fees.

If a school institutes a "pay-to-play" policy, it should make sure that the fee charged is reasonable, that disadvantaged students (those who are finan-

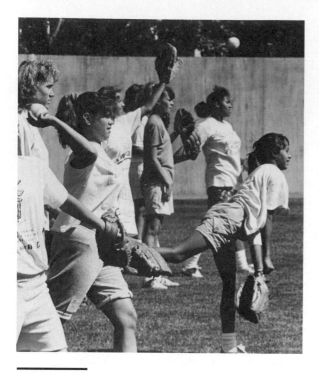

Many sport programs have instituted a "pay-to-play" policy.

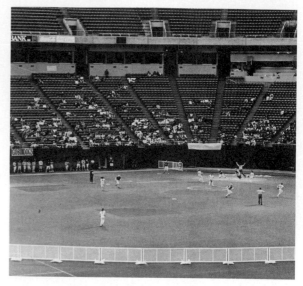

Stands such as those at the Metrodome in Minneapolis must be filled to meet budget projections.

cially unable to pay) are exempt, and that fees are used solely to cover program operation costs.

TRADITIONAL SOURCES OF INCOME

General school or college fund. In elementary and secondary schools, the physical education and sport program usually is financed through the general fund (e.g., local taxes and state appropriation) to a large extent. At most colleges and universities, the general fund of the institution also represents a major source of income, especially for physical education and recreational sport programs.

Gate receipts. Gate receipts play an important part in some schools in financing at least part of the physical education and sport program. Although gate receipts are usually less important at lower educational levels, some colleges and universities finance a large share of their sports programs includ-

ing recreational sports and physical education programs through such a method. At a few high schools throughout the country, gate receipts have been abolished because of the feeling that if sports represent an important part of the education program, they should be paid for in the same way that science and mathematics programs are financed. Table 10-1 shows a general organization financial statement of expenses and receipts.

General organization and activity fees. Some high schools either require or make available to students separate general organization or activity fees and tickets or some other inducement that enables them to attend sporting, dramatic, and musical events. In colleges and universities a similar plan is generally employed sometimes as a part of a student activity fee, thus providing students with reduced rates to the various extracurricular activities offered by the institution.

ESTIMATING RECEIPTS/CREDITS

Some steps that might be followed for projecting receipts in the general school budget that also have ap-

TABLE 10-1.   General organization athletic account—financial report (Sept-Dec)

Program	Expenses
Football	
Officials (four home games)	$ 480.00
Equipment and supplies	2364.02
Transportation	175.00
Supervision (police, ticket sellers and takers)	952.00
Reconditioning and cleaning equipment	1313.20
Medical supplies	125.40
Scouting	60.00
Film/video	31.36
Guarantees	520.00
Football dinner	231.00
Miscellaneous (printing tickets, meeting)	172.00
TOTAL	$6423.98
Cross country	
State and county entry fees	$ 10.00
Transportation	64.00
TOTAL	$ 74.00
Basketball	
Supervision (three games)	$ 36.00
Custodian (three games)	26.00
Security (one game)	12.00
TOTAL	$ 74.00
Cheerleaders	
Transportation	52.20
Sixteen new uniforms	320.00
Cleaning uniforms	96.00
TOTAL	$ 468.20
Total expenses	7040.18

Program	Receipts
Football games	
Newburgh	$1311.70
Norwalk	1819.60
Yonkers	1129.50
Bridgeport	1100.00
Guarantee (New Haven)	120.00
Total receipts	$5480.80

plication to physical education and sport budgeting include gathering and analyzing all pertinent data, estimating all income based on a comprehensive view of income sources, organizing and classifying receipts in appropriate categories (e.g., gate receipts, parking, concessions), estimating revenue from all gathered data, comparing estimates with previous years, and computing a final draft of credits as well as debits.

EXPENDITURES

In physical education and sport budgets, typical examples of expenditures are items of *capital outlay,* such as a swimming pool or weight room; *expendable equipment,* such as badminton shuttlecocks and soccer balls; and a *maintenance and repair provision,* such as towel and laundry service and the refurbishing of equipment and uniforms. See Appendix F for a sample list of expenditures for various interscholastic sport programs.

Some expenditures are easy to estimate, but others are more difficult, requiring accurate inventories, past records, and careful analysis of the condition of inventoried equipment. Some items and services will need to be figured by averaging costs over a period of years, such as equipment cleaning and repair. Awards, new equipment needs, transportation, guarantees to visiting teams, insurance, and medical services for emergencies are other expenditures that must be projected.

Some sound procedures to follow in estimating expenditures include determining objectives and goals of program; analyzing expenditures in terms of program objectives; preparing a budgetary calendar that states what accomplishments are expected and by what date; estimating expenditures by also considering past, present, and future needs; comparing estimates with expenditures from previous years; and thoroughly evaluating estimates before preparing a final draft.

Cost-Cutting Procedures

In light of current economic problems some managers are cutting costs. This is being accomplished by such means as doing away with low participation

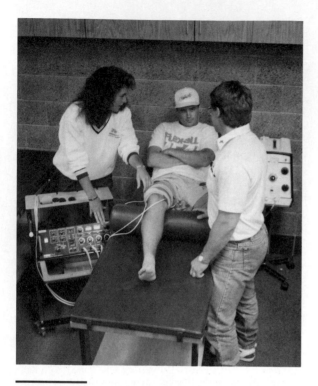

Medical personnel and equipment costs must be part of physical education and sport programs.

sented to him or her for approval. Good management means, furthermore, that the budgetary items have been reviewed with the principal during their preparation, so that approval is usually routine.

In colleges and universities, the proper budgeting channels should be followed. This might mean clearance through a dean or other management officer. Each person who is responsible for budget preparation and presentation should be familiar with the proper working channels.

For successful presentation and adoption, the budget should be prepared in final form only after careful consideration and consultation so that little change will be needed. Requests for funds should be justifiable, and ample preliminary discussion of the budget with persons and groups most directly concerned should be held so that needless difficulty will be avoided.

BUDGET MANAGEMENT

After the presentation and approval of the budget, the next step is to see that it is managed properly. This means it should be followed closely with periodic checks (audits) on expenditures to see that they fall within the budget appropriations provided. The budget should be a guide to economical and efficient management.

Budget time frames such as Program Evaluation Review Techniques (PERT) and Critical Path Method (CPM) are often applied in budget management to assist in time expectation management.

To employ these management techniques the project must (1) have a clear objective and end point, (2) be divided into a series of stages or phases, (3) have projected due dates assigned to completed tasks, and (4) have a kick off or starting date.

sports, reducing referees' pay, eliminating insurance, permitting fewer contests, using volunteer coaches, discontinuing the purchase of personally used equipment (e.g., bats, hockey sticks), reducing the number of coaches, lowering coaches' salaries, eliminating sports where rental facilities are used, and scheduling teams (e.g., girls' and boys' soccer) on the same day and combining transportation and coaches for these teams. Management must be creative to keep programs intact.

BUDGET PRESENTATION AND ADOPTION

After being prepared, school physical education and sport budgets are usually submitted to the superintendent through the principal's office. The principal is the person in charge of his or her particular building; therefore subdivision budgets should be pre-

BUDGET APPRAISAL

Periodic appraisal calls for an audit of the accounts and an evaluation of the school program resulting from the management of the current budget. Such appraisal should be done honestly and with a view to eliminating weaknesses in current budgets and strengthening future ones. It should also be remembered that the budget will be only as good as management makes it and that the budget will improve only as management improves.

ZERO-BASE BUDGETING

Zero-base budgeting (ZBB)[5] is a procedure and system based on a justification for all expenditures of an organization at the time the budget is formulated. It allows management to in effect start over and not be influenced by previous budgets. ZBB was developed and introduced by the Texas Instruments Company in 1969.

The traditional method of developing a budget is to use the previous year's budget as a base and then require a justification for any increase that is requested for the ensuing year. For example, if $500 had been allocated for recreational sports the previous year and the recreational sports director asked for $600 this year, then only the $100 increase would have to be justified.

Zero-base budgeting, on the other hand, requires a justification of all expenditures that are requested. In the example above, the entire $600 would have to be justified. In other words, each element or subdivision of an organization that is allocated funds starts from zero and any and all funds requested must be justified in light of their contribution to the achievement of the objectives of the organization.

Zero-base budgeting requires each subdivision or program of an organization to justify its request for funds. It requires planning regarding how these subdivisions can contribute to the achievement of the organization's goals and brings decision making into the procedure. Zero-base budgeting could mean that some elements of an organization have outgrown their usefulness and will no longer receive any funds whatsoever. Also, it could mean that new programs would be more likely to receive funds if they can be shown to be in line with, and capable of contributing to, organizational goals.

The steps followed in zero-base budgeting include identifying the goals of the organization, planning a program to meet goals, identifying alternative ways to achieve goals in light of budgetary constraints, performing a cost analysis of the alternatives, and then arriving at a decision concerning what functions or alternatives should receive funding.

Zero-base budgeting could be especially valuable to organizations so steeped in tradition that they are not capitalizing on current trends and developments and need to implement new and creative ideas, programs, and projects. This type of budgeting can also make it possible to see that funds are used in the most effective way to achieve organizational goals.

PPBES: PLANNING-PROGRAMMING-BUDGETING-EVALUATION SYSTEM

PPBES came about as a solution to problems of fiscal accountability and optimal use of scarce inputs or limited resources.

A History of PPBES

PPBS, as it was originally known, started in 1949 when the Hoover Commission report on the organization of the executive branch recommended that the government adopt a budget based on function, activities, and objectives. In 1954 the Rand Corporation developed a performance budget for use in military spending. Planning-Programming-Budgeting System (PPBS) was the title given to this system. The DuPont Corporation and the Ford Motor Company were among the first to implement PPBS. In the early 1960s Robert McNamara introduced the system to the Defense Department. The reults of the system were so impressive that President Johnson ordered all federal departments and agencies to adopt PPBES by August 1965. At present, many schools, colleges, and other organizations are using this system, and many more are researching the feasibility of using it in their particular cases. PPBS became PPBES when the function of *evaluation* was added.

Definition of PPBES

PPBES (Figure 10-1) may be defined as a long-range plan to accomplish an organization's objectives, using continual feedback and updating of information to allow for greater efficiency in the decision-making process. The four elements of PPBES are as follows:

1. Planning—establishing objectives
2. Programming—combining activities and events to produce distinguishable results
3. Budgeting—allocating resources; the financial plan for meeting program needs and objectives
4. Evaluation—determining how adequately the budget fits the program and the program meets the objectives, and evaluating the relationship of accomplishments to cost.

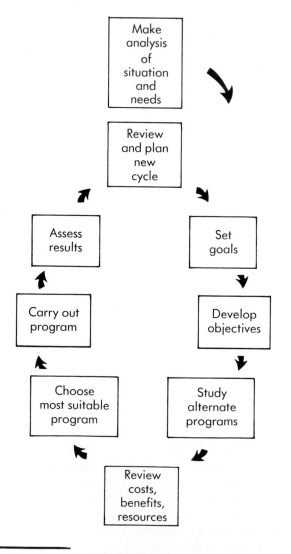

FIGURE 10-1 The PPBES cycle.

To implement PPBES, the objectives of the organization must be clearly defined. All activities that contribute to the same objective, regardless of placement in the organization, are clustered or grouped together. A financial plan designed to reach these objectives is formulated for a particular time period (PERT or CPM techniques may be utilized). An analysis document assesses long-range needs and evaluates the adequacy, effectiveness, costs, benefits, and difficulties inherent in the proposed program. Under PPBES, funds must be used with definitive goals in mind. In this way accountability for expenditures is stressed. In using PPBES each activity and educational program is considered, not only by itself, but also with respect to other educational programs that make up the whole system. In this way the needs of the entire school system or organization are considered.

The following are the steps necessary to apply PPBES:

1. *Goals and objectives.* Goals and objectives should be stated in terms of behavior and performance outcome. The results of the program should also be determined in relation to knowledge, skills, and attitudes.
2. *Statement of needs and problems.* Needs and problems of the particular organization and user group must be adequately defined.
3. *Determination of expected satisfaction of needs.* Numbers of persons and skills needed must also be determined.
4. *Constraints and feasibility.* Both of these items must be evaluated to determine whether the system can overcome certain limitations (personnel, materials, facilities). The system may need modification in terms of needs or objectives to overcome existing limitations and barriers.
5. *Alternative programs.* These programs outline the different ways the organization can reach its goals. Alternative programs should be evaluated in terms of needs, goals, and constraints of the system.
6. *Resource requirements.* The resource needs of each alternative must be computed. One way to accomplish this might be to derive the faculty teaching cost per student credit hour

and then add department overhead costs such as counseling, management, equipment, and clerical support.

7. *Estimate of benefits.* The benefits of the program must be determined in relationship to student accomplishment at present and in the future.

8. *Development of an operating plan.* From the data collected, all alternatives should be weighed against fixed criteria such as cost of implementation and risk involved, estimated benefits, and future budget allocations.

9. *Pilot implementation of best alternative.* A pilot program should be conducted at a level where it could be modified or changed without involved or costly effort.

10. *Evaluation.* The data from the pilot program should be used to determine whether it is meeting the objectives of the organization. The program should be modified accordingly.

11. *Feedback and further modification.* Once PPBES is in process, it should be continually reevaluated and modified to ensure that the goals and objectives agreed on are being met.

12. *Situational analysis.* This is both a beginning and end process determined by the present state of the situation. This is a crucial and meaningful assessment of needs.

Advantages and Disadvantages of PPBES

Before implementing PPBES in an institution, management must be thoroughly familiar with the advantages and disadvantages of such a system. Each situation differs, and careful situational analysis before and after implementation is essential. Some of the advantages of PPBES follow.

1. The system assists in formulating goals, objectives, and skills.

2. Curriculum can be designed to meet the objectives formulated.

3. Staff members can be provided with prior planning experience and resource materials.

4. Alternative plans can be more systematically analyzed.

5. Costs, accomplishments, and risks may be systematically compared.

6. Staff members are more involved in decision making, and morale, motivation, and productivity may be increased.

7. Instructional and operational costs may be easily identified.

8. Innovation and coordination can be promoted in programs as well as within the entire organization.

9. New, creative ideas that have been scrutinized and tested are continually applied to the system.

10. Public awareness, understanding, and communication are increased.

Some disadvantages of such a system follow.

1. Staff time is limited, and staff members with sufficient technical skills in these areas may also be limited.

2. Implementation may lead to conflict and resistance from community members and sometimes from within the organization.

3. Cost-benefit analysis is difficult to quantify; some benefits from education are not easily measurable.

4. Communication among staff members may be limited as a result of centralization of system planning.

5. PPBES is a method of indicating the best use of funds; however, in doing so, funds are also expended, and limited budgets may not be able to justify implementation of such a system.

6. The vocabulary is vague to those who are not directly involved in using such a system.

7. PPBES may be mistakenly seen as a substitute for management rather than a tool of management.

8. Alternatives with great potential are passed up because of their high risk or chance of failure according to PPBES criteria.

9. Some persons may feel that they are answerable to the "system" for their program; however, the "system" should be an aid, not a deterrent.

Using PPBES

Surveys indicate that more than 1000 schools in the United States employ PPBES with their budgets. Michigan and California are two examples.

The Michigan program. Michigan has adopted PPBES in its publicly funded institutions of higher education. Although the system costs more money, it enables managers to have greater information for decision making and provides taxpayers a better indication of where their money is being spent.

The California program. Under the direction of the Advisory Commission on School District Budgeting and Accounting, 15 school districts piloted PPBES. They simplified plans so that they were readily understandable to voters in the hope that the public's understanding would help the passage of school bond issues. When explained in terms of objectives and expected outcomes and accomplishments, budgets and programs were supported and approved.

It is obvious from the California and Michigan examples that PPBES is a process that can help organizations use available funds wisely, identify problem areas, and improve program weaknesses. In addition, the public is not only given input into the process, but also is offered clear and understandable data to assist in adopting and supporting sound fiscal budgeting.

How Can PPBES Be Applied to Physical Education and Sport Programs?

Physical education and sport have much to gain by implementing PPBES. If this system is used, physical education and sport programs and budget requests cannot be arbitrarily dropped or refused because of inadequate funding. Each segment of the program must be given equal emphasis according to objectives and benefits derived from meeting these objectives.

Pre-PPBES physical education and sport budgets were considered in terms of bats and balls rather than total program and user needs, objectives, and benefits. PPBES provides management with a situation assessment, a detailed list of goals and objectives, an analysis of problems and barriers, alternatives, solutions, and recommendations. The most important attribute of PPBES is the way it relates program costs and risks to expected outcomes and accomplishments.

COST ANALYSIS

Cost analysis of resources used in a program is a derivative of cost accounting. Cost analysis is needed to help the manager evaluate present operations and project future planning and budgets. Cost analysis is limited to the types of accounting systems being used as well as designating the unit to be compared. It is particularly applicable to schools and colleges. For example, some schools operate on K-12, others K-6 or K-8 or some other educational pattern. Naturally, a great difference in expenditures per student would occur depending on the various patterns of organization.

Various units are employed in cost analysis in a school's general education fund. The number of students in attendance, the census, average daily attendance, and average daily membership are some of those numbers used. Each of the various units has advantages and disadvantages.

As a raw measure of educational costs, the average daily membership is better than the average daily attendance. Teachers' salaries must be paid whether pupils are in 90% or 100% attendance, and desks and school books must be available whether pupils are in attendance or not. With respect to raw per capita units, the average daily membership is a better unit to measure the educational costs than the more commonly used average daily attendance unit. Tradition, however, has favored the average daily attendance unit over average daily membership.

Cost analysis as it relates to equipment and supplies for physical education and sport may be simply handled by allowing a certain number of dollars per pupil or per participant, depending on whether one is concerned with a school or another organizational program.

Some experts in fiscal management feel a per capita expenditure allocation for physical education and sport represents a good foundation program. However, they recommend in addition (1) an extra percentage allocation for program enrichment, (2) an extra percentage allocation for variation in enrollment, and (3) a reference to a commodity index (current prices of equipment and supplies) that may indicate need for changes in the per capita expenditure because of current increase or decrease in the value of the items being purchased.

To determine the amount of money needed for physical education and sport programs, the following example can be used as a guideline. The director of physical education or athletic director submits and substantiates the needs for the coming school year; increased expenditures—a sound estimate of projected increases regarding student program participation based on increased enrollments, student interest, program changes, and the anticipated cost of equipment and supplies to be used; inventory—equipment and supplies on hand and the condition of these items; and the previous year's budget—amounts allocated in the previous year or years. These items represent the basis on which most allocations of funds to physical education and sport programs are determined.

Directors of physical education and sport programs surveyed believed that when they were granted increases in per capita allocations it was the result of such factors as increase in the number of participants, a careful evaluation of the number of participants and the time they spent using the equipment and supplies, the cost per hour, and an excellent working rapport with the Board of Education.

THE EXECUTIVE DIRECTOR OF FINANCE OR BUSINESS MANAGER: FISCAL MANAGEMENT IN SCHOOLS AND COLLEGES

Schools and colleges today are in the business of education. The size of the physical plant and the large expenditures require the talents of a qualified executive director of finance or business manager. The school or college business manager is an integral part of the entire management team and ideally should possess experience in both business administration and education. Most business managers have earned a master's or a doctor's degree, usually in business administration. Some are certified public accountants, and others have taken courses from management institutes. Many college and university business managers are recruited from outside the academic world. The manager is primarily responsible for the efficient and economic management of business matters concerning the educational institution and often its physical education and sport programs.

Physical education and athletic directors must understand and appreciate the vital role of the business manager. Many management functions of physical educators, including fiscal management, fall within the responsibility of the business manager. The business manager is a specialist in this area, and educators and coaches should work closely with this individual in reference to business-related matters. It is up to teachers and coaches to supply the business manager with an accurate and up-to-date database (debits, receipts, equipment costs, etc.).

The school or college business manager is responsible for budget preparation and fiscal accounting, investment of endowment and other "gift" monies, planning and construction of buildings, data processing, management of research and other contracts, business aspects of student loans, and intercollegiate activities.

Regardless of who performs the role of "business manager" or what title he or she assumes, the functions outlined and the working relationship with physical education and sport personnel are similar to or have implications for physical educators in colleges as well as other public- and private-sector organizations.

Function

The business manager's function is strictly limited by the size of the educational triangle—program, receipts/credits, expenditures/debits (Figure 10-2). The greater the perimeter of the triangle, the larger the sphere of operations. This applies to all departments within the system. Likewise, in times of inflation, the expenditures and receipts may increase, but the program side may remain stable. Hence it is obvious that the business manager must project both expenditures and receipts if a physical education or sport program is going to be maintained or grow.

The business office represents a means to an end, and it can be evaluated in terms of how well it contributes to the realization of the objectives of education.

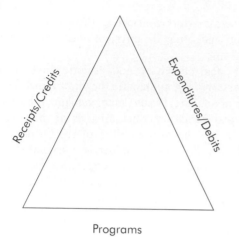

Receipts/Credits

Expenditures/Debits

Programs

FIGURE 10-2 The business manager's isosceles triangle.

Objectives

In serving schools and colleges, the business manager constantly has the goal of helping them obtain the greatest educational service possible from each tax or other dollar spent. He or she should take a democratic approach to decisions affecting others. A decision will then be reached that will be for the best, with the assurance that the educational benefits are worth the cost and risks.

The business manager or finance director is part of the management team—along with principals, superintendents, board members, presidents, directors, and chairs—who may be expected to look into the years ahead and present long-term ideas regarding the future plans of the school or college as well as its programs.

Responsibilities

The business manager's responsibilities are varied. He or she must be familiar with employee health insurance problems as well as with state and federal allocations for education. In the smaller school district the business responsibilities may be incorporated into the duties of the chief school administrator. As districts enlarge, they need to hire a person to oversee all the nonteaching areas of the district so

that the chief school administrator is free to devote more time to the educational programs of the district. No two districts are alike in handling business responsibilities.

The following are some of the business manager's duties as listed by Frederick W. Hill, past president of the Association of School Business Officials:

Budget and financial planning. This is an area in which the business manager has to be sensitive to the needs of staff members to carry out a program. One also must have a sixth sense to understand how much the community can expend on the program. This can be related to the accompanying isosceles triangle. A direct relationship must exist among all the components that make up the three sides of the triangle.

Purchasing and supply management. The business manager must use the best purchasing techniques to obtain maximal value for every dollar spent. After purchases are made and goods received, he or she is responsible for warehousing, storage, and inventory control. Equipment offered at the lowest bid price is not always the most economical to purchase.

Plans. The business manager works with administrators, teachers, coaches, architects, attorneys, and citizens of the community in developing plans for expansion, renovation, and construction of new facilities.

Personnel. The business manager's duties vary in relation to the size of the district. In a large district he or she may be in charge of the nonteaching personnel, and in a small district he or she may be in charge of all personnel. In this capacity the manager has to maintain records and pay schedules, initiate payroll and retirement reports, and keep other personnel records.

Staff improvement. The business manager is always interested in upgrading the people under his or her jurisdiction by providing workshops and in-service courses concerning the latest developments in the field of fiscal management and services.

Community relations. Without community support the school would not operate. Some managers tend to forget this when they become too far removed from the community. There is always a need to interpret the financial responsibility and accountability of the institution and program to the public.

Transportation. It has often been said that Boards of Education find themselves spending too much time on the three Bs—buses, buildings, and bonds. When this occurs, it is time to look into hiring a business manager. Transportation is vital but also one of the most complex and costly line items to control.

Food services. The business manager is responsible for the efficient and effective management of food services.

Accounting and reporting. The business manager establishes and supervises the financial records and accounting procedures.

Debt service. The business manager is involved with various capital developments and financial planning through short-term and long-term programs. The financial rating of a school district is judged in part based on the way its debt service is handled.

Insurance. The business manager must be familiar with a large schedule of insurance provisions ranging from fire and liability to health and injury insurance. He or she must maintain records for proof in case of loss.

Legal matters. The business manager has to be familiar with education and school law, and he or she must know when to consult with attorneys who are typically retained by most school districts, colleges, corporations, and other public- and private-sector organizations.

Money raising. The business manager is frequently called on to lead or organize fund-raising drives for schools, colleges, and universities.

Grants and financial aid. The business manager must be aware of money available for programs through private, state, and federal agencies. Grants and aid and other monies available for scholarships from private and public sources should also fall into his or her domain.

Systems analysis. The business manager must constantly question and challenge existing systems to see if they can be improved so that managerial tasks can be performed more efficiently and effectively.

In the Lexington, Massachusetts public schools most of the "collectibles" and "accountables" are transferred via computer to the business manager's centralized database. Thus the role of the teacher and coach is to feed specialized information (e.g., equipment types and prices) to the central office. The business manager via computer can then check out the item, comparison shop, project and audit the existing equipment budget, evaluate alternative purchase offers, and produce vendor requisitions and purchase orders, as well as update the existing equipment inventory and provide documentation back to the physical education chair or athletic director.

Similar procedures for budgeting exist, ensuring increased accuracy and standardized budget request forms, providing appropriate copies to affected management, and continually tracking and auditing the existing budget area.

FINANCIAL ACCOUNTABILITY

The large amount of money involved in physical education and sport programs makes strict account-

From budgeting to data storage, computerization helps all dimensions of physical education and sport programs to maintain accountability.

ability mandatory. This includes the maintenance of accurate records, proper distribution of materials, and adequate appraisal and evaluation of procedures. Financial accounting should provide a record of receipts and expenditures for all departmental transactions. With help from the computer the process should also provide permanent records of all financial transactions, which can help form a pattern of expenditures as related to the approved budget. Documenting compliance with mandates and requests imposed either by law or by administrative action, evaluating and accounting to ensure that funds are dealt with honestly, and managing properly with respect to control, analysis of costs, and reporting all fall within the domain of the business manager (see the box below).

 REASONS FOR FINANCIAL ACCOUNTING

To provide a method of authorizing expenditures for items that have been included and approved in the budget. This means proper accounting records are being used.

To provide authorized procedures for making purchases of equipment, supplies, and other materials and to let contracts for various services.

To provide authorized procedures for paying the proper amounts (a) for purchases of equipment, supplies, and other materials, which have been checked upon receipt; (b) for actual labor; and (c) for other services rendered.

To provide a record of each payment made, including the date, to whom, for what purpose, and other pertinent material.

To provide authorized procedures for handling various receipts and sources of income.

To provide the detailed information essential for properly auditing accounts, such as confirmation that money has been spent for accurately specified items.

To provide material and information for the preparation of future budgets.

To provide a tangible base for developing future policies relating to financial planning.

Management Policies for Financial Accounting

Management has the final responsibility for accountability for all monies, equipment, and supplies (see the box on p. 301). Departments should establish and enforce policies covering loss, damage, theft, misappropriation, or destruction of appropriate departmental resources. A system of accurate record keeping should be established and uniformly applied throughout the organization. The person to whom equipment and supplies are issued can be held accountable for these materials, and accurate inventories can be maintained. Once again the computer is user friendly for these types of systems.

Accounting for Receipts and Expenditures

A centralized accounting system is advantageous, with all funds being deposited with the business manager, treasurer, or other responsible person. Purchase orders and other forms are usually then countersigned or certified by the proper official, thus better guaranteeing integrity in the use of funds. A system of bookkeeping wherein books and databases are housed in the central office by the business manager helps ensure better control of finances and allows all subdivisions or departments in a system to be uniformly controlled. The central accounting system fund accounts, in which the physical education and sports funds are located, should be audited annually by qualified persons. Last, an annual financial report should be developed and publicized to indicate receipts, expenditures, and other pertinent data associated with the enterprise.

All receipts and expenditures should be recorded in the ledger or computer properly, providing such important information as the fund in which it has been deposited or from which it was debited; the money received from sources such as sport participation fees and organization dues should be shown with sufficient credit cross references and detailed information. Supporting vouchers should also be maintained and readily accessible for inspection. Tickets to sports and other events should be numbered consecutively and checked to get an accurate record of ticket sales. Students should not be permitted to handle funds except under the supervision of the management staff or faculty.

A. Preliminary considerations in preparing the budget
1. Program additions or deletions
2. Staff changes
3. Inventory of equipment on hand

B. Budget preparation: additional considerations
1. Athletic gate receipts and expenditures—athletic association fund
2. Board of Education budget—allocations for physical education, including athletics and recreational sport
3. Coaches' request and requests of teachers and department heads
4. Comparison of requests with inventories
5. Itemizing and coding requests
6. Budget conferences with administration
7. Justification of requests

C. Athletic association funds: considerations
1. Estimated income
   a. Gate receipts
   b. Student activities tickets
   c. Tournament receipts
2. Estimated expenditures
   a. Awards
   b. Tournament fees
   c. Films and videos
   d. Miscellaneous
   e. Surplus

D. General budget: considerations
1. Breakdown
   a. By sport or activity
   b. By gender and per student
   c. Transportation
   d. Salaries of personnel
   e. Insurance
   f. Reconditioning of equipment
   g. Supervision
   h. General and miscellaneous
   i. Equipment
   j. Officials
2. Codes
   a. Advertising
   b. Travel
   c. Conferences
   d. Others

E. Postbudget procedures
1. Selection of equipment and supplies
2. Preparation of list of deals to bid
3. Request for price quotations
4. Requisitions

5. Care of equipment
6. Notification of teachers and coaches of amounts approved

F. Ordering procedures
1. Study the quality of various products
2. Accept no substitutes for items ordered
3. Submit request for price quotations
4. Select low quotes or justify higher quotes
5. Submit purchase orders
6. Check and count all shipments
7. Record items received on inventory cards or computer printouts
8. Provide for equipment and supply accountability

G. Relationships with management
1. Consultation—program plans with building principal and/or superintendent
2. Make budget recommendations to administration
3. Advise business manager of procedures followed
4. Discuss items approved and deleted with business manager
5. Advise teachers and coaches of amounts available and adjust requests

H. Suggestions for prospective directors of physical education and sport programs
1. Develop a philosophy and approach to budgeting
2. Consult with staff for their suggestions
3. Select quality merchandise
4. Provide proper care and maintenance of equipment and supplies
5. Provide for all programs on an equitable basis
6. Budget adequately but not elaborately
7. Provide a sound, well-rounded program of physical education and sport
8. Emphasize equality for girls and boys
9. Provide for basic instruction, adapted, intramural and extramural, and interscholastic parts of the program
10. Conduct a year-round public relations program
11. Try to overcome these possible shortcomings:
    a. Board of Education not oriented to needs of physical education and sport
    b. Program not achieving established goals
    c. Staff not adequately informed and involved in management process

◆ **CHECKLIST FOR BUDGETING AND FINANCIAL ACCOUNTING**

	Yes	No
1. Has a complete inventory been taken and itemized on proper forms as a guide in estimating equipment needs?	___	___
2. Does the equipment inventory include a detailed account of the number of items on hand, size and quantity, type, condition, etc.?	___	___
3. Is the inventory complete, current, and up-to-date?	___	___
4. Are budgetary estimates as accurate and realistic as possible without padding?	___	___
5. Are provisions made in the budget for increases expected in enrollments, increased student participation, and changes in the cost of equipment, supplies, and insurance?	___	___
6. Have supply house and the business manager been consulted on the cost of new equipment?	___	___
7. Has the Director of Physical Education and Athletics consulted with the staff on various budget items?	___	___
8. Has the Director of Physical Education and Athletics consulted with the school business manager in respect to the total budget for the department?	___	___
9. Are new equipment and supply needs for physical education and sport determined and budgeted at least 1 year in advance?	___	___
10. Was the budget prepared according to the standards desired by the chief school administrator?	___	___
11. Are data bases and information for previous years indicated as a means of comparison?	___	___
12. Is there a summary of receipts and expenditures listed concisely on one page so that the total budget can be quickly seen?	___	___
13. If receipts from sport or other funds are to be added to the budget, is this shown?	___	___
14. Are there alternate program plans with budgetary changes in the event the budget is not approved?	___	___
15. Has a statement of objectives of the program been included that reflects the overall educational philosophy and program of the total school and community?	___	___
16. Has the budget been prepared so that the major aspects may be viewed readily by those persons desiring a quick review and also in more detail for those persons desiring a further delineation of the budgetary items?	___	___
17. Is the period of time for which the budget has been prepared clearly indicated?	___	___
18. Is the physical eduation and sport budget based on an educational plan developed to attain the goals and purposes agreed on by management and staff within the framework of the total school's philosophy?	___	___
19. Is the physical education and sport plan a comprehensive one reflecting a healthful environment, physical education class, adapted, recreational sports, and interscholastic program?	___	___
20. Does the plan include a statement of the objectives of the physical education and sport programs, and are these reflected in the budget?	___	___
21. Are both long-range and short-range plans for achieving the purposes of the program provided?	___	___
22. Have provisions been made in the budget for emergencies?	___	___
23. Are accurate records kept on such activities involving expenditures of money as transportation, insurance, officials, laundry and dry cleaning, awards, guarantees, repairs, new equipment, medical expenses, and publicity?	___	___

◆ **CHECKLIST FOR BUDGETING AND FINANCIAL ACCOUNTING—cont'd**

	Yes	No
24. Are accurate records kept on the receipt of monies from such sources as gate receipts and advertising revenue?	____	____
25. Once the budget has been approved, is there a specific plan provided for authorizing expenditures?	____	____
26. Are specific forms used for recording purchase transactions?	____	____
27. Are purchases on all major items based on competitive bidding?	____	____
28. Are requisitions used in obtaining supplies and equipment?	____	____
29. Are requisitions numbered and do they include such information as the name of the person originating the requisition, when the item to be purchased will be needed, where to ship the item, the description and/or code number, quantity, unit price, and amount?	____	____
30. With the exception of petty cash accounts, is a central purchasing system in effect?	____	____
31. Is the policy of quantity and cooperative purchasing followed whenever possible and desirable in the interest of economy?	____	____
32. If quantity purchasing is used, are advanced thought and planning given to storage and maintenance facilities and procedures?	____	____
33. Are performance tests made on items purchased? Are state, regional, or national testing bureaus or laboratories utilized where feasible?	____	____
34. Are receipts of equipment and supplies checked carefully?	____	____
35. Is an audit made of all expenditures?	____	____
36. Are specific procedures in effect to safeguard money, property, and employees?	____	____
37. Is there a check to determine that established standards, policies, and procedures have been followed?	____	____
38. Are procedures in operation to check condition and use of equipment and supplies?	____	____
39. Is a financial report made periodically?	____	____
40. Are there proper procedures for the care and maintenance and accountability of all equipment and supplies?	____	____
41. Are accurate records kept on all equipment and supplies, including condition, site, and age?	____	____
42. Have established procedures been developed and are they followed in regard to the issuance, use, and return of equipment?	____	____
43. Have provisions been made for making regular notations of future needs?	____	____

Purchase orders on regular authorized forms issued by the organization should be used so that accurate and standardized records may be kept. To place an order verbally is a questionable policy. Preparing written purchase orders on regular forms and according to sound accountability procedure better ensures legality of contract together with prompt delivery and payment (see the box on pp. 302-303).

SUMMARY

The management of physical education and sport programs must be concerned with proper fiscal man-agement. The lack of money from traditional sources such as a school district's general fund is prompting many organizations to look to government, foundations, the corporate sector, and other sources for help in meeting their fiscal needs and budgetary requirements. Other organizations are engaging in special fund-raising projects ranging from raffles to T-shirt sales in order to secure the financial help they need to conduct quality programs. Management of funds also requires a knowledge of such things as how to prepare and implement budgets; how to determine proper costs of supplies and equipment; how to apply zero-base budgeting, PPBES, and PERT; and how to provide for fiscal accountability within the organization. Computerization should also come into play to ensure greater accuracy and to streamline operations.

♦ **SELF-ASSESSMENT ACTIVITIES**

These activities will assist students in determining if material and competencies presented in this chapter have been mastered.

1. What are the reasons for fiscal management in physical education and sport programs?
2. Outline the procedure you would follow in preparing a zero-base budget if you were the chair of a department of recreational sports for a city-wide program.
3. Develop a detailed PPBES plan for a department of athletics at the junior high school level.
4. As a business manager in a school system, what aspects of fiscal management would involve you and the management of a physical education and sport program?
5. Formulate ten policies to ensure sound financial accounting.
6. Design and defend a pay-to-play policy for an interscholastic varsity sport program.

REFERENCES

1. American Management Association, *Financial management,* New York, 1986, American Management Association.
2. Apostolou NG, Crumbley DL: *Handbook of government accounting and finance,* New York, 1988, John Wiley and Sons.
3. Athletic Purchasing and Facilities: What happens when the money runs out? *Athletic Purchasing and Facilities* p. 44, July 1981.
4. Clegg AA, Jr: The teacher and manager of the curriculum, *Educational Leadership* p. 308, Jan 1973.
5. Dirmith MW, Jablonsky SF: Zero-base budgeting as a management techique and political strategy, *Academy of Management Review* 4(4):555-565, Oct 1979.
6. Klappholz LA: Involving the staff in the budget-making process, *Physical Education Newsletter* Nov 1980.
7. Parkhouse BL, Dennison M: Pay for play: solution or stopgap? *Athletic Business* p. 12, Apr 1984.
8. Roe WH: *School business management,* New York, 1961, McGraw-Hill.

SUGGESTED READINGS

▪ Austin DA: Economic impact on physical education, *Journal of Physical Education, Recreation and Dance* 55:35, May/June 1984.

Discusses how sources of funds that affect physical education and sport programs have been cut back. It lists strategies for a lifetime game plan, the principle of which stresses that the way to sustain physical education is to provide excellent instructional programs. The value of being taught to actively engage in physical exercise should be continually stressed since the public is willing to supply funds to accomplish the objectives that result from such programs.

▪ Bronzan R: Fund raising today demands better ideas, *Athletic Business* p. 12, May 1984.

Accentuates the need to raise funds for physical education and sport programs in schools and colleges. Such outside sources need to be tapped if these programs are to survive. Provides suggestions for procuring external funds.

▪ Dougherty NJ, Bonanno D: *Management principles in sport and leisure services,* Minneapolis, 1985, Burgess Publishing.

Financial management is discussed, including such aspects as operating versus capital budgets, types of budgets, preparing and presenting the budget, and sources of funding.

▪ DuBrin AJ, Ireland RD, Williams JC: *Management and organization,* Cincinnati, Oh, 1989, South-Western Publishing.

Presents control methods and techniques relative to budgeting and finance. Discusses various network analysis techniques such as PERT and cost-profit schemes.

▪ Lewandowski DM: Shoestrings and shoeboxes, *Journal of Physical Education, Recreation and Dance* 55:34, Aug 1984.

Provides suggestions for how a school without sufficient cash can, through ingenuity, effort, and time, come up with solutions for insufficient space and equipment. It also provides suggestions in chart form for homemade equipment, how items can be constructed, and in what activities they can be used.

▪ Needler BE, Jr, Anderson HR, Caldwell JC: *Financial and managerial accounting,* Boston, 1988, Houghton Mifflin.

Presents procedures and policies in accounting, as well as budget guidelines and format.

CHAPTER 11

Purchase and Care of Supplies and Equipment

▶ **Instructional Objectives and Competencies To Be Achieved**

After reading this chapter the student should be able to

- Explain why sound supply and equipment management is important and explain the basis on which supplies and equipment should be selected for physical education and sport programs.
- Discuss the various procedures and principles that should be followed in purchasing supplies and equipment.

- List guidelines for the selection of an equipment manager and for the management of the equipment room.
- Establish a system for checking, issuing, and maintaining supplies and equipment.
- Justify the need for various types of audiovisual supplies and equipment for physical education and sport programs.

In the chapter on fiscal management it was shown that a large portion of the budget is allocated for the purchase of supplies and equipment for physical education and sport programs. Management is responsible for seeing that the supplies and equipment that are purchased will meet program needs and be of good quality, and are acquired via a procedural pattern that reflects efficient and effective practices.

Physical education and sport programs use supplies and equipment that cost thousands of dollars. *Supplies* are those materials that are expendable and have to be replaced at frequent intervals, such as shuttlecocks, tennis balls, and adhesive tape. *Equipment* refers to those items that are not considered expendable, but are used for a period of years,

such as parallel bars, volleyball standards, canoes, and videotape recorders.

Because so much money is spent on supplies and equipment and such materials are vital to the health and safety of participants, to good playing conditions, and to values derived from the programs, it is important that the management aspects related to supplies and equipment are well planned and carefully developed. In addition, the purchase of supplies and equipment should be related to achieving program objectives designated by PPBES. Physical educators, coaches, and equipment room personnel should express their needs for supplies and equipment in terms of these programmatic goals.

Many different sources for purchasing equipment

High school gymnastics room with equipment.

Specialized equipment for basketball being assembled.

exist, many grades and qualities of materials are available, and many methods of storing and maintaining such merchandise are prevalent. Some of these sources, grades, and methods are good, whereas others are extremely questionable. To obtain the best value for the investment of scarce financial inputs, basic principles of selecting, purchasing, and maintaining need to be understood and applied.

DETERMINING SUPPLY AND EQUIPMENT NEEDS

Supply and equipment needs vary according to a wide range of factors, including the level of the program and the activities being offered. Other factors are the facilities and physical plant, training rooms

(see Chapter 12), playing space available, and number of activities or sports being offered. Some organizations have only limited physical education and sport programs and facilities. Under such conditions the supplies and equipment needed differ from those required in settings where more spacious and sophisticated accommodations exist. Other factors to consider are the nature of the clientele (age, gender, and number), the financial resources available, the length of playing seasons, the environment, and health and safety provisions. Those responsible for purchasing supplies and equipment should carefully study their own particular situations and estimate and project their needs objectively and realistically.

In the physical education instructional domain, all types of balls, apparatus, nets, standards, implements (e.g., gloves, bats, racquets), and racks will be needed for the conduct of individual and team sports, as well as for aquatics, dance, and other physical activities. These same types of supplies and equipment are also used in the recreational sport program. Many times, in fact, the same human and physical (facility, supplies, equipment) resources are utilized.

Physical education supply and equipment needs,

Rolling equipment carts make it easy to transport, store, and account for costly equipment.

and the manner by which they are determined, vary from organization to organization. For example, an elementary school may be given an equipment budget based on the number of students enrolled. Then, within the parameters of the budget, teachers request at the end of each year the equipment and supplies they will need the following year. Another procedure that might be followed in a high school, where various units of different activities constitute the program, would be to have an inventory of supplies at the conclusion of each teaching unit. A third procedure followed in cities and school districts such as Wayzata, Minnesota is, in the interest of economy, ordering all supplies and equipment through a central office computer system for all schools within the city or district. In such cases, items are frequently kept in a warehouse where they can be obtained as needed.

In sport programs, inventories are usually taken and purchase requests instituted at the end of each respective sport season such as at the end of the football season. In this process, the sport-specific coach, equipment manager, and athletic director usually cooperate to ensure that the necessary supplies and equipment are available for the beginning of the next season.

GUIDELINES FOR SELECTING SUPPLIES AND EQUIPMENT

Selection should be based on local needs. Supplies and equipment should be specified and selected because they are needed in a particular situation and by a particular user group. Items should be selected that represent materials needed to carry out the program as outlined and that represent essentials to fulfilling program objectives.

Selection should be based on quality. In the long run, the item of good quality is the least expensive and the safest. Bargain goods too often represent inferior materials that wear out much earlier and perhaps do not supply the protection needed for safe participation. Only the best grade of football equipment should be purchased. A study conducted on football deaths that occurred during a 25-year period revealed that many of these deaths resulted from the use of inferior helmets and other substandard equipment. What is true of football is also true of other activities.

Selection should consider whether the product is both budget and maintenance friendly. From uniforms to artificial surfaces, management must consider not only the initial capital outlay for an item (e.g., shoulder pads, ice hockey breezers, pool lane dividers, golf mats), but also the maintenance and upkeep. If possible, managers should avoid buying the "label" of, for example, training equipment (Cybex, Nautilus, Sports Medicine Industries, OEI, Med X, Keiser, Polaris, Randall, etc.),[3] since alternate equipment may be found at significant savings without compromising quality.

Equipment that has readily replaceable parts that are "recommended by the manufacturer" for liability purposes should be the only type of equipment purchased and maintained.

Selection should be made by professional personnel. The persons selecting the supplies and equipment needed in physical education and sport programs should be knowledgeable and competent. Performing this responsibility efficiently means examining many types and brands of products; conducting comparative experiments to determine economy, durability, and safety; listing and weighing the advantages and disadvantages of different items; and knowing how each item is going to be used. The person selecting supplies and equipment should be interested in this responsibility, have the time to do the job, be a member of the Athletic Equipment Managers Association, and be able to perform the function efficiency. Some organizations have purchasing agents who are specially trained in these matters, whereas others use athletic equipment managers. In small organizations the department chair, director, coach, or equipment commit-

Weight training equipment is costly, yet if maintained properly, it can last for many years.

tee frequently performs this responsibility. One other point is important: regardless of who the responsible person may be, the staff member who uses these supplies and equipment in his or her particular facet of the total program should have direct input concerning the specific items being considered for selection.

Selecting should be continuous. A product that ranks as the best available this year may not necessarily be the best next year. Manufacturers are constantly conducting research to develop and produce a safer and improved product. There is keen competition in the marketplace; management, therefore, cannot be complacent, thinking that because a certain product has served well in the past, it remains the best buy for the future. The search for the best product available must be a continuous process. With the help of the computer, these trends can be tracked.

Selection should consider service and replacement needs. Supplies and equipment may be difficult to obtain in volume. On receipt of merchandise, sizes of uniforms may be wrong, and colors may be mixed up. Additional materials may be needed on short notice. Therefore one should select items that will be available in volume, if needed, and deal with business firms that will service and replace materials with manufacturer's approved parts and take care of emergencies without delay or controversy. Local merchants should be strongly considered in the purchasing process.

Selection should consider whether old equipment can be reconditioned successfully or whether new equipment should be purchased. Management should make this decision based on factors such as safety, cost, and suitability for effective use in activities in which the item is required. In some cases, if old equipment is repaired, it may be costly; therefore it may be more beneficial to buy new equipment. If the safety of participants is in question, the decision definitely should be in favor of new equipment.

Selection should consider those persons with disabilities. Members of various special-population user groups may need special types of equipment to participate in some of the activities that are a part of the physical education and sport program. Equipment may be needed for such aspects of the program

as perceptual-motor activities or correction of postural deviations. For the most part, however, regular equipment can and should be adopted for those with disabilities, since the trend is to have students with disabilities integrated into as many regular classes as possible. This notion holds true with sport participation as well.

Dunn and Fait[4] discuss equipment and supplies for special populations. They include information concerning topics such as ordering and maintenance of equipment, safety, supervision required, and storage space, and also provide a list of equipment suppliers.

Selection should consider acceptable standards for athletic equipment.[2] The stamp of approval of the National Operating Committee on Standards for Athletic Equipment (NOCSAE) should be on football helmets. This will ensure that the helmet has been properly constructed and injury will be less likely to occur. NOCSAE researches sports equipment and encourages acceptable standards in manufacturing. They also distribute information concerning sport standards and safety to various organizations and individuals in the interests of safety, utility, and legal considerations. Furthermore, they provide an opportunity for individuals and organizations to consider problems regarding various aspects of sports equipment and how they can be solved.

Selection should consider trends in sports equipment and uniforms.[6] The emerging trends in sports equipment and uniforms also should be taken into consideration. Some significant changes include ventilated mesh cloth, and waterproof and breathable Gore-Tex–like materials, screen-printed lettering, and one-piece wrestling uniforms, not to mention the myriad fabrics (e.g., such as nylon filament, stretch nylon, lycra, cotton, acrylic, polypropylene, and polyester). Additional accessories to basketball uniforms (e.g., T-shirts might be worn under the uniform shirt, and spandex tights under the pants) are also popular.

Developments in equipment are improving both safety and sport performance. Modifications in equipment ranging from ice hockey skate blades to composite tennis racquets and from eye protection to high-tech ski bindings have made continuous up-

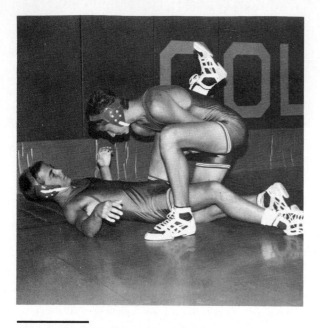

Equipment and uniform selection should be up to date;
University of Colorado, Boulder.

SELECTED MANAGEMENT GOALS RELATING TO THE PURCHASE OF SUPPLIES AND EQUIPMENT

- Try to standardize supplies and equipment as much as possible.
- Supervise the entire process of selection, specification, purchase, storage, and maintenance.
- Maintain an inventory of materials on hand (via computer database).
- Prepare specifications for items to be purchased.
- Secure bids for large purchases and those required by law.
- Decide on or recommend distribution where materials and supplies are to be purchased.
- Test products to see that specifications are satisfactorily met.
- Check supplies and equipment to determine if all that were ordered have been delivered and are in top condition.
- Expedite the delivery of purchases so that materials are available as needed.
- Seek new products that meet the needs of the program.
- Try to order NOCSAE and other approved equipment where appropriate.

dating requisite to providing the most current and safe equipment for the physical activity and sport consumer.

GUIDELINES FOR PURCHASING SUPPLIES AND EQUIPMENT

Purchases should meet the organization's requirements and have management approval. Each organization has its own policy providing for the purchase of supplies and equipment. It is essential that the prescribed pattern be followed and that proper management approval be obtained. Requisition forms that contain descriptions of items, amounts, and costs (Figure 11-1), purchase orders that place the buying procedure on a written or contract basis (Figure 11-2), and voucher forms that show receipt of materials all should be used as prescribed by regulations. The physical education and sport manager and staff should all be familiar with and adhere to the purchasing policies of the organization, and be

sure that their policies include standards such as those of NOCSAE and the U.S. Consumer Product Safety Commission.

Purchasing should be done in advance of need.[1] The majority of supplies and equipment for physical education and sport programs should be ordered in bulk, and well in advance of the time the materials will be used. Late orders, rushed through at the last moment, may mean mistakes or substitutions on the part of the manufacturer. When purchase orders are placed early, manufacturers have more time to carry out their repsonsibilities efficiently. Goods that do not meet specifications can be returned and replaced, and many other advantages result. Items needed in the fall should be ordered not later than the preceding spring, and items desired for spring use should be ordered not later than the preceding fall (see the box above).

REQUISITION FORM
BLOOMINGTON SCHOOL DISTRICT 271

REQUISITION NO. 158236

ALL REQUISITIONS MUST BE TYPEWRITTEN

Name & Address of Vendor

Required Delivery Date

SHIP TO:

Today's Date

Source of Price:
Estimate ☐   Catalog ☐   Contract ☐
Verbal Quote ☐   Written Quote ☐   (Attach copies of all quotes received)
Requisitions in excess of $1,000.00 require competitive written quotes.

(Vendor Information Below This Line)

Quantity	Unit of measure	Catalog Number	Give complete information as to color, size, dimensions, copyright date, edition, etc. — state if book, film, magazine, etc.	Unit Price	Total Price Each
1.					
2.					
3.					
4.					
5.					
6.					
7.					
8.					
9.					
10.					
				TOTAL	

PURCHASE REQUISITION

Purchase requisitions are generally initiated by a school or department to cover requirements which are needed during the school year that are to be purchased from a supplier. Requisitions should be made in duplicate:

1. Original sent to business office for processing
2. Duplicate retained by initiating school or department

ADDITIONAL INFORMATION — (INFORMATION SHOWN BELOW THIS LINE WILL NOT GO TO VENDOR)
COMMENTS:

DIST.	SCHOOL & DEPT.	REQUESTED BY	DATE	PURCHASE ORDER	T	VEVDOR
4			39 44	45 50	51	52
271						

G/E	FD	ORG	PRG	FIN	OBJ	CRS	CR	PURCHASE ORDER AMOUNT	POC	BLT	CR	AMOUNT	TP1	TP2	INVOICE NUMBER	PTL
	9 10	11 13	14 16	17 19	20 22	23 25	26 27		37 36	26 27			37 38	58		68
						000										
						000										
						000										
						000										
						000										
						000										

Principal _____

District Administrator _____

PURCHASE ORDER

45   50

DATE OF ORDER

39   44

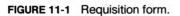

FIGURE 11-1 Requisition form.

FIGURE 11-2 Purchase order.

Supplies and equipment should be standardized. Ease of ordering is accomplished and larger quantities of materials can be purchased at a saving when standardized supplies and equipment are used. Standardization means that certain colors, styles, and types of material are ordered consistently. This procedure can be followed after careful research to determine which are the best, most reliable, and most serviceable products for the money. However, standardization of supplies and equipment should never mean termination of further study and research to find the best materials to meet program objectives.

Specifications should be clearly set forth. The trademark, item number, catalog number, type of material, and other important specifications should be clearly stated when purchasing supplies, equipment, and other materials to avoid any misunderstanding of what is being ordered. This procedure ensures that quality merchandise will be received when it is ordered. It also makes it possible to objectively compare bids of competing business firms. For example, if a particular brand of baseball, basketball, or football is desired, the trademark, item number, and catalog number should be clearly stated. Also, it should be noted in writing that no substitutes will be accepted.

Cost should be kept as low as possible without loss of quality. Quality of materials is a major consideration. However, among various manufacturers and business concerns, prices vary for products of equal quality.[3] Because supplies and equipment are usually purchased in considerable volume, a few cents per unit could represent a saving of many hundreds of dollars to departments and taxpayers. Therefore if quality can be maintained, materials should be purchased at the lowest cost figure.

Purchases should be made from reputable business firms. In some cases, higher management authorities decide the firm from which supplies and equipment are to be purchased. In the event of such a procedure, this principle is academic. However, when the business firm from which purchases will be made is determined by physical education and sport personnel, it is wise to deal with established, reputable businesses that are known to have reasonable prices, reliable materials, ample manufacturer-approved inventory for replacement, and good service. In the long run, this is the best way to conduct business.

Central purchasing can result in greater economy. Some school districts and other organizations purchase supplies and equipment for several schools or other groups. In this way they can buy larger amounts at a reduced price per unit. In some cases, large school districts even go so far as to standardize their uniforms' colors, thus enabling them to purchase uniforms at lower prices. These systems also usually computerize their purchase orders, contracts, and other records, not to mention their entire budgetary and purchasing process. Databases for maintaining inventory and equipment lists are also made immediately available. The physical educator and coach are called on for their valuable input.

Local firms should be considered. Management's main concern must be to obtain good value for money expended. If local firms can offer equal values, render equal or better service for the same

money, and are reliable, then preference should probably be given to local dealers. In some cases, it is advantageous to use local dealers, because they are more readily accessible and can provide quicker and better service than firms located farther away. It also makes for good public relations.

Bids should be obtained. A sound management procedure that helps eliminate any accusation of favoritism and helps obtain the best price available is competitive bidding. This procedure requires that special forms be distributed to the many dealers who handle the supplies and equipment desired (Figure 11-3). In such cases the specifics regarding the description (e.g., kind, make, model), amount, and quality of articles desired should be clearly stated. After bids have been obtained, the choice of vendor can be made. Low bids sometimes do not have to be accepted; however, a decision not to honor one must be justified. Such justification could be that a company's reputation is in question, the service rendered is poor, delivery cannot be made on time, or that the company is situated at such a great distance that communication and service are hampered.

Horine[5] discusses the question of whether the competitive bidding process is desirable. He points out that this process sometimes increases costs, slows down the purchasing process, discourages bids from local dealers, and encourages dealers to cut corners in order to submit lower bids. Often times the result leads to an inferior product being delivered.

Advantages of the bidding system are that it may stimulate honest competition, resulting in lower prices; it may promote on-time delivery; it can provide for better and more reliable service; it spreads the purchasing among more vendors; it eliminates favoritism; and it reduces the risk of poor quality merchandise.

Gifts or favors should not be accepted from dealers. Some dealers and their representatives (reps) are happy to present management or staff members with a set of golf clubs, a nice training outfit, tennis racquet, or other gifts if, by so doing, they believe it is possible to acquire an account. In most cases, it is poor policy to accept such gifts or favors. The reason is that it may place a person under obligation to an

NOTICE TO BIDDERS

(For use in advertising)

The board of education of ____(legal name)____ School District
No. ____ of the Town(s) of _____ popularly known
as _____ , (in accordance with Section 103 of
Article 5-A of the General Municipal Law) hereby invites the sub-
mission of sealed bids on _____ for use in the
schools of the district. Bids will be received until _____ on the
                                                        (hour)
_____ day of _____ , 19 ____ , at _____
(date)   (month)   (place of bid
_____ , at which time and place all bids will be publicly opened.
opening)
Specifications and bid form may be obtained at the same office. The
board of education reserves the right to reject all bids. Any bid
submitted will be binding for _____ days subsequent to the date of
bid opening.

                                     Board of Education

                        _____ School District No. ____

                        of the Town(s) of _____

                        County(ies) of _____

                        _____
                                (Address)

                        By _____
                                    (Purchasing Agent)

_____
    (Date)

Note: The hour should indicate whether it is Eastern Standard or
       Eastern Daylight Saving Time.

FIGURE 11-3   Sample notice to bidders form.

individual or firm and can result only in difficulties and harm to the program. A manager or staff member should never profit personally from any materials purchased for use in the programs. Therefore such gifts or favors should be scrutinized carefully in light of professional ethics.

A complete inventory analysis is essential before purchasing. Before purchases are made, the amount of supplies and equipment on hand and the condition of these items should be known. This knowledge prevents overbuying and having large stockpiles of ma-terials that may be outdated when they become needed. Inventories in some cases are taken period-ically, whereas in other cases, computerization en-sures that a perpetual inventory is maintained. In some organizations inventories are taken at such times as the end of a sport season or semester, or on an annual basis. In other organizations the inventory is kept up to date on a continuing basis. Computer-ized inventories for departments, school districts, and other organizations are now in use in many places[7] (see the box on p. 315).

STEPS IN PURCHASING SUPPLIES AND EQUIPMENT

Need	Staff identifies need for equipment in program.
Consultation	Staff consults with management supporting need for equipment.
Initiation	A request is made for equipment to fulfill, augment, supplement, or improve the program.
Review of request	The proper management personnel approve or disapprove request after careful consideration of need.
Review of budget allocation	A budget code number is assigned after availability of funds in that category has been determined.
Preparation of specifications	Specifications are prepared in detail, giving exact quality requirements, and made available to prospective contractors or vendors.
Receipt of bids	Contractors or vendors submit price quotations.
Comparisons	Careful evaluation is made to determine exact fulfillment of quality requirements.
Recommendations	The business manager prepares specific recommendations for approval.
Purchase order to supplier	After approval, a purchase that fulfills the requirements at a competitive price is made.
Follow-up	Purchasing agent makes a follow-up inquiry if equipment is not received when due.
Receipt of goods	Warehouse receives goods, checks according to specifications, and returns purchase order with approval.
Payment	Purchasing agent and Board of Education approve purchase for payment, and accounting office pays.
Accountability	Goods are sent to the department that is held accountable for equipment.
User receives	Staff picks up equipment at designated place and inspects before payment.

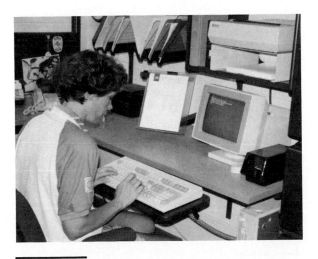

Computers connected to centralized data banks help determine equipment needs as well as inventory.

GUIDELINES FOR THE EQUIPMENT ROOM AND THE EQUIPMENT AND SUPPLY MANAGER

The equipment and supply manager's position is very important. The money spent on uniforms, supplies, and equipment amounts to a large part of an organization's budget. Therefore the person in charge of the equipment and supply room, whether a student or a paid employee, should be selected with care. A qualified person will be able to help make equipment and supplies last longer through proper maintenance, storage, cleaning, and care. Accountability for equipment will be better assured because a system of good record keeping will be established and less equipment will be lost (Figures 11-4 and 11-5). Also, a qualified manager will be able to make sound recommendations regarding the purchasing

---

EQUIPMENT ISSUE

Date...

I .... have

accepted school property ....

.... (write in article and its number)

and agree to return it clean and in good condition or pay for said uniform.

Signed ....

H. R. #

Home Phone #   Home Address...

FIGURE 11-4   Form for checking out physical education and athletic equipment.

---

of athletic equipment. In light of such important responsibilities, an equipment manager should be selected who has qualifications that include technical equipment skills, organizational ability, an interest in keeping equipment in excellent condition, an understanding of the care and maintenance of sports equipment and supplies, a willingness to learn, the ability to get along with people, trustworthiness, patience, the ability to supervise other people effectively, and communication skills. The equipment manager should also possess thorough understanding of the philosophy, goals, and objectives of the program and where this position fits in the total process.

The equipment and supply room is an important facility in physical education and sport programs. It is important to have sufficient space with proper ventilation to take care of the various purposes for which such a room exists (e.g., laundry, drying, storage). Space should be sufficient to store, label, and identify the equipment and supplies needed in the program. Adequate bins, shelves, and racks for equipment are needed. Space should be sufficient to

permit movement for handling the routine functions of issuing equipment and supplies. People working in the room should be able to move with ease throughout the facility. Space should be provided for drying equipment, such as football or soccer uni-

Qualified equipment personnel are required for efficient and effective management.

EQUIPMENT CHECKOUT RECORD

Player_____ Home Room_____

Address_____ Phone_____

Class_____ Height_____ Weight_____ Age_____

Parents Waiver_____ Examination_____ Insurance_____

Football   Cross Country   Basketball   Swimming   Wrestling

Baseball   Track   Tennis   Golf

	Out	In	Game Equipment	Out	In
Blocking pads			White jersey		
Shoulder pads			Maroon jersey		
Hip pads			White pants		
Thigh pads			Maroon pants		
Knee pads			Warm-up pants		
Helmet			Warm-up jacket		
Shoes			Stockings		
Practice pants					
Practice jersey					

I hereby certify that I have received the above-listed athletic equipment and will return same not later than the day following the last game of the season for the sport checked.

Signature_____

FIGURE 11-5 Equipment checkout record.

forms that have become wet when practices or games are held in the rain. The equipment and supply room should be well organized and a model of efficiency and sound organization.

GUIDELINES FOR CHECKING, STORING, ISSUING, AND MAINTAINING SUPPLIES AND EQUIPMENT

All supplies and equipment should be carefully inspected upon receipt. Equipment and supplies that have been ordered should not be paid for until they have been thoroughly inspected and inventoried as to amount, type, quality, size, and other specifications listed on the purchase order. If any discrepancies are noted, they should be corrected before payment is made. This is an important responsibility and should be followed carefully. It represents sound and prudent business practice in an area requiring business aptitude.

Supplies and equipment requiring organization identification should be labeled. Equipment and supplies are often moved from location to location and sometimes are part of an integrated (e.g., physical education, recreational sports) locker room system. It is a good practice to stencil or stamp inventory with the organization's logo in order to identify it. This also helps to trace and locate missing articles, discourage misappropriation of such items, and determine what is and what is not departmental property.

Procedures should be established for issuing and checking in supplies and equipment. Considerable loss of material can result if poor accounting procedures are followed. Procedures should be established so that items are issued as prescribed, proper forms are completed, records are maintained, and all materials can be traced and located. Articles should be listed on the records according to various specifications of amount, size, or color, together with the name of the person to whom the item is issued. The individual's record should be classified according to name, street address, telephone, locker number, social security number, student ID, or other information important for identification. In all cases, the person or persons to whom the supplies and equipment are issued should be held accountable.

Equipment should be in constant repair. Equipment should always be maintained in a serviceable condition. Maintenance procedures for equipment should be routinized so that repairs are provided as needed. All used equipment should be checked and then repaired, replaced, or serviced as needed. Repair can be justified, however, only when the cost for such is within reason and manufacturer's approved parts can be obtained. Supplies should also be replaced when they have been depleted.

Equipment and supplies should be stored properly. Equipment and supplies should be handled efficiently so that space can be properly organized for storing. A procedure should be established for identification and location, and proper safeguards should be taken to protect against fire and theft. Convenient bins, racks, shelves, hangers, and other accessories should be available. Temperature, humidity, and ventilation are also important considerations. Items going into the storeroom should be properly checked for quality and quantity before acceptance is confirmed. An inventory should be readily available for all items on hand in the storeroom. Computerization is strongly recommended for this function. Every precaution should be taken to provide for the adequate care of all materials so that investments are properly maintained and protected.

Garments should be cleaned and cared for properly. According to the Rawlings Sporting Goods Company, the care of garments should be considered in four categories: (1) New garments should be kept in original packing boxes and stored in a cool, dry area with low humidity. (2) During the season, garments should be cared for immediately after a game. Before being sent to the cleaner, they should be inspected for tears or other defects and repaired immediately. (3) For away contests, garments should be packed for the trip and then hung up as soon as possible on arrival as well as on return. If an extended trip is being made, or if the trip home will not take place until the following day, the garments should be hung up for drying after each game. (4) Upon completion of the season, final cleaning, repair, and storage of the garments are crucial. If followed, proper cleaning and storing procedures will extend the life of the garments, help maintain attractiveness, and save time and money (see the boxes on pp. 319-321).

AUDIOVISUAL SUPPLIES AND EQUIPMENT

Audiovisual aids and materials have become an important part of physical education and sport programs.

A survey among 100 schools, colleges, and other sport-related organizations revealed that more than one half of them used some form of audiovisual assistance in their programs. All of the persons surveyed believed that audiovisual media are valuable supplements to instruction for acquiring motor skills and encouraging and motivating people to be physically fit. The survey also revealed that videotaping and computer simulation are on the increase as instructional tools, and that wall charts, slides, video cassettes, and instructional television were often utilized.

The most recent trends in the video realm, however, are computer simulation and the interactive video disc. Computer simulation (e.g., golf and bowling) is beginning to earn its place in the classroom and gymnasium, while the interactive video disc, which facilitates self-paced practice and learn-

ing, will most certainly have a tremendous impact on physical education and sport programs in the 90s.

Reasons for Increased Use of Audiovisual Materials in Physical Education and Sport Programs

They enable the viewer to better understand concepts concerning the performance of a skill, event, game, and other experiences. Use of video, laser discs, graphics, or other materials provides a clearer idea of the subject being taught, whether it is how a heart functions or how to groove a golf swing.

They help provide variety to teaching. When audiovisual aids are used in addition to other teaching techniques, structures, and strategies, motivation is enhanced and the attention span is prolonged. The subject matter comes alive and is more exciting and meaningful.

They increase motivation on the part of the viewer. To see a game played, a skill performed, or an experiment conducted in clear, understandable, graphic representation helps motivate a person to engage in a game, perform a skill more effectively, or want to know more about the relationship of physical activity to health. This is particularly true in video replay or computer simulation, whereby a per-

---

 SUGGESTIONS FOR CLEANING SPORTS EQUIPMENT

- The person responsible for cleaning should be informed concerning the need for special handling of the garments.
- Dry cleaning usually will remove dirt and stains but normally will not remove perspiration. Therefore, garments that can be cleaned by soap and water rather than by dry cleaning should be purchased.
- Garments of different colors should not be laundered together.
- Strong chemicals or alkalies should not be used because they will fade colors and may damage the material.
- Chlorine bleach should not be used.
- Water levels in washing equipment should be kept

high if lower mechanical action is desired, but kept low if uniforms are badly soiled, to increase mechanical action. Do not overload washing equipment.
- When using commercial steam press, it is recommended that garments should be stretched back to original size.
- Uniforms and other garments should be dry before being stored.
- Water temperatures above 120° F may fade colors and cause shrinkage.
- Specialized all-automatic athletic laundry facilities that are owned by the organization are recommended as a means of protecting garments against shrinkage, color fading, snags, and bleeding.

ATHLETIC EQUIPMENT BUYERS' ALMANAC

MONTH	TYPE OF SPORTS EQUIPMENT			
	FOOTBALL	BASEBALL	BASKETBALL	TRACK
JANUARY	ORDER NEW EQUIPMENT	ORDER NEW EQUIPMENT	PRACTICE FREE THROWS	ORDER NEW EQUIPMENT
FEBRUARY	ORDER NEW EQUIPMENT	TIME IS RUNNING OUT		TIME IS RUNNING OUT
MARCH	ORDER NEW EQUIPMENT	DELIVERY	TAKE INVENTORY	
APRIL	TIME IS RUNNING OUT	MARK AND SAFETY CHECK EQUIPMENT	ORDER NEW EQUIPMENT	
MAY	PRINCIPAL'S RETREAT		ORDER NEW EQUIPMENT	ATTEND TAC MEETING
JUNE	ATTEND SCHOOL BOARD PICNIC	TAKE INVENTORY	ORDER NEW EQUIPMENT	TAKE INVENTORY
JULY	DELIVERY		ORDER NEW EQUIPMENT	
AUGUST	MARK AND SAFETY CHECK EQUIPMENT	ATTEND COUNTRY FAIR	TIME IS RUNNING OUT	
SEPTEMBER		SECURE METRODOME	DELIVERY	DELIVERY
OCTOBER		ORDER NEW EQUIPMENT	MARK AND SAFETY CHECK EQUIPMENT	MARK AND SAFETY CHECK EQUIPMENT
NOVEMBER	TAKE INVENTORY	ORDER NEW EQUIPMENT	FINAL FOUR MEETING	ORDER NEW EQUIPMENT
DECEMBER	ORDER NEW EQUIPMENT	ORDER NEW EQUIPMENT		ORDER NEW EQUIPMENT

ORDER NEW EQUIPMENT   TIME IS RUNNING OUT   YOU MAY BE TOO LATE

MANAGEMENT'S CODE OF ETHICS FOR PERSONNEL INVOLVED IN PURCHASING	
1. To consider first the interests of the organization and the betterment of the program. 2. To be receptive to advice and suggestions of colleagues, both in the department and in management, and others insofar as advice is compatible with legal and moral requirements. 3. To endeavor to obtain the most value for every dollar spent. 4. To strive to develop expertise and knowlege of supplies and equipment that ensure recommendations for purchases of best value and user impact. 5. To insist on honesty in the sales representation of every product submitted for consideration for purchase.	6. To give all responsible bidders equal consideration in determining whether their product meets specifications and the educational needs of the program. 7. To discourage and to decline gifts that in any way might influence a purchase. 8. To provide a courteous reception for all persons who may call on legitimate business missions regarding supplies and equipment. 9. To counsel and help others involved in purchasing. 10. To cooperate with governmental or other organizations or persons and help in developing sound business methods in the procurement of equipment and supplies.

son sees how he or she performs a skill and then can compare the performance to a model program or movement pattern.

The recent innovation of the interactive video disc carries the video concept one step further. Students not only view the video, but also are asked to respond to questions concerning strategies or skill execution. Correct responses allow the program to proceed, whereas incorrect answers key the disc to repeat the learning sequence. This instructional strategy provides immediate feedback of results, is student-paced, and offers out-of-class learning options for students who need additional practice time.

They provide an extension of what can normally be taught in a classroom, gymnasium, or playground. Audiovisual aids enable the viewer to experience other countries and cultures as well as to view sporting events in other parts of the United States. All of these are important to the objectives of physical education and sport programs.

They provide a historical reference for physical education and sport. Outstanding and sometimes traumatic events (e.g., the 1972 Munich Olympics, Magic Johnson, Arthur Ashe) in sports, physical education, and health that have occurred in past years

can be brought to life before the viewer's eyes. In this way the person obtains a better understanding of these events and the important role they play in our society and other cultures of the world.

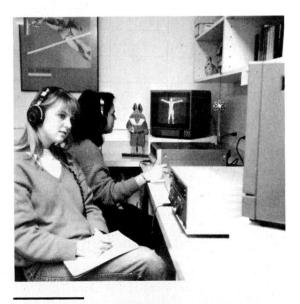

Instructional systems and audiovisual aids assist students to learn at their own pace.

CHECKLIST OF SELECTIVE ITEMS TO CONSIDER IN THE PURCHASE AND CARE OF SUPPLIES AND EQUIPMENT

	Yes	No
1. Selection of equipment and supplies is related to the achievement of the goals of physical education and sport.		
2. Equipment and supplies are selected in accordance with the needs and capacities of the participants, including consideration for age, gender, skill, disability, and interest.		
3. A manual or written policies have been prepared regarding the procedure for purchasing and care of all supplies and equipment.		
4. Mechanics of purchasing such as the following are used: requisitions, specifications, bids and quotations, contracts and purchase orders, delivery data, receipt of merchandise, vendor invoices, and payment.		
5. The relationship of functions such as the following to purchasing is considered: programming, budgeting and financing, auditing and accounting, property maintenance, legal regulations, ethics, and philosophy of education.		
6. Principles of purchasing such as the following are adhered to: quality, safety, quantity, storage, inventory, and salvage value.		
7. A close working relationship exists between the department chairperson and school or college business manager or athletic director.		
8. Girls and boys provide their own equipment and supplies when appropriate.		
9. Merchandise is purchased only from reputable manufacturers and distributors, and consideration is also given to replacement and the services provided.		
10. The greatest value is achieved for each dollar expended.		
11. Management possesses current knowlege of equipment and supplies.		
12. Management is receptive to advice and suggestions from colleagues who know, use, and purchase equipment and supplies.		
13. The coach of a sport is contacted when ordering merchandise for his or her activity, and specifications and other matters are checked.		
14. The director of physical education and athletics consults with the business manager when equipment and supplies are needed and ordered.		
15. Local regulations for competitive purchasing are followed.		
16. Equipment and supply purchases are standardized whenever possible to make replacement easier.		
17. Management is alert to improvements and advantages and disadvantages of various types of equipment and supplies.		
18. Brand, trademark, and catalog specifications are clearly defined in the purchase requisitions.		
19. Purchase orders are made on standardized school forms.		
20. Functional quality of merchandise and the safety it affords are major considerations.		
21. The inventory is used to plan for replacements and additions.		
22. Complete and accurate records are kept on all merchandise purchased.		
23. New equipment and supply needs are determined well in advance.		
24. New materials and equipment are tested and evaluated before being purchased in quantity lots.		
25. New equipment complies with minimal safety requirements.		
26. Honesty is expected in all sales representation.		
27. State contracts are used when they are available.		
28. Management is prompt and courteous in receiving legitimate salespeople and businesspeople.		

CHECKLIST OF SELECTIVE ITEMS TO CONSIDER IN THE PURCHASE AND CARE OF SUPPLIES AND EQUIPMENT—cont'd

	Yes	No
29. All competitors who sell merchandise are given fair and equal consideration.		
30. Gifts or favors offered by salespeople or manufacturers are refused.		
31. Materials received are checked with respect to quality and quantity and whether they meet specifications that have been indicated in school requisitions.		
32. Prompt payment is assured on contracts that have been accepted.		
33. All orders are checked carefully for damaged merchandise, shortages, and errors in shipment.		
34. Policies have been established for designating procedures to be followed when there is theft, loss, or destruction of merchandise.		
35. People who are issued equipment and supplies are held accountable for them.		
36. Inventories are taken periodically to account for all materials.		
37. A uniform plan is established for marking equipment and supplies.		
38. A written procedure has been established for borrowing and returning equipment and supplies.		
39. A procedure has been established for holding students accountable for merchandise that is not returned.		
40. Proper storage facilities have been provided.		
41. Equipment is cleaned and repaired when necessary before replacements are ordered.		

Guidelines for Selecting and Using Audiovisual Aids

Audiovisual materials should be carefully selected and screened before purchasing and use. Appropriateness for age and maturity level of students and others, accuracy of subject matter, technical qualities, inclusion of current information, cost, and other factors are important to ascertain before selecting audiovisual materials.

Management should see that the presentation of materials is carefully planned to provide continuity in the subject being taught. Instructors should select and use materials that amplify and illustrate some important part of the material being covered. Furthermore, audiovisual aids should be employed at a time that logically fits into the presentation of certain material and concepts.

Management should see that the materials are carefully evaluated after they have been used. Whether materials are used a second time should be determined on the basis of their worth the first time they were implemented. Therefore they should be evaluated carefully after their use. Evaluation records should be maintained by the teacher, coach, media resource center, or other personnel.

Management should realize that slow-motion and stop-action projections are best when a pattern of coordination of movements in a skill is to be taught. When teaching a skill, the physical educator or coach usually likes to analyze the various parts of the whole and also to stop and discuss aspects of the skill with the students.

Management should see that equipment is properly maintained and repaired. Videotape players, computers, projectors, record and disc players, television equipment, and other materials need to be maintained in good operating condition and serviced on a regular basis. The operator should be qualified to ensure the longevity of equipment. It is vital to have an efficient and cost-effective audiovisual program in every physical education and sport setting (see the box on pp. 322-323).

SUMMARY

Physical education and sport programs spend thousands of dollars on supplies and equipment in order to provide a meaningful and varied program of activities for their user groups. Since a large expenditure of funds is made for supplies and equipment, it is important that this management responsibility be carried out in a business-like manner. Supply and equipment needs must be accurately determined, selection accomplished according to sound guidelines (e.g., user or organization needs and goals), and purchasing conducted within organizational requirements. Storage, maintenance, and repair of these items are also crucial to the effective and efficient operation of a well-managed physical education and sport program. The computer should be utilized in this vital management function.

♦ SELF-ASSESSMENT ACTIVITIES

These activities will assist students in determining if material and competencies presented in this chapter have been mastered:

1. Why is supply and equipment management important, and what factors need to be considered regarding this management responsibility?
2. List and discuss five guidelines for selection of equipment that should be followed before buying or tendering competitive bids.
3. Discuss the steps that should be considered in purchasing supplies and equipment.
4. Establish a job description for the position of equipment manager.
5. Prepare a management plan that you as chair of a physical education department would recommend for checking, issuing, and maintaining physical education supplies and equipment.
6. Prepare a volleyball lesson plan that includes the use of audiovisual aids and explain how and when audiovisuals could be used most effectively.
7. Design a model equipment room facility.

REFERENCES

1. Equipment innovations: how they've changed the way we play, *Athletic Business* 40, Jan 1985.
2. Protective equipment: getting the right fit makes the difference, *Athletic Business* 36, Mar 1985.
3. *1991 Buyers guide, Madison, Wisconsin,* Feb 1991, Athletic Business Publications Inc.
4. Dunn J, Fait H: *Special physical education,* Dubuque, Ia, 1989, Wm C Brown.
5. Horine L: *Administration of physical education and sport programs,* Philadelphia, 1991, Wm C Brown.
6. Roberts J: Investigate the market before purchasing uniforms, *Athletic Business* 78, May 1985.
7. Williams H, Chiasson G: Computerized information retrieval: options and issues for physical education and sport, *Journal of Physical Education, Recreation and Dance* 54:21-24, 1983.

SUGGESTED READINGS

▪ How to select and care for your wrestling, gym mats, *Athletic Purchasing and Facilities* 60, Sept 1982.
  Shows how the materials and manufacturing methods that go into today's wrestling and gym mats have made tremendous gains. It also describes how the best mat will break down if not given proper care. The article outlines several suggestions for keeping mats in good repair.
▪ Athletic Business: *1991 Buyers Guide, Madison, Wisconsin,* Feb 1991, Athletic Business Publications.
  Provides a purchasing resource and reference base for physical education, sport, recreation, and fitness. Includes a facility specification guide, a manufacturers and suppliers directory, and a directory of associations to explore equipment purchase opportunities.
▪ Miller G: A completion to purchasing, *College Athletic Management,* 3(1):15-19, Jan 1991.
  Presents a procedure of setting goals and priorities, tracking performance, and power purchasing. Also explores various cost-cutting measures and multiple utilization of equipment.
▪ Rosentsweig J: Homemade strength equipment, *Journal of Physical Education, Recreation, and Dance* 55:45, Jan 1984.
  Illustrates how homemade strength equipment can be inexpensively constructed. Provides a means whereby many organizations that cannot afford expensive strength training machines and devices can create and develop functional equipment on their own.

CHAPTER 12

Management and the Athletic Training Program

▶ **Instructional Objectives and Competencies To Be Achieved**

After reading this chapter the student should be able to

- Summarize the incidence of injuries among athletes.
- Understand the role of prevention and care of injuries in physical activity and sport programs.
- Discuss the qualifications, duties, and responsibilities of team physicians and athletic trainers.

- Discuss some risk management procedures that should be undertaken to emphasize safety in a school or other organized physical activity or sport program.
- Understand the functions and role of the athletic trainer.
- Identify the appropriate supplies that should be included in an athletic trainer's kit.

In addition to the functions of fiscal and facility management, the health and safety of students, student-athletes, and other user groups must be provided for by physical educators, directors of athletics, and other members of the management team. With the increasing number of participants in sports programs, it becomes particularly important to provide proper training, conditioning, protective techniques, and other preventive measures to reduce the number of injuries that may occur in both physical education and sport programs. This chapter is concerned with the nature and scope and the responsibilities of management in providing a quality athletic training program.

The number of athletes injured increases each year. It is estimated that 1 million sport injuries requiring hospital treatment occur each year, and that

50% of the 1.85 million girls and 3.5 million boys participating in interscholastic sport in 24,000 high schools will incur injury and that one sixth of these injuries will be time-loss classified (1 to 2 lost days per year).[7] A survey by the Department of Health, Education, and Welfare reported that at least 111,000 serious sports-related injuries occur each year that cause students to miss 3 weeks of school or more; however, most injured athletes return to school within a few days of their injury.[8]

Each year, more than 1 million boys participate in high school football, another 75,000 play at college, and still another estimated 300,000 participate in other community-based organizations (e.g., Pop Warner). There are an estimated 300,000 football injuries per year alone—injuries caused by things such as poor-quality football helmets, pads, and other equipment; hazardous playing surfaces; and players returning to action before fully recovered from injuries.[1]

Basketball has the second highest injury rate of competitive sports. Injuries to the knee, sprained ankles, stress fractures, and other serious contusions (hip, thigh, leg) are most prominent. In baseball and softball, most injuries occur to the hands, wrist, and arm (hit by the ball), and some are caused by improper sliding techniques, as well as associated spike injuries. With the tremendous growth of youth soccer, injuries in this sport have also increased. Lower extremity injury (ankle and knee ligaments, fractures), not to mention occasional heat exhaustion and dehydration, seem to cause the most problems.

Chandy and Grana[3] studied seven sports over a 3-year period in 130 Oklahoma secondary schools. The study included 24,485 male and 18,289 female athletes. The results revealed that female athletes had not only more injuries, but their injuries were also more severe than those of their male counterparts. Girls had injuries such as sprains and dislocations, whereas boys sustained more strains and fractures. Knee injuries requiring surgery were more common among girls than boys. Of the sports studied, basketball had the highest injury rate.

Other research indicates that, with the exception of collision sports in which males suffer more injuries, females seem to be more susceptible to injury, although the well-trained, conditioned female athlete is no more likely to sustain injury than is a male athlete. Therefore to reduce the number of injuries, researchers recommend that, particularly among female athletes, a sound conditioning program be established to develop strength of the major muscle groups in the lower extremities, particularly those muscle groups that protect the joints.[8]

With the tremendous increase of individuals involved in physical education and sport (e.g., 5.3 million interscholastic, and more than 30 million children between ages 6 and 12 in out-of-school activities), and subsequent reported and projected injury rates, the crucial need to provide quality sports medicine services at all levels of participation is evident. John L. Marshall, orthopedic surgeon at the Hospital for Special Services in New York City,

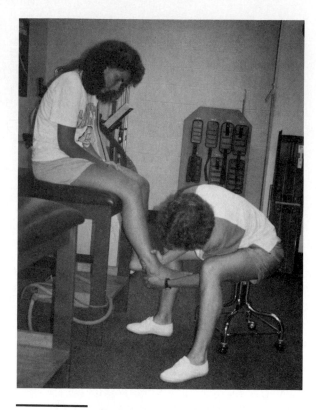

A student-athlete receives attention from a certified athletic trainer for an ankle injury.

however, reports that fewer than 10 out of every 100 of the nation's 24,000 high schools provide proper medical care for their student-athletes. Stopka and Kaiser[7] support Marshall's contention and report that fewer than 10% of the nation's high schools (1 for every 5500 student-athletes) employ certified athletic trainers.

Although Division I and professional level sports are keeping pace with the needs of athletes, the picture in corporate and private-sector physical education, sport, and fitness is, at best, dismal. The National Athletic Trainer Association (NATA), however, projects that thousands of certified athletic trainers will be filling this void in the decade of the 1990s. The need and challenge are evident, and sound and prudent management practice mandates providing quality sports medicine services to all who are engaged in physical activity and sport programs.

THE SPORTS MEDICINE MANAGEMENT TEAM

Although this chapter has strong implications for all persons who participate in physical education and recreational sport at all levels and ages, sports medicine services are especially important for student-athletes. Not only does the growth of sport programs support this notion, but the legal community does as well. School systems would be less likely to be held liable for injuries if a certified trainer was on staff. Even more crucial is the fact that contemporary management philosophy makes the individual student-athlete a high priority that mandates accessibility to quality sports medicine services. The complexities of student-athletics (e.g., physical, psychological) and the rigor of training regimens, ranging from pre-season to off-season, make it requisite that a team approach to management of sports medicine services be applied (Figure 12-1).

THE TEAM PHYSICIAN

A team physician must be selected with care. He or she must not neglect team responsibilities because of a growing practice or other commitments. The physician should remain objective and avoid being influenced by student-athletes, parents, and coaches. If a physician is needed and none is available, the local medical society, medical school, or HMO should be consulted for a recommendation of one or perhaps two physicians who will jointly care for the team. A team dentist and physical therapist may also be identified in the same fashion. Some of the duties of the team physician are located in the box to the right.

Although it might be impossible to have a physician present for all sport contests, some suggestions for sport management in such cases might include the following:

- At contests or matches where a physician cannot be present, have a telephone or beeper number where he or she can be contacted on short notice.
- Provide a certified athletic trainer.
- Refer the injured student-athlete to the family physician at parents' request.

- Provide for emergency and ambulance service to the closest medical center emergency room.
- Prepare and keep on hand a complete athletic trainer's kit.
- Prepare and keep on file an accident report containing all essential injury-related information, including nature and extent of injury, date, time, place, and witnesses.

◆ THE TEAM PHYSICIAN'S DUTIES

- Preparing and compiling medical histories of students, noting injuries and other health conditions.
- Examining athletes, reporting to coaches the results of such examinations, and making recommendations regarding whether the player can participate, or under what conditions he or she can play.
- Supervising and counseling athletic trainers and working with coaches, student-athletes, and parents in determining the best course of action to follow.
- Attending home games and also practice, if possible.
- Working cooperatively with the athletic trainer and the athletic director in preparing emergency procedures.
- Examining all injuries and making recommendations about the future play of the athlete. The player must receive the physician's approval to play.
- Providing time for students' queries regarding such matters as nutrition, conditioning, substance abuse, and injuries.
- Engaging in in-service self-education to keep abreast of the latest developments in prevention and care in sports medicine.
- Making recommendations to the athletic director and coaches regarding injury prevention and care.
- Verifying injuries when required for insurance settlements.
- Making recommendations regarding and helping to select proper protective equipment.

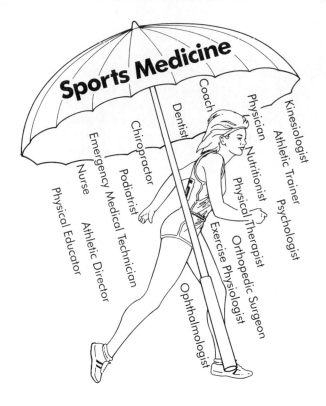

FIGURE 12-1 *Sports medicine* is an umbrella term that includes all professionals who are concerned with enhancing the performance and health care of individuals.

ATHLETIC TRAINERS

The importance of athletic trainers in sports injury prevention, treatment, and rehabilitation cannot be overlooked by management. It is unfortunate that in the secondary schools where athletic trainers are most needed, they are poorly represented.[6] Compounding this situation is the inadequate medical and injury prevention training of most coaches (i.e., 50% have not taken a first aid course). Even if the coach has been well schooled in sports medicine, he or she simply does not have sufficient time to carry out both coaching duties and the responsibilities of an athletic trainer.

In 1980, 10.9% of public secondary schools had athletic trainers, but only 5% were certified by the National Athletic Trainers Association. Of the private secondary schools 15.4% had trainers, but only 5% of them were NATA approved. On the college level 16.1% of the 2-year colleges had trainers, but

The physician plays an important part in the sports medicine team.

only 7% were NATA approved; 40% of the 4-year colleges had trainers, with 28% of them NATA approved. Those figures have remained status quo up to the present for the more than 24,000 high schools in the United States. Only at major Division I colleges and universities and at the professional level do we seem to find acceptable athlete-to-trainer ratios.

In the past the athletic trainer simply wrapped ankles and administered first aid to athletes. He or she usually had no special preparation for this role, but had learned through on-the-job training. Often such an individual had little scientific knowledge concerning the prevention and care of sports injuries.

Today, however, sports medicine and athletic training in particular has become a science as well as an art. The functions of the athletic trainer have become varied and complex, and the "on-the-job training" philosophy, although crucial, is no longer all that is required. An explosion of scientific information concerning physiology, nutrition, biomechanics, sport psychology, and sociology, as well as sophisticated rehabilitation and treatment equipment, make it advantageous for the athletic trainer to have an undergraduate major in physical education, kinesiology, and/or sports medicine with graduate work in physical therapy and/or athletic training.

The qualifications for an athletic trainer[1] are both personal and professional. Personal qualifications include poise, good health, intelligence, maturity, emotional stability, compassion, cleanliness, ethics,

fairness, and stamina. Professional qualifications include a knowledge of anatomy and applied physiology, psychology and sociology of sport, conditioning and training, taping, methods for preventing injury, substance abuse, counseling, and protective equipment. Furthermore, the athletic trainer should have qualities that provide a harmonious and productive rapport with the team physician, coaches, sports managers, student-athletes, and the public in general. The trainer must be able to practice good human relations, as well as protect the athletes' well-being. It is also strongly recommended that the NATA Code of Professional Practice be adopted[4] (see the box below).

NATA CODE OF PROFESSIONAL PRACTICE

Ethical principles

1. Athletic trainers should neither practice nor condone discrimination on the basis of race, color, sex, age, religion, or national origin.
2. Athletic trainers should not condone, engage in, or defend unsportsmanlike conduct or practices.
3. Athletic trainers should provide care on the basis of the needs of the individual athlete. They should not discriminate on the basis of athletic ability.
4. Athletic trainers should strive to achieve the highest level of competence. They should use only those techniques and preparations which they are qualified and authorized to administer.
5. Athletic trainers should recognize the need for continuing education to remain proficient in their practice. They should be willing to consider new procedures within guidelines that assure safety.
6. Athletic trainers should recognize that personal problems and conflicts may occur, which may interfere with professional effectiveness. Accordingly, they should refrain from undertaking any activity in which their personal problems are likely to lead to inadequate performance or harm to an athlete or colleague.
7. Athletic trainers should use care to be truthful and not misleading when stating their education, training, and experience.

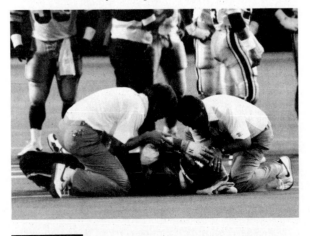

Qualified trainers look after an injured student-athlete.

The National Athletic Trainers Association's basic minimum requirements for the professional preparation of athletic trainers are recommended by most experts in the field. These standards include graduating from an approved undergraduate or graduate program that meets specific criteria set forth by NATA, having a physical therapy degree (such preparation meeting the specific requirements set forth by NATA), or serving an apprenticeship that meets NATA specifications. Persons preparing for positions in athletic training should also be certified by NATA. To do this, they must have proper training and pass the NATA certification examination. Other important courses (including those previously mentioned) in preparing to be an athletic trainer include kinesiology/biomechanics, first aid and safety, CPR, nutrition, remedial exercises, health and disease, techniques of athletic training, psychosocial behavioral disorders (e.g., bulimia, anorexia nervosa), and communication.

Just as the traditional functions of the athletic trainer have changed, so has the opportunity for women to enter the profession. At present, 50% of the student trainers involved in the athletic training educational process are women.

The athletic trainer's function is crucial and rewarding, but it is also very demanding and entails long hours and total commitment.

THE TRAINING ROOM

Elaborate training rooms and equipment are not always essential in sports programs. Indeed, most high schools do not have much in the way of a training room. A well-lighted and properly ventilated private room with an examining table, a desk, shelf space, phone, and a few chairs is the minimal requirement. However, a training room should be provided if possible, for it will serve both physical education and sport programs as a multipurpose place for first aid, physical examinations, bandaging and taping, rehabilitation, treating athletes, keeping records, and other functions concerned with the health of students, athletes, and staff members. The training room should be near the dressing room, shower, and playing areas. A telephone, proper lighting, ice machine or refrigerator, whirlpool and, if possible, equipment for thermal and mechanical therapy, electrotherapy, and hydrotherapy, should be provided.

If the sport program involves a great number of participants, it is recommended that special service sections or areas be separated by low walls or partitions. For those institutions that desire more sophisticated facilities, separate sections would include those for taping, bandaging, and orthotics; thermal and mechanical therapy; electrotherapy; hydrother-

An athletic trainer assists in rehabilitation.

A well-organized athletic training room is an important part of all physical education and sport programs.

apy; and a reconditioning and rehabilitation area with equipment such as Cybex, Stairmaster, and exercise bicycles. Of course, there should be an area for storage so that adequate training supplies and well-stocked training kits would always be readily available. The box on pages 332-333 provides a checklist of requisite supplies for the athletic trainer's kit.

The training room is crucial to any sport program. It is a meeting place, a safe haven for the student-athlete, and a place to share problems and gain counsel. The training room should be accessible, open and staffed year round, and fully supported by management with the appropriate financial, physical, informational, technical, and human resources.

MANAGEMENT'S RESPONSIBILITY IN ATHLETIC TRAINING

What is the management's responsibility in providing quality sports medicine services and preventing sports injuries? The first responsibilty is to hire or subcontract, when possible, fully qualified and certified physicians, coaches, and athletic trainers who understand sports injuries and know how to prevent,

Water, rest, and sound training and conditioning procedures help prevent injury.

as well as treat, them. These persons should be aware of the latest preventive measures necessary for sports safety. The American Medical Association's Committee on Medical Aspects of Sport and the National Federation of State High School Associations provide further elaboration on this topic, which may be found in the box on page 334.

Other key elements of injury prevention are complete and thorough medical examinations, including blood and urine tests, for every athlete. Athletes who are immature physically, who have sustained previous injuries, or who are inadequately conditioned are prone to sports injuries. Crash diets and dehydration (routinely practiced in wrestling and gymnastics) are injurious to an athlete's health and should be abolished. Training practices based on sound physiological principles are one of the best ways to avoid sports injuries. Of course, proper protective equipment must be used in appropriate sports. Facilities and equipment must be developed with safety in mind, and sport safety and legal regulations must be reviewed. Research also must be conducted to improve sport safety.

Proper conditioning of athletes. Conditioning of athletes helps prevent sport injuries. This means preseason training, as well as proper conditioning maintenance during the season. Certified educators and coaches who know how to coach fundamentals and how to convey proper athletic training procedures are crucial to this process. Careful selection and fitting of equimcnt, protective strapping, and counseling athletes about nutrition and rest also play an important part in the total conditioning package.

Conditioning exercises for athletics should be compatible with the athlete's capacity and fitness level and include a warmup, a progressive exercise routine both in-season and out-of-season, and special exercises to increase muscular strength and endurance, flexibility, and relaxation.

Protective sports equipment. Sports equipment that protects vulnerable parts of the athlete's body from injury is important, particularly in such collision sports as football, ice and field hockey, soccer, and lacrosse. For example, football helmets should be purchased in accordance with standards established by NOCSAE. The NOCSAE seal on a football helmet indicates that the manufacturer has

Checklist for athletic trainer's kit*[1]

Item	Amount	Football-rugby	Basketball-volleyball-soccer	Wresting	Baseball-softball	Track and cross-country	Water polo and swimming	Gymnastics	Tennis-squash
						Activity			
Accident reports		X	X	X	X	X	X	X	X
Adhesive tape									
½-inch (1.25 cm)	1 roll	X	X	X	X	X		X	X
1-inch (2.5 cm)	2 rolls	X	X	X	X	X		X	X
1½-inch (3.75 cm)	3 rolls	X	X	X	X	X		X	X
2-inch (5 cm)	1 roll	X	X	X	X	X		X	X
Alcohol (isopropyl)	4 ounces	X	X	X	X	X	X	X	X
Ammonia ampules	10	X	X	X	X	X	X	X	X
Analgesic balm	½ pound	X	X	X	X	X	X	X	
Ankle wraps	2	X	X		X	X			X
Antacid tablets or liquid	100	X	X	X	X	X	X	X	X
Antiglare salve	4 ounces	X			X				
Antiseptic powder	4 ounces	X	X	X	X		X	X	X
Antiseptic soap (liquid)	4 ounces	X	X	X	X	X	X	X	X
Aspirin tablets (with physician permission)	100	X	X	X	X	X	X	X	X
Band-Aids (assorted sizes)	2 dozen	X	X	X	X	X	X	X	X
Butterfly bandages (sterile strip)									
Medium	6 dozen	X	X	X	X	X		X	
Small	6 dozen	X	X	X	X	X		X	
Contact case		X	X	X	X	X	X	X	X
Cotton (sterile)	1 ounce	X	X	X	X	X	X	X	X
Cotton-tipped applicators	2 dozen	X	X	X	X	X	X	X	X
Elastic bandages									
3-inch (7.5 cm)	2 rolls	X	X	X	X	X		X	X
4-inch (10 cm)	2 rolls	X	X	X	X	X		X	X
6-inch (15 cm)	2 rolls	X	X	X	X	X	X	X	X
Elastic tape roll (3-inch)	2 rolls	X	X	X	X	X		X	X
Eyewash	2 ounces	X	X	X	X	X	X	X	X
Felt									
¼-inch (0.6 cm)	6 × 6 sheet	X	X	X	X	X		X	X
½-inch (1.25 cm)	6 × 6 sheet	X							
Flexible collodion	2 ounces	X	X	X	X	X		X	
Foot antifungus powder	2 ounces	X	X	X	X	X	X	X	X

*Extra amounts of items such as tape and protective padding are carried in other bags.

Checklist for athletic trainer's kit*[1]—cont'd

Item	Amount	Football-rugby	Basketball-volleyball-soccer	Wrestling	Baseball-softball	Track and cross-country	Water polo and swimming	Gymnastics	Tennis-squash
Forceps (tweezers)	1	X	X	X	X	X	X	X	X
Fungicide (salve)	2 ounces	X	X	X	X	X	X	X	X
Germicide (solution)	2 ounces	X	X	X	X	X	X	X	
Grease (lubrication)		X	X	X	X	X			X
Gum rosin (adherent)	1 ounce	X	X		X	X			X
Heel cups	2			X		X		X	
Insurance information		X	X	X	X	X	X	X	X
Instant cold pack	2	X	X	X	X	X	X	X	X
Liniment	2 ounces	X	X	X	X	X	X	X	X
Medicated salve	2 ounces	X	X	X	X	X	X	X	X
Mirror (hand)	13	X	X	X	X	X	X	X	X
Moleskin	6 × 6 sheet	X	X	X	X	X		X	X
Nonadhering sterile pad (3 × 3)	12	X	X	X	X	X		X	X
Oral screw	1	X	X	X	X	X	X	X	X
Oral thermometer	1	X	X	X	X	X	X	X	X
Paper and pencil		X	X	X	X	X	X	X	X
Peroxide	2 ounces	X	X	X	X	X	X	X	X
Plastic cups		X	X	X	X	X	X	X	X
Salt tablets	50	X	X	X	X	X		X	X
Shoehorn	1	X	X	X	X	X			X
Sponge rubber									
⅛-inch (0.3 cm)	6 × 6 sheet	X	X	X	X	X		X	X
¼-inch (0.6 cm)	6 × 6 sheet	X	X	X	X	X		X	X
½-inch (1.25 cm)	6 × 6 sheet	X							
Sterile gauze pads (3 by 3)	6	X	X	X	X	X		X	X
Sun lotion	2 ounces	X	X	X	X	X	X	X	X
Surgical scissors	1	X	X	X	X	X	X	X	X
Tape adherent	6-ounce spray can	X	X	X	X	X		X	X
Tape remover	2 ounces	X	X	X	X	X	X	X	X
Tape scissors (pointed)	1	X	X	X	X	X	X	X	X
Tongue depressors	5	X	X	X	X	X	X	X	X
Triangular bandages	2	X	X	X	X	X	X	X	X
Waterproof tape (1-inch)	1 roll						X		

SAFEGUARDING THE HEALTH OF THE ATHLETE

A joint statement of the Committee on the Medical Aspects of the American Medical Association and the National Federation of State High School Athletic Associations.
A checklist to help evaluate five major factors in health supervision of sport.

Participation in sport is a privilege involving both responsibilities and rights. The athlete's responsibilities are to play fair, to train and to conduct themselves with credit to their sport and their school. In turn they have the right to optimal protection against injury as this may be assured through good conditioning and technical instruction, proper regulations and conditions of play, and adequate health supervision.

Periodic evaluation of each of the factors will help assure a safe and healthful experience for players. The checklist below contains the kinds of questions to be answered in such an appraisal.

PROPER CONDITIONING helps prevent injuries by hardening the body and increasing resistance to fatigue.

1. Are prospective players given directions and activities for preseason conditioning?
2. Is there a minimum of 3 weeks of practice before the first game or contest?
3. Are precautions taken to prevent heat exhaustion and heat stroke?
4. Is each player required to warm up thoroughly before participation?
5. Are substitutions made without hesitation when players evidence disability?

CAREFUL COACHING leads to skillful performance, which lowers the incidence of injuries.

1. Is emphasis given to safety in teaching techniques and elements of play?
2. Are injuries analyzed to determine causes and to suggest preventive programs?
3. Are tactics discouraged that may increase the hazards and thus the incidence of injuries?
4. Are practice periods carefully planned and of reasonable duration?

GOOD OFFICIATING promotes enjoyment of the game and protection of players.

1. Are players, as well as coaches, thoroughly schooled in the rules of the game?
2. Are rules and regulations strictly enforced in practice periods as well as in games?
3. Are officials qualified both emotionally and technically for their responsibilities?
4. Do players and coaches respect the decisions of officials?

CORRECT EQUIPMENT AND FACILITIES serve a unique purpose in protection of players.

1. Is the best protective equipment provided for use in collision sports?
2. Is careful attention given to proper fit and adjustment of equipment?
3. Is equipment properly maintained and worn, with outmoded items discarded?
4. Are proper areas for play provided and carefully maintained?

ADEQUATE MEDICAL CARE is a necessity in the prevention and control of injuries.

1. Is there a thorough preseason health history and medical examination?
2. Is a physician present at contests and readily available during practice sessions?
3. Does the physician make the decision as to whether an athlete should return to play following injury during games?
4. Is authority from a physician required before an athlete can return to practice after being out of play because of disabling injury?
5. Is the care given athletes by coach or trainer limited to first aid and medically prescribed services?

complied with prescribed standards for protection of the head. Mouth guards and head or eye protection should be worn, when appropriate, in a number of sports (e.g., baseball, basketball, ice hockey, squash, racquetball).

Protective equipment must be tested for adequacy, maintained in good repair, and must in essence be as good as new to prevent injury and avoid legal problems. Furthermore, proper equipment to protect the chest, ribs, elbows, knees, and shins is required in certain sports (e.g., volleyball, soccer, team handball). Shoes and all other equipment should always be carefully selected to ensure proper fit, comfort, and maximal protection.

Taping, bandaging, and padding. Protective taping, bandaging, and padding can help prevent, as well as provide care for, injuries. Bandaging is needed at times to protect wounds from infection, to immobilize an injured area, to protect an injury, to support an injured part, to hold protective equipment in place, and to make arm slings and eye bandages. Padding and orthotic devices (e.g., usually made from malleable plastics such as polyethylene) are needed to cushion against injury, to restrict the athlete's range of joint motion, and to be used as foot pads. Orthotic devices can help in knee supports and shoulder braces. Taping, bandaging, padding, and shaping and fitting orthotic devices requires special skill and knowledge.

Nutrition. Proper nutrition is important to the health of the athlete for physical fitness and stamina, recuperation from fatigue, energy, and the repair and regeneration of damaged tissues. Athletes should include proper amounts of carbohydrates, fats, proteins, minerals, vitamins, and water in their

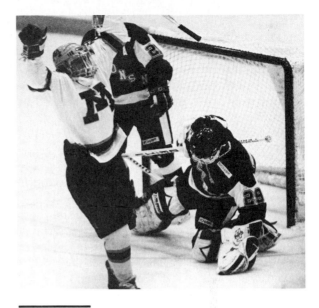

Protective equipment that fits well is crucial to all collision sports, including ice hockey.

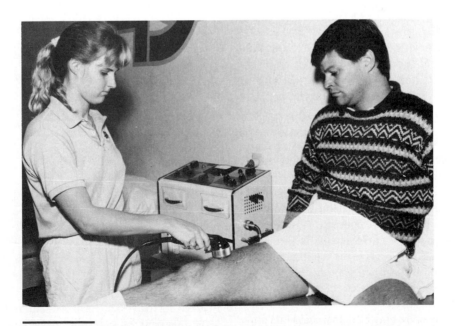

Prescribed ultrasound therapy is performed by a qualified athletic trainer.

diets. Eating disorders appear to be prevalent in sport and should be discussed.

Ergogenic aids. Ergogenic aids are supplements or agents that supposedly enhance sport performance. In other words, they are work-producing aids and are supposed to improve physical effort and performance outcome. They include drugs, food, physical stimulants such as thermal packs or electrical devices, and hypnosis. Some of these agents are questionable and unethical. The trainer should be familiar with the ramifications of such methods and substance use and abuse.

Coaches, athletic trainers, and physical educators should endorse only ethically and morally sound training practices.[4] Under no circumstances should chemical substances, including over-the-counter (OTC) drugs (e.g., Doan's pills, Tylenol, aspirin, diet pills), be administered to student-athletes for ingestion. Usually OTC first aid preparations for skin wounds such as topical antibiotics are permitted, but the trainer should refer to school policies.

Some athletic associations (e.g., NCAA, NFSHSA) and sports medicine organizations have taken a strong stand against the use of agents or drugs that enhance performance through artificial means. Substances ranging from Benzedrine (to reduce fatigue) to anabolic steroids (to gain weight and strength) and from dimethyl sulfoxide (DMSO) to crack cocaine have been placed on the banned substance list. The procedures and policies described in Chapter 5 and Appendix C fall well within the domain of those involved in athletic training.

SAFETY IN PHYSICAL EDUCATION AND SPORT

In light of the increased participation in physical education and sport, management must give attention to providing for the health and safety of persons engaging in these activities. Besides those maladies that might restrict active participation, injury to the participant is the paramount concern. Injuries are related not only to actual participation in these activities, but also to things such as the equipment provided, conditions of athletic and playing fields, lighting, and myriad other factors associated with safe play.

Sport participation results in many accidents and injuries. For example, there are an estimated 7.5

million racquetball players and more than 850 registered racquetball clubs. The increase in injuries to the eyes and the facial area has been dramatic. Approximately 8000 swimmers drown each year, and fatal or paralyzing football injuries which, although not numerous, are traumatic to all involved. Injuries in basketball (640,755), bicycling (580,119), baseball (433,799), roller skating (97,842) and skate boarding (82,428) all contribute their fair share to the estimated more than two million amateur athletes to visit United States emergency rooms each year. Given the large number of participants and accidents, it is recommended that one of the first management steps (risk management) taken should be to set an accident and injury policy that is prepared by each subunit involved in specific activities. Written policy has been a valuable tool in not only enforcing safety regulations, but in lowering incidence of injury as well.

Another management recommendation is the appointment of an individual who will be responsible for the safety compliance program of the organization. In large organizations such a position would pay for itself by reducing the accident rate and therefore the loss of production and other costs related to accidents and injuries. If a full-time profes-

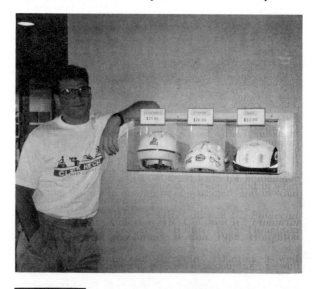

Helmets for bicycling, roller skating and blading, and skate boarding, among other activities, are commonplace and help prevent injury.

sional cannot be employed, this responsibility should be assigned to a staff member (e.g., athletic trainer). This professional would have responsibilities such as developing policies and procedures, inspecting facilities and equipment, conducting safety research, and reporting accidents to appropriate networks.

One such network organization that collects data on athletic injuries is the National Athletic Injury Illness Reporting System (NAIIRS). Participating schools receive periodic reports about the number and types of injuries in various sports. Another organization that is very much concerned with equipment standards and injury reduction in sports is the American Society for Testing and Materials (ASTM), an organization composed of manufacturers, consumers, and technical experts. One of the technical committees of this organization is NOCSAE. They have a subcommittee concerned with helmets and face guards for sports such as football, baseball, softball, and ice hockey. The organization also researches the number and types of injuries suffered by both male and female athletes. The NCAA Injury Surveillance System (ISS), developed in 1982, also provides current and reliable data on injury trends in intercollegiate sport. It provides a sport breakdown injury rate both in practice and in game situations.

The development of a proper accident reporting system is another important management recommendation. According to the National Safety Council, a well-organized reporting system is essential to a safety program. The council points out that use of accident reports, along with other systematic reporting, helps prevent further accidents by getting at the causes of unsafe acts and unsafe conditions and by developing a program that results in the removal of such acts and conditions.

In schools, mandatory preparation of a school safety handbook is recommended. The handbook should contain specific guidelines for maintaining a safe physical activity and sporting environment, can identify individual responsibilities (e.g., student-athlete, parent, coach, athletic director, athletic trainer), and can initiate and facilitate safety awareness and other creative risk management strategies.

A concluding management recommendation is the establishment of a safety committee. Safety committees have proved helpful in gaining organizational support for sound safety practices and awareness. The functions of such a committee are to develop procedures and implement safety recommendations, to hold regular meetings to discuss safety promotion, to conduct periodic inspections and safety audits, to investigate accidents, to recommend changes in equipment and physical plant in order to eliminate hazards and reduce injury incidence, and to promote health and safety in all phases of the physical education and sport program.

SUMMARY

An important responsibility in physical education and sport management is to provide for the health and safety of participants. This requires establishing policies and procedures that will provide for proper sports medicine services, seeing that coaches have an understanding and skill in sound athletic training procedures, providing a full-time certified athletic trainer when possible, and ensuring that proper equipment and safe sport environs are provided.

The number of injuries that occur in sports programs today requires management to oversee the programs to make sure that sound sports medicine and athletic training policies, procedures, and practices exist so that such injuries are kept to a minimum and are treated effectively and efficiently. Risk management awareness is also crucial to sound physical education and sport programs.

◆ SELF-ASSESSMENT ACTIVITIES

These activities will assist students in determining if material and competencies presented in this chapter have been mastered.

1. Prepare an accident report, including the nature and scope of the injuries that have just occurred at your junior high school volleyball match. Outline the procedures that were followed.
2. As a coach of a soccer team, what steps should you take in preventing injuries to your players? Describe the procedures you would follow if a player broke a leg in practice.
3. What are the duties of a team physician?
4. Prepare a list of arguments to present to the Board of Education to justify the addition of an athletic trainer to the school staff.

5. List the desirable qualifications and functions of the athletic trainer.

6. Construct a risk management checklist for your university physical education department.

REFERENCES

1. Arnheim DD: *Modern principles of athletic training,* ed 7, St Louis, 1989, Mosby–Year Book.
2. Booher JM, Thibodeau GA: *Athletic injury assessment,* ed 2, St Louis, 1989, Mosby–Year Book.
3. Chandy TA, Grana WA: Secondary school athletic injury in boys and girls: a three-year comparison, *The Physician and Sports Medicine* 13:106, Mar 1985.
4. Mangus B, Ingersoll C: Approaches to ethical decision making in athletic training, *Athletic Training, Journal of National Athletic Trainer Association* 25(4):340-343, Winter 1990.
5. National Athletic Trainers' Association: The future of athletic training, *NATA News* 1(1):5, 1988.
6. Porter M, Noble H, Bachman D, Hoover R: The faculty athletic training program: a model, *The Physician and Sports Medicine* 10:85, Apr 1982.
7. Stopka C, Kaiser D: Certified athletic trainers in our secondary schools: the need and the solution, *Athletic Training, Journal of National Athletic Trainer Association* 23(4):322-324, Winter 1988.
8. Whieldon TJ, Cerny F: Incidence and severity of high school athletic injuries, *Athletic Training, Journal of National Athletic Trainer Association* 25(4):344-350, Winter 1990.

SUGGESTED READINGS

- Avoiding aerobics injuries, *Athletic Business* 9:10, Mar 1985.
  Discusses the fast-growing physical activity of aerobic dance and how overcrowded class conditions result in rising injury rates.
- What's new in training room aids? *Athletic Business* 8:58, Sept 1984.
  A comprehensive look at what is available for training rooms, from tape to training tables to therapeutic, protective, and rehabilitation devices.
- Clain MR, Hershman EB: Overuse injuries in children and adolescents, *The Physician and Sports Medicine* 17(9):111-123, Sept. 1989.
  Discusses the implications of overuse injury in young athletes in regard to growth plate damage, which can result in such problems as traction apophysitis and Little League elbow. Provides information about appropriate interventions that can prevent potential long-term complications.
- Kent F: Athletes wait too long to report injuries, *The Physician and Sports Medicine* 10:127, Apr 1982.
  A survey of 450 Canadian amateur athletes with injuries found that nearly one of every two waited 5 days or more before seeing a physician. The delay can have serious consequences.
- Morris AF: *Sports medicine: prevention of athletic injuries,* Dubuque, Ia, 1984, Wm C Brown.
  A text for physical educators and exercise science persons who wish to study the emerging field of sports medicine; the text is written from a physical education perspective.
- Mueller FO, Blyth CS: Fatalities and catastrophic injuries in football, *The Physician and Sports Medicine* 10:135, Oct 1982.
  Compares football fatalities and injuries for the years 1976 through 1981 with earlier data, drawing implications for rule and equipment changes that have taken place since 1976.
- Olson JR, Bauer RP: Safety guidelines for gymnastic facilities, *Athletic Business* 8:28, July 1984.
  Sets forth guidelines for a safe gymnastic program that includes maintaining constant supervision, conducting regular safety inspections, and making all repairs promptly.
- Olson JR, Hunter GR: Weight training safety guidelines, *Athletic Purchasing & Facilities* 7:29, Jan 1983.
  Guidelines for weight training facilities that guard against unsafe practice, hazardous conditions, and dangerous equipment.
- Rankin J: Athletic trainer education: new directions, *Journal of Physical Education, Recreation, and Dance* 60(6):68-71, 1989.
  A curriculum that provides prospective athletic trainers with a background in human performance as opposed to the traditional background in teaching is presented.
- Roy S, Irvin R: *Sports Medicine,* Englewood Cliffs, NJ, 1983, Prentice-Hall.
  A text that is concerned with the prevention, evaluation, management, and rehabilitation of athletic injuries.
- Sports medicine groups of 1990. *The Physician and Sports Medicine* 18:131-142, 1990.
  Provides a comprehensive listing of professional organizations and resource groups. More than 40 organizations and 21 groups including government agencies, sport federations, and statistic gathering groups are referenced.
- Wilmore JH: *Training for sport and activity,* Boston, 1982, Allyn & Bacon.
  Designed to provide the sport practitioner, coach, athlete, team trainer, and team physician with a basic understanding of physiological principles underlying physical conditioning and performance in physical education and sport.

CHAPTER 13

Legal Liability, Risk, and Insurance Management

▶ **Instructional Objectives and Competencies To Be Achieved**

After reading this chapter the student should be able to

- Define each of the following terms: *legal liability, tort, negligence, in loco parentis, save harmless, assumption of risk, attractive nuisance, immunity,* and *risk and insurance management.*
- Indicate the legal basis for physical education programs throughout the United States and the implications this has for making physical education a requirement for all students.
- Discuss recent court interpretations regarding sport product liability, violence, and physical education activities held off campus.
- Describe what constitutes negligent behavior on the part of physical educators and coaches and what constitutes defense against negligence.

- Identify common areas of negligence in the conduct of physical education and sport programs, and explain what can be done to eliminate such negligence.
- Appreciate the relationship of Title IX to legal liability in the conduct of physical education and sport programs.
- Discuss precautions that physical educators can take to prevent accidents and provide for the safety of students and other individuals who participate in their programs.
- Recommend sound insurance and risk management plans for physical education and sport programs.

Among the most important management responsibilities of physical education and sport programs is conducting programs within limits provided by legislation and the law. Unlike other programs that relate to academic pursuits, physical education and sport programs take place in a variety of high-risk settings where injuries may occur. Therefore every

effort must be taken to provide preventive safety measures (i.e., risk assessment) that will keep such injuries to a minimum. This includes hiring competent, qualified, and certified personnel to plan, conduct, and oversee programs and activities; purchasing approved and quality equipment; providing facilities and play areas that are safe and well main-

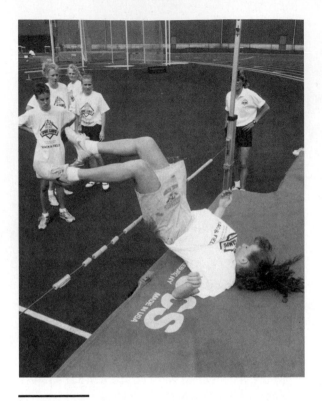

Physical activity and sport injuries can lead to questions of legal liability.

tained; and acquiring and recommending appropriate liability insurance to protect participants and personnel as well as the institution, organization, or program. Establishing procedures concerning skill progression, health status, and use of protective gear; educating the students to the risk of the activity; and selecting opponents to avoid dangerous mismatches are also factors to be fully considered. This chapter explores those aspects of legal liability, risk, and insurance management that are pertinent to the prudent management of physical education and sport programs.

According to Bouvier's *Law Dictionary,* liability is "the responsibility, the state of one who is bound in law and justice to do something which may be enforced by action." Other definitions describe liability as the condition of affairs that gives rise to an obligation to do a particular thing to be enforced by court action.[7,11,14]

The tremendous increase in participation in all physical education and sport endeavors across the Physical Activity and Sport Continuum (e.g., youth sport, increased women's participation, lifetime sport, Sport for All) concomitant with our contemporary "legal climate" make it requisite that all physical education and sport professionals be knowledgeable not only of injury incidence reduction, but also the legal ramifications that are intimately interwoven with the profession (e.g., program, facilities, supervision, and safety policies).

The fact that physical educators are involved in more than 50% of the injuries sustained by students each year, and that approximately 65% to 70% of all school jurisdiction accidents involving boys and 59% to 65% involving girls occur in physical education and sport-related programs provide evidence that professional awareness must be increased. Furthermore, the fact that millions of boys and girls and adults will continue to participate in physical activity, that an estimated 1 out of 30 to 35 students attending school will be injured, and that public and private sector as well as corporate- and community-based physical education and sport programs involve millions of people where accidents and injuries will occur, make it mandatory to be more than just "familiar" with the topic.

When an accident resulting in personal injury occurs, the question often arises about whether damages can be recovered. All employees run the risk of being sued by injured persons on the basis of alleged negligence that caused physical injury. Such injuries occur on playgrounds and sports fields (including the stands), in parks and ski areas, golf courses, gymnasiums and fitness laboratories, and in the myriad places where physical education and sport activities take place.

The legal rights of the individuals involved in such cases are worthy of study. Although the law varies from state to state and case to case, it is possible to discuss liability in a way that has implications for most settings in which physical educators and coaches work.* First, it is important to understand

---

*If a legal issue does arise, seeking advice from the school, institutional, or association legal counsel or hiring a private attorney is recommended.

Most injuries in schools occur in physical education classes.

the legal basis for physical education and sport, and for those domains that fall under the Physical Education and Sport Continuum that was presented in Chapter 1.

LEGAL LIABILITY IN PHYSICAL EDUCATION AND SPORT

There has been a trend over the last decade concerning physical education and sport legal liability cases. Some experts have pointed to increased availability of legal services (e.g., more lawyers, contingency fees), a more sophisticated public concerning their legal rights, the modification of the doctrine of governmental immunity (e.g., the state and local government can now be sued), a public attitude that groups such as insurance companies and schools have endless sources of revenue, and the movement (approximately 39 states) toward the doctrine of comparative rather than contributory negligence wherein pro-rated settlements evolve between liti-

gious parties, as the main reasons for increased legal action. Other contributory litigious trends that directly affect physical education and sport management include litigation involving discrimination in respect to persons with disabilities, and increased legal negligence or foreseeability cases wherein participants were not properly warned that injury could result from their participation.[7]

Some years ago the courts recognized the hazards involved in the play activities that are a part of the educational program. A boy sustained an injury while playing tag. The court recognized the possibility and risk of some injury in physical education programs and would not award damages. However, it pointed out that care must be taken by both the participant and the authorities in charge. It further implied that the benefits derived from participating in physical education activities such as tag offset the risk that occasional injury might occur.

The decision regarding the benefits derived from participating in physical education programs was handed down at a time when the attitude of the law was that no governmental agency (e.g., federal, state, local, public school or college) could be held liable for the acts of its employees unless it so consented. Since that time a changing attitude in the courts has been evident. The immunity derived from the old common-law rule that "the King or Sovereign could do no wrong" and that a government agency cannot be sued without its consent is changing so that federal, state, and local governments may be sued (*Russell v. Men of Devon,* 100 Eng. Rep 359, 1788).[14]

In 1959 the Illinois Supreme Court (*Molitor v. Kaneland Community Unit,* District No. 302, 163 N.E. 2nd 89) overruled the immunity doctrine. The supreme courts of Wisconsin, Arizona, and Minnesota legislature followed suit; however, in 1963 the Minnesota legislature restored the rule, but provided that school districts that had liability insurance were responsible for damages up to the amount of coverage. The principle of governmental immunity has also been put to the test in courts in states such as Colorado, Iowa, Kansas, Oregon, Pennsylvania, and Utah. However, the courts in some of these states have been hesitant to depart from the precedent and insist that it is the legislature of the state rather than the courts that should waive the rule.[18]

There also have been incidences in which immunity has been upheld. In the case of *Cerrone v. Milton School District,* 479 A. 2nd 675 (Pa. 1984) Cerrone received an injury while wrestling in high school. As a result of a suit against the Milton School District in Pennsylvania the court ruled that the school district was immune from suit as provided by the Tort Claims Act.[4]

In another case, *Kain v. Rockridge Community Unit School District #300,* 453 N.E. 2nd 118 (Ill. 1983), a football coach was granted immunity when Kraig Kain sued the Rockridge Community Unit School District for alleged negligent conduct by the coach who let him play in a game without observing the required number of practices before participation.[2]

In most cases governmental immunity has been modified, abrogated, or subjected to exceptions by either legislation or judicial decision. Schools and school districts may legally purchase liability insurance (many states expressly authorize school districts to carry liability insurance), protecting themselves when they become involved in lawsuits, although this does not necessarily mean governmental immunity has been waived. Of course, in the absence of insurance and *save harmless* laws (laws requiring that school districts assume the liability of the teacher, whether negligence is proved or not), any judgment rendered against a school district must be met out of personal funds. School districts in states such as Connecticut, Massachusetts, New Jersey, and New York have *save harmless* laws. Wyoming also permits school districts to indemnify or financially protect employees.

A strong feeling exists among educators and many in the legal profession that the doctrine of sovereign immunity should be abandoned. In some states students injured as a result of negligence are assured recompense for damages directly or indirectly, either because governmental immunity has been abrogated or because school districts are legally required to indemnify school employees against financial loss. In other states, if liability insurance has been secured, a possibility exists that students may recover damages incurred.

Although school districts have been granted governmental immunity in many states, teachers do not have such immunity. A 1938 decision of an Iowa court provides some of the thinking regarding teachers' responsibilities for their own actions (*Montanick v. McMillin,* 225 Iowa 442, 452-453, 458, 280 N.W. 608, 1938):

[The employee's liability] is not predicated upon any relationship growing out of his [her] employment, but is based upon the fundamental and underlying laws of torts, that he [she] who does injury to the person or property of another is civilly liable in damages for the injuries inflicted ... The doctrine of *respondeat superior,* literally, "let the principle answer," is an extension of the fundamental principle of torts, and an added remedy to the injured party, under which a party injured by some act of misfeasance may hold both the servant and the master liable. The exemption of governmental bodies and their officers from liability under the doctrine of *respondeat superior* is a limitation of exception to the rule of *respondeat superior* and in no way affects the fundamental principle of torts that one who wrongfully inflicts injury upon another is liable to the injured person for damages. ... An act of misfeasance is a positive wrong, and every employee, whether employed by a private person or a municipal corporation owes a duty not to injure another by a negligent act of commission.

Factors and Special Situations That Influence Legal Liability

Sports managers have the responsibility and the duty to be aware of salient factors and special situations that can lead to litigation. Some potential litigious factors include: ignorance of the law, ignoring the law, failure to act, failure to warn, and time and expense.[15] Failing to provide accessibility for persons with disabilities to programs, ignoring Title IX mandates concerning equal opportunity, failure to check facilities and equipment on a regular basis, omitting warning and hazard signs or failing to issue warning statements during strenuous and potentially hazardous activities, and failure to properly repair and regularly inspect equipment are domains of litigation that have produced individual awards in excess of $1 million.

Most often, the physical educator, coach, or athletic director is responsible for many of the ministerial or operational acts cited. This notion was upheld in the Michigan Court of Appeals in *Ross v. Consumer Power Company* (1984), in which it was contended that individual government employees are immune from liability only when they are

A. Acting during the course of their employment, and are acting, or reasonably believe that they are acting, within the scope of their authority

B. Acting in good faith

C. Performing discretionary-decisional, as opposed to ministerial-operational, acts

Hence, when a student in a beginning swimming class, as in *Webber v. Yio,* 383 N.W. 2nd 230 (1985), dove into a pool and failed to surface and efforts to revive him failed, the court held that the system of rescue was a discretionary act from which the instructor was immune from liability; however, the instructor's failure to warn participants and negligent supervision and resuscitation procedures were ministerial acts for which the instructor may be held liable.[11]

The courts have also heard legal liability cases dealing in such areas as sport product liability, violence, travel, and off-campus physical education and sport activities.

Sport product liability. The sale of sporting goods is a multibillion-dollar industry. As a result, the subject of sport product liability has arisen. The

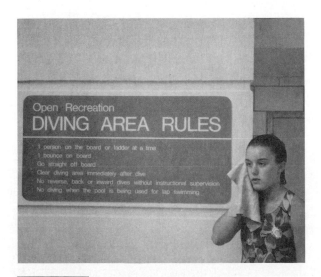

Signs with rules are important for activity areas.

term *sport product liability,* according to Arnold,[5] refers to the liability of the manufacturer to the person who uses the manufactured product and who sustains injury or damage as a result of using the product. Physical educators, coaches, and athletic directors are being named as codefendants in approximately one third of all sport product liability suits.

In the past, the buyer was responsible for inspecting the product before making the purchase. He or she assumed the risk of injury or damage to property. Today, however, the courts are placing more and more responsibility on the manufacturer to provide a reasonable standard of product to the market and to discover weaknesses and defects in the product. It is reasoned that the manufacturer or seller is in a better position than the consumer to become aware of, and to correct or eliminate, the defect. The manufacturer is required to exercise due care in designing, manufacturing, and packaging of the product, including new replacement parts. The manufacturer guarantees the product to be safe for consumer use. Failure to do so is negligence in product liability.

According to Arnold,[5] within the last 30 years an estimated 42 states have used the strict liability doctrine for some products. Under this doctrine the plaintiff must establish proof that the product contained a defect causing the injury or damage. In addition to this doctrine, a breach of the manufacturer's warranty where the product or object fails to function according to its written specifications can also be just cause for awarding damages. In breached warranty, there is no need for the injured party to prove negligence or recklessness.

The number of suits involving product liability has increased dramatically in the last few years. One reason is the possibility of large monetary settlements, especially in football cases in which an injury has occurred. A result of these large awards is skyrocketing insurance rates that are passed on to the institution, organization, user, or sport consumer.

Sporting goods manufacturers are now calling for a national product liability standard that would stabilize the rules under which they operate. However, legislators are having difficulty finding a solution acceptable to both consumers and business. At present

---

◆ **REDUCING THE RISKS ASSOCIATED WITH SPORT PRODUCT LIABILITY**

Arnold has listed 10 ways that the risks associated with sport product liability may be reduced and that will help when faced with product liability litigation.

- Become involved in collecting pertinent facts and information associated with illness and injury. This procedure can result in discouraging unwarranted claims.
- Purchase the best quality equipment available. Equipment should be carefully evaluated and tested. When equipment is purchased, records should be kept regarding such items as date of purchase. Also, reconditioned and repaired items should be recorded.
- Purchase only from reputable dealers. Reputable dealers stand behind their products and provide replacements when called for.
- Use only reputable reconditioning equipment companies that have high standards. For example, the NOCSAE stamp of approval should apply to reconditioned football helments.

- Follow manufacturer's instructions regarding fitting, adjusting, and repairing equipment, particularly protective equipment. Also, urge participants to wear protective equipment regularly.
- Be careful not to blame someone or something for the injury without just cause. Furthermore, it is best to confine such remarks to the accident report.
- Good teaching and supervising are important. Do not use any drills or techniques not approved by professional associations and respected leaders in the field.
- An emergency care plan should be prepared and ready to be implemented when needed.
- Insurance coverage for accident and general liability should be purchased or be available to all parties concerned, including students, athletes, staff members, and schools.
- When and if serious injuries occur, preserve items of evidence associated with the injury, such as pieces of equipment.

Adapted from Arnold DE: *Journal of Physical Education and Recreation* 49:25, Nov/Dec 1978.

---

the lack of certainty about how cases will be treated contributes to the high cost and the availability of product liability insurance (see the boxes on pp. 344 and 345).

Violence and legal liability. An increasing number of injuries that occur in sport contests are not accidental but intentional. These acts are referred to as intentional torts (e.g., assault, battery, reckless misconduct), and involve the harmful, unpermitted contact of one person by another. Awards for violence in sport such as the case of the professional basketball player who was punched in the face and was awarded $3.3 million in damages capture the headlines; however, reckless misconduct is evident in cases ranging from *Nabozny v. Barnhill,* 31 Ill. App. 3rd, 212, (1975) in which a goalie was kicked in the head during a high school soccer match to *Oswald v. Township High School District,* 84 Ill. App. 3rd, 723, (1980) in which a student sued another for

kicking him while participating in a physical education basketball class.

The coach or teacher is not necessarily free from liability in such cases of violence. Carpenter and Acosta[10] cite two theoretical situations in which the coach may be held liable. The first situation is when a coach knows a player is likely to commit a violent act in a sport-specific situation, but still inserts the player into the lineup. In this case the coach is not taking the necessary precautions to protect opponents from harm and injury, and in the event injury occurs, the coach may be found negligent. The second situation is when a coach may instruct a player "to take Player X out of the game." In this case, the player who follows such an instruction is acting as an agent of the coach; as a result, a person who causes battery to be committed (in this situation, the coach) is just as negligent as the player who commits the act. In incidents such as these, which too fre-

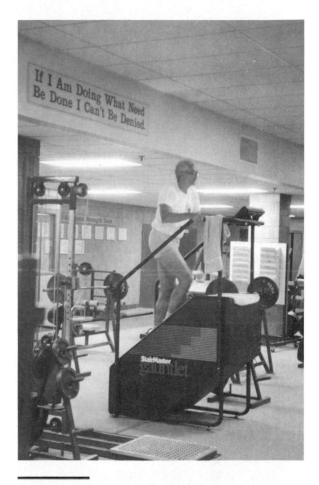

APPENZELLER AND ROSS'S RECOMMENDATIONS REGARDING HELMETS

- Purchase only the best equipment.
- Ensure that *all* players have the best equipment.
- The coach should see that helmet fits properly.
- The helmet should be inspected weekly.
- In event of injury see that no one removes the helmet during transportation to the hospital.
- See that helmet is removed safely.
- Both players and parents should be informed about risk involved in using helmet.

Adapted from Appenzeller H, Ross CT: *Sports and the Courts,* Charlottesville, VA, 1983, The Michie Company.

Careful selection of quality equipment keeps potential product liability suits to a minimum.

---

quently occur in the sporting process, coaches need to exercise common sense and sound ethical judgment to ensure that they and their team will conduct themselves in accordance with the proper standards, rules, and spirit of the game.

Off-campus activities and legal liability. Off-campus physical education and sport course offerings have become popular in many communities, schools, and colleges. In such cases, instruction in the activity may be provided by faculty members, or faculty members may provide only limited supervision, with the activity being instructed by a specialist not associated with the organization, school, or university. In fact, no faculty or staff member may even be present on a regular basis during the conduct of the off-site activity.

Although instruction may take place in off-campus settings by non-faculty members, considerable responsibility and control still rests with the management and staff members of the organization sponsoring these activities. Arnold[6] cites the case of a college that had a person not affiliated with the college teach a course at an off-campus equestrian center. The plaintiff was injured in a fall from a horse while receiving instruction. The plaintiff's attorney argued that the college was vicariously liable for the negligence of the riding academy. The court's ruling

went in favor of the college, which did not have to pay damages on the grounds that a master-servant relationship did not exist between the plantiff and the college. To show such a relationship the plaintiff would have had to prove that, among other things, the college could control the instruction taking place. Furthermore, the court ruled that the agency relationship did not result in the college authorizing the fall leading to the injury and that no complaints had been supplied regarding the instruction given.

When off-campus physical education activities are conducted (bowling, skiing, sailing, sport climbing, swimming), it is of primary concern whether *due care* is provided. The type of activity offered would indicate the amount of care that should be provided. For example, conducting a bowling class in a town bowling alley may not require as much care in most cases as an alpine skiing class. It is the responsibility of the organization and its management to exercise care and prudence in selecting the

Off-campus activities, such as horseback riding, skiing, and outdoor pursuit, add increased risk to physical education programs.

sites to be used for off-campus activities, providing quality personnel to see that proper instruction is being given, and ensuring that proper supervision is provided.[6]

Required physical education.   One legal implication for schools is that of requiring students to enroll in physical education classes. The schools should be flexible enough to provide alternatives for those cases in which activities such as dancing or swimming may be against a participant's sociocultural principles or religion.

Supervision.   Legal experts estimate that almost 80% of all court cases concerning sports injuries deal with some dimension of supervision. Whether checking on the health status of the participant or managing a weight room, supervision is vital. In Michigan, a high school principal and athletic director were sued for allegedly breaching their duty to a 15-year-old boy who was severely injured when weights fell on him (*Vargo v. Svitchan,* 301 N.W. 2nd 1, Mich. 1981). The boy accused the administration of negligence for failing to supervise his coach, provide for proper ventilation in the weight room, and observe rule violations for illegal summer football practice. The boy further charged the school's athletic director with negligence for failing to supervise the sports program. The Michigan court noted that the athletic director had the responsibility of enforcing the rules and supervising activities because of his specialized training in sports. It also reasoned that the athletic director had the authority to eliminate unsafe practices engaged in by the coaches under his direction.

Personnel.   Although covered in Chapter 7, personnel issues deserve another mention. Too often management employs unqualified and incompetent personnel to support their programs. Personnel reflect directly on management in all settings, and the courtroom is no exception. Whether at the school, college, or corporate level or with volunteer youth coaches, management retains the responsibility and liability to provide competent, certified, and well-trained personnel.

Equipment, facilities, and physical plant.   Those responsible for the conduct of physical education and sport programs should set policies and proce-

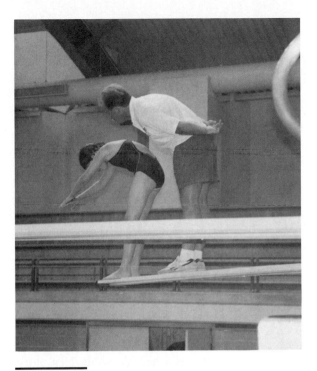

Proper supervision is required for safe participation in physical activity and sport.

dures concerning the inspection of equipment, facilities, and other associated physical plant systems (e.g., pool filters, heating, ventilation). Safety audits and periodic inspections, maintenance, repair, and status reports should all be included on database file. Names, areas, times, places, purchase and requisition orders, serial and catalog numbers, and manufacturers' warnings should all be a matter of record.

It is hoped that these legal liability suggestions will serve to eliminate risks before they become injurious, as well as potential legal entanglements.

TORT

A *tort* is a legal wrong resulting in direct or indirect injury to another individual or to property. A tortious act is a wrongful act, and damages can be collected through court action. Tort can be committed through *omission* or *commission*. An act of omission results when the accident occurs during failure

to perform a legal duty, such as when a teacher fails to obey a fire alarm after he or she has been informed of the procedure to be followed. An act of commission results when the accident occurs while an unlawful act, such as assault, battery, or reckless misconduct, is being performed. (An example was previously provided in the legal liability and violence section.)

The National Education Association[16] points out that:

A tort may arise out of the following acts: (a) an act which without lawful justification or excuse is intended by a person to cause harm and does cause the harm complained of; (b) an act in itself contrary to law or an omission of specific legal duty, which causes harm not intended by the person so acting or omitting; (c) an act or omission causing harm which the person so acting or omitting did not intend to cause, but which might and should, with due diligence, have been foreseen and prevented.

The teacher, coach, or other sport manager (e.g., fitness club, ski area) not only has a legal responsibility as described by law, but also has a responsibility to prevent injury. This means that in addition to complying with certain legal regulations such as proper facilities (e.g., lighting, pool depth), the teacher must comply with the principle that children should be taught without injury to them and that prudent care, such as a parent would give, must be exercised. The term *legal duty* does not mean only those duties imposed by law, but also the duty owed to society to prevent injury to others. A duty imposed by law would be one such as complying with housing or traffic regulations. A duty that teachers and coaches owe to society, in general, consists of teaching children without injury to them.

It is important to understand the legal meaning of the word *accident* in relation to the topic under discussion. According to the Black's *Law Dictionary,*[9]

An accident is an unforeseen event occurring without the will or design of the person whose mere act causes it. In its proper use, the term excludes negligence. It is an event which occurs without fault, carelessness, or want of proper circumspection for the person affected, or which could not have been avoided by the use of that kind and degree of care necessary to the exigency and in the circumstance in which the person was placed.

Stehn v. Bernarr McFadden Foundation, Inc., 434 F. 2nd 811 (6th Cir. Tenn., 1970) showed that omission of a legal duty was involved in an inexperienced volunteer wrestling coach's failure to teach a wrestling escape. An eighth-grade wrestler's spinal cord was severed during a match, and the pivotal legal question involved the qualifications of the volunteer coach. The paralyzed youth was awarded $385,000.

In another tort example, *Bourque v. Duplechin,* 331 So. 2nd 40 (La., Ct. App. 1976), in a recreational league softball game Duplechin slid into second base, breaking the jaw and seven teeth of second baseman Bourque. The umpire ejected Duplechin from the game. The court found for Bourque for intentional tort and against Duplechin's contestment of assumption of risk.

The courts are now taking a hard look at assumption of risk (20 states have abolished or extensively modified it), and if a player violates the rules and if the act injures another, that individual as well as the teacher, coach, official, and athletic director who enforce the rules may be held liable.

NEGLIGENCE

Questions of liability and negligence occupy a prominent position in connection with the actions of those involved in physical education and sport programs. Negligence is the failure to exercise reasonable or ordinary care.

The law in America pertaining to negligence is based on common law, previous judicial rulings, or established legal procedure. This type of law differs from statutory law, which has been written into the statutes by lawmaking bodies.

Negligence implies that someone has not fulfilled his or her legal duty or has failed to do something that according to common sense reasoning should have been done. Negligence can be avoided by acting reasonably and being prudent in various situations. One of the first things that must be determined in the event of an accident is whether there has been negligence.[7] Negligence is "the ommission to do something which a reasonable (person), guided by those ordinary considerations which ordinarily reg-

ulate human affairs, would do, or the doing of something which a reasonable and prudent (person) would not do."[9]

The National Education Association's report[16] elaborates further:

Negligence is any conduct which falls below the standard established by law for the protection of others against unreasonable risk of harm. In general, such conduct may be of two types: (a) an act which a reasonable person would have realized involved an unreasonable risk of injury to others, and (b) failure to do an act which is necessary for the protection or assistance of another and which one is under a duty to do.

The National Education Association's report[16] includes the following additional comment:

The law prohibits careless action; whatever is done must be done well and with reasonable caution. Failure to employ care not to harm others is a misfeasance.

Negligence may be claimed when the plaintiff has suffered injury either to self or to property, when the defendant has not performed his or her legal duty and has been negligent, and when the plaintiff has constitutional rights and is not guilty of contributory negligence. Negligence is sometimes defined in degrees such as negligence, gross negligence, and willful, wanton, and reckless misconduct. The teacher, coach, fitness specialist, or leader (even volunteer) of children in such cases is regarded as *in loco parentis,* that is, acting in the place of the parent in relation to the child, and this relationship is sufficient to create a legal duty (see the box on p. 349).

Because negligence implies failure to act as a reasonably prudent and careful person, necessary precautions should be taken, danger should be anticipated, and common sense exercised. For example, if a teacher permits a group of very young children to venture up a high slide alone and without supervision, he or she is not acting prudently.

Four factors of negligence must be proved before a lawsuit can be decided. First, there must be conformance to a standard of behavior that avoids subjecting a person to reasonable risk or injury. Second, a breach of duty must be shown. Third, the breach of legal duty must be the proximate cause of injury to the victim. The final factor that must be proved is

---

◆ **A SCHOOL EMPLOYEE MAY BE NEGLIGENT BECAUSE OF THE FOLLOWING REASONS:**

- Appropriate care was not taken.
- Although due care was exercised, he or she acted in circumstances that created risks.
- His or her acts created an unreasonable risk of direct and immediate injury to others.
- He or she set in motion a force that was unreasonably hazardous to others.
- He or she created a situation in which third persons such as students or inanimate forces, such as gymnastic equipment, may reasonably have been expected to injure others.
- He or she allowed students to use dangerous devices although they were incompetent to use them.
- He or she did not control a third person such as a special child, whom he or she knew to be likely to inflict intended injury on others.
- He or she did not give adequate warning.
- He or she did not look out for persons, such as students, who were in danger.
- He or she acted without sufficient skill and care.
- He or she did not make sufficient preparation to avoid an injury to students before beginning an activity in which such preparation is reasonably necessary.
- He or she failed to inspect and repair mechanical devices to be used by students.
- He or she prevented someone, such as another teacher, from assisting a student who was endangered, although the student's peril was not caused by his or her negligence.

Adapted from Garber LO: *Law and the School Business Manager,* Danville, IL, 1957, Interstate Printers and Publishers.

that injury did occur. A student in the Chatham Junior High School, Chatham, New Jersey, was severely injured in an accident while participating in physical education class. The testimony revealed that the physical education teacher was not present when the accident occurred but was treating another child for a rope burn. However, the teacher had continually warned the class not to use the springboard at any time he was out of the room. (The student was trying to perform the exercise in which he would dive from a springboard over an obstacle and finish with a forward roll.) The prosecution argued that the warning had not been stressed sufficiently and that the teacher's absence from the gymnasium, leaving student aides in charge, was an act of negligence. The court ruled negligence and awarded the boy $1.2 million for injuries. His parents were awarded $35,140. On appeal, the award to the boy was reduced to $300,000, and the award to the parents remained fixed.

Concerning negligence, considerable weight is given in the law to the *foreseeability of danger.* One authority points out that "if a danger is obvious and a reasonably prudent person could have foreseen it and could have avoided the resulting harm by care and caution, the person who did not foresee or failed to prevent a foreseeable injury is liable for a tort on account of negligence.[7] If a person fails to take the needed precautions and care, he or she is negligent. However, it must be established on the basis of facts in the case. It cannot be based on mere conjecture.

Physical educators must realize that children will behave in certain ways, that juvenile acts will cause injuries unless properly supervised, and that hazards must be anticipated, reported, and eliminated. The question raised by most courts of law is: "Should the physical educator have had enough prudence to foresee the possible dangers or occurrence of an act?"

Two landmark court actions point to legal reasoning on negligence as interpreted in one state. In *Lane v. City of Buffalo* in 1931, the board of education was found not liable. In this case a child fell from a piece of apparatus in the schoolyard. It was found that the apparatus was in good condition and that proper supervision was present. In a similar court action, the defendant was found liable. The City of Buffalo owned a park supervised by the park department. While skating on the lake in the park, a boy playing crack-the-whip hit a 12-year-old boy who was also skating. Workers and a guard had been assigned to supervise activity and had been instructed not to allow rough or dangerous games.

The ability to foresee potential danger is crucial to physical educators and coaches.

Although there are no absolute, factual standards for determining negligence, certain guides have been established that should be familiar to teachers, coaches, and others engaged in physical education and sport programs. Attorney Cymrot,[17] in discussing negligence at a conference in New York City, suggested the following:

1. The person must be acting within the scope of his or her employment and in the discharge of his or her duties in order to obtain the benefits of the statute.
2. There must be a breach of a recognized duty owed to the participant.

3. There must be a negligent breach of such duty.
4. The accident and resulting injuries must be the natural and foreseeable consequence of the person's negligence arising from a negligent breach of duty.
5. The person must be a participant in an activity under the control of the instructor, or, put in another way, the accident must have occurred under circumstances where the instructor owes a duty of care to the participant.
6. A person's contributory negligence, however modified, will bar his or her recovery for damages.
7. The plaintiff must establish the negligence of the instructor and his or her own freedom from contributory negligence by a fair preponderance of evidence. The burden of proof on both issues is on the plaintiff.
8. Generally speaking, in a school situation, the Board of Education alone is responsible for accidents caused by the faulty maintenance of physical plant and associated equipment.

Some states have a *save harmless* law that provides for protection of their employees. For example, in New Jersey the law reads:

Chapter 311. P.L. 1938 Boards assume liability of teachers. It shall be the duty of each board of education in any school district to save harmless and protect all teachers and members of supervisory and administrative staff from financial loss arising out of any claim, demand, suit or judgment by reason of alleged negligence or other act resulting in accidental bodily injury to any person within or without the school building provided such teacher or member of the supervisory or administrative staff at the time of the accident or injury was acting in the discharge of his duties within the scope of his employment and/or under the direction of said board of education; and said board of education may arrange for and maintain appropriate insurance with any company created by or under the laws of this state, or in any insurance company authorized by law to transact business in this state, or such board may elect to act as self-insurers to maintain the aforesaid protection.

Negligence Concerning Instruction

Many cases result from situations concerning improper instruction or educational malpractice in an activity. For example, if a child is injured in a basketball game or diving from a diving board, in physical education class, his or her parents may try to show that instruction had been either inadequate or unreasonable. These cases are often found in favor of the student because of the inherent danger of the activity. Other students and their families have sued teachers because they did not follow a class syllabus that many states require of their teachers. Such a syllabus outlines the course content and proper progression, and if injury occurs in an unlisted activity, then a basis for suit is apparent. Teachers have also been held liable when joining in on class activity.

In *Dibortolo v. Metropolitan School District of Washington Township,* 440, N.E. 2nd 506 (1982), a student injured her mouth performing a preliminary run as part of the jump-and-reach test. The jury found for the plaintiff due to erroneous instruction, as the student should have begun the test from a stationary position, and the teacher should have demonstrated the skill.

Negligence Concerning Equipment and Facilities

Defective or otherwise hazardous equipment or inadequate facilities are often the cause of injuries that lead to court action. If a physical educator or coach has noted the equipment is defective, he or she

Expert teaching, careful supervision, and excellent equipment make for fun as well as safe participation.

should put this observation in writing for personal future protection. A letter should be written to the principal and superintendent of schools or other responsible managerial personnel stating that danger exists and noting the areas and specifics of such danger. A copy should be maintained on file. In these cases, the courts tend to agree with the student, even if dangerous conditions had been noted. Conditions cannot only be recognized, but also must be corrected or removed. Therefore physical educators and coaches should see to it that defective equipment (e.g., frayed ropes, splintered bats, warped arrows, holes in field) is either repaired, appropriately stored, or destroyed and discarded.

Negligence in Sport Participation

Many injuries are related to participation in sport. Unequal competition is often the cause of sport accidents. Physical educators should consider gender, age, size, and skill of students in grouping players for an activity, especially one classified as collision or contact.

In *Benitez v. City of New York,* Bronx Supreme Court, Index No. 7407/85 (May 29, 1986), a 19-year-old was injured in a high school football game. The plaintiff, who injured his neck, received a 70% contributory award of $875,000 because A vs. B teams had been scheduled.

Negligence in Supervision

Failure to properly supervise physical activity is another frequently litigated situation. Whether it be failure to warn students about activities, failure to provide competent spotters, or failure to render immediate and adequate first aid, professionals should be aware of their responsibilities. The defendant in these incidents must have been able to prevent the injury that has occurred.

Defenses Against Negligence

Despite the fact that an individual is negligent, to collect damages the plaintiff must show the negligence resulted in or was closely connected with the injury. The legal question in such a case is whether or not the negligence was the *proximate* cause (legal cause) of the injury. Furthermore, even though it is determined that negligence is the proximate cause of the injury, a defendant may base his or her case on certain defenses (see the box below).

Proximate cause. The negligence of the defendant may not have been the proximate cause of the plaintiff's injury. In most cases, the test for actual causation is whether the plaintiff has established that the harm would not have occurred but for the negligent conduct of the defendant. Thus, in *Markowitz v. Arizona Parks Board,* 705 P. 2nd 937 (Ariz. 1985), in which the plaintiff dived into shallow water and sued for failure to post warning signs, the lack of signs was found not to be the proximate cause of injury so as to impose liability for the injury on the Parks Board. Negligence requires that there be some causal connection between the defendant's conduct and the plaintiff's injury.

 MEASURES TO BE TAKEN TO AVOID CHARGES OF NEGLIGENCE

- Be familiar with the health status of players.
- Require medical clearance of players who have been seriously injured or ill.
- Render services only in those areas where fully qualified and certified.
- Follow proper procedures in the case of injury.
- See that medical personnel are available at all games and are on call for practice sessions.
- See that all activities are conducted in safe areas.
- Be careful not to diagnose or treat players' injuries.
- See that protective equipment is properly fitted and worn by players who need such equipment.
- See that coaching methods and procedures provide for the safety of players.
- See that only qualified personnel are assigned responsibilities.
- See that proper instruction is given before players are permitted to engage in contests.
- See that a careful and accurate record is kept of injuries and procedures followed.
- Act as a prudent, careful, and discerning coach whose players are the first consideration.

From *The Coaches Handbook* of the AAHPERD.

Act of God. An act of God is a situation that exists because of certain conditions beyond the control of human beings. For example, a lightning storm, gust of wind, cloudburst, tornado, or other such factor may result in injury. However, this assumption applies only in cases where injury would not have occurred had prudent action been taken. Emergency procedures in these cases should be outlined and followed.

Assumption of risk. Assumption of risk is especially pertinent to games, sports, and other phases of the physical education and sport program. It is assumed that an individual takes a certain risk when engaging in various games and sports, especially where collision and contact are frequent, and where balls, implements, and apparatus are used. Participation in such activity indicates that the person assumes a normal risk. Only the risk created by negligent conduct of the defendant can be litigated. The participant, however, must know, be forewarned and informed of, and fully appreciate the risk involved.

Assumption of risk is a defense to negligence and strict liability. There are several dimensions to assumption of risk, including express consent, implied consent, duty, and misconduct. Express consent is when the user, student, or player relieves the defendant of obligation, usually by signing a waiver form; implied consent is present when a ticket to a game is purchased (and is sometimes printed on the back of the ticket). Duty means that the plaintiff voluntarily entered into an agreement such as an employee contract knowing that risks were involved, and misconduct is when the plaintiff knows the risk, but continues to play in an unsafe environment.

In *Scala v. City of New York,* 102 N.Y.S. 2nd 709, the plaintiff was injured when playing softball on a public playground, but at the same time was aware of the risks caused by curbing and concrete benches near the playing field. It was decided that the plaintiff must be held to have voluntarily and fully assumed the dangers and, having done so, must abide by the consequences.

In an action by Maltz (*Maltz v. Board of Education of New York City,* 114 N.Y.S. 2nd 856, 1952) for injuries, the court held that a 19-year-old (who was injured when he collided with a doorjamb

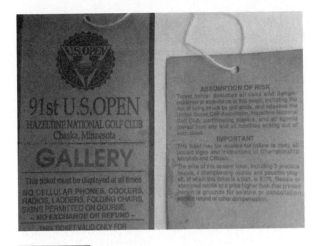

Assumption of risk is not as clear as it seems.

in a brick wall 2 feet from the backboard and basket in a public school basketball court and who had played on that same court several times before the accident) knew the basket and backboard were but 2 feet from the wall, had previously hit the wall or gone through the door without injury, was not a student at the school but a voluntary member of a team that engaged in basketball tournaments with other clubs, knew or should have known the danger, and thus assumed the risk of injury.

Rutter v. Northeastern Beaver County School District, 496 Pa. 590, 437 A. 2nd 1198 (1981), in which a 16-year-old lost an eye during summer football practice, indicates that the decision to assume the risk must be free and voluntary, and that the participant needs to clearly understand what dangers exist in order to be able to assume such a risk.

Contributory and comparative negligence. Another legal defense is contributory and comparative negligence. A person who does not act as a normal individual of similar age and nature thereby contributes to the injury. In such cases, negligence on the part of the defendant might be ruled out. Individuals are subject to contributory negligence if they expose themselves unnecessarily to dangers. The main consideration that seems to turn the tide in such cases is the age of the individual and the nature of the activity.

Contributory negligence, an all-or-nothing concept, has been modified to include the concept of comparative negligence; that is, the fault is prorated. In other words, the plaintiff and the defendant both share at times some of the fault for the injury or damage. In such cases where comparative negligence exists, damages are awarded on a pro-rated basis.

Appenzeller[2] reports that 39 states have adopted the comparative negligence doctrine and that other states are trying to adopt this concept. Contributory negligence is usually a matter of defense, and the burden of proof is placed upon the defendant to convince the jury of the plaintiff's fault and of causal connection with the harm sustained. Minors may not be held to the same degree of care as is demanded of adults.

Contributory and comparative negligence have implications for a difference in the responsibility of elementary and high school teachers. The elementary school teacher, because the children are immature, has to assume greater responsibility for the safety of the child. That is, accidents in which an elementary school child is injured are not held in the same light from the standpoint of negligence as those involving high school students who are more mature. The courts might say that a high school student was mature enough to avoid doing the thing causing him or her to be injured, whereas if the same thing occurred with an elementary school child the courts could say the child was too immature and that the teacher should have prevented or protected the child from doing the act that caused the injury.

Sudden emergency. Sudden emergency is pertinent in cases in which the exigencies of the situation require immediate action on the part of a teacher or coach and as a result, an accident occurs. For example, an instructor in a swimming pool is suddenly alerted to a child drowning in the water. The teacher's immediate objective is to save the child. He or she runs to help the drowning person and in doing so knocks down another student who is watching from the side of the pool. The student who is knocked down is injured. This would be a case of sudden emergency and, if legal action is taken, the defense may be based on this premise.

LAWSUITS

Lawsuits need only a complaint to exist. The NCAA Committee on Competitive Safeguards and Medical Aspects of Sports assumes that those who sponsor and govern sport programs have accepted the responsibility of attempting to keep the risk of injury to a minimum. Because lawsuits are apt to occur in cases of injury, despite the efforts of teachers, coaches, athletic directors, and event managers, attempts should be made to ensure legal protection. The committee contends that the principal defense against an unwarranted complaint is documentation that adequate measures have been taken and programs have been established to minimize the risk inherent in sport. No checklist is ever complete, but the checklist that follows should serve as a review of safety considerations for those responsible for the management of interscholastic and intercollegiate sport programs. The list can also certainly be extrapolated for use in all physical activities.

LEGAL AVOIDANCE CHECKLIST

Preparticipation medical examination. Before a student or athlete is permitted to participate in physical education, organized sport, or physical activity, he or she should have a health status evaluation. An annual update of a student's health history with the use of referral exams when warranted is sufficient. The NCAA Committee on Competitive Safeguards and Medical Aspects of Sports and the National Interscholastic Athletic Administrators Association (NIAAA) have developed health questionnaires and guidelines to assist in conducting a preparticipation medical examination, as well as other sports medicine procedures.

Health insurance. Each student-athlete should have, by parental or guardian coverage or institutional plan, access to customary hospitalization and physician benefits for defraying the cost of a significant injury or illness.

Preseason preparation. Particular practices and controls should protect the candidate for the team from premature exposure to the full rigors of the sport. Preseason conditioning recommendations from the coaching staff will help the candidate arrive at the first practice in good condition. Attention to heat stress, dehydration, and cautious competitive matching of candidates during the first weeks are additional considerations.

Acceptance of risk. "Informed consent" or "waiver of responsibility" by student-athletes, or their parents if the athlete is a minor, should be based on an informed awareness of the risk of injury being accepted as a result of the student-athlete's participation in the sport involved. Not only does the individual share responsibility in preventive measures, but also he or she should fully appreciate the nature and significance of the risk involved. The forms should be discussed with the student, and both students and parents should sign the forms.

Planning and supervision. Proper supervision of a sizable group of energetic and highly motivated student-athletes can be attained only by appropriate planning. Such planning should ensure both general supervision and organized instruction. Instruction should provide individualized attention to the progressive refinement of skills and conditioning. First aid evaluation should also be included with the instruction. Planning for specific health and safety concerns should take into consideration conditions encountered during travel for competitive purposes.

Equipment. As a result of the increase in product liability litigation, purchasers of equipment should be aware of impending, as well as current, safety standards recommended by authoritative groups and should purchase materials only from reputable dealers. In addition, attention should be directed to the proper repair and fitting of equipment.

In accordance with the preceding paragraph, one should know, for instance, that NOCSAE has established a voluntary football helmet standard that has been adopted by the NCAA, the National Association for Intercollegiate Athletics (NAIA), the National Junior College Athletic Association (NJCAA), and the National Federation of State High School Associations. All new helmets purchased by high schools and colleges must bear the NOCSAE seal. According to NCAA football rules, if a helmet is in need of repair, it must be reconditioned according to the NOCSAE Football Helmet Standard recertification procedures.

Facilities. The adequacy and condition of the facilities used for all sports should not be overlooked. The facilities should be examined and inspected regularly. Inspection should include warm-up and adjacent spectator areas, as well as the actual competitive area.

Emergency care. The NCAA guidelines state that attention to all possible preventive measures will help to eliminate sports injuries. At each practice session or game, the following should be available:

- The presence or immediate availability of a person qualified and delegated to render emergency care to an injured participant.
- Planned access to a physician by phone or nearby presence for prompt medical evaluation of the situation when warranted.
- Planned access to a medical facility—including a plan for communication and transportation between the sport or event site and medical facility—for prompt medical services when needed.
- A thorough understanding by all persons involved in the contest, including the management of visiting teams, of the personnel and procedures involved.

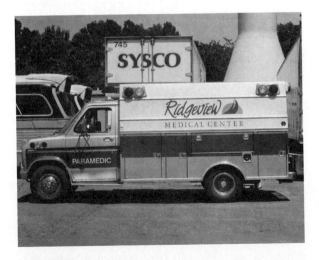

Paramedics and immediate medical transportation should be available at all sporting events.

Records. Documentation is fundamental to management. Authoritative sports safety regulations, standards, and guidelines should be kept current and on file. Permission slips and waiver forms may not prevent lawsuits, but they help reflect organizational control and attention to injury control. These need to be kept up-to-date together with the student-athletes' health status and eligibility forms (see the box below).

NUISANCE

Action can be instituted for nuisance when the circumstances surrounding the act are dangerous to life or health, result in offense to the senses, are in violation of the laws of decency, or cause an obstruction to the reasonable use of property.

 PRECAUTIONS TO BE TAKEN BY THE PHYSICAL EDUCATOR TO AVOID POSSIBLE LEGAL LIABILITY

- Be familiar with the health status of each person in the program.
- Inform students of the potential risk involved in the activity.
- Consider each individual's skill level when teaching new activities.
- Group participants together on equal competitive skill, fitness, and developmental levels.
- Perform proper progression leading up to all activities.
- Be sure equipment, uniforms, facilities, and environs are safe.
- Organize and carefully supervise the class. Never leave the class unattended—even in emergencies. If an emergency occurs, secure a replacement before leaving the room.
- Administer only first aid and CPR—never prescribe or diagnose.
- Use only qualified personnel to aid in classrooms.
- Keep accurate accident records.
- Provide adequate instruction, especially in potentially dangerous activities.
- Make sure any injured person receives medical attention.

The National Education Association[16] states the following regarding a nuisance:

There are some conditions which are naturally danger-ous and the danger is a continuing one. An inherent danger of this sort is called by law a "nuisance;" the one respon-sible is liable for maintaining a nuisance. Liability may be predicated upon negligence in permitting the continuing danger to exist, but even without a showing of negligence the mere fact that a nuisance does exist is usually sufficient to justify a determination of liability. For example, a junk pile in the corner of the grounds of a country school was considered a nuisance for which the district was liable when a pupil stumbled over a piece of junk and fell while playing at recess (*Popow v. Central School District No. 1, Towns of Hillsdale et al.,* New York, 1938). Dangerous playground equipment available for use by students of all ages and degrees of skills has also been determined to be a nuisance (*Bush v. City of Norwalk,* Connecticut, 1937).

On the other hand, allegations that the district has maintained a nuisance have been denied in some cases; for example, when a small child fell into a natural ditch near the schoolyard not guarded by a fence, the ditch was held not to be a nuisance for which the district would be liable (*Whitfeld v. East Baton Rouge Parish School Board,* Louisiana, 1949). The court said this ditch did not consti-tute a nuisance; nor did the principle of *res ipsa loquitur* apply. Under this principle the thing which causes the in-jury is under the management of the defendant and the ac-cident is such that in the ordinary course of events, it would not have happened if the defendant had used proper care.

In addressing the Health Education Division of the New York City Schools, Cymrot[17] had the fol-lowing to say about an "attractive nuisance":

Teachers need to be aware of decisions of the courts pertaining to "attractive nuisance," . . . an attractive con-trivance which is maintained, alluring to children but in-herently dangerous to them. This constitutes neglect. But it is not every contrivance or apparatus that a jury may treat as an "attractive nuisance." Before liability may be imposed, there must always be something in the evidence tending to show that the device was something of a new or uncommon nature with which children might be supposed to be unfamiliar or not know of its danger. Many courts have held, however, that for children above the age of 10 years the doctrine of "attractive nuisance" does not hold. Children are expected to exercise such prudence as those of their age may be expected to possess.

The following cases present representative court rulings concerning nuisance. In *Iacono v. Fitzpat-rick* in Rhode Island in 1938, a 17-year-old boy, while playing touch football on a playground, re-ceived an injury that later resulted in his death. He was attempting to catch a pass and crashed into a piece of apparatus. The court held the apparatus was in evidence and the deceased knew of its pres-ence. It further stated the city had not created or maintained a nuisance.

A 7-year-old child playing with his friends on a golf course had his eye put out when hit by a golf ball (*Lyshak v. Detroit,* 351 Mich. 230. 88 N.W. 2nd 596, 1958). The court found that signs and fences were inadequate in this example of attractive nui-sance.

GOVERNMENTAL VERSUS PROPRIETARY FUNCTIONS

The government in a legal sense is engaged in two types of activity: governmental and proprietary.

The *governmental function* refers to particular activities of a sovereign nature. This theory dates back to the time when kings ruled under the divine right theory, were absolute in their power, and could do no wrong. As such, sovereigns were granted im-munity and could not be sued without their consent for failing to exercise governmental powers or for negligence. Furthermore, a subordinate agency of the sovereign could not be sued. The state college or university, public high school, and municipality, ac-cording to this interpretation, acts as an agent of the state in a governmental capacity. The logic behind this reasoning is that the municipality is helping the state govern the people who live within its geo-graphic limits.

Many activities are classified under the govern-mental function. Functions such as education, police protection, and public health fall in this category.

Regarding public education, the courts hold this is a governmental function and therefore is entitled to state's immunity from liability for its own negli-gence. As has previously been pointed out, however, the attitude of the courts has changed and, for the most part, the doctrine of immunity has been neu-tralized.

Proprietary function pertains to government functions similar to those of a business enterprise. Such functions are for the benefit of the constituents within the corporate limits of the governmental agency. An example of this would be the manufacture, distribution, and sale of some product to the public. Renting a school's gymnasium or skating rink to the private sector is a proprietary function. In proprietary functions a governmental agency is held liable in the same manner as an individual or a private corporation would be held liable.

In *Watson v. School District of Bay City,* 324 Mich. 1, 36 N.W. 2nd 195, a decision was handed down by the supreme court of Michigan in February 1949. In this case a 15-year-old girl attended a high school night football game. In going to her car she was required to walk around a concrete wall. As she attempted to do this, she fell over the wall and onto a ramp. She suffered paralysis and died 8 months later. The parking area was very poorly lighted. The supreme court held that staging a high school football game was a governmental function and refused to impose liability on the district.

From this discussion it can be seen that education, recreation, and health are governmental functions. The distinction between governmental and proprietary functions precludes a recovery from the governmental agency if the function was governmental. However, if the high school had rented its stadium to another entity and the same action occurred, the outcome might have been different, because a proprietary function would have been involved.

FEES

Most public recreation activities, facilities, and the like are offered free to the public. However, certain activities, because of the expenses involved, necessitate a fee to stay in operation. For example, golf courses and ice arenas are expensive, and charges are usually levied so that they may be maintained. This is sometimes also true of facilities such as camps, bathing beaches, and swimming pools.

The fees charged have a bearing on whether the activity is a governmental or a proprietary function. The courts in most states have upheld recreation as a governmental function, because of its contribution to public health and welfare and also because its programs are free to the public at large. When fees are charged, however, the whole or conceptual picture takes on a different aspect.

The attitude of the courts has been that the amount of the fee and whether or not the activity was profit making are considerations in determining whether recreation and sport is a governmental or a proprietary function. Incidental fees used in the conduct of the enterprise do not usually change the nature of the enterprise. If the enterprise is run for profit, however, such as a health spa, the function changes from governmental to proprietary.

LIABILITY OF THE MUNICIPALITY

It has been previously noted that a municipality as a governmental agency performs both governmental and proprietary functions.

When the municipality is performing a governmental function, it is acting in the interests of the state, receives no profit or advantage, and is not liable for negligence on the part of its employees or for failure to perform these functions. However, this would not hold if there was a specific tort claim statute imposing liability for negligence. When the municipality is performing a proprietary function— some function for profit or advantage of the agency or people it comprises—rather than the public in general, it is liable for negligence of those carrying out the function. As previously pointed out, many states and municipalities have instituted specific statutes and permitted purchase of insurance recognizing the trend to permit injured citizens to recover damages from the managing agency for the torts of its employees.

LIABILITY OF THE SCHOOL DISTRICT

As a general rule the school district is not held liable for acts of negligence on the part of its management or employees, provided a state statute does not exist to the contrary. The reasoning behind this is that the school district or school board in maintaining public schools acts as an agent of the state. It performs a purely public or governmental duty imposed on it by law for the benefit of the public and, in so doing, it receives no profit or advantage.

Some state laws, however, provide that school districts may be sued in cases of negligence in the performance of certain duties, such as providing for a safe environment and competent and qualified leadership. Furthermore, the school district's immunity in many cases does not cover acts that bring damage or injury through trespass of another's premises or where a nuisance exists on a school district's property, resulting in damage to other property. Just as protection of the state and municipality is on the wane, so too is that of the school district.

LIABILITY OF SCHOOL BOARD MEMBERS

In general, school board members are not personally liable for any duties in their corporate capacities as board members that they perform negligently. Furthermore, they cannot be held personally liable for acts of employees of the district or organization over which they have jurisdiction on the theory of *respondeat superior* (let the master pay for the servant). Board members act in a corporate capacity and do not act for themselves. For example, in the state of Oregon the general rule about the personal liability of members of district school boards is stated in 56C.J., page 348, section 223, as follows:

School officers, or members of the board of education, or directors, trustees, or the like, of a school or other local school organization are not personally liable for the negligence of persons rightfully employed by them in behalf of the district, and not under the direct personal supervision or control of such officer or member in doing the negligent act, since such employee is a servant of the district and not of the officer or board members, and the doctrine of *respondeat superior* accordingly has no application; and members of a district board are not personally liable for the negligence or other wrong of the board as such. A school officer or member of a district board is, however, personally liable for his own negligence or other tort, or that of an agent or employee of the district when acting directly under his supervision or by his direction.

However, a board member can be held liable for a ministerial act (an act or duty prescribed by law for a particular administrative office) even though he or she cannot be held for the exercise of discretion as a member of the board. If the board acts in bad faith and with unworthy motives, and if this can be shown, it can also be held liable. Furthermore, acts of individual board members beyond their legal scope of duties are *ultra vires* (beyond their authority) acts, for which they may be held liable.

LIABILITY OF THE ADMINISTRATOR/SUPERVISOR

The doctrine of *respondeat superior* does not apply to administrators and supervisors, and thus in the absence of a statute imposing liability, such officials are not liable for the tortious conduct of their subordinates when liability is based solely on supervising responsibility.[14] The administrator/supervisor may, however, be liable if improper training or negligence in hiring is found.

LIABILITY OF TEACHERS, COACHES, AND LEADERS

The individual is responsible for negligence of his or her own acts. With the exception of specific types of immunity, the teacher, coach, or leader in programs of physical education and sport is responsible for what he or she does. The Supreme Court has reaffirmed this principle, and all should recognize its important implications. Immunity of the government agency such as a state, school district, or board does not release the teacher, coach, or leader from liability for his or her own acts.

In New York (*Keesee v. Board of Education of City of New York,* 5 N.Y.S. 2nd 300, 1962), a junior high school girl was injured while playing line soccer. She was kicked by another player. The Board of Education syllabus listed line soccer as a game for boys and stated that "after sufficient skill has been acquired two or more forwards may be selected from each team." The syllabus called for 10 to 20 players on each team and required a space of 30 to 40 feet. The physical education teacher divided into two teams some 40 to 45 girls who did not possess any experience in soccer. An expert witness in such matters testified that to avoid accidents, no more than two people should be on the ball at any time and criticized the board syllabus for permitting the use of more than two forwards. The expert also testified that students should have experience in kicking, dribbling, and passing before being permitted to play line soccer. The evidence showed the teacher permitted six to eight inexperienced girls to be on the ball at one time. The court held that possible injury was at least reasonably foreseeable under such conditions, and the teacher's negligence was the cause of the student being injured.

Teachers and leaders are expected to conduct their various activities carefully and prudently. If this is not done, they are exposing themselves to lawsuits for their own negligence. The National Education Association[16] has the following to say regarding management:

> The fact that administrators (speaking mainly of principals and superintendents) are rarely made defendants in pupil-injury cases seems unjust to the teachers who are found negligent because of inadequate supervision, and unjust also to the school boards who are required to defend themselves in such suits. When the injury is caused by defective equipment, it is the building principal who should have actual or constructive notice of the defect; when the injury is caused by inadequate playground supervision, the inadequacy of the supervision frequently exists because of arrangements made by the building principal. For example, a teacher in charge of one playground was required to stay in the building to teach a make-up class; another teacher was required to supervise large grounds on which 150 pupils were playing; another teacher neglected the playground to answer the telephone. All of these inadequacies in playground supervision were morally chargeable to administrators; in none of these inadequacies in playground supervision did the court action direct a charge of responsibility to the administrator. Whether the administrator in such cases would have been held liable, if charged with negligence, is problematical. The issue has not been decided, since the administrator's legal responsibility for pupil injuries has never been discussed by the courts to an extent that would make possible the elucidation of general principle; the administrator's moral responsibilities must be conceded.

Many schools and agencies in states that have passed indemnification statutes allow the district or agency to pay tort damage judgments against their employees. This is not mandatory, however, and includes only those actions that are within the scope of the job. Actions outside the scope of their job that

result in negligent behavior may find even the volunteer (who is classified as an employee) personally liable. All teachers, coaches, and leaders (even if volunteers) should check with their employers to determine the type and extent of liability coverage and plan accordingly for complete professional coverage.

ACCIDENT-PRONE SETTINGS

Because many accidents occur on the playground, during recess periods, in physical education classes, and at sport events, some pertinent remarks are included here from the National Commission on Safety Education.[16]

Playground and Recess Games

The unorganized games played during recess and noon intermissions are more likely to result in injuries than the organized games played in physical education class. Playground injuries may be pure accidents, such as when a student ran against the flagpole while playing (*Hough v. Orleans Elementary School District of Humboldt County,* California, 1943), or when a student was hit by a ball (*Graff v. Board of Education of New York City,* New York, 1940). The courts have said in connection with this type of injury that every act of every student cannot be anticipated. However, the school district should make rules and regulations for students' conduct on playgrounds so as to minimize dangers. For example, it was held to be negligence to permit students to ride bicycles on the playground while other students were playing (*Buzzard v. East Lake School District of Lake County,* California, 1939).

Playgrounds should be supervised during unorganized play and such supervision should be adequate. One teacher cannot supervise a large playground with more than 100 students playing (*Charonnat v. San Francisco Unified School District,* California, 1943), and when the supervision is either lacking or inadequate, districts that are not immune are liable for negligence in not providing adequate supervision (*Forgnone v. Slavadore Union Elementary School District,* California, 1940). Students are known to engage in fights and may be expected to be injured in fights; it is the responsibility of the school authorities to attempt to prevent such injuries. The misconduct of other students could be an intervening cause to break the chain of causation if the supervision is adequate; but when the supervision is not adequate, misconduct of other students is not an intervening superseding cause of the injury.

If a student wanders from the group during playground games and is injured by a dangerous condition into which he or she places himself or herself, the teacher in charge of the playground may be liable for negligence in student supervision (*Miller v. Board of Education, Union Free School District,* New York, 1943), although the district would not be liable in a common-law state because of its immunity (*Whitfield v. East Baton Rouge Parish School Board,* Louisiana, 1949).

Supervision of unorganized play at recess or noon intermission should be by competent personnel. A school janitor is not qualified to supervise play (*Garber v. Central School District No. 1 of Town of Sharon,* New York, 1937).

When children of all ages share a playground, extra precautions should be taken to prevent acci-

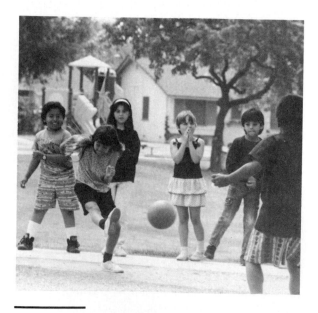

Playground activities also need to be supervised.

dents, since some children are more adept in using equipment than others and some playground equipment is dangerous to the unskilled.

Physical Education and Sport Events

Student injuries in this area occur when playground or gymnasium equipment is defective, when students attempt an exercise or sport for which they have not been sufficiently trained, when there is inadequate supervision of the exercise, when other students conduct themselves in a negligent manner, and even when the students are merely spectators at sports events.

It has been held that physical education teachers, coaches, or the school district in states where the district is subject to liability are responsible for injuries caused by defective equipment. For example, there was liability for the injury to a student who was injured in a tumbling race when the mat, not firmly fixed, shifted on the slippery floor (*Cambareri v. Board of Education of Albany,* New York, 1940).

Defects in equipment should be known to the physical education teacher or coach. There may be either actual knowledge or constructive notice of the defect. The term *actual knowledge* is understood; *constructive notice* means that the defect has existed for a sufficient time so that the instructor should have known of its existence, whether he or she did or not. Physical education teachers and coaches should make periodic examination of all equipment at frequent intervals and maintain appropriate records; otherwise, they may be charged with negligence in not having corrected equipment defects that have existed long enough that ignorance of the defect is a presumption of negligence.

Physical education teachers may also be liable for injuries that occur to students who attempt to do an exercise that is beyond their skill level. A running-jump somersault is one such instance (*Govel v. Board of Education of Albany,* New York, 1944), and a headstand exercise is another (*Gardner v. State of New York,* New York, 1939). These exercises were found to be inherently dangerous by the courts, and the evidence showed that previous instruction had been inadequate and the students had not been warned of the dangers. However, when the previous instruction and the supervision during the exercise are both adequate, there is no liability so long as it cannot be proved that the teacher is generally incompetent (*Kolar v. Union Free School District No. 9, Town of Lenox,* New York, 1939). These cases suggest that teachers should not permit students to attempt exercises for which they have not been fully prepared by warnings of the dangers and preliminary exercises to develop the required fundamental lead-up skills.

As in other types of student injury, the physical education teacher is not liable if the injury occurred without his or her negligence. If caused by the negligence of another student, the teacher will likely be relieved of liability, if the other student's misconduct was not foreseeable. Pure accidents occur in both physical education and sport; if there is no negligence, there is no liability (*Mauer v. Board of Education of New York City,* New York, 1945).

Sports events to which nonparticipating students and even the public are invited raise other problems of liability for the district or the physical education teacher, coach, or sport manager in charge. If the locality is in a common-law state where the district is immune, the charge of an admission fee does not nullify the district's immunity or make the activity a proprietary function as an exception to the immunity rule (*Watson v. School District of Bay City,* Michigan, 1949). If a spectator is accidentally hit by a ball, there is no liability; even when a student was injured by being hit by a bottle at a game, there was no liability because the misconduct of the other spectator was not foreseeable (*Weldy v. Oakland High School District of Alameda County,* California, 1937).

COMMON AREAS OF NEGLIGENCE

Common areas of negligence in physical education and sport activities listed by Begley[8] include situations involving poor selection of activities, failure to take protective procedures, hazardous conditions of buildings or grounds, faulty equipment, inadequate supervision, and poor selection of play area. Cases involving each of these common areas of negligence follow:

Poor selection of activities. The activity must be suitable to the child or youth. In *Rook v. New York,* 4 N.Y.S. 2nd 116 (1930), the court ruled that tossing a child in a blanket constituted a dangerous activity.

Failure to take protective measures. The element of foreseeability enters here, and proper protective measures must be taken to provide a safe place for children and youth to play. In *Roth v. New York,* 262 App. Div. 370, 29 N.Y.S. 2nd 442 (1942), inadequate provisions were made to prevent bathers from stepping into deep water. When a bather drowned, the court held the state was liable.

Hazardous conditions of buildings or grounds. Buildings and grounds must be safe. Construction of facilities and their continual repair must have as one objective the elimination of hazards. In *Novak et al. v. Borough of Ford City,* 141 Atl. 496 (Pa., 1928), unsafe conditions were caused by an electric wire over the play area. In *Honaman v. City of Philadelphia,* 185 Atl. 750 (Pa., 1936), unsafe conditions were caused by failure to erect a backstop.

Faulty equipment. All play and other equipment must be in good condition and properly maintained at all times. In *Van Dyke v. Utica,* 203 App. Div. 26, 196 N.Y. Supp. 277 (1922), concerning a slide that fell over on a child and killed him, the court ruled that the slide was defective.

Inadequate supervision. Qualified supervisors must be in charge of all play activities. In *Niles v. San Rafael,* 116 Cal. Rptr. 733 (Ca 1974), a city park was held responsible for failure to properly supervise a physical activity when a student was hit over the head with a bat during a softball game. The nature, location, training, and number of supervisors should also be of concern to prudent management.

Poor selection of play area. The setting for games, sport, and physical activity should be selected with the safety of the participants in mind. In *Morse v. New York,* 262 App. Div. 324, 29 N.Y.S. 2nd 34 (1941), when sledding and skiing were permitted on the same hill without adequate barriers to prevent participants in each activity from colliding with each other, the court held that the state was liable for negligence.

SUPERVISION

Children are entrusted by parents to physical education and sport programs, and parents expect adequate supervision will be provided to minimize the possibility of accidents.

Questions of liability regarding supervision pertain to two points: (1) the extent of the supervision (number and location) and (2) the quality of the supervision (certification and experience).

Concerning the first point, the question is raised about whether adequate supervision was provided. This is difficult to answer because it varies from situation to situation. However, the answers to these questions help determine this: "Would additional supervision have eliminated the accident?" and "Is it reasonable to expect that additional supervision should have been provided?"

Regarding the quality of the supervision, it is expected that competent personnel should handle specialized programs in physical education and sport. If the supervisors of such activities do not possess proper training in such work, the question of negligence can be raised.

It is crucial to have pre-service, in-service, and continual professional development for all employees to ensure that proper training is an ongoing feature of the management scheme.

WAIVERS, PERMISSION SLIPS, AND CONSENT FORMS

Waivers and consent forms are not synonymous. A waiver is an agreement whereby one party waives a particular right. A consent form or permission slip is an authorization, usually signed by the parent, permitting a child to take part in a particular activity.

Regarding a waiver, a parent cannot waive the rights of a minor. When a parent signs such a slip, he or she is merely waiving his or her right to sue for damages. Kaiser[14] points out that although the courts have a penchant not to enforce liability waivers, such waivers are still helpful in risk management programs since they may discourage lawsuits and enhance legal defense of assumption of risk by increasing the participant's awareness of programmatic risk, rigors, and hazards.

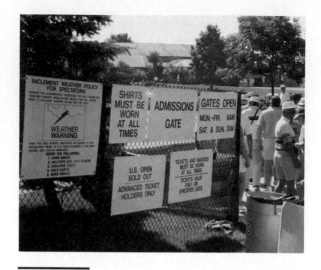

Sport events where weather may play a factor should be noted and posted.

Consent forms offer protection from the standpoint of showing the child has the parent's permission to engage in an activity.

THE COURTS AND ELIGIBILITY RULES

When eligibility regulations have been challenged, courts have traditionally been reluctant to substitute their judgment for the judgments of school athletic associations.[1] In recent years, however, federal judges have been finding eligibility rules unconstitutional (*Regents of University of Minnesota v. NCAA*, 1976). Physical educators and sport managers have noted this change in court attitude and rulings, and many colleges have employed compliance officers, as well as legal counsel, to ensure due process concerning eligibility issues.

Due process refers to the rights guaranteed under the Fourteenth Amendment that entitles the accused (e.g., student, teacher, coach, athletic director) to (1) the name of the accuser and witnesses, (2) an oral or written report on the facts to which each testified, (3) an opportunity to present a defense, and (4) an opportunity to produce witnesses or testimony on his or her behalf. The right to due process is the right to be treated fairly, the right to a standardized procedural process, to be heard, if needed to have counsel and, if found guilty, the right that the penalty imposed be proportional to the offense committed. It is interesting to note that denial of participation in sport as a punishment can be as serious as school suspension and may be regarded as the denial of a student's legitimate entitlement to public education as found in the landmark due process case of *Goss v. Lopez,* 419 U.S. 565, 1975.[13]

Court decisions in which eligibility rules have been found to be segregationist have been consistently found unconstitutional. For example, a ruling in Alabama found that having racially based athletic associations was unconstitutional. The United States Circuit Court has also ordered the Louisiana High School Athletic Association to admit private black high schools.

Sample rulings concerning eligibility include a recent federal court order voiding the Indiana High School Athletic Association rule that prohibited married students from sport participation. Another significant decision involved the Iowa High School Athletic Association and the suspension of a student-athlete because he was riding in a car that was transporting beer. The student was not drinking, and the event occurred in the summer when school was not in session. In addition, no state or federal law was broken. The eligibility law was found to be unreasonable, and the student was reinstated.

TITLE IX AND THE COURTS

Recent years have found the media reporting on numerous cases involving discrimination against women in sport. In 1978 a federal judge in Dayton, Ohio ruled that girls may not be barred from playing on boys' school sport teams, even in such collision sports as football and wrestling. In the decision the judge pointed out there might be many reasons why girls would not want to play on boys' teams, such as "reasons of stature or weight, or reasons of temperament, motivation, or interest. This is a matter of choice. But a prohibition without exception based on sex is not." The judge also indicated the ruling would have national implications.

A ruling by the State Division on Civil Rights of New Jersey requires Little League baseball teams to permit girls to play. New Jersey was the first state to have such a ruling. The order also requires that both boys and girls be notified of team tryouts and that children of both sexes be treated equally.

An amendment to the Education Law of New York State provides that no one may be disqualified from school sports teams because of sex, except by certain regulations of the state commissioner of education.

In *Yellow Springs Exempted Village School District v. Ohio High School Athletic Association,* 647 F. 2nd 651 (1981), it was found that the OSAA rule preventing girls from playing on boys' teams was unconstitutional. The Indiana Supreme Court has also ruled that it is discriminatory for a high school to sponsor a boys' team and not a girls' team.

A Michigan judge's court ruling (*Othen v. Ann Arbor School Board,* 507 F. Supp. 1376 E.D. Mich. [1981]) had serious implications for the implementation of Title IX. Federal District Court Judge Joiner ruled that Title IX can apply only to programs that directly receive federal funds. In the case in question, the judge ruled the U.S. Department of Education could not enforce Title IX in the Ann Arbor School District's interscholastic sports program because the program itself did not receive any federal funding. A similar finding was upheld in *Bennett v. West Texas State University* in 1981 and 1986.

The United States Court of Appeals for the First Circuit also ruled Title IX is programmatic, and not institutional, in scope. The Court of Appeals ruled that "the only meaningful interpretation of Title IX is that it prohibits sex discrimination in a federally funded education program offered by an educational institution." In support of its decision, the court relied on the language of the statute (including its definition of the term *educational institution*), the legislative history of Title IX, and previous court rulings that have addressed the question.

The Supreme Court of the United States ruled on February 24, 1984, that Title IX was intended to apply only to education "programs and activities" that receive direct federal aid. Before this decision

Title IX ensures that physical education and sport opportunities are open to all. Coeducational flag football is popular at many schools.

the interpretation was that if an institution received federal aid all programs within that institution were subject to Title IX regulations. As a result of this decision (*Grove City College v. Bell,* 465 U.S. 555, 79 L.Ed. 2nd 516, 104 S.Ct. 1211 [1984]), the status of Title IX enforcement remained uncertain until passage of the 1988 Civil Rights Restoration Act, which served notice that Title IX was to be returned to its prior interpretation.

Discriminatory action, however, is still taking place concerning due process, opportunity, equal financial aid, and support (*Haffer v. Temple University of the Commonwealth System of Higher Education,* 1987); *Lantz v. Ambach,* 620 F. Supp. 663 (D.C. N.Y., 1985); and *Ridgeway v. Montana High School Association,* 633 F. Supp. 1546, (1986). These actions, however, are being filed, for the most part, under Fourteenth Amendment claims.

SAFETY

It is important to take every precaution possible to prevent accidents by providing for the safety of students and other individuals who participate in physical education and sport programs (see the box above). If such precautions are taken, the likelihood of a lawsuit diminishes and the question of negli-

SAFETY CODE FOR THE PHYSICAL EDUCATION INSTRUCTOR OR COACH

The following safety codes should be followed by the physical education instructor or coach:

Have a proper and current teaching certificate and coaching license.

Operate and teach at all times within the scope of employment as defined by the rules and regulations of the employing board of education and within the statutory limitations imposed by the state.

Provide the safeguards designed to minimize the dangers inherent in a particular activity.

Provide the required amount of supervision for each activity to ensure the maximal safety of all the students.

Inspect equipment and facilities periodically to determine whether they are safe for use.

Notify the proper authorities forthwith concerning the existence of any dangerous condition as it continues to exist.

Provide sufficient instruction in the performance of any activity before exposing students to its hazards.

Be certain the task is one approved by the employing board of education for the age and abilities of the students involved.

Do not force a student to perform a physical feat the student obviously feels incapable of performing.

Act promptly and use discretion in giving first aid to an injured student, but nothing more.

Exercise due care in practicing his or her profession.

Act as a reasonably prudent person would under the given circumstances.

Anticipate the dangers that should be apparent to a trained, intelligent person (foreseeability).

This material is reprinted with permission from the JOPERD (Journal of Physical Education, Recreation & Dance), Volume 33, 1962, p. 28. JOPERD is a publication of the American Alliance for Health, Physical Education, Recreation and Dance, 1990 Association Drive, Reston, VA 22091-1599.

gence will be minimized. The following are recommended precautions to which the teacher, coach, or sport manager should adhere:

- Be properly trained, licensed, certified, and qualified to perform specialized work.

- Be present at all organized activities in the program.
- Organize classes properly according to class size, activity, physical fitness level, and other factors that have a bearing on safety and health of the individual.
- Require medical examinations of all participants.
- Have a planned, written program for proper disposition of participants who are injured or become sick or in case of other emergencies.
- Make regular inspections of items such as equipment, apparatus, ropes, or chains, placing extra pressure on them, and taking other precautions to make sure they are safe. They should also be checked for deterioration, looseness, fraying, and splinters.
- Avoid overcrowding at sport and other events, adhere to building specifications and codes and fire regulations, and provide adequate lighting and proper safety signs for all facilities.
- Use protective equipment, such as mats, wherever needed. Any hazards such as projections or obstacles in an area where physical activity is taking place should be eliminated. Floors should not be slippery. Shower rooms should have surfaces conducive to secure footing. Appropriate eye and mouth protection must be used.
- Require the wearing of gym shoes on gymnasium floors and provide adequate space for each activity.
- Adapt activities to the age and developmental, maturity, and fitness level of the participants; provide proper and competent supervision; and use trained spotters in gymnastics and other similar high-risk activities.
- Instruct students and other participants in the correct use of apparatus and performance of physical activities, and duly warn them of the risk involved. Any misuse of equipment should be prohibited.
- Inspect the buildings and other facilities regularly for safety hazards, such as loose tiles, broken fences, cracked glass, and uneven pavement. Defects should be reported immediately

to responsible persons and necessary precautions taken.

- In planning play and other instructional activities the following precautions should be taken: Space should be sufficient for all games. Games using balls and other equipment that can cause damage should be conducted in areas where there is minimal danger of injuring someone. Quiet games and activities requiring working at benches, such as arts and crafts, should be undertaken in places that are well protected.
- In the event of an accident, the following or similar procedure should be followed:
  a. The nearest teacher, coach, or sport manager should immediately proceed to the scene, notifying the person in charge, and medical personnel, if available, by phone or messenger.
  b. A primary first aid survey of the injured person will provide some idea of the nature and extent of the injury and the emergency of the situation. If necessary, the person in charge should call 911 for emergency medical services (EMS).
  c. If the teacher or coach at the scene is well versed in first aid, assistance should be given, paying particular attention to the ABCs of first aid (Airway, Breathing, and Circulation). A current first aid and CPR certificate and undertaking proper procedures will usually absolve the teacher of negligence.

     Every teacher, coach, and sport manager should hold first aid and CPR certification. In any event, everything should be done to make the injured person comfortable until emergency medical services (EMS) or care by a physician can be secured.
  d. After the injured person has been provided for, the person in charge should fill out the appropriate accident report forms, take the statements of appropriate witnesses, and file the report for future reference. Reports of accidents should be prepared promptly and sent through appropriate managerial channels.

e. There should be a complete follow-up of the accident, an analysis of the situation, and an eradication of any existing hazards.

The Standard Student Accident Report Committee of the National Safety Council listed the following reasons why detailed injury reports are important for school authorities:

1. They aid in protecting school personnel and school districts from associated publicity and from liability suits growing out of student injury cases
2. They aid in evaluating the relative importance of the various safety areas and the time each merits in the total school safety effort
3. They suggest modification in the structure, use, maintenance, and repair of buildings, grounds, and equipment
4. They suggest curriculum adjustments to meet immediate student needs and safety requirements

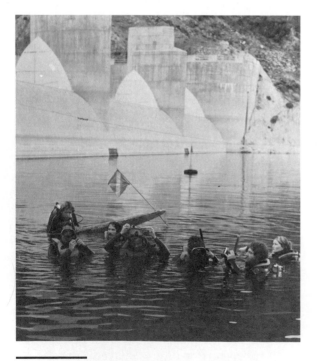

Special care should be provided for activities such as scuba.

5. They provide significant data for individual student guidance
6. They give substance to the school managers' appeal for community support of the school safety program
7. They aid school management in guiding the school's safety activities for individuals and user groups

INSURANCE MANAGEMENT

Schools and other organizations employ three major types of insurance management to protect themselves against loss. The first is insurance for property. The second is insurance for *liability protection* when there might be financial loss arising from personal injury or property damage for which the school district or organization is liable. The third is insurance for *crime protection* against a financial loss that might be incurred as a result of theft or other illegal act. This section on risk and insurance management is concerned primarily with liability protection.

A definite trend can be seen in school districts toward having some form of school accident insurance to not only protect students against injury, but to shield teachers, coaches, and staff against injury and liability as well. The same is true wherever physical education and sport programs are conducted. Along with this trend can be seen the impact on casualty and life insurance companies that offer insurance policies. The premium costs of accident policies vary from community to community and also in accordance with the age of the insured, type of plan offered, and sport to be covered. Interscholastic sport has been responsible for the development of many state athletic protection plans, as well as the issuance of special policies by commercial insurance companies, ranging from basic athletic injury to lifetime catastrophic injury. Because accidents are the primary cause of death among students between the ages of 5 and 18, it is apparent that adequate and ample protection is requisite to a well-managed program of physical education and sport (see the box on p. 367).

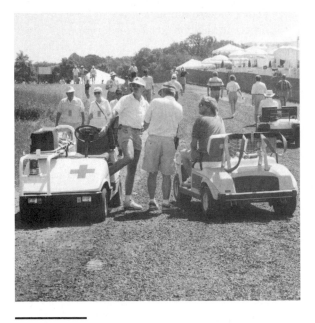

Accident procedures and care should be well managed.

Common Features of School Insurance Management Plans

Some school boards have found it a good policy to pay the premium on insurance policies because full coverage of students provides peace of mind for both parents and teachers. Furthermore, many liability suits have been avoided in this manner.

Other school officials investigate the various insurance plans available and then recommend a particular plan, and the student-athlete's parents or guardians deal directly with the company or through the school to guarantee coverage. Such parent-paid plans are frequently divided into two options: (1) they provide coverage for the student on a door-to-door basis (to and from school, while at school, and in school-sponsored activities) and (2) they provide 24-hour accident coverage with premiums usually four times higher than those of the school-only policy. The school-only policy rates are based on age, with rates for children in the elementary grades lower than for high school students. These policies usually run only for the school year.

SOME COMMON FEATURES OF INSURANCE MANAGEMENT PLANS ACROSS THE UNITED STATES

Premiums are paid for by the school, by the parent, or jointly by the school and parent.

Schools obtain their money for payment of premiums from the Board of Education, general organization fund, or a pooling of funds for many schools taken from gate receipts in league games.

Schools place the responsibility on the parents to pay for any injuries incurred.

Blanket coverage is a very common policy for insurance companies to offer.

Insurance companies frequently offer insurance coverage for athletic injuries as part of a package plan that also includes an accident plan for all students.

Most schools have insurance plans for the protection of athletes.

Most schools seek insurance coverage that provides for benefits whether x-ray examinations are positive or negative.

Hospitalization, x-ray examinations, emergency transportation, medical fees, and dental fees are increasingly becoming part of the insurance coverage in schools.

Student accident insurance provides coverage for all accidents regardless of whether the insured is hospitalized or treated in a doctor's office. Some medical plans such as Blue Cross and Blue Shield, as well as various HMOs, may be limited in the payments they make. Student accident insurance policies, as a general rule, offer reasonable rates and are a good investment for all concerned. Parents should be encouraged, however, to examine their existing family policies before taking out such policies to avoid overlapping coverage.

A survey of nine school districts in Ohio disclosed the following practices and problems concerned with selecting an insurance policy for sport:

1. The chief school administrator was the person

who usually selected the insurance company from whom the policy would be purchased.

2. Medical coverage on policies purchased ranged from $30 to $5000 and dental coverage from zero to $500.

3. Companies did not follow through at all times in paying the amount for which the claim was made.

4. Most insurance companies writing sport policies have scheduled benefit plans.

5. Catastrophe clauses were absent from all policies.

6. Athletes' coverage ranged from 80% to 100%.

7. In most cases part of each athlete's premium was paid for from a school athletic fund.

8. Football was covered by a separate policy.

As a result of this survey the following recommendations were made:

1. Some person or group of persons should be delegated to review insurance policies and, after developing a set of criteria, should purchase the best one possible.

2. Where feasible, cooperative plans with other schools on a county, district, association, state high school league, or other basis should be encouraged to secure less expensive group rates.

3. Criteria for selecting an insurance policy should, in addition to cost, relate to such important benefits as maximum medical, excluded benefits, maximum hospital, dental, dismemberment, surgical, x-ray and MRI examinations, and physical therapy.

4. The greatest possible coverage for cost involved should be an important basis for selecting a policy.

5. For football programs especially, a catastrophic clause should be investigated as possible additional coverage.

6. Deductible clause policies should not be purchased, if possible.

7. Dental injury benefits are an important consideration.

8. Determine what claims the insurance company will and will not pay.

9. The school should insist on 100% enrollment in the athletic insurance program.

10. Schools should have a central location for keeping insurance records, and there should be an annual survey to ascertain all the pertinent facts about the cost effectiveness and quality of coverage.

Procedure for Insurance Management

Every school should be covered by insurance. Five types of accident insurance may be obtained: (1) commercial insurance policies written on an individual basis, (2) student medical benefit plans written on a group basis by commercial insurers, (3) state high school athletic association benefit plans, (4) medical benefit plans operated by specific city or district school systems, and (5) self-insurance. Before adoption by any school, each type of insurance should be carefully explored and weighed so that the best coverage is obtained for the type and scope of program sponsored.

Sport and Insurance Coverage

Some schools and colleges do not provide a sport insurance program. If a student is injured in a sporting event, the family is then responsible for all medical expenditures. No provision is made for the school or college to reimburse the family for its expense. Of course, the school or college is always open to a lawsuit by the parents, as well as the student, in an effort to reclaim expenses. This is expensive for the school or college, for if the claim is settled in favor of the parents, the school's or college's insurance premiums for the next few years are increased, not to mention the intangible effect to the school's or college's reputation and public image. In these cases, the high school is, usually, through its membership in a state high school association, supplied with catastrophic insurance to supplement the individual's personal coverage.

An alternative is to provide an opportunity for students to purchase athletic insurance (many high schools provide this) or, better yet, for the school or college to purchase a policy for student-athletes (most collegiate athletic departments provide insurance). Of course, the latter is the best method because all students are then covered, regardless of their economic status, and the students' liability policy is not subject to suit. Most parents are interested only in recovering monies actually spent, and they are satisfied accordingly. Usually a blanket policy purchased by the school or college can be obtained at a lower unit cost than a policy purchased by individuals. The athletic insurance program can be managed through the business office of the school district or by a local or regional broker, relieving the school or college of going into the insurance business.

It is the responsibility of the director of physical education or athletics to maintain and supply accurate lists of participating students to the business office before the beginning of the various sport seasons. It is also imperative that the coaches and athletic trainers be made aware of the types of insurance coverage plans so that when accidents happen, they can inform the athletes of the proper procedure to follow in seeking appropriate care, as well as in filing reports and claims. Usually the business or athletic office will supply policies for every participant in a covered sport team or program.

The coach should not only be knowledgeable concerning insurance coverage, but he or she should also show concern for accident victims as well as injured players. This is not only a form of good public relations, but it may also make the difference in the parents' minds concerning potential litigation. The coaches must also be instructed by management in the proper attitude to take when such mishaps occur. Legal counsel, if required, should be made available through the school, institution, or agency. If not, a private attorney should be retained (see the box on pp. 370-371).

School Sport Insurance

Sport protection funds usually have these characteristics: they are a nonprofit venture, they are not compulsory, a specific fee is charged for each person registered with the plan, and provision is made for recovery for specific injuries. Generally the money is not paid out of tax funds, but instead is paid either by participant fee or by the school or other agency.

In connection with such plans, after receiving benefits an individual could in most states still bring action against the coach or other leader whose negligence contributed to the injury.

In respect to paying for liability and accident insurance out of public tax funds, states vary in their practices. Some states do not permit tax money to be used for liability or accident insurance to cover students in physical education and sport activities. On the other hand, the state legislature of Oregon permits school districts to carry liability insurance. This section is stated as follows in the revised code, O.R.S.:

332.180 Liability insurance; medical and hospital benefits insurance. Any district school board may enter into contracts of insurance for liability coverage of all activities engaged in by the district, for medical and hospital benefits for students engaging in athletic contests and for public liability and property damage covering motor vehicles operated by the district, and may pay the necessary premiums thereon. Failure to procure such insurance shall in no case be construed as negligence or lack of diligence on the part of the district school board or the members thereof.

Some athletic insurance plans in use in the schools today are entirely inadequate. These plans indicate a certain amount of money as the maximum that can be collected. For example, a boy may lose the sight in one eye. According to the athletic protection fund, the loss of an eye will draw $1500. This amount does not come even remotely close to paying for such a serious injury. In this case, as a hypothetical example, the parents sue the athletic protection fund and the teacher for $30,000. In some states, if the case is lost, the athletic fund will pay the $1500 and the teacher the other $28,500. It is evident that some of these insurance plans do not give complete and adequate coverage and protection to all concerned.

In many states physical educators and coaches need additional protection against being sued for accidental injury to students and student-athletes. Legislation is needed permitting school funds to be used as protection against student injuries. In this way a school would be legally permitted, and could

◆ THE PRUDENT MANAGER

The following exercise should provide personal guidance for management as to the establishment of an appropriate degree of prudence commensurate with the professional, as well as legal, responsibility of the contemporary manager in physical education and sport.

Degree of compliance

	Always	Frequently	Rarely	Never

The prudent manager:

1. Seeks to prohibit the situation that may lead to litigation through constant foresight and care inherent in the professional role he or she holds.

2. Assigns instuctional and supervisory duties concerning an activity to only those people who are qualified for that particular activity.

3. Conducts regular inspections of all equipment used and insists on full repair of faulty items before use.

4. Establishes procedures and enforces rules concerning safe use of equipment and proper fitting of all uniforms and protective gear.

5. Has written plans with adequate review procedures to ensure that participants do not move too rapidly into areas of skill performance beyond their present skill level.

6. Selects opponents for each participant/team with care to avoid potentially dangerous mismatching.

7. Establishes and scrupulously enforces rules regarding reporting of illness or injury, to include compilation of written records and names and address of witnesses.

8. Does not treat injuries unless professionally prepared and certified to do so.

9. Regularly updates first aid, CPR, and emergency medical care credentials.

10. Does not permit participation in any activity without medical approval following serious illness or injury.

11. Readily recognizes the presence of any attractive nuisance, and initiates firm control measures.

12. Posts safety rules for use of facilities, then orients students and colleagues to danger areas in activities, facilities, and personal conduct.

◆ **THE PRUDENT MANAGER—cont'd**

Degree of compliance

	Always	Frequently	Rarely	Never
13. Does not place the activity area in the control of unqualified personnel for *any* reason.	___	___	___	___
14. Relies on waiver forms, not as a negation of responsibility for injury, but only as a means of assuring that parents/guardians recognize students' intent to participate.	___	___	___	___
15. Does not permit zeal for accomplishment or emotion of the moment to suppress rational behavior.	___	___	___	___
16. Provides in letter and spirit nondiscriminatory programs for all students.	___	___	___	___
17. Cancels transportation plans if unable to be thoroughly convinced of the personal and prudent reliability of drivers, means of transportation, and adequacy of insurance coverage.	___	___	___	___
18. Does not conduct a class or practice or contest without a plan for medical assistance in the event of injury, regardless of the setting.	___	___	___	___
19. Holds professional liability insurance of significant dollar dimensions and pertinent applicability to professional pursuits involving physical activity.	___	___	___	___
20. Does not permit excessive concern about legal liability to prohibit the development of a challenging and accountable physical education/sport experience for each participant.	___	___	___	___

This material is reprinted with permission from the JOPERD (Journal of Physical Education, Recreation & Dance), January, 1979, p. 45. JOPERD is a publication of the American Alliance for Health, Physical Education, Recreation and Dance, 1990 Association Drive, Reston, VA 22091-1599.

---

be required, to purchase liability insurance to cover all students, teachers, and coaches.

SUMMARY

Legal liability, risk, and insurance management are important functions of management of physical education and sport programs. It is important that in managing such programs the persons in charge be familiar with the laws and legal basis for physical education and sport programs and the responsibilities associated with things such as product liability, negligence in the conduct of activities, common areas of negligent behavior, safety precautions necessary to prevent accidents, and the provisions that need to be implemented for a sound insurance management program. Furthermore, management should be aware that citizens (e.g., parents and student-athletes) are becoming increasingly aware of the meaning of laws that concern their programs, as well as their individual rights, including due process in such matters. As a result, the prospect of litiga-

The most inexpensive insurance policy is the employment of master teachers and coaches.

tion has significantly increased. Management, therefore, should be prepared to do all it can to prevent not only injury, but also possible litigation.

♦ SELF-ASSESSMENT ACTIVITIES

These activities will assist students in determining if material and competencies presented in this chapter have been mastered.

1. Without consulting your text, construct a definition for each of the following terms: *legal liability, tort, negligence, in loco parentis, save harmless law, assumption of risk, attractive nuisance, immunity,* and *insurance and risk management.*

2. Prepare a legal brief for a case in your state that justifies a rule that requires all students in grades K-12 to participate in physical education.

3. Discuss sport product liability and the methods you would take to ensure adequate protection for your ice hockey team.

4. Arrange a mock trial in your class. Have a jury, prosecutor, plaintiff, defendant, witnesses, and other features characteristic of a regular court trial. The case before the court is that the coach of a high school football team in the final minutes of a game used a player who had incurred a brain concussion in the first quarter. The player later suffered brain damage.

5. Survey the physical education and sport programs at your college and identify any areas of negligence that might exist in the conduct of the programs. If any are found, recommend how they can be eliminated.

6. Prepare a step-by-step list of emergency safety procedures that should be followed by every physical education teacher and coach to provide for the welfare of all students and student-athletes.

7. Take a field trip to a local community playground and chart the various safety concerns observed.

REFERENCES

1. Appenzeller H: *The right to participate,* Charlottesville, VA, 1983, The Michie Company.
2. Appenzeller H: *Sports and the courts: trends in tort liability,* Physical Education and Sports Law Quarterly, Summer Law and Sports Conference, Guilford College, Greensboro, NC, June 1983.
3. Appenzeller H, Ross CT: *Sports and the courts,* Summer Law and Sports Conference, Guilford College, Greensboro, NC, June 1983.
4. Appenzeller H, Ross CT: Sports and the courts, 6:15 Spring 1985.
5. Arnold DE: Sport product liability, *Journal of Physical Education and Recreation* 49:25, Nov/Dec 1978.
6. Arnold DE: Legal aspects of off-campus physical education programs, *Journal of Physical Education and Recreation* 50:21, Apr 1979.
7. Baley JA, Matthews DL: *Law and liability in athletics, physical education and recreation,* Boston, 1984, Allyn and Bacon.
8. Begley RF: Legal liability in organized recreational playground areas, *Safety Education Digest,* 1955.
9. Black HC: *Black's Law Dictionary,* ed 5, St Paul, Mn, 1979, West Publishing.
10. Carpenter LJ, Acosta RV: Violence in sport—is it part of the game or the intentional tort of battery? *Journal of Physical Education and Recreation* 51:18, Sept 1980.
11. Clement A: *Law in sport and physical activity,* Carmel, In, 1989, Benchmark Press.
12. Garber LO: *Law and the school business manager,* Danville, Il, 1957, Interstate Printers & Publishers.
13. Huggins HC Jr, Vacca RS: *Law and education: Contemporary issues and court decisions,* Charlottesville, Va, 1979, The Michie Company.
14. Kaiser RA: *Liability and law in recreation, parks, and sport,* Englewood Cliffs, NJ, 1986, Prentice Hall.

15. Lewis G, Appenzeller H: *Successful sport management,* Charlottesville, Va, 1985, The Michie Company.

16. National Education Research Division for the National Commission on Safety Education: *Who is liable for pupil injuries?* Washington, DC, 1950, National Education Association.

17. *Proceedings of the City Wide Conference With Principals' Representatives and Men and Women Chairmen of Health Education,* City of New York Board of Education, Bureau of Health Education, Brooklyn, NY, 1953.

18. Shapiro FS: Your liability for student accidents, *National Education Association Journal* 54:46, 1965.

SUGGESTED READINGS

- Berg R: Catastrophic injury insurance: an end to costly litigation? *Athletic Business* 8:10, Nov 1984.

  Discusses the Ruedlinger Plan, a plan endorsed by 48 state high school athletic associations that is designed to provide lifetime care for catastrophically injured athletes and protection from lawsuits for the schools.

- Bayless MA, Adams SH: A liability checklist, *Journal of Physical Education, Recreation and Dance* 56:49, Feb 1985.

  Provides guidelines for coaches to assist them in evaluating the adequacy of their program to avoid liability-producing circumstances.

- Kaiser RA: Program liability waivers, *Journal of Physical Education, Recreation and Dance* 55:54, Aug 1984.

  Discusses the pros and cons of liability waivers and shows how they can discourage lawsuits and enhance legal defenses by increasing participant awareness.

- Krotee ML, Lincoln ES: Sport and law, *Choice* 18:1055-1065, 1981.

  Delves into sport and law in regard to sports injuries, sex discrimination, education, contracts, and taxation. Describes the role of law in society and its effect on prudent management.

- Ross CT: *Sports and the courts,* P.O. Box 2836, Winston-Salem, NC.

  A physical education and sports law newsletter that provides information concerning various legal issues, concerns, and cases.

- Stotlar DK, Butkie SD: Who's responsible when a spectator gets hurt? *Athletic Purchasing and Facilities* 7:22, Apr 1983.

  Explains how the courts have ruled that spectators at sports events assume certain risks. However, there are steps managers can take to reduce potential negligence on their part.

- van der Smissen B: *Legal liability and risk management for public and private entities,* Vol I-III, Cincinnati, 1990, Anderson Publishing.

  A three-volume exploration of physical education and sport and the law. Thoroughly treats legal liability and risk management for public and private sports-related organizations.

- Wong GM: *Essentials of amateur sports law,* 1988, Dover, MA, Auburn House Publishing.

  Presents an overview of the court systems in the United States along with those entities that govern amateur sport. Contract law, tort law, drug testing, and sex discrimination cases are explored.

- Wong GM, Ensor RS: Torts and tailgates, *Athletic Business,* 9:46, May 1985.

  Pre- and post-game tailgating are popular among sport fans, but institutions can be held liable if reasonable precautions are not taken, particularly those related to alcohol.

CHAPTER 14

Public Relations

▶ **Instructional Objectives and Competencies To Be Achieved**

After reading this chapter the student should be able to

- Define the term *public relations* and its purpose and importance to physical education and sport programs.
- Understand the relationship of marketing to a public relations program.
- Recognize the constituents and needs of various publics in physical education and sport.
- Describe key principles that should guide a sound public relations program.

- Be familiar with various public relations media and how they can best be used to promote physical education and sport programs.
- Be familiar with the construction of a news release.
- Identify some professional organizations that can serve as resources for the conduct of public relations programs.

Abraham Lincoln once said, "Public sentiment is everything. With public sentiment, nothing can fail; without it, nothing can succeed." The management teams of physical education and sport programs need positive public recognition that the programs under their jurisdiction are meeting the needs of consumers. To accomplish this, the consumer and the public in general should be familiar with, understand, and support the services these programs render. Therefore, to have sound public relations, quality programs must exist, effective promotion must take place, communication channels with the various publics must be kept open, and media must be utilized in a manner that effectively presents the objectives of the organization to the public at large.

Public relations is an all-encompassing term. It is commonly defined as the planned effort to influence

opinion through good character and responsible performance, based on mutually satisfactory two-way communications.[1] It indicates the positive relationship of the institution or organization and its total complement of personnel as well as its public constituencies.[6] *Public Relation News* further adds that it is the management function that evaluates public attitudes, identifies the policies and procedures of an individual or organization with the public interest, and plans and executes a program of action to earn public understanding and acceptance. Two characteristics of public relations are careful planning and proper conduct, which in turn will result in public understanding and confidence. Public relations includes attempts to modify the attitudes and actions of the public through persuasion and to integrate the attitudes and actions of the public with those of the organization or people who are conducting the public relations program. Public relations is the entire body of relationships that makes up our impressions of an individual, institution, organization, or idea.

These concepts of public relations help clarify its importance for any organization, institution, or group of individuals trying to develop an enterprise, profession, or business. Public relations considers important factors such as consumers' interest, human relationships, public understanding, and goodwill. In business it attempts to show the important place that specialized enterprises have in society and how they exist and operate in the public interest. In education, it is concerned with improving public opinion, proclaiming the needs of the school or college, and acquainting constituents with what is being done in the public interest. It also should acquaint the community with problems and challenges that must be solved and overcome for education to render a greater service.

Purposes of school relations include: (1) serving as a public information source concerning school activities; (2) promoting confidence in the schools or school-related organizations; (3) gathering support for school or organizational funding and programs; (4) stressing the value of education for all individuals; (5) improving communication among students, teachers, coaches, parents, and community members; (6) evaluating school and organization programs; and (7) correcting misunderstandings and misinformation concerning the aims and objectives of the school, its programs, and other organizations.

Physical education and sport need public relations because the public does not always understand the positive contributions that these programs make to all the people of a community. Many persons feel that these programs are appendages to schools' academic programs and are sources of entertainment rather than education. Sound public relations programs both internally (e.g., faculty, staff, students, parents, alumni) and externally (e.g., community, business) are needed to correct these misunderstandings.

The goals of physical education and sport as presented in Chapter 2 are educational in nature and can be achieved through well-planned and effec-

Public relations promotes everyone involved in physical education and sport.

tively and efficiently managed programs. These facts should be communicated to the public, both internal and external, through various media, as well as through the pursuit of excellence in the programs.

The practice of public relations has been related to education since a publicity bureau was established at Harvard in 1900. Since that time, public relations has invaded all areas of human endeavor, including education, business, politics, religion, military, government, and labor, as well as physical education and sport (e.g., AAHPERD's Physical Education Public Information Commission, or PEPI). A sound public relations program is not hit-or-miss. It is planned with considerable care, employing the steps outlined previously in the planning process. Great amounts of time and effort are necessary to produce meaningful results. Furthermore, it is not something in which only top management, executives, or administrative officers should be interested. For any organization to have a good program, all members must be conscious of public relations.

The extent to which interest in public relations has grown is indicated by the number of individuals specializing within its domain. A recent edition of the *Public Relations Directory and Yearbook* listed more than 5000 directors of public relations with business firms, approximately 2000 of whom are associated with trade and professional gorups, and nearly 1000 associated with social organizations. Some of these people are involved in physical education and sport programs. Indeed, almost every NCAA Division I institution designates a school official to manage its public relations efforts (e.g., sports information, public or external affairs or relations).

Public relations is steadily being recognized for the impact it may have in not only the business or corporate world, but also the realm of physical education and sport. All programs need public support and understanding to survive. A sound program of public relations helps to not only sustain our programs, but also to make them grow and flourish. A lot of work has yet to be accomplished in this regard.

National Girls and Women in Sports Day in Minnesota.

MARKETING PHYSICAL EDUCATION AND SPORT PROGRAMS

In the past, U.S. corporate structures manufactured goods and then made every effort to sell them. Today management teams adhere to a strict policy of marketing analysis or identifying needs of the consumer, and then trying to satisfy these desires. Management is marketing oriented, rather than production oriented. In other words, nothing should be manufactured or supplied unless there is a demand for it. This concept applies to physical education and sport, as well as to the corporate arena.

The term *marketing* includes areas such as analysis (including identifying recurring market patterns, frequencies, and tendencies), promotion, and coordination. It involves a strategic game plan for the various factors that relate to persuading the public to endorse, purchase, support, and utilize a product or service. In so doing, it tries to find out things such as what products and services customers want, the target population (e.g., opinion research), and how best to present the product to the targeted public. In practical terms marketing has several dimensions, sometimes called the *marketing mix.* These dimensions include consumer research, product planning, pricing, public relations, advertising or positioning, promotion, packaging, distribution, and servicing. Management is responsible for coordinating all of these dimensions into an effective program.

A marketing-oriented organization starts with the consumer and his or her needs, which have been identified by sound marketing research. A determination is made between specialization and diversification—whether to stress one or several services or products.

In essence, marketing refers to the relationship of the producer to the consumer. In physical education and sport programs it relates to the various services provided and programs implemented and how well these services and programs meet the needs of the consumer (students, administration, alumni, faculty, community, and the population in general) as well as the "non-consumer." Marketing is the process by which the objectives of the physical education and sport programs can be best achieved. A marketing strategy that will enable the organization

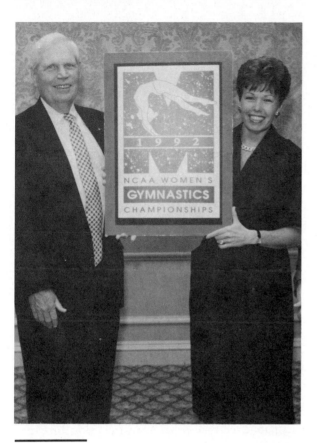

Successful marketing campaigns bring championship meets, as well as revenue and recognition, to programs, schools, and communities.

to accomplish its objectives as efficiently and effectively as possible should be developed. Marketing therefore has a significant relationship with the conduct of an effective public relations effort.

THE MANY PUBLICS

For a public relations program to be successful, accurate facts must be gathered and articulated to the public in a meaningful fashion. To establish what facts are to be packaged and presented to the public, management needs to identify the consumers, or target population, of the product or service.[2] Marketing people call this *market segmentation*. In identifying

the target population, such factors as socioeconomic status, age, proximity, transportation, parking, and other product-service needs play a significant role in selecting which population the management wishes to direct its efforts toward.

A public is a group of individuals drawn together by common interests who are in a specific geographic location or area, or are characterized by some other common feature (e.g., age, interest). The United States, because of its diversity, is made up of hundreds of different publics—farmers, senior citizens, organized workers, students, professional and blue-collar workers, veterans, and so on. The various publics may be national, regional, and local. They can be classified according to race, gender, ethnicity, age, religion, occupation, politics, disability, income, profession, economic level, or background (business, fraternal, or educational). Each organization or group with a special interest represents a public. Regardless of the public, all possess common elements to which public relations efforts must be sensitive. Each public (e.g., internal, external, immediate, associated) usually needs to belong, wants to have input, and desires to be included (psychosocial ownership) in order to maintain its interest and enhance its reputation. Public relations–minded and dependent organizations (e.g., education, physical education, sport) should always think in terms of the publics with which they wish to interact and serve in order to promote understanding as well as to determine how those publics can best be reached and satisfied.

To have a meaningful and purposeful community relations program, it is essential to visit and interact with the community; obtain accurate facts about these publics; and gain an understanding of their needs, interests, lifestyle practices, and hobbies, as well as other essential information. It is also important to consider what is good for most of the people in the community.

Public opinion, along with other factors, helps determine whether a profession (e.g., physical education and sport) is important or not, whether it meets an essential need, and whether it is making a contribution to society. Public opinion can influence the success or failure of a department, program, school, institution, business, bond issue, or, indeed, an entire profession. It is dynamic and results from the interaction of people, the media, and all those involved with the physical education and/or sporting process. Public opinion has great impact, and any group, institution, or organization that wants to survive, sustain, and succeed should learn as much about its process as possible.

To gather information on what the public thinks, why it thinks as it does, and how it reaches its conclusions, various techniques may be explored. Surveys, questionnaires, opinion polls, interviews, expert opinion, discussions, town meetings, observations, and other techniques have proved valuable. Anyone interested in community relations should be acquainted with these various techniques.

Some forms of public opinion are shaped as a result of influences in early life, such as the effect of parents, peers, coaches, and school and community environment. Individuals' everyday lifestyles and what they see, hear, and experience in other ways also contribute to the establishment of public opinions. Furthermore, the media, including newspapers, radio, and television, play a significant role in influencing the formation and strength of our opinions. It is important not only to be aware of these facts, but also to remember that one is dealing with many different publics (e.g., unaware non-consumer, aware non-consumer, media consumer, light user, dropout), each requiring a special source of research data gathering and study in order to plan the most meaningful way to develop, organize, and manage an effective, efficient, and meaningful public relations campaign.

PLANNING THE PUBLIC RELATIONS PROGRAM

Public relations programs are more effective when they are planned by a team of interested and informed individuals and groups.[5] Individuals and groups such as school boards, management personnel, teachers, students, administrators, coaches, and citizens' committees can provide valuable input and assistance in certain areas of the community relations program. These people, serving in an advisory capacity to physical education and sport profession-

Wheelchair athletes at the Marine Corps Marathon, Washington, DC.

als, can help immeasurably in planning a community public relations program by following these specific steps:

- Establish a sound public relations policy.
- Identify the services, programs, and products that will yield the greatest dividends.
- Obtain facts about what consumers and non-consumers do and do not know and believe about educational values and needs.
- Decide what facts and ideas will best enable consumers and non-consumers to understand the benefits obtained from quality programs.
- Decide what program or personnel improvements will improve service or programs.
- Make full use of effective planning techniques to generate mission statements, policies, goal setting, understanding, and appreciation.
- Relate cost to opportunity for participants to learn, experience, maintain, and improve health and achieve fitness.
- Decide who is going to perform specific communication tasks at particular times.

After the public relations plan is put into operation, it is important to assess and evaluate its results to see if its goals are being met and to improve the quality of the program.

PRINCIPLES OF PUBLIC RELATIONS

The role of management to provide sound public relations is vital to any institution or organization. The following are common principles to observe in developing a good public relations program:

- Public relations should be considered internally before being developed externally. The support of all substructures and representatives within the organization, from top management to operational staff, should be obtained. A team effort is crucial! Furthermore, such items as mission and purpose of program, person or persons responsible, funding sources, media involvement, and self-controlled communication tools to carry on the program should be primary considerations before implementation.
- A public relations program should be outlined and put in writing, and members of the organization should have meaningful input, as well as the responsibility to become familiar with the program. The better its mission, goals, and objectives are known and understood, the better chance the program has of succeeding.
- The persons directly in charge of the public relations program must have thorough knowledge of the professional services being rendered, the attitudes of members of the profession and of the organization represented, and the nature and reaction of the consumers and of all the publics directly or indirectly related to the task at hand.
- After all relevant information has been gathered, a program that meets the needs of the organization and the public or community should be developed. It should be based on this market or opinion research and not on the whims of management.
- Adequate funds should be made available to do the job. Furthermore, all support services necessary to allow the public relations program to succeed should be mobilized to ensure the campaign a fair chance to meet its stated objectives.
- The formation of a public relations staff will be determined by the needs of the organization, the amount of money available, the attitude of the management, and the size and resources of the organization. If additional staff members are needed, specific job descriptions should be developed so that talented individuals can be sought for the PR team.
- Individuals assigned public relations work should stay in the background if deemed appropriate by the nature of the program, instead of seeking the limelight.
- Public relations workers should keep abreast of the factors and influences that affect the program and develop and maintain a wide sphere of contacts.
- As a public relations program is developed, the following items should be checked. Is there a handbook, manual of guidelines, or newsletter to keep members of the organization informed as to both their role and place in the overall picture? Is there a system for disseminating information to local electronic (i.e., radio and television) and newsprint outlets? Is there a booklet, flyer, or printed matter that tells the story of the organization? Do members of the organization participate in community activities? Are there provisions for a speakers' bureau so that civic and service clubs, schools and other organizations may obtain someone to speak on various topics? Does the organization hold open house, clinics, or seminars for interested persons? Does the organization have a video or other visual or printed material that can be shown and distributed to interested groups that explains and interprets the work of the organization? Is interinstitutional or intrainstitutional E-mail utilized to its fullest capacity?
- A good public relations program will employ all available human, technical, and informational resources to disseminate crucial information to the public to ensure adequate dialogue between the consumer, potential consumer, and the organization.

PUBLIC RELATIONS AND THE MEDIA

Many media (e.g., electronic and newsprint) can be employed in a public relations campaign. Some have more significance in certain localities (e.g., your local sports writer) than others, and some are more readily accessible than others (e.g., local cable television). Physical educators, athletic directors, and coaches should survey their communities to determine the media networks to which they have access, and that which can be used most effectively and meaningfully to promote their programs and the institutions and communities they represent.

Program and Staff

The program and the staff represent perhaps the best medium for establishing an effective public relations program. Through activities and experiences (e.g., clinics, presentations, workshops, health fairs) provided and the leadership given, much goodwill may be built for any school, college, department, or profession.

Another important consideration is that some of the most effective community relations occurs on a person-to-person basis. This might be teacher to student, student to parent, teacher to citizen, or physical educator to coach to participant. Research concerning communication, persuasion, and voter patterns indicate that one-to-one communication is a very effective tool. Sport managers must enter and experience the community if this profession is to be meaningful and sustained.

Print Media/News Releases

The newsprint medium is one of the most common and useful means for disseminating information. It reaches a large audience and can be helpful in presenting and interpreting physical education and sport to the public at large. Some questions that might be asked to determine what makes a good news story are the following: Is the news of interest to the public? Are the facts correct? Is the style direct? Is it written in the third person in nontechnical terms, and is it well organized? Does it include news about individuals who are closely related to the local school, college, or other organization? Does the article have a goal, theme, or plan of action, and does

```
                    PROCLAMATION

      WHEREAS, the City of Wayzata, Minnesota is
 actively concerned and involved in nurturing and
 supporting the educational and physical development
 and achievements of its natives and residents; and

      WHEREAS, the achievements academically and
 athletically of our native citizen, Libby Nelson, are
 a source of great community pride and interest as she
 represents our hometown in the nation and at the
 University of Minnesota as an accomplished athlete and
 scholar; and

      WHEREAS, she will be especially honored during
 ceremonies at the University of Minnesota; and
 "Hometown Days" celebration of her achievements is
 representative of the recognition our City supports:

      NOW, THEREFORE, BE IT RESOLVED, as Mayor of the
 City of Wayzata, Minnesota, I hereby do declare the
 date of

      APRIL 5, 1991 AS OFFICIAL LIBBY NELSON
      WAYZATA HOMETOWN DAY IN THE CITY

 Proclaimed by the City Council of the City of Wayzata
 this 2nd day of April, 1991.


                              _____
                              Robert D. Gisvold, Mayor
```

Many communities are recognizing the contributions of student-athletes.

it play a significant part in interpreting the program?[1]

When a story or news release is going to be submitted to a newsprint medium, phone contact should take place prior to the preparation of the manuscript. In some cases, a news advisory is preferable to a story or news release.

The following guidelines[1] should be followed when formulating a news release to promote an event:

- Complete the news release, "the message."
- Use Associated Press (AP) writing style.
- Be concise; one page should to it!
- Identify the market segment (target population) you wish to address.
- Identify the primary players (e.g., media experts, local feature editors) to whom you should mail or fax your releases.

- Contact these media "keys" and explain the importance of the news release both to the program and community, as well as the society.
- Avoid the "majority fallacy" and target your release to the appropriate following (e.g., heavy consumer, light consumer, non-consumer).
- Mail your release in plenty of time (2 to 3 weeks before the event). Events like National Physical Education and Sports Week (May 1-7), the Great American Workout, or National Employee Health and Fitness Day are just a few of the themes that may be utilized.
- Include any other relevant materials (e.g., program, brochure, media guide).
- Follow up your mailed news release with a call to be sure it is "on-line" and to answer any questions.
- Send a note of thanks.

There are no guarantees when dealing with the newsprint media. Many times, a supposedly great story may be submitted and will never appear before the public. Some of the most common reasons for rejecting material include limited reader interest, poor writing, inaccuracies, and insufficient information. The discretion that the media exercises over the public relations domain can be discouraging. The best bet is to just be persistent; get to know the "key" media people and learn who you can and cannot rely on for the release of important information (e.g., stories, features, events). Mixing up your strategies for releasing information may be helpful. Use word of mouth, press releases, personal letters, phone calls, etc. Never give out incorrect information or information based solely on hearsay; memories are long in the media business and serious repercussions often result in subsequent negative publicity.

There are also thousands of popular magazines, professional journals, trade publications (e.g., *Sports Market Place*), and other periodicals that provide another challenging outlet for building sound public relations. National newsprint media such as *Newsweek, Sport Magazine, Sports Illustrated,* and *Reader's Digest* are excellent for publicity purposes. So are journals such as *JOPERD, NIRSA, National Aquatic Journal, Parks and Recreation, the Journal of Sport and Social Issues,* and

National Strength and Conditioning Association Journal, just to name a few. However, just like breaking into a major daily newspaper, it is difficult to get manuscripts or notices in such publications because of their rigid requirements.

Many of the major media outlets like to cover the stories with their own staff writers. Many times it is better to suggest ideas to these sources rather than to submit a manuscript. The public relations person can attempt to interest the editors in some particular work being done and ask them to send a staff writer to cover the story. It might be possible to get a freelance writer interested in the organization, program, or event and have him or her develop a story. Someone on the department staff with writing skill can also be assigned to write a piece for newsletter or magazine consumption and then also submit the story to various periodicals for consideration.

In many cases, however, it is not necessary to get a story in a national magazine. Many local and community outlets provide excellent exposure and are geared specifically to one community or a specific topic. Sound public relations must be built, and working with your local paper, magazine, cable, radio, or television outlet will provide an extra personalized boost to your physical education or sport program.

The newsprint media can be used effectively by any school or other organization. To be most effective, however, the information must be related to the readership of that particular publication and meet the needs of the target population. To this end, the focal point of public relations is still providing crucial information to the target audience at the most opportune time.

Pictures and Graphics

Pictures represent an effective medium for public relations. Two words should be kept in mind by the persons who take and select the pictures for publication: *action* and *people*. Pictures that reflect action are more interesting and appealing than stills. Furthermore, pictures with people in them are more effective than those without people. Usually a few people are better than many. Finally, such considerations as background, accuracy in details, clarity, and educational significance should be taken into consideration. Some newspaper outlets require that photographs be taken by union or newspaper-employed photographers. Permission should always be secured and rules checked (e.g., NCAA, agents) to ensure the photo is within all legal and jurisdictional guidelines.

Educational matters, such as budgets, statistical and demographic information regarding growth and diversity of school population, information about participation in various school or college activities, and many other items relating to schools and other organizations can be made more interesting, intelligible, and appealing if presented through colorful and creative graphics. Pictures, flow charts, and graphs should relate specifically, of course, to the age, grade, gender, and level of activity that is being publicized. The computer software packages now available have increased and enhanced the visual effects employed by public relations personnel.

Public Speaking

Public speaking can be an effective medium for achieving good public relations. Addresses to schools and civic and social groups in the community, as well as at public affairs, gatherings, and professional meetings afford good opportunities for interpreting a profession to the public. However, it is

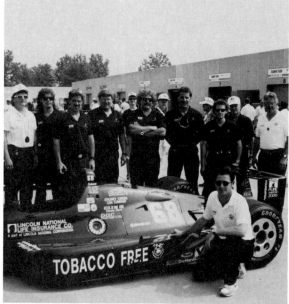

Public relations concepts can sweep a nation and the world.

important to do a commendable job, or the result can be poor, rather than good, community relations.

To make an effective speech, a person should observe many fundamentals, including mastery of the subject, sincere interest and enthusiasm, interest in putting thoughts rather than the speaker across to the public, directness, straightforwardness, preparation, brevity, and clear and distinct enunciation.

If the educational or sport organization is large enough and it has several qualified speakers within it, a speakers' bureau may also be an asset. Various civic, school, college, church, and other leaders within a community can be informed of the services the organization has to offer. Then, when the requests come in, speakers can be assigned on the basis of qualifications and availability. The entire department or organization should set up facilities and make information and material available for the preparation of such presentations. If desired by the members of the organization, in-service training, seminars, or courses could even be worked out in conjunction with the English or Communications department or some experienced person in developing this particular phase of the community relations program. Public speaking is not easy, and young professionals and student-athletes should all be exposed to such positive experiences, although only after appropriate "practice."

In many high schools and colleges, student-athletes are being mobilized to speak at local K-12 schools concerning academics, reading, "Just-Say-No," substance abuse, and other crucial topics. Public speaking skills are requisite for all those involved in physical education and sport programs.

Discussion and Advisory Groups

Discussion groups, forums, coffee klatches, and other similar meetings are frequently held in educational institutions and communities. At such gatherings, representatives from the community, including educators, industrialists, business people, physicians, lawyers, clergy, labor leaders, politicians, and others discuss topics of general interest. This is an excellent setting to enlighten civic leaders, clarify issues, clear up misunderstandings, and discuss the pros and cons of your programs and projects. Physical educators, coaches, and public- and private-sector sport managers should play a larger role in such meetings than in the past. Much good could be done for all through this medium of public relations.

Someone once said, "there is no such thing as an original idea." With time, ideas, methodologies, and concepts are refined over and over again. Do not be afraid to listen to people who are in the community. One of the most effective ways to keep current on the "pulse" of community sentiment is to form an advisory group. The purpose of the group is simple— to stay in touch with community needs, feelings, and desires. Members of your group will invariably be from all walks of life. You may start with friends in the business community or parents of children in your organization who have an interest in certain opportunities your program can offer.

The group should meet as often as is reasonable to discuss and brainstorm concerning the possibilities that exist in the immediate community to promote your programs and attract others who may be interested. You may be surprised at the results achieved by information relayed through company newslet-

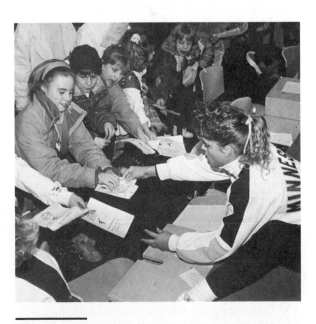

Public image and interaction help to promote physical education and sport.

ters, word of mouth, payroll envelope stuffers, and other ideas that have been generated at these informal meetings. In addition, allowing "ownership" in your program by including outside parties can only serve to expand your programmatic and informational resource base for the future.

Radio and Television

Electronic media such as radio and television are powerful media because of their universal appeal. These media are well worth the money spent for public relations. However, the possibilities of obtaining free time should be thoroughly explored. The idea of public service will influence some radio and television station managers to grant free time to an organization. This may be in the nature of an item included in a newscast program, a spot public service announcement (PSA), or a public service program that might range from 15 to 60 minutes.

Some radio and television stations reserve, and make available, spots for educational purposes. One example is the "Kids and Arnold" PSA developed by the President's Council on Physical Fitness and Sports, which has captured an estimated $2.8 million in comparative advertising value. This possibility should be investigated. Many local communities, schools, and colleges have stations (e.g., cable, radio) of their own that may be used.

Sometimes a person must take advantage of these media on short notice; therefore it is important for an organization to be prepared with written plans that can be put into operation immediately. The following include some short list items of preparation that might be kept on file:

- Know your message—health, Physical Best, Fit to Achieve, stop smoking, Jump Rope for Heart, National Youth Sports Program (NYSP)
- Know the program—style, format, audience participation, time
- Know the audience—seniors, teens, up-scale, non-consumers, fans
- Tailor the message—construct and target according to audience interest
- Tailor the presentation—to the show, time, audience

- Practice—rehearse, speak in lay terms, be brief and concise

Being prepared to contribute might make the difference between being accepted or rejected for a media opportunity. The organization must also be prepared to assume the work involved in rehearsing, gathering research and background materials, preparing scenery, arranging facility availability, or other factors essential in presenting such a program.

Radio and television offer some of the best means of reaching a large number of people at one time. Organizations concerned with physical education and sport should continually translate their message into material that can be used by the media. This, in turn, will assist in the building and maintaining of quality programs.

Films and Video

Film and video productions can present dramatic and informative stories ranging from an organization's public service to highlights concerning the training of its student-athletes. They constitute an effective medium for presenting a story briefly. A se-

Student-athletes get an opportunity to voice their opinions concerning sport at the University of Minnesota.

ries of visual impressions will remain long in the minds of the viewers.

Because a vast majority of Americans enjoy films and videos, it is important to consider them in any public relations program. Film and video are not only a form of entertainment, but also an effective medium to use to inform, educate, and motivate. They stimulate attention, create interest, and provide a way of getting across information not inherent in printed material. They can be a powerful tool if effectively incorporated in your public relations campaign.

Movies, videos, slide films, educational television, and other visual aids have also been used by a number of physical education and sports organizations to present their programs to the public and to interest individuals in their message (e.g., health, fitness, school and community togetherness).

Posters, Exhibits, Brochures, Demonstrations, Miscellaneous Media

Posters, exhibits, and brochures are important in any public relations program concerned with physical education and sport. Well-illustrated, brief, and attractive brochures can visually and informatively depict activities, facilities, projects, opportunities, and services that a department or organization has to offer as part of its total program.

Drawings, paintings, charts, graphics, pictures, and other aids, when placed on posters and properly distributed, will illustrate activities, show progress and concern, and present information visually. These media will attract and interest the public.

Exhibits, when properly prepared, placed, and presented, such as in store window or gymnasium entryway or some other prominent spot, can do much to demonstrate work being done by the school or organization.

Demonstrations that entertain, inform, and present the total program of an organization or profession are a unique aspect of any community relations program. The main objectives for a physical education or sport demonstration are (1) to inform the public and provide an outlet for interest in physical education and sport programs by community members, (2) to provide an opportunity for members of an organization to work together toward a common goal, (3) to demonstrate the need and benefit of physical education and sport to all participants, (4) to provide opportunities for the general public to see the physical education and sport program in action, (5) to contribute to the objectives of the organization, (6) to include all participants in the activities, (7) to reflect the needs of the consumer in the present and in the future, and (8) to contribute to the health, and social and emotional well-being of participants and spectators.

Other miscellaneous media, such as correspondence in the forms of letters and messages to parents, student publications, and newsletters and reports, offer opportunities to develop good relations and favorable understanding concerning schools, colleges, and other organizations and the work they are doing. Every opportunity must be used to build and sustain positive public relations.

PUBLIC RELATIONS IN ACTION

Many examples exist that indicate that effective public relations programs are a vibrant aspect of the profession of physical education and sport. The President's Council on Physical Fitness and Sports distributes materials designed to make physical educators, community-based program leaders, and the public in general aware of the value of physical fitness and sport. Some of the Council's programs include Spring into Action, NYSP, and the Presidential Sports Award. One of the Council's publications, "A School Physical Education Performance Checklist," provides students, parents, physical educators, and others a guide concerning the effectiveness of their programs in light of the desired objectives (see the box on p. 386).

The PEPI Project

The Physical Education Public Information (PEPI) project is designed to educate the public regarding the vital contribution of physical education to children, youths, and adults. Through the project the use of local media—print, radio, and television—is emphasized as a means of gaining greater public understanding concerning physical education.

◆ **PERFORMANCE CHECKLIST**

Yes	No		
☐	☐	Physical fitness is not a part-time agenda. Does your school provide at least one period per day of instruction in vigorous physical activity?	
☐	☐	Play alone won't develop physical fitness. Is a part of each physical education period devoted to activities like running, calisthenics, agility drills, and weight training?	
☐	☐	Skill in sport is a valuable social and health asset. Does your school program offer instruction in lifetime sports like tennis, swimming, golf, skiing, and jogging?	
☐	☐	Most physical problems can be alleviated if discovered early enough. Does the school give a screening test to identify those students who are weak, inflexible, overweight, or lacking in coordination?	
☐	☐	All children can improve with help. Are there special physical education programs for students with varying disabilities?	
☐	☐	Testing is important to measure achievement. Are all students tested in physical fitness at least twice a year?	

What to do to change the "No" answers to "Yes"

First: Make sure you know what your local school code says about physical education, and what is specified in state laws or regulations.

Then:

1. Speak to the physical education instructor in your child's school. You will find him or her very cooperative and willing to answer your questions.

2. If the physical education instructor can't help, speak to the school principal.

3. If significant changes are needed in the school's priorities or scheduling, try to encourage your parent/teacher organization to support a regular physical education program with an adequate emphasis on physical fitness.

4. If the problem is one of policy in the entire school district, take up the issue with your local Board of Education.

5. If your school is doing all it can at this time, make certain your child gets at least one-half hour of vigorous physical activity every day before or after school.

For additional information or help in setting up a program of vigorous physical activity for your child, write:

THE PRESIDENT'S COUNCIL ON
PHYSICAL FITNESS AND SPORTS
701 Pennsylvania Ave., NW
Washington, DC 20004

In its initial phase the project identified a local PEPI coordinator for each of the nation's 100 largest metropolitan listening and viewing areas (there are now more than 600 PEPI coordinators). The PEPI coordinator's responsibility is to organize and report PEPI activity in his or her area. This means such things as arranging with local radio and television stations for programming, contacting local newsprint media about physical education initia- tives such as Fit to Achieve, and finding appropriate outlets for PEPI posters (e.g., malls, schools, supermarkets).

PEPI was developed by NASPE and funded by AAHPERD. The basic concepts of the PEPI program include: (1) physical education is a form of health insurance, (2) physical education contributes to academic achievement, (3) physical education contributes to lifetime sport skills, and (4) physical

A student-athlete gymnastics exhibition at Northrop Mall, University of Minnesota.

education helps develop a positive self-concept and an ability to both compete and cooperate with others.

The PEPI Action Corps (PAC) was organized to aid PEPI coordinators with public information and media contact. PAC consultants were selected on the basis of their enthusiasm and outstanding achievements on behalf of physical education. Some of the consultants have their own television and radio programs and serve in an advisory capacity to further the objective of publicizing the benefits of physical education.

PEPI is currently 1 of 20 arms of the National Association for Sport and Physical Education (NASPE) and will be undergoing reorganization to become more effective and efficient in order to better meet long-term AAHPERD aims and objectives.

National Physical Fitness and Sports Month

National Physical Fitness and Sports Month was established in 1983 by the President's Council on Physical Fitness and Sports and is endorsed by the President of the United States. May is usually designated as the month, and various public relations plans are utilized to motivate the public into action. Slogans such as "Shape up America" and "Spring Into Action" and public relations messages delivered by the President and governors, as well as celebrities such as Arnold Schwarzenegger, are used to alert people of all ages that physical education and fitness remain a top priority and a national concern. As a result of this promotion many communities, schools, and businesses across the country sponsor various physical education and sport activities and other health-related fitness events during the month of May.

Jump Rope for Heart

One of the most successful public relations activities of AAHPERD is the Jump Rope for Heart (JRFH) program. The American Heart Association and AAHPERD cooperate to sponsor rope-skipping exhibitions, Jump Rope for Heart, and Jump-Rope-a-Thons to raise funds. Student groups who have been involved in demonstrations have been very well received. This project has raised considerable money to benefit the AHA, as well as to augment AAHPERD funds, and remains a tremendous public relations vehicle that focuses on community involvement. JRFH has completed more than 10 years of providing students with jump rope skills as well as

Jump rope provides a good cardiovascular workout and also serves as an AAHPERD public relations initiative.

knowledge, attitudes, and understanding concerning heart disease and the positive effects that cardiovascular fitness can play in prevention. The Alliance provides a thorough Media Training Supplement that is helpful to any educator.

FIT TO ACHIEVE

The recent Fit to Achieve[4] initiative by NASPE focuses on why children need physical education. With the continuing fiscal problems facing our school system, this program provides the professional pertinent information concerning the 1987 H. Con. Res. 97 that encourages all K-12 schools to provide quality, daily physical education. NASPE provides the following recommendations concerning quality physical education:

- It should be taught daily.
- It should be taught by a certified physical education teacher.
- It provides logical progression, K-12.
- It allows for all children, including those with disabilities, to participate and succeed at their own level.
- It encourages students to use the skills and knowledge acquired in class.

The Alliance also provides a kit that includes models for presentations, news releases, public service announcements, contemporary fitness facts, and a 12-minute video that will be a service to any professional in the field. Indeed, all K-12 teachers should be familiar with NASPE's initiatives such as Physical Best, Sport Sense, and the Hershey Youth Project.

PUBLIC RELATIONS IN SCHOOL AND COMMUNITIES

Research conducted in various school systems concerning the nature and scope of their public relations programs has revealed the following concerning physical education and sport.

The policies that govern the programs indicated that the director of physical education and/or athletics was usually directly responsible for all public relations press releases. All printed material needed

National Physical Education and Sport Week • May 1-7

Fit to Achieve

Through Quality Daily Physical Education

1900 Association Drive • Reston VA 22091 • (703) 476-3410

Poster used in public relations effort to promote National Physical Education and Sport Week and quality daily physical education.

the approval of the director and/or the superintendent of schools before being released. The coaches of interscholastic sport were responsible for preparing all sport-specific releases regarding their programs. Each physical educator and coach was urged to recognize that his or her activities were part of the professional and public relations programs of the school district.

Communications media employed included the physical education and sport program, newspaper, posters, films, videos, public speaking, school publications, newsletter, letters to parents, demonstrations and exhibits, personal contact, pictures, radio, television, window displays, brochures, sports days, and bulletin boards. The five media found to be the most effective in their professional and public rela-

tions programs were (1) the total physical education and sport program, (2) personal contact, (3) newspapers, (4) public speaking, and (5) demonstrations and exhibits (see the box on p. 390).

All the directors of physical education and sport indicated that sport received more publicity than the physical education program. When asked why they thought this was so, some typical comments were: "The public demands it," "Because of public interest," and "The newspapers will only accept and print releases on athletics."

When the directors were asked what message they were trying to convey to the public, the following were typical answers: the value of the total physical education and sport programs, the importance of the programs to the student, recognition and achievement of all students in all areas of physical education and sport, efforts and energies being expended to give each person a worthwhile experience in physical education and sport, the role of the physical education and sport programs in enhancing the health and welfare of the participant, and the aims and objectives of the total physical education and sport programs.

In summary, the professional and public relations programs in the school districts surveyed by the authors were conducted in light of the following principles:

- Each physical education and sport department recognized the importance of an active public relations program.
- Sound policies guided the program.
- Responsibility for public relations was shared by all members of the department, with central authority residing with the director.
- Many different communications media were used to interpret the program to the numerous publics.
- The total physical education and sport program was recognized as being the most effective medium of professional and community relations.
- Efforts were made to interpret accurate facts about physical education and sport to the public.
- Considerable planning was needed for the effective use of public relations media.

◆ PUBLIC RELATIONS AND FUND-RAISING PROMOTIONAL IDEAS

Art auction	Cross-country skiing marathon	Reading marathon
Arts and crafts fair	Garage sale	Roller skating marathon
Backgammon tournament	Golf tournament	Sailing regatta
Bake sale	Greeting card sales	Showing films and videos
Ballroom dancing	Guest speakers	Silent auction
Basketball marathon	"Guiness" risk activities	Skating marathon
Bicycle marathon	Hay rides	Soccer clinic
Bingo	Historical and/or house tour	Softball tournament
Book sale and fair	Holding a dance	Spaghetti or chili dinners
Bowling contest	Marathon—10K, 5K, walking	Sport camp
Candy, cookie, or fruit sales	Monopoly marathon	Swimming marathon
Canoe race	Night golf	T-shirt and sweatshirt sales
Car wash	Pageant (male or female)	Talent show
Carnivals	Pancake breakfast	Tennis tournament
Church supper	Picture taking	Used equipment swaps
Club exhibitions	Pizza sales	Weiner and pig roasts
Concert	Radio marathon	
Coupon book sales	Raffles	

Partners of the Americas in cooperation with the University of Minnesota and Special Olympics International play host to a Uruguayan coach and gold medal winning athlete.

Communities have also assisted schools and other public- and private-sector organizations and associations in the promotion of physical education and sport. Rotary Clubs, Lions Clubs, American Legion Posts, Junior Chambers of Commerce, Partners of the Americas, and Special Olympics International, among other service organizations, have a long tradition of assisting in the positive public relations of physical education and sport programs.

SUMMARY

Public relations is an important responsibility for all who manage physical education and sport programs. Public support for these programs is essential if the necessary funds, facilities, staff, and other support essentials are to be provided. Therefore sound principles should guide the public relations program in a way that will communicate the objectives of these programs to the various publics who are interested. Furthermore, all of the faculty, staff, and members of the organization should be involved in the public relations program.

T-shirt, sweat shirt, and boxer short sales are a top fund-raising enterprise.

◆ SELF-ASSESSMENT ACTIVITIES

These activities will assist students in determining if material and competencies presented in this chapter have been mastered:

1. As a manager you are conducting a staff meeting in your school. Explain to the staff why you believe that an in-service program in public relations would be valuable to staff members and managers alike.

2. What is meant by the term *marketing,* and what are its implications for promoting physical education and sport programs?

3. What is meant by the fact that physical education and sport are dealing with not just one, but many publics? Identify two different publics and indicate what type of public relations program you would employ with each and how they differ.

4. List the principles that should be observed in a public relations program. Apply five of these principles in communicating the importance of a strong physical education program in your school.

5. Prepare a 2-minute news release to be published or broadcast to the public about some event or phase of a physical education or sport program. Present it to the class and have the class evaluate it.

6. Present a fund-raising plan that would serve to build public relations in your elementary physical education program.

REFERENCES

1. Cutlip SM, Center AH: *Effective public relations,* Englewood Cliffs, NJ, 1978, Prentice Hall.
2. Dougherty NJ, Bonanno D: *Management principles in sport and leisure services,* Minneapolis, Mn, 1985, Burgess Publishing.
3. Kraus RG, Curtis JE: *Creative management in recreation and parks,* St Louis, 1986, Mosby–Year Book.
4. NASPE: *Fit to Achieve grassroots kit,* Reston, Va, 1988, AAHPERD.
5. Pangrazi RP, Darst PW: *Dynamic physical education curriculum and instruction for secondary school students,* New York, 1991, Macmillan.
6. Williams J: Public Relations. In Lewis G, Appenzeller H, editors: *Successful sport management,* Charlottesville, Va, 1985, The Michie Company.

SUGGESTED READINGS

■ American Alliance for Physical Education, Recreation and Dance: *Jump Rope for Heart and Fit to Achieve publicity kits,* 1900 Association Drive, Reston, VA 22091.
The Alliance and NASPE provide excellent materials by way of publicity kits that assist in forming vigorous promotion for physical education and sport programs.
■ American Alliance for Physical Education, Recreation and Dance: *Shaping the body politic: legislative training for the physical educator,* Reston, Va, 1985, AAHPERD.
A new publication prepared by the American Alliance Public and Legislative Affairs Office. It offers some helpful advice for educators charged with developing a school public relations program.
■ Buturusis D: Gaining and keeping support for physical education, *Journal of Physical Education, Recreation and Dance* 55:44, Aug 1984.
Discusses various ways physical education can achieve public support. Stresses such requisites as direct communication with parents and other segments of public, staff involvement, assessing community needs, and prudent media utilization.

- Jackson JJ: *Sport administration,* Springfield, Il, 1981, Charles C Thomas.
  Presents the theoretical base for various aspects of management, including public relations, then links it with specific situations in physical education, sport, and recreation.
  Marken GA: Thirteen ways to make enemies of the press, *Public Relations Quarterly* 32:30-31, Winter, 1987.
  Discusses guidelines for management when dealing with the press. Provides information on how to work in cooperative spirit with the media.
- Roloff BD: Public relations: objectives for physical education, *Journal of Physical Education, Recreation and Dance* 56:69, Mar 1985.
  Sets forth 15 objectives for public relations that, when properly implemented, will achieve public understanding and support for physical education.
- Sutton W, Migliore E: Strategic long-range planning for intercollegiate athletic programs, *The Journal of Applied Research in Coaching and Athletics* 3(4), 233-261, 1988.
  Presents an environmental or climate assessment approach to various marketing strategies. Topics ranging from priority seating to internal and external sport competitions are examined in order to facilitate better strategic market planning processes.
- Tenoschok M, Sanders S: Planning an effective public relations program, *Journal of Physical Education, Recreation and Dance* 55:48, Jan 1984.
  Describes how concerned parents and administrators are more willing to offer support if they know how the physical education program helps their children, what concepts are developed, and why activities are offered. Various techniques are suggested for accomplishing these goals.
- Yiannakis A: Some contributions of sport sociology to the marketing of sport and leisure organizations, *Journal of Sport Management* 3:103-115, 1989.
  Presents a detailed analysis of critical concerns involving sport marketing, consultative assistance, target market identification, and product marketing. Also discusses the marketing mix of product, price, place, promotions, and people.

CHAPTER **15**

Office Management

▶ **Instructional Objectives and Competencies To Be Achieved**

After reading this chapter the student should be able to

- Appreciate the importance of office management in a physical education and sport program.
- Understand and appreciate the role of the computer in accomplishing management tasks.
- Justify the need for office personnel in the management of a physical education and sport program.

- Identify basic office management procedures that should be used in carrying out the tasks of a physical education and sport program.
- List the records and data bases that should be maintained in a physical educator's and athletic director's office.

Managers of physical education and sport programs know that efficient office management determines to a great extent the success of their programs. Therefore, along with functions such as public relations, facility management, and fiscal accountability, office management is a crucial management component.

Office management has often been neglected by physical educators, coaches, and other sport managers. Efficient office management indicates a well-run department. The office is the place for first impressions, communication between student and teacher or athlete and coach, the focus of management duties and functions, and a point of contact for the management and staff and, often times, the public.

OFFICE MANAGEMENT TASKS

Although many office management tasks have been moved to a centralized location (e.g., principal's or district business manager's office) and the computer has enabled office personnel to instantly retrieve relevant information (e.g., student medical status, eligibility, equipment inventory, schedule), office personnel are still responsible for many important tasks including the following:

Communication. The office is the nerve center of the organization, where information is received and transmitted to staff members and others by means such as face-to-face conferences, telephone, fax, correspondence, intercom, and electronic mail systems.

Correspondence. The office is the setting for preparing and filing letters and reports for managers and staff members and for handling and sorting their incoming and outgoing mail.

Supplies and equipment. The office is the place for requesting, receiving, and disbursing supplies and equipment needed for conducting the organization's various activities. It should be a place that safeguards programmatic assets.

Processing materials. The office is a central point for recording, duplicating, typing, and word processing data, information, and materials pertinent to the management of the program.

Record keeping. The office is the place where records containing information on staff, students, athletes, and other materials are housed or made available via computer database. Calendars, schedules, attendance, and medical status reports are usually priorities of well-run offices. The computer has made centralized housing of student records more accessible and efficient.

Personnel concerns. The office serves as a central location for employment interviews, counseling, and small conferences.

Report preparation. The office is a place for preparing and retrieving data and information, and for finalizing reports for various faculty and staff members and other personnel to whom the management is required to report.

Budget preparation and implementation. The office is where budget information is prepared, payrolls are initiated and may be distributed, revenues and expenditures are recorded, and financial reports and summaries are compiled and stored or electronically filed and fed to a central database.

Community and public relations. The office is a key communications center for the conduct, planning, and management of community-based and professional projects that are closely related and important to the achievement of the goals and functions of the organization. Reception of visitors as well as other personnel is crucial to the program.

Emergencies. The office is a focal point for meeting day-to-day emergency situations that call for immediate action. Instant communication and location of personnel and students necessitate precise record keeping.

IMPORTANCE OF OFFICE MANAGEMENT

Colleagues, community leaders, business contacts, new staff members, potential employees, students, and other visitors frequently have their initial contacts with physical education and sport departments in the central office.[6] Their reception, the courtesies they are shown, the efficiency and attitude with which the office work is conducted, and other covert operational details leave lasting impressions. Friends, alumni, employees, and recruits are often made or lost at this strategic control point.

Communications Center

Office work, broadly defined, is the handling and management of information. The office is usually the place where schedules are arranged and distributed; telephone calls made and received; reports

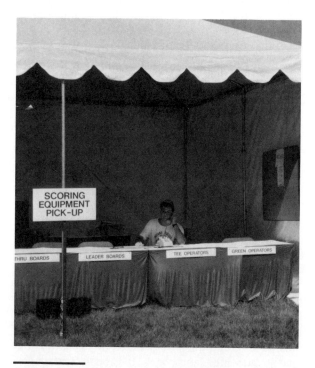

Offices can take on many shapes and forms, but they are always crucial to communication, US Open; Chaska, MN.

typed or word processed and duplicated; mail received, opened, and distributed; bulletins prepared and issued; conferences arranged and held; appointments made and confirmed; and greetings voiced and exchanged. The office represents the hub of activity around which revolves the effective and efficient functioning of the physical education and coaching personnel. Unless these functions are carried out with dispatch, accuracy, and courtesy, the entire management process begins to break down.

Focus of Management Duties

The chief management personnel, secretarial assistants, and clerical help constitute the office staff. The filing system (e.g., computer), key records, and reports are usually housed in the office. When inventories need to be examined, letters pulled from files, or the program chair or director consulted on important matters, the office is frequently the point of contact. Management responsibilities are carried out in the office, making this space a point of focus for the entire organization.

Point of Contact for Management and Staff Members

Staff members visit the office regularly. Mailboxes are located there, and telephone calls may be taken and transferred by the office. Conferences and appointments with students and visitors often bring staff members to the office. Constant communication and dialogue take place between the management and staff members in this setting. The atmosphere in the office can and should create high staff morale, efficiency, a friendly climate, and a feeling of working toward common goals.

RELATIONSHIP OF MANAGEMENT TO OFFICE STAFF MEMBERS

The management should establish a good working relationship with office staff members. Secretaries and other personnel should have a feeling of belonging and a recognition that they are an important part of the organization. The work each one performs is essential to the achievement of the organization's goals.

Most managers depend heavily on their office staff members to carry out day-to-day duties and routines efficiently and productively. Furthermore, managers (e.g., teachers, athletic directors, coaches) are frequently away from their desks on organization assignments, and in their absence the office must function in the same manner as when the manager is present. These goals cannot be achieved unless there is an excellent working relationship between the management and office staff members.

In-service education of office staff members. The management should encourage office staff members to engage in in-service education and be aware of the updating of any office procedures. Areas in which improvement might take place include word processing skills, computer programming, shorthand skills, answering telephones, updating the filing system, simplifying record keeping, and human relations skills (e.g., assertiveness and self-development training).

Office staff should also be encouraged to continue their education and keep in good physical condition; it is hoped that management will see that these might be built into the office staff's busy schedule.

Sexual harassment. Sexual harassment is a problem that has been highlighted in recent years. Newspaper stories and court cases have described how sexual harassment in educational settings has resulted in dismissals as well as psychological trauma. Managers must recognize that such conduct cannot be tolerated. Departmental procedures should be established, and staff should be encouraged to attend workshops concerning this crucial issue.

OFFICE SPACE

The central office for the physical education and sport departments should be readily accessible. If physically possible, the office should be near health service and athletic training offices, gymnasiums, exercise rooms, locker rooms, fields, pools, and other departmental facilities.

Most central offices for physical education and sport should consist of at least three divisions including (1) a general reception area, (2) a clerical space, and (3) private offices. Other desirable features to be considered are a rest room, storage and duplicating room, and conference room for staff and other meetings and functions.

General Reception Area

The general reception area is used by visitors as a waiting room or information center; for staff members to pick up their mail, conduct appointments, or acquire information; and for office services in general. The area should be attractive and well maintained, with comfortable chairs, current and attractive bulletin boards, and other items essential to carrying out necessary management routines. It should create a warm, friendly, professional atmosphere. A counter, railing, or desk divider should separate the general waiting room from the rest of the office facilities. This helps ensure greater privacy and security and more efficient conduct of office responsibilities.

Clerical Space

The clerical space should be separated from the general waiting and reception room. It should be equipped with computer, typewriters, files, tables,

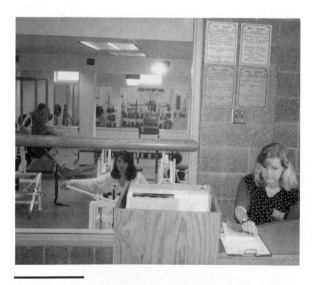

Reception areas with viewing windows are popular in health and fitness centers.

telephones, and fax machine. It is often desirable to have a private alcove or office for one or more of the secretaries, depending on the size of the department and office space demands. Privacy is often needed for word processing, typing, preparing reports, or for the convenience of visitors and other personnel. There should be ample lighting and sufficient space for freedom of movement so that duties can be carried out comfortably and with minimal confusion and difficulty.

Private Offices

The chairperson or director of the department or program and possibly other staff members, depending on the school size and educational domain (college, university), should have private offices. The offices should be large enough so that the persons in managerial positions can concentrate on their work without interruptions, conduct private conferences and tutorials with students, interact with staff members or visitors, and in general carry out their duties as efficiently as possible. The offices should be equipped appropriately and well maintained. Desks should be functional, and calendars, schedule pads for appointments and conferences, and other essential organizational materials should be provided. Filing and storage cabinets, book shelves, resource material, and other office equipment (e.g., computer, laser printer, and scanner) should be provided as needed.

OFFICE PERSONNEL

The number of office personnel depends on the size and mission of the program or department. The staff can consist of secretaries, stenographers, transcribing and fax machine operators, receptionist, switchboard operator, and word processors in a large department. However, most offices, especially at the school level, usually consist of one secretary. In some small schools, student help may be the only office personnel available. This is why the selection and qualities of office personnel (usually only a secretary) are vital to any physical education and sport program.

The following are brief descriptions of the roles of

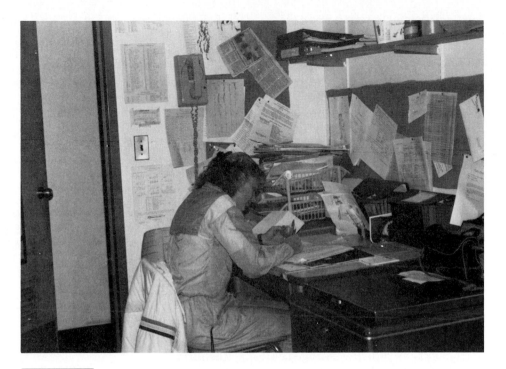

Private staff offices are necessary for maximal efficiency.

various specialized office personnel, realizing that these duties are usually collapsed into one or, if fortunate, two top-notch secretaries.

The *secretary* should be a solid contributor to the chairperson and to the department as a whole. To be most helpful, he or she will be a master typist and word processor, a stenographer, a public relations representative, an expert computer operator, and be efficient at photocopying, faxing, and duplicating. He or she will see that the office runs smoothly. The secretary should know where documents and materials are filed and be able to obtain them quickly, assist management with minor details (e.g., appointments, calendar, copying), and see that accurate records are maintained, databases established, and that reports are sent out on time. Without question, the secretary is crucial to a well-managed office.

The duties and functions of an outstanding secretary range from keeping managerial calendars to maintaining public relations, from taking minutes to control and security (e.g., keys, locks), and from completing endless forms to laboring over reports and manuscripts. The secretary is the backbone of most departments and should both command and show a great deal of respect from and for all involved in the managerial process.

A *stenographer* is a typist who can also take shorthand. A stenographer, however, does not usually have the confidential duties a secretary maintains. Large departments frequently have stenographic or word processing pools of individuals who are on call to do work for any staff member requesting their services.

A *transcribing word processing operator* listens to dictated material on a playback mechanism, then word processes the material in accordance with the instructions provided. This technical skill usually carries over into the operation of the facsimile (fax) machine and general office duties as well.

The positon of *receptionist* will vary with the program. In some departments a receptionist is a greeter who presents an attractive appearance and is polite, courteous, and helpful to visitors and callers. Some departments also assign to this person certain typing, filing, and duplicating responsibilities.

Large departments frequently have *switchboard operators* who answer and direct calls and answer the phones for staff members and other personnel who are not available. Calls may also be rolled over and messages relayed by the switchboard operator through the prescribed channels, including voice mail. The courteous, efficient, and accurate handling of information is crucial to the functioning of an efficient organization.

Office personnel should be selected very carefully. Experience, intelligence, character, personality, honesty, common sense, appearance, and ability should play important roles in the selection process. The secretary should be well educated, exposed to a secretarial course of study or experienced, and possess a solid background in word processing, book-keeping, and English, as well as the requisite psychosocial qualities (e.g., discretion, loyalty, integrity) to function well with the management team.

In small elementary schools, high schools, and colleges, the manager may have to rely partially or entirely on students (e.g., work study) to perform much of the clerical work. In-service education should take place for these student workers to ensure that acceptable procedures are followed in the conduct of their work. Student help is a necessary part of most management teams and should provide a meaningful experience for the employee. This responsibility usually resides with the senior secretary, but sometimes the manager must embrace this important duty.

EQUIPMENT AND SUPPLIES

Whether an office is efficient and effective sometimes depends on the equipment and supplies available. The materials needed vary with the size of the organization. In smaller organizations equipment such as computers and duplicating machines might be centrally located rather than in departmental offices. The following are some of the physical resources that should be considered when conducting a functional analysis of office requirements (FAOR):

Calculator
Bookcases
Bulletin boards
Buzzers
Calendars
Camera
Chairs
Clips
Coat racks
Clock
Computer package and stand (laser printer, mouse, modem, appropriate software such as spreadsheet, database, word processor, graphics package)
Copying machine
Desk baskets and dividers
Desk lamps
Desk pads
Desks
Dictionaries
Facsimile machine
First aid cabinet
Letter trays
Magazine racks
Paper cutter
Paperweight
Paste, glue
Pencil sharpeners (manual and electric)
Pencils and pens
Reproducing machines
Rulers
Safe
Scanner
Scissors
Scrapbooks
Stamps
Stapling machine
Stationery and paper
Tables
Telephone
Typewriters
Umbrella rack
Wardrobe cabinets
Wastebaskets

Although physical resources (e.g., equipment, supplies and other materials) are vital for effective and efficient office functioning and/or communicating and for maintaining records, recording appointments, and controlling supplies and equipment, the human resource is still the most crucial commodity and is the key to successful office management.

COMPUTER APPLICATIONS IN OFFICE MANAGEMENT

In 1983 sales of personal computers reached approximately 3.5 million units. The number of desktop computers in schools is estimated to be at least 2 million. In the 1990s, 65% of all professional, managerial, and administrative jobs will depend on computers, and expenditure relating to computer utilization will reach to almost 13% of our gross national product (GNP).[2]

The Department of Parks and Recreation in Hartford, Connecticut, realized the potential of the computer in its project Leisure Match. The department developed a computer information service for Hartford residents to familiarize them with the leisure opportunities the city was offering. It enabled interested individuals to match leisure interests to leisure opportunities, helped people to better understand and enjoy new and different leisure experiences, and provided management with a computerized information system that not only resulted in a better program but also contributed to future planning and resource allocation.[2]

Tenneco Incorporated maintains a computer system to help achieve the goals of its corporate health and fitness program. The computer has been particularly helpful in areas such as providing demographic, fitness, and medical testing data on employees, as well as in exercise logging—the employee keeps a daily record of activity workouts.

Computers are useful not only in parks and recreation programs and the corporate fitness setting, but they also play a significant role in the operation of physical education and sport programs.

The Lexington, Massachusetts public schools have used their computer system to link all physical education staff members to an electronic mail system. This enables physical education teachers and their supervisors to communicate instantaneously within all school buildings through the use of desktop computers linked to the school system's mainframe computer. This eliminates delays caused by use of interoffice mailing systems and provides for immediate communication to individuals or specified groups on the network.

Lexington has also developed a computerized program for tracking students in grades 3 through 12 in regard to the AAHPERD Physical Best. Teachers in each school, upon completion of the testing, enter the raw data from their desktop computer into a user-friendly, menu-driven mainframe program.

Computer literacy is required for all future managers.

This program converts entered data instantaneously to national normed percentiles, maintains a progressive student database, and provides an individualized fitness report card, as well as offering pre-designed graphics packages to utilize in program evaluation and public relations.

Another feature of the Lexington program allows each physical education teacher and coach, after being assigned a predetermined budget amount, to enter a computerized catalog of physical education and sport equipment and purchase requirements. These orders are sorted and compiled into a singular bid list and sent to a variety of vendors. When the bids are returned and analyzed, the computer writes the purchase orders automatically. The manager or supervisor can keep up to date on purchases and budget expenditures and their projected implications through specified procedures and continuous staff input concerning needs (e.g., equipment, travel, tournaments, etc.).

Computer Contributions to Management

A computer is a machine that can, among other things, program managerial functions in areas such as physical education and sport.[5] It possesses a memory and will carry out a given set of instructions almost instantaneously. It can use data concerning physical education and sport programs (e.g., budget, test scores) and process that information by performing mathematical and logical operations.

The main advantages for management in using a computer include *speed;* it saves a considerable amount of time (e.g., the addition that one person could do in 100 days can be done in 5 seconds or less via computer). A second advantage is *accuracy;* the computer does not make errors if the correct input is applied. A third advantage is that it *imposes discipline;* a person must thoroughly understand a problem before programming the computer to arrive at the correct answer. A fourth advantage is *versatility;* the computer can score, add, subtract, multiply, divide, sort, compare, correct, simulate, draw, and store information, as well as perform a variety of other potentially helpful operations.[2]

The computer processes most likely to be applied by management include word processing, database, spreadsheets, desktop publishing, and networking.

Word processing is the computer function most called upon by management. Letters, memos, and other correspondence; manuscripts; curriculum guides; playbooks; forms; and evaluations, among other items, are common word processing outcomes that can be stored, mailmerged, spellchecked, and graphically represented.

Database has transformed worn phone books, old student records, and past scouting reports, as well as any other "collectible" into functional bits of information for the business manager, teacher, coach, and athletic director.

Spreadsheets assist the manager with inventory, facility utilization and scheduling, and budgeting among other "countables." They permit the manager to see how the future (forecasting) will be affected by potential decisions such as budget reduction or attendance gain.

Desktop publishing allows the user to write newsletters and produce fliers and overheads, as well as curriculum guides and playbooks with graphics. Scanners transfer data from texts, ledgers, and videos onto disks for editing and storage.

Networking is a means to link the staff to a centralized data bank. Depending on the software, this may range from departmental electronic mail to national computer conferencing and electronic bulletin board. Modems or devices that enable you to send and receive files across telephone lines between your computer and a mainframe or a colleague's computer also assist in networking. Curriculum and instructional programs, scouting services, reference materials (library resources), laptop computer evaluation, and exchange of documents are the trend for the 1990s.

Computer Utilization in Physical Education and Sport

The computer can be used effectively in physical education and sport programs. It can be programmed to aid in management decision making at all levels. The bottom line is recognizing that many management tasks—whether concerned with bookkeeping, class scheduling, record keeping, talent assessment, or direct mail public relations—can be handled by the computer at a far more accurate and efficient pace than by the clerical staff.

REPT FIN333 16

BLOOMINGTON ISD #271
INSTRUCTIONAL SUPPORT SERVICES
ACCOUNTING PERIOD 12

SORT KEYS: NBR-PRG-EXP

OBJ	DESCRIPTION		YTD-EXPENDED	A YTD-EXPENDED	B YTD-ENCUMBER	C BUDGET	C − (A + B) BUDGET-BALANCE	% EXP
200	DISTRICT CONTEST	TOTAL	0.00	1,315.82	0.00	3,500.00	2,184.18	37.6
220	ATHLETIC DIR OFFICE	TOTAL	18,579.35	72,336.13	0.00	264,540.00	192,203.87	27.3
221	FOOTBALL-BOYS	TOTAL	2,984.03	70,129.30	0.00	90,010.00	19,880.70	77.9
222	BASKETBALL-BOYS	TOTAL	5,131.51	6,139.85	0.00	42,980.00	36,840.15	14.3
223	HOCKEY-BOYS	TOTAL	6,626.46	7,371.31	0.00	49,360.00	41,988.69	14.9
224	BASEBALL-BOYS	TOTAL	0.00	994.00	0.00	34,880.00	33,886.00	2.8
226	SOCCER-BOYS	TOTAL	1,182.73	34,109.46	0.00	37,580.00	3,470.54	90.8
227	GYMNASTICS-BOYS	TOTAL	197.00	12,144.11	0.00	17,480.00	5,335.89	69.5
228	SWIMMING-BOYS	TOTAL	2,883.37	5,987.47	0.00	24,760.00	18,772.53	24.2
229	CC-SKIING-BOYS	TOTAL	797.64	797.64	0.00	5,640.00	4,842.36	14.1
230	WRESTLING-BOYS	TOTAL	2,568.20	3,560.79	0.00	27,960.00	24,399.21	12.7
231	TRACK-BOYS	TOTAL	265.26	1,283.61	0.00	26,570.00	25,286.39	4.8
232	CC-RUNNING-BOYS	TOTAL	5.82	4,219.30	0.00	5,360.00	1,140.70	78.7
233	GOLF-BOYS	TOTAL	373.43	389.48	0.00	9,980.00	9,590.52	3.9
234	TENNIS-BOYS	TOTAL	0.00	82.20	0.00	12,540.00	12,457.80	.7
235	SLALOM/SKIING-BOYS	TOTAL	520.55	520.55	0.00	6,320.00	5,799.45	8.2
240	VOLLEYBALL-GIRLS	TOTAL	803.90	24,915.16	0.00	34,780.00	9,864.84	71.6
241	BASKETBALL-GIRLS	TOTAL	6,303.42	9,886.92	0.00	41,380.00	31,493.08	23.9
242	GYMNASTICS-GIRLS	TOTAL	2,724.62	2,724.94	0.00	16,980.00	14,217.06	16.2
243	CC-SKIING-GIRLS	TOTAL	717.66	717.66	0.00	5,380.00	4,662.34	13.3

FIGURE 15-1 A school district sport budget control document.

The computer can be especially valuable in the areas of budget and finance, personnel, program and scheduling, and facilities. In the area of budget and finance, the computer can be helpful in such management tasks as handling payrolls, inventories, budget control and allocation (Figure 15-1), cost analysis, purchasing, and general accounting. In the area of personnel, the computer can save much cler-

ical work and be of help in such areas as student registration, grade reporting and recording, faculty assignments, and staff retention. In the area of programming and scheduling, the computer can assist management in designing curricula and instructional strategies, as well as in scheduling students (e.g., demand analysis) or other clientele for particular classes or activities (Figure 15-2). It can record

FIGURE 15-2 Computer activity report used in health and fitness program at Tenneco Inc.; Houston, TX.

facts concerned with students' interests, faculty availability, complex scheduling, and staff use.[3]

To be more specific, physical educators and sport managers are interested in having complete demographic records on faculty and staff regarding names, addresses, phone numbers, teaching background, health status, and teaching loads. The computer is a tremendous asset in having such records filed and immediately accessible. Registration of students and class scheduling can be better accomplished. The computer can accurately report which gymnasiums, swimming pools, tennis courts, weight rooms, basketball courts, baseball fields, and other facilities are in use at any particular time. The computer can be used to keep physical fitness, health status, and accident reports on every student or member of an organization.

Instead of keeping individual cards on each person, the computer would generate a master file of physical fitness data for each person, compare the data to state and national norms and print out a "report card." The computer can keep attendance records, compare prices for equipment and supplies, and locate every book and periodical related to physical education and sport in the library.[4]

In the area of facilities the computer will be an asset for management in providing the best use of building space, availability of facilities, equipment inventory, cost of building maintenance and energy, and projected future needs of buildings and other facilities. This is crucial to long-range planning as well as efficient and effective facility usage.

Uses for the computer in sport programs include scheduling games and facilities, gathering data on players in a school or organization, and identifying their tendencies, weaknesses, and strengths. It can also keep individual statistics on every team member, as well as on the opponents.[1]

Other database uses of the computer in physical education and sport may include long-range scheduling, newsletter construction, travel arrangements and transportation schedules, news releases, fitness forms, grade or report cards, locker and lock assignments, media guides, injury reports, playbooks, ticket generation, eligibility lists, potential sponsors for fund raising, trend analysis, scoreboard graph-

ics, maintenance inventory, and a host of other applications that can reduce time and increase the efficiency and effectiveness of office and program operation.[1]

Without question office management and the profession of physical education and sport have been revolutionized by the computer. From desktop curricular guides to E-Mail, from computer-assisted instruction and simulation to MEEC's Sports XL Collection (e.g., Athletic Director, Club/League Organizer, Soccer), and from mass mailings to spellcheck, the computer has permeated contemporary society, including the arena of physical education and sport. The box on p. 404 provides samples of popular software programs, as well as a beginning computer software reference list.

The functions described are only some of the applications of the computer to physical education and sport. The challenge of the 1990s is to become computer literate and conversant in order to be able to function more effectively and to better contribute to society. Computer literacy is requisite for all students and should play an ongoing role in the professional development of all teachers, coaches, athletic directors, and sport managers.

MANAGEMENT ROUTINE[7]

The management routine or manner in which the day-to-day business of the organization, center, or department is carried out by the organization's office personnel represents the basic reason why such a facility exists. Although the computer has reduced labor intensity and time and has even omitted some office procedures, there are still offices and "management" in transition; therefore the following should continue to receive careful consideration and attention for maximal office efficiency and effectiveness.

Office Hours

The office should be open during regular hours. This usually means from 7:30 or 8 AM to 4:30 or 5 PM in most school and institutional settings. During this time someone should always be present to answer the telephone, greet visitors, field questions, and

◆ COMPUTER SOFTWARE

Popular programs and beginning software

Word processing: Retype (Apple), MultiScribe (Apple), Word (Macintosh), MacWrite II (Macintosh), WordPerfect (IBM), and PFS: First Choice (IBM).

Database: Retype (Apple), PFS: File (Apple), HyperCard (Macintosh), Microsoft Works (Macintosh, IBM), and dBASE (IBM).

Spreadsheets: Retype (Apple), Excel (Microsoft Works), and Lotus 1-2-3 (IBM).

Fitness Testing: Comp-Tech "Health Related Fitness," Cramer "Fit-N-Dex," Campbell Soup "Fitnessgram," AAHPERD's "Physical Best," Dauer/Pangrazi Fitness Assessment," "AAU," "Fit-America," and "Dino*Fit."

Desktop Publishing: MultiScribe (Apple) and PageMaker (IBM and Macintosh).

Graphics: MacPaint, MacDraw Pro (Apple).

Scheduling: MacProject II (Apple).

Partial reference list of computer software

Heartbeat 2020: A Vision of the Future. American Heart Association, Greater Los Angeles Affiliate, 3550 Wilshire Blvd., Los Angeles, CA 90010

Award Maker. Baudville, 1001 Medical Park Dr. SE, Grand Rapids, MI 49506

Sport Stats. Big G. Software, Rt. 2 Box 111, Alleyton, TX 78935

Print Shop. Broderbund Software, 17 Paul Drive, San Rafael, CA 94903

Athletic Department Packages. Paciolan, 2875 Temple Ave., Long Beach, CA 90806

Appleworks. Claris Corp., 5201 Patrick Henry Drive, Santa Clara, CA 95054

Health Clubs. Club Runner, 1 Devika Drive, Englewood, NJ 07631

Bike Series, Bowling Series, Cardiovascular Fitness Lab, Health-Related Physical Fitness, Heart and Exercise, Orienteering, Paddle Power, Physical Education Management System (PEMS), Physics of Sport, Sport Challenge Series, Up the Creek, Volleyball, Wilderness: A Survival Game. Comp Tech Systems Design, P.O. Box 516, Hastings, MN 55033

Fitness Clubs. Inter Visions Inc., 9001 Airport Blvd., Suite 209, Houston, TX 77061

Fit-N-Dex. Cramer Software Group, 153 W. Warren, Gardiner, KS 66030

Club/League Organization. MGCC, 1775 Old Hwy. 8, Suite 110, New Brighton, MN 55112

ComputerEyes. Digital Vision, 66 Eastern Avenue, Dedham, MA 02026

Campbell Soup Fitnessgram. Institute for Aerobics Research, 12330 Preston Rd., Dallas, TX 75230

Motor Skill Assessment Training Module. Luke Kelly and Associates, Curry School of Education, University of Virginia, Charlottesville, VA 22903

Puzzles and Posters: Sport Series. MECC, 3490 Lexington Avenue No., St. Paul, MN 55126

Crossword Magic. Mindscape, Inc., 3444 Dundee Road, Northbrook, IL 60062

Certificate Maker. Springboard Software, 7808 Creekridge Circle, Minneapolis, MN 55434

Physics of Sport. Videodiscovery, P.O. Box 85878, Seattle, WA 98109

Your local university or college bookstore.

---

carry out the regular functions of the office. Some exceptions to these hours may be made (e.g., flex time), but in all cases office hours should be posted and publicized as widely as possible.

Staff members should also post regular office hours concerning when they will be accessible, and these, too, should be on file in the central office. Office personnel should be kept informed, and office

hours carefully observed by staff. Alternative times should be supplied to the central office if for some circumstance (e.g., attendance at national meeting, professional growth seminar) office hours cannot be observed; the result will be that requests for information and assistance can be properly handled and staff members can be reached if necessary.

Assignments

All assignments for office personnel should be in writing with tasks clearly outlined and appropriately publicized. Office personnel may be required to turn on and check office machines; duplicate materials; prepare weekly bulletins; distribute and account for supplies; check, update, and prepare the calendar of events; recycle office materials; contact students; deliver mail; and assist in general office clean-up. These duties, among others, should be clearly understood and carried out at the proper time. Specific responsibilities should be fixed, appropriate work priorities established, and a schedule of duties prepared to prevent any misunderstanding. Any misunderstandings should be quickly and amicably resolved because respect, pride, cooperative spirit, and efficiency of the organization must be maintained.

Correspondence

Correspondence represents a most effective public relations medium. Letters and messages can be written and transmitted in a cold, impersonal manner, or they can carry warmth, respect, and courtesy and help interpret what a program reflects and is trying to accomplish for a student, staff, faculty, or other person or organization. Letters, memos, and mes-

Office professionalism and conduct are important for all personnel.

sages should be prepared carefully, using proper grammar and a format that meets the highest standards of secretarial practice. If a staff member must prepare his or her own letters, these same standards should be met. All correspondence should convey the feeling that the department is anxious to assist, support, and serve wherever possible. Letters and memos should be distributed promptly, and follow-up memos should be sent in a timely fashion. Copies of all important correspondence should be stored for future reference. Creative office personnel should also improve and refine appropriate office forms, as well as keep a word processing file of standard correspondence in order to reduce turn-around time.

Files and Filing

The office should contain steel filing cases that can be secured for vertical filing. The filing system employed depends on the number of personnel involved and the person doing the filing, but in any case it should be simple and functional and should be used for storing only the most current information. Other records, data, and information should when possible be stored on computer or microfiche. Files usually consist of correspondence and informational material. For ease of retrieving material, some form of alphabetical filing should be applied, although numerical filing may at times be practical. The alphabetical files utilize a name or subject designator (e.g., "Brown, Charles A." or "Medical Examinations") using a manila or hanging folder for all the material to be filed under the name or subject. Cross-references should be included to facilitate locating material. Guide cards can be used to show which divisions of the file pertain to each letter of the alphabet, thus facilitating the search for material.

Office files should be maintained accurately. The person filing should be careful to see that any letter or other material borrowed from a file is returned to the proper folder and that the folder is returned to its correct location. Filing should also be kept up to date. A periodic review of the files should be made to cull material that is no longer pertinent to the department. Files that for any reason are removed from the file cabinet should be signed out and signed in on return.

Telephone and Facsimile Machine

The use of the office telephone or fax machine is a major consideration for good departmental public relations. A few simple rules that should be observed follow.

Promptness. The telephone should be answered as promptly as possible. Answering promptly reflects efficient office practice and consideration for the person calling. Answering machines, voice mail, and phone rollover to the central office should be considered.

Professional purposes. The telephone is installed in an office for professional purposes. Office personnel should not be permitted to talk for long periods of time about personal matters. The telephone should be kept clear for business important to the achievement of organizational objectives.

Courtesy, friendliness, and helpfulness. The person answering the phone should be pleasant and courteous and should desire to be of assistance to the caller. This manner represents a professional responsibility that should be standard procedure at all times.

Messages. At times staff members who are being called will not be available. A memo pad should be kept at hand for recording day, time, name, and phone number of callers in such cases. A definite procedure should be established for relaying these messages (e.g., fax, telex) to the proper persons. Voice and electronic mail have become popular to assist in this procedure.

Appointments

Appointments should not be made unless it is believed they can be kept. Furthermore, all appointments should be kept as close to the time scheduled as possible. Many times the person making an appointment has arranged his or her day with the understanding that the conference will be at a certain time. If this time is not adhered to, it means the schedule has to be altered, and complications frequently arise as a result. The secretary should keep an accurate list of appointments. If no secretary is available, the staff member should keep his or her own schedule of appointments and check it regularly to see that it is met.

RECORDS AND REPORTS

At times, records and reports are not prepared and maintained accurately because the directions given by management or staff members are not clear and definite. When complicated reports are to be prepared, oral instructions alone will usually not be sufficient. Instead, directions (e.g., format, style, computer compatibility) should be written, typed, and distributed. The preparation of a sample method and preferred style will also help ensure better results.

Managers are often responsible for poorly kept records, inaccurate reports, and late submissions. Directions should be clear, with announcements at regular intervals, reminders of when reports are due, and a prompt checking of report status to see if they have been submitted or are "on-line." Any omissions or other inaccuracies concerning records and reports should be corrected immediately.

A survey was conducted of 21 school systems to determine the types of records that were kept in departmental files for physical education (Figure 15-3). The results of this survey showed that some of the schools were conscientious in record keeping and others were not.

The survey also revealed that in some schools records concerning health status, fitness level, and attendance were kept in the physical education department, whereas in others records were kept in the central office. The same was true regarding budgetary and inventory records. Some heads of departments kept these records, whereas in other schools the business manager and principal kept them.

Most department heads and teachers admitted they should put more time and effort into this phase of management. The result of the survey indicated that office management procedures are in a state of transition and contemporary management must lead the way to build effective, efficient functioning at this crucial management level (see the box on pp. 408-409).

SUMMARY

Office management is an important consideration in the management of physical education and sport

X denotes records kept	Accident	Adapted program	Application for participation in interscholastic sports	Attendance	Cumulative class record	Equipment	Extracurricular activities	Game reports	Health	Interscholastic sports	Intramurals	Inventory	Medical form for interscholastic sports	Medical form for physical education	Parental permission Sports participation	Physical fitness
School 1	×			×	×				×	×	×					×
School 2					×			×			×	×			×	×
School 3	×	×		×					×	×			×	×	×	×
School 4	×			×		×						×	×		×	×
School 5					×			×		×			×		×	×
School 6		×		×	×						×				×	×
School 7	×			×								×			×	×
School 8	×		×	×	×		×			×	×	×				×
School 9				×	×				×				×			
School 10	×			×							×			×	×	×
School 11	×	×	×	×						×	×	×			×	×
School 12				×		×				×	×	×				×
School 13	×			×		×					×	×			×	×
School 14		×		×			×	×		×	×					
School 15	×	×		×											×	×
School 16	×			×					×					×		
School 17			×		×	×			×			×			×	
School 18														×	×	×
School 19				×					×							×
School 20	×			×											×	×
School 21	×		×	×	×	×	×		×	×	×					×

FIGURE 15-3   Physical education records used in 21 school systems.

| ◈ CHECKLIST OF SOME IMPORTANT CONSIDERATIONS FOR OFFICE MANAGEMENT |

Space and working conditions   Yes   No

1. Does the reception room provide ample space for waiting guests?   ____   ____
2. Is the clerical space separated from the reception room so that office work is not   ____   ____
   interrupted by the arrival of guests?
3. Are there private offices for the director of physical education and athletics and as   ____   ____
   many staff members as possible?
4. Is there an up-to-date health suite that provides an office and other essential facil-   ____   ____
   ities for medical personnel?
5. Are there adequate space and equipment for filing?   ____   ____
6. Are file drawers arranged so that papers can be inserted and removed easily and   ____   ____
   with space for future expansion?
7. Is the office arranged so that as many workers as possible get the best natural light,   ____   ____
   with glare from sunlight or reflected sunlight avoided?
8. Has the office space been painted in accordance with the best color dynamics?   ____   ____
9. Have provisions been made so that unnecessary noise is eliminated, distractions are   ____   ____
   kept to a minimum, and cleanliness and a smoke-free environment prevail?
10. Are there good ventilation, appropriate artificial lighting, and satisfactory heating   ____   ____
    conditions?
11. Is the value of the computer fully integrated?   ____   ____

Personnel

12. Is a receptionist available to greet guests and answer queries?   ____   ____
13. Is there a recorded analysis of the duties of each secretarial position?   ____   ____
14. Are channels available for ascertaining causes of dissatisfaction among office per-   ____   ____
    sonnel?
15. Do secretaries dress neatly and conservatively?   ____   ____
16. Do secretaries maintain a desk that has an orderly appearance and clear their desks   ____   ____
    of working papers each day?
17. Do secretaries concern themselves with the efficiency of the office?   ____   ____
18. Are secretaries loyal to the department and staff members?   ____   ____
19. Do staff members have regular office hours?   ____   ____
20. Are appointments kept promptly?   ____   ____
21. Is up-to-date and appropriate reading material furnished for waiting guests?   ____   ____
22. Does the office help continually pay attention to maintaining offices that are neat,   ____   ____
    with papers, books, and other materials arranged in an orderly manner?
23. Are the secretaries knowledgeable about departmental activities so that they can   ____   ____
    answer intelligently queries about staff members and activities?
24. Do secretaries assist guests promptly and courteously?   ____   ____
25. Is work arranged neatly, free from errors, and presented appropriately?   ____   ____
26. Is correspondence handled promptly?   ____   ____
27. Is the filing system easily learned and is the filing done promptly so that the work   ____   ____
    does not pile up?
28. Does the office routine use human resources efficiently, eliminating duplicate oper-   ____   ____
    ations?
29. Are the most effective and efficient office methods used?   ____   ____

◆ **CHECKLIST OF SOME IMPORTANT CONSIDERATIONS FOR OFFICE MANAGEMENT—cont'd**

Procedures

30. Is the clerical output satifactory, with work starting promptly in the morning and after lunch, breaks taken according to schedule, and work stoppage taking place as scheduled?

31. Has a streamlined procedure been developed so that telephones are answered promptly, guests are treated courteously, and personal argument and gossiping are eliminated?

32. Are essential records properly maintained and kept up to date?

33. Have procedures for typing, word processing, and duplicating course outlines, committee reports, examinations, bulletins, fliers, letters, and announcements been developed to eliminate uncertainty or confusion on the part of staff members?

34. Are regular office hours for staff posted and known so that office staff members can make appointments as needed?

35. Are secretaries acquainted with such details as securing films and other visual aids, obtaining reference material, helping in registration, duplicating material, and obtaining additional forms and records?

36. Is the office staffed continuously during working hours?

programs. It concerns such matters as communication, correspondence, processing materials, record keeping, and public relations. It is the nerve center of the operation; therefore if the group, center, program, department, or other unit of the organization is to be efficiently run, much attention must be given to office management. Things such as space, personnel, human relations, equipment, computers, management routine, records, evaluations, and reports must receive continual and careful attention.

◆ **SELF-ASSESSMENT ACTIVITIES**

These activities will assist students in determining if material and competencies presented in this chapter have been mastered.

1. Why is sound office management essential to effective public relations?

2. What are some important reasons why office management is important to a department of intercollegiate athletics?

3. In what ways can the computer be used in physical education and sport programs?

4. As a manager of a large high school physical education program, describe the office personnel and equipment you would need and then justify your request.

5. Establish a set of rules for an effective management routine with respect to (a) office hours, (b) assignments, (c) correspondence, (d) files and filing, (e) telephone, and (f) appointments.

6. Prepare a set of sample records you would want to maintain as part of a junior high or middle school physical education program.

REFERENCES

1. Andrus S, Lane SA: Computerizing the athletic department, *College Athletic Management,* 1:30-34, Mar 1989.

2. Jensen MA: Computer applications: an introduction, *Journal of Physical Education, Recreation, and Dance,* 55:32, Apr 1984.

3. Minor RO: Computer technology can manage curriculum, link learning to instruction, *NASSP Bulletin* 73(521):75-79, 1989.

4. Mohnsen B: Using computers—helping physical education administrators, *Journal of Physical Education, Recreation, and Dance* 62:40-43, Jan 1991.

5. Sardinas JL: *Computing today: an introduction to business data processing,* Englewood Cliffs, NJ, 1981, Prentice-Hall.

6. Schaffer G: *Functional analysis of office requirements: a multiperspective approach,* NY, 1988, John Wiley and Sons.
7. Tedesco EH, Mitchell RB: *Administrative office management systems,* New York, 1987, John Wiley and Sons.

SUGGESTED READINGS

- Asbury G: Bringing your operations into the computer age, *Athletic Purchasing and Facilities* 7:20, Mar 1983.
  An assistant athletic director at a large university describes a computer-based system for managing facility operations and maintenance, and how it has helped turn a $1 million annual budget deficit into a surplus.
- Baun WB, Baun M: A corporate health and fitness program: motivation and management by computers, *Journal of Physical Education, Recreation, and Dance* 55:42, Apr 1984.
  Describes how Tenneco Inc. uses computers in its corporate fitness program to achieve departmental goals and objectives.
- Cicciarella CA: Getting into the computer game: guidelines and pitfalls, *Journal of Physical Education, Recreation, and Dance* 55:46, Apr 1984.
  Suggests procedural guidelines for selecting, acquiring, and installing computer hardware and software.
- Coventry WF, Burstiner I: *Management: a basic handbook,* Englewood Cliffs, NJ, 1977, Prentice-Hall.
  A book devoted to management procedures and function with many implications for office management.
- MECC/University of Minnesota: *Improving the use of technology in schools: what are we learning?* Research Bulletin #1, Minneapolis, Mn, 1988, Center for the Study of Educational Technology.
  Covers the impact of technology on education. Focuses on computer-based programs, desktop procedures, and pursuing quality instructional software.
- Tontimonia TL: Choosing a computer that fits your needs, *Athletic Business* 8:32, Oct 1984.
  Tells how to choose a computer that fits the needs of any particular organization or program.
- Turner JA: A personal computer for every freshman: even faculty skeptics are now enthusiasts, *Chronicle of Higher Education,* Feb 1985.
  Describes how some colleges and universities are providing students with computers and how they are being integrated throughout campus.

The Role of the Parent

Notice of an Educational Assessment/Reassessment Plan for Parent's Permission

Referral Review and Assessment Determination for Parent's Information

Notice of Special Education Services Presented to Parents for Their Consent

Parent's Rights Form

Individual Education Progress Plan

Educational Service Center
I.S.D. 279
11200 93rd Avenue North
Maple Grove, Minnesota 55369

**NOTICE OF AN EDUCATIONAL
ASSESSMENT/REASSESSMENT
PLAN**

Learner's Full Name: _____

ID: ☐☐☐☐–☐☐☐–☐☐–☐☐☐☐ Birthdate: ☐☐–☐☐–☐☐

Month / Day / Year: _____

School: _____ Grade: _____

Dear_____:

We are requesting your permission to assess your child's current educational functioning in order to determine your child's possible eligibility for special education services. The specific reasons and plans for assessment are on the next page.

☐ This notice is for an **Initial Assessment.** The district must receive your signed permission before we can begin.

☐ This notice is for a **Reassessment.** The school will begin the assessment unless you object in writing within 10 school days after receiving this request. If you sign and return this form right away, it will allow us to do the assessment without waiting.

The assessment will be conducted at _____
and is provided at no cost to you. The assessment procedures may include a review of school records, diagnostic teaching, observation of your child's activities, personal interviews, and consultation with you or others you recommend, along with individual testing as outlined. *(See next page)*

It is important to know your rights. Please read the enclosed **Parent Rights and Procedural Safeguards** brochure.

If you have questions, please contact me.

Sincerely,

Name	*Position*	*Telephone*

Address

PARENT RESPONSE

DIRECTIONS TO PARENT: Please **check** one of the options below, **sign** this form, and **return** the original of this page.

A. ☐ I give permission to the district to proceed as proposed.

B. ☐ I need further information. Please contact me to schedule a meeting to explain the reasons for the assessment.

C. ☐ I do not give permission for the district to proceed with the assessment as proposed. I understand that you will be contacting me to offer a conciliation conference where my concerns will be discussed. I also understand that I may choose not to participate in the conciliation conference and may proceed directly to a due process hearing.

X _____

| *Parent Signature (or Learner, if of legal age)* | *Daytime Telephone* | *Month, Day, Year* |

ED-01956-02

Educational Service Center I.S.D. 279 11200 93rd Avenue North Maple Grove, Minnesota 55369	**REFERRAL REVIEW AND ASSESSMENT DETERMINATION**

Learner's Full Name: _____

ID: ☐☐☐☐–☐☐☐–☐☐–☐☐☐☐ Birthdate: ☐☐–☐☐–☐☐

Month / Day / Year: _____

School: _____ Grade: _____

Person Referring: _____ Title: _____

A. Review of Referral

1. Briefly describe the reason for referral. *(You may attach district referral form.)*

2. Attach documentation of the two required interventions for learning and/or behavior problems, including their design and outcome. *(Interventions are not required for reassessment.)*

3. If the interventions have been waived, please check here ☐ and attach rationale.

4. Does the learner have limited proficiency in English? ☐ Yes ☐ No ☐ Previously received LEP services

B. Review of Learner's Performance

Review each of the following areas and determine if there is a need to assess.	Do we need to assess?
1. Intellectual Functioning	☐ Yes ☐ No
2. Academic Performance	☐ Yes ☐ No
3. Communicative Status	☐ Yes ☐ No
4. Motor Ability	☐ Yes ☐ No
5. Sensory Status	☐ Yes ☐ No
6. Health/Physical Status	☐ Yes ☐ No
7. Emotional and Social Development and Behavior Skills	☐ Yes ☐ No
8. Functional Skills	☐ Yes ☐ No
9. Vocational, Occupational Potential, and Transition	☐ Yes ☐ No

Comments:

C. Assessment Determination

As a result of our review, the team has decided that:

☐ 1. No special education assessment is necessary.

☐ 2. An Initial Assessment Plan is needed. (Complete Notice of an Educational Assessment/Reassessment Plan form.)

☐ 3. A Reassessment Plan is needed. (Complete Notice of an Educational Assessment/Reassessment Plan form.)

D. Persons Who Reviewed the Referral

_____   _____

_____   _____

_____   _____

SS 12

Educational Service Center I.S.D. 279 11200 93rd Avenue North Maple Grove, Minnesota 55369	**NOTICE OF** **SPECIAL EDUCATION SERVICES**

Learner's Full Name: _____

ID: ☐☐☐☐–☐☐☐–☐☐–☐☐☐☐   Birthdate: ☐☐–☐☐–☐☐

Month / Day / Year: _____

School: _____ Grade: _____

Dear _____.

This notice is required whether or not you attended the Individual Education Program (IEP) Team meeting on
_____ *(month/day/year)*.

The team recommends that:

1. ☐ your child begin to receive special education services. The school district will not proceed without your written consent. *(IEP attached)*

2. ☐ your child's special education placement or services be changed as noted in the IEP. The school district will proceed with this change unless you object in writing within 10 school days of receiving this notice. *(IEP attached)*

3. ☐ all current special education services be discontinued. The school district will proceed with this change unless you object in writing within 10 school days of receiving this notice. *(Supporting documentation attached)*

4. ☐ all special education services be discontinued. Your child is graduating from high school with a diploma. *(Supporting documentation attached)*

The reasons for the above recommendations, the basis upon which they are made, and all factors affecting this decision are in the attached documents.

Comments:

Please read the enclosed **PARENT RIGHTS AND PROCEDURAL SAFEGUARDS,** complete the "Parent Response" portion of this form, and return the original to me. Sincerely,

_____   _____   _____
Signature of IEP Manager   *Position*   *Telephone*

_____
Address

PARENT RESPONSE

DIRECTIONS TO PARENT: Please **check** one of the options below, **sign** this form, and **return** the original.

A. ☐ I give permission for the district to go ahead as proposed above.

B. ☐ I need further information. Please contact me to schedule a conference.

C. ☐ I do not give permission for the district to proceed with this recommendation for my child's special education services. I understand that you will be contacting me to offer a conciliation conference where my concerns will be discussed. I also understand that I may choose not to participate in the conciliation conference and may proceed directly to a due process hearing.

X _____   _____   _____
Parent Signature (or Learner, if of legal age)   *Daytime Telephone*   *Month, Day, Year*

Date Received by District	**COPIES:** Learner File Parent IEP Manager

ENCLOSED: **PARENT RIGHTS AND PROCEDURAL SAFEGUARDS**
IEP PLAN or SUPPORTING DOCUMENTATION

GRIMSBY COLLEGE

LIBRARY

NUNS CORNER, GRIMSBY

Educational Service Center
I.S.D. 279
11200 93rd Avenue North
Maple Grove, Minnesota 55369

Parent Rights

and

Procedural Safeguards

*presented to protect
the rights of you and your child*

DISTRICT 279

DEDICATED
TO LEARNING
FOR ALL

Dear Parent:

This pamphlet is designed to explain your rights when planning for your child's education. As a partner in making educational decisions for your child, it is important that you read and understand your rights. The information in this pamphlet is taken from federal and state laws, rules, and regulations. Some of the items may not relate directly to you because they are intended to cover a number of actions.

You may contact "Parents Advocacy Coalition for Educational Rights," (PACER) for consultation.

PACER Center, Inc.	(612) 827-2966
4826 Chicago Avenue So.	(TTY & Voice)
Minneapolis, MN 55417-1055	(800) 537-2237

Also, the following are low-cost legal services:

Legal Advocacy for Persons	(612) 332-1441
with Developmental Disabilities	(800) 292-4150
or **Client Assistance Project**	TTY: ⇃
or **Mental Health Law Project**	(612) 332-4668
222 Grain Exchange Building	
323 Fourth Avenue South	
Minneapolis, MN 55415	

Legal Advocate for the Blind	(612) 339-1431
NorthStar East Center	
608 2nd Ave. So., Suite 380	
Minneapolis, MN 55402	

Other resources:

Minnesota Dept. of Education	(612) 297-2843
Office of Monitoring & Compliance	
Administrative Review & Complaint Specialist	
550 Cedar Street	
Capitol Square Building	
St. Paul, MN 55101	

We are committed to serving all children with handicapping conditions who live in the district. If you have questions or concerns, please call. Your interest and communication are appreciated.

Be Informed of Your Rights

1. You have the right to review and receive copies of all records or other written information regarding your child which are in the school's possession.

2. You have the right to participate as a team member in developing and determining your child's educational program, including special education services, and/or to provide information relative to his or her assessment and the development of the program plan. *A convenient time to meet will be set with you and you will be informed of the procedures for planning your child's program.*

3. You have a right to have an interpreter present if you do not speak or understand English well, are hearing impaired or use some other mode of communication. You may also invite an advocate.

4. You have the right, prior to the meeting and upon request, to receive interpretations of assessment or reassessment procedures, instruments and data or results, and of the program plan from a knowledgeable school employee. You also have the right for this meeting to be held in private. *The specific procedures and time for this meeting will be explained following your request.*

5. You have the right to have included, on the team that interprets the assessment data and/or develops the individual education program (IEP) plan, a person who is a member of the same minority or cultural background or who is knowledgeable concerning the racial, cultural, or handicapping differences of your child. *The specific procedures and time for this team meeting will be explained following your request.*

6. You have the right to obtain an independent assessment at your own expense. You also have the right to request information from the district about where an independent assessment may be obtained. You may obtain an independent assessment at public expense if you disagree with an assessment obtained by the district. However, a district

may initiate a due process hearing to show that its assessment is appropriate after the offer of at least one conciliation conference. If you refuse the offer of conciliation or if the matter is not resolved in conciliation, the district shall initiate a due process hearing to show that its assessment is appropriate. If the hearing officer's final decision is that the district's assessment is appropriate, you still have the right to an independent assessment, but not at public expense. *Whenever an independent evaluation is at public expense, the criteria under which the evaluation is obtained, including the location of the evaluation and the qualifications of the examiner, must be the same as the criteria which the district uses when it initiates an evaluation.*

7. You have the right to know that the district will not proceed with its proposed initial formal assessment or proposed initial placement without your prior written consent. "Initial" means the first time the district has proposed to assess your child or place your child in any special education program in this district. *If you do not respond to the initial assessment or placement, a conciliation conference will be offered by the school. If this is not the first assessment or first placement by the district, the district will proceed with the proposal within ten school days of your receipt of the notice unless you object in writing.*

8. You have the right to discuss placement and service options which are available for your child.

9. You have the right to know that your consent for assessment or placement is voluntary and that you may revoke it at any time. If you do revoke your consent, however, the district may not agree, in which case the due process procedures on the reverse side of this sheet would be followed.

If you disagree with the school proposal, see other side.

Note to Non-Custodial Parent:
Please contact your child's school for information regarding your rights.

Procedural Safeguards Available to Parent

If you disagree with what the school is proposing, please be informed that:

- You have the right to object to the district's proposed action (assessment or placement) in writing. If you object, you will be requested to attend a conciliation conference which will be held at a mutually agreeable time and place. If this is an initial assessment or placement and you do not respond to the notice, a conciliation conference will be offered to you by the district.

- You have a right to proceed directly to an impartial due process hearing and bypass the conciliation conference. Even if you do attend a conciliation conference, if you do not agree with action proposed by the school you always have a right to a due process hearing.

- You have the right to be represented by counsel or another person of your choosing at the conciliation conference or the impartial due process hearing.

- You have the right to be assured that, unless you and the district agree otherwise, your child will not be denied initial admssion to school and your child's educational program will not be changed as long as you object in writing to the proposed action.

- You have the right to be represented in preparation for, and at, the hearing by legal counsel or other representatives of your choice.

- You have the right, in accordance with laws relating to confidentiality, to examine and receive copies of your child's school records before the hearing, including tests, assessments, reports, or other information concerning the educational assessment or reassessment upon which the proposed action may be based.

- You have the right to call your own witnesses and to present evidence, including expert medical, psychological, and educational testimony and relevant records, tests, assessments, reports or other information.

- You have the right to request the attendance of any official or employee of the providing or resident school district or any other person who may have evidence relating to the proposed action and you have the right to be informed of the manner and time in which to do so.

- You have the right to present evidence and cross-examine any employee of the school district(s) or other persons who present evidence at the hearing.

- You have the right to have your child, who is the subject of the hearing, present at the hearing.

- You have the right to a closed hearing unless you want to request an open hearing.

- You have a right to obtain a record of the hearing, including the written findings of fact and decisions, whether or not you appeal.

- You have the right to be informed that, if a due process hearing is held and your position is upheld, you may be awarded attorney's fees and costs.

- You have the right to be informed of any free or low cost legal service.

- Each form you receive from the district proposing action will have a place for your response. The form will also identify the district employee to whom it should be returned and to whom questions may be directed.

SE-90-PRPS

Educational Service Center I.S.D. 279 11200 93rd Avenue North Maple Grove, Minnesota 55369	**INDIVIDUAL EDUCATION PROGRAM (IEP) PLAN**

A.   LEARNER INFORMATION

Learner Name (Last, First, M.I.)			Birthdate
Doe, Lisa			2/15/80

Current Address (Street, City, State, Zip)	Learner's Primary Language	Sex	Grade
301 Maple Lane Maple Grove, MN 55069	English	M F **X**	4

ID# 5 5 4 4 - 2 3 3 - 1 2 - 3 7 8 9

School of Enrollment	School Telephone Number	District No.
Crest View	(612) 555-4230	#279

Learner's Permanent Residence Address (If Different Than Above) — District No.

B.   PARENT/GUARDIAN INFORMATION

Name(s) of Parent(s)	Home Telephone Number	Other Telephone Number
Glenn and Carol Doe	(612) 555-4230	( )

Address (If other than Learner's Permanent Residence Address) — District No.

Guardian(s)/Surrogate Parent(s) Name(s)	☐ Guardian(s) ☐ Surrogate Parent(s)

Address (if other than Learner's Permanent Address)	Home Telephone No.	Other Telephone No.	District No.
	( )	( )	

C.   IEP INFORMATION

Federal Child Count Information

3 Learning Disabilities

IEP Manager Name	Telephone Number	Date IEP Written
Leslie Childs	(612) 555-3629	1/3/92

IEP Type	Date of Last Comprehensive Assessment	Periodic Review Date
☐ Initial ☒ Annual ☐ Interim	12/18/91	Month 6 / Year 92

D.   IEP PLANNING MEETING

Date of Planning Meeting 1/5/92	**List Names of All Team Members**	**Indicate Attendance**
Parent	Glenn Doe	☒ Yes ☐ No
Parent	Carol Doe	☒ Yes ☐ No
Administrator/Designee	Dan James	☒ Yes ☐ No
Special Education Teacher	Leslie Childs	☒ Yes ☐ No
Regular Education Teacher	Judy Black	☒ Yes ☐ No
Speech/Lang. Teacher	Renee Green	☒ Yes ☐ No
Adap. PE Teacher	Mary Brown	☒ Yes ☐ No
Occup. Therapist	Kris Smith	☒ Yes ☐ No
		☐ Yes ☐ No
		☐ Yes ☐ No
		☐ Yes ☐ No
		☐ Yes ☐ No

Date _____ 1/3/92 _____   Learner's Name: _____ Lisa Doe _____

E.

PRESENT LEVELS OF PERFORMANCE AND SPECIAL EDUCATION NEEDS

Carefully consider and document data from all sources in the following areas: (Include information and observation provided by parent(s).)

1. Intellectual Functioning
2. Academic Performance
3. Communicative Status
4. Motor Ability
5. Sensory Status
6. Health/Physical Status
7. Emotional and Social Development and Behavior Skills
8. Functional Skills

* 9. Vocational, Occupational Potential, and Secondary Transition
   A. Jobs and Job Training
   B. Recreation and Leisure
   C. Home Living
   D. Community Participation
   E. Post-Secondary Training and Learning Opportunities

* Area Number 9 must be summarized for all learners who have reached the 9th grade or age 14 and younger learners for whom the team determines it is applicable.

Present Levels of Performance	**Special Education Needs**

In years when an initial assessment or reassessment is conducted, attach the Assessment Team Summary Report for performance level information.

1. Intellectual Functioning
   Lisa scored in the low average range on the WISC-R and Columbia Mental Maturity Scale. (12-6-91)

2. Academic Performance
   Lisa's reading skills are approximately 2 years delayed; math skills are approximately 1 year delayed; spelling and written language approximately 2 years delayed. Other content area courses (i.e. science, health, and social studies) are modified for her. (12-18-91)

    2. Academic Performance
      a. Lisa needs to improve her decoding and comprehension reading skills.
      b. Lisa needs to improve her math computation and problem solving skills.
      c. Lisa needs to improve her written language and spelling skills.

3. Communicative Status
   Lisa scored in the moderately low range for vocabulary and concept understanding and usage. Her expressive language has made great gains. Her articulation has made continued growth. (11-16-91)

    3. Communicative Status
      a. Lisa needs to improve her articulation skills.
      b. Lisa needs to improve her vocabulary and concept usage and understanding.

4. Motor Ability
   Lisa has difficulty in the areas of balance, bilateral coordination, muscular strength, and endurance. (11-20-91)

    4. Motor Ability
      a. Lisa needs to improve her physical fitness level in the areas of muscular strength and endurance.
      b. Lisa needs to improve gross motor areas of balance, motor planing, coordination, and mainstream curriculum skills.

5. Sensory Status
   Lisa's visual perception skills in the areas of form and space perception, sequencing, and visual memory are low. Her auditory memory is in the low average range. (12-3-91)

    5. Sensory Status
      a. Lisa needs to improve visual perceptual skills in the areas of form and space perception, sequencing, and visual memory.

6. Health/Physical Status
   Lisa has been diagnosed as having Attention Deficit Hyperactivity Disorder without hyperactivity or impulsiveness and is not receiving medication. (11-12-91)

7. Emotional and Social Development and Behavior Skills (11-6-91).
   Lisa is a well-adjusted child without social or emotional deficits.

Page 2 of IEP
Date _____ 1/3/92 _____   Learner's Name: _____ Lisa Doe _____

| E. | PRESENT LEVELS OF PERFORMANCE AND SPECIAL EDUCATION NEEDS |

Carefully consider and document data from all sources in the following areas: (Include information and observation provided by parent(s).)

1. Intellectual Functioning
2. Academic Performance
3. Communicative Status
4. Motor Ability
5. Sensory Status
6. Health/Physical Status
7. Emotional And Social Development and Behavior Skills
8. Functional Skills

* 9. Vocational, Occupational Potential, and Secondary Transition
    A. Jobs and Job Training
    B. Recreation and Leisure
    C. Home Living
    D. Community Participation
    E. Post-Secondary Training and Learning Opportunities

* Area Number 9 must be summarized for all learners who have reached the 9th grade or age 14 and younger learners for whom the team
  determines it is applicable.

Present Levels of Performance	**Special Education Needs**

**In years when an initial assessment or reassessment is
conducted, attach the Assessment Team Summary Report for
performance level information.**

8. Functional Skills
   Lisa's functional skills are age
   appropriate.   (11-19-91)

9. Vocational, Occupational Potential,
   and Secondary Transition

   This area will be addressed when l
   turns 14 years old or when she ente
   the 9th grade.

Date _____1/3/92_____   Learner's Name: _____Lisa Doe_____

F.

ANNUAL GOALS, SHORT-TERM INSTRUCTIONAL OBJECTIVES

Use one **PAGE 3** for each goal. Thoroughly state the goal. List objectives for the goal, including attainment criteria for each objective.	GOAL #__7__ OF __8__ GOALS

GOAL:
Lisa will improve her physical fitness level in the areas of muscular strength and endurance.

Short-Term Instructional Objectives

1. Given activities to improve abdominal strength and endurance, Lisa will perform 30 correct curl-ups in 60 seconds.

2. Given activities to improve upper body strength and endurance, Lisa will perform 12 mature push-ups in 30 seconds.

3. Given activities to improve cardiovascular endurance, Lisa will run/walk 1 mile at the 15% level for her age-group norms.

G.

IEP PERIODIC REVIEW

Date Reviewed:__6-4-92__   Progress made toward this goal and objectives:

The learner's IEP:

[X] Meets learner's current needs and will be continued without changes.

[ ] Does not meet learner's current needs and the modifications (not significant) **listed below** will be made without an IEP meeting unless you contact us.

[ ] Does not meet learner's current needs and the **significant changes listed below** require a revised IEP. We will be in contact soon to schedule a meeting.

NOTE TO PARENT(S): You are entitled to request a meeting to discuss the results of this review.

Page 4 of IEP

ED-01878-02

Learner's Name:_____ Lisa Doe

H. ADAPTATION OF REGULAR AND SPECIAL EDUCATION

Describe changes in regular and special education that will be made to permit successful accommodation and education of this learner: e.g., grading, credits, staff, transportation, facilities, materials, equipment, technology, adaptive devices, curriculum, methods, and other services.

```
Transportation - small bus
Classroom - Self-Contained
Curriculum methods/grading - modified
```

Describe use of regulated behavioral interventions. *Attach more information, if necessary.*

```
Not applicable for Lisa at this time.
```

Describe any regular education secondary graduation standards modified for this learner.

```
This will be addressed when Lisa enters 9th grade.
```

I. SPECIAL EDUCATION AND RELATED SERVICES

* SERVICE(S)	MIN./WEEK Indirect	MIN./WEEK Direct	STARTING DATE	SERVICE PROVIDER AND TELEPHONE		BUILDING NAME AND ROOM (If another school district, provide district name)
SCLD		900	1/5/92	Leslie Childs	555-3629	Crest View 9
Speech		90	1/5/92	Renee Green	555-3629	Crest View 15
OT		60	1/5/92	Kris Smith	555-3629	Crest View 12
APE		60	1/5/92	Mary Brown	555-3629	Crest View 8

* The duration of these services may not exceed 1 year from the date of this IEP. This IEP is in effect for:
[X] a normal school year.
[ ] an extended school year. Explain:
[ ] less than a normal school year. Explain:

Learner's Name:_____ Lisa Doe _____   ED-01878-02

J.

LEAST RESTRICTIVE ENVIRONMENT (LRE)

Check all sites and settings in which special education and related services will be provided:

SITE
- [X] School building learner would attend if did not have handicapping condition(s)
- [ ] Alternative regular school within the district
- [ ] Alternative regular school outside of the district
- [ ] Alternative special school within the district
- [ ] Alternative special school outside of the district
- [ ] Home-based/Homebound
- [ ] Community-based site other than a school or home
- [ ] Residential school
- [ ] Hospital or treatment center
- [ ] Other _____

> **NOTE:** Please use this setting and site information to determine the federal child count placement category for all learners, birth through age 21, and enter in Part C. on front page of IEP Plan.

SETTING

[X] Regular education	840	min./week
[X] Special education	1110	min./week
[ ] Integrated community		min./week
[ ] Other _____		min./week

Explain why options selected above are the most appropriate and the least restrictive.

Due to Lisa's academic deficits, she requires structured, small group instruction so that she may experience academic gain.

Describe any other options considered, and provide reasons those options were rejected.

LENGTH OF DAY   [ ] Check here if the learner's school day is shorter or longer than peers without handicapping conditions. *If checked, Commissioner of Education approval is required.*

K.

DESCRIPTION OF ACTIVITIES WITH LEARNERS WITHOUT HANDICAPPING CONDITIONS

For a learner who is served more than half-time in a special education setting, include any activities in which the learner will be participating with learners who do not have handicapping conditions (e.g., lunch, assembly periods, club activities, field trips, and other special events).

Lisa interacts with her mainstream peers in science, health, art, physical education, music, media, and social studies. She also participates in other special activities as they are appropriate.

NOTE: **Attach Notice of Special Education Services form when needed.**

Approaches to Crowd Control

The Sixth National Conference of City and County Directors of AAHPERD spent considerable time on the subject of crowd control at sport contests. A summary of their discussions follows.

APPROACHES TO CROWD CONTROL: SUMMARY OF REPORTS FROM SMALL GROUP DISCUSSIONS

The nature and seriousness of the problems in crowd control have recently become more drastic and bizarre as they have occurred with increasing frequency. They take on the collective character of a deliberate attempt to either ignore or confront the system. This social problem may be impossible to eliminate completely, but an attempt must be made to cope with the immediate symptoms. Our only hope is for imaginative and coordinated efforts by the school and sport management, the majority of students, and community authorities to promote standards of conduct conducive to continuing spectator sports in comparative tranquility. The alternatives are to allow a disruptive element to completely negate the nature of school sport, to play with no spectators, or to abandon the activity.

The following will present some causes of crowd control problems and some approaches to solutions.

Some Causes of Problems

- Lack of anticipation of, and preventive planning for, possible trouble
- Lack of proper facilities
- Poor communication resulting in lack of information
- Lack of involvement of one or more of the following: school administration, faculty, student body, parents, community, press, and law enforcement agencies
- Lack of respect for authority and property
- Attendance at games of youth under the influence of illegal substances
- Increased attitude of permissiveness
- School dropouts, recent graduates, and outsiders

Some Approaches to Solutions

Develop written policy statements, guidelines, and regulations for crowd control
1. Consult the following before writing policy statements or promulgating regulations: school administration, athletic director, coaches, faculty members involved in the school sports program, school youth organizations, local police departments and community leaders

2. Properly and efficiently administer regulations and provide for good communications
3. Constantly evaluate regulations and guidelines for their relevance and effectiveness
4. Make guidelines and regulations so effective that the director of athletics who follows them is secure in knowing he or she has planned with the staff for any eventuality and has sufficient help to cope with any situation that may arise

Provide adequate facilities
1. Plan and design stadiums, fieldhouses, and gymnasiums for effective crowd control
2. Provide for adequate rest room facilities
3. Establish a no smoking and drug-free school and promote these during contests
4. Provide for complete preparation of facilities before game time

Teach good sportspersonship throughout the school and the community
1. Begin education in good sportspersonship in the earliest grades and continue it throughout the school life
2. Make frequent approving references to constructive and commendable behavior
3. Arrange for program appearances by faculty members and students jointly to discuss the true values of sport competition including good sportspersonship
4. Make use of all news media through frequent and effective television, radio, and press presentations and interviews, commentaries, and frequent announcement of good sportspersonship slogans and awards
5. Distribute a printed Code of Ethics for Good Sportspersonship
6. Include the good sportspersonship slogan in all printed programs at sports events
7. Urge the use of sports events as an example in elementary school citizenship classes, stressing positive values of good conduct at games, during the raising of the flag, and singing of the national anthem; also emphasize courtesy toward visitors
8. Involve teachers in school athletic associations, provide them with passes to all sports events, and stress the positive values of their setting an example of good sportspersonship

Intensify communications before scheduled games
1. Arrange for an exchange of speakers at school assembly programs; the principals, coaches, or team captains could visit the opposing school
2. Discuss with appropriate personnel of the competing school the procedures for the game, including method and location of team entry and departure
3. Provide superintendent or principal, athletic director, and coach with a copy of the written policy statement, guidelines, and regulations
4. Meet all game officials and request them to stress good sportspersonship before, during, and after all contests
5. Meet with coaches and instruct them not to question officials during a contest; stress the importance of good sportspersonship and that their conduct sets the tone for spectator reaction to game incidents
6. Instruct students about what to expect and what is expected of them
7. Schedule preventive planning conferences with local police to be assured of their full cooperation and effectiveness in spectator control

Inform the community
1. Request coaches and athletic directors to talk to service groups and other community groups
2. Invite community leaders (nonschool people) to attend sports events on a regular basis
3. Post on all available notice boards around town, in businesses, factories, and other public places, posters showing the Sportspersonship Code of Ethics and Guidelines in brief
4. Release constructive information and positive statements to news media and request publication of brief guidelines on sports pages
5. Provide news media with pertinent information as to ways in which the community may directly and indirectly render assistance in the crowd control problem

Involve law enforcement personnel
1. Police and other security personnel should be strategically located so as to afford the best possible control
2. Law enforcement professionals should handle *all* enforcement and disciplining of spectators

3. Strength in force may be shown by appearance of several police officers, motorcycles, police cars, etc., at and near the site of the game
4. Police may be stationed in rest rooms
5. Civil Defense organizations could patrol parking areas
6. A faculty member from the visiting school may be used as a liaison with police and local faculty in identifying visiting students
7. Attendants, police, county sheriffs, and deputies should be in uniform. Uniformed authority figures command greater respect

Use supervisory personnel other than police
1. Carefully select teacher supervisors who are attentive and alert to signs of possible trouble
2. Identify faculty members by arm bands, T-shirts, or other means
3. Provide for communication by means of walkie-talkie systems
4. Assign some faculty members to sit behind the visiting fans; this reduces verbal harassment of visitors
5. Employ paid ticket takers and paid chaperones to mingle strategically among the crowd and to remain on duty throughout the game, including half-time
6. Issue passes to elementary and junior high physical education teachers and coaches to provide more adult supervision

Plan for ticket sales and concession stands
1. Arrange for advance sale of student tickets to avoid congestion at the gate
2. Sell tickets in advance only to students in their own schools, and avoid sale of tickets to outsiders and nonstudents
3. Provide for a close check at the gate or entrance
4. Arrange for concession stands to be open before the game, during half-time, and after the game
5. Channel the flow of traffic to and from concession stands using ropes or other means; keep traffic moving and away from the playing area

Prepare spectators and contestants
1. Encourage as many students as possible to be in the uniforms of the athletic club, pep club, booster clubs, band, majorettes, cheerleaders

2. Bus participants to and from the game site
3. Have participants dressed to play before leaving for a game or contest
4. Adhere to established seating capacity of stadiums and gymnasiums
5. Request home team fans to remain in their own stands until visiting team fans have left
6. Try to arrange for a statewide athletic association regulation prohibiting all noise makers including musical instruments except for the school band or orchestra under professional supervision
7. Request the assistance of visiting clubs
8. Educate cheerleaders, student leaders, band captains, pep squads, and faculty supervisors by means of a 1-day conference program
9. Keep spectators buffered from the playing area as much as practical
10. Request that elementary school children be accompanied by an adult

Miscellaneous
1. Inform and involve school superintendents when problems arise in connection with sports events
2. Impose appropriate penalties on faculty, coaches, and students guilty of poor conduct
3. Publish the identity of offenders at games and notify parents if possible; any penalties inflicted should also be noted (Note: If the offense leads to juvenile court action, care should be taken not to contravene laws about publishing names of juvenile offenders)
4. Consistently enforce rules and regulations; this is a necessity
5. Work toward the assumption of responsibility for strong regulation and enforcement of team behavior on the part of the state athletic associations
6. Attempt to work with the courts toward greater cooperation
7. Avoid overstressing the winning of games
8. Discontinue double and triple headers
9. After-game incidents away from the proximity of the stadium or gymnasium are out of the control of school officials, but they do cause bad public relations

Summary

Safety and crowd controls at school sport functions are imperative! Greater concentration on treating the causes of the problem is essential. Preliminary groundwork is the key to good crowd control. Coordination and cooperation of school, community, and law enforcement agencies are keys to success.

Youths should be taught to know what to expect and what is expected of them. Consistent enforcement of rules and regulations is a necessity if youth are to respect authority. Adult behavior should be such that it may be advantageously and admirably emulated by youth whose actions may result in deserving praise instead of negative criticism and disapproval.

The sport program is a constructive and valuable school activity. It should be permitted to function in a favorable, healthful, and friendly environment.

Drugs and Alcohol

Intercollegiate Drug and Alcohol Program

High School Pledge of Honor

Junior High School Rules Concerning Mood-Altering Chemicals

U OF M INTERCOLLEGIATE ATHLETIC DRUG AND ALCOHOL EDUCATION, TESTING, AND REHABILITATION PROGRAM

Illicit drug use and alcohol abuse are major problems in America today, and they are present on all college and university campuses. Student-athletes are as prone to the ills of drug use and alcohol abuse as anybody else and the Department of Men's and Women's Intercollegiate Athletics believe it is their responsibility to do everything possible to protect the health and welfare of the student-athletes and to eradicate the problem. Drug testing is appropriate to help ensure the safety of student-athletes while they participate in athletic contests. In addition, a program to prevent the use of performance-enhancing drugs promotes fair competition in intercollegiate athletics. The NCAA has established a drug testing program for participants in national championship events. The University of Minnesota program serves the same purposes for in-season competition. It is reasonable for the University to require a student to submit to drug testing as a condition of the privilege of participating in intercollegiate athletics. Toward that end, the Men's and Women's Athletic Departments have formulated a comprehensive drug and alcohol program that focuses on Education, Testing, and Rehabilitation.

PURPOSES OF THE INTERCOLLEGIATE ATHLETIC DRUG PROGRAM

1. To adhere to NCAA, Big Ten, and University of Minnesota rules and procedures regarding licit or illicit drug use by student-athletes.
2. To disseminate information and educate student-athletes about problems associated with drug and alcohol abuse.
3. To identify student-athletes who are using illicit drugs or abusing alcohol or other illicit drugs and provide avenues for remediation.
4. To assure all athletes, parents, and University officials that the University of Minnesota Men's and Women's Intercollegiate Athletic Departments are committed to providing a drug-free environment for the conduct of all athletic programs.

DRUG EDUCATION

At least once each academic quarter a Chemical Dependency Consultant, physician, and/or Head Coach will meet with all departments to discuss drug and alcohol use and to review the University of Minnesota Intercollegiate Athletic Drug Program, including all policies and procedures. Behavioral responsibilities and disciplinary expectations will also be fully discussed at that time.

NOTE: All freshman student-athletes will meet as a group in the fall with a drug counselor and Head Coaches to discuss in detail the University of Minneosta Intercollegiate Athletic Drug and Alcohol Program.

In addition, a resource pool of educational materials, films, videos, and speakers will be made available for use by the coaches and student-athletes at any time throughout the year.

Each fall, a copy of the drug and alcohol program will be mailed to the parents or legal guardians of each newly entering student-athlete. Parents or guardians will be encouraged to contact the athletic department regarding any questions they might have.

Finally, each student-athlete will be asked to sign and return to the Head Trainer a "Consent to Participate" form relative to the Athletic Drug Testing Program.

VOLUNTARY PARTICIPATION

Any athlete who feels that he/she has a problem with alcohol or other drugs, and who has not had a previous positive test, may request assistance through the Trainer, Team Physician, Chemical Dependency Consultant, or other staff member. Such a request *shall not* be treated as a positive test, and the athlete shall be treated/counseled in a manner appropriate to his/her problem. Any positive test (or equivalent) occurring after such voluntary participation shall be treated as a first positive test.

ATHLETES' RESPONSIBILITY

As a member of any University of Minnesota Athletic Department team participating in any events or activities authorized by the department, you are required to provide proof of compliance with the U of M Drug and Alcohol Education, Testing, and Rehabilitation Programs. It is your responsibility to present a urine specimen free from banned substances or evidence of inappropriate use of alcohol or illicit medications. Any urine sample testing positive will be considered valid and that of an active user.

Selection of the athlete or team for testing will be determined by the Athletic Director of the University of Minnesota Men's/Women's Intercollegiate Athletic Department or their designate. In NCAA Big 10 post-season competition and championship or bowl games, each athlete/team selected to represent the University of Minnesota will undergo testing. If an athlete's test is positive for a banned substance the athlete will be disqualified and another athlete may replace him/her. The athlete's replacement must likewise be tested. If tests are conducted more than 30 days prior to the game, those athletes/teams are subject to re-testing closer to the time of the games. Athletes/teams with a previous positive test will also be tested.

Athletes participating in NCAA, WCHA, etc. are subject to further testing by those organizations. Tests will be conducted on the top three athletes/teams and three other athletes/teams at random. Both the University of Minnesota and the NCAA will honor State and Federal confidentiality laws.

ALCOHOL AND PRESCRIPTION (LICIT) MEDICATION

The University recognizes that alcohol and prescription medications are two of the most commonly used and abused drugs in our society. For this reason any use of alcohol that results in harmful consequences (i.e. assault, theft, public intoxication, property destruction, underage drinking, and others) to the athlete or others, shall be treated as a positive drug test and dealt with according to the conditions of this drug program. *Athletes are reminded that the legal age for consumption of alcohol in the State of Minnesota is 21.*

DRUG COUNSELING STAFF

The drug counseling staff shall consist of:
   Team Physician
   Chemical Dependency Consultant
   Associate Director or Designate
   Head Coach
   Sports Medicine Coordinator/Director of Student Services
The Team Physician and the Chemical Dependency Consultant shall be the overall coordinators for the counseling staff. Physicians and counselors who are responsible for direct patient care shall be qualified in their respective fields in accordance with community standards and regulations. All members of the counseling staff are expected to have training in the field of alcohol and other drug use/abuse appropriate to their job description.

SCREENING FOR ILLICIT DRUG USE

As part of the fall physical examination and at subsequent unannounced dates throughout the academic year, student-athletes may be asked to give urine samples as part of the drug testing program. *Refusal to provide a urine specimen will be considered as a positive test.*

Each athlete should expect to be tested at least once a year for selected drugs including, but not limited to:

alcohol	heroin
amphetamines	LSD
anabolic steroids	marijuana
barbiturates	PCP
cocaine	quaaludes
diuretics	

Use of any of the above drugs by a student-athlete at the University of Minnesota is prohibited, except as may be prescribed by a licensed physician to treat specific medical conditions. Athletes should declare all medications routinely taken, prescription or nonprescription, to their team trainer prior to their season's beginning.

TESTING PROCEDURES

All urine samples for testing will be collected under direct observation to eliminate substitutions. Procedures will be designed to preserve the integrity, accuracy, and confidentiality of the testing process.

Containers, samples, and identification sheets will remain under constant supervision of the Athletic Training Staff members or Team Physician until they are delivered to the Hennepin County Toxicology Laboratory or other appropriate facility for testing.

Upon completion of testing, the Director of the Laboratory will submit a written report of test results to the Team Physician and Athletic Director, who in turn will notify the respective Head Coach of each sport and Sports Medicine Coordinator/Director of Student Services. Summary statistical reports will also be submitted to the Central Officer responsible for intercollegiate athletics.

POLICY REGARDING POSITIVE TESTS

All positive results will be re-tested from a reserve sample for verification. If the positive test is verified, the Head Coach or Team Physician will notify the athlete of the results and explain the procedure to be followed.

1. First Positive Test

The Sports Medicine Coordinator/Director of Student Services will arrange an appointment with the Team Physician or Drug Counselor for the purposes of evaluation, education, and if necessary, treatment or counseling. The evaluation will include a diagnosis using standard diagnostic instruments, history, and if necessary, physical examination. Information from other sources will be solicited for the purposes of the evaluation. These sources include, but are not limited to, coaches, academic advisors, trainers, dormitory personnel, other athletes, and members of the athletic department staff. Such information shall be used for the purposes of obtaining the clearest view possible of the athlete's clinical picture. Upon completion of the interview, a diagnosis will be formulated, which will characterize the athlete in one of five general categories with respect to alcohol/drug use. These categories include experimental use, social use, chemical abuse, chemical dependency, and an indeterminate category. In the case of the chemical abuse and dependency categories, diagnosis shall be made in accordance with the Diagnostic and Statistical Manual (current edition) or the criteria of the National Council on Alcoholism.

In some cases disposition may include simple education and limit-setting techniques. In the case of chemical dependency, structured treatment will be a prerequisite to the athlete's continued participation in athletics. When problems other than chemical use/abuse are uncovered, the physician/counselor may refer the athlete to other appropriate resources. The athlete will also be subject to periodic re-tests on any given date throughout the calendar school year of the first positive test. These tests will be done under the supervision of the drug counselor and/or team physician.

In addition to the evaluation process, the athlete will be required to participate in a conference call with his/her parents, guardian, or spouse, the Athletic Director (or designee), Head Coach, and Physician or Counselor.

Refusal or failure of the athlete to meaningfully participate in the evaluation/counseling process, as defined by the counselors, shall result in immediate suspension from the team until such time as the athlete shall cooperate with counseling and evaluation measures.

Before implementation of any suspension, or as soon thereafter as is practical, the athlete will have the opportunity to fully discuss the matter with the drug counseling staff and present evidence contesting the accuracy of the test or any mitigating circumstances the athlete believes are important.

2. Second Positive Test

A second positive test, by its very nature, indicates a more serious problem requiring more formal intervention. Upon confirmation of the second positive test the athlete will be suspended from all competition for a period equivalent to 10% of his/her regular season games. The suspension shall be served starting with the next scheduled game and will be in effect for both regular and playoff competition. If the infraction occurs at the end of the season or during the off-season, the suspension will be served in the next season. If the infraction occurs at the end of the regular season but before a playoff, it shall be served during the playoff.

In addition, the player will be reevaluated by the team physician or drug counselor and will be referred to appropriate treatment on or off campus. Athletes who receive treatment for chemical dependency will be required to attend weekly meetings of an appropriate self-help group such as Alcoholics Anonymous or Cocaine Anonymous. In addition, the athlete will be responsible for carrying out the discharge plans of the treatment facility. Athletes will sign appropriate authorization forms to ensure that results of treatment, treatment plans, etc. are available to the Team Physician, Drug Counselor, and Athletic Director. Failure to comply with Athletic Department Drug Policy or treatment program recommendations will result in immediate suspension from all competition, practice, and training until compliance is achieved. A second positive test could result in the suspension of the athlete from related financial aid.

The athlete will also be subject to periodic re-tests on any given date throughout the calendar school year of the second positive test. These tests will be done under the supervision of the drug counselor and/or team physician.

Before implementation of the treatment/penalties, or as soon thereafter as is practical, the athlete will have the opportunity to fully discuss the matter with the drug counseling staff and present evidence contesting the accuracy of the test or any mitigating circumstances he/she believes are important.

3. Third Positive Test

Upon confirmation of a third positive test the athlete will be suspended from all competition, practice, and training for 1 year. In addition, athletic financial aid will be revoked for the same period. The athlete's parents, guardian, or spouse will be notified by the athletic director or designee concerning said suspension.

After appropriate treatment and aftercare (including regular attendance at AA, CA, etc.), and at the end of the suspension, the athlete shall be eligible to apply for reinstatement to the athletic program. Reinstatement will not be considered automatic. A panel including the Athletic Director (or designee), Team Physician, Drug Counselor, Head Trainer, Head Coach, and others deemed appropriate by the Athletic Director shall review and determine the outcome of the petition for reinstatement. Participation in and cooperation with treatment goals, maintenance of sobriety, academic performance, and social functioning shall be considered as requirements for reinstatement. During this conference, the athlete will have appropriate opportunity to present his/her case for reinstatement.

Before implementation of the suspension, or as soon thereafter as is practical, the athlete will have the opportunity to fully discuss the matter with the drug counseling staff and present evidence contesting the accuracy of the test or any mitigating circumstances he/she believes are important.

RELAPSE

The University of Minnesota recognizes that chemical dependence (as opposed to chemical use or abuse) is a chronic disease requiring abstinence from all mood-altering chemicals (including alcohol) and is associated with the possibility of relapse. Any athlete having been diagnosed as having the disease of chemical dependency, and having cooperated with appropriate treatment, who sustains a relapse, may not be treated as having a third positive test if the athlete reacquires his/her sobriety, cooperates with relapse treatment recommendations, or if necessary, reenters treatment and aftercare. If a second relapse occurs, the athlete will be subject to the consequences of a third positive test.

APPEAL PROCESS

Along with an appeal or presentation of mitigating circumstances to the Drug Education Committee, any athlete who is found to test positive for a banned substance has the right to register an appeal to the Athletic Director. The Athletic Director will implement appropriate procedures to review the appeal. This procedure involves discussions with the athlete involved, the Drug Counseling Staff, the athlete's Head Coach and appropriate Assistant Coaches, and any other person the Athletic Director feels has bearing on the appeal.

REINSTATEMENT

Reinstatement of the athlete to athletic participation would be made possible only after the provision of proof of successful completion of appropriate Certified Drug Education and/or Rehabilitation Program (on or off campus), drug testing results, and approval by the counseling staff and athletic department.

Refusal of the student-athlete to meaningfully participate and cooperate in the evaluation and counseling program will result in *immediate suspension from the team, immediate revocation of aid, and non-eligibility for athletic aid for the subsequent year.*

VIOLATIONS OF CRIMINAL LAW

Any athlete arrested and convicted for violations of city, county, state, or federal criminal statutes related to alcohol or illegal drug use shall be immediately suspended from participation in athletics pending the outcome of an investigation of the charges against the individual. Conviction for any felony offense shall result in a 1-year suspension from athletic participation. At the end of said period, the athlete may apply to the Athletic Director for reinstatement. Reinstatement shall be contingent on the satisfactory serving of any sentence applied by the court system, including completion of treatment for chemical dependency and cooperation with aftercare recommendations.

CONCLUSION

It is believed and hoped that the implementation of this University of Minnesota Intercollegiate Athletic Drug Education and Testing Program will serve to benefit all connected with intercollegiate athletics at the University of Minnesota.

**NCAA DIVISION I, BIG TEN
U OF M INTERCOLLEGIATE ATHLETIC
DRUG AND ALCOHOL EDUCATION, TESTING,
AND REHABILITATION PROGRAM**

CONSENT TO PARTICIPATE

I certify by my signature below that I have read and reviewed the University of Minnesota Intercollegiate Athletics Drug Program. I recognize and understand that I will be asked to provide urine for drug analysis. I consent to any such testing conducted as a part of the University of Minnesota Intercollegiate Athletics Program and agree that I will not refuse to take any such test or otherwise dispute the University's right to perform such tests. Likewise, I hereby agree to abide by the treatment program and guidelines set forth in the University of Minnesota Intercollegiate Athletics Drug Program for a *First Positive Test, a Second Positive Test, and a Third Positive Test.*

I understand that the University will abide by State and Federal Laws and the Data Privacy Act to maintain the confidentiality of all matters related to drug tests and other information to be performed pursuant to this policy.

I further agree to inform the Team Physician or Head Trainer of any and all medications I may take from time to time, either under prescription or self-administered. I recognize that this information is necessary to assist my Team Physician and Trainer in providing me with the best possible care, should such care be needed.

I also authorize the Team Physician to make a confidential release to the Athletic Director, Head Coach, and Head Trainer, and to contact my parents, legal guardian, or spouse with information relating to positive test results, in accordance with terms of the University of Minnesota Intercollegiate Athletics Drug Program.

I understand that the University of Minnesota's Counseling Center and other help is available to me should I have any difficulty with drugs, alcohol, or any other personal matter, or with any questions regarding the University of Minnesota Intercollegiate Athletics Drug Program.

To the extent set forth in this document and the University of Minnesota Intercollegiate Athletics Drug Program, I waive any privileges I may have in connection therewith.

The Regents of the University of Minnesota, its officers, employees, and agents are hereby released from legal responsibility or liability and the release of such information and records as authorized by this form.

_____   _____

Print Full Name   Signature/Date

Signature of legal guardian if student-athlete is not 18 by September 1.

_____

Signature/Date

TROJAN HOCKEY
PLEDGE OF HONOR

I, _____Rob Krotee_____, as a member of Wayzata High School's hockey team, recognize my responsibility to my teammates and coaches to follow the training rules set forth by the Minnesota State High School League and any other rules set by my coaches for the 1990-91 hockey season. By signing this contract, I pledge and promise not to use or possess alcoholic beverages, illegal drugs, or tobacco products during the 1990-91 hockey season.

If I am tempted to break training, I will gain the strength to abstain by remembering the trust my teammates and coaches have in me, my own self respect, and the pride I take in being a member of the Wayzata Trojan hockey team.

_____   _11/23/90_
Player's Signature   Date

_____
_____   Team Captains
_____

I have read this contract signed by my son.

_____
Parent's Signature

OLSON JUNIOR HIGH SCHOOL
ELIGIBILITY INFORMATION BULLETIN
FOR INTERSCHOLASTIC ATHLETICS

SCHOLARSHIP RULES

1. First semester 7th graders must have been promoted from the 6th grade.
2. Second semester 7th graders and 8th graders must be making satisfactory progress in completing course work toward promotion.

MOOD-ALTERING CHEMICALS

1. **Philosophy and Purpose**
   The Bloomington Schools recognize the use of mood-altering chemicals as a significant health problem for many adolescents, resulting in negative effects on behavior, learning, and the total development of each individual. The misuse and abuse of mood-altering chemicals for some adolescents affect extracurricular participation and development of related skills. Others are affected by misuse and abuse by family, team members, or other significant persons in their lives.
2. **Rule**
   During the school year, regardless of the quantity, a student shall not (1) use a beverage containing alcohol, (2) use tobacco, or (3) use or consume, possess, buy, sell, or give away any other controlled substance (including steroids).
   A. The rule applies to the entire school year and any portion of an activity season that occurs before the start of the school year or after the close of the school year.
   B. It is not a violation for a student to be in possession of a controlled substance specifically prescribed for the student's own use by her/his doctor.
3. **Penalties for Athletic Activities**
   A. First Violation
      Penalty: After confirmation of the first violation, the student shall lose eligibility for the next two (2) consecutive interscholastic contests or two (2) weeks of a season in which the student is a participant, whichever is greater. No exception is permitted for a student who becomes a participant in a treatment program.
   B. Second Violation
      Penalty: After confirmation of the second violation, the student shall lose eligibility for the next six (6) consecutive interscholastic contests or two (2) weeks of a season in which the student is a participant, whichever is greater. No exception is permitted for a student who becomes a participant in a treatment program.
   C. Third and Subsequent Violations
      Penalty: After confirmation of the third or subsequent violation, the student shall lose eligibility for the next twelve (12) consecutive interscholastic contests in which the student is a participant. If after the third or subsequent violations, the student on his/her own volition becomes a participant in a chemical dependency program or treatment program, the student may be certified for reinstatement in MSHSL activities after a minimum period of six (6) weeks. Such certification must be issued by the director or a counselor of a chemical dependency treatment center.

D. Penalties shall be accumulative beginning with and throughout the student's participation on Junior High and Senior High athletic teams.

E. A student shall be disqualified from all interscholastic athletics for nine additional weeks beyond the student's original period of ineligibility when the student denies violation of the rule, is allowed to participate, and is subsequently found guilty of the violation.

Statements to be Signed by Participant & Parent or Guardian

I have read, understand, and acknowledge receiving the Athletic Eligibility Information, which contains a summary of the eligibility rules for interscholastic athletics at Olson Junion High School.

Informed Consent for Athletes: By its nature, participation in interscholastic athletics includes risk of injury, which may range in severity. Although serious injuries are not common in supervised school athletic programs, it is impossible to eliminate the risk. Participants can and have the responsibility to help reduce the chance of injury. Players must obey all safety rules, report all physical problems to their coaches, follow a proper conditioning program, and inspect their own equipment daily.

_____

Student's Signature   Grade in School   Date

_____

Parent or Guardian's Signature   Date

Tear off and return signed statement to your school prior to practice or participation.

Associations for Athletes with Disabilities

ASSOCIATIONS FOR ATHLETES WITH DISABILITIES

American Athletic Association of the Deaf
Richard Caswell
3916 Lantern Drive
Silver Springs, MD 20902
(301) 942-4042

American Hearing Impaired Hockey
Irvin G. Tianhnybik
1143 West Lake Street
Chicago, IL 60607
(312) 226-5880

American Wheelchair Bowling Association
Daryl Pfister
N54W15858 Larkspur Lane
Menomonee Falls, WI 53051
(414) 781-6876

Amputee Soccer Association
Al Becker
25 North 14th Street #50
San Jose, CA 95112
(408) 293-2342

Canadian Wheelchair Sports Association
333 River Road
Ottawa Ontario, Canada K1L 8H9
(613) 748-5685

Comite International Des Sports Des Sourds
Jerald Jordan
Gallaudet College
Washington, DC 20002
(202) 651-5000

Eastern Amputee Athletic Association
Jack Graff, President
Jim Coffey, Vice President
2080 Ennabrock Road
North Bellmore, NY 11710
(516) 221-0610

Handicapped Scuba Association
Jim Gatacre
1104 El Prado
San Clemente, CA 92672
(714) 498-6128

International Foundation for Wheelchair Tennis
Peter Burwash, International
2203 Timberlock Place, Suite 126
The Woodlands, TX 77738
(713) 363-4707

International Wheelchair Road Racers Club, Inc.
Joseph M. Dowling, President
30 Mayano Lane
Stamford, CT 06902
(203) 967-2231

National Beep Baseball Association
James Mastro
Director of Braille Sport Foundation
7525 North Street
St. Louis Park, MN 55426
(612) 920-9363

National Association of Handicapped Outdoor
   Sportsmen, Inc.
P.O. Box 25
Carterville, IL 62918
(618) 985-3579

National Foundation of Wheelchair Tennis
Brad Parks, Director
15441 Redhill Ave., Suite A
Tustin, CA 92680
(714) 259-1531

National Handicapped Sports and Recreation
   Association
Ron Hernley, President
Farragut Station
P.O. Box 33141
Washington, DC 20033
(301) 652-7505

National Wheelchair Athletic Association
Pat Karman, Chairperson
3617 Betty Drive, Suite S
Colorado Springs, CO 80907
(303) 597-8330

National Wheelchair Basketball Association
Stan Lebanowich
110 Seaton Building
University of Kentucky
Lexington, KY 40506
(606) 257-1623

National Wheelchair Softball Association
Jon Speake, Commissioner
P.O. Box 22487
Minneapolis, MN 55422
(612) 437-1792

Your State Special Olympics

North American Riding for the Handicapped
   Association
Leonard Warner, Executive Director
Box 100
Ashburn, VA 22011
(703) 471-1621 or (703) 777-3540

Ski for Light, Inc.
1455 West Lake Street
Minneapolis, MN 55408
(612) 827-3232

Special Olympics International
Joseph P. Kennedy, Jr., Foundation
1350 New York Avenue, NW, Suite 500
Washington, DC 20005
(202) 737-1937

United States Amputee Association
Richard Bryant
149 Abelle Forest Circle
Nashville, TN 37221
(615) 670-2323/2325

United States Cerebral Palsy Athletic Association,
   Inc.
Grant Peacock, President
34518 Warren Road, Suite 264
Westland, MI 48185
(313) 425-8961

United States Quad Rugby Association
Tommie Willard
811 Northwestern Drive
Grand Forks, ND 58201
(701) 775-0790

United States Wheelchair Racquet-Sports
   Association
Chip Parmelly
1941 Viento Verano Drive
Diamond Bar, CA 91765
(714) 861-7312

United States Association for Blind Athletes
Dr. Roger Neppl, Executive Director
33 North Institute, Brown Hall
Colorado Springs, CO 80903
(719) 630-0422

Checklist for Facility Planners

◆ **CHECKLIST FOR FACILITY PLANNERS**		

	Yes	No
General		
1. A clear-cut statement has been prepared concerning the nature and scope of the program and the special requirements for space, equipment, fixtures, safety, and facilities dictated by the activities to be conducted.	_____	_____
2. The facility has been planned to meet the total requirements of the program as well as the special needs of those who are to be served, including those with disabilities.	_____	_____
3. The plans and specifications have been checked by all governmental agencies (city, county, state, and federal) whose approval is required by law.	_____	_____
4. Plans for areas and facilities conform to local, state and federal regulations and to accepted standards and practices.	_____	_____
5. The areas and facilities planned make possible the programs that serve the interests and needs of all people.	_____	_____
6. Every available source of property or funds has been explored, evaluated, and used whenever appropriate.	_____	_____
7. All interested persons and organizations concerned with the facility have had an opportunity to share in its planning (professional educators, users, consultants, administrators, engineers, architects, program specialists, building managers, and builder—a team approach).	_____	_____
8. The facility and its appurtenances will fulfill the maximal demands of the program. The program has not been curtailed to fit the facility.	_____	_____
9. The facility has been functionally planned to meet the present and anticipated needs of specific programs, situations, and publics.	_____	_____
10. Future additions are included in present plans to promote economy of construction.	_____	_____

◆   **CHECKLIST FOR FACILITY PLANNERS—cont'd**

	Yes	No

11. Lecture classrooms are isolated and insulated from sources of distracting noises. _____ _____
12. Storage areas for indoor and outdoor equipment are adequately sized. They are located adjacent to the gymnasiums. _____ _____
13. Shelves in storage rooms are slanted toward the wall. _____ _____
14. All passageways are accessible: free of obstructions; fixtures are recessed. _____ _____
15. Facilities for health services, athletic training, health testing, health instruction, and the first aid and emergency-isolation rooms are suitably interrelated. _____ _____
16. Buildings, specific areas, and facilities are clearly identified and hazards noted. _____ _____
17. Locker rooms are arranged for accessibility and ease of supervision. _____ _____
18. Offices, teaching stations, and service facilities are properly interrelated. _____ _____
19. Special needs of persons with disabilities are met, including a ramp into the building at a major entrance and accessibility to all floors and areas. _____ _____
20. All "dead space" is used. _____ _____
21. The building is compatible in design and comparable in quality and accommodation to other organizational structures. _____ _____
22. Storage rooms are accessible to the play area. _____ _____
23. Workrooms, conference rooms, and staff and administrative offices are interrelated. _____ _____
24. Shower and dressing facilities are provided for professional staff members and are conveniently located. _____ _____
25. Thought and attention have been given to making facilities and equipment as durable and vandalproof as possible. _____ _____
26. Low-cost maintenance features have been adequately considered. _____ _____
27. This facility is a part of a well-integrated master plan. _____ _____
28. All areas, courts, facilities, equipment, climate control, security, etc., conform rigidly to detailed standards and specifications. _____ _____
29. Shelves are recessed and mirrors are supplied in appropriate places in rest rooms and dressing rooms. Mirrors are not placed above sinks. _____ _____
30. Dressing space between locker rows is adjusted to the size and age level of participants. _____ _____
31. Drinking fountains are conveniently placed in locker room areas or immediately adjacent thereto. _____ _____
32. Special attention is given to provision for the locking of service windows and counters, supply bins, carts, shelves, and racks. _____ _____
33. Provision is made for the repair, maintenance, replacement, and off-season storage of equipment and uniforms. _____ _____
34. A well-defined program for laundering and cleaning of towels, uniforms, and equipment is included in the plan. _____ _____
35. Noncorrosive metal is used in dressing, drying, and shower areas except for enameled lockers. _____ _____
36. Antipanic hardware is used where required by fire regulations. _____ _____
37. Properly placed hose bibbs and drains are sufficient in size and quantity to permit flushing the entire area with a water hose. _____ _____
38. A water-resistant, coved base is used under the locker base and floor mat, and where floor and wall join. _____ _____

	Yes	No
39. Chalkboards and/or tackboards with map tracks are located in appropriate places in dressing rooms, hallways, and classrooms.	_____	_____
40. Book shelves are provided in toilet areas.	_____	_____
41. Space and equipment are planned in accordance with the types and number of participants.	_____	_____
42. Basement rooms, being undesirable for dressing, drying, and showering, are not planned for those purposes.	_____	_____
43. Spectator seating (permanent) in areas that are basically instructional is kept at a minimum. Rollaway bleachers are used primarily. Balcony seating is considered as a possibility.	_____	_____
44. Well-lighted and effectively displayed trophy cases enhance the interest and appearance of the lobby.	_____	_____
45. The space under the stairs is used for storage.	_____	_____
46. Department heads' offices are located near the central administrative office, which includes a well-planned conference room.	_____	_____
47. Workrooms are located near the central office and serve as a repository for department materials and records.	_____	_____
48. The conference area includes a cloak room, sink, and toilet.	_____	_____
49. In addition to regular secretarial offices established in the central and department chairperson's offices, a special room to house a secretarial pool for staff members is provided.	_____	_____
50. Staff dressing facilities are provided. These facilities may also serve game officials.	_____	_____
51. The community and/or neighborhood has a planning "round table."	_____	_____
52. All those (persons and agencies) who should be a party to planning and development are invited and actively engaged in the planning process.	_____	_____
53. Space and area relationships are important. They have been carefully considered.	_____	_____
54. Both long-range plans and immediate plans have been made.	_____	_____
55. The physical comfort of the student and other participants, a major factor in securing maximal learning, has been considered in the plans.	_____	_____
56. Plans for quiet areas have been made.	_____	_____
57. In the planning, consideration has been given to the need for adequate recreation areas and facilities, both near and distant from the homes of people.	_____	_____
58. Plans recognize the primary function of recreation as being enrichment of learning through creative self-expression, self-enhancement, and the achievement of self-potential.	_____	_____
59. Every effort has been exercised to eliminate hazards.	_____	_____
60. The installation of low-hanging door closers, light fixtures, signs, and other objects in traffic areas has been avoided.	_____	_____
61. Warning signals, both visible and audible, are included in the plans.	_____	_____
62. Ramps have a slope equal to or less than a 1-foot rise in 12 feet.	_____	_____
63. Minimum landings for ramps are 5 feet $\times$ 5 feet, they extend at least 1 foot beyond the swinging arc of a door, have at least a 6-foot clearance at the bottom, and have level platforms at 30-foot intervals on every turn.	_____	_____
64. Adequate locker and dressing spaces are provided.	_____	_____
65. The design of dressing, drying, and shower areas reduces foot traffic to a minimum and establishes clean, dry aisles for bare feet.	_____	_____

◆ CHECKLIST FOR FACILITY PLANNERS—cont'd

	Yes	No
66. Teaching stations are properly related to service facilities.		
67. Toilet facilities are adequate in number. They are located to serve all groups for which provisions are made.		
68. Mail services, outgoing and incoming, are included in the plans.		
69. Hallways, ramps, doorways, and elevators are designed to permit equipment to be moved easily and quickly.		
70. A keying design suited to management and instructional needs is planned.		
71. Toilets used by large groups have circulating (in and out) entrances and exits.		

Climate control

1. Provision is made throughout the building for climate control—heating, ventilating, humidity control, and air conditioning.		
2. Special ventilation is provided for locker, dressing, shower, drying, and toilet rooms.		
3. Heating plans permit both area and individual room control.		
4. Research areas where small animals are kept and where chemicals are used have been provided with special ventilating equipment.		
5. The heating and ventilating of the wrestling and combatives gymnasium have been given special attention.		

Electrical

1. Shielded, vaporproof lights are used in moist areas.		
2. Lights in strategic areas are key controlled.		
3. Lighting intensity conforms to approved standards.		
4. An adequate number of electrical outlets are strategically placed.		
5. Gymnasium lights are controlled by dimmer units.		
6. Locker room lights are mounted above the space between lockers.		
7. Natural light is controlled properly for purposes of visual aids and other avoidance of glare.		
8. Electrical outlet plates are installed 3 feet above the floor unless special use dictates other locations.		
9. Controls for light switches and projection equipment are suitably located and interrelated.		
10. All lights are shielded. Special protection is provided in gymnasiums, court areas, and shower rooms.		
11. Lights are placed to shine between rows of lockers.		

Walls

1. Movable and folding partitions are power-operated and controlled by keyed switches.		
2. Wall places are located where needed and are firmly attached.		
3. Hooks and rings for nets are placed (and recessed in walls) according to court locations and net heights.		
4. Materials that clean easily and are impervious to moisture are used where moisture is prevalent.		

	Yes	No

5. Shower heads are placed at appropriate heights—4 feet (elementary) to 7 feet (university)—for each school level.

6. Protective matting is placed permanently on the walls in the wrestling room, at the ends of basketball courts, and in other areas where such protection is needed.

7. An adequate number of drinking fountains is provided. They are properly placed (recessed in wall).

8. One wall (at least) of the dance studio has full-length mirrors.

9. All corners in locker rooms are rounded.

Ceilings

1. Overhead-supported apparatus is secured to beams engineered to withstand stress.

2. The ceiling height is adequate for the activities to be housed.

3. Acoustical materials impervious to moisture are used in moist areas.

4. Skylights, being impractical, are seldom used because of problems in waterproofing roofs and the controlling sun rays (gyms).

5. All ceilings except those in storage areas are acoustically treated with sound-absorbent materials.

Floors

1. Floor plates are placed where needed and are flush-mounted.

2. Floor design and materials conform to recommended standards and specifications.

3. Lines and markings are painted on floors before sealing is completed (when synthetic tape is not used).

4. A coved base (around lockers and where wall and floor meet) or the same water-resistant material used on floors is found in all dressing and shower rooms.

5. Abrasive, nonskid, slip-resistant flooring that is impervious to moisture is provided on all areas where water is used—laundry, swimming pool, shower, dressing, and drying rooms.

6. Floor drains are properly located, and the slope of the floor is adequate for rapid drainage.

Gymnasiums and special rooms

1. Gymnasiums are planned so as to provide safety zones (between courts, end lines, and walls) and for best use of space.

2. One gymnasium wall is free of obstructions and is finished with a smooth, hard surface for ball-rebounding activities.

3. The elementary school gymnasium has one wall free of obstructions, a minimum ceiling height of 18 feet, a minimum of 4000 square feet of teaching area, and a recessed area for housing appropriate equipment and teaching aids.

4. Secondary school gymnasiums have a minimum ceiling height of 22 feet; a scoreboard; electrical outlets placed to fit with bleacher installation; wall attachments for apparatus and nets; and a power-operated, sound-insulated, and movable partition with a small pass-through door at one end.

5. A small spectator alcove adjoins the wrestling and combatives room and contains a drinking fountain (recessed in the wall).

6. Cabinets, storage closets, supply windows, and service areas have locks.

7. Provisions have been made for the cleaning, storing, and issuing of physical education and sport uniforms.

◆ **CHECKLIST FOR FACILITY PLANNERS—cont'd**

	Yes	No
8. Shower heads are placed at varing heights in the shower rooms for each school level.	_____	_____
9. Special equipment is provided for use by persons with disabilities.	_____	_____
10. Special provision has been made for audio and visual aids, including intercommunication systems, radio, television, and interactive video disk linkage.	_____	_____
11. Team dressing rooms have provisions for:		
a. Hosing down room	_____	_____
b. Floors pitched to drain easily	_____	_____
c. Hot- and cold-water hose bibbs	_____	_____
d. Windows located above locker heights	_____	_____
e. Chalk, tack, and bulletin boards, and movie and video projection	_____	_____
f. Lockers for each team member	_____	_____
g. Drying facility for uniforms	_____	_____
12. The indoor rifle range includes:		
a. Targets located 54 inches apart and 50 feet from the firing line	_____	_____
b. 3 feet to 8 feet of space behind targets	_____	_____
c. 12 feet of space behind firing line	_____	_____
d. Ceilings 8 feet high	_____	_____
e. Width adjusted to number of firing lines needed (1 line for each 3 students)	_____	_____
f. A pulley device for target placement and return	_____	_____
g. Storage and repair space	_____	_____
13. Dance facilities include:		
a. 100 square feet per student	_____	_____
b. A minimum length of 60 linear feet for modern dance	_____	_____
c. Full-height viewing mirrors on one wall (at least) of 30 feet; also a 20-foot mirror on an additional wall if possible	_____	_____
d. Acoustical drapery to cover mirrors when not used and for protection if other activities are permitted	_____	_____
e. Dispersed microphone jacks and speaker installation for music and instruction	_____	_____
f. Built-in cabinets for record, tape, and video players, microphones, and amplifiers, with space for equipment carts	_____	_____
g. Electrical outlets and microphone connections around perimeter of room	_____	_____
h. An exercise bar (34 inches to 42 inches above floor) on one wall	_____	_____
i. Drapes, surface colors, floors (maple preferred), and other room appointments to enhance the room's attractiveness	_____	_____
j. Location near dressing rooms and outside entrances	_____	_____
14. Training rooms include:		
a. Rooms large enough to adequately administer proper health services	_____	_____
b. Sanitary storage cabinets for medical supplies	_____	_____
c. Installation of drains for whirlpool, tubs, etc.	_____	_____
d. Installation of electrical outlets with proper capacities and voltage	_____	_____
e. High stools for use of equipment such as whirlpool, ice tubs, etc.	_____	_____
f. Sink, toilet, and shower	_____	_____
g. Extra sink in the trainer's room proper	_____	_____
h. Adjoining dressing rooms	_____	_____

	Yes	No

i. Installation and use of hydrotherapy and diathermy equipment in separate areas

j. Space for the trainer, the physician, and the various services of this function

k. Corrective exercise laboratories located conveniently and adapted to the needs of persons with disabilities

15. Coaches' room should provide:

    a. A sufficient number of dressing lockers for coaching staff and officials

    b. A security closet or cabinet for athletic equipment such as timing devices

    c. A sufficient number of showers and toilet facilities

    d. Drains and faucets for hosing down the rooms where this method of cleaning is desirable and possible

    e. A small chalkboard, scheduling chart, and tackboard

    f. A small movie screen, video monitor, and projection table for use of coaches to review films and videos

Persons with disabilities

Have you included those considerations that would make the facility accessible? These considerations include:

1. The knowledge that persons with disabilities will be participants in almost all activities, not merely spectators, if the facility is properly planned.
2. Ground-level entrance(s) or stair-free entrance(s) using inclined walk(s) or inclined ramp(s).
3. Uninterrupted walk surface; no abrupt changes in levels leading to the facility.
4. Approach walks and connecting walks no less than 4 feet wide.
5. Walks with gradient no greater than 5%.
6. A ramp, when used, with rise no greater than 1 foot in 12 feet.
7. Flat or level surface inside and outside of all exterior doors, extending 5 feet from the door in the direction that the door swings, and extending 1 foot to each side of the door.
8. Flush thresholds at all doors.
9. Appropriate door widths, heights, and mechanical features.
10. At least 6 feet between vestibule doors in series, i.e., inside and outside doors.
11. Access and proximity to parking areas.
12. No obstructions by curbs at crosswalks, parking areas, etc.
13. Proper precautions (handrails, etc.) at basement window areas, open stairways, porches, ledges, and platforms.
14. Handrails on all steps and ramps.
15. Precautions against the placement of manholes or barriers in primary or major sidewalks.
16. Corridors that are at least 60 inches wide and without abrupt pillars or protrusions.
17. Floors that are nonskid and have no abrupt changes or interruptions in level.
18. Proper design of steps.
19. Access to rest rooms, water coolers, telephones, food-service areas, lounges, dressing rooms, play area, elevators, and auxiliary services and areas.
20. Elevators in multiple-story buildings.
21. Appropriate placement of controls to permit and prohibit use as desired.

	CHECKLIST FOR FACILITY PLANNERS—cont'd

	Yes	No
22. Sound signals for the blind, and visual signals for the deaf as counterparts to regular sound and sight signals.	_____	_____
23. Proper placement, concealment, or insulation of radiators, heat pipes, hot water pipes, drain pipes, etc.	_____	_____

Swimming pools

	Yes	No
1. Has a clear-cut statement been prepared on the nature and scope of the design program and the special requirements for space, equipment, safety, and facilities dictated by the activities to be conducted?	_____	_____
2. Has the swimming pool been planned to meet the total requirements of the program to be conducted, as well as any special needs of the clientele to be served?	_____	_____
3. Have all plans and specifications been checked and approved by the local board of health?	_____	_____
4. Is the pool the proper depth to accommodate the various age-groups and types of activities it is intended to serve?	_____	_____
5. Does the design of the pool incorporate the most current knowledge and best experience available regarding swimming pools?	_____	_____
6. If a local architect or engineer who is inexperienced in pool construction is employed, has an experienced pool consultant, architect, or engineer been called in to advise on design and equipment?	_____	_____
7. Is there adequate deep water for diving (minimum of 12 feet for 1-meter boards and 3-meter boards, and 18 feet for 10-meter towers)?	_____	_____
8. Have the requirements for competitive swimming been met (7-foot lanes; 12-inch black or brown lines on the bottom; pool 1 inch longer than official measurement; depth and distance markings)?	_____	_____
9. Is there adequate deckspace around the pool? Has more space been provided than that indicated by the minimum recommended deck/pool ratio?	_____	_____
10. Does the swimming instructor's office face the pool? And is there a window through which the instructor may view all the pool area? Is there a toilet-shower-dressing area next to the office for instructors?	_____	_____
11. Are recessed steps or removable ladders located on the walls so as not to interfere with competitive swimming turns?	_____	_____
12. Does a properly constructed overflow gutter extend around the pool perimeter?	_____	_____
13. Where skimmers are used, have they been properly located so that they are not on walls where competitive swimming is to be conducted?	_____	_____
14. Have separate storage spaces been allocated for maintenance and instructional equipment?	_____	_____
15. Has the area for spectators been properly separated from the pool area?	_____	_____
16. Have all diving standards and lifeguard stands been properly spaced and anchored?	_____	_____
17. Does the pool layout provide the most efficient control of traffic from showers and locker rooms to the pool? Are toilet facilities provided for wet swimmers separate from the dry area?	_____	_____

	Yes	No

18. Is the recirculation pump located below the water level?

19. Is there easy vertical access to the filter room for both people and material (stairway if required)?

20. Has the proper pitch to drains been allowed in the pool, on the pool deck, in the overflow gutter, and on the floor of shower and dressing rooms?

21. Has adequate space been allowed between diving boards and between the diving boards and side walls?

22. Is there adequate provision for lifesaving equipment? Pool-cleaning equipment?

23. Are inlets and outlets adequate in number and located so as to ensure effective circulation of water in the pool?

24. Has consideration been given to underwater lights, observation windows, and speakers?

25. Is there a coping around the edge of the pool?

26. Has a pool heater been considered in northern climates in order to raise the temperature of the water?

27. Have underwater lights in end racing walls been located deep enough and directly below surface lane anchors, and are they on a separate circuit?

28. Has the plan been considered from the standpoint of persons with disabilities?

29. Is seating for swimmers provided on the deck?

30. Has the recirculation-filtration system been designed to meet the anticipated future bathing load?

31. Has the gas chlorinator (if used) been placed in a separate room accessible from and vented to the outside?

32. Has the gutter waste water been valved to return to the filters, and also for direct waste?

33. Can a computer be used to control chemical balance?

Indoor pools

1. Is there proper mechanical ventilation?

2. Is there adequate acoustical treatment of walls and ceilings?

3. Is there adequate overhead clearance for diving (20 feet above low springboards and 3-meter boards, and 15 feet for 10-meter platforms)?

4. Is there adequate lighting (50 footcandles minimum)?

5. Has reflection of light from the outside been minimized by proper location of windows or skylights (windows on side walls are not desirable)?

6. Are all wall bases coved to facilitate cleaning?

7. Is there provision for proper temperature control in the pool room for both water and air?

8. Can the humidity of the pool room be controlled?

9. Is the wall and ceiling insulation adequate to prevent "sweating"?

10. Are all metal fittings of noncorrosive material?

11. Is there a tunnel around the outside of the pool, or a trench on the deck that permits ready access to pipes?

◆ **CHECKLIST FOR FACILITY PLANNERS—cont'd**

	Yes	No

Outdoor pools

1. Is the site for the pool in the best possible location (away from railroad tracks, heavy industry, trees, and dusty open fields)? _____ _____

2. Have sand and grass been kept the proper distance away from the pool to prevent them from being transmitted to the pool? _____ _____

3. Has a fence been placed around the pool to ensure safety when not in use? _____ _____

4. Has proper subsurface drainage been provided? _____ _____

5. Is there adequate deck space for sunbathing? _____ _____

6. Are the outdoor lights placed far enough from the pool to prevent insects from dropping into the pool? _____ _____

7. Is the deck of nonslip material? _____ _____

8. Is there an area set aside for eating, separate from the pool deck? _____ _____

9. Is the bathhouse properly located, with the entrance to the pool leading to the shallow end? _____ _____

10. If the pool shell contains a concrete finish, has the length of the pool been increased by 3 inches over the official size in order to permit eventual tiling of the basin without making the pool too short? _____ _____

11. Are there other recreational facilities nearby for the convenience and enjoyment of swimmers? _____ _____

12. Do diving boards or platforms face north or east? _____ _____

13. Are lifeguard stands provided and properly located? _____ _____

14. Has adequate parking space been provided and properly located? _____ _____

15. Is the pool oriented correctly in relation to the sun? _____ _____

16. Have windscreens been provided in situations where heavy winds prevail? _____ _____

Adapted and updated from National Facilities Conference, *Planning Areas and Facilities for Health, Physical Education, and Recreation,* Washington, D.C., 1965, AAHPER.

APPENDIX **F**

Sample Budgets

Typical Suburban School District Budget and Funding
  Sources

Typical High School Varsity Sport Budget

Intercollegiate Recreational Sport Budget

Community-Based Youth Sport Budget

Typical suburban school district budget and funding
(1 High School and 2 Junior High Schools)

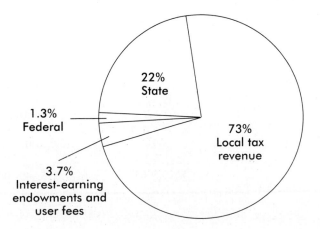

1.3%
Federal

22%
State

73%
Local tax
revenue

3.7%
Interest-earning
endowments and
user fees

Total budget: $45,000,000 - $75,000,000

Physical education and recreational sports:
  $400,000 - $600,000

Varsity sport: $400,000 - $600,000
  (Less than 2% of budget)

Typical High School Varsity Sport Budget

Fund: General

Location: INSTRUCTIONAL SUPPORT SERVICES—003

	Budget code	Actual expenditures	Budget	Proposed budget
Interscholastic athletics—221 boys				
*Casual	132		$ 4,374.00	$ 4,920.00
*Extra assignment	152		-0-	-0-
*Athletics	155		158,196.00	177,880.00
General supplies	330		23,100.00	25,450.00
Postage and express	332		-0-	-0-
Printing and publishing	422		1,810.00	2,400.00
Rental equipment	432		1,050.00	1,300.00
Use of vehicles	447		31,260.00	33,000.00
Facility use	450		51,550.00	54,050.00
Telephone and fax	452		200.00	300.00
Repair equipment	462		-0-	3,700.00
Laundry	486		2,500.00	2,650.00
Official expense	492		16,270.00	16,270.00
*Other contract services	499		17,430.00	20,270.00
Travel and expense	902		800.00	800.00
Dues and memberships	905		-0-	-0-
TOTAL DEPARTMENT			$308,540.00	$342,990.00
Interscholastic athletics—240 girls				
*Casual	132		$ 3,070.00	$ 3,450.00
*Extra assignment	152		-0-	-0-
*Athletics	155		126,784.00	143,976.00
General supplies	330		14,550.00	16,700.00
Postage and express	332		-0-	-0-
Printing and publishing	422		270.00	500.00
Rental equipment	432		500.00	600.00
Use of vehicles	447		22,360.00	23,480.00
Facility use	450		38,850.00	40,850.00
Telephone and fax	452		100.00	150.00
Laundry	486		1,500.00	1,850.00
Official expense	492		12,510.00	12,510.00
*Other contract services	499		8,432.00	10,090.00
Travel and expense	902		800.00	800.00
Dues and memberships	905		-0-	-0-
Repair equipment	462		-0-	500.00
TOTAL DEPARTMENT			$230,596.00	$255,456.00

*Negotiated—increase pending

Intercollegiate Recreational Sport Budget Management Summary Income/Expenses

| Expenses | Current fiscal year | | | | |
Item Name	Month	%	YTD	%	Budget
Planning and operations	26,286.14	6	106,615.66	27	387,338.00
Intramurals	18,331.12	7	59,551.53	25	232,771.00
Fitness and open recreation	11,547.36	6	58,031.02	33	171,881.00
Sport clubs	8,707.33	5	101,777.11	69	147,237.00
Facilities	33,036.08	10	96,087.53	31	309,027.00
Instructional	15,747.30	8	63,121.88	34	183,652.00
Aquatics	27,434.09	10	73,438.59	28	259,386.00
Special events	6,871.91	14	13,743.95	29	46,438.00
SUBTOTAL	$147,961.33		$572,367.27		$1,737,730.00

| Income | Current fiscal year | | | | |
Item Name	Month	%	YTD	%	Budget
Planning and operations	15,660.00	*	323.06	*	0.00
Intramurals	955.00	0	17,803.85	14	123,475.00
Fitness and open recreation	8,065.62	10	17,392.24	22	77,800.00
Sport clubs	2,227.00	26	2,244.00	26	8,500.00
Facilities	26,812.03	11	89,178.94	39	227,500.00
Instructional	10,253.44	11	31,780.83	35	89,500.00
Aquatics	950.00	2	15,332.00	36	42,500.00
Special events and student service fees	354,127.40	31	464,344.28	41	1,168,455.00
SUBTOTAL	$387,730.49		$638,399.20		$1,737,730.00

Community-based youth sport budget

WAYZATA YOUTH HOCKEY ASSOCIATION

Gross Receipts/Sales

Registrations (726)	$17,170.00	
Sponsors	5,750.00	
Blue Line Boosters	31,138.19	
Ice time	10,699.07	
Wayzata Tournament (2)	10,607.12	
General donations	250.00	$75,614.38

Expenses and Cost of Sales

League fees, referees, and ice time	$13,523.38	
Registration expense	1,269.50	
Equipment	14,462.21	
Rink and arena maintenance	5,260.58	
Outside tournaments and playoffs	3,265.00	
Wayzata tournament costs	3,892.68	
Insurance	694.00	
Interest on loan	347.59	
Loan payment	2,000.00	
Blue Line Boosters	20,525.41	
Concession commission to school district	1,732.18	
Travel team coaches' expense	1,487.30	
Miscellaneous administrative expense	517.35	68,977.18
Net results of Operations—Gain		$6,637.20
Beginning cash: Association Checking Account	$11,113.53	
Blue Line Boosters Accounts	1,804.39	
Savings Account (Capital Improvement)	7,072.34	$19,990.26
Plus Interest on Savings		478.56
		$20,468.82
Ending cash: Association Checking Account	$18,043.81	
Blue Line Boosters Accounts	1,511.31	
Savings Account (Capital Improvement)	7,550.90	27,106.02
Net cash increase		$6,637.20

NOTE: The savings account is held as collateral for the $3000 loan at Wayzata Bank.

The Association Account and Blue Line Account are held for capital improvements and season start-up costs.

Index

Credits

Chapter 1 UF1-2, President's Council on Physical Fitness and Sports; UF 1-7, Bob Thomason, Tenneco, Inc.; UF 1-9, From Nichols B: *Moving and learning: the elementary school physical education experience,* ed 2, St Louis, 1990, Mosby–Year Book.

Chapter 2 UF 2-5, Ralph Lord, Lexington Public Schools, Lexington, MA; UF 2-7, University of Nevada, Las Vegas.

Chapter 3 UF 3-2, Omaha Public Schools, Omaha, NE; UF 3-8, John Tasker, Arnold College Division, University of Bridgeport, CT. Parents and Friends Association of Mentally Retarded Children; UF 3-13, From Nichols B: *Moving and learning: the elementary school physical education experience,* ed 2, St Louis, 1990, Mosby–Year Book; UF 3-14, Cramer Products, Inc., Gardner, KS.

Chapter 4 UF 4-4, Beth Kirkpatrick, Tilford Middle School, Vinton, IA; UF 4-5, Youth Services Section, Los Angeles City Schools, CA; UF 4-8, Youth Services Section, Los Angeles City Schools, CA; UF 4-9, Hope College, Holland, MI; UF 4-10, Division of Municipal Recreation and Adult Education, Milwaukee Public Schools, Milwaukee, WI.

Chapter 5 UF 5-5, From Coakley J: *Sport in society: issues and controversies,* ed 4, St Louis, 1990, Mosby–Year Book; UF 5-10, Cramer Products Inc., Gardner, KS; UF 5-18, Courtesy of Special Olympics International; UF 5-19, From Wuest D, Bucher C: *Foundations of physical education,* ed 11, St Louis, 1991, Mosby–Year Book.

Chapter 6 Part III Opener, Martha Swope, Pepsi Co., Inc., Purchace, NY; UF 6-3, Martha Swope, Pepsi Co., Inc., Purchace, NY; UF 6-5, William B. Baun and Evelyn Navarr, Tenneco Management Company, Houston, TX; UF 6-6, William B. Baun and Evelyn Navarr, Tenneco Management Company, Houston, TX; UF 6-7, William B. Baun and Evelyn Navarr, Tenneco Management Company, Houston, TX; UF 6-10, From Wuest D, Bucher C: *Foundations of physical education,* ed 11, St Louis, 1991, Mosby–Year Book; UF 6-16, Westwood Home, Clinton, MO.

Chapter 7 UF 7-7, From Wuest D, Bucher C: *Foundations of physical education,* ed 11, St Louis, 1991, Mosby–Year Book.

Chapter 8 UF 8-2, From Nichols B: *Moving and learning: the elementary school physical education experience,* ed 2, St Louis, 1990, Mosby–Year Book; UF 8-5, American Alliance for Health, Physical Education, Recreation and Dance; UF 8-7, Omaha Public Schools, Omaha, NE; UF 8-8, From Nichols B: *Moving and learning: the elementary school physical education experience,* ed 2, St Louis, 1990, Mosby–Year Book; UF 8-9, From Mood D, Musker F, Rink J: *Sports and recreational activities for men and women,* ed 10, St Louis, 1991, Mosby–Year Book.

Chapter 9 UF 9-3, William B. Baun, Tenneco Management Company, Houston, TX; UF 9-4, Photo by Dave Black; UF 9-5, Trinity College, Hartford, CT; UF 9-6, HOK Sports Facilities Group, Kansas City, MO; UF 9-

13, Courtesy of Donald Krotee Partnership, Planning and Architecture, Santa Ana, CA; UF 9-14, Courtesy of Scholastic Coach; UF 9-17 A, B, C, D, HOK Sports Facilities Group, Kansas City, MO.

Chapter 11   UF 11-3, University of California at Irvine; UF 11-5, From Mood D, Musker F, Rink J: *Sports and recreational activities for men and women,* ed 10, St Louis, 1991, Mosby–Year Book; UF 11-9, From Wuest D, Bucher C: *Foundations of Physical Education,* ed 11, St Louis, 1991, Mosby–Year Book.

Chapter 12   UF 12-1, From Coakley J: *Sport in society: issues and controversies,* ed 4, St Louis, 1990, Mosby–Year Book; UF 12-3, From Arnheim D: *Modern principles of athletic training,* ed 7, St Louis, 1989, Mosby–Year Book; UF 12-7, From Booher J, Thibodeau G: *Athletic injury assessment,* ed 2, St Louis, 1989, Mosby–Year Book; UF 12-9, From Wuest D, Bucher C: *Foundations*

of physical education, ed 11, St Louis, 1991, Mosby–Year Book; UF 12-11, From Coakley J: *Sport in society: issues and controversies,* ed 4, St Louis, 1990, Mosby–Year Book.

Chapter 13   UF 13-2, Tom and Faye Sitzman, Omaha NE; UF 13-5, Courtesy of United Cerebral Palsy Association, Inc.; UF 13-15, University of Nevada, Las Vegas.

Chapter 14   UF 14-4, Courtesy of President's Council on Physical Fitness and Sports; UF 14-10, From Nichols B: *Moving and learning: the elementary school physical education experience,* ed 2, St Louis, 1990, Mosby–Year Book; UF 14-11, From Wuest DA, Bucher CA: *Foundations of physical education,* ed 11, St Louis, 1991, Mosby–Year Book.

Chapter 15   UF 15-4, From Wuest DA, Bucher CA: *Foundations of physical education,* ed 11, St Louis, 1991, Mosby–Year Book.